# AMERICA
## A TO Z

AMERI

# CA A TO Z

PEOPLE, PLACES

CUSTOMS

AND CULTURE

Reader's Digest

THE READER'S DIGEST ASSOCIATION, INC.
PLEASANTVILLE, NEW YORK/MONTREAL

# AMERICA A TO Z

## STAFF

*Project Editor*
Alma E. Guinness

*Project Art Editor*
Judith Carmel

*Senior Research Editor*
Eileen Einfrank

*Editor*
Carolyn Chubet

*Research Editors*
Barbara Guarino Lester
Linda Ingroia

*Associate Editors*
Jeff Akellian
Troy Dreier
Tracy O'Shea
Marianne Wait

*Associate Art Editor*
Andrew Ploski

*Picture Research Editors*
Romy Charlesworth
Linda Patterson Eger
Sue Israel

*Art Production Associate*
Wendy Wong

*Assistant Production
Supervisor*
Mike Gallo

## CONTRIBUTORS

*Editorial Assistant*
Andrew Boorstyn

*Picture Research Editors*
Lois Safrani
Dee Shapiro

*Copy Editor*
Gina Grant

*Production Coordinator*
Tracey Grant

*Writers*
Ashton Applewhite
Edward S. Barnard
Stephen L. Barnard
Carol Bergman
Neill Bogan
David Brownell
Rachel Carley
Michael Cox
Justin Davidson
Brian Dillon
Jack El-Hai
Marjorie Flory
Andrew Frothingham
Alice Gordon
Christopher Gordon
Reily Hendrickson
Sydney Johnson
Tony Kaye
Carlotta Kerwin
Guy A. Lester
Harvey B. Loomis
Jill McManus
Dallas Murphy
Wendy B. Murphy
Tod Olson
Christopher F. Packard

Paul Pierog
David Reilly
Rosemary G. Rennicke
Nancy Shepherdson
Justin Smith
John S. Tompkins
David Veinot
James S. Wamsley
Melissa Wanamaker
Densie Webb
Carol Weeg
Stephen Weinstein

*Indexer*
Sydney Wolfe Cohen

## READER'S DIGEST
## GENERAL BOOKS

*Editor-in-Chief, Books and
Home Entertainment*
Barbara J. Morgan

*Editor, U.S. General Books*
David Palmer

*Executive Editor*
Gayla Visalli

*Editorial Director*
Jane Polley

*Art Director*
Joel Musler

*Research Director*
Laurel A. Gilbride

The credits and acknowledgments that appear on pages 414–416 are hereby made a part of this copyright page.

Library of Congress Cataloging-in-Publication Data
America A to Z.
    p.        cm.
  ISBN 0-89577-900-5
  1. United States—Civilization—Miscellanea—Encyclopedias.
2. Popular culture—United States—Miscellanea—Encyclopedias.
3. Americana—Encyclopedias.    I. Reader's Digest Association.
E169.1.A444 1997
973'.03—dc20
          96-2685

Printed in the United States of America.

Address any comments about *America A to Z* to Editor, U.S. General Books, c/o Customer Service, Reader's Digest, Pleasantville, NY 10570. To order copies of *America A to Z*, call 1-800-846-2100.

## About This Book

**R**emember ant farms? Uncle Milton was the brains behind those green plastic plantations, which now occupy a fixed place in our collective memory. How about the Keystone Kops, the Model T, and Burma-Shave? Like the bells of the Good Humor truck, they are instantly recognized. And they are distinctly ours, along with hot dogs and jazz and icons like "American Gothic," the painting of the farmer and his daughter that is said to be known to more people than the "Mona Lisa." These are the things that make America American. And they are what *America A to Z* is all about.

In this book we pay tribute to foods such as Spam and Wonder Bread, Eskimo Pies and Häagen-Dazs (so named because it sounds expensive; it doesn't mean a thing in any language). We open our closets to reveal leisure suits and elevator shoes; hail monuments to excess, like monster trucks and the Mall of America; and relive fads like mood rings and dance marathons. We tune in when deejay Alan Freed coins the phrase *rock and roll*. On television, Dick Clark finds his calling, *Candid Camera* catches "unsuspecting folks in the act of being themselves," and *Dallas* has the entire nation asking, "Who shot J. R.?" At the movies, *Gone With the Wind* lingers indefinitely, and Bogie's toast, "Here's looking at you, kid," still sends shivers.

Like any album worth its salt, *America A to Z* is packed with pictures. And people. There's Ella Fitzgerald and Fred Astaire; American originals such as Will Rogers and Walt Whitman; and the man who invented Post-it notes because he wanted an easy way to mark the pages of his hymnal. Al "Scarface" Capone is here, along with our favorite entertainers, including Jimmy Durante ("The Schnozzola") and Betty Grable, who once said, "There are two reasons why I'm in show business and I'm standing on both of them." And, of course, heroes like Babe Ruth and Martin Luther King, Jr. A special nod to Irving Berlin, who played piano in only one key, yet still managed to write the song that says it all: "God Bless America."

*The Editors*

Rainy weather has turned a typical dirt road into a quagmire, causing an AAA excursion car to sink. AAA strove to upgrade the country's roads, literally paving the way for the automobile.

## AAA

Before the first expressway, before the first gas station, even before the Model T, there was the American Automobile Association. Founded in 1902 by nine auto clubs, AAA offered motoring enthusiasts outings, auto shows, and tours. Long-distance driving tours were intended to demonstrate the reliability of the automobile, but because the roads were unmarked, part of the challenge was finding the way. One method was to follow the chicken feathers that had scattered when other cars chased the birds out of the way. And talk about potholes: it often took a team of horses to extract a car from a nasty ditch.

Not everyone welcomed the horseless carriage. One group, the Farmers' Anti-Automobile Association, demanded that cars traveling on country roads at night send up a rocket every mile. Drivers were also asked to cover their machine with blankets when a team of horses was approaching and, if a horse refused to pass the vehicle, to take the car apart quickly and hide the parts in the bushes.

Today AAA's tow trucks have replaced the four-legged rescue teams of yore. And their nifty Triptiks—custom-made strip maps—are a big improvement over chicken feathers.

## A&P

Two young men bargaining with clipper ship captains for tea and coffee on the wharves of New York in the 1860s took a step toward creating the supermarket. Noting the brisk sales of their "cargo-priced" wares, George Huntington Hartford and George Gilman (founders of the A&P, or The Great Atlantic and Pacific Tea Company) launched the first chain of grocery stores in 1869. And in 1917 another innovation crucial to the evolution of the supermarket occurred in Memphis: Clarence Saunders, owner of the Piggly Wiggly store, decided to let his customers serve themselves—no more waiting for a clerk to assemble an order item by item, one customer at a time. The latest twist in the supermarket chain is the presence of warehouse-size stores.

## AARON, HANK

He did what most baseball fans had thought was impossible: he beat Babe Ruth. On April 8, 1974, in front of an excited home crowd in Atlanta, Hank Aaron hit his 715th home run, surpassing the Babe's record of 714. He also made the game

A young customer follows the store's instructions to "Serve Yourself." This 1940 *Saturday Evening Post* cover by artist Albert W. Hampson rings a bell with anyone who has ever shopped with a toddler.

Renowned for the strongest wrists in the game, Aaron waited until the last possible moment before flicking his bat at the oncoming pitch.

look easy. At bat he had a relaxed stroke, and on the bases he ran smoothly and gracefully.

During his 23-year career, Aaron rarely drew attention to himself. Because he was so quiet on and off the field, his name isn't always included when the names of the greatest players are mentioned. Still, by the time he retired from baseball, he had hit 755 home runs, an all-time record, and he had set major league career records for runs batted in and games played. No one since has come close to matching him.

## ABBOTT, GEORGE

Director, actor, writer, producer, and play doctor, George Abbott had the longest (82 years) and most prolific career in the American theater. Involved in more than 120 productions, he won four Tony Awards, a Pulitzer Prize, and the Kennedy Center Lifetime Achievement Award. When asked to explain the famed Abbott touch, which turned his shows to gold, he said, "Keep the action alive." As good as his word, he delivered plays that were funny, fast-paced, and full of life.

A no-nonsense director, he once silenced Carol Channing's "Why?" with "Because I say so!" He launched the careers of such stars as Gene Kelly, Kirk Douglas, Shirley MacLaine, and Carol Burnett, among many others. Tall and lean, he invariably wore a jacket and tie, walked everywhere, and scorned cocktail parties and showbiz phonies. His courtliness prompted Tallulah Bankhead to rumble, "I could never be mad about you, dahling. You're too reliable." Mister Abbott, as he was universally called, liked Mallomar cookies, dancing, and golf. At 75 he had three hit plays running on Broadway; at 76 he dashed off his autobiography; at 96 he married his third wife; at 106 he had his pacemaker replaced; and at 107 he died, shortly after completing a revision of his 1954 hit, *The Pajama Game*.

## ABBOTT AND COSTELLO

As familiar as the knuckleheads down the street, but with better gags, Bud Abbott and Lou Costello became the favorite comedy team of the 1940s. Their first low-budget surprise hit, *Buck Privates*, established the formula for later movies: two average Joes confronting a big, scary world, with only each other to depend on. Tall, fast-talking Abbott acted like a con man but was really a softy at heart; roly-poly Costello got them both in Dutch but always looked like a hero by the end of the movie.

Combining the rough physical style of burlesque with a vocal approach honed in radio, Abbott and Costello's humor was broad but highly polished. Many of their routines, developed with writer John Grant, featured inspired verbal confusion—Abbott: "Didn't you go to school, stupid?" Costello: "Yeah, and I came out the same way." Such twisted cross talk, like their famous "Who's on First" routine, keeps audiences roaring to this day.

Portrait of the dapper George Abbott during the 1955 revival of *The Skin of Our Teeth* (above). Gwen Verdon and Buzz Miller dance in his *Damn Yankees* (right).

### MISTER ABBOTT'S MAJOR PRODUCTIONS

Broadway 1926
Three Men on a Horse 1935
Boy Meets Girl 1935
On Your Toes 1936
Room Service 1937
All That Glitters 1938
The Boys from Syracuse 1938
Too Many Girls 1939
Pal Joey 1940
Best Foot Forward 1941
Sweet Charity 1942
On the Town 1944
Billion Dollar Baby 1945
High Button Shoes 1947
Look Ma, I'm Dancin' 1948
Where's Charley? 1948
Call Me Madam 1950
A Tree Grows in Brooklyn 1951
Me and Juliet 1953
Wonderful Town 1953
The Pajama Game 1954
Damn Yankees 1955
Fiorello! 1959
Once Upon a Mattress 1959
A Funny Thing Happened on the Way to the Forum 1962
Flora, the Red Menace 1965
How Now Dow Jones 1967

In *Buck Privates* (1941) Lou Costello (left) and Bud Abbott portray two hapless soldiers who learn to cope with life in the U.S. Army.

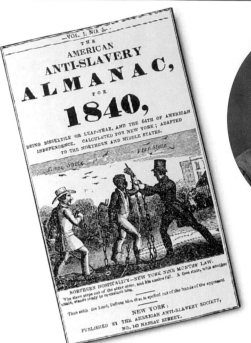

Such publications as the *Almanac* (left) documented the horrors of slavery and stirred public indignation. Frederick Douglass (above) wrote about his life as a slave and later founded an antislavery newspaper, *The North Star.*

## ABOLITIONISTS

The most prominent advocate of the antislavery movement in the North was the fiery William Lloyd Garrison, who in 1831 founded the abolitionist newspaper *The Liberator.* In the first issue Garrison pledged that he would not rest until slavery was ended. "I will not excuse—I will not retreat a single inch—*and I will be heard,*" he wrote.

Perhaps the most eloquent and convincing spokesman for the abolitionist movement was Frederick Douglass, a runaway slave from Maryland. He made impassioned speeches throughout the North against slavery, telling audiences, "I expose slavery...because to expose it is to kill it. Slavery is one of those monsters of darkness to whom the light of truth is death."

## ACADEMY AWARDS

Oscar is 13½ inches tall, weighs about eight pounds, and is gold-plated and numbered. A naked knight holding a sword, he stands on a reel of film whose spokes represent the five original branches of the Academy of Motion Picture Arts and Sciences: actors, directors, writers, technicians, producers. Founded in 1927 by Louis B. Mayer to mediate labor disputes, improve the industry's image, and hold annual banquets, the academy incidentally formed an awards committee. At a small dinner the silent film *Wings* inaugurated the Best Picture category. Since 1937 the academy's other activities have been overshadowed by its popular annual awards. In 1953 the ceremony was nationally televised for the first time; it is now carried to the world by satellite.

The Big Night has been a showcase for political and fashion statements, emotional outbursts, and, in 1974, a streaker. On occasion, voting has reflected internal politics: the 1941 *Citizen Kane,* an innovative film, lost because its creator, Orson Welles, had made enemies in the industry. A Best Picture award can add millions to a movie's gross, but for some winners, such as Louise Fletcher (Nurse Ratched in *One Flew Over the Cuckoo's Nest*), it is not a milestone on the road to stardom. As Johnny Weissmuller, famed as Tarzan but a perennial loser, remarked, "Me sit in tree for 17 years. Me watch 'em come and go."

## WINNING FACTS

**1934:** *It Happened One Night* is the first picture to win the top five awards: Best Picture, Best Actor (Clark Gable), Best Actress (Claudette Colbert), Best Director (Frank Capra), and Best Screenplay.

**1934:** At age six, Shirley Temple wins a special Academy Award.

**1939:** *Gone With the Wind* wins Best Picture, beating *The Wizard of Oz.* Hattie McDaniel is the first African-American to win an Oscar, for her role as Mammy.

**1959:** *Ben-Hur* wins the most Oscars—11.

**1973:** 10-year-old Tatum O'Neal is the youngest performer to win an Oscar for a supporting role (*Paper Moon*).

**1976:** Peter Finch is the first actor to win posthumously (*Network*).

**1979:** George C. Scott refuses to accept his award (*Patton*).

**1986:** After seven nominations, Paul Newman wins his first Best Actor award (*The Color of Money*).

Comic Billy Crystal, host of the 1990 Academy Awards show, hams it up with Oscar.

## ACRONYMS

What a *snafu*! (Situation Normal: All Fouled Up!) Why say five words when one will do? No reason at all, at least in America. An acronym is a word created by stringing together initial letters. For example, *laser* is short for Light Amplification by Stimulated Emission of Radiation. (Note, however, that initials that are pronounced letter by letter, such as VIP—Very Important Person—don't really qualify as acronyms.)

Acronyms began to take hold in America during World War II with AWOL (Absent Without Leave), WAAC

(Women's Army Auxiliary Corps), and WAVES (Women Appointed for Voluntary Emergency Services). Sometimes groups are named by working backward—first the catchy acronym, then the words to match (VISTA, or Volunteers In Service To America). Will all this lead to a new Quick-Speak language? Perhaps. Meanwhile, HAND (Have A Nice Day)!

## ADAMS, JOHN AND ABIGAIL

"Fly to the Woods with our children!" John Adams wrote to his wife as the battles of the Revolutionary War edged closer to the family's farm. Instead, Abigail stayed put, lodging homeless refugees who had fled British-occupied Boston. Pledged to public service regardless of the outcome, the Adamses would raise their children to do the same.

When John Adams worked at the Continental Congress in Philadelphia, Abigail wrote to urge him and his fellow lawmakers to end slavery, educate children, and tax whiskey. An early feminist, she even pressed for laws upholding women's rights. John was astonished ("I cannot but laugh ... you are so saucy"), but he was unmoved by her pleas.

After his stint in the U.S. Congress, he served as a diplomat in France, Holland, and Great Britain. Loneliness tore at Abigail while John spent all those years away from home. The two were happily reunited in 1788, when he was elected vice-president under Washington. After eight years, he became America's second president (and first one-term president).

For the next three generations, many descendants of John and Abigail felt a responsibility to follow in their footsteps. Their son, John Quincy Adams, also became a diplomat and later our sixth president. Grandson Charles Francis Adams fought to abolish slavery and persuaded Britain to remain neutral during the Civil War. Great-grandson Henry Adams became an eminent historian. "They were," wrote historian Daniel J. Boorstin, "a rare and spectacular example of the continuity of talents in a single family."

## ADDAMS, CHARLES

Cartoonist Charles Addams delighted America with his good-natured ghoulishness and the humor he injected into everyday life. In his cartoons a young witch asks her mother, "Can I have the broom tonight?" and Prince Charming complains to a marriage counselor, "We're not living happily ever after."

Addams's fiends and demons sprang from the glossy pages of *The New Yorker*, where his work was first published in 1932 and where he worked until his death in 1988. His most popular cartoons featured a creepy bunch that became known as the Addams Family. Readers saw the Addams children prepare for Santa's visit by lighting a roaring fire in the fireplace, and the whole family greet holiday carolers with a vat of boiling oil. This outlandish family was so well liked that it starred in its own television show in the 1960s and later in two movies.

Charles Addams's world: the Addams family's butler, Lurch, carries a bound and gagged Pugsley out to meet his school bus (top); on a *New Yorker* cover, a mountain climber is surprised to find Easter eggs in a nest (center); a portrait of the artist with the family and friends (bottom).

Powered by a long-lasting battery, Eveready's tireless Energizer Bunny marches in and out of commercials as the announcer boasts, "Still going... and going..."

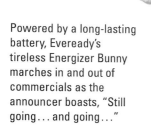

An airborne model demonstrates Wings, a fragrance for men by Giorgio Beverly Hills. The magazine insert also offers a sniff sample and promises to "set your spirit free."

Little Miss Coppertone of 1953 (left) shows a deep tan once believed to be healthy. By 1994 (right) she is careful to wear a lot of Coppertone sunscreen, a T-shirt, and a hat.

## ADVERTISING

Whether it's in print or on television, radio, or billboards, advertising profoundly influences our lives. The ads we see, hear, and smell (in the case of open-and-sniff perfume inserts in magazines) affect how we feel and what we think about a wide range of products. Companies pay a lot of money (up to $1 million for a 30-second Super Bowl spot) to persuade us that their products are the best.

Advertising has a long history in North America. As early as the 1600s, ads were used to attract English settlers to the Colonies. According to historian Daniel Boorstin, these brochures contained "hopeful overstatements, half-truths, and downright lies...." Nonetheless, the sales campaign was effective; people came. In the 1700s famous figures were involved in the advertising business, among them Benjamin Franklin, who ran ads in his publications, and Paul Revere, who advertised his handmade false teeth. But it wasn't until the late 1800s, with the boom in mass-circulation magazines, that advertising became the powerful force it is today. Television arrived in the 1940s and created a new, action-packed advertising medium. Creative writers at advertising agencies have dreamed up amazing scenarios, such as a tornadolike cleanser whirling through a kitchen (The White Tornado) and beer bottles playing football (The Bud Bowl).

Creating a good ad isn't as easy as it might seem. One key is to find the right spokesperson. An effective approach is to have the company president speak. In the 1980s Chrysler's Lee Iacocca urged viewers, "If you can find a better car, buy it." Another is to hire an athlete, such as sure-handed quarterback Dan Marino (Isotoner gloves) and superstar Michael Jordan (McDonalds, Gatorade, and Nike). Still another option is to create unforgettable characters, such as the dancing California raisins, the Speedy Alka-Seltzer fellow, or an animated parrot (Gillette).

A memorable slogan is helpful as well: "I can't believe I ate the *whole* thing"; "Where's the beef?"; "You deserve a break today"; "It's finger-lickin' good"; "I shoulda had a V8"; "Good to the last drop"; "Get a piece of the rock"; "Just do it"; "See the USA in your Chevrolet"; "We try harder"; "When it absolutely, positively has to be there overnight."

## AEROBICS

Before 1968 Americans' idea of exercise was doing push-ups and pumping iron. But Dr. Kenneth H. Cooper changed all that when he wrote his revolutionary book *Aerobics.* He touted the benefits of workouts that raise the heart rate and improve cardiovascular fitness—the cornerstone of a healthy body. The fitness craze was born.

Aerobics brought people to health clubs in droves, spawning the spandex revolution. Jane Fonda, among the gurus who championed the cause, challenged her followers to "go for the burn!" In the 1990s people increasingly brought fitness into their own homes, exercising to videotapes that promised "abs of steel" and other taut body parts.

Thin thighs aside, the healthful aim of aerobics is to raise the pulse to within a certain "target zone" in order to increase the body's intake of oxygen and boost blood circulation. To calculate your target zone, subtract your age from the number 220. Multiply the resulting figure by both 70 percent and 85 percent. Your pulse rate after exercising should fall between these two numbers. Check with a doctor before starting a program, especially if you are sedentary, over 35, or have any physical infirmity, such as shortness of breath.

## AIR CONDITIONERS

The air conditioner may be one of the most welcome appliances in the world, but it was invented almost by accident. In 1902 a young engineer named Willis Carrier was trying to figure out a way to lower the humidity in a Brooklyn printing plant. To keep the presses from stalling on humid days, he devised a machine that reduced humidity by cooling the air. Recognizing his invention's potential, Carrier was soon in business for himself. Movie theaters were among the first businesses to install air conditioners. The idea was to boost attendance in summer by offering a cool refuge to moviegoers. The appeal was strong—it was often more of a draw than the film itself.

When air conditioners became more affordable, in the '50s, the stifling heat of the South could at last be overcome. Businesses rushed down there to take advantage of the lower operating costs and lower taxes in Southern states, and workers soon followed. So great was the shift in population that the 1970 census was dubbed "the air conditioned census" by *The New York Times*.

## AIR FRESHENERS

Airwick, the first deodorant designed for the home, was tested in the late 1930s at the Lion House of the Bronx Zoo. Proved strong enough to tame the air there, Airwick was deemed by its inventor a "valuable contribution to public welfare," and flowery fragrances began to emanate from abodes everywhere.

Our enthusiasm for perfumed sprays and shrinking solids actually mirrors centuries of efforts to sweeten the air around us. Alexander the Great directed his servants to douse his marble floors with perfume. Women in the 1600s used a bellows to blow powdered flowers, herbs, and spices around a room. And Victorian homes featured wall-mounted posy holders. Today we can tuck away any number of devices that stick on, clip on, pop up, and even plug in for that balmy illusion of piney glades, country gardens, vanilla vines, and the sweet life.

To get the most from aerobics, move your arms and legs vigorously. And if you are in tip-top shape, you may strap light weights to your wrists and ankles.

### A SAMPLING OF VIDEO TITLES

Abs of Steel 2000
Cherfitness: A New Attitude
Dance! Workout with Barbie
Dancing Grannies
David Carradine's Kung Fu
Idrea Says, The Larger
Woman's Workout
Sweatin' to Country
Sweatin' to the Oldies 1 & 2
Thighs of Steel

The air-cooled atmosphere of this movie theater got star billing in 1935 because the public would buy a ticket just to spend an afternoon or evening out of the heat.

The chapel is all that remains of the Alamo, in the heart of downtown San Antonio. The former mission is considered the cradle of Texas liberty.

Against impossible odds, the defenders of the Alamo held out over 13 days of siege. N. C. Wyeth painted his vision of their last stand.

A total of 36 prisoners have attempted to escape from Alcatraz. Most were quickly recaptured; the others are presumed drowned.

## ALAMO

It was the most celebrated battle of our nation's youth—a lost cause whose story never grows old. The plot: a band of frontiersmen, hopelessly outnumbered, fights to the last man against a vast encircling army and is propelled into immortality by the battle waged at a crumbling Spanish mission.

Of course, if William Travis, the local army commander at San Antonio, had listened to Sam Houston, chief of the fledgling Texas Army, and had fled the Alamo, then he, Davy Crockett, Jim Bowie, and the other heroes of the March 6, 1836, encounter might have lived to see Texas win its independence. But Travis was certain that San Antonio was the key to Texas. As Mexican dictator Antonio López de Santa Anna advanced, Travis disobeyed Houston and stood fast, promising, "I shall never surrender or retreat." Some 185 defenders met an attacking force of 1,500. More than 600 Mexicans died. One victor reported that when Santa Anna saw the body of Davy Crockett surrounded by Mexican dead, he ran his sword through the Tennesseean.

The defenders' heroism was not entirely for naught. It bought time for Houston to prepare his troops, and less than two months later he annihilated Santa Anna's army at San Jacinto with the famous battle cry "Remember the Alamo!"

## ALCATRAZ

Located on a rocky outcrop in the middle of San Francisco Bay, Alcatraz was the site of a lighthouse and a military stockade long before it became a penitentiary in 1934. As a prison, its security was so tight that the first inmates arrived in San Francisco aboard a specially designed armored train.

Life was hard for the inmates of Alcatraz. They were allowed to converse only at meals and during recreation, and they received only two eight-minute breaks from their labor each day. They lived under constant surveillance, and even minor infractions brought long stays in solitary confinement.

Alcatraz proved to be the perfect place to stash the nation's worst offenders. Celebrity inmates, such as Al Capone, focused public attention on the institution—publicity that, the government hoped, might deter renegades in other prisons from disruptive behavior, for which they could be sent to "The Rock." Icy currents made escape virtually impossible. Alcatraz was closed as a prison in 1963 after only 29 years. It was reopened for visitors in 1973.

## ALCOHOLICS ANONYMOUS

"Keep it simple" were the dying words of Alcoholics Anonymous co-founder Dr. Bob Smith to Bill Wilson in 1950, 15 years after they started AA. True to Smith's wishes, AA has stuck to its simple formula. Part of its success comes from knowing what not to do: the organization does not set up large bureaucratic offices or raise funds, but it does offer support meetings at which members can turn to one another for help and advice. Smith and Wilson, both recovered alcoholics, realized that the best way for alcoholics to stay sober was to talk with other people who understood their problems. AA's 12-step approach, a kind of road map to spiritual recovery, has proved so successful that it has been adopted by other recovery programs, such as Gamblers Anonymous.

## ALGER, HORATIO JR.

America loves a good rags-to-riches tale, and no one penned more of them than Horatio Alger, Jr. To please his father he became a Unitarian minister, but in 1866 he left his Brewster, Massachusetts, congregation and moved to New York to pursue his real dream: writing.

Alger's volunteer work at the Newsboys' Lodging House for orphans and runaways became his ticket to success when he began patterning his stories on the lives—highly sentimentalized—of the boys he met there. Series with such titles as *Ragged Dick*, *Luck and Pluck*, and *Tattered Tom* convinced an entire generation of boys that hard work and virtue lead to wealth and honor. In fact, Alger wrote so many novels on this theme—more than 100 in all—that a "Horatio Alger story" became synonymous with any triumph over humble beginnings. Now deemed trite and poorly written, these novels nevertheless made Alger one of the best-selling authors of all time.

## ALGONQUIN ROUND TABLE

"I saw the play under unfortunate circumstances," remarked George S. Kaufman. "The curtain was up." Kaufman, author of the hit play *The Man Who Came to Dinner*, was a member of the Round Table, a group of writers and theater people who for 12 years met for lunch at the Algonquin Hotel in Manhattan. Sometimes called the Vicious Circle, it began by chance in 1919, when *New York Times* drama columnist Alexander Woollcott (described by foes as "a butterfly in heat"), impressed by the Algonquin's cuisine, urged his friends to join him there. The group grew larger, and the lunches became a daily ritual. The hotel manager, recognizing the group's enormous publicity value, reserved a prominent table for its exclusive use.

Among those who networked at the Algonquin were critic Dorothy Parker (who once dismissed a book as "in four volumes, suitable for throwing") and writers F. P. Adams, Robert Benchley, Edna Ferber, Robert Sherwood, and Ring Lardner. Witty and ambitious, the Round Table reflected well on its members. Although the group disbanded in the early 1930s, their bons mots are legendary. Playwright Charles MacArthur and his wife, actress Helen Hayes, asked Woollcott to be their baby's godfather. At the christening Woollcott was heard to sigh, "Always a godfather, never a god!"

Alger wrote quickly, sometimes completing a book in a matter of weeks. Among his works was a biography of Abraham Lincoln, but his dream was to write a serious adult novel.

Members of the Algonquin Round Table included, clockwise from bottom left, Dorothy Parker, Robert Benchley, Alexander Woollcott, Heywood Broun, Marc Connelly, F. P. Adams, Edna Ferber, George S. Kaufman, and Robert Sherwood. Seated at the smaller table are Alfred Lunt and Lynn Fontanne, with Frank Crowninshield standing nearby.

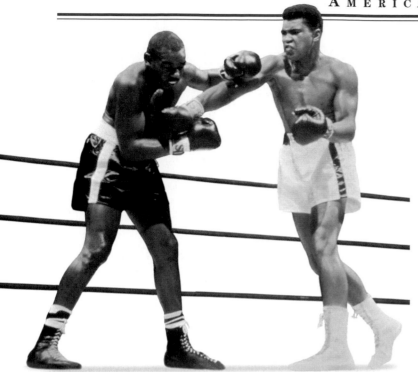

Ali (above right), fighting Doug Jones in 1963, was noted not only for his power and agility but for saying he was "the best-looking, the fastest, the cleverest...." He won this championship belt (right) for beating George Foreman in 1974.

Ethan Allen, aided by Benedict Arnold, stormed Fort Ticonderoga at dawn. The Continental Congress, far from pleased, ordered an inventory taken so that all the guns and stores could be returned to the British.

## ALI, MUHAMMAD

The most controversial boxer in American history, Muhammad Ali often proclaimed, "I am the greatest," and recited poems that mocked his opponents. Born Cassius Marcellus Clay, he was 17 when he won the national Golden Gloves championship in 1959. He went on to join the 1960 Olympic team in Rome, winning the gold and turning pro the same year. In 1964 Clay took the championship from Sonny Liston after promising to "float like a butterfly, sting like a bee." Soon afterward, Clay joined the Nation of Islam and changed his name to Muhammad Ali.

Ali was stripped of his title in 1967 when he refused to be inducted into the army. He returned to the ring in 1970 and won back the title by beating George Foreman in 1974. In 1978 he lost to Leon Spinks in a major upset but beat him later that year, dancing the famous "Ali shuffle" in the last round. In 1996, the ailing sports figure surprised and delighted the world when he lit the Olympic flame in Atlanta.

## ALL-AMERICA

All-America teams have been a favorite of football fans for more than 100 years, yet they've never played a single game. That's because they are "dream teams," lists compiled annually by sports writers and former coaches of the year's finest college athletes. The first All-America team was devised in 1889 by Walter Camp and Caspar Whitney, and published in Whitney's paper, the *Week's Sport*. The list proved so popular that the idea spread to other newspapers and to other sports.

The expression *all-American* has even become a part of everyday speech and refers to someone who epitomizes basic American virtues. The idealistic young hero of *Jack Armstrong, the All-American Boy*, a radio program of the 1930s and '40s, was just such a character.

## ALLEN, ETHAN

On May 10, 1775, Ethan Allen and his Green Mountain Boys captured Fort Ticonderoga from some 45 sleeping British soldiers. Their mission: to seize the cannons and use them to drive the British from Boston. Although this event is recorded as an early victory of the Revolutionary War, it was not appreciated at the time by the Continental Congress, which had not authorized the attack. Allen had organized the Green Mountain Boys five years earlier to protect his "homeland," now Vermont. Britain had decreed that the disputed land belonged to New York. Allen sought to evict the New Yorkers, prompting New York's governor to put a price on his head.

After attacking Fort Ticonderoga, Allen botched an unauthorized attack on Canada and became a British prisoner. Upon his release, he petitioned the Continental Congress to make Vermont a state. When his request was denied, he conspired with Britain to make Vermont a part of Canada, a plot so confused that he was never tried for treason.

## ALLEN, WOODY

"When we played softball, I'd steal second, then feel guilty and go back." So said Woody Allen in the early 1960s while making his name as a stand-up comedian. He was already known as a brilliant comedy writer for *Your Show of Shows* and the *Garry Moore Show*. But he was petrified of performing. On some nights he literally had to be pushed onstage. Still, audiences loved the comic's sheepish demeanor. "My parents sent me to interfaith camp one summer," he joked. "That meant I got beat up by kids of all faiths."

Success for Allen meant his exit from the stand-up stage and his emergence in Hollywood. In 1969 he wrote and directed *Take the Money and Run*, in which he played a bumbling burglar. Originally released in only one theater, it was launched into the limelight by a smash review in *The New York Times*. *Bananas* and *Sleeper*, screwball comedies that remain favorites among fans, followed. Ultimately Allen became known for such urban romantic comedies as *Annie Hall*, which won four Academy Awards.

## ALUMINUM FOIL

If it weren't for cigarettes, we might not have aluminum foil. Wraps made of lead and tin were first used by R. R. Reynolds to protect cigarettes from moisture. After Reynolds's nephew, Richard, started the U.S. Foil Company, he noticed that the price of a new metal called aluminum was beginning to drop. He gave it a try, creating the first aluminum wrap.

During World War II the young Reynolds turned to the mass production of aluminum for aircraft. After the war, rather than shut down his sprawling new plants, he searched for consumer uses for this remarkably lightweight metal. One company executive recalled a Thanksgiving day when his wife was unable to find a roasting pan for the turkey. He improvised a pan from some commercial foil samples, and the idea for aluminum foil as we know it was born.

## AMERICA

By rights, the New World should have been named for Christopher Columbus or, perhaps, Lief Erikson. Instead it was named for Amerigo Vespucci, a Florentine navigator who journeyed west a few years after Columbus and returned to amaze all of Europe with his tales.

Columbus thought he had found a route to Japan, but Vespucci realized otherwise. He wrote, "These regions we may rightly call Mundus Novus, a new world, because our ancestors had no knowledge of them.... I have found a continent more densely peopled and abounding in animals than our Europe, Asia, or Africa." His colorful letters satisfied the public's thirst for stories of the fabled new lands. And because Vespucci was widely believed to have crossed the ocean before Columbus did, there was little challenge when the New World was named for him.

Woody Allen's *Annie Hall* mirrored a real-life romance between Allen and Diane Keaton. His humorous brand of romantic skepticism also fueled a syndicated newspaper cartoon.

### MAJOR FILMS OF WOODY ALLEN

Take the Money and Run 1969
Bananas 1971
Play It Again, Sam 1972
Sleeper 1973
Love and Death 1975
Annie Hall 1977
Interiors 1978
Manhattan 1979
Stardust Memories 1980
Zelig 1983
Broadway Danny Rose 1984
The Purple Rose of Cairo 1985
Hannah and Her Sisters 1986
Radio Days 1987
September 1987
Crimes and Misdemeanors 1989
Alice 1990
Shadows and Fog 1992
Husbands and Wives 1992
Manhattan Murder Mystery 1993
Bullets Over Broadway 1995

Aluminum foil, advertised as the wrap with "1001 kitchen miracles in every roll," proved to have myriad uses. Here, a foil-wrapped mummy makes the Halloween scene.

A quarter century before MTV, *American Bandstand* spotlighted the latest rock and roll hits as teens danced the jitterbug, the pony, and the stroll. Early on, host Dick Clark admitted, "I don't understand this music."

## AMERICAN BANDSTAND

In the late 1950s and early '60s, teenagers across America raced home from school to watch *American Bandstand*, a show about, by, and for them. It featured real-life teens from Philadelphia who strolled, jitterbugged, and twisted to popular songs. Every weekday afternoon and, later, on Saturday, the show's young audience learned to dance by imitating the smooth moves of their favorite "stars," taking note of who was dancing with whom (a change in steady partners was a sure sign that a certain romance was on the rocks). Not only did the on-screen teens have the most extraordinary after-school jobs, but many even received fan mail.

*American Bandstand* conferred instant stardom on singers who had been virtually unknown before they appeared on the program. Host Dick Clark, who remained youthful-looking during his 30 years on the show, greeted everyone who was going to be anyone. In turn, Chubby Checker, Frankie Avalon, Fabian, Bobby Rydell, Simon and Garfunkel, and even Prince (among many others) lip-synched the songs they wanted to promote.

## AMERICAN DREAM

People everywhere have hopes, but America is the only nation to claim its own collective dream. Politicians have invoked the American Dream ever since historian James Truslow Adams first coined the phrase in 1931. In his best-selling book, *The Epic of America*, he described the dream as the average American's "Star in the West which led him on...in search of a home where toil would reap a sure reward, and no dead hands of custom or exaction would push him back into 'his place.'" The phrase caught on like wildfire and endures still, though its meaning is often vague. To some the "sure reward" is a luxury car. To others it's a college degree, a steady job that pays the bills, or a house in the suburbs and a family of four à la Ozzie and Harriet. But the dream is above all America's own brand of optimism, which was brought over by the first settlers and which presumes no limits to what anyone can have or achieve.

## AMERICAN GOTHIC

"American Gothic" is said to be more widely recognized than the "Mona Lisa." This painting, which depicts not a married couple but a farmer and his daughter, is so familiar that it has inspired countless spoofs.

When Grant Wood entered "American Gothic" in a contest at the Art Institute in Chicago in 1930, it not only won a $300 prize but ended up hanging in the museum. The painting was popular from the start, although its fame did cause unexpected trouble. Some of Wood's neighbors in Cedar Rapids, Iowa, thought the image of the sour-faced woman was intended to make fun of them. They were mollified only when Wood revealed that the model had been his own sister, Nan. The farmer pictured with her was Wood's dentist.

Wood painted at a time when many of his contemporaries were enamored of impressionist art from Paris. In his early days he himself had dabbled with a more impressionis-

tic style but ultimately chose to buck the trend. He looked to the fertile fields of Iowa for inspiration, painting ordinary folks and celebrating rural life. Many art critics of the day dismissed his work, but average Americans loved it. Wood's popularity endures to this day, and "American Gothic" remains one of the best-known paintings in American art.

## AMERICAN GRAFFITI

Coming of age is seldom easy, as George Lucas affirmed in his movie classic *American Graffiti*, a poignant autobiographical look at growing up in small-town America in the early 1960s. Filmed in 28 nights on a budget of $700,000, it rode into 1973 on a wave of nostalgia, with a rock and roll soundtrack that featured Bill Haley and the Comets and a howling cameo by Wolfman Jack. After the Broadway success of *Grease*, it was the first of many films to look back on simpler times.

The movie follows four high school friends on the brink of adulthood as they spend their last night together joyriding and girl chasing. Hanging over them is the knowledge that their once-carefree lives are about to change forever. As a paean to pop culture in a long-gone age of innocence, *American Graffiti* was a surprise success, earning five Oscar nominations and launching the careers of George Lucas, Richard Dreyfuss, and Ron Howard. It also inspired the television series *Happy Days*, in which Howard starred.

## AMERICA'S CUP

In 1851 the schooner yacht *America* sailed all the way across the Atlantic Ocean from New York to challenge a group of English yachtsmen who thought that they had the world's fastest boats. They were stunned when *America* handily beat 17 British boats to win the trophy: an ornate silver ewer that became known as the America's Cup.

For about a century and a half, yachtsmen from all over the world have competed for the cup in what is considered to be the longest-running international sporting event. It is held approximately every three years. Only twice has the trophy left the United States: in 1983, when Australia ended the United States' 132-year winning streak, and again in 1995, the year of New Zealand's first victory.

America's Cup racing is not for those with skinny wallets. In 1995 the average cost to a syndicate campaigning for the cup was reckoned to be about $30 million. Nor is it a sport for the fainthearted. Using the newest materials and technology, yacht designers make the boats as light and fast as allowed by the rules; sailors push the boats to the limits. The 75-foot yacht *One Australia*, racing in rough water off San Diego in March 1995, suddenly broke up and, within two and a half minutes, sank. (All 17 crew members survived to race again.) It was the first time in 144 years that an America's Cup yacht had sunk on the racecourse—a stern reminder that however tough the competition may be, the sea can be tougher still.

Many of the scenes in *American Graffiti* take place in a car. Director George Lucas was turned down by every major studio before Universal agreed to back the film. It was Lucas's first hit.

Today's yachts are built with space-age technology and weigh a fraction of the *America's* 170 tons. The cup was crafted in 1848 by a silversmith of the British court.

Amish clothing resembles European peasant garb. These simple outfits are fastened with hooks and eyes rather than buttons.

Marian Anderson said of her long struggle, "I had become, whether I liked it or not, a symbol representing my people."

In the 1938 film *Love Finds Andy Hardy*, Mickey Rooney shared a malted with co-star Judy Garland. She would return for two more Andy Hardy films.

## AMISH

Part of the larger community of Mennonites, also known as the Pennsylvania Dutch, the Amish migrated from Switzerland to Pennsylvania beginning in the 18th century to escape religious persecution. Called the Plain People, they live almost completely apart from the modern world. Farming is the lifeblood of their community. They cook their food on gas stoves, and they travel by horse-drawn buggy. Even the buggy's design is prescribed by church law.

The more conservative Amish largely ignore American civil life. On the grounds of religious freedom, they decline to vote, serve in the military, or send their children to school beyond the eighth grade. They even fought for, and won, exclusion from the Social Security program. The rare individual who strays outside the fold is subject to shunning, a severe form of discipline that denies the person any social contact with the community, even with his or her spouse.

## ANDERSON, MARIAN

After hearing her sing in 1935, conductor Arturo Toscanini told Marian Anderson, "A voice like yours is heard once in a hundred years." Anderson, one of the finest opera singers of her time, found her first great success playing before European audiences. When she returned to America, racial prejudices still barred her path, but she confronted them with her own quiet dignity. In 1939 she was refused a booking at Constitution Hall in Washington, D.C., by the owners of the hall, the Daughters of the American Revolution. During the protests that followed, Anderson received approval to perform an outdoor concert in front of the Lincoln Memorial. More than 75,000 people attended, and Anderson was overcome by their enthusiastic response.

Anderson's career was marked by another historic moment when, in 1955, she became the first black performer to sing at New York's Metropolitan Opera. Music lovers from across the country traveled to be there for that memorable occasion. Anderson was honored with a standing ovation before she sang a single note.

## ANDY HARDY

As played by Mickey Rooney, Andy Hardy was the happy-go-lucky teenage son of a small-town judge in a popular series of MGM movies. The 16 Hardy films became one of the most successful series ever produced by Hollywood.

Rooney's exuberant portrayal of Andy Hardy was the key to the series's appeal. A taller actor was almost chosen by the studio, but the producer, Carey Wilson, decided that a shorter boy would be funnier. Rooney's irrepressible energy and boy-next-door looks were a perfect combination. In 1938 he was awarded an Oscar for "bringing to the screen the spirit and personification of youth." In 1942 the series itself won an Oscar for "representing the American way of life."

## ANIMAL CRACKERS

In 1902 the "Greatest Show on Earth" went edible. The first boxes of Barnum's Animals, printed with a circus-cage motif and housing a menagerie of animal-shaped cookies, were sold at Christmastime by the National Biscuit Company. Each box had a string for hanging it on the tree. These colorful five-cent cartons fast became a year-round favorite. Children delighted in taking a bite out of 17 different beasts, from lions and camels to hippos and kangaroos. (Some of the original animals, such as the dog, have been replaced.) So popular were these cookies that they inspired the title of the 1930 Marx Brothers comedy, *Animal Crackers*. Five years later, Shirley Temple sang their praises in the movie *Curly Top*.

The Animal Crackers box was changed temporarily in 1995 to raise awareness of endangered animals. New cookies were shaped as Komodo dragons and giant pandas.

## ANNAPOLIS

Prior to the opening of the U.S. Naval Academy in 1845, formal training of the navy's midshipmen was a haphazard affair. Cadets had been trained at sea, and only when other shipboard duties were finished. The first class at Annapolis, a former army post, was made up of 50 men. Classes concentrated on engineering, to meet the demands of running the newly introduced steamships. Today, in coed courses ranging from engineering to English, more than 4,000 students are prepared for assignments on land and sea.

Candidates for Annapolis must be appointed by members of Congress or the executive branch or by certain other officials; vacancies are also reserved for navy and marine corps members and children of Medal of Honor recipients. Famous graduates include former president Jimmy Carter, billionaire H. Ross Perot, and football star Roger Staubach.

## ANT FARMS

Other 1950s fads have come and gone, but the ant farm continues to fascinate. A mail-order merchant named Milton Levine, known as Uncle Milton, first created this nature toy in 1956, after going on a picnic reminded him of the simple joy of watching ants dig tunnels in a dirt-filled Mason jar. Millions of ant farms later, Levine's design—two transparent walls containing a green plastic farmscape and plenty of sand—is still selling. The ants themselves are not enclosed. Customers have to send in a certificate that comes with the ant farm; they are then mailed a colony of red harvesters (one of the few species that work during the daytime).

Marketed as a "living TV screen," the farm is a window on the busy life of an ant. Observers can watch soldiers, laborers, nurses, and pallbearers carry out their tasks as bridges are built, tunnels are dug, and food is stored. Feeding the insects is easy enough, as one cornflake every few days will do nicely. After the colony has expired, the farm owner can ask Uncle Milton for more ants or get some the old-fashioned way—by foraging in the backyard.

Hats aweigh! The tradition of tossing their caps skyward helps launch new graduates into their navy or marine corps commissions. The caps are then kept as souvenirs by guests at the ceremony.

One of the great American nature toys, Uncle Milton's ant farm has changed remarkably little since it was introduced in 1956.

Collectibles don't have to be hundreds of years old to be valuable. Whether buying cameos or coon-skin caps, we search out the things that are important to us.

The Apollo was the place the Beatles most wanted to visit when they made their first trip to New York. For decades this theater has been a mecca for fans of jazz and r&b.

Computers were complicated, room-size machines tended by white-coated technicians before Apple introduced its easy-to-use models.

## ANTIQUE HUNTING

No matter how strange an old machine, a gizmo, or a product may be, there are at least a few Americans scouring city cellars and country barns for more of them. Casual shoppers show up at yard sales at the time specified on the flyer. Wily pros show up an hour early so they can bargain for the lawn jockey, the fringed flapper gown, the milk-glass goblet, or the Tiffany lamp before the competition arrives.

Every year a few people are taken in by washstands or bureaus artificially aged with shotgun-added "wormholes." But for every unhappy buyer, there are hundreds who find a milk can that would make a perfect plant stand, or a green copper weathervane that would add just the right touch of quaintness to a renovated house. And every so often someone finds a valuable original Stickley Mission oak bench hiding under a few coats of paint or a document signed by George Washington stuffed behind a picture in an old frame.

## APOLLO THEATRE

This Harlem landmark on West 125th Street in New York City has been a major showcase for top black entertainers since the 1930s. Built in 1913, it began as a burlesque house that didn't allow blacks in the audience. By the 1920s it was offering shows that usually included jazz. In 1932 it became a black vaudeville house.

It wasn't until renovations were made in the mid-1930s that the Apollo became a world-renowned venue for jazz musicians. "Lady Day" (Billie Holiday) was a sensation when she opened with Count Basie's orchestra in 1937. Duke Ellington, the elegant dancing Nicholas Brothers, and pianist Nat "King" Cole also held court there. In later years rhythm and blues, gospel, and soul prevailed; among the popular headliners were James Brown, Aretha Franklin, and Smokey Robinson and the Miracles. Recently the Apollo has been operating as a nonprofit performance center. Its famous Wednesday night amateur show continues its tradition of discovering future stars and booing the unready offstage.

## APPLE COMPUTER

In 1975 two young college dropouts started the personal-computer revolution. Working out of a garage, Steven Jobs, a video game designer, and Stephen Wozniak, a self-taught electronics wizard, built a small tabletop machine that they called the Apple Computer.

The next year they introduced the handmade Apple I and sold 600 of them, mostly to hobbyists. In 1977 they came out with Apple II, a typewriter-size machine that led the industry for five years. Those who were trained on old-fashioned, room-size computers simply could not take Apple seriously. For some, it seemed too easy to use. But that didn't stop Jobs and Wozniak from coming out with the Macintosh in 1984. Because this radically different computer came with a hand control called a mouse, users didn't have to type commands. It took only hours, rather than weeks, to learn how to use the Mac. Computers of the future will certainly become even smaller and more portable. To the next generation, even today's machines may look enormous.

## APPLE PIE

It's said that nothing is as American as apple pie. That phrase may have gotten its start in colonial New England, where apples could be found at every meal. Our ancestors made them into fritters, puddings, tarts, and all manner of pies. They especially enjoyed apple pie with a slice of cheese for breakfast. A saying of the time was "Apple pie without the cheese is like a kiss without the squeeze."

Today apple pies are baked with raisins, dates, nuts, or cranberries. For some, the ultimate apple pie has a lattice crust, just like Mom used to make; for others, no pie is complete unless it is served à la mode.

Tart apples, such as Granny Smith, Macoun, and Baldwin, make the best pies. Other varieties, such as Red Delicious and McIntosh, don't do as well, because they tend to become mushy when cooked.

## APPLESEED, JOHNNY

Johnny Appleseed was a legendary, if eccentric, folk hero almost from the time he planted his first apple seed. Often dressed in an old coffee sack, with a tin pan for a hat (in which he also cooked), Appleseed (whose real name was John Chapman) spread apple seeds—and the word of Swedish mystic Emanuel Swedenborg—across the American frontier from 1803 until his death in 1847. Indians regarded him as a medicine man. Settlers welcomed him for his gentle ways and respected his unselfish love of nature. Since it's impossible to know just how far his planting extended, Americans enjoy thinking that just about any apple tree around today might be descended from a seed sown by Johnny Appleseed.

A genuinely kind man, Johnny Appleseed grew trees from seeds rather than by grafting because he believed it was cruel to cut a tree.

## ARCHIE BUNKER

Archie Bunker was the inspired creation of character actor Carroll O'Connor and producer Norman Lear. A bigoted 50-year-old loading-dock foreman, he was the central character of *All in the Family*, which originated on CBS in 1971. Feisty, outspoken, and easily outraged, Archie turned situation comedy on its ear. Goaded by his liberal son-in-law, Mike (Rob Reiner), whom he called meathead, Bunker took on the political issues of the day, from Watergate to women's liberation. Even Archie's wife, Edith (Jean Stapleton), wasn't exempt from his scorn. "I'm talkin' English... you're listenin' in dingbat," he would complain. Fed up with an argument, he would shout, "Stifle yourself!" or "It's just a pigment of your imagination!" Viewers understood that beneath the bluster was an old-fashioned man trying to cope with a rapidly changing world. The show was one of the most popular in television history and spawned several spin-offs, including *The Jeffersons*, *Maude*, and *Good Times*.

"We lost a daughter, Edith, but we gained a meathead." Liberal son-in-law Mike kept Archie Bunker's home life in an uproar.

The press loved to joke about Marcel Duchamp's *Nude Descending a Staircase*, calling it "a lot of disused golf clubs" and "an explosion in a shingle factory." The cartoon below is from a *New York World* article entitled "Nobody Who Has Been Drinking Is Let In to See This Show."

Hello, Satchmo! An American jazz legend, Louis Armstrong traveled the world over, spreading good cheer and his own joyous musical mayhem.

## ARMORY SHOW

One woman was so overcome with laughter that she rolled on the floor. Theodore Roosevelt strode through the exhibition, pointing at paintings and muttering, "That's not art! That's not art!" An article in *The New York Times Magazine* was titled "Cubists and Futurists Are Making Insanity Pay."

What ignited this firestorm of invective was the International Exhibition of Modern Art of 1913, or The Armory Show, as it was soon called. This epic event, held in the cavernous Armory at Lexington Avenue and 25th Street in New York City, gave Americans their first look at European avant-garde artists, such as Marcel Duchamp, Pablo Picasso, Wassily Kandinsky, Henri Matisse, and Constantin Brancusi. Organized by a group of American artists looking for a wider audience, The Armory Show included approximately 1,500 works of art, two-thirds of which were actually by Americans. Despite all the raucous criticism their work received, however, the European artists stole the show. Almost overnight America became a market for modern art, ending forever its isolation from the international art world.

## ARMSTRONG, LOUIS

A crowd pleaser and jazz innovator, Louis Armstrong was one of the great American showmen. With his trumpet in hand, he could entertain packed houses all night long, pausing only to wipe his brow with a white handkerchief.

Armstrong took to music early; as a boy, he would follow his favorite performers around the streets of New Orleans. He received his first formal instruction, on the cornet, while in a boys' home, where he had been sent for a minor offense. That cornet gave Armstrong his direction in life. In a few short years, he was playing with the best band in town, led by cornetist Joe "King" Oliver. Armstrong was so talented that later, when Oliver took his band to Chicago, he sent for the young man. The following years were a whirlwind for Armstrong as he traveled between New Orleans, Chicago, and New York, playing and recording with some of the biggest stars of the time. He also organized his own band, the legendary Hot Five (later enlarged to the Hot Seven).

Well-known to jazz fans, Armstrong came to national attention after he hit New York in 1929. He had incredible endurance and played two shows daily, first performing in the Broadway revue *Hot Chocolates* (where he played his showstopper, "Ain't Misbehavin'"), then returning to Harlem's famous Connie's Inn for a late show. Before long he was traveling the country and performing in Hollywood films, such as *High Society*, with Bing Crosby and Grace Kelly. When he began touring worldwide in the mid-1950s, he earned the unofficial title of America's Ambassador of Goodwill. Armstrong died in 1971 and was remembered, appropriately, with a lively jazz funeral in New Orleans.

## ARMY-NAVY FOOTBALL GAME

Sportswriter Grantland Rice called the army-navy football game "the heavyweight boxing championship, the World Series, and the Kentucky Derby rolled into one." Since 1890 the cadets and the midshipmen have battled for service-academy supremacy before crowds as large as 100,000. In years past these games have featured Heisman Trophy winners like Felix "Doc" Blanchard and Glenn Davis for the army and Roger Staubach for the navy. Pregame hijinks are a tradition: army cadets have kidnapped the navy goat, and midshipmen have spread Limburger cheese on the cadets' stadium seats.

## ARNOLD, BENEDICT

Before he became our country's most notorious traitor, Benedict Arnold was a Revolutionary War hero with a reputation as a skilled tactician and a brave leader. Not one to remain behind the lines, Arnold fought alongside his men, earning their respect and loyalty. But he was also a proud and arrogant man who argued with other officers and felt slighted when he was passed over for a promotion.

After being crippled by two wounds in his left leg, Arnold received an easy assignment and was placed in command of Philadelphia in 1778. Owing to his new marriage and the couple's extravagant social life, Arnold was often low on funds. His bride supported the British, and before long Arnold, angry and now poor, made an offer to sell his services. For £20,000 he was to surrender West Point, a stronghold on the Hudson River. When his plot was revealed, he fled to the British, who refused to give him a satisfactory command because they didn't trust him. Eventually Arnold took his family to England, bitterly believing that he never got all that he deserved. Most Americans agreed.

## ASHCAN SCHOOL

In 1908 the shabbiness of New York's alleys and side streets was showcased in a notorious exhibition by eight young painters. "The Eight" rebelled against genteel impressionism by showing the gritty side of urban life. Critics later labeled them the Ashcan School. Four of them had been newspaper artists and were adept at illustrating stories of accidents, murders, and fires with a few quick strokes of the pen.

Like their literary counterparts Theodore Dreiser and Frank Norris, the Ashcan painters described city life with the realism of journalists. John Sloan loved backyards and New York streets; Everett Shinn showed the theater in all of its gaudy gaiety; George Luks painted laborers; and William Glackens depicted bustling parks with a colorful simplicity.

The Ashcan School would greatly influence such later painters as George Bellows and Edward Hopper. By the middle of the century, the portrayal of crowded, dehumanizing cities became commonplace. In retrospect, the works of the Ashcan School no longer seem so harsh.

The rivalry of the army-navy game began in 1890, when some midshipmen challenged the cadets to a football game.

Benedict Arnold was forced to flee after his plan to help the British capture West Point was uncovered.

John Sloan called himself a spectator of life and was adept at painting intimate portraits of New York. *Backyards, Greenwich Village* shows his observant eye and his tender feelings for the big city.

Notably cool on the court, Arthur Ashe said, "Always have the situation under control, even if losing. Never betray an inward sense of defeat."

Fred and Ginger danced with debonair grace in *Swing Time.*

The Houston Astrodome was so posh it prompted one pitcher to ask, "Is it all right to chew tobacco?" Only one game there was ever rained out—it rained so hard that no one could get to the stadium.

## ASHE, ARTHUR

In 1955 a 12-year-old black tennis player was turned away from a Richmond, Virginia, city tournament because of his color. His name was Arthur Ashe, and 13 years later he would win the U.S. Open. A top-rate tennis player and a consummate gentleman, he was among the last of that breed. In a sport once noted for its refinement but more recently dominated by the quick-tempered, Ashe was special.

In total contrast to his calm demeanor, Ashe played a passionate game. Quietly brilliant in a quintessentially white sport, he encouraged young blacks to join the ranks. Ashe won Wimbledon in 1975. Four years later, at age 36, he suffered the first of several heart attacks. In 1985 he was named to the International Tennis Hall of Fame. He contracted AIDS from a blood transfusion, and died in 1993.

## ASTAIRE AND ROGERS

Fred: "Every once in a while I suddenly find myself dancing." Ginger: "I suppose it's some kind of an affliction."

From *Top Hat*, this exchange—his nonchalant delivery, her sassy response—typified the on-screen chemistry between Fred Astaire and Ginger Rogers that delighted movie audiences almost as much as their dancing did. Also from *Top Hat*, one of 10 Astaire and Rogers dance musicals made between 1933 and 1949, is their legendary number "Cheek to Cheek," she wearing the famous feathered dress, he dancing the title song in his trademark white tie and tails.

Before he met Rogers, Astaire had danced onstage, partnering his sister Adele. Unlike Rogers, who had been playing supporting screen roles, he was unknown to moviegoers. The two were first teamed in *Flying Down to Rio*, followed by such classics as *The Gay Divorcée* and *Swing Time*. Alone, Astaire was a dancer of unmatched grace and elegance; with Rogers, his best partner, he was sublime. Although each pursued separate careers, together Fred and Ginger (as they were universally known) made one of the best-loved performing couples in movie history.

## ASTRODOME

When the $36.5 million Houston Astrodome opened in 1965, baseball fans were agog at the steel-and-Lucite "eighth wonder of the world." Not only could they watch a major league game indoors for the first time in history, they could do it in air-conditioned comfort from upholstered seats, to which they had been led by pretty "spacettes." "Sky boxes" came with ornate private suites complete with a Dow Jones ticker and a fully stocked bar.

The only problem was that on sunny days the glare was so intense that the outfielders couldn't see the fly balls. This was solved by tinting part of the dome gray. But then the pampered grass turned brown. Ultimately a remedy was found in the unlikely form of synthetic grass, now known as AstroTurf.

## ASTRONAUTS

America's first men in space were the seven astronauts of Project Mercury, all of whom became instant superheroes. They were chosen in 1959 from among the best of the country's military test pilots. Each passed a grueling battery of tests, physical and mental, designed to search out those "for whom spaceflight will impose no stress at all."

The astronauts then underwent an intensive training program. They rode in a simulated space capsule on the end of a 50-foot centrifuge arm that whirled them around and thrust them back in their seats with up to seven times the force of gravity. To get them used to weightlessness, they were piloted through parabolic flight paths in C-131 transports and F-100s that included more than half a minute of free fall.

On May 5, 1961, Alan Shepard was sealed into a tiny space capsule—so small it was dubbed a "garbage can"—high atop a Redstone rocket. The nation held its breath as he was launched into space. On returning safely from a 15-minute suborbital flight, Shepard was flown to Washington, D.C., and presented with a medal in the rose garden of the White House. On February 20, 1962, John H. Glenn, Jr., became the first American to orbit the earth. During his flight, which lasted five hours, he ate applesauce and watched for Perth, Australia, where residents had turned on all the lights in the city to greet him.

In 1968 Project Apollo sent three men around the moon. Then on July 20, 1969, Neil Armstrong became the first man to set foot on the moon, remarking to a live television audience, "That's one small step for man, one giant leap for mankind."

## ATLANTIC CITY

For 150 years Atlantic City has been a mecca for pleasure seekers. Built on the barren sand dunes of southern New Jersey, it strove mightily to become the definitive national resort. Its streets were named after the states of the union, and the annual Miss America beauty pageant was first held there, in 1921. In 1946 the United Nations considered Atlantic City for its temporary headquarters. It was even the inspiration for the playing board of one of America's favorite board games, Monopoly.

Atlantic City's fabled boardwalk was constructed in 1870 at the instigation of disgruntled innkeepers, who tired of visitors' tracking sand into their lobbies. The city fathers decided on a short, 10-foot-wide wooden walkway that could be removed during the winter. By 1896 a permanent boardwalk stretched four miles long and 60 feet wide.

Decorum was relaxed under the influence of sun and sand, and visitors swam in the ocean, strolled along the beach, rode roller coasters and carousels, and gobbled hot dogs and cotton candy. After World War II the seaside resort fell on hard times, only to reemerge as a glittering fantasy land of extravagant hotels and casinos.

**THE MERCURY SEVEN**

Scott Carpenter
Gordon Cooper
John Glenn
Virgil Grissom
Walter Schirra
Alan Shepard
Donald Slayton

America's brightest spotlight shone on the three who flew to the moon: Neil Armstrong, Edwin "Buzz" Aldrin, and Michael Collins (above). An astronaut takes a clumsy walk in space (top).

The boardwalk was invented in Atlantic City, as was the rolling chair, which first appeared in 1884 for the convenience of those who wished to "stroll" the walkway with a minimum of exertion.

This legendary Charles Atlas ad gave hope to 97-pound weaklings everywhere.

Audubon's *Birds of America* pictured 1,065 birds. Shown here are loons in non-breeding (left) and breeding (right) plumage.

Clean and even elegant, Automats offered diners a taste of the good life for the price of the change in their pockets.

## ATLAS, CHARLES

In 1907 skinny Charles Atlas really did get sand kicked in his face. Back then he was Angelo Siciliano, a 15-year-old kid visiting Coney Island with a pretty girl. Humiliated by the experience, he started bodybuilding at the YMCA, with impressive results. Siciliano chose his stage name after seeing a classical sculpture of Atlas and began a career in Coney Island sideshows, driving nails into boards with his bare hands and tearing phone books in half.

Not until he was named America's Most Perfectly Developed Man in 1921 and 1922 did Atlas decide to sell his secrets. With his system of "Dynamic-Tension," people could build strength by pitting one muscle against another. But orders for the fitness manual were slow until he hired adman Charles Roman, who turned Atlas's experiences into one of the best-known advertisements of all time, "The Insult That Made a Man Out of Mac."

## AUDUBON, JOHN JAMES

John James Audubon was born in Haiti in 1785, the son of a French sea captain and his Creole mistress. Throughout his life in France, Pennsylvania, Kentucky, and Louisiana, he devoted himself to his one abiding passion: birds. As a young boy he spent hours in the woods, observing and sketching. Eventually he would shoot and mount the birds, finally drawing life-size renditions complete with the appropriate foliage.

Realizing that he would never get a book of his drawings published in America, Audubon traveled to England in 1826 to find a publisher for his series, *Birds of America*. First printed in 1827, it was completed in 1838 as a set of four enormous volumes called elephant folios because of their size: three feet by two feet. Wrote Audubon: "I have labored like a cart Horse for 30 years on a Single Work, have been successful almost to a miracle in its publication thus far, and now am thought a—a—a (I dislike to write it, but no matter here goes)... a Great Naturalist!!!"

## AUTOMAT

Roast beef with mashed potatoes and gravy, hot rolls, and homemade apple pie, all from coin-operated slot machines—that was the Automat, a beloved New York institution. Coffee flowed from ornate silver spigots in a setting where a future Broadway star might be at a nearby table and a banker didn't mind sitting next to a bum.

Known as Horn & Hardart after its founder, the Automat actually originated in Philadelphia in 1902 with German-made vending equipment. It came to New York 10 years later, and in the 1930s expanded to more than 40 branches. But it took as many people to fill the vending machines as to service a cafeteria, and after World War II more practical fast-food chains replaced the Automat. Still mourned by some, the last Automat closed its doors in 1991.

# BABY BOOM

If the Depression brought small hopes and smaller families, the end of World War II brought boundless optimism and a renewed zeal for procreation. People married younger than they had at any other time during the century, settled down in spiffy new suburban homes, and began producing babies in record numbers. In 1957 the birthrate reached an all-time high of 4.3 million, or one new baby every seven seconds.

Born between 1946 and 1964, this bumper crop of kids swept through the second half of the century, in the words of demographers, "like a pig moving through a python." They made record demands for everything from diapers to nursery schools. And they shaped the economy with every dollar they spent on clothes, cars, and entertainment. When they entered the job market, they created fierce competition. All in all, their influence was so great that in 1965 *Time* magazine named the entire generation Man of the Year.

# BAKELITE

The word *plastic* may lack that nostalgic ring, but say "Bakelite" and images of glossy radios from the 1930s spring to mind, as do Bakelite telephones from the '40s and '50s.

The "miracle material of a thousand uses," Bakelite was the first entirely synthetic plastic. Patented in 1907 by a Belgian immigrant named Leo Baekeland, it was first used to insulate electrical components, then made its way into the kitchen in the form of pot handles that never got hot. Soon it was molded into everything from ashtrays to billiard balls. The 1920s and '30s brought Bakelite "kitchen jewelry," art deco flatware that was both fun and affordable. In the '30s and '40s, Bakelite fashion jewelry adorned even the well-to-do. Ironically, the plastic baubles, as well as the flatware, are now high-priced collector's items.

# BALANCHINE, GEORGE

George Balanchine is to ballet what Picasso is to art. His bold experiments with form and abstraction set new directions for dance in the 20th century. By freeing classical ballet movements from their storytelling contexts, Balanchine was able to reinvent the language of dance: speeding it up, sharpening it, infusing it with new meaning. His neoclassical style piqued America's interest in ballet, perhaps because the pace of his dances matched the pace of America itself.

Considered a privileged bunch, baby boomers grew up in new suburbs and were twice as likely as their parents to go to college.

Sleek Bakelite radios once heralded the future, just as they now recall the past.

"Ballet is woman," said Balanchine, whose protégées included many of the greatest stars of the dance world.

27

Bald eagles gather near the Chilkat River in Alaska. With the success of the Endangered Species Act of 1973, similar gatherings can once again be seen in the lower 48 states.

## WHERE TO SEE BALD EAGLES

**Here's a partial list of migration stops and wintering areas.**

**Northwest:** Klamath Basin in northern California and Oregon; Skagit River, Washington

**National Parks:** Glacier, Grand Teton, and Yosemite

**Mississippi River:** From Minneapolis through Illinois

**West:** Cedar and Rush valleys, Utah

**Southeast:** Florida Everglades; Reelfoot Lake, Tennessee

With practice, little fingers can peel and stick on a Band-Aid. Small fry love the ones with Sesame Street characters and neon designs.

Born in Russia in 1904, Balanchine trained at the Imperial School of Ballet in St. Petersburg and danced, as a child, for the czar. On the urging of businessman Lincoln Kirstein, he came to the United States in 1933, and the two formed the American Ballet and, later, the New York City Ballet. There "Mr. B," as his dancers called him, popularized the "Balanchine ballerina"—wafer-thin, with long legs, a long neck, and superior technical skills—epitomized by Maria Tallchief and Suzanne Farrell. The dancers gave life to Balanchine's choreography, which in turn shed new light on the music it embodied. Although Balanchine died in 1983, his influence, like Picasso's, may prove immortal.

## BALD EAGLE

Benjamin Franklin objected to the choice of the bald eagle as our national bird because, as he wrote, the eagle is "a bird of bad moral character; he does not get his living honestly.... Too lazy to fish for himself, he watches the labor of the fishing hawk and...takes [its fish] from him." Franklin suggested choosing the wild turkey instead, but he was outvoted by colleagues, who saw the bald eagle as a symbol of freedom and power—one that could use its impressive 7½-foot wingspan to soar effortlessly across the sky and use its keen eyes and razor-sharp talons to hunt.

No matter what their hunting habits may be, bald eagles have admirable domestic qualities. A male and a female stay together for life, and males share in the care of the young. Once faced with extinction, mainly because of pollution, the eagle has made a comeback. It was reclassified in 1995 from "endangered" to "threatened" on the endangered-species list.

## BAND-AIDS

A Johnson & Johnson employee, Earle Dickson, created the first Band-Aid to help his bride tend to the minor cuts and burns she sometimes got as she prepared their meals. She (and anyone else who was injured) had been using clumsy bandages that wouldn't stay in place. Dickson came up with a neater, more reliable combination of gauze and surgical tape. J&J marketed the product in 1921, and it soon became one of the company's biggest sellers.

J&J kept improving the Band-Aid over the years, making it ever more user-friendly. In 1932 the company wrapped each Band-Aid individually, thus making it more portable. In 1940 the easy-to-open red string appeared, to be replaced in 1993 with an even easier pull tab.

And because many of the Band-Aid's best customers are children, J&J added some fun to its product. In 1957 boxes of "Charmers" had colorful patterns of stars, dogs, and even a closed zipper. These were fun for kids to wear—even if they didn't have a boo-boo. Families also loved the "ouchless" Band-Aids that arrived in the 1970s, which peeled the strip from sensitive skin without pulling the hair.

## BANKHEAD, TALLULAH

The bourbon-soaked, husky "Dah-h-ling" is still imitated; Tallulah, the tawny-haired Alabama beauty, was one of the best-known theater personalities of her era. Her stage successes included a scheming Regina in Lillian Hellman's *The Little Foxes* (1939) and a seductive Sabina in *The Skin of Our Teeth* (1942). Of a flop one critic snapped, "Only Mae West as Snow White could have been more miscast."

As a young actress she was a big hit in London, where actress Mrs. Patrick Campbell observed: "Watching Tallulah Bankhead onstage is like watching somebody skate over very thin ice." Flamboyant, profane, witty, she was supremely Tallu. Said to be Bette Davis's inspiration for Margo Channing in *All About Eve*, she growled: "Bette and I are good friends; there's nothing I wouldn't say to her face—both of them."

## BARBECUE

Throughout the American South and Southwest, cooks, gourmets, and gourmands agree that *barbecue* means "meat that's been slow-cooked in pits over a cool (not flaming) fire." But that's all they agree on. Everything else about barbecue is the subject of passionate debate, with various states, cities, and tin-roofed shacks claiming to be the home of the world's best, and genuine, barbecue.

In Texas beef is the meat of choice. In Kentucky it's mutton. But in the Carolinas barbecue almost always means pork. Still, even if there's agreement on the meat, there are arguments about which cuts to use and whether the meat should be minced, chopped, sliced, or pulled off the bone. Many also have fervent beliefs about the correct barbecue sauce or marinade. Some use vinegar, mixing it with tomatoes or peppers; others swear by mustard-based sauces.

As Southerners and Southwesterners moved to the North and the West, they started barbecuing in their own backyards, using charcoal grills instead of hickory-filled pits and bottled sauces instead of homemade marinades. These days barbecue experts populate the entire country.

## BARBER, RED

Walter "Red" Barber broadcast major league baseball for 33 years, but during his 15 years in Brooklyn, his conversational style, salted with homespun phrases, found a special niche. Radio was king in the 1940s, and the "old redhead's" voice wafted across Brooklyn and the nation. When stringing base hits, the Dodgers were "tearin' up the pea patch" and when they loaded the bases, they were "FOB" (full of Brooklyns). A pitcher stifling the opposition was "sitting in the catbird seat." Barber's credo was objectivity and preparation.

During the 1980s Barber reached new audiences each Friday morning on National Public Radio, where the talk ranged from camellias and cats to baseball and football.

Tallulah Bankhead powders her nose in a scene from *Life Boat* (1944) as she and her fellow survivors await rescue. They are (clockwise from left) John Hodiak, Mary Anderson, Hume Cronyn, and Henry Hull.

Barbecued shish kebabs, easy to make and festive, are well suited to a party.

Red Barber was one of the first sportscasters elected to the Broadcasters Wing in the Baseball Hall of Fame.

Members of a barbershop quartet (circa 1974) wear the traditional striped jackets, boater-style hats, and handlebar mustaches of an earlier era. The last will be peeled off after the show is over.

Barbie wears a striped bathing suit to celebrate her 35th anniversary in 1994. She also poses for the cover of *Barbie Bazaar,* a collector's magazine. In her free time, Barbie buzzes around town in a sports car.

## BARBERSHOP QUARTETS

In the 19th century men who were waiting for a haircut or a shave at the barbershop would often sing in harmony, following a tradition of 16th-century England. In barbershop music, the lead tenor carries the melody, another tenor harmonizes above him, and a baritone and a bass fill in the low notes. At the turn of the century, professional quartets had such hits as "Sweet Adeline," "In the Good Old Summertime," and "Let Me Call You Sweetheart." These professional quartets died out, but thousands of amateurs have kept the tradition alive.

## BARBIE

In 1959 American girls said bye-bye to baby dolls and hello to Barbie, the curvaceous "Teenage Fashion Model" that was to become the best-selling doll in history. Ruth and Elliot Handler, the founders of Mattel Toys, created Barbie after noting how much their daughter, Barbara, loved dressing up paper dolls in stylish cut-out wardrobes.

Barbie's own wardrobe, as hip as it is vast, is updated annually by a team of fashion designers. But her glamorous world extends beyond ball gowns, pajama sets, and shopping ensembles. She also has a dream house, a sports car, her own hair salon, and a recording studio. A modern woman at heart, she has had careers ranging from surgeon to Olympic athlete and astronaut, for which she is always smartly dressed. But her most popular outfit remains the wedding gown, to be worn in the event of her marriage to Ken. He debuted in 1961, followed by a wide circle of friends. In 1976 Barbie was sealed in a time capsule. It is to be opened in 2076—possibly the first time she is caught sporting an outdated look.

## BARCALOUNGER

After World War II, if a man's home was his castle, his throne was a BarcaLounger. One of the first reclining chairs, it was designed by Dr. Anton Lorenz to mimic the feeling of floating on water by tilting back the head, raising the legs, and letting the arms go limp.

A bedding maker named Edward Barcalo first manufactured the chair in 1947, and though clunky-looking, it was an instant hit. Men returning home to the suburbs after a hard day's work loved to loll in its cushioned comfort at every degree of reclinement. Later on, competitors came out with vinyl-covered models that vibrated and gave the "TV chairs" a bad name. But makers rushed to repair their reputation, developing styles elegant enough for the living room and daintier, scaled-down models for women. Features now include a fold-down snack tray, a built-in cup holder, a telephone jack, and a drawer for videotapes and magazines, all of which conspire to make these chairs even harder to leave.

## BARN RAISING

When a farmer was ready to build a barn in the 19th century, he would enlist his neighbors' help. Together they would erect a sturdy post-and-beam structure. Hard work and planning preceded that barn-raising day, however. A site that would make the best use of the land had to be chosen; the pieces of the framework had to be crafted and numbered; and a foundation had to be laid. On the big day neighbors would swarm at the site like well-organized bees, securing the posts, beams, braces, siding, and roof—all in one day!

## BARNUM, P. T.

Phineas Taylor Barnum, the self-proclaimed Prince of Humbug, never failed to fleece a crowd—to its infinite delight and amusement. At the age of 25, he used his savings to take over a tour featuring Joice Heth, who claimed to be the 160-year-old former nurse of George Washington. Sensing no end to the public's gullibility, he later opened Barnum's American Museum in New York, filled with "historical relics," so-called freaks of nature, such as the Feejee Mermaid (part monkey, part fish tail), and, in Barnum's words, "innumerable other attractions of a minor though nevertheless a most interesting, instructive, and moral character." Another exhibit was a door marked Egress, which was only an exit; visitors were amazed to find themselves suddenly outside the museum.

Barnum charmed audiences with a midget in uniform he called General Tom Thumb. At one point, he gambled all of his assets to sign on Jenny Lind, the soprano known as the Swedish Nightingale, whose voice he had never heard. The pride of Europe, Lind was virtually unknown in America. But thanks to Barnum and his ingenious publicity stunts, a crowd of 40,000 was waiting to greet her when her ship docked.

Not until 1871, at the age of 61, did Barnum create the Greatest Show on Earth, for which he is best remembered. Its biggest attraction, literally, was Jumbo the elephant, who traveled in his own railroad car. When Jumbo died, Barnum turned this setback into an opportunity: Jumbo's stuffed hide and his skeleton went on tour.

## BARRYMORES

Known as the royal family of the American stage, the Barrymores could trace their theatrical heritage to Elizabethan England. Ethel, who made her stage debut at age 15, was known for her beauty, her velvety voice and imperious manner, and her curtain line: "That's all there is; there isn't any more."

Of John—dashing, handsome, amorous—one critic marveled, "His Hamlet was alive with vitality and genius." Potentially the greatest classical actor of his generation, John left the stage for Hollywood and became a legendary star. Eventually he dissipated his talents. His brother, Lionel, also left the theater, becoming a character actor in countless films.

This poster (circa 1918) offers innocent amusement, a notion that was dear to founder P. T. Barnum. It boasts of bears that are clever enough to be comic actors.

John Barrymore, known as the Great Profile, and sister Ethel strike a pose in a scene from the 1912 production of *A Slice of Life.*

"I am with the wounded," Clara Barton cabled from Havana. A tireless relief worker, Barton went to Cuba at the age of 77 to help the injured and fever-stricken during the Spanish-American War.

"Take Me Out to the Ball Game," goes the song, calling up memories of days at the ballpark. It's always better when you bring another fan along.

## BARTON, CLARA

Clara Barton was one of the most admired figures of her time, receiving a host of honors and decorations. She began her lifesaving efforts during the Civil War, when she became known as "the angel of the battlefield." Despite the vehement opposition of military authorities, she worked in hospitals at the front, preparing meals, comforting sick and dying soldiers, and distributing relief supplies. She followed the war closely, saying that her place was "anywhere between the bullet and the battlefield."

After the war, Barton learned about the International Committee of the Red Cross, which had been established by the Geneva Convention. In 1881 she founded the American branch of the Red Cross, which responded to 21 major disasters during her presidency.

## BASEBALL

Baseball was invented in New York City in 1845. Although similar games existed, it was Alexander Cartwright of the Knickerbockers, an early baseball team, who formalized many of the rules that give baseball its distinctive character. Walt Whitman, who would see it played as he walked the streets of Brooklyn, thought the game might "... relieve us from being a nervous, dyspeptic set." In 1856 the Sunday *New York Mercury* dubbed baseball "America's Pastime."

The first baseball teams were local and represented businesses and organizations. By the late 1800s several professional leagues developed. At first blacks played alongside whites, but in the 1880s they were banned from white teams. Blacks formed their own leagues but received little attention from the media. More than 400 exhibition games were played between white major league and Negro league players, with the blacks winning close to three-quarters of them. Despite this, baseball had to wait until 1950 to see Jackie Robinson become the first black player to join the major leagues.

Professional baseball had nearly evolved into the form it takes today by 1903, when the year's two best teams from the two biggest leagues played the first World Series. Baseball players became popular, and their salaries began to reflect their status. When Babe Ruth was asked how he could justify making more money than the president of the United States, he quipped, "I had a better year than him."

The history of professional baseball in the 20th century is replete with heroes and heroics, scoundrels and scandals. But baseball's significance for American culture transcends its function as an entertaining spectator sport. It has served as an intergenerational thread of memories and hopes. Most Americans have some memory of baseball: the smell of the glove, the feel of the ball, the sound of the bat striking the ball, the first visit to a major league park. These are experiences that will continue to help define what it is to be an American.

## BASEBALL CARDS

Thousands of middle-aged Americans are convinced that they'd be millionaires today if only their mothers hadn't thrown out their baseball cards. For years baseball cards were the most prized possessions of the all-American boy. They were collected, traded, and gambled in schoolyards across the country.

Baseball cards didn't start out as toys, though. They first appeared in the 1880s as bonuses in packs of cigarettes. In the 1930s baseball cards were used to sell chewing gum instead of tobacco. By the '50s the cards had become more popular than the gum, and in 1991 gum was phased out altogether, as collectors felt that the sugar damaged the cards.

By the 1980s baseball cards had become big business, and the prices for rare cards skyrocketed. The Holy Grail for collectors is the legendary T206 Wagner, a card featuring Honus Wagner, a Pittsburgh shortstop, that was issued in 1910. In 1989 hockey superstar Wayne Gretzky and a partner paid $451,000 for a mint-condition T206 Wagner, the highest price ever paid for a baseball card.

## BASKETBALL

Although basketball was first played in Springfield, Massachusetts, in 1891, fans know that it wasn't invented all at once. Basketball evolved into the game we know today.

Early basketball games were slow. After every point, someone had to climb a ladder and fish the ball out of the peach basket. Switching to a bottomless net eliminated that delay. The backboard was added in the late 1890s to stop fans in balconies from interfering with the ball. Such innovations as the pivot play, give-and-go offense, and switching on defense are credited to the Original New York Celtics, founded in 1912. After a rule change in 1937, players no longer had to return to the center line for a new tip-off after each basket.

The modern basketball era began in 1949, when the merger of two feuding leagues created the National Basketball Association (NBA). The 24-second shot clock was added in 1954, making faster-paced games and higher scores inevitable. The score of the first basketball game, in 1891, was 1–0; today teams regularly break 100 points.

Basketball's growth was fueled by legendary rivalries. In the late 1960s the fast-breaking Boston Celtics, with Bill Russell, sparred with the Los Angeles Lakers, led by Wilt Chamberlain. In 1979 the rivalry was revived as Larry Byrd led the Celtics against the Lakers' Magic Johnson and Kareem Abdul-Jabbar.

In 1976 the NBA absorbed four franchises from the American Basketball Association (ABA), and Julius Erving helped bring the airborne showmanship of schoolyard hoops to professional basketball. The sport continues to evolve as Michael Jordan, one of the most recognized and popular athletes, sets new standards with his gravity-defying leaps.

Once simply a kids' collectible, the baseball card has become big business. Enthusiasts meet each year at dozens of conventions to buy and sell.

### GREAT MOMENTS

The history of basketball is full of amazing feats: astonishing acrobatic leaps, long-distance three-point shots, and bone-crunching dives to keep the ball in bounds. Here are a few of the sport's greatest moments:

**1947**—Philadelphia's Joe Fulks becomes the first NBA player to score over 1,000 points in a season.

**1956**—Bob Petit of the St. Louis Hawks is named the NBA's first Most Valuable Player.

**1962**—Wilt "The Stilt" Chamberlain, playing for the Philadelphia Warriors, scores 100 points in a single game.

**1967**—Future U.S. senator Bill Bradley begins his professional career with the New York Knickerbockers after a spectacular college career at Princeton.

**1970**—Nearly crippled by injuries, Willis Reed nevertheless leads the Knicks to victory over the Lakers.

**1992**—Olympic basketball is dominated by America's Dream Team, led by Michael Jordan and brash Charles Barkley.

The greats make it look easy. Here, Kareem Abdul-Jabbar displays his trademark "skyhook," an elegant and altogether unstoppable shot.

Baton twirling's heyday was during the 1940s and '50s, when nearly 1 million youngsters were involved in this colorful pastime.

## BATON TWIRLING

Baton twirlers are a part of the American cultural landscape. Every Fourth of July parade needs a twirler to lead the band, and no college football game is complete without a sideline twirling display. In its early days, however, twirling was a man's sport, as batons were longer and heavier. When they were made smaller, the wave of interest swelled. After World War II, girls and boys across the nation learned how to strut, spin, and step gracefully while performing intricate twirls with one baton or two.

Today there are fewer twirlers, since young women are more likely to play high school or college sports. That hasn't stopped twirling routines from becoming more elaborate, however. National competitions are held regularly, and if twirlers hope to win, they must combine dance and gymnastic moves in flawless performances.

## BEACH BOYS

Sun and teen fun were the province of this 1960s California pop-rock group. Brian, Dennis, and Carl Wilson, cousin Mike Love, and a friend, Al Jardine, first got together in high school. Soaking up The Everly Brothers and The Four Freshmen, they began performing locally as Carl and the Passions and were managed by the Wilsons' father, Murray.

Singing good-natured pop songs about sun, sand, and surfing, The Beach Boys became a symbol of California and teenagers' golden days.

Their first recording as The Beach Boys, "Surfin'" (1961), glowed with their rich vocal harmonies. They took off with "Surfin' Safari" and "Surfin' U.S.A.," which was simply Chuck Berry's "Sweet Little Sixteen" with new lyrics. Other number one hits followed, including "I Get Around" (1964) and "Help Me, Rhonda" (1965). Brian, the creative eldest brother, had begun experimenting with overdubbing techniques on "Surfer Girl," and the result was their biggest hit, the million-selling "Good Vibrations" (1966). The track, to which were added the sounds of a harpsichord, a Jew's harp, and sleigh bells, took six months to produce.

## BEAN, ROY

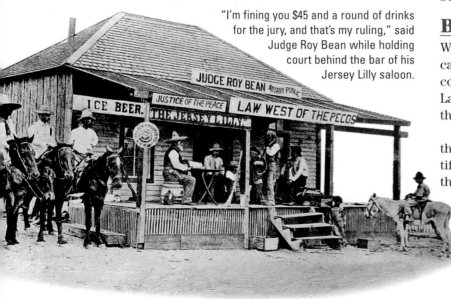

"I'm fining you $45 and a round of drinks for the jury, and that's my ruling," said Judge Roy Bean while holding court behind the bar of his Jersey Lilly saloon.

When the West became too wild, the Texas Rangers would call on Roy Bean, saloon keeper and justice of the peace. A colorful character, Bean moved to the trackside town of Langtry in 1882, claiming that he was the only "law West of the Pecos."

Bean held court from behind the bar. Patrons comprised the jury, and a trusty six-shooter enforced his rulings. To justify his decisions, he read from the only law book he owned, the *1879 Revised Statutes of Texas*, which he occasionally held upside down. Some of his rulings are legendary. When $40 and a pistol were found in the pockets of an unidentified corpse, Bean fined the cadaver $40 for carrying a concealed weapon. Horse thieves might be stripped of gun, horse, and anything else of value, then forced into the desert to try to reach the next town.

Although he had never met British actress Lily Langtry, Bean declared his devotion to her and even claimed to have named the town after her. He wrote to the actress often, inviting her to visit "her" town. When she finally did, 10 months after Bean's death, she was honored with a celebration and presented with Bean's pistol.

## BEAT GENERATION

Typing on a 150-foot roll of Teletype paper to speed the flow of his spontaneous prose, Jack Kerouac wrote *On the Road* in just three weeks. This burst of words matched the pace of his novel's bohemian characters. Entirely autobiographical, the book followed Kerouac ("Sal Paradise") as he hitchhiked across the country, looking for adventure. Largely because of a favorable review in *The New York Times*, *On the Road* became a best-seller, capturing the minds of restless young Americans in the 1950s and '60s. It would become one of the defining works of the writers and poets called the Beat Generation, a group who saw themselves as literary rebels. To them, being a beat meant being outside the mainstream and not bound by tradition.

But public reaction to the beats was hostile. People didn't understand their writings and labeled them beatniks. Critics heaped scorn on their work. The more controversial works of Allen Ginsberg and William S. Burroughs were even called obscene. Lawrence Ferlinghetti, a fellow beat and the publisher of Ginsberg's *Howl and Other Poems*, was arrested for selling the book in San Francisco. He was acquitted of an obscenity charge, though, when a judge found *Howl* to be a legitimate work of art, not pornography.

## BEATLEMANIA

The British press warned of "Beatlemania" after the group's London Palladium concert in 1963. America, however, was unprepared for the tidal wave of adolescent enthusiasm that would be unleashed by their appearance on *The Ed Sullivan Show* in February 1964. The "Fab Four" from Liverpool, with their long hair and irreverent high spirits, knocked the socks off teenagers who came of age during the Vietnam War.

The Beatles's music, largely written by John Lennon and Paul McCartney, had an irresistible quality that immediately appealed to its listeners. Songs like "I Want to Hold Your Hand" and "She Loves You" filled the airwaves and topped the charts. The Beatles were like nothing that American audiences had heard or seen before.

Soon a multimillion-dollar business mushroomed in Beatles trading cards, wigs, jewelry, and dolls. Fans chose their favorite band member: Paul was boyishly cute, John had a bad-boy arrogance, George seemed shy and spiritual, and Ringo was happy-go-lucky. When their first film, *A Hard Day's Night*, became a hit in 1964, the group showed that they could impress serious movie critics as well.

A restless spirit and an acute observer, Jack Kerouac wrote about his own adventures in *On the Road,* a book that helped define the Beat Generation.

The Beatles swept America with their fresh sound and likable personalities. In March 1964 they claimed all five top spots on the *Billboard* Hot 100 chart. Screaming fans followed them wherever they went. Some carried scissors, hoping to snip a lock of their favorite's moptop.

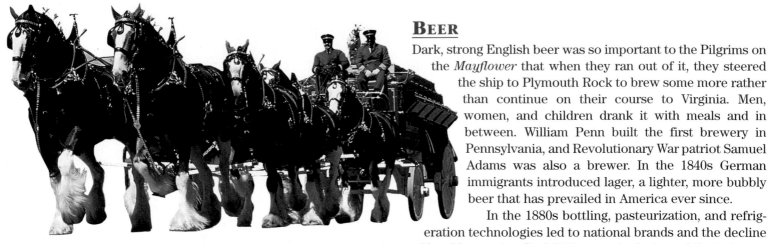

In the 19th century draft horses, such as these Clydesdales, pulled beer wagons from town to town, expanding the businesses of local brewers.

## BEER

Dark, strong English beer was so important to the Pilgrims on the *Mayflower* that when they ran out of it, they steered the ship to Plymouth Rock to brew some more rather than continue on their course to Virginia. Men, women, and children drank it with meals and in between. William Penn built the first brewery in Pennsylvania, and Revolutionary War patriot Samuel Adams was also a brewer. In the 1840s German immigrants introduced lager, a lighter, more bubbly beer that has prevailed in America ever since.

In the 1880s bottling, pasteurization, and refrigeration technologies led to national brands and the decline of local breweries. Prohibition nearly destroyed the industry, although a few brewers survived by making weak near beer, malt syrups, soft drinks, and ice cream. In the 1990s microbreweries came into vogue, offering more flavorful brews and bringing a part of the business back to its beginnings.

## BELAFONTE, HARRY

Harry Belafonte's recordings of "Jamaica Farewell," "Day-O (The Banana Boat Song)," and "Matilda" popularized West Indian calypso and folk music in the United States. The catchy, lilting rhythms of calypso evolved from the work songs of slaves, who chanted them in French-based patois to a drumbeat. They often slipped in personal messages, which resulted in the type of ribald and humorous songs performed by steel bands today, especially at the carnival in Trinidad.

Belafonte, born to West Indian parents in New York City, spent several years in Jamaica as a child. His lasting interest in world folk music led him to several film roles and, in 1985, to a key part in organizing the "We Are the World" recording for famine relief in Africa.

Belafonte, called the King of Calypso, sparked a West Indian folk song craze. His album *Calypso* was the first to sell a million copies.

Jack Benny's screechy violin performances were fodder for an endless series of barbs.

## BENNY, JACK

For millions of Americans in the 1930s and '40s, Sunday night at 7:00 meant listening to *The Jack Benny Program*. The running gags that centered on Benny's dismal violin playing and his vanity are etched into the nation's memory, along with his long-standing feud with comedian Fred Allen and his perpetually claiming to be 39 years old. But it was Benny's stinginess that was most often the butt of jokes. Each week his chauffeur and valet, Rochester, complained bitterly of poor pay for driving Benny's sputtering automobile, the Maxwell, which Benny begrudgingly filled with gas one gallon at a time. A classic routine involved an armed robber confronting Benny and demanding his money or his life. After pausing, he would answer, "I'm thinking it over."

Benny's humor relied on his impeccable timing; his drawn-out pauses were often more important than any punch line. He moved successfully to television in 1950 with a weekly series on CBS that aired until 1965.

## BENTON, THOMAS HART

One of the foremost regionalist painters and the best-known muralist of the 1930s and '40s, Thomas Hart Benton rebelled against the "general cultural inconsequences of modern art." Unlike most of his peers, he chose to paint art that ordinary people could identify with, and he found his inspiration in scenes from America's heartland.

Benton dramatized life in the Midwest with a flowing realism that captured the American imagination. His depictions were often controversial—some critics objected to his choice of subjects—but his works were popular and led to commissions to paint murals for public buildings. One of his most famous, a depiction of Missouri history on the walls of the state capitol, upset lawmakers because it focused on common men and thieves instead of on politicians and heroes. Benton responded: "The ordinary mule had more to do with the growth of this state than any number of favorite sons."

## BERLE, MILTON

Milton Berle was in the right place at the right time. The former vaudeville comedian landed a spot as host of NBC's *Texaco Star Theater* in 1948, just as the new medium of television emerged. During the show's first year, the number of television sets in America doubled, thanks in large part to Uncle Miltie—thereafter known as Mr. Television. Adults and children alike tuned in on Tuesday nights to watch his latest madcap routine. Over the years he was joined by such top comedians as Harpo Marx, Dean Martin, and Jerry Lewis.

Berle worked seven days a week as producer, director, co-writer, and chief talent of the show. During its heyday, from 1948 to 1956, he stockpiled some 2 million gags "borrowed" from other comics. In 1951 he signed a 30-year contract with NBC that prevented him from working for another network, even after his show went off the air.

## BERLIN, IRVING

"Irving Berlin has no place in American music," wrote fellow composer Jerome Kern. "He *is* American music." Born in Temun, Siberia, as Israel Baline, Berlin came to the U.S. with his family in 1893. He first sang with his father, a cantor.

Only eight when his father died, Berlin went out to fend for his family, singing for pennies in the street and in saloons. Later he plugged songs for others before writing his first hit, "Alexander's Ragtime Band." He went on to score blockbuster musicals, including *Annie Get Your Gun*.

Berlin played piano in only one key, relying on a special device to help him transpose. He was shrewd enough early in his career to obtain the rights to his songs and even started his own music-publishing company. Among his more than 1,000 songs were "God Bless America" and "White Christmas," an instant favorite. In 1977 he received the Presidential Medal of Freedom for his musical contributions.

"Cradling Wheat," 1938, is Benton's forceful tribute to the hardworking farmers of the Midwest and the beauty of the Great Plains.

Irving Berlin had a gift for writing memorable melodies that expressed the American spirit.

Standing atop a pile of rubble, a crowd of German children waves exuberantly at an American cargo plane during the 1948 Berlin airlift.

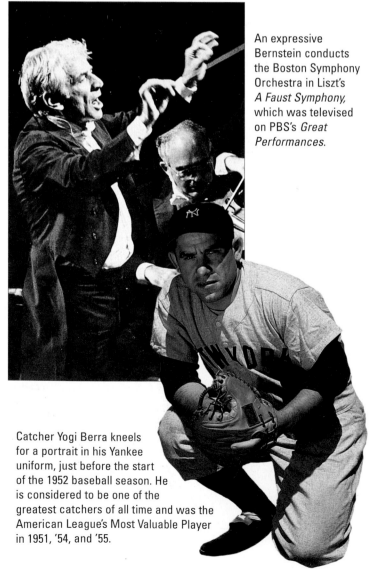

An expressive Bernstein conducts the Boston Symphony Orchestra in Liszt's *A Faust Symphony,* which was televised on PBS's *Great Performances.*

Catcher Yogi Berra kneels for a portrait in his Yankee uniform, just before the start of the 1952 baseball season. He is considered to be one of the greatest catchers of all time and was the American League's Most Valuable Player in 1951, '54, and '55.

## BERLIN AIRLIFT

On June 24, 1948, three years after the Cold War had begun, the Soviet Union attempted to deny the United States, France, and Great Britain access to Allied sections of Berlin. It blockaded the city, threatening 2.5 million Berliners with starvation. In response to the crisis, President Harry Truman decided not to use arms or to surrender. Instead, he ordered what became known as the Berlin airlift, supplying that city by air with everything from baby food to coal. It was a logistical miracle that demonstrated America's dedication to the defense of the free world.

Cargo planes, landing every minute and a half in all kinds of weather, delivered as much as had once been brought in by road and rail. After 321 days, the Soviets quietly ended the blockade. This heroic display of American power—277,264 flights in all—earned lasting goodwill for the nation.

## BERNSTEIN, LEONARD

The popular maestro, known for his genius and dramatic persona, shone like a beacon at the gate of American music. His vigorous conducting style offended some—"Bernstein rose vertically à la Nijinsky, and hovered there 15 seconds," wrote one critic—but by shattering the stodgy image of classical music, he attracted new audiences.

After studying conducting, Bernstein became a protégé of Serge Koussevitzky at Tanglewood, a center of music in Massachusetts. Soon thereafter, he was appointed assistant conductor of the New York Philharmonic. He rose to fame overnight in 1943, when he stepped in for the ailing Bruno Walter and conducted a nationally broadcast performance.

A bravura pianist who often conducted from the keyboard, Bernstein also composed. He wrote three symphonies, the ballet *Fancy Free,* two operas, an operetta, four musicals, and a film score. His most popular work was *West Side Story* (1957), choreographed by Jerome Robbins.

In 1958 Bernstein became music director of the New York Philharmonic, which, inspired by his bristling energy, took on new life. Bernstein toured the world as a guest conductor, earning respect for American music. He educated American audiences through televised lectures on classical music and jazz, and after teaching music to his own children, he developed the innovative Young People's Concerts (1958–73). When he retired from the Philharmonic in 1969, he was named conductor laureate for life.

## BERRA, YOGI

Despite the fact that Yogi Berra wore a catcher's mask throughout most of his 19 years with the New York Yankees, his grinning face became one of the most recognizable visages in America. Berra's squat physique belied his catlike reflexes and his uncanny ability when batting to hit a pitch thrown anywhere between his neck and his ankles.

With a deadpan delivery, he uttered malapropisms and truisms that have since entered the language. As a young player with the Yankees, he credited coach and former Yankee catching legend Bill Dickey for "learning me my experience." After achieving stardom, Berra explained his success by saying, "Baseball is 90 percent mental. The other half is physical." Searching for the cause of a rare batting slump, he wondered, "How can I hit and think at the same time?" Also attributed to Berra is "It's déjà vu all over again," a comment on the fortunes of one of his teams. When he managed the New York Mets, carrying them to an improbable pennant in 1973, he coined "It ain't over till it's over."

## BETTY BOOP

A style sheet shows Betty Boop's "skeleton" of intersecting ovals. To inspire artists, she obligingly strikes a few poses.

BASIC CONSTRUCTION

"I wanna be loved by you...oo, oo, oo...boop-boop-a-doop," sang Betty Boop in her cutie-pie voice while rolling her huge eyes. Her creator, animator Grim Natwick, was inspired by the flapper girls of the 1920s. He modeled her face after that of singer Helen Kane and her body after Mae West's, coiffing her in spit curls and dressing her in a mini.

She was to become the first female cartoon star to receive top billing. Debuting in 1930 in "Dizzy Dishes," she starred in nearly a hundred Fleischer Studio cartoons. In her films (1930–39) she was pursued by lechers but was never compromised. These days she makes cameo appearances on ties, T-shirts, boxer shorts, and at the Macy's Thanksgiving Day parade in New York, where she is a towering presence.

## BEVERLY HILLBILLIES

When the Clampetts moved from their Ozarks Mountain home of Sibly to fancy Beverly Hills, California, Granny rode in the back of the truck in her rocking chair, holding a jar of moonshine in one hand and a bottle of mountain medicine in the other. Many critics groaned, but audiences loved *The Beverly Hillbillies*.

Created and produced by Paul Henning, the show aired on September 26, 1962, on CBS and soon shot to the top of the ratings. The comic acting, anchored by television veterans Buddy Ebsen (Jed) and Irene Ryan (Granny), was superb. However, the dialogue was corny—the Clampetts would not relinquish their country ways and values, despite their newfound riches (oil had been found in their backyard) and their fancy new mansion.

The plot was full of misunderstandings between the rubes and their snobbish neighbors. Asked by a stuffed shirt if they liked Kipling, one Clampett replied, "I don't know—I ain't never kippled." When Jed admired his pretty daughter, Elly May, dressed up for a date, he said, "She was slicker'n a cow's belly." And when a young man tried to kiss Elly May's hand, she decked him, explaining that "he was fixin' to bite me." The show was canceled in 1971, but the Clampetts made a successful comeback in 1993 as stars of a full-length movie.

The Clampetts tour Beverly Hills in their hillbilly-style convertible. Jethro drives as Jed rides shotgun; Granny and Elly May sit in back.

## BIBLE BELT

When H. L. Mencken coined the phrase *Bible Belt* in the 1920s, he was, as usual, being critical. Today, however, many use the term with pride. In the Bible Belt, Sunday schools and Bible classes are full. Ministers are a powerful force both in politics and on television. A strong emphasis on traditional morals and on rural and small-town values is prevalent.

The phrase *Bible Belt* generally refers to the Central and Southern United States but is also used to describe any area where people, many of whom are fundamental and evangelical Christians, read their bibles regularly.

## BICENTENNIAL

With flags fluttering, bands a-fifing, and fireworks blazing across the sky, America threw itself a glorious 200th birthday bash to salute the British colonies' declaration of independence from the Crown in 1776. The bicentennial unleashed a wave of patriotic spirit that swept people of various races, creeds, and ethnic origins into a swirl of celebration—from picnics and pageants in the heartland to glittering extravaganzas in the big cities.

Although festivities were held all year, the biggest party took place on July 4th, beginning with a flag-raising ceremony at 4:31 A.M. at Mars Hill, Maine, as dawn broke over America. Among the events cherished in national memory was the striking of the Liberty Bell in Philadelphia, its call answered by a chorus of bells tolling throughout the country. In Washington, D.C., the U.S. Army Band played "Happy Birthday" at the National Archives, and in Los Angeles the day's largest parade wended its way along 11 miles of palm-lined streets. Perhaps the most stirring spectacle was the majestic procession of more than 200 tall-masted ships in New York Harbor, their sails billowing as they passed in review beneath the approving gaze of Lady Liberty.

As part of the bicentennial celebration, the square-rigger *Christian Radich* sails past the Statue of Liberty. More than 30,000 boats of all sizes jammed New York Harbor during Operation Sail. Meanwhile, the citizens of Washington, D.C., celebrated with a giant cake (right).

## BIG BANDS

Benny Goodman's band, appearing at the Palomar Ballroom in Los Angeles in August 1935, officially kicked off the Big Band swing era. The band went for broke during a live broadcast and played such hard-swinging arrangements as "King Porter Stomp" and "Blue Skies."

Soon bands from hot to sweet were sprouting everywhere, adding more horns, recording their music, and riding buses to play to packed houses. "They lifted you high in the air with them," recalled former *Metronome* critic George T. Simon, "filling you with an exhilarated sense of friendly well-being... in one of the happiest, most thrilling rapports ever established between the givers and takers of music."

These bands—and their leaders—became famous. The Dorsey Brothers formed a band together, then separately. Clarinetist Artie Shaw led a hot band; Harry James's trumpet blazed at the head of his own ensemble.

King of Swing Benny Goodman (pictured here with his band in the movie *Sweet and Low Down*) thrilled jitterbuggers with his soaring clarinet solos.

And Count Basie's jumping, blues-based band cut the deepest groove of all.

On the sweet side, no one was more beloved than Guy Lombardo and his orchestra. Meanwhile, trombonist Glenn Miller's smooth band delighted dancers with "In the Mood." The Big Band sound waned in the mid-1940s as gas shortages and economic troubles brought on by the war forced bands to fold, leaving the airwaves to dulcet crooners.

## BIGFOOT

Bigfoot, a popular figure in American folklore, was first sighted in 1784 in Alberta, Canada. According to a newspaper report, a group of Indians had captured one and then tried to sell it to a traveling circus.

Believers point to footprints, some up to 16 inches long, and eyewitness accounts as proof that Bigfoot exists. Most encounters are reportedly brief, and the few alleged photographs of the creature are of poor quality. Bigfoot is said to be between six and seven feet tall and to weigh some 450 pounds. Also called Sasquatch, it is hairy and may exude a repugnant odor. Bigfoot has been sighted mostly in the mountain forests of the Northwest, although skeptics maintain that its true habitat is our imagination.

## BIG TEN

Located in the Midwest, a part of the country that especially loves college sports, the Big Ten is the oldest conference in the U.S. and boasts fierce rivalries. Founded in 1895 as the Intercollegiate Conference of Faculty Representatives (with seven members), it became the Big Ten in 1949.

The group's original goal was to regulate college sports by putting them under the control of the faculties instead of the students. It set rules that required athletes to meet entrance requirements and determined who was eligible to play. Other college conferences followed in the Big Ten's wake, creating a more level playing field in college sports.

## BILL OF RIGHTS

If a poll of Americans had been taken in 1787, a majority would probably have opposed ratification of the newly drafted Constitution. Older citizens in particular feared the strong central government that the Constitution set forth. They worried that the presidency might become "an American throne."

In order to have the Constitution ratified, its supporters agreed to add amendments that would spell out individual freedoms. These 10 amendments, known as the Bill of Rights, became law in 1791. Although there will always be debate over how the Supreme Court interprets its provisions, the Bill of Rights is unquestionably the foundation of the American concept of limited government, individual freedom, and rule of law.

This still from a 1968 film catches an alleged Bigfoot as it steps into a clearing.

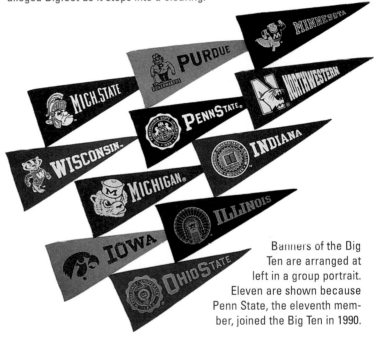

Banners of the Big Ten are arranged at left in a group portrait. Eleven are shown because Penn State, the eleventh member, joined the Big Ten in 1990.

## RIGHTS HIGHLIGHTS

**Everyday life:** guarantees free speech, a free press, free assembly, and the right to petition the government

**Personal property:** prohibits "unreasonable searches and seizures" of persons and property; allows "people to keep and bear arms" for the purpose of "a well-regulated militia"

**You and the law:** sets up grand juries for "infamous crimes"; prevents double jeopardy (being tried for the same offense twice); says that an accused may not be forced to testify against himself; guarantees "a speedy and public trial," as well as a jury; provides that a suspect be informed of his rights; prohibits excessive bail and fines and "cruel and unusual punishments"

**Loophole amendments:** provide that any right—that is either not mentioned specifically or not given to the federal government—cannot be denied to the people or to the states

Sheriff Pat Garrett's "authentic" biography of Billy the Kid contains many tall tales about the outlaw, despite the fact that Garrett said he was going to set the record straight. At right is a rare photo of Billy himself.

The appeal of bingo is that it's simple to play and there's always a winner. A home version of the game (below) includes a cage for spinning the calling balls and a board for holding them after they are selected by the caller.

## BILLY THE KID

Billy the Kid was dead by the age of 21, but he will live forever in Western mythology—either as a bloodthirsty desperado who killed 21 people or as a gallant frontier knight who defended his mother's honor, had a way with women, and killed only when he had to.

Even his real name is in question. Born either Henry McCarty or William H. Bonney in 1859, he was first arrested—and first escaped from jail—at the age of 16, for theft. A year later he killed a bully in a brawl and escaped to New Mexico, where he got embroiled in the bloody Lincoln County range war. Now known as Billy the Kid, he rode with the Regulators, a vigilante posse that dispensed justice ruthlessly, although semi-legally. After the Regulators' leader was gunned down, Billy turned outlaw, rustling cattle and killing a saloon braggart and two deputies. Sheriff Pat Garrett vowed to catch him, and after tracking the Kid for months, Garrett shot him dead in the darkness of a bedroom. The first biography of Billy the Kid hit the newsstands a few weeks later.

## BINGO

The most popular game in America isn't baseball or football or golf. It's B-I-N-G-O. To play, all you have to do is walk into any church hall or community center where a group has a bingo night going. Millions of women and men spend their evenings buying and filling up bingo cards as a caller calls out numbers. Players listen carefully and try to complete a line down, across, or diagonally as quickly as possible. The first to cry "Bingo!" gets the cash in the pot.

While many groups that run these evenings are volunteer organizations, some, such as the Seminole tribe in Florida, view bingo as a business. The tribe has increased its annual bingo revenue from $900,000 to over $45 million in 15 years. No matter who hosts it, bingo night is popular. Says a woman who has played for 40 years, "It's a social event!"

## BIRTH OF THE BLUES

"From a whippoorwill.../ They took a new note / Pushed it through a horn / 'Til it was a blue note." This line, from a 1926 popular song called "The Birth of the Blues," offers one theory of blues music's origins. Scholars debate just how African rhythms, slaves' work songs, English ballads, and Southern spirituals mixed together to form the blues. The musicians themselves tell a simpler story. Says one, "Love makes the blues. That's where it comes from."

Many of the earliest blues guitarists were traveling street performers who, because many could not read either words or music, developed patterns that were ideal for improvisation. "Playing the blues" meant repeating one of these patterns many times while a singer made up rambling stories filled with vivid imagery. The anguish of love lost, the perils of gambling and liquor, and a longing for the open road were widely known to cause someone to sing the blues. Listeners could nurse their heartache to a slow blues melody or enjoy raucous tales of no-good men and loose women.

W. C. Handy, who started publishing his own compositions and those of others in 1912, was one of the first to recognize the commercial potential of the blues. But it wasn't until a 1920 recording of "Crazy Blues" by Mamie Smith sold a million copies that the music industry realized how popular the blues could be. Soon many performers who had established themselves as brilliant musicians were going into the recording studio. Foremost among these was Blind "Lemon" Jefferson, whose "Long Lonesome Blues" became a classic.

Bessie Smith gained a reputation as one of the finest blues singers when she began recording in 1923. She actually started out as a dancer, having joined a traveling vaudeville troupe that passed through her hometown of Chattanooga, Tennessee, in 1912. That tour featured Gertrude "Ma" Rainey, the "Mother of the Blues." Smith was soon a headliner herself, transfixing audiences with her impassioned, sometimes ribald singing and performing the definitive versions of such songs as "Nobody Knows You When You're Down and Out" and "Backwater Blues."

"Whatever pathos there is in the world, whatever sadness she had, was brought out in her singing," one theater owner recalled of Smith at the height of her fame. Once the Depression set in, however, the blues lost out; people preferred to be cheered up. The blues never regained the popularity it had enjoyed in the mid-1920s, but its raw feeling and rhythmic energy have greatly influenced rhythm and blues, rock, and jazz. Musicians like B. B. King, John Lee Hooker, and Eric Clapton continue to keep the blues tradition alive.

## BLACK TUESDAY

The stock market crash of October 29, 1929, known as Black Tuesday, signaled the end of the Roaring Twenties, a time when it seemed that anyone could become rich. And even though the crash became the enduring symbol of the Great Depression, it did not actually cause it.

In the months prior to that dire October day, there were omens of disaster: a slowing economy, Federal Reserve warnings of overspeculation, and sharp price declines in March, July, and August. But the market kept rallying to new highs. On October 3 stocks broke sharply in the worst loss of the year, and then continued to sink. By October 24, panic set in and a group of bankers spent millions buying key stocks in an attempt to stabilize prices. This worked briefly, but the market soon dropped again. The bottom finally fell out on Tuesday. The ticker-tape lagged hours behind trading as 16.4 million shares were dumped at any price. Brokers on the floor wept. Trinity Church was jammed with worshipers. Doctors treated men acting like shell-shocked soldiers. No one, however, anticipated the Depression that was to come.

Huddie "Leadbelly" Ledbetter sang his way out of jail. The singer was released in 1934 so that he could record for the Library of Congress. "Goodnight, Irene" is his best-known song.

Influenced by 1930s blues legend Robert Johnson, Muddy Waters (right) was a spirited performer known for his commanding "shout" voice and loudly amplified bands.

B. B. King, shown here with his guitar, "Lucille," was named "King of the Blues" in the '50s. Still one of the most popular performers, he has been inducted into both the blues and the rock Hall of Fame.

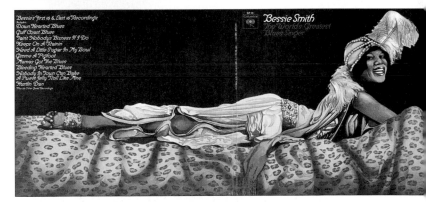
This double album reissue offers a sampling of the rich trove of recordings that earned Bessie Smith the title Empress of the Blues.

The music of such string bands of the 1930s as J. E. Mainer's Mountaineers was the forerunner of bluegrass.

Former president Jimmy Carter relaxes in blue jeans, the comfortable favorites that were advertised in the early days as "famous patent riveted clothing." Levi Strauss priced his first "waist-high overalls" at a mere 22 cents.

In the darkness of a cold December night, patriots tossed tea overboard in a defiant gesture that presaged the War of Independence.

## BLUEGRASS

As a term for a singular style of Southern hill-country music, *bluegrass* is a relative newcomer. It came into general usage in the late 1940s and early '50s on the coattails of Bill Monroe's popular string band, the Blue Grass Boys, which became a favorite on the Grand Ole Opry's Saturday-night broadcasts from Nashville. The original group included Cleo Davis on guitar, Art Wooton on fiddle, and Monroe on mandolin. In 1945 a sensational banjo picker named Earl Scruggs joined the group, and what is known as bluegrass became fixed in American musical tradition.

Classic bluegrass bands consist of four to seven musicians. The melody is played on such unamplified instruments as the mandolin, banjo, and fiddle; rhythm is supplied by the guitar and string bass. Today Bill Monroe's own "high, lonesome sound" continues to be the admired standard by which all bluegrass singers are measured.

## BLUE JEANS

When Levi Strauss first began peddling "waist-high overalls" to California's gold prospectors in the 1860s, he never imagined that he was altering the course of fashion history. The blue jean originated as sturdy, natural-colored pants cut from tenting canvas. When the supply of canvas ran out, Strauss switched to indigo-dyed cotton, which was more comfortable and less likely to show dirt. In 1872, on the suggestion of retailer Jacob Davis, he began to reinforce the seams with copper rivets. Strauss brought Davis into the business, patented his riveted clothing, and never looked back.

## BOSTON TEA PARTY

Long-brewing resentment among Massachusetts patriots against Britain's colonial trade practices culminated in the Boston Tea Party. The impetus was Parliament's 1773 Tea Act, which had given the financially troubled East India Company a monopoly on the importation of tea, to the detriment of many American merchants. Three East India Company ships were about to unload their cargo in Boston, and the patriots decided to act.

Gathering just before midnight on December 16, 1773, some 100 Sons of Liberty, led by Samuel Adams, plotted to destroy the tea before it could be brought ashore. Thinly disguised as Mohawk Indians, the men boarded the ships. With only token resistance from the crews, they broke open and jettisoned 342 chests of tea.

Emboldened by this radical act, patriot resisters throughout the Colonies began to call for united action. Parliament retaliated with the punitive Intolerable Acts, one of which, the Massachusetts Government Act, virtually nullified the Massachusetts Colony's charter. The colonists' resolve only stiffened, however, and they pressed on in the march toward independence.

## BOWLING

The 10-pin version of bowling, developed in 19th-century America, was the descendant of a game popular in medieval German churchyards. There, players gathered to roll a ball at a pin-shaped Kegel that represented Satan. To hit the target was to "knock the Devil." Evolving into ninepins and shedding its symbolism, the sport eventually came to America. The tenth pin was added around 1800, and a century later the American Bowling Congress standardized the rules of the game.

## BOY SCOUTS

Since 1910, when the Boy Scouts of America was founded, millions of American youngsters have climbed the ladder toward manhood, each of them steadied by the mottos "Be prepared" and "Do a good turn daily." The words, and the practices that the BSA follows to this day, are those of Robert Baden-Powell, a British officer, who is credited with founding the original organization in England in 1908. But, as he would be the first to say, many of his ideas were really born in turn-of-the-century America, through the work of two Americans, Daniel Carter Beard and Ernest Thompson Seton.

Concerned about the poor survival skills of the conscripts under his command, Baden-Powell resolved to teach youngsters how to cope in unfamiliar situations. He eventually came upon the efforts of Beard and Seton, whose separate organizations, the Sons of Daniel Boone and the Woodcraft Society, taught urban American boys frontier skills, wildlife stewardship, and self-reliance. Neither group gained much of a following, but recast in Baden-Powell's Boy Scouts and reintroduced to America in 1910, Beard's and Seton's goals of training boys to be responsible and physically fit were given new life. By 1916, when a federal charter recognized the Boy Scouts of America as "a genuine contribution to the welfare of the nation," more than 500,000 boys had joined. Inspired by Baden-Powell, Juliette Low founded the Girl Scouts in Savannah in 1912.

## BUBBLE GUM

Seeking to improve chicle-based chewing gum, Frank Fleer came up with the first bubble gum recipe in 1906. It was too sticky and crumbly, however, and Fleer abandoned the project. But when an employee, Walter Diemer, presented Fleer with "Dubble Bubble" in 1928, an instant candy store sensation was born. The elasticized confection led to many imitations, including the Bowman Company's Blony, the first gum to be packaged with picture cards. In the decades since, the pink stuff has become part of American culture, and blowing bubbles, a competitive sport. The reigning champion is said to be a Californian who blew a bubble measuring 22 inches on the official "gumputer."

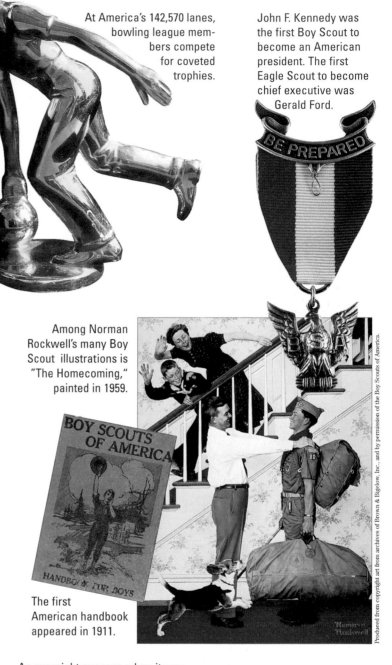

At America's 142,570 lanes, bowling league members compete for coveted trophies.

John F. Kennedy was the first Boy Scout to become an American president. The first Eagle Scout to become chief executive was Gerald Ford.

Among Norman Rockwell's many Boy Scout illustrations is "The Homecoming," painted in 1959.

The first American handbook appeared in 1911.

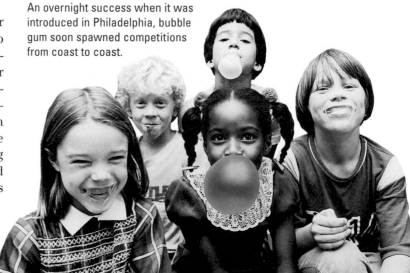

An overnight success when it was introduced in Philadelphia, bubble gum soon spawned competitions from coast to coast.

# BUILDING STYLES
## OF THE 20TH CENTURY

*Old traditions and new technology help solve problems, celebrate space, and create well-loved public monuments.*

### JOHN HANCOCK CENTER
Form follows function in a 1960s minimalist megatower soaring 1,127 feet (100 stories) above the Chicago skyline. Tapered sides and exterior cross braces not only help bear weight and wind loads but also express the building's structure visually.

### CHRYSLER BUILDING
New York's famous 1930 art deco skyscraper—complete with radiant stainless-steel arches, futuristic spire, and gargoyles modeled after a 1929 Chrysler radiator cap— is a joyous monument to automotive technology and machine-age materials. Inlaid wood-veneer elevator doors (above) display an exotic lotus pattern that is typical of the art deco building style.

### THE SUPREME COURT
The classically inspired Beaux Arts style endows this 1935 temple to law and order with a deliberate sense of ceremony and tradition. Monumental Corinthian columns (inset) establish an imposing scale for the Washington, D.C., landmark.

## TRANSAMERICA BUILDING

Although it looks as solid and permanent as an ancient pyramid, this 1972 office tower in San Francisco is designed to survive earthquakes by safely swaying during tremors. The non-load-bearing curtain walls comprise 3,000 individual concrete slabs attached to an interior frame.

## SPACE NEEDLE

Decades after it served as the centerpiece of the 1962 Century 21 Exposition in Seattle, this 607-foot tower remains a familiar city landmark. The space-age design features a revolving saucer-shaped restaurant that appears to hover above the skyline like an alien spacecraft. A pod-like elevator cab (inset) carries visitors from the ground.

## DULLES AIRPORT

Capturing the spirit of flight in a sweep of glass and concrete, Chantilly, Virginia's 1962 terminal, is a triumph of modernist design—at once an oversize sculpture appearing poised for takeoff and an efficient gateway for travelers.

*The Bullwinkle Show* featured humor that went right over the heads of young viewers. After one obscure joke, Bullwinkle asked Rocky, "Did you get it?" Rocky: "I got it." Bullwinkle: "Millions won't!"

Bumper cars, like Ferris wheels, have a timeless appeal. An early version seated 10 people and was driven by a motorman. The ride was so boring, it was quickly abandoned.

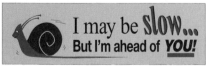

For every sentiment there's a bumper sticker. There's even one for those sick of the stickers, which reads: "I Don't Care What You Love, What Your Other Car Is, or What You'd Rather Be Doing."

## BULLWINKLE

Jay Ward created Crusader Rabbit and George of the Jungle, but his most enduring cartoon characters were Rocky, Bullwinkle, and their friends and enemies. *The Bullwinkle Show*, which featured the same dim-witted moose and flying squirrel that premiered in 1959 in *Rocky and His Friends*, became a cult favorite. Although the show's animation was never great, its writing, which layered shameless puns on historical allusions and sly satire, made it irresistible.

In the two episodes of each show, Bullwinkle J. Moose and Rocket J. Squirrel, from Frostbite Falls, Minnesota, waged a cold war against Pottsylvania's nefarious spies, Boris Badenov and Natasha Fatale. Whether the mission was to protect the gravity-defying upsidaisium mine, to guard the formula for mooseberry jet fuel, or to play football for Wossamotta U. against the Mud City Manglers, our heroes won the day with all-American exuberance and innocence.

Each episode featured a clever title ("The Ruby Yacht of Omar Khayyam" was about a bejeweled toy boat). Special segments included Peabody's Improbable History, in which a smart dog, Mr. Peabody, and his pet boy, Sherman, time-traveled in the "Wayback Machine" and put a new spin on historical events. On a trip to England to visit Shakespeare, they encountered Francis Bacon, who claimed to be the author of Shakespeare's plays, prompting the bard to threaten, "Bacon, you'll fry for this!" Fractured Fairytales were tongue-in-cheek versions of familiar classics. In "Sleeping Beauty," a prince turns Beauty's castle into a theme park and is vexed by the wicked witch, who demands half the profits.

## BUMPER CARS

"Keep your hands inside the cars!" What child hasn't heard those words of caution while settling eagerly into a bumper car? Bumper cars first appeared in the nation's amusement parks in the early 1920s, when competing firms introduced the Skooter and the Dodgem cars. Powered with electricity from a charged ceiling, they glide smoothly across a metal floor. Impact is the goal, and kids love the ensuing free-for-all, complete with harmless head-on collisions. The ride proved so popular that it inspired an aquatic spin-off: bumper boats.

## BUMPER STICKERS

Bumper stickers have been around for a long time. In 1935 many visitors to Canada came home with "I Saw the Dionne Quintuplets" plastered on their cars. But the stickers didn't take off until after World War II, when self-sticking paper was invented. Soon such political sentiments as "I Like Ike" were displayed on highways. In 1964 "AuH$_2$O" (the chemical symbols for gold and water) boosted Barry Goldwater's candidacy. In 1966 "Draft Beer, Not Boys" showed up.

Bumper stickers comment on everything from travel ("Carlsbad Caverns: 22 Percent More Cavities") to consumer complaints ("If You Could Squeeze This Car You'd Get Lemonade") to family relationships ("Sibling Rivalry Is Kid Stuff"). They often carry serious messages, too, such as "School's Open, Drive Slowly." Tailgating is discouraged with "If You Can Read This, You're Too Close." Horn blowers are zinged with "Honking Is for Geese." And then there's the ultimate grump: "Ban Bumper Stickers."

## BUNGEE JUMPING

In the 1980s thrill seekers looking for an extreme adrenaline rush discovered a new sport: bungee jumping. Jumpers hook themselves up to an elastic bungee cord and jump headfirst from a cliff, tower, crane, or hot-air balloon. The cords, which were originally designed to attach tanks and jeeps to parachutes for airdrops from cargo planes, stretch to about twice their length. Then they recoil, yanking jumpers back almost to their starting point.

Forerunners of these daring jumpers include the "land divers" of Pentecost Island in the South Pacific archipelago of Vanuatu, who as part of a ritual jumped with liana vines tied to their ankles from platforms in banyan trees. Circus acrobats introduced bungee jumping to America in the 1920s, but it didn't become a sport until 1979, when the Oxford Dangerous Sports Club jumped from the Clifton Bridge in Bristol, England, and the Golden Gate Bridge in San Francisco. Bungee jumping has resulted in a few deaths, but tens of thousands, including couples who took the plunge together after exchanging marriage vows, have jumped safely.

In the latest death-defying pursuit to take hold in America, bungee jumpers hurtle earthward at speeds of up to 60 m.p.h. They are suspended by a bungee cord, made of 365 strands of rubber enclosed in a sheath about five-eighths of an inch in diameter.

## BURMA-SHAVE SIGNS

Car trips took longer when highways had only two lanes, but the boredom was relieved by the makers of Burma-Shave, who from 1925 to 1963 spread their ads across a series of roadside signs. The verses were divided among six or more 18-inch-by-40-inch boards set 100 feet apart and angled so that drivers could read only one at a time. Everyone in the car read along: "WITHIN THIS VALE...OF TOIL...AND SIN...YOUR HEAD GROWS BALD...BUT NOT YOUR CHIN—USE...BURMA-SHAVE."

The signs, and the first jingles, were created by the Odell family of Minnesota to sell their brushless shaving cream. By the end of the 1920s, Americans across the country were writing the signs. An annual contest offered $100 for any jingle used, and thousands of entries poured in, including one from the novelist Vladimir Nabokov. The verses that won were full of folksy good humor, such as "BEN...MET ANNA...MADE A HIT...NEGLECTED BEARD...BEN-ANNA SPLIT...BURMA-SHAVE." Some offered such advice as "PAST...SCHOOLHOUSES...TAKE IT SLOW...LET THE LITTLE...SHAVERS GROW...BURMA-SHAVE."

The signs worked when, at 35 miles an hour, it took 18 seconds to pass six of them. They were discontinued when highways got bigger and traffic got faster.

Burma-Shave signs made family car trips more fun during the Great Depression. The last remaining signs were taken down in 1963.

Burma-Shave
If Ida used
Ida won my Ida
Ida refused
To Ida
I proposed

George Burns and Gracie Allen got laughs for Paramount in such movies as *The Big Broadcast* (1932). After Allen's death, Burns withdrew from the limelight but returned 11 years later, when he won an Academy Award for *The Sunshine Boys* (1975).

George Bush and his wife, Barbara, often retreated to their home in Kennebunkport, Maine, with First Dog Millie, a best-selling "author."

## BURNS AND ALLEN

George Burns was delighted to play straight man and second fiddle to his wife, Gracie Allen, on the *Burns and Allen* radio show. But on the air he played a man exasperated by her scatterbrained ways. Gracie, famous for her misuse of language, was the show's comic inspiration. When George asked what a wizard was, she replied, "A snowstorm." "Then what is a blizzard?" "A blizzard is the inside of a chicken. Anybody knows that." And when Burns tried to put her down, saying, "You ought to live in the home for the feebleminded," Allen retorted, "Oh, I'd love to be your houseguest sometime."

After nearly 20 years on radio, the two moved to *The George Burns and Gracie Allen Show* on CBS television. When Gracie died in 1964, George floundered, but he reemerged as a solo performer admired for his dry humor. He was 92 when he starred in the movie *18 Again.*

## BURR, AARON

Revolutionary soldier and one-term vice president Aaron Burr is best remembered for his 1804 duel with political rival Alexander Hamilton. Four years earlier, Hamilton had thwarted Burr when flawed voting procedures nearly handed Burr the presidency instead of the vice presidency. Burr lost the position of chief executive largely because Hamilton distrusted him. Hamilton foiled Burr again during Burr's campaign for governor of New York, calling him "the most unfit and dangerous man in the community." Bitter, Burr challenged his foe to a duel that left Hamilton mortally wounded.

Although he was wanted by the law, Burr finished his term as vice president, plotting all the while to seize territory in the West and the South in order to establish a new republic. He was charged with treason but was later acquitted. Politically ruined, he fled to Europe, where he tried to gain Napoleon's support for invading Louisiana and Florida.

## BUSH, GEORGE

"Any definition of a successful life must include service to others," said George Bush, echoing the values instilled in him by his father, a former U.S. senator. After graduating from Yale and founding a company in the Texas oil fields, he fulfilled this obligation through a 25-year political career that led from the House of Representatives to the White House.

Bush's code of decency and loyalty were the underpinnings of both his public and his private roles. Calling for a "kinder, gentler America," the 41st president replaced official pomp with personalized diplomacy, whether chatting with tourists through the South Lawn fence or assembling troops for the Gulf War. Outside the media glare, where he often appeared aloof, Bush is known and loved as the down-to-earth "Poppy," who cherishes his wife, "Bar," and their extended family—dogs included—and who enjoys such simple pleasures as horseshoes, country music, and pork rinds.

## CABBAGE PATCH KIDS

In 1983, to the utter dismay of many marketers, a national craze erupted for a new line of homely dolls that didn't talk, cry, or wet their pants. Xavier Roberts, a young man from Georgia experimenting with soft sculpture, had drawn on Appalachian folk traditions to create his handmade dolls with yarn for hair—the antithesis of modern, high-tech toys. After promoting his creations successfully at crafts fairs, Roberts approached several toy companies about large-scale production. Only one, Coleco, was interested.

Coleco's Cabbage Patch Kids were a monumental hit, possibly because they appealed to a nostalgia for simpler times. Each Kid or Baby (the makers didn't call them dolls) was unique. "Adopted" by a child "parent," it arrived with adoption papers from the "hospital" in Cleveland, Georgia, after it had been "born" in a cabbage patch. Adults seeking to buy Cabbage Patch Kids as Christmas presents actually rioted when supplies ran short. Ironically, Coleco ultimately went bankrupt, and another company now sells the dolls.

## CAESAR, SID

Albert Einstein was so taken with Sid Caesar's ersatz German expert, Professor Ludwig von Knowitall, that he asked to meet the star of *Your Show of Shows*. The 90-minute variety show, which ran from 1949 to 1954, has long been considered the acme of live television comedy.

Caesar worked with some of the best writers in the business on a grueling schedule that involved creating six new sketches each week for 39 weeks. But when the cameras rolled, Caesar, his costar, Imogene Coca, and their supporting cast, including Carl Reiner and Howard Morris, were on their own. Caesar spoke gibberish in several foreign languages and played a wide spectrum of characters, from Cool Cees, a sax player, to a six-month-old baby. In one sketch about a cheap date, he played the pay phone, taxicab, French maître d', and Italian waiter, who, delighted with his 10-cent tip, says rhapsodically, "She's a-come in at last, my ship."

But the man behind the comedy was not a happy person, and after the show ended, he faded from view to battle his personal demons. In his 1982 autobiography, *Where Have I Been?* he admitted to depression and drug use. His humor may in fact have been fueled by despair. Caesar himself pointed out that comedy verges on tragedy: "Laugh too hard and you cry. Cry too hard and you laugh."

In 1983 Cabbage Patch Kids were so in demand that one store manager put his last seven dolls in a vault and held a lottery for would-be buyers.

Sid Caesar and Imogene Coca set the standard for live television comedy in *Your Show of Shows*. In 1992 the two reprised their best sketches in a successful stage show, *Together Again*.

The Cajuns, with their exuberant festivals, 24-hour liquor licenses, and colorful Mardi Gras celebrations, are well known for their zest for life. There are few reminders of their tragic early history as narrated by Longfellow in his poem "Evangeline."

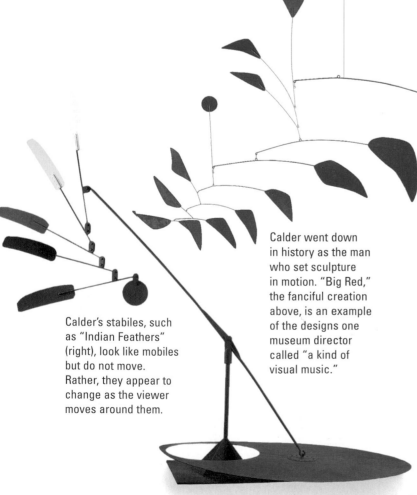

Calder's stabiles, such as "Indian Feathers" (right), look like mobiles but do not move. Rather, they appear to change as the viewer moves around them.

Calder went down in history as the man who set sculpture in motion. "Big Red," the fanciful creation above, is an example of the designs one museum director called "a kind of visual music."

## CAJUN CULTURE

Cajun culture lends a unique flavor to parts of southern Louisiana and Texas. Ancestors of the Cajuns left western France in the 1600s to settle in Acadia, in the region now called Nova Scotia, Canada. After the British captured Acadia in 1755, many exiled Acadians fled to the bayous and prairies of southern Louisiana, then still owned by France. There, in relative isolation, they maintained their customs, cuisine, and dialects and became known as Cajuns, short for Acadians.

Throughout the 19th century, most Cajuns made their living by farming, trapping, and fishing, and they continued to speak their own language. But in the early 20th century, their isolation ended with the building of highways and the influence of radio. In schools, Cajun children were not allowed to speak French. The Cajun heritage seemed to be eroding. Eventually, however, the importance of preserving Cajun folkways was realized, and in 1968 the Council for the Development of French in Louisiana was founded.

Today visitors flock to New Orleans and outlying parishes to sample gumbo, jambalaya, and spicy boudin sausage, and to waltz and two-step in packed dance halls to music played on fiddles, accordions, and triangles. And the Cajuns are proudly showing them how to *laissez les bon temps rouler*, or "let the good times roll."

## CALDER, ALEXANDER

Born into a family of respected academic artists, Alexander Calder sought less traditional outlets for his own talents. He earned a degree in mechanical engineering before entering a New York art school. Then, as an illustrator for the *National Police Gazette*, he delighted in sketching circus performers. All of these experiences influenced Sandy Calder's witty, deceptively simple creations, including wire sculptures, a miniature circus, jewelry, and kitchen utensils.

Calder was also influenced by the painters he met in Paris in the 1920s. Captivated by Piet Mondrian's brightly colored geometric designs, he determined to make these designs vibrate. His first mobiles were motor-driven, but he soon learned to suspend metal shapes on a wire frame so precisely that, when stirred by a breeze, they turned in ever-changing patterns. This invention not only secured Calder's reputation as America's leading sculptor, it inspired an industry. Mobiles now grace public spaces—and nurseries—everywhere.

## CALL-IN SHOWS

People love to hear themselves talk—one reason for the popularity of call-in shows, which date back to the early days of radio. *The Answer Man*, which debuted in 1937, was actually a "write-in" show: the host responded to questions that listeners had mailed in, such as "Is is true that only the male cricket chirps?" On *The Goodwill Hour*, John J. Anthony, whose real name was Lester Kroll, took questions from listeners who were selected to come to the studio. His credentials—three doctoral degrees—were as fictitious as his name, but still people were eager to "ask Mr. Anthony."

Today talk radio has seemingly taken over the airways. Some shows, especially those on A.M. radio, offer advice on everything from investments to car repairs. But call-in shows on radio and television have also become America's 24-hour town halls. They offer listeners the chance to share their views on the hot topics of the day, fostering what has been called "dial-in democracy." Most feature sharp-tongued hosts and debates that double as entertainment. Ultraconservative Rush Limbaugh, dubbed the "King of Call-ins," never fails to light up the switchboard.

## CAMPBELL, JOSEPH

Like a mythic hero himself, Joseph Campbell assumed a herculean task: to examine and interpret world mythology. Tracing eons-old tales through diverse civilizations, Campbell found that myths express our efforts to understand life's mysteries. He discovered a deep-seated impulse for storytelling and ceremony that persists today. In the *Star Wars* trilogy, Campbell felt, director George Lucas had "put the newest and most powerful spin" on the concept of the hero's journey. In presidential funerals he saw an "illustration of the high service of ritual to a society."

With some 20 books to his credit, Campbell rose to fame —posthumously—when he appeared in 1988 with journalist Bill Moyers in the PBS series *The Power of Myth*, taped during the last years of Campbell's life. Their conversations touched on everything from Australian aborigines to Santa Claus. Bringing mythology to widespread public attention formed a capstone to Campbell's work, for he believed that the goal of experience, in myth or in real life, is not self-aggrandizement but the attainment of wisdom.

## CANDID CAMERA

The television show *Candid Camera* used a simple formula: make absurd things happen to unsuspecting people and film their reactions. Then, when they are at the peak of frustration, let them in on the gag by saying, "Smile, you're on *Candid Camera*." Average Americans were caught talking back to mailboxes, puzzling over bowling balls without finger holes, and working themselves into a fury as some stranger not only read the newspaper over their shoulder but turned the pages, too.

Allen Funt, who introduced the show in 1948, hosted most of the episodes and took part in many setups. He often relied on women as accomplices. Few men would have stopped to help Funt with his luggage, but a series of eager gentlemen did rush to help a pretty woman— whose suitcase just happened to be filled with concrete.

Larry King's guests have ranged from Barbra Streisand to Ross Perot, who announced his intention to run for president right there on CNN.

Durward Kirby (left) joined Allen Funt (right) as cohost of *Candid Camera*. As the program itself put it, *Candid Camera* caught "unsuspecting folks in the act of being themselves."

Bootlegger Al Capone said he only supplied a legitimate demand: "Some call it bootlegging. Some call it racketeering. I call it a business."

The dean of children's entertainers, Captain Kangaroo delighted children for 29 years with the help of Bunny Rabbit, Dancing Bear, and Mr. Green Jeans.

## CAPONE, AL

Four members of Al Capone's gang dressed as police officers and staged a "raid" on a rival Chicago mobster's headquarters on February 14, 1929. Their target, George "Bugs" Moran, wasn't there, but seven of his men were shot. The slayings, dubbed the St. Valentine's Day Massacre, were brutal even for Chicago in the 1920s. With the Moran gang out of business, Capone became the undisputed boss of the city's underworld. He had complete control of the illegal liquor trade, as well as of much of the city's legitimate business. "Scarface Al," as the tabloids called him, raked in up to $100 million a year. He became a law unto himself, ultimately controlling the police, the politicians, and the press.

Capone had flashy taste and liked to flaunt his power. He wore an 11-carat diamond ring and drove around the city in an armor-plated Cadillac. But Capone's notoriety was his undoing. While Justice Department agent Eliot Ness and his Untouchables raided Capone's warehouses and speakeasies, IRS agents launched an investigation that led to his conviction in 1931 for income tax evasion. Freed in 1939, the ailing Capone spent his final years in Florida.

## CAPTAIN KANGAROO

The Captain respected children, and they adored him. Created and played by Bob Keeshan, Captain Kangaroo was a gray-haired, gentle host who always had another surprise hidden in his many coat pockets. The show premiered in 1955 and stood in marked contrast to another popular children's television show, *Howdy Doody*. While *Howdy Doody* had a peanut gallery of frenzied kids responding to nonstop gags and pranks, the Captain calmly invited children to imagine themselves visiting his Treasure House. There they met Mr. Green Jeans, a farmer friend, as well as a cast of puppets that included the mischievous Mr. Moose and the introspective Bunny Rabbit.

Although each show had an educational theme, there were always plenty of jokes. Millions of children watched the show, but because Keeshan refused to allow the airing of commercials for products he considered inappropriate, CBS executives claimed that the network was losing money. Reluctant to make American mothers angry, CBS eased the show off the air by cutting it to 30 minutes and changing its time slot to 6:30 A.M. When it was canceled in 1984, it had been the longest-running children's program on television.

## CARNEGIE, ANDREW

Andrew Carnegie spent half his life struggling to become the richest steelmaker on earth and the other half giving his money away. The son of poor Scottish immigrants, Andrew Carnegie started out as a bobbin boy in a Pennsylvania textile mill at age 13 and was paid $1.20 a week. When he was 18, he impressed a railroad baron with the quality of his work and was hired as a secretary and personal telegraph operator. Before long, Carnegie began investing and reinvesting his earnings in such industries as bridge building and the manufacture of iron products and telegraph equipment. At the age of 66, Carnegie was able to sell his Carnegie Steel Company for $447 million, the largest liquid fortune of the time.

"A man who dies rich dies disgraced," declared Carnegie in his 1889 essay, "Wealth." Determined to dispose of his fortune as carefully as he had earned it, he made donations to universities, libraries, hospitals, parks, and concert halls. By 1917, his wealth had been used to establish more than 2,500 libraries and the first charitable foundation.

## CARNEGIE, DALE

In 1912 Dale Carnegie was an unemployed actor living in New York City. Trying to change his luck, he talked the director of a YMCA into letting him teach a night course in public speaking. With that job, Carnegie took his first step toward a phenomenal career as America's master of persuasion. His comforting message to the socially unskilled was that shyness, fear, and lack of confidence could all be overcome. He taught that people wanted to be liked and that anyone could be won over by a warm and genuine smile. His book, *How to Win Friends and Influence People*, became the first paperback to sell a million copies, and it is still in print in dozens of languages.

Carnegie died in 1955, but the corporation that bears his name continues to teach his course to millions of people, including an impressive roster of CEOs. In fact, many of America's Fortune 500 companies pay for their executives to take the Dale Carnegie course.

## CAROL BURNETT SHOW

Carol Burnett would do anything for a laugh. In an era when most comedy-variety shows were failing, *The Carol Burnett Show* was a huge success. An inspired comedian, Burnett was also a talented singer and dancer. Each week, she performed skits and satires with her regular cast, which featured Harvey Korman, Vicki Lawrence, and Tim Conway.

Burnett began each show by taking questions from the studio audience, usually while wearing a glittering Bob Mackie gown. A series of sketches followed, many of which featured that night's guest star. Some favorites include "Mr. Tudball and Mrs. Wiggins," in which a boss was continually frustrated by his inept secretary, and "Ed and Eunice," about the home life of a lowbrow married couple. The cast also parodied soap operas in the recurring sketch "As the Stomach Turns." During its run, the show won wide acclaim and 20 Emmys. It was canceled in 1978, lasting only one season after Korman left. For Burnett, going off the air ended a brilliant 11-year run. The show was later syndicated as *Carol Burnett and Friends*, in a half-hour version.

Part of Andrew Carnegie's generous legacy, Carnegie Hall plays host to great orchestras and performers from around the world.

Appearing as Cleopatra in this 1975 skit, Carol Burnett showed the right way to walk like an Egyptian. Regular cast member Harvey Korman provided the backup.

## CARPETBAGGERS

For many Southerners after the Civil War, the most hated symbol of Northern "oppression" was the carpetbagger. The Yankees who carried everything they owned in bags made of carpeting were viewed as scoundrels who roamed the South, fleecing impoverished whites of their last possessions. This portrayal says more about the Southerners' bitterness about losing the war than about the Northerners who moved south, many of whom—ex-soldiers, teachers, merchants, and preachers—were looking for opportunities to work and build a future. Their energy and capital were frequently welcome.

One carpetbagger who made a name for himself was the Ohio-born Willard Warner. After moving to Alabama to plant cotton, he was soon elected to the Senate. He also started the Tecumseh Iron Company with money from his Northern associates. When he moved to Tennessee, where he owned blast furnaces, he was voted into the state legislature. Still, despite his work and that of others like him, the image of the predatory carpetbagger persisted for long afterward.

This Thomas Nast cartoon shows the commonly held opinion of carpetbaggers as greedy and unprincipled men who preyed on the South after the Civil War.

## CARSON, RACHEL

Rachel Carson was a gifted ecologist who expressed her findings in beautiful prose. Born in Pennsylvania in 1907, Carson worked as an aquatic biologist with the U.S. Fish and Wildlife Service for many years. She wrote three highly regarded books about the sea, but she is best remembered for *Silent Spring*, published in 1962, in which she warns about the dangers of indiscriminate use of pesticides.

*Silent Spring* was an immediate best-seller and one of the most influential books of the 20th century. It helped to launch the ecology movement and to establish the Environmental Protection Agency. The book's argument that fat-soluble pesticides were interfering with reproduction in birds was strongly disputed by the chemicals industry. Studies proved, however, that long-lasting substances in DDT weakened the eggshells of such birds of prey as bald eagles and peregrine falcons, thus threatening the species' very survival. DDT was finally banned in 1971, and many once-dwindling American bird populations are now recovering.

"Spring now comes unheralded by the return of the birds," Rachel Carson wrote, "and the early mornings are strangely silent where once they were filled with the beauty of bird song." Carson's inspiring work helped ensure the survival of a variety of birds, including the warbler (above).

## CARTER, JIMMY

When Jimmy Carter announced that he planned to run for president, even his mother asked, "President of what?" As the governor of Georgia, Carter had attracted some national attention as a symbol of the "new South," but his name was hardly a household word. In the wake of Watergate, however, Americans responded to this peanut farmer from Georgia precisely because he wasn't part of the establishment.

Carter won strong international approval for limiting aid to countries with a record of human rights abuses and for pushing through the Panama Canal treaties. His greatest accomplishment was brokering the historic 1979 peace agreement that ended 30 years of enmity between Israel and Egypt. Still, Carter's achievements were overshadowed by problems, especially the energy crisis, that caused inflation to soar into double digits. The worst moment of his administration came in November 1979, when Iranian militants seized 52 American hostages in Tehran. An attempted rescue ended in failure, and Americans showed their frustration by voting Carter out of office in the next election.

Instead of retiring, however, he founded the Carter Center of Emory University in 1986. As its emissary, he has served as mediator in international crises in places as diverse as Bosnia, Nicaragua, and North Korea, with results so impressive that one commentator called him "one of the greatest ex-presidents America has had."

## CARVER, GEORGE WASHINGTON

In 1896 George Washington Carver received a letter from Booker T. Washington, founder of the Tuskegee Institute in Alabama. Washington had heard of Carver's reputation as an expert in horticulture at the Iowa Agricultural College and wanted him to head the agriculture department at Tuskegee. "I can't offer you money, position, or fame," he wrote. "I offer you in their place...the task of bringing a people from degradation, poverty, and waste to full manhood." "I am coming," Carver wrote back, and for the next 47 years, he taught at and directed the only all-black agricultural-experiment station.

Carver tried to lift black sharecroppers out of poverty by persuading them to rotate their crops. But it was his work with peanuts that would bring him fame. When he appeared before a congressional tariff hearing on peanuts in 1921, congressmen who had at first merely patronized him were in the end fascinated by the products he had derived from the lowly peanut, including candy, cosmetics, and ink.

## CASABLANCA

A classic tale of love and sacrifice, *Casablanca* turned Humphrey Bogart and Ingrid Bergman into legends and became one of the timeless favorites of the silver screen. Many of its oft-quoted lines have become common expressions, from "Round up the usual suspects" to "I think this is the beginning of a beautiful friendship." But the line "Play it again, Sam" is never spoken in the film. "Play it, Sam," says Ilsa to the piano player at Rick's Café Américain.

Among other ironies, the Oscar-winning screenplay was hastily cobbled together. Until the last day of filming, no one knew whether Rick or Ilsa's husband, Victor Laszlo (Paul Henreid), would get the girl. The exotic locale was actually a Hollywood lot. The fog in the final scene was essential to shroud a blatantly fake plywood airplane. And an early publicity release listed the stars as Ronald Reagan and Ann Sheridan—casting that might have changed history.

Jimmy Carter's postpresidential career included building houses for the homeless. In 1992 he and Rosalynn lent a hand in Washington, D.C.

George Washington Carver's achievements as an educator and an inventor were honored in 1948, when the U.S. Postal Service issued this three-cent stamp.

"Here's looking at you, kid." As time goes by, the enduring romance of Casablanca never loses its magic.

Cassatt's visiting nephews and nieces inspired the first of her mother-and-child paintings. This theme would ultimately make up one-third of her work.

*The Catcher in the Rye* has been a favorite since its release in 1951. Teenage readers, especially, identify with Holden Caulfield and his efforts to come to terms with the ambiguities of life.

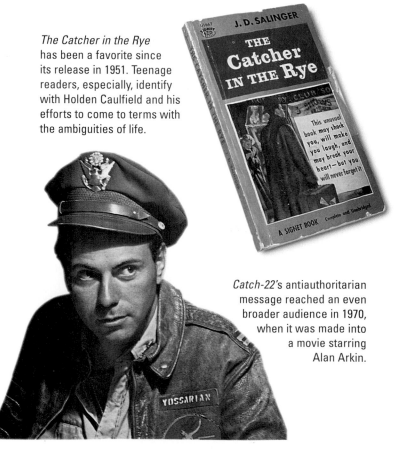

*Catch-22*'s antiauthoritarian message reached an even broader audience in 1970, when it was made into a movie starring Alan Arkin.

## CASSATT, MARY

Mary Cassatt is widely considered to be America's finest woman painter and perhaps the finest American painter of her generation. Juxtaposing bright colors, she flooded her canvases with warmth and light. Her favorite subjects were mothers and children, shown unsentimentally but sympathetically in everyday situations.

Enthralled by art since early childhood, Cassatt attended the prestigious Pennsylvania Academy of Fine Arts. She then persuaded her father, a Philadelphia stockbroker who thought upper-class women needed only "polite accomplishments," to let her pursue her studies in Paris. Recognition came after she joined the group of painters later known as the Impressionists (including Monet, Renoir, Pissarro, and others). Edgar Degas, in particular, admired Cassatt's work, observing, "I am not willing to admit that a woman can draw that well." The two strong-willed artists formed a close but stormy lifelong friendship. Although based in France, Cassatt influenced American taste by encouraging wealthy friends to collect outstanding new works of European art.

## CATCHER IN THE RYE

Teenage alienation never found a truer voice than that of Holden Caulfield, the malcontent hero of J. D. Salinger's classic coming-of-age novel, *The Catcher in the Rye*. After flunking out of three East Coast prep schools, Caulfield makes a poignantly funny journey from a room in a fleabag hotel in New York City to a spiritual crisis involving his failure to save a down-and-out prostitute and to a disastrous marriage proposal to his former girlfriend. Alternately profound and profane, Caulfield is often called a 20th-century Huck Finn because of his sardonic wit, his straightforward philosophy, and his heartbreaking sensitivity to the pain of others.

Salinger himself is one of America's best-known recluses. "Publishing is a terrible invasion of my privacy," remarked the author of just four slim books. In 1965 Salinger abruptly stopped writing for publication, although he continues to write for himself. He lives in seclusion in New Hampshire.

## CATCH-22

In his darkly humorous novel *Catch-22*, Joseph Heller describes a World War II air force bombardier, Captain John Yossarian, who wants to quit the war but can't because of a bureaucratic booby trap he calls Catch-22. This fictional military regulation stipulates that you don't have to fight if you're insane, but since wanting to live is normal, asking for a discharge means that you're sane and therefore must stay.

Although the setting is World War II, to critics of war the novel seemed to apply equally well to the Korean War and, later, to the Vietnam War. Yossarian became a role model for war resisters. The term *Catch-22* now refers to any arbitrary regulation by which those who are regulated can't win.

## CATHER, WILLA

In *My Antonia*, one of Willa Cather's most popular novels, she writes about the joys of creating a homestead on the sweeping expanse of the Great Plains during the late 1800s. "That is happiness; to be dissolved into something complete and great," muses one of the novel's main characters.

Cather left her rural hometown of Red Cloud, Nebraska, as a young woman and eventually settled in New York City. Once there, she led a sophisticated life, indulging her passion for opera, fine food, and the latest fashions. She worked for the influential *McClure's* magazine from 1906 to 1912 before deciding to devote her time to writing. Her first novel, *Alexander's Bridge*, is set in the cultured worlds of Boston and London, but she returned to her roots with a saga of immigrants who create a prosperous farm out of the unforgiving sod of the Nebraska prairie, *O Pioneers!*

Cather's concern was for the universal truths that underlie all of human experience. As one character in *O Pioneers!* puts it, "There are only two or three human stories, and they go on repeating themselves as fiercely as if they had never happened before."

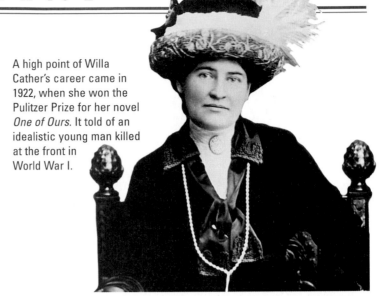

A high point of Willa Cather's career came in 1922, when she won the Pulitzer Prize for her novel *One of Ours*. It told of an idealistic young man killed at the front in World War I.

## CATLIN, GEORGE

In 1837 artist George Catlin's "Indian Gallery" exhibition created a sensation when it toured the East Coast. Crowds thronged for a closer look at his extraordinary paintings and to hear his unconventional plea for appreciation of Indian cultures.

Trained as a lawyer, Catlin left his practice to become a portrait painter. He had a strong interest in American Indians, and at the age of 34, he began his artistic expeditions into the West, traveling by horse and canoe and on foot. In all, he visited 48 Southwestern tribes in six years and painted more than 600 portraits. He found that the Indians were just as curious about him as he was about them. A Blackfoot medicine man known as White Buffalo was so delighted with the portrait of him in full bearskin dress that he presented the costume to Catlin as a gift.

George Catlin's love for American Indian culture shows in this painting, "Archery of the Mandan." His mission, he said, was to rescue "from oblivion the looks and customs of the vanishing races of native man in America."

## CATSKILL RESORTS

Before the stand-up comics of the 1950s reached *The Ed Sullivan Show*, many of them had perfected their timing in the Borscht Belt, the circuit of hotels in the Catskill Mountains that catered to Jewish vacationers. The Catskill resorts drew crowds by providing endless activities. Golf, tennis, miniature golf, softball, volleyball, horseshoes, shuffleboard, swimming, and more went on throughout the day; movies, dancing, and stage shows were offered each night. And through it all, especially at the bountiful meals in the cavernous dining halls, there was the incessant joking of comics working what many of them have called the toughest—and most rewarding—audience they would ever face.

Big-name comics like Buddy Hackett (left), Danny Kaye, Milton Berle, Red Buttons, and Sid Caesar began their careers performing at Catskill resorts.

## CATTLE KINGS

At the end of the Civil War, it seemed that just about any Western rancher could get rich practically overnight. Millions of unbranded cattle roamed the plains, most grazing land was in the public domain, and the price of beef kept rising. Wyoming cattleman Alexander Hamilton Swan parlayed one herd into a $50 million company. Financiers from Wall Street and Europe rushed to buy out ranches and combine them into vast spreads, some covering entire counties. Many European owners built elegant mansions and social clubs, while homegrown barons, such as John Chisum, built sprawling ranch houses surrounded by irrigated fields in the desert.

By the early 1880s, homesteaders had begun to crowd the plains. The cattle kings protected "their" ranges by setting prairie fires, starting stampedes, and worse: one rancher formed a vigilante band aptly called the Stranglers. But even the cattle kings could not fight Mother Nature. When the winter of 1886–87 killed cattle by the thousands, many fortunes disappeared even faster than they were made.

## CENSUS

In August 1790 some 650 census takers set out on horseback and on foot to count the "Whole Number of Persons" for the nation's first census. They asked residents six simple questions and tallied the results on loose sheets of paper. Taking the census was no easy job. One census taker complained that he was "riding horses almost to Death" in mountainous back country while looking for isolated families. Some suspicious families even refused to cooperate.

Today the census, mandated by the Constitution, is more than just a head count. It offers a snapshot of life in America by providing information on housing, income, employment, and ethnic origin. Politicians watch the results, in the words of one journalist, "like a mother hawk with a fragile egg" because the census figures determine the number of congressional representatives allowed each state and help dictate how government money will be spent. Citizens are generally obliging. One man, asked how many children he had, replied, "How many do you need to meet your quota?"

## CEREALS

Scorning breakfasts of syrupy pancakes and home-cured hams, self-proclaimed health experts at the turn of the century urged a regimen of toasted bits of corn, oats, rice, or wheat. Dr. John Kellogg developed flaked cereals in 1894 for patients at his sanatorium in Battle Creek, Michigan, as part of a program aimed at "getting the stomach right." One patient, C. W. Post, was so impressed that he later marketed a wheat-flake cereal to the public. He also created Grape Nuts, advertised as a "remedy for consumption, malaria, and loose teeth." Each box included a pamphlet titled "The Road

Many cattle barons began with nothing but a few cowhands and a herd—often of longhorns—rounded up on the open prairie.

The census turns up such facts as the number of centenarians, which recently jumped from the hundreds to the tens of thousands.

Many cereals vie for children's attention by using cartoon characters and plenty of sugar. Adults are more likely lured by nutrition.

to Wellville." Housewives were taken with the convenience of breakfast in a box. Soon Battle Creek became known as the Cereal City, producing 108 brands of cornflakes alone.

Ironically, some children's cereals—in an array of colored loops, puffs, and even cookie shapes—attract buyers more for the fun packaging and small prizes than for nutrition. "I tell kids they should throw away the cereal and eat the boxes," says one dentist. "At least they'd get some fiber."

## CHAPLIN, CHARLIE

The Little Tramp, with his derby hat, baggy pants, twirling cane, and toddling gait, was the diminutive creation of one of this century's towering film geniuses. Charlie Chaplin was born in London into a miserable childhood from which he escaped via the stage. While on tour in the U.S. with a variety troupe, he signed a contract with the Keystone Company, which cranked out one- and two-reel silents. Within a year, he had assumed his now-familiar screen persona and, as director, introduced to Keystone's slapstick films the crafts he had learned onstage: characterization, pantomime, and pathos. In short, he humanized movie comedy.

By 1915 Chaplin was already being copied by other screen comics. At Mutual Film Corporation, where he had been given complete creative control, he directed such gems as *The Rink* and *The Cure*. At United Artists, which he co-founded, Chaplin produced *The Gold Rush*, often considered his greatest masterpiece. But divorce and scandal marred his private life. He was attacked for not being a citizen and was accused of being a Communist. Many clamored for his deportation, and, vowing never to return to the U.S., Chaplin moved to Switzerland with his fourth wife and their eight children. In 1972 he accepted a special Academy Award for "making motion pictures the art form of this century." In 1975 the former street kid was knighted by Queen Elizabeth.

## CHARLES, RAY

"Soul," explained Ray Charles, "is when you can take a song and make it a part of yourself, a part that is so true, so real, people think it must have happened to you." And when he sang in his gritty voice over his romping jazz piano, punctuating the rhythms with moans, grunts, and manic "testifying" of gospel music, "The Genius" revealed to popular audiences the emotional intensity of the black church experience.

Born poor in Georgia, Charles went blind at age six from untreated glaucoma. At a school for the blind, he learned to play several instruments and to write music in Braille. Eventually he started a jazz trio in Seattle, singing smoothly in Nat "King" Cole style. But by the time he recorded his first big hit, "I Got a Woman," based on a gospel hymn, he had found—and begun to popularize—soul. Hits poured forth in a range of styles, from rock to blues to country. In 1986 Charles was inducted into the Rock and Roll Hall of Fame.

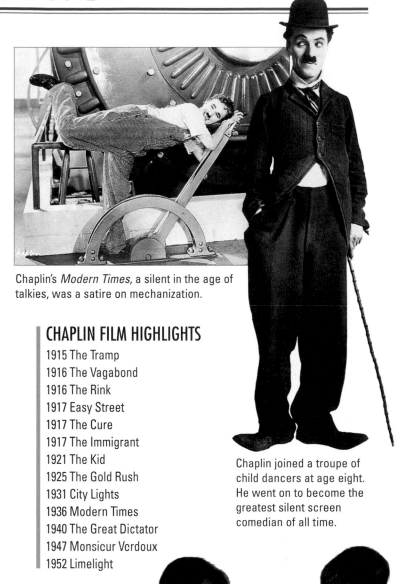

Chaplin's *Modern Times,* a silent in the age of talkies, was a satire on mechanization.

### CHAPLIN FILM HIGHLIGHTS
1915 The Tramp
1916 The Vagabond
1916 The Rink
1917 Easy Street
1917 The Cure
1917 The Immigrant
1921 The Kid
1925 The Gold Rush
1931 City Lights
1936 Modern Times
1940 The Great Dictator
1947 Monsicur Vcrdoux
1952 Limelight

Chaplin joined a troupe of child dancers at age eight. He went on to become the greatest silent screen comedian of all time.

Soul superstar Ray Charles plugged Pepsi in the 1980s. In his prime during the 1950s and '60s, he influenced such major performers as Aretha Franklin and Stevie Wonder.

Sidney Toler played the invincible and courteous B-movie detective in *Charlie Chan at the Wax Museum* (1940). After Toler's death the role of Charlie Chan was played by Roland Winters.

Charlie McCarthy was king of the snappy comeback, with Edgar Bergen as the straight man. Charlie seemed so lifelike that no one seemed to care if Bergen's lips moved.

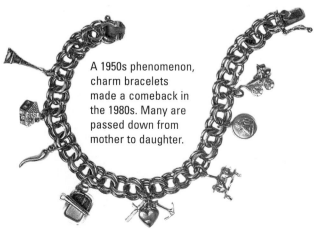

A 1950s phenomenon, charm bracelets made a comeback in the 1980s. Many are passed down from mother to daughter.

## CHARLIE CHAN

America's favorite Asian sleuth, Charlie Chan was modeled on a real-life Honolulu policeman. After Chan's debut in a 1925 *Saturday Evening Post* serial by Earl Derr Biggers, he appeared in some 46 movies. He trapped criminals through cleverness and was often helped—or hindered—by his eager young sons. He was never played by a Chinese actor, but his two main portrayers, Swede Warner Oland and American Sidney Toler, were immensely popular. Oland was so convincing, in fact, that he was greeted in Chinese when he visited China.

Reacting to charges of racial stereotyping, defenders of the Charlie Chan films point out that while earlier screen Asians were ridiculous villains, Chan was dignified and even heroic, frequently outsmarting Caucasian cops. Some Asian-Americans have complained that Chan "talks like a fortune cookie," but moviegoers of the 1930s and '40s loved such "witticisms" as "Bad alibi like dead fish—cannot stand test of time" and "Mind like parachute—only function when open."

## CHARLIE MCCARTHY

"I'll clip you, Bergen. So help me, I'll mow-w-w you down!" This threat, along with the top hat, white tie, tails, and monocle, was one of Charlie McCarthy's trademarks. The debonair dummy with the amused chuckle was known for his quick wit and seemed to have a life of his own. In 1938 his creator, Edgar Bergen, received a special Academy Award, a wooden statuette, for his "outstanding comedy creation."

Bergen and McCarthy reached the height of their popularity on the radio with *The Charlie McCarthy Show*, trading quips with guest stars. (When W. C. Fields threatened to carve Charlie into a venetian blind, Charlie came back with "That makes me shudder.") The duo also made several films, notably *You Can't Cheat an Honest Man*.

## CHARM BRACELETS

Jingling sweetly, imbued with sentiment, charm bracelets have an appeal that never quite fades away. One of the hottest fashion trends of the 1950s, the bracelets served as tender reminders of one's girlhood. Travels, interests, and milestones were chronicled by gold or silver Eiffel towers, minuscule musical instruments, tiny tennis rackets, and photo lockets. All the rage were itsy-bitsy banks for storing mad money in the form of a tightly folded bill.

Like a scrapbook, a collection of charms is highly personal. Mamie Eisenhower wore a bracelet with 21 charms representing events in the life of the president, including a miniature key to the executive mansion. At the height of the charm bracelet craze, Tiffany's carried some 4,000 different charms. More affordable were those sold by Woolworth's in the 1980s, when the bracelets made their way back into style.

## CHAUTAUQUA MOVEMENT

Chautauqua Lake in western New York was the birthplace of a unique adult-education and self-improvement movement that uplifted and entertained millions of Americans from the 1870s to the 1920s. Chautauqua was founded by John Heyl Vincent, a Methodist minister, and Lewis Miller, a businessman, as a summer training center for Protestant Sunday school workers. It rapidly expanded to include a university, a massive summer camp for adults, and a Book-a-Month Club, probably the first of its kind. Religion was, in the beginning, a main focus, but there were also lectures on topics from science to social reform as well as concerts and plays.

Chautauqua proved so popular that several traveling schools were organized, along with home-study courses that brought enlightenment to rural residents. The movement is said to have reached one-third of all Americans by 1924.

## CHAVEZ, CESAR

As a child, Cesar Chavez experienced the misery and poverty suffered by one of the most exploited groups in the United States: workers who moved from job to job harvesting crops. In 1962 Chavez quit his job as a labor organizer and dedicated himself to organizing a union for migrant farm workers.

Chavez recruited a group of grape pickers to form what became the United Farm Workers (UFW). In 1965 the union organized a strike against grape growers near the town of Delano, California. Chavez drew attention to the issue by fasting for 25 days. He used the ensuing publicity to alert the nation to the scandalous conditions his workers endured. As a result, civil rights groups, national leaders, and ordinary citizens began to boycott grapes. In 1968 *New York* magazine wrote, "Most liberals . . . would rather eat a cyanide pellet than a California grape." In 1970 Chavez scored a historic victory when the grape growers signed a contract with the UFW.

## CHEERLEADING

Cheerleading began at Ivy League colleges as a men's activity. In 1878 D. A. Rollings of Dartmouth College led yells of "Wah-hoo-wah," and in the 1880s Princeton men offered cheers of "Sis, boom, bah." When the men went off to fight in World War II, women took over the cheering chores.

By the 1950s, the cheerleading impulse had seized high schools. Tryouts became an annual test of skill, beauty, and popularity. Many hopefuls attended summer cheerleading camps to increase their chances of making the squad. Practice became increasingly necessary as acrobatic stunts became more daring. In 1972 cheerleading became a paying job when the Dallas Cowboys football team hired the first professional cheerleaders, the Dallas Cowgirls. Critics felt that the scantily clad Cowgirls detracted from cheerleading's wholesome image, but fans liked them and other teams were quick to hire professional cheerleaders of their own.

Described as a cross between a camp meeting and a county fair, traveling Chautauquas brought an array of musical programs, plays, and lectures to eager townsfolk. Local reading circles also proved popular.

At the Rose Bowl, cheerleaders not only stir up the crowd but entertain television viewers at halftime.

Enthusiasm for cheeseburgers takes many forms, including a phone that came on a sesame-seed bun. For the truly burger-obsessed, there are a host of toys and knickknacks available, including this wind-up hopping cheeseburger (left).

## CHEESEBURGER

The cheeseburger is the quintessential American food. It's quick and filling, and you can usually get one at the nearest eatery. This meal-on-a-bun tastes great whether the cheese used is American, cheddar, Swiss, or Monterey Jack.

The cheeseburger is believed to have originated in the late 1930s as a double-decker burger at one of the Bob's Big Boy restaurants. Despite criticism of its high fat content, the cheeseburger remains a favorite. McDonald's alone has sold billions since they opened their doors in the 1950s (the company stopped counting after it hit the 100 billion mark).

## CHICAGO

Chicago isn't called "The Windy City" just because of the gales that come off Lake Michigan. Surprisingly, the city first got its nickname from its long-winded boosters. But Richard J. Daley, "de Mare" who presided over Chicago for 21 years, simply christened it "the city that works."

At the heart of Chicago is the Loop, a ring of elevated train tracks that carry tens of thousands of workers to the business district every weekday. Surrounding the downtown area is a variety of ethnic neighborhoods, from Chinatown to Greektown, established by immigrants who brought their muscle to the city's stockyards and steelworks. Other newcomers, blacks from the South, brought their music, mixing Delta blues with Chicago's gritty urban edge to create a new style. Legendary performers like Muddy Waters and Elmore James built their careers in Chicago's smoky nightclubs.

Gilded Age magnates also left their mark. Their mansions and monuments line the avenues, and their millions subsidized such institutions as the Field Museum of Natural History and the Art Institute of Chicago. The city's hustle attracted less legitimate entrepreneurs as well; it was here that Al Capone and his fellow mobsters bootlegged their way through Prohibition.

The Great Fire of 1871, which consumed 2,000 acres and killed 300 citizens, hardly broke Chicago's stride. The city bounded back with the world's first metal-framed skyscraper. Soon Chicago was known for its innovative architecture, from Beaux Arts jewel boxes to glass monoliths.

Long suffering under its census ranking of "Second City," Chicago has labored to amass superlatives. "Make no little plans," advised the Chicago architect Daniel Burnham. "They have no magic to stir men's souls." Accordingly, the city boasts the biggest aquarium, busiest airport, tallest building with the fastest elevator (the 110-story Sears Tower), and greatest number of Nobel laureates. It was the site of the first nuclear chain reaction and home to the first *Playboy* magazine. Even the ever-optimistic Cubs bear a singular distinction: they have had the longest World Series drought in baseball history.

Chicago *go bragh*! Every year for St. Patrick's Day, the mighty Chicago River is dyed green. At right, one of the four pylons that flank the river's Michigan Avenue Bridge.

## CHILD, JULIA

With her commanding presence, high-pitched voice, unpretentious manner, and unabashed passion for good food, Julia Child has popularized haute cuisine by bringing it into everyone's home. Her first television show, *The French Chef*, premiered on Boston's educational channel, WGBH, in 1963 and paved the way for the many cooking shows on the air today.

One of Child's culinary pet peeves is the growing obsession with diet among Americans. She believes that food should be a source of joy, not suspicion. Her desire to spread the gospel of good food led her to become cofounder of the American Institute of Wine and Food in 1981. Today there are more than 30 local chapters around the country.

When Julia Child first appeared on television, she earned a mere $50 for each show. However, she quickly gained a following, becoming America's favorite chef.

## CHINATOWN

*Tangrenbu* was the name newly arrived Chinese immigrants gave to their community, but the rest of America knew it as Chinatown. In this teeming ten-block area in the shadow of San Francisco's Nob Hill, they created a world reminiscent of Canton. For example, residents called one street *Tak Wo Gaai*, "Street of Virtuous Harmony," not Washington Place, as did city maps. On Chinatown's cobbled streets, flower vendors jostled for space with toy peddlers and fortune-tellers. Shops with brightly lit lacquered lanterns offered exotic merchandise from Asia. Other Chinatowns have since grown up in Los Angeles, New York City, and, in recent years, the Seattle-Vancouver area. All have the same appeal: fragrant herb shops, Chinese delicacies, Eastern medicines, and a glimpse at the color and vitality of an ancient Asian culture.

A Chinese New Year celebration provides a 10-day spectacle of parades, floats, and dances like the Dragon Dance. A haze of blue smoke rises from long strings of firecrackers, which are set off on every corner.

## CHISHOLM TRAIL

When the Chisholm Trail was completed in 1867, ranchers hailed it as a safe route for cattle drives from Texas to the railhead in Abilene, Kansas, from which cattle were shipped east. The original trail followed the wagon tracks of Jesse Chisholm, a trader who had hauled skins between San Antonio and Wichita in the early 1860s. Livestock dealer Joseph McCoy extended it to Abilene so that drivers could easily reach the cattle depot he had established there.

Although the trail avoided mountainous terrain and the lands of hostile Indians, cowboys still found that skill and endurance were necessary. In Indian Territory (now Oklahoma), local tribes tried to extort a toll ranging from 10 cents to one dollar a head. At the Kansas border, bands of marauders lay in wait. Cowboys often had to shoot their way past angry Kansas farmers, who were determined to keep out the longhorns, carriers of the fatal Texas fever. Stampedes and treacherous river crossings also claimed many lives.

In the early 1880s the railroads came to southern Texas, and the long cattle drives ended. But by then the Chisholm Trail was worn deep and up to 400 yards wide, leaving a permanent mark on the land as well as on Western history.

*Red River*, a classic 1948 Western starring John Wayne and Montgomery Clift, was based on a story in the *Saturday Evening Post*. The film's action takes place on the Chisholm Trail and recounts the hardships of the first of many long cattle drives.

## CHOCOLATE CHIP COOKIES

Legend has it that the chocolate chip cookie was created around 1930 by Ruth Wakefield, proprietor of the Toll House Inn in Massachusetts. Wakefield's Toll House cookies were made with brown sugar, flour, eggs, butter, and small pieces broken from a Nestlé's chocolate bar.

As the cookie's popularity grew, Nestlé obtained Wakefield's permission to print her recipe on the wrappers of its chocolate bars. The company soon began to look for ways to make their chocolate easier to use in recipes. In 1939 the chocolate drops Americans know and love were introduced as Nestlé Toll House Morsels, and today the recipe for Toll House cookies can still be found on every package.

## CHOP SUEY

While chop suey might sound Chinese, the dish is unknown in China. A cross-cultural concoction, it was invented in San Francisco during the mid-1800s by cooks responsible for feeding Chinese railroad workers. While building the Pacific railroad lines, the workers were often fed this mixture of bean sprouts, water chestnuts, bamboo shoots, and small pieces of meat. Roughly translated from the Mandarin dialect and twisted by the unaccustomed American tongue, *tsa sui*, or "bits and pieces," sounded like "chop suey."

## CHRISTMAS IN AMERICA

American Christmas customs, derived from many cultures, were given a special setting when Clement Clarke Moore wrote his famous poem "An Account of a Visit from St. Nicholas" in 1823. Moore's poem—better known by its first line, "'Twas the night before Christmas"—portrays St. Nick as a "jolly old elf," not the austere churchman of European tradition. He rides in a sleigh pulled by "eight tiny reindeer" instead of a horse-drawn wagon. Children's stockings are "hung by the chimney with care," recalling the clogs left by Dutch youngsters to be filled by Sint Nikolass—a name transformed in New Amsterdam to Sinterklass, then Santa Claus. Indeed, Moore's poem provides a scenario for the elaborate Christmas rituals now enacted by multitudes of Americans.

Songs celebrating the miraculous birth of Christ include such favorites as "Silent Night" and "O Little Town of Bethlehem." Over the years new songs have been added to the repertoire, from "The Little Drummer Boy" and "Rudolph the Red-Nosed Reindeer" to "White Christmas."

Christmas trees, introduced by German immigrants, were first embellished with electric lights by an associate of Thomas Edison. Christmas cards, which were first sold commercially in England, have been taken over by Americans. We now send nearly 4 billion cards each year. And the offering of gifts from the Magi to the Christ Child has inspired such an explosion of gift giving that the Christmas shopping season is now the mainstay of American retailing.

Many of us grew up licking the batter and eating the chocolate morsels right out of the bag. Baking chocolate chip cookies is one of the most popular of family activities—everyone can lend a hand.

The quintessential Santa Claus was given to us by illustrator Thomas Nast. Today many people decorate their homes with ceramic miniatures, such as this charming replica of Old North Church.

## CITIZEN KANE

"Rosebud..." whispers Orson Welles in the famous opening moments of *Citizen Kane*, a film that since its release in 1941 has appeared on every list of best films ever made. The 25-year-old Welles, dubbed "the boy wonder," had already formed his prestigious Mercury Theatre when he was summoned to Hollywood. Under contract to RKO, he was given complete artistic control (and a stingy budget) to produce, direct, and star in this thinly veiled biography of newspaper tycoon William Randolph Hearst. The innovative story structure, sound, and camera techniques of the resulting work transformed the way we look at movies and has influenced filmmakers ever since. The picture enraged Hearst, who fought for its suppression through his papers. *Citizen Kane* took only one Academy Award, for Best Original Screenplay—the only Oscar that the controversial Welles would ever win. Years later he said, "Two percent moviemaking and 98 percent hustling is no way to spend a life."

## CIVIL RIGHTS MOVEMENT

The South became a battleground after the Supreme Court's landmark 1954 decision, *Brown* v. *Board of Education of Topeka*. The court concluded that "'separate but equal' has no place. Separate educational facilities are inherently unequal."

The elimination of the legal basis for segregation made integration the law of the land and accelerated the demand for full civil rights for all Americans. Blacks were joined by sympathetic nonblacks as they challenged discrimination in a series of protests, including the Montgomery bus boycott, the Greensboro lunch-counter sit-ins, the freedom rides, and the Mississippi Freedom Summer voter-registration drive. The South's old guard, which included politicians, community leaders, and members of the Ku Klux Klan, opposed the protesters. The police assaulted them with fire hoses, attack dogs, mass arrests, and even murder.

Their brutality backfired, as television coverage of these violent attacks shocked the nation and rallied public support for the protesters. On August 28, 1963, a quarter of a million Americans joined in a "March on Washington," demanding racial justice. The federal government responded with a series of laws aimed at eliminating a legacy of oppression.

The Civil Rights Act of 1964 outlawed discrimination in facilities that were open to the public, such as hotels, restaurants, and swimming pools. It also prohibited racial discrimination in public and private employment. The Voting Rights Act of 1965 outlawed literacy tests and other measures that had been used to deny voting rights. The Civil Rights Act of 1968 ended discrimination in the sale, rental, financing, and advertising of housing. It took a long time, but because of the civil rights movement, the nation's laws finally reflected the statement in the Declaration of Independence that "all men are created equal."

In the role of Charles Foster Kane, Orson Welles presented a searing portrait of a ruthless man utterly consumed by ambition.

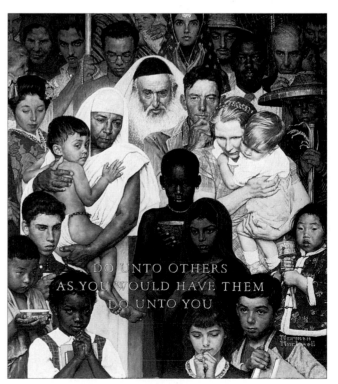

Norman Rockwell's April 1961 *Saturday Evening Post* cover depicted the civil rights movement in religious terms: "Do unto others as you would have them do unto you."

# CLASSIC *American* CARS

*For 100 years Americans have embraced the automobile as a symbol of freedom, style, and status.*

### 1931 MODEL A FORD

The successor to Henry Ford's ubiquitous Model T sold over 4 million cars from 1928 through 1931. Attractive, reliable, and tough as an anvil, it still enjoys an avid following.

### 1937 CORD 812 BEVERLY SEDAN

This brilliantly unique design bristled with fresh ideas, such as disappearing headlights, front-wheel drive, vacuum-assisted shifting, and stunning styling, that would influence other carmakers for years to come.

### 1934 LA SALLE CONVERTIBLE COUPE

Cadillac's companion car carried its owners through the Great Depression in style and comfort. Decades later, the theme song to the TV show *All in the Family* included the nostalgic lyrics, "Gee, our old LaSalle ran great . . ." And that it did.

## 1955 CHEVROLET BEL AIR

In 1955 the sturdy, steady, low-priced Chevrolet became "The Hot One," thanks to a new high-performance V-8 engine and daring stylistic features, such as a Ferrari-inspired grille.

## 1959 CADILLAC SERIES 62

This outrageous expression of the tail-fin school of design became a symbol of postwar American prosperity. It marked the beginning of the end of extremism in automotive styling.

## 1957 FORD THUNDERBIRD

Ford's sleek two-seat roadster was hailed as a timeless design from its debut. The 1957 edition kept up with the style of the day by combining the chrome-encased taillight with a sporty canted fin.

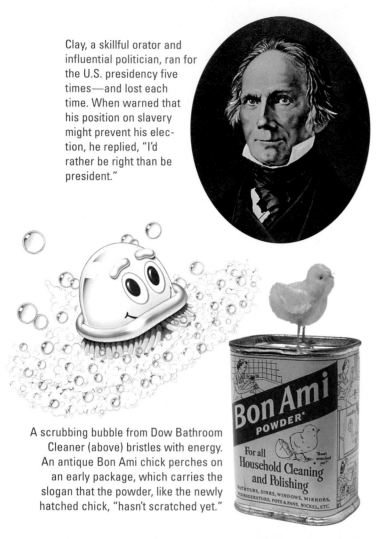

Clay, a skillful orator and influential politician, ran for the U.S. presidency five times—and lost each time. When warned that his position on slavery might prevent his election, he replied, "I'd rather be right than be president."

A scrubbing bubble from Dow Bathroom Cleaner (above) bristles with energy. An antique Bon Ami chick perches on an early package, which carries the slogan that the powder, like the newly hatched chick, "hasn't scratched yet."

Van Cliburn plays in concert in 1968, 10 years after his triumph in Moscow. A child prodigy, he made his debut at four and won his first competition at 13. Until age 17, his only teacher was his mother.

## CLAY, HENRY

Henry Clay occupied center stage in American politics for more than 40 years, as a senator and congressman from Kentucky and as Secretary of State under John Quincy Adams. He was called "The Great Compromiser" because he negotiated three landmark compromises that managed to stave off the bloodbath of the Civil War for 10 years.

His masterpiece was the "American System," a bold idea that would unify the country with federally funded roads and canals and impose tariffs to protect fledgling industries. But Clay's vision of an active central government was out of step with the independent spirit of the young states, and his plan was not implemented. His ideas outlived him, though, and many were eventually put into action at a later time.

## CLEANSERS

The American obsession with cleanliness is no accident. It was fostered by social reformers who wanted to clean up the "great unwashed" masses of immigrants, and by manufacturers who wanted to clean up by selling their cleansers.

Backed by women's clubs, health educators, and manufacturers, the Cleanliness Institute was founded in 1927. The Institute supplied schools with thousands of posters, flyers, pamphlets, and textbooks that promoted washing as the key to good health. It also ran coupon-bearing advertisements and sent out more than a million free booklets on "cleanliness problems." These advertisements, coupled with manufacturers' ads, convinced the public that soap-based personal hygiene and housecleaning were essential to success at climbing America's social and occupational ladders. Although machines began to handle many tasks that had once covered people in sweat and coal dust, Americans were sure they were dirty, and the tradition of the once-a-week Saturday-night bath gave way to daily bathing.

New and improved products are introduced every year, but some of the early brands are still going strong. One of the best known is Ivory, which has sold well since 1879, when a factory worker left a machine running while he went to lunch and accidentally invented an air-filled soap that floats.

## CLIBURN, VAN

A tall, good-looking young man from Texas, Van Cliburn was the first American to win the Tchaikovsky Competition in Moscow. The year was 1958; the 23-year-old pianist was hailed as a hero of the Cold War. New York City welcomed him home with a ticker-tape parade, and he went on to perform in many other cities. Later, Cliburn toured the Soviet Union, where he drew huge crowds. In 1962 he founded an international piano competition.

Nonetheless, the pianist, seemingly shackled forever to Tchaikovsky's *First Concerto*, for which he'd won the prize, fell into a rut and suffered from stage fright. In 1978 he retreated to his home in Fort Worth, emerging only to play for Gorbachev at the White House in 1987 and a few concerts after that. Then, at age 60, Cliburn undertook a U.S. tour with the Moscow Philharmonic. His many fans were thrilled to discover that a full ringing tone was still at his command and that his Romantic virtuosity was as powerful as ever.

## CLIFFS NOTES

It's entirely possible that the *Cliffs Notes* study guide for *A Tale of Two Cities* has been read by more students than the book itself. We'll never know, because people rarely admit that they have taken a literary shortcut. But *Cliffs Notes* have been bailing out time-pressed students since 1958, and currently some 5 million of them are sold each year.

When they first came out, *Cliffs Notes* were frowned on, and possession of one of these hard-to-hide yellow-and-black-striped booklets was enough to get a student in trouble. Now, however, many teachers and professors accept them, in part because they are written by experts.

Two students struggle with their books and crumpled notes in Norman Rockwell's 1931 *Saturday Evening Post* cover. If only they'd had *Cliffs Notes*...

## CNN

From its first transmission in June 1980, the Cable News Network has drawn attention for the speed and thoroughness of its news coverage. Owner Ted Turner's plan was simple: Beam live coverage from around the world, 24 hours a day, to growing cable systems, bypassing the three networks that dominate TV news. These networks, tied to stationary phone lines and a commitment to a variety of programming, could not match his mobile, news-only system.

CNN often has the first—perhaps the only—pictures of history as it happens; other broadcasters are often forced to buy its footage. It televised the explosion of the space shuttle *Challenger* and the revolt of Chinese students at Tiananmen Square—live. During the Gulf War of 1991, kings and presidents joined home viewers in watching the war on the network's exclusive live feed from Iraq. CNN's heroic presence behind the lines became part of the news itself.

Peter Arnett
Baghdad, Iraq

Correspondent Peter Arnett reported live from Baghdad during the Gulf War. Even the U.S. Secretary of Defense watched CNN.

## COBB, TY

Ty Cobb, the Georgia Peach, achieved the highest career batting average (.367) in major league history. A driven competitor, Cobb turned every game into a struggle for survival. Opposing players hated him, and his Detroit Tiger teammates barely tolerated his irascible behavior. Except for his hometown boosters in Detroit, fans roundly disliked Cobb and regularly unleashed torrents of abuse in his direction.

A brilliant batter, Cobb used an odd split-grip to lace line drives. He won 12 American League batting titles (nine from 1907 to 1915). Possibly the best player in baseball history, he was the first to be elected to the Baseball Hall of Fame.

Ty Cobb poses in his sliding position and shows how his carefully sharpened spikes are exposed to any opposing player in his path.

Coca-Cola's graceful lettering was penned in 1887 by the inventor's bookkeeper and is still used on the product and in advertising. The classic curvaceous glass bottle debuted in 1916.

Soda fountains and diners were supplied with signs, trays, napkin holders (above), and other paraphernalia—all with soda-pop logos. Originals of these are now collectibles.

An advertisement for Scott's Emulsion of Pure Cod Liver Oil made the incredible claim that it was as "palatable as milk."

## COCA-COLA

Coca-Cola devotees might be surprised to learn that the world's best-known soft drink was originally imbibed as a medicine. Concocted in 1886 by Atlanta pharmacist John S. Pemberton, the syrupy mixture of kola nuts, coca leaves, caffeine, and other ingredients was said to cure headaches and dyspepsia and was sold for five cents a glass. A year later Pemberton sold the rights to the syrup—the precise recipe is still a closely guarded secret—to another pharmacist, Asa G. Candler, who successfully marketed the brew as a refreshing drink. With pervasive advertising, distinctive packaging, and such catchy slogans as "Have a Coke and a Smile," "Things Go Better With Coke," and "The Pause That Refreshes," Coca-Cola gained widespread recognition.

So did Pepsi-Cola with its slogans: "Pepsi Hits the Spot" and "You're the Pepsi Generation." The beverage, first called Brad's Drink after its inventor, pharmacist Caleb D. Bradham, got its start in 1898, also as a tonic for dyspepsia. Dr. Pepper, first brewed in 1885, carries the name of a pharmacy owner as well. As for Dr. Brown's famous cream and celery-tonic sodas, no one knows if there really was a Dr. Brown.

## COCHISE

Cochise, a chief of the fierce Chiricahua Apaches during the 19th century, was admired for his courage and wisdom and dreaded as a foe. Although the Chiricahua had fought with Mexicans along the border for centuries, they had lived in peace with the settlers. That changed in 1861, when a band of Pinal Apaches kidnapped a boy from a southern Arizona ranch. Cochise was arrested as the culprit.

Although he was innocent, Cochise and his family were held by Army Lieutenant George Bascom as hostages until the boy was returned. However, Cochise escaped and took his own hostages. When Bascom unwisely refused an exchange, Cochise killed his prisoners, whereupon Bascom hanged three members of the chief's family. In retaliation, Cochise set off on a bloody campaign that terrorized southern Arizona for a decade.

The Chiricahua attacked stagecoaches, miners, and soldiers and emptied entire towns of frightened pioneers. The cavalry and the settlers fought back, at one point murdering 128 unarmed Apaches. In the end, more than 4,000 people on both sides had been killed. In 1872 the government sought a truce, and the battle-weary warrior agreed. The result was the establishment of an enormous Chiricahua reservation in southeastern Arizona, where the man who had lived by war died in peace two years later.

## COD LIVER OIL

If you had to swallow doses of cod liver oil as a child, you can blame Dr. Johann Schenk. In 1824 the German doctor found that the oil helped prevent rickets, a childhood bone disease.

The major drawback was its terrible taste. Nevertheless, cod liver oil soon became a popular home remedy in America. A century later scientists discovered that mothers who swore by the oil were actually giving their children vitamin supplements. Cod liver oil is rich in vitamins A and D, which help ward off colds and strengthen bones and eyesight. Mothers continued to coax their children into taking the awful-tasting oil for much of the 20th century. Nowadays, however, a balanced diet provides whatever vitamins most people need.

## CODY, BUFFALO BILL

William Frederick "Buffalo Bill" Cody embodied the Wild West to people all over the world, and even though he was a master showman, he wasn't just acting. Born in 1846, Cody had had a remarkable string of jobs that included Pony Express rider, horse thief, buffalo-hunting guide, and scout for the frontier cavalry, where his sharpshooting skills were prized in battles against the Indians.

A sensationalized version of his exploits—the first of many Buffalo Bill dime novels—was so popular that in 1872 Cody appeared in a melodrama in Chicago and found his true calling. He organized Buffalo Bill's Wild West show, presenting "actual scenes, genuine characters" from the West. There were "historical" depictions of Custer's last stand and the attack on the Deadwood stagecoach. "Little Sure Shot" Annie Oakley shot cigarettes out of the mouth of fellow sharpshooter (and husband) Frank Butler, and cowboys rode bucking broncos and performed rope tricks. Sitting Bull, the legendary Sioux chief, even appeared one season. Enthralled audiences flocked to performances, eagerly accepting the show's glory and adventure as the genuine West and Buffalo Bill as its undisputed hero.

For the next 30 years, the show toured all over America and Europe. Eventually, having been supplanted by rodeos, it folded its tents for good. Buffalo Bill, showman to the end, gave his last performance three months before his death.

## COHAN, GEORGE M.

European-style operettas dominated Broadway theater until George M. Cohan introduced his uniquely American brand of musical entertainment. A performer in his family's vaudeville act, the enterprising song-and-dance man became a star with *Little Johnny Jones*, his 1904 musical comedy that featured the song "Give My Regards to Broadway." Cohan, who wrote, produced, or starred in some 200 shows, soon became known as the man who built Broadway. Of his more than 500 songs, Cohan is best remembered for such patriotic gems as "You're a Grand Old Flag." "Over There," written the morning after America entered World War I, earned him a congressional medal. Cohan has been immortalized by a statue in Times Square and by James Cagney in the award-winning 1942 film biography *Yankee Doodle Dandy*.

In a poster for his Wild West show, Buffalo Bill Cody (center foreground) rides with his cast of characters. When Buffalo Bill started his show, he held roping and riding auditions to find the best in the West.

Although George M. Cohan's birth certificate reads July 3, 1878, his mother always maintained (as do the lyrics of his signature song, "The Yankee Doodle Boy") that he was born on the fourth of July.

The world shared the joy of these East and West Germans when the Berlin Wall was torn down in 1989. One year later the two halves of the city were legally reunited.

## COLD WAR

Americans returning home from World War II thought they had secured world peace. But a new danger emerged when the Soviet Union installed communist regimes throughout Eastern Europe. In a 1946 speech at Westminster College in Fulton, Missouri, former British prime minister Winston Churchill said that the Soviets "had drawn an Iron Curtain across the continent."

Antagonism between the communist East and the democratic West never resulted in direct fighting between the superpowers. However, Soviet rhetoric, such as Premier Khrushchev's vow that "we will bury you," caused fear that the Soviets might start a nuclear war. Tensions heightened during the Cuban Missile Crisis of 1962, when the U.S. discovered that the Soviets had installed ballistic missiles in Cuba.

From the outset, the Soviets strove to isolate the communist bloc from capitalist influences. However, radio broadcasts by the Voice of America, a U.S. government agency, undermined their efforts. Ordinary people behind the iron curtain were fascinated by Western culture, its democratic system, and its economic freedoms; they bought American blue jeans on the black market and listened avidly to Western music. In the late 1980s, economic collapse throughout the communist world led to the disintegration of the Soviet empire. Destruction of the Berlin Wall symbolized the end of the cold war.

## COLE, NAT "KING"

Singer Billy Eckstine said of Nat "King" Cole: "He's one of the two guys who took a style and made a voice out of it—the other was Louis [Armstrong]." Cole's breathy, purring baritone had only a two-octave range, but when it caressed a ballad like "The Christmas Song" ("Chestnuts Roasting on an Open Fire") or "Mona Lisa," the song shimmered.

Jazz aficionados remember Cole's early band, the trendsetting King Cole Trio. Sparked by Cole's swinging piano, it influenced such pianists as Erroll Garner and Oscar Peterson. Soon Cole was drawn to the more lucrative role of popular singer. He sold millions of records while still in his thirties and was one of the first black artists to have a sponsored radio show. In the 1950s, his heyday, he had his own TV show, appeared in films, and toured the country. His gentle smile and gracious manner won fans worldwide. In 1991 his Grammy-winning daughter, Natalie Cole, found a unique way to revive her father's memory. Using studio wizardry, she sang a duet with her father on his classic hit "Unforgettable."

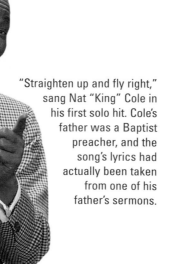

"Straighten up and fly right," sang Nat "King" Cole in his first solo hit. Cole's father was a Baptist preacher, and the song's lyrics had actually been taken from one of his father's sermons.

## COLUMBUS, CHRISTOPHER

Christopher Columbus became the first explorer to alert Europe to the vast lands that could be found by sailing west. In 1492 King Ferdinand and Queen Isabella of Spain gave

Columbus three small ships—the *Niña*, the *Pinta*, and the *Santa Maria*—and in a remarkable feat of courage and seamanship, he led 88 sailors across the Atlantic, finally landing in what is now the Bahamas. Columbus believed he was on the coast of Asia and that he had discovered a new route to the Orient. He left 44 members of his crew to start a colony and returned to Europe with gold, plants, and even natives, but without the *Santa Maria*, which had run aground.

In three subsequent voyages, and with larger fleets, Columbus explored several Caribbean islands and the coast of South America. Schoolchildren still memorize the date of his first voyage with the rhyme "In fourteen hundred and ninety-two / Columbus sailed the ocean blue."

## COMICS

During a newspaper strike in 1937, Mayor Fiorello LaGuardia made sure that New Yorkers weren't deprived of their favorite fare—he read the comics on the radio.

The first comic-strip character, Richard Felton Outcault's Yellow Kid, appeared in Joseph Pulitzer's *New York Sunday World* in 1895 and was an instant hit. In fact, rival publisher William Randolph Hearst soon hired Outcault away for his *New York Journal*. In 1896 Hearst created the first color comics section, which he billed as "eight pages of polychromatic effulgence that make the rainbow look like a lead pipe."

More comics soon appeared. Rudolph Dirks created *The Katzenjammer Kids* in 1897, the first strip to use word balloons. Readers were delighted with the slapstick mischief of its two young hellions, Hans and Fritz, as they played pranks on their elders. This golden age of comics also saw the birth of such classics as *Bringing Up Father* (1913), with the contentious Maggie and Jiggs, and *Blondie* (1930), featuring Dagwood, Blondie's bumbling, sandwich-making husband.

Most of the comics were simple line drawings, but a few contained undeniably fine artwork. *Little Nemo in Slumberland*, created in 1910, was drawn as well as were the finest book illustrations. In 1937 *Prince Valiant*, a medieval tale with high-quality illustrations, made its debut.

Each successful comic strip had its own appeal. The characters in *Gasoline Alley* have the same problems as its readers do and age along with them. *Dick Tracy*, on the other hand, never seems to change. Details in Milton Caniff's *Terry and the Pirates* are realistic, but his worldwide adventures are fantastic. When Walt Kelly's *Pogo* appeared, it brought political satire to the cartoon page. Modern favorites, such as *Doonesbury* and *Bloom County*, carry on this tradition.

Some people predicted that comics would die out as TV became ever more popular. But comics have already made the jump onto the information superhighway. Cartoonist Scott Adams distributes his *Dilbert* comics over the Internet.

Pogo and Albert mixed goofy puns with sharp political satire. Below, the Postal Service commemorated 100 years of comics with a special line of stamps in 1995.

Dick Tracy never lost a case. Armed with such gadgets as his two-way wrist TV, his skills were every bit as sharp as his classic profile. Junior detectives once played at fighting crime with this toy badge (left).

Fat cat Garfield was an instant hit when he appeared in 1978. Here, a plush Garfield poses with his pal, Odie.

The breathtaking parachute jump (left) was scary but very popular. A grinning symbol of fun adorns the entrance of Steeplechase Park (below).

President Jefferson Davis bore a resemblance to Abraham Lincoln. The battle flag of the Confederacy has 13 stars, which stand for the Confederacy's 11 states and two territories.

## CONEY ISLAND

Sigmund Freud once called Coney Island the only place in America that interested him. Located at the southwest corner of Brooklyn, facing the Atlantic Ocean, Coney Island was a fantasy world where millions came to have fun in summer.

At the turn of the 20th century, Coney Island offered independent rides as well as the three magical amusement parks—Steeplechase, Dreamland, and Luna Park—for which it was best known. The main attractions were mechanical rides that combined speed with a hint of danger. For example, in the Steeplechase Race, riders were strapped into seats shaped like horses that made a circuit around the Pavilion of Fun, rising and dipping along the way at heights of up to 35 feet. At the end of the race, clowns whacked the participants with paddles as bystanders howled with laughter.

The Human Roulette Wheel was a spinning wooden disk to which people clung, trying to avoid being thrown off. In the Blowhole Theatre, jets of air shot up from beneath iron grills, sending women's dresses skyward. Elsewhere, people tried to walk upright through large revolving barrels.

At night, Luna Park was ablaze with a million incandescent bulbs that lit up its entire facade. The Steeplechase symbol, a Funny Face with an enormous, toothy smile, captured its zany, eccentric appeal. Coney Island's role as the amusement-park capital of America waned in the mid-1960s, and today the crowds come mostly for the sun and surf.

## CONFEDERACY

"The South will never submit to such humiliation and degradation as the inauguration of Abraham Lincoln," one Atlanta newspaper declared. On December 20, 1860, South Carolina proved the prediction accurate by seceding from the United States, an action soon taken by 10 other Southern states. Together they formed the Confederate States of America to preserve the slavery that Lincoln opposed, to protect states' rights, and to ensure freedom from domination by the North. With Jefferson Davis of Mississippi as president, the Confederacy sought to secede peacefully, but the United States refused, and on April 12, 1861, the Civil War began.

From the outset, President Davis faced overwhelming problems. Southern nationalists blamed him for not creating the strong central government the South needed to win the war, while most governors jealously guarded states' rights. Some would not even allow their men to fight in states other than their own.

Lack of money was an even bigger problem. With only $27 million in its coffers, the Confederacy had to resort to increasingly unpopular measures, printing paper money unbacked by gold and sending soldiers to seize crops and livestock, paying for the goods with worthless scrip. One farmer said he would "prefer seeing Yankees to our Cavalry," and many others began hiding their produce and animals.

As the war dragged on and enthusiasm waned, the Confederate Congress instituted the first draft in American history. But by exempting men who owned at least 20 slaves, it prompted cries of "rich man's war, poor man's fight." The governors of Georgia and North Carolina ignored the draft.

After losing 50,000 men at Gettysburg and Vicksburg in July 1863, the Confederacy suffered one defeat after another. The Confederate armies finally lost by attrition, their country torn by internal dissension and drained of resources. When the war ended, the Confederacy was dissolved and its member states were gradually readmitted into the Union.

## CONVENIENCE FOODS

It all began in 1857 with Borden's condensed milk. Then in the 1920s commercial sliced bread was developed. No more mixing, kneading, or baking—just open the package and serve. With this modest beginning, convenience foods gained a foothold in American kitchens and paved the way for further innovations. In the 1950s pre-sliced cheese arrived. Mixes followed, offering flavorful, surefire cakes, muffins, and brownies. A cook could serve delicious baked desserts at a moment's notice and with very little effort.

In the post-World War II era, the advent of the home freezer brought about an enormous change in American cooking habits. Food manufacturers provided new ways to make life easier for the cook, and time saving became a priority. A barrage of frozen foods resulted: the frozen dinner, for example, supplied a complete meal. That was followed by boil-in-a-bag items in the 1960s. Everything from Salisbury steak to broccoli in cheese sauce could be ready to eat in minutes. On the dessert front, Cool Whip (just thaw and serve) arrived to take the place of whipped cream. In the 1970s and '80s, the microwave oven came into its own. Just about any food product was packaged so it could be zapped.

The latest in convenience, with a nod to the trend of healthful eating, are the fresh salad mixes in a bag. Just pour the precut salad into a bowl, pour on the dressing, and toss. Voilà! a Caesar salad with no fuss or muss.

## COOLIDGE, CALVIN

Calvin Coolidge probably holds the record for saying the fewest words per year of any politician. He gained fame when, as governor of Massachusetts, he used the state guard to end a police strike. Coolidge served as vice president under Warren G. Harding and as president from Harding's death in 1923 through 1929. This was an era when most voters wanted politicians to keep government and taxes to a minimum and allow business to have a free hand.

According to one story, a woman once said to Silent Cal, "I just bet someone I can make you say more than two words." Coolidge replied, "You lose."

Dinner is served—instantly—when Mom or Dad twists open a little jar of baby food. Such manufacturers as Gerber and Beech-Nut pioneered easy-to-serve, take-anywhere food for infants. The tower at left shows some of the many products that busy cooks can use to build a meal.

Calvin Coolidge donned a headdress when he became an honorary Sioux Indian chief. A popular president who kept his own counsel, he once said, "I have noticed that nothing I never said ever did me any harm."

Copland, whose *Third Symphony* was called the greatest American symphony, also wrote the scores for *Our Town* and *The Heiress*.

*The Cosby Show*, said Bill Cosby, was "based on my personal experience as a husband, as a parent." Syndicated reruns brought a record $4.4 million per episode.

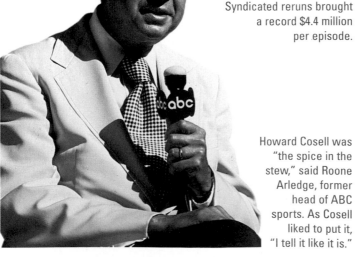

Howard Cosell was "the spice in the stew," said Roone Arledge, former head of ABC sports. As Cosell liked to put it, "I tell it like it is."

## COPLAND, AARON

In his thirties, the "dean of American composers" recalled this of his early music career: "I occasionally had the strange sensation of being divided in half—the austere, intellectual modernist on the one side, the accessible popular composer on the other." After studying in Paris and hearing the music of Stravinsky and the French impressionists, Copland longed to create a purely American music that would mirror the soul of his native land. From that time on, his many pursuits— composing, encouraging young composers, writing, lecturing, and conducting—reflected this overriding ambition.

Some of his pieces incorporated jazz elements; others were indeed "austere." In the 1930s and '40s, touched by populism, he opted to compose "in the simplest possible terms." Of these efforts, the best-loved are *El Salón México* and the ballets *Billy the Kid*, *Rodeo*, and *Appalachian Spring*, his most famous work. Copland was, as critic Arthur Berger wrote, "at last an American we may place unapologetically beside the recognized creative figures of any other country."

## COSBY, BILL

In Bill Cosby's early days as a stand-up comic, his most effective material came from his ability to re-create the dilemmas of his childhood. Audiences would howl as he described how he got into trouble when, terrified by a scary radio show, he set the couch on fire to ward off monsters.

After winning three Emmys for his role in the series *I Spy*, Cosby won the nation's heart with *Fat Albert and the Cosby Kids*, an animated show based on his comedy routines about childhood. In 1984, frustrated by the lack of quality sitcoms, he created *The Cosby Show*, which featured an upper-middle-class black family. Parenting issues were grist for the humor mill. Part of what made the show work were Cosby's engaging personality and a clear affection for his young costars. As Cliff Huxtable, whose delusions of hipness got out of hand, he was often deflated by his son, sighed at by his eldest daughter, or soothed by wise words from the mouth of a tiny child.

## COSELL, HOWARD

Wearing a bad toupee, chomping on a cigar, and describing sports events in a high-pitched, staccato voice, Howard Cosell blazed a trail as the most opinionated broadcast reporter in sports. When he didn't like a football play, a baseball pitch, or a boxer's punch, he said so—insultingly. A 1970s poll found him to be both the most-despised and the best-loved sportscaster in America. He was *Monday Night Football* incarnate.

Called The Mouth That Roared, Cosell (born Cohen) left a successful law practice in 1954 for a job taping locker-room interviews. Self-described as "arrogant, pompous, obnoxious, vain, cruel, verbose, a showoff," he was a defender of Muhammad Ali's refusal to serve in the armed forces and a goad to higher ethical standards in sports.

## Cosmetic Surgery

Plastic surgery can literally be a lifesaver. Modern surgical techniques make it possible to reconstruct bodies—and lives—shattered by injuries or deformed by birth defects. Skin grafts can rehabilitate burn victims, and breast reconstruction can restore self-esteem after a mastectomy.

But cosmetic surgery, which is elective, attracts healthy people seeking slimness, beauty, and eternal youth. Why diet or exercise, many ask, when you can have excess fat siphoned from your thighs by liposuction, one of the most popular cosmetic operations in the nation? Dissatisfied with your looks? You can have your nose reshaped, your face, lips, or eyelids lifted, your ears pinned back, your cheekbones filled out, or your wrinkles smoothed by injections of collagen. Breasts can be enlarged or reduced, and bald spots, covered by hair implants. Although none of these costly, sometimes risky procedures will transform ordinary mortals into a young Elizabeth Taylor or Paul Newman, more than a million Americans turn to them each year in the hopes of realizing their dreams, or at least in feeling better about themselves.

## Cotton Candy

When Americans went to the 1904 World's Fair in St. Louis, Missouri, one of the delights they discovered was Fairy Floss. Previously, spun-sugar confections had been laboriously made by hand and used to decorate exotic desserts. But an "electric candy machine" patented in 1903 made it possible for the fair's concessionaires to sell more than 68,000 boxes of the cottony stuff. The machines simply melt sugar and spin it out through pinholes, turning it into airy fibers that stick to paper serving cones—and to anything else they touch.

Cotton candy, now in a rainbow of colors and flavors, remains one of the treats associated with fairs and amusement parks. Children love the sweet, melt-in-your-mouth taste and quickly learn not to take the fluffy cones on fast rides.

## Couch Potato

In the 1980s people exhausted by demanding jobs and hectic social lives planted themselves in front of the television and declared themselves "couch potatoes." The phrase was popularized by Robert Armstrong of Dixon, California, who cofounded the original Couch Potato Club after realizing that he and his friends, who watched "the boob tube" all the time, could be called "tubers." He praised passive viewing as "transcendental vegetation."

A series of technologies, among them the remote control and cable television, encouraged the couch-potato lifestyle. The VCR, an essential accessory, and microwave popcorn brought the movie experience home. In 1987 a wave of couch-potato paraphernalia, including a potato-shaped doll and a game, hit the market. But the craze soon died down—the marketers had probably gone back to watching television.

The sweet treat called cotton candy was popularized in the United States but is loved the world over. Each cone contains about 110 calories.

Rooted in front of the tube, remote control within reach, couch potatoes ate a steady diet of snacks and made couch sales and video rentals soar.

Known as the Man in Black, Johnny Cash has had 58 top-40 country hits. He wears black for the downtrodden who live in the "hopeless hungry side of town."

The Judds, featuring Naomi and daughter Wynonna, became one of the most successful mother-daughter duos in history.

Willie Nelson was at the center of a group of musicians in Austin known as The Outlaws. *Wanted: The Outlaws* was the first country album to sell a million copies.

Popular for her full figure as well as her music, Dolly Parton proved herself a queen of musical crossover, with songs on both the country and the pop charts.

## COUNTRY MUSIC

Explaining the appeal of country music, Nashville hit maker Carlene Carter said that people may like rap, but they still need country to tug at their heartstrings. Carlene's great-uncle, A. P. Carter, was one of the industry's pioneers, collecting such folk tunes as "Amazing Grace" and "Wildwood Flower" from his Appalachian neighbors in the 1920s. His wife, Sara, sang the songs, and his sister-in-law, Maybelle, set them to her distinctive rhythmic guitar.

In 1923 record companies began to court musicians like the Carters in order to serve a new market: Southern rural folk who had recently emigrated to the cities. Soon "hillbilly" music was picked up by radio and spread by such shows as Nashville's *Grand Ole Opry*. In 1927 a railroad worker from Mississippi named Jimmie Rodgers became the first country-music superstar. He melded blues with a yodel that, as Merle Haggard put it, "displayed his real feeling better than any lyric could have." Alabaman Hank Williams, the granddaddy of country writers, sang of the "hopes and prayers and dreams of the common people" in such songs as "I Saw the Light" and "I'm So Lonesome I Could Cry."

In the 1930s and '40s, regional styles called western swing and honky-tonk came to the fore. Honky-tonk dominated country music until the mid-'50s. In 1952 Kitty Wells sang "It Wasn't God Who Made Honky-Tonk Angels," her answer to men's songs about cheating wives. That recording opened the way for other women country singers. Patsy Cline conveyed an aching vulnerability in such ballads as "Crazy" but also sang scorchers like "Lovesick Blues." She died in a plane crash at age 30 and remains a country legend.

As country music became more popular, it also became more homogenized. Although some singers, Johnny Cash among them, continued to portray gritty realism with songs like "Folsom Prison Blues," many others chose a softer mainstream approach that came to be called the Nashville sound. Willie Nelson left Nashville to escape it, but others, including Dolly Parton, rode the wave to stardom. In the 1990s country music reached new heights of popularity. Reba McEntire topped the charts with a mixture of old and new country styles. And in 1992 singer Garth Brooks outsold every other pop musician in the country.

## COURT TV

Trials in the United States were always intended to be public; every courtroom has a spectators' gallery. Not one, however, could begin to accommodate the millions who now tune in to watch real trials unfold on *Court TV*. The 24-hour cable channel went on the air after most states began to allow cameras in the courtroom. Its founder, Steven Brill, saw it as an antidote to Hollywood's fast-forward versions of judicial proceedings and to the snappy summations recounted by television news. Part entertainment, as was *The People's Court* before it, *Court TV* also educates viewers about how the judicial system handles the human affairs—from the mundane to the monstrous—that find their way into the courtroom.

Americans watching *Court TV* witnessed the acquittal of William Kennedy Smith of the charge of rape, the deadlocked jury in the parricide trial of the Menendez brothers, and the Rodney King verdict, which would incite riots. During the O. J. Simpson trial, millions were glued to the television set day after day, proving that *Court TV* fulfilled Brill's vision of a "C-SPAN with soap operas."

## COVERED WAGONS

To cries of "Westward, Ho!" a flood of prairie schooners washed over the plains in 1843, carrying restless emigrants along the Oregon–California Trail. Pulled by three yoke of oxen, each boat-shaped wagon held up to 3,000 pounds of possessions and provisions for the five-month trip. Only necessary supplies were packed, including at least a barrel of flour, about 200 pounds of bacon, and 25 pounds of coffee.

Wagon trains set out in late May, when grass for grazing was plentiful. The heavy wagons faced danger at river crossings; in the mountains, four men and a winch might be needed to edge a wagon over a steep pass. Still, the greatest peril came at the end of the trip. Emigrants headed to western Oregon had to navigate the roiling Columbia River on rafts. Those going to California had to get across the Sierra Nevada before the way was blocked by the snows of October or risk the gruesome fate of the Donner party.

Today we realize that the voyagers wreaked havoc on the land they passed through, stripping it of grass and trees. The same caravans that promised new fortunes to the emigrants killed bison herds and exposed Indian tribes to cholera, causing great hardship for the Plains Indians.

## COWBOYS

Cowboys are as tall in western mythology as they are in the saddle, soft-spoken heroes with fiercely independent spirits. Their heyday came after the Civil War, when cattle drives reaped big profits and dime novels glorified the cowboy's life. Thousands of young war veterans were drawn westward, along with Indians, blacks (who made up a quarter of all cowboys), and Mexicans. What they found was a hard life of riding and roping that required skill and grit. A few years on the range, wrote Theodore Roosevelt, "leaves printed on their faces certain lines which tell of dangers quietly fronted and hardships uncomplainingly endured."

The greatest hardships were found on the cattle drive, when 10 drovers would trail some 2,000 steers from Texas to market in Missouri or Kansas. They covered up to 15 miles a day—or less if rustlers or angry farmers set off deadly stampedes. By 1888 the plains were fenced in and crosshatched by railroads, ending 20 colorful years of the open-range cowboy.

The O. J. Simpson trial, featuring the former football star and his "dream team" of lawyers, mesmerized viewers of *Court TV*.

Hot tempers on the road are nothing new. In 1849 two wagon drivers shot each other over who was first in line.

Frederic Remington's "The Bronco Buster" was the first of 24 bronze sculptures, most of which captured lone men on horseback.

In Indian folk tales the coyote was a wily trickster (and sometimes a fool) with animal, human, and supernatural traits.

Cracker Jack prizes included magnifying glasses, toy cars, and baseball cards. Many have become collector's items. One, a Joe Jackson baseball card, is said to be worth more than $7,000 today.

## COYOTE

"In the beginning of the world, the coyote was more foolish than he is now," begins one Native American legend. Many North American tribes recognize Coyote as a trickster who sometimes does good, sometimes bad. The Hopis blame him for ruining the night sky. Coyote, they say, saw Grandmother Spider carefully arranging the Milky Way and sparkling constellations with a handful of stars drawn from her clay pot. Coyote wanted to put stars in the sky, too, so he pawed at the pot, knocking it sideways and scattering stars hither and thither. A few stars fell and burned his nose, which explains how coyotes got their black noses.

Coyote's tricks often backfire. In fact, his failings are what endear him to tribal children and their elders. He steals a horse and brags that his bravery won him the mount; but the moment he gets off the horse, it walks back to its owner. Coyote nearly drowns trying to retrieve the reflection of red berries from a stream. Tribal lore insists that Coyote stories be recited aloud, but only on winter nights between the first killing frost and the first spring thunderstorm. Calamity comes to those who break tradition: they lose their voices.

## CRACKER JACK

A number of ingredients went into building America's affection for the snack called Cracker Jack. The combination of candy-coated popcorn and peanuts was invented in 1893, and it was a big hit that year at the World's Colombian Exposition in Chicago. The mix was named in 1896, when someone tasting it for the first time exclaimed, "That's a cracker jack!" a popular slang expression of approval.

Cracker Jack was shipped to retailers in large wooden tubs until the development in 1899 of the moisture-proof wax-sealed box. The box not only kept the snack fresh but allowed the addition of the one ingredient that ensured Cracker Jack's popularity with generations of children: the prize. At first the company experimented with printing gift coupons on the box, but a surprise inside proved to be more popular. In 1908 Cracker Jack's immortality was secured when its name was included in the words of the song "Take Me Out to the Ball Game." The mix has remained almost unchanged for a century. The box, too, has changed very little since 1918, when, in a patriotic gesture, the company introduced a red-white-and-blue box that featured a boy—Sailor Jack—and his dog, Bingo.

## CRANE, STEPHEN

At age 22, Stephen Crane had never been on the battlefield. But that didn't stop him from writing a war novel so realistic that veterans swore he had seen action. After spending the winter of 1893 reading books on the Civil War, he set out to capture on paper the thoughts and feelings of soldiers in battle. A penniless author, Crane had to write parts of the story on butcher paper because he could not afford to buy stationery. When *The Red Badge of Courage* was published two years later, it was an instant success.

The first American novel to question romantic notions of war, *The Red Badge of Courage* examines a soldier's struggle with fear during his first days of combat. Henry Fleming flees his first battle but then returns to the front. He finds that he is neither a coward nor a hero but, like the soldiers around him, a man controlled by the overwhelming forces of war. Crane became a war correspondent and covered conflicts in Mexico and Cuba. He died of tuberculosis at 28.

## CRATER, JUDGE JOSEPH

As a prominent Democrat and a justice of the New York State Supreme Court, Joseph Crater was important enough when he was around. But—like Atlantis, free lunch, and 18½ minutes of Watergate tapes—he is most famous for being absent.

On August 6, 1930, Judge Crater had dinner with friends in New York's theater district. At about 9:30 P.M. he got into a taxi, ostensibly to go to a Broadway show that was only a few blocks away and that had already begun. As the cab pulled away, a snazzy double-breasted brown suit, Panama hat, and 185 pounds of judge vanished into the damp air of a Manhattan summer night. A nationwide hunt produced plenty of hoaxes but no missing jurist, either dead or alive. A grand jury, after listening to testimony from 95 witnesses, concluded that it had no idea where Joseph Crater was. Graffiti artists began leaving messages for him on walls. "Judge Crater, call your office" was a popular one.

## CRAZY HORSE

Crazy Horse was the legendary military leader of the Oglala Sioux. He inherited his name from his father after proving himself as a warrior. But warriors had no place in reservation life, and when Sioux leaders signed a treaty to settle their people in the Black Hills, Crazy Horse became a "hostile," hunting buffalo on the old ranges and fighting with soldiers.

In 1876 Crazy Horse ignored a War Department order that all Sioux return to their reservations, then handed a crushing defeat to the troops sent to bring him in. He moved to the valley of the Little Bighorn to join Sitting Bull's encampment shortly before General Custer made his fateful assault on the camp. Crazy Horse and Chief Gall of the Hunkpapa Sioux swept down on Custer's troops and decimated them, a victory that would prove disastrous for the Indians.

Crazy Horse was pursued relentlessly in Montana. After nearly a year he surrendered, one of the last important chiefs to do so. While he waited to be assigned to a reservation, a rumor spread that he was plotting an escape. In the struggle to lock him up, Crazy Horse was stabbed by a soldier. Whether his death was planned by the army or not, it remains a symbol of the white man's campaign to crush the Indians' spirit.

*The Red Badge of Courage* so accurately portrayed Civil War battles that many veterans insisted they had fought in the same regiment as the author.

Despite offers of a reward, no trace of Judge Crater was ever found. For decades police continued to receive tips as to his whereabouts. Crater's wife insisted he was a victim of foul play.

**$5,000.00 REWARD**

JOSEPH FORCE CRATER
JUSTICE OF THE SUPREME COURT, STATE OF NEW YORK

The CITY of NEW YORK offers $5,000.00 reward to any person or persons — Any information should be forwarded to the Detective Division of the Police Department of the City of New York

In the Black Hills of South Dakota, visitors can inspect a small-scale replica of the Chief Crazy Horse sculpture (foreground). The actual work in progress (background) was begun in 1948 and measures 56 stories high.

Zydeco music sets toes tapping to its irresistible beat. Here, Nathan and The Zydeco Cha-Chas use an accordion and a washboard to offer up a traditional spicy sound.

With his long rifle in hand, Fess Parker played "Davy Crockett, king of the wild frontier" in a TV series about the woodsman in a coonskin cap.

After his retirement from network news, Walter Cronkite occasionally hosted TV specials, such as this one on anthropology.

## CREOLE

It's hard to pin down the exact meaning of the word *Creole*. It used to mean North American–born descendants of the early French or Spanish settlers in Louisiana, Mississippi, Alabama, and Florida. Then it was used to refer to their slaves. It's even been used to refer to any native of Louisiana. But the simplest definition is Louisiana's own: "A Creole can be anyone who says he is one."

Creole culture is known especially for its cooking, which combines elements of fine European cuisine (the use of butter-and-flour-based sauces) with flavors borrowed from that of black and Native American cultures. Unlike the informality of Cajun cooking—which specializes in one-pot dishes and finger foods—Creole cooking is more formal and apt to be served in courses.

Zydeco, a popular style of Creole music played at parties called *la las*, also borrows from several traditions. (The word *zydeco* means "snap bean" in Creole.) It mixes African, Caribbean, and European influences to create a sound with one purpose: to keep people dancing.

## CROCKETT, DAVY

Adventure-loving television viewers in the 1950s saw Davy Crockett as a frontier hero who could grin raccoons out of trees and whip his weight in wildcats. Though the legend was created by Crockett himself, it's somewhat shy of the truth.

Born in 1786 in Tennessee, Crockett grew up with little schooling, which suited his lackadaisical nature just fine. That same nature kept him from making much of a mark throughout most of his adult life. On his wedding day, his intended ran off with a rival. He joined the Tennessee militia in the 1813 campaign against Creek warriors, but wasn't present for the famous battles. And although he served in Congress, he usually backed legislation that didn't pass.

All that changed, however, with the publication in 1834 of his "autobiography," tall tales in backwoods lingo that depicted Crockett as a larger-than-life folk hero. The book was a huge success. Two years after its release, Crockett traveled to Texas, where he fought at and died defending the Alamo, an act of bravery that fueled his fame.

Hollywood discovered Crockett in the 1940s, and television periodically rediscovers him, ensuring that the legend of the "ring-tailed roarer" from Tennessee will never die.

## CRONKITE, WALTER

For millions of Americans in the 1960s and '70s, a good reason to believe that the unbelievable had happened—that Martin Luther King, Jr., John Kennedy, and Robert Kennedy had been killed; that astronauts had landed on the moon; that Nixon had resigned—was that Walter Cronkite had told them so. During his 20 years at the helm of the *CBS Evening News*, Cronkite's name had become synonymous with television reporting: the Swedish word for "anchorman" is *Cronkiter*. His stamina, skillful ad-libbing, sharp editorial eye, and authoritative delivery made him a fixture of television news. In fact, he was such a permanent presence that his colleagues complained of "Walter to Walter coverage." The public had an enormous amount of trust in and respect for Cronkite because he was rigorously objective in his reporting. When he ended each broadcast with "and that's the way it is," his viewers had faith that it was indeed so.

## CROONERS

The use of radio microphones in the early 1920s helped create a popular new style of singing. "Crooning" took off because this sensitive new microphone favored smooth, understated baritone vocals. Rudy Vallee, with his romantic voice, was the first to be labeled a crooner. The good-looking Yale grad, who sang in four languages, made college girls swoon. But Vallee was upstaged in 1931 by Bing Crosby's full-bodied, conversational tones, which set the standard for a new style. Crosby's closest rivals were Russ Columbo, a big-band singer, and Buddy Clark, who had his own radio show.

Crooners who lasted beyond the big-band era included such stars as Dick Haymes, Bob Eberle, and, of course, Frank Sinatra. Known in later years as "The Velvet Fog," Mel Tormé had a unique sound caused, it is said, by tonsils that had partially grown back after surgery in childhood.

Following World War II, crooners brought their laid-back style to TV audiences. New stars included Eddie Fisher, Andy Williams, Pat Boone, and Perry Como. Johnny Mathis was a wildly popular crooner from the Nat "King" Cole school of singing. He's known for lending his purring vibrato to such hits as "Chances Are" and "Misty."

## CROSBY, BING

Affectionately called "Der Bingle" or just plain Bing by his fans, Harry Lillis Crosby had a much-emulated singing voice —a mellow croon interspersed with an occasional "buh-buh-buh-boo." He was usually photographed wearing a hat (to hide his baldness) and holding a pipe between his teeth.

Crosby began his career in a trio called The Rhythm Boys that performed with the great Paul Whiteman Band. Soon he had his own radio show (which ran for 30 years), adopting "Where the Blue of the Night" as his theme song.

One of the most popular entertainers of all time, Crosby also became one of the richest. In the 1940s his light comedies, such as the famous *Road* movies, in which he starred with Bob Hope, were perfect wartime escapist fare. Although nobody's idea of a heartthrob, Crosby had considerable charm on-screen. In 1944 he won an Oscar for playing a priest in *Going My Way*, and a year later he was nominated for his role in another family film, *The Bells of St. Mary's*. At the age of 73, Bing died while playing golf, his favorite game.

"I'm just a vagabond lover," sang Rudy Vallee, the first of the crooners. This romantic style of singing, from the tender ballads of Johnny Mathis (above) to the relaxed sounds of Perry Como (right), would be popular for years.

Despite his great popularity, Bing Crosby always considered himself an average guy: "If I've achieved any success as a warbler, it's because I've managed to keep the kind of naturalness in my style…which any Joe Doakes possesses."

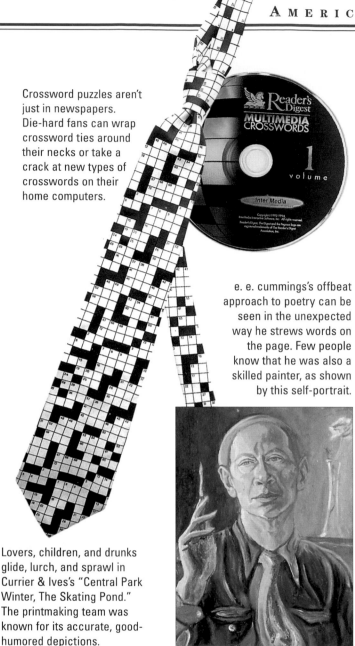

Crossword puzzles aren't just in newspapers. Die-hard fans can wrap crossword ties around their necks or take a crack at new types of crosswords on their home computers.

e. e. cummings's offbeat approach to poetry can be seen in the unexpected way he strews words on the page. Few people know that he was also a skilled painter, as shown by this self-portrait.

Lovers, children, and drunks glide, lurch, and sprawl in Currier & Ives's "Central Park Winter, The Skating Pond." The printmaking team was known for its accurate, good-humored depictions.

# CROSSWORD PUZZLES

In 1913 a *New York World* newspaper editor devised the first crossword puzzle as a whimsical Christmas-season page filler. Quickly pulling together clues and answers (18 Across: What this puzzle is—HARD), he named the puzzle a "word-cross" and gave it a diamond-shaped design. Surprisingly, readers asked for more. The *World*, however, played down the puzzle by setting it in very small type.

When the first crossword book came out in 1924, its publishers, Dick Simon and Max Schuster, were afraid that it would be laughed off the shelves. Far from being a failure, however, the book started a craze overnight. National tournaments sprang up, attracting thousands of fans. Women wore dresses and stockings patterned with crossword designs. And Los Angeles librarians, swamped by enthusiasts, placed a five-minute limit on the use of the dictionary.

## CUMMINGS, E. E.

Writing a poem a day from the age of eight, e. e. cummings became one of the most innovative and prolific poets of his day. He combined words playfully and experimented with typography. An example of his whimsical phrasing appears in this poem: "in Just- / spring when the world is mud- / luscious the little / lame balloonman / whistles far and wee / and eddieandbill come / running from marbles and / piracies and it's / spring / when the world is puddle-wonderful."

Called by admirers a "poet of immediacy and feeling" and by critics a poet of "baby talk," cummings is known by many people only for signing his name in lowercase letters. Although he dropped this idiosyncrasy in the 1930s, he never compromised his resistance to tradition. He reveled in the sheer fun of playing with language and structure.

## CURRIER & IVES

The age of pictorial journalism began in January 1840, when a New York penny daily printed a shocking picture of the steamboat *Lexington* burning, a disaster that cost 123 lives. Nathaniel Currier, a lithographer, commissioned an illustration from news reports and his own vivid imagination. That edition quickly sold out, making Currier famous.

Soon Currier hired bookkeeper James Merrit Ives as a partner, and the firm of Currier & Ives was born. Self-proclaimed "publishers of cheap and popular pictures," they printed both sentimental landscapes and images of terrible catastrophes. Victorian-era homemakers bought pictures of children, bowls of fruit, pastoral country lanes, and depictions of the ravages of alcohol. Other subjects included Civil War battles, horse races, and farm, village, and country life.

Currier & Ives prints have found unexpected uses in our own times. Since the early days of the motion picture, set and costume designers have used these prints for reference when designing period clothing, artifacts, and furniture.

## DALLAS

What do you get when you combine double-crossing relatives, a philandering husband who tries to have his wife institutionalized, and characters who won't die even after being shot? Well, when you put all that on a sprawling ranch thick with Texas oil, you've got *Dallas*, the highest-rated prime-time soap since *Peyton Place*. Much of *Dallas*'s popularity was due to Larry Hagman, who played J. R. Ewing, the villainous oil tycoon everyone loved to hate. When the show first aired in 1978, audiences were slow to tune in, but after a spellbinding first season, the show was a hit. The second season ended with a cliffhanger: Who shot J. R.? Millions of people wanted to find out, and not even the cast knew the answer, as several possibilities had been filmed. The culprit (one of J. R.'s ex-mistresses) was revealed on November 21, 1980, in one of the highest-rated episodes in history.

*Dallas* soon inspired other prime-time soaps slithering with wealthy schemers, including *Dynasty*, about the glittering Carrington clan, and *Falcon Crest*, set in the wine country of northern California. *Dallas* started losing steam, however, in 1987, when viewers learned that the lust, murder, and greed of the previous year had been merely the bad dream of one of the characters. Four years later, *Dallas* at last hung up its ten-gallon hat.

## DANCE MARATHON

Feats of endurance, such as flagpole sitting, were joined in the early 1920s by the dance marathon, a punishing event in which couples competed for prize money by dancing until they dropped. Although each marathon began with excitement and fanfare, the dancing deteriorated into artless shuffling after a few days. Spectators came to watch dancers use smelling salts or slap each other to stay awake. Competitors got a 15-minute rest break every hour, less as time went on.

Despite efforts by police and health authorities to curb them, dance marathons flourished all over the country, sometimes as many as 40 at a time. The madness peaked in the 1930s as more people than ever danced for prizes. The record was set at Chicago's Merry Garden Ballroom in the winter of 1930–31, when one couple danced for 214 days in order to win $2,000. The dance-marathon craze caused three known deaths, one in Atlantic City when a weary dancer went for a short swim and drowned.

Larry Hagman's J. R. Ewing was conniving and selfish—and the viewers loved it! *Time* called him "that human oil slick," while Hagman labeled J. R. "a WASH—a White Anglo-Saxon Hedonist."

Dance marathons quickly turned into grueling tests of endurance. In the 1969 movie *They Shoot Horses, Don't They?* a referee checks that a sleeping contestant's knees aren't touching the floor.

Irene and Vernon Castle (right) first danced together at private parties. Vernon, who was also an aviator, flew combat missions during World War I. Irene was one of the first women to bob her hair.

New dances come and go, but elegant ballroom dancing is here to stay.

A breakdancer's needs are simple: a street corner and a portable stereo.

## DANCING

From the mambo to the mashed potato, the bunny hug to the funky chicken, dancing has kept America on its toes. The earliest dances enjoyed in the colonies were group endeavors, such as contredanses and quadrilles, that involved little body contact. After the waltz swept Europe in the mid-1800s—shocking solid citizens with the closeness required of partners—Americans eagerly embraced it, along with the polka, another imported "social dance."

At the turn of the century, though, Americans took the lead with the two-step, and subsequently taught the world to move to a different beat with each changing era. The elegant Vernon and Irene Castle epitomized the new age, popularizing not only their own Castle walk but also the fox-trot and the tango—mainstays of tea dances and ballrooms. Their refined style competed with such lively ragtime rages as the turkey trot and the kangaroo dip. Then the Roaring Twenties took over, as sheiks and flappers Charlestoned, shimmied, and rumbaed at speakeasies to frenzied jazz rhythms.

The swing bands and big bands of the 1930s and '40s set the tempo for the jitterbug. Hipsters jived in dance halls to the lindy hop and the big apple, whose energetic steps were punctuated with through-the-legs slides and over-the-shoulder rolls.

Hot on their heels came the '50s Latin craze, which introduced the cha-cha and the merengue.

Then rock rolled in, and suddenly soda shops were packed with bobby-soxers bopping to a jukebox spinning 45s. The top tune of 1960 was "The Twist," performed by Chubby Checker, who revolutionized social dancing. "I'm the guy that started people dancing apart," said Checker. No longer did partners need to touch each other or learn prescribed patterns—they simply "did their own thing" at discotheques and go-go clubs. Just as their parents had watched TV's *The Arthur Murray Party* to brush up on their ballroom dancing, baby boomers tuned in to *American Bandstand* for the latest on the locomotion, the swim, the jerk, the pony, and countless other pop dances.

Except when twirling to the intricate choreography of disco in the '70s, Americans continued dancing separately in free-form interpretations of the music. And in the trend of the '80s—break dancing—partners were dispensed with altogether, letting hip-hop dancers shine solo with electrifying dives, spins, and glides to the driving drone of rap.

## DARE, VIRGINIA

On a wilderness seacoast, on August 18, 1587, Eleanor Dare gave birth to a daughter, Virginia, the first American child born of English parents. They had arrived just weeks before with 115 other colonists to establish the first English settlement in the New World, a tiny outpost on Roanoke Island in what is now part of North Carolina.

Days after Virginia's birth, her grandfather, Governor John White, left for England. Three years later, he returned and found the settlement deserted. He beseeched the Almighty "to helpe & comforte" his daughter and grandchild, who he believed still lived. The fate of the so-called Lost Colony was never determined. One theory holds that friendly natives took in the colonists.

## DARROW, CLARENCE

By the opening day of the sensational 1925 Scopes Monkey trial, Clarence Darrow's reputation as a relentless defender of the underdog was widespread. In 1895, when Darrow had defended the railroad union's right to strike, a railroad magnate skipped town to avoid both a subpoena and Darrow's questions about strikebreaking tactics. In 1924 Darrow had taken on the Leopold-Loeb murder case and created an innovative insanity defense to save his clients from execution.

When Tennessee schoolteacher John Scopes was put on trial for teaching evolution, a violation of state law, Darrow led the defense. Crowds of spectators listened to Darrow, an agnostic, and to the eloquent William Jennings Bryan, a champion of fundamentalism, as they argued the case. Darrow called Bryan to the witness stand and challenged his belief in a literal interpretation of the Bible. Bryan's testimony was impassioned but not effective; the judge actually ruled that what Bryan said be stricken from the record. However, the trial was not about evolution, just whether or not the law had been broken; the jury found Scopes guilty. Although the prosecution won the legal contest, many felt that the moral victory had gone to Darrow for his defense of free speech.

## DAVIS, BETTE

"Oh, Jerry, don't let's ask for the moon, we have the stars!" The actress who immortalized this line from the movie *Now, Voyager* was neither beautiful nor particularly charming; she had pop-eyes, an awkward mouth, and a strutting gait. Yet in an almost 60-year screen career, she made more than 80 films and is still considered the quintessential movie star.

Bette Davis was a contract player at Warner Brothers who had made a series of lackluster pictures when, in 1934, she got her big break in *Of Human Bondage*, playing a part no other actress wanted. This role led the way to other difficult roles, which were her specialty. When she walked out on Jack Warner in 1936, he sued and won. Realizing her star value, however, he upgraded her films. In the late '40s she gave what is considered her greatest performance: as Margo Channing in *All About Eve*. Her career faltered in the late '50s, but she made a comeback in 1962 with *What Ever Happened to Baby Jane?* Accepting the Lincoln Center Film Society Award, she brought down the house with her much-imitated line from the 1949 film *Beyond the Forest*: "What a dump!"

Virginia Dare was christened with this name because, as her grandfather wrote, "this childe is the first Christian borne in Virginia."

Clarence Darrow (left) was prompted to defend Scopes when William Jennings Bryan (right), a man of great stature, joined the prosecution.

In *All About Eve* Margo Channing (Davis, above) suddenly realizes that she is one step behind Eve (Anne Baxter), her scheming protégée.

Troops waded ashore in the greatest amphibious assault in history. Some 155,000 men landed on five beaches along 60 miles of Normandy coastline. The code names of the beaches were Omaha and Utah (American forces), Gold and Sword (British), and Juno (Canadian).

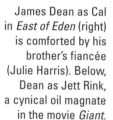

James Dean as Cal in *East of Eden* (right) is comforted by his brother's fiancée (Julie Harris). Below, Dean as Jett Rink, a cynical oil magnate in the movie *Giant*.

## D DAY

Aware that the Allies would invade occupied France in the summer of 1944, Hitler was convinced they would cross at Pas-de-Calais, the narrowest part of the English Channel. The Allies had set up dummy tanks and guns on the British coast and had created phony radio traffic to foster this illusion. The Allies, able to decode German radio dispatches, knew the deception was working. On June 6, 1944—code-named D Day—the date chosen for the massive attack on German-occupied France, the weather was so stormy that German reconnaissance planes were grounded.

As the Allied troops poured ashore, Hitler continued to believe the attack was a feint and held sizable German forces in reserve for the invasion he expected 200 miles to the north. Rough seas made the landings a near disaster, as tanks sank and many soldiers drowned. The Germans had fortified Omaha Beach with bunkers and barbed wire, and for long, desperate hours, nearly 35,000 Americans were pinned down. When at last the Americans broke through, men and machines poured onto French soil: the Allies had their foothold.

## DEAN, JAMES

The cult of James Dean, American icon of teenage rebellion, is based on exactly three films: *East of Eden*, *Rebel Without a Cause*, and *Giant*. Of these, *Rebel*, a film about youthful alienation, is the one with which he is most strongly associated. Dean, originally from Indiana, went to New York in 1951, where he eked out a living. He audited classes at the Actors Studio, made famous by Marlon Brando, whose intense acting style Dean emulated. A Broadway appearance resulted in a screen test at Warner Brothers and a movie career that lasted just over a year.

On September 30, 1955, while driving his Porsche Spider to a car race in Salinas, California, he was killed in a highway crash. To this day his burning good looks and rebellious manner are adored by teenagers worldwide. James Dean posters proliferate, and books about him keep the legend alive.

## DEAR ABBY, DEAR ANN

Abigail Van Buren and Ann Landers, identical twins, were housewives when they began their journalistic careers as personal-advice columnists. Their similar writing styles have confused readers, who often can't remember which sister provided a particular piece of advice, but that hasn't diminished their popularity. Conservative about sex and women's roles, they are political liberals who blend humor with practicality. Neither Ann nor Abby hesitates to take issue with her readers, calling them "buster" or "kiddo." When one man wrote to Ann, whining that his "kindness" had resulted in a pregnancy, she advised him to get an attorney and to ask for a paternity test. But "if it's sympathy you're looking for," she continued, "you'll [find] it in the dictionary."

## DEATH VALLEY

In 1849 a party of prospectors entered this desert furnace, hoping for a shortcut to the gold mines of California. Months later the survivors staggered out of the valley, their harrowing story written in a tangled trail of oxen carcasses, burned wagons, and human skeletons. "Good-bye, Death Valley!" one of them is supposed to have shouted, and so it was christened.

One forty-niner brought out a piece of silver—a powerful lure for prospectors. Over the next 50 years, rumors of gold and other valuable minerals brought fortune seekers to the valley. But true to Death Valley's stingy reputation, these mines were expensive to work and seldom yielded any profit. An exception was borax, which was mined profitably in the 1880s and hauled out by the famous 20-mule-team wagons.

Some unscrupulous miners hit pay dirt by bilking eager investors, but none did so as successfully as the flamboyant Walter Scott. Scott persuaded dozens of financiers to invest in his "secret" gold mine, sight unseen. And although "Death Valley Scotty" was eventually forced to admit that there was no such mine, he built a luxurious mansion in the valley and lived out his dreams of grandeur until his death in 1954.

Two people trudge over the rocky Devil's Golf Course in Death Valley. The valley itself is a deep trough; its lowest point is 282 feet below sea level, the lowest in the Western Hemisphere. Summer temperatures reach 125°F.

## DECLARATION OF INDEPENDENCE

The opening volleys of the Revolutionary War had already been fired when the Continental Congress appointed John Adams, Benjamin Franklin, Robert R. Livingston, Roger Sherman, and Thomas Jefferson to write a formal declaration of independence from Great Britain. The young Jefferson was asked to do the actual writing because of his "peculiar felicity of expression." He produced an eloquent draft in two weeks; Congress approved the declaration on July 4, 1776.

The declaration was engrossed, or written in beautiful script, on parchment. "It compleats a Revolution, which will make as good a Figure in the History of Mankind, as any that has preceeded it," wrote an enthusiastic John Adams.

Clockwise from top: Two bass decoys aid ice fishers in the Midwest; a swan shows off its long carved neck; three shorebirds, a long-beaked curlew and two black-bellied plovers, balance on wooden sticks that can be inserted into the ground.

## DECOYS

Anyone who has ever started to ask for directions from a mannequin in a department store can sympathize with a duck lured to its death by a decoy. Southwestern Native Americans made the first fake fowl out of reeds and feathers about 1,000 years ago to persuade airborne flocks to alight within range of their bows and arrows. European colonials borrowed the technique, and by the end of the 19th century, American factories were churning out wooden decoys by the gaggle.

Today shooting waterfowl is a restricted sport, and pricey decoys may outnumber the protected ducks. Hand-carved and intricately painted mallards, pintails, drakes, mergansers, redheads, whistlers, and old-squaws— some of which may never have been outdoors—have become highly prized collectible folk art.

Alan Freed (right) introduced music by the likes of Chuck Berry and Fats Domino to white audiences. Here were tunes that teens could dance to without taking lessons. Wolfman Jack (below) was a mystery to listeners until a role in *American Graffiti* gave his famous voice a face.

The "long green line" of equipment by Deere & Co. included this 1935 tractor, designed for farmers' vegetable gardens. Dozens of other tractors were tailored for use on specific crops.

## DEEJAYS

It was a voice on the radio in Cleveland, belonging to Alan Freed, that in 1951 slapped the phrase *rock and roll* on the latest rhythm and blues songs. The establishment damned the music as rites of a "pagan culture," capable of inducing "prehistoric rhythmic trances," but disc jockeys like Freed helped make it the sound track to a period of American history. Freed, known as Moon Dog, growled and wailed at the night and thumped a phone book to the music's beat, giving voice to the rebelliousness of teens all over Ohio and, after 1954, New York. Listeners learned colorful street jive from Lavada Durst (Dr. Hepcat): to have "a pony to ride" was to have a job; to "cop some presidents" meant to earn money.

Disc jockeys had the power to make or break new talent. Freed's Cleveland rival, Bill Randle, brought Elvis fame outside Memphis by playing his songs every 15 minutes. Most deejays were local celebrities; but in the early 1960s, Wolfman Jack took over a powerful station in Mexico and sent his howls, music, and love-potion ads across the border and through America with the help of "the skip," an atmospheric phenomenon that enables radio waves to travel farther at night. The 1980s brought notoriously vulgar "shock jocks," such as Howard Stern, and trendy "morning zoos," featuring "zookeepers" who specialized in parodies of songs and offbeat humor, which all but eclipsed the music they played.

## DEERE, JOHN

A simple broken saw blade revolutionized American agriculture. John Deere, a struggling blacksmith, had been trying to solve a problem for his neighbors: how to run a smooth plow through the heavy, moist Midwestern farmland. Cast-iron blades were not slick enough, and because the steel blades that existed were poorly designed, farmers had to stop frequently to scrape them clean. When Deere spotted a discarded Sheffield blade in a sawmill, he decided to experiment with the English steel. The result: a specially curved blade that enabled the plow to "self-scour."

The Deere plow, pulled by only one horse instead of a team, was launched in 1837 in Grand Detour, Illinois. About 10 years later, the business Deere had started was selling 1,000 plows each year. Deere & Company is now one of the world's largest producers of farm equipment.

## DELICATESSENS

"Send a Salami to Your Boy in the Army," blared the neon sign at Katz's Deli. Founded in 1888, Katz's is the oldest deli in New York. For more than a century, the city's Jewish delis have been an institution. Pastrami, corned beef, brisket, tongue on rye, sour and half-sour pickles, potato knishes, and Dr. Brown's sodas—that was deli heaven. Orders for lean corned beef brought a rude response: "Corned beef isn't lean. If you don't like fat, don't order corned beef."

Fortunately for fans of mile-high sandwiches, a few classic delis remain. The Stage Deli, now open in several cities, names its sandwiches after politicians and celebrities. (An Oprah Winfrey is a triple-decker, and a Dolly Parton comes on twin rolls.) The late owner of New York's Carnegie Deli knew the value of his pastrami. After being robbed, he laughed, "Stupid fools! they took the money and left the pastrami."

## DE MILLE, CECIL B.

When Cecil B. De Mille was directing *King of Kings* (1927), he was shocked to discover that H. B. Warner, who played Jesus, was being distracted by one of the nubile slave girls of Mary Magdelene. "If she must fool around," thundered De Mille, "let it be with Pontius Pilate!" De Mille, wearing riding breeches and issuing orders via megaphone from his director's chair, was the very model of an old-style director. His specialty was biblical spectacles with huge sets, thousands of extras, and legendary special effects. Before filming the 1923 version of *The Ten Commandments*, he chortled, "We'll be the first studio in history to part the Red Sea!" After seeing the movie, Will Rogers wrote, "It's easy to see where God left off and Cecil De Mille began."

The public adored De Mille's pictures, although critics accused them of vulgarity. Sneered one: "A movie for De Millions if there ever was one!" By using little-known actors, De Mille had money to spend on the production opulence that made his name a household word. During the filming of *The Ten Commandments*, his partner, Jesse Lasky, expressed alarm at how much of the studio's money was being sunk into the film. De Mille replied, "What do they want me to do? Stop now and release it as *The Five Commandments?*"

## DEMPSEY, JACK

With "a neck like a bull, a granite jaw, and fists like iron," an ex-copper miner, lumberjack, and dance-hall bouncer named Jack Dempsey came out of the West in 1914 and changed boxing forever. His electrifying violence ended the upright defensive sparring style that had dominated the sport.

A brutally efficient brawler, Dempsey rarely had to fight more than four rounds. He won the heavyweight title in 1919, defeating in just three rounds a larger, heavier Jess Willard, who quit with a broken jaw, a closing eye, and missing teeth. In 1921 Dempsey beat Georges Carpentier of France in Jersey City, drawing boxing's first million-dollar gate. Ironically, Dempsey was defeated in 1926, on points, by "Gentleman Gene" Tunney, a phenomenal but colorless boxer who lacked a killer instinct and was known to quote Shakespeare. Tunney outpointed him again the next year with the help of the notorious "long count." Dempsey was hated for avoiding military service in World War I. He served in the Coast Guard during World War II and ultimately became America's favorite ex-champ.

At classic delis such as Katz's, sandwiches typically include a pound or more of meat. Pickles are often the only green vegetable in sight.

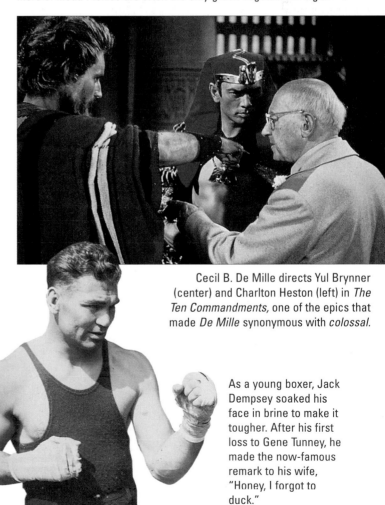

Cecil B. De Mille directs Yul Brynner (center) and Charlton Heston (left) in *The Ten Commandments*, one of the epics that made *De Mille* synonymous with *colossal*.

As a young boxer, Jack Dempsey soaked his face in brine to make it tougher. After his first loss to Gene Tunney, he made the now-famous remark to his wife, "Honey, I forgot to duck."

Using the "look, say" method, the *Dick and Jane* primers introduced one new vocabulary word per page. They were the first readers to include stories by established children's writers and drawings by prominent artists.

With characteristic brevity, Emily Dickinson wrote:
"'Hope' is the thing with feathers
That perches in the soul—
And sings the tune without words
And never stops—at all."

As Norman Rockwell illustrated, dieting is not just the purview of svelte supermodels. And it is anything but easy: 90 percent of dieters regain some or all of the weight they lost.

## DICK AND JANE

The first step toward reading for more than 40 million American children involved three short words: "See Spot run." From the early 1930s to the '60s, *Fun with Dick and Jane* entertained first-time readers with the playful antics of Dick and his younger sister Jane and baby sister Sally. Father sometimes had to temper Dick's mischievousness, but Mother always had a little helper in Jane. The family pets, Spot and Fluff, completed the "perfect" nuclear family.

Edited by William Gray, an educational psychologist, and reading expert May Hill Arbuthnot, the series replaced earlier children's primers with readers that featured more contemporary settings and progressive education values. Although later accused of being classist, sexist, and racist, the books were a big improvement over their predecessors.

## DICKINSON, EMILY

The "Belle of Amherst," Emily Dickinson composed most of her 1,775 poems during an intense two-year period when she was in her early 30s. She published—anonymously—only seven of them. By that point she was a virtual recluse, dressing only in white and rarely leaving her father's house. Some of her habits, too, were peculiar. She assembled a few of her poems into hand-sewn packets and hid many of these packets in a box in her bedroom. Many were meditations on love, death, and other enduring truths. She wrote: "Because I could not stop for Death / He kindly stopped for me; / The carriage held but just ourselves / and Immortality."

Early critics were alarmed by her strange syntax, irregular rhymes, and her unique mixture of rebellious and reverent sentiments. Today, however, both students of American literature and casual readers of poetry appreciate her genius for revealing deep, abiding wisdom in a few simple words.

## DIETING

Many Americans believe that "you can never be too rich or too thin." In the 1960s and '70s, diet pills were all the rage. Today the weight-loss business is a multibillion-dollar industry. Most commercial diets are based on a particular theory of how weight is lost. Metabolisms are measured, calories are counted, food groups are separated. Many diets include prepackaged-food plans. Gimmicks range from eating on smaller plates to gulping gallons of water to feel full. Radically unbalanced diets, such as all-grapefruit diets, can be as dangerous as they are, ultimately, ineffective. Furthermore, research shows that "yo-yo dieting," or constantly losing and gaining weight, may be more harmful than obesity.

The key to weight loss is a balanced diet combined with regular exercise. Exercise works, in part, by speeding up the metabolic rate so that calories are burned more quickly and efficiently. As Dr. G. A. Sheehan said, "Man was not made to remain at rest."

## DILLINGER, JOHN

John Dillinger, a machinist from Indiana and one of the most infamous gangsters of the 1930s, was the first and only man named Public Enemy Number One. (After Dillinger, the FBI created the "Ten Most Wanted List.")

Dillinger's life of crime began in earnest after he served nearly nine years for assault while robbing a local grocery store. After his release from prison in 1933, he went on a 14-month spree of robbing small-town banks throughout the Midwest. His gang included Charles "Pretty Boy" Floyd and George "Baby Face" Nelson, an impulsive killer whose murders were blamed on Dillinger. Daring, clever, and polite to victims, Dillinger was admired for breaking out of an "escape-proof" jail with a handmade wooden gun. Betrayed by a woman he knew, he was shot to death in 1934 by FBI agents outside a Chicago movie theater.

John Dillinger was described by J. Edgar Hoover, chief of the FBI, as "a cheap, boastful, selfish, tight-fisted plug-ugly." But he was courteous to his victims. Once when he broke out of jail with two hostages, he gave the men carfare home.

## DiMAGGIO, JOE

Even more than a baseball legend, Joe DiMaggio was an American hero. A reluctant superstar, he shunned publicity and preferred to let his on-field performance speak for him. At the plate, his wide stance and short, ferocious batting stroke were immediately recognizable to fans everywhere. DiMaggio patrolled the vast outfield of Yankee Stadium with characteristic ease. His greatest achievement in baseball came in 1941, when he hit safely in a record 56 consecutive games. His hitting streak gripped America at a time when war waged in Europe. Fans across the nation would ask, "Did he get one today?"

DiMaggio achieved a legendary presence in the Yankee clubhouse. In June 1949, after missing the first two months of the season because of painful heel spurs, he played in a crucial series in Boston and smashed clutch home runs in a Yankees sweep. It was the Yankee Clipper's swan song to a fabulous career. Beset by injuries, DiMaggio retired following the 1951 season.

"Joltin' Joe," a nine-time World Series champion and one of baseball's greatest outfielders, is remembered for the grace of his game— and of his character.

"True" diners were factory-built, often with steel siding and Formica ceilings, and modeled after railway cars. Modern diners often copy the look but not the outdated menus.

## DINERS

In the 1940s and '50s there was nothing quite like a roadside diner. About 5,000 of them welcomed hungry Americans driving on the open road. Truckers and families alike stopped at the streamlined, stainless-steel eateries, where fast-talking waitresses called customers Hon while dispensing advice and serving large portions of simple food. Sitting at the sleek counters or at black Formica tables, people from all walks of life ordered BLTs on whiskey (bacon, lettuce, and tomato on rye bread), with rice pudding for dessert.

In the 1960s diners lost out to the development of interstate highways: rest stops are generally serviced by fast-food franchises. Still, urban diners, such as San Francisco's Fog City Diner and New York's Empire Diner, have flourished by offering an upscale setting and more sophisticated fare.

John Travolta (right) helped America catch a fever—a *Saturday Night Fever*—during the height of the disco craze. Donna Summer (below), the Queen of Disco, also led the way with her 17-minute disco hit "Love to Love You Baby."

With her new top-loader, this 1950s housewife makes doing the dishes look almost glamorous. Dishwashers went from being a luxury to a necessity in a matter of a few decades.

## DISCO

Before it became a national craze, disco was popular in inner-city nightclubs, where deft disc jockeys wove songs together to keep customers dancing all night long. While this new style had its fans, it didn't become a national mania until 1977, when John Travolta starred in *Saturday Night Fever*, a movie about a working-class kid who, come the weekend, trades in his blue collar for the splayed lapels of a white suit. That same year, Studio 54 opened in New York City. Admission depended on celebrity status and the whim of the doorman.

Suddenly, it seemed, disco's thumping beat was everywhere. Van McCoy's single "The Hustle" sold 10 million copies, and Donna Summer made the cover of *Newsweek*. An Australian trio called the Bee Gees became one of the best-selling groups in history. Disco fashions became more outrageous as club regulars wore polyester pants, sequins, and platform shoes. A club in Iowa hosted disco weddings, airports installed disco lounges, and Ethel Merman recorded a disco version of "There's No Business Like Show Business."

## DISHWASHER

The dishwasher was invented as a dish-saving appliance, not a laborsaving one. In 1886 socialite Josephine Cochrane invented a machine to help clean up after her lavish dinner parties without—as her maids would invariably do—breaking the china. She crafted a wheel of wire compartments, to hold plates and cups, that lowered into a large copper boiler. Muscle power was still needed to turn the hand crank that made the machine spray the dishes with soapy water.

Impressed with the "steam servant girl," hotels and restaurants began placing orders. But because early home models could cost up to $1,000 and could use up a whole tank of hot water for one load, sales to housewives were not brisk. Most surprising to dishwasher manufacturers was women's claim that they enjoyed washing dishes by hand. As machines got quieter, more efficient, and better at removing stains, and as attitudes toward housework began to change, sales picked up. Today more than half the homes of America have dishwashers, and we wouldn't have it any other way.

## DISNEY, WALT

Walt Disney was just another young hopeful in Hollywood when he arrived in 1923 to produce animated cartoons. It wasn't long, however, before his sense of fun—this was a man who could see magic in mice—made his short features wildly popular. When he set out to create his first full-length film, *Snow White and the Seven Dwarfs*, people warned him that it was bound to bomb. But Disney was right to trust his instincts—the movie broke attendance records and won a special Academy Award in 1939.

In 1940 Disney made *Fantasia*, a distant ancestor of today's music videos that interpreted classical music with brilliantly creative animation. Although the film was not a commercial success, it helped solidify Disney's reputation as a creator of entertaining and educational movies. In the following years, he would make such all-time classics as *Bambi*, *Dumbo*, and *Sleeping Beauty*.

Disney was recognized as a preeminent source of family entertainment throughout the postwar baby boom. In addition to his animated features, he made nature documentaries and *The Wonderful World of Disney*, a weekly TV show that presented lively adventures, including Disney's version of the life of Davy Crockett.

In 1955 he opened Disneyland, a theme park in southern California that brought his magical world to life. Realizing that seediness kept people away from some parks, he designed Disneyland to be unquestionably clean and wholesome. Trash was collected constantly and quickly removed so that guests would never see it. A strict employee dress code was enforced: women's hair could not be frosted or streaked, and they could not wear colored nail polish; men had to be clean-shaven. Disneyland quickly became one of the most popular destinations in the world.

Disney began planning an even bigger park in Florida, but he died five years before Walt Disney World opened in 1971. EPCOT Center, which was finished in 1982, reflects Disney's belief that education can be made entertaining.

In the years since Disney's death, his company has continued to expand, and new parks have been created in Japan and France. And it still has a stable of characters that are beloved—and licensed—throughout the world. With the release of such films as *Beauty and the Beast*, *Aladdin*, and *Pocahontas*, the Disney empire continues to grow.

## DR. KILDARE

Good doctors are hard to find, so it's not surprising that audiences fell in love with *Dr. Kildare*. Fans of the NBC series, which ran from 1961 to 1966, may not have been aware that Richard Chamberlain was not the first idealistic young intern to seek success at bustling Blair General Hospital. Lew Ayres popularized the character in the MGM movie series of the 1930s and '40s; Lionel Barrymore played the demanding head of internal medicine, Dr. Leonard Gillespie, a master diagnostician who felt that his interns should take their work seriously: "Remember, a doctor is a doctor 24 hours a day."

Raymond Massey filled in ably as the curmudgeonly Dr. Gillespie when the series moved to TV. But the focus was on Kildare, and the show made Richard Chamberlain a star. *Ben Casey*, which premiered on ABC that same year, was also a huge success. Audiences continue to be fascinated by what goes on behind the scenes in hospitals, as evidenced by the success of *Marcus Welby, M.D.* and *Medical Center* in the 1970s, *St. Elsewhere* and *Trapper John, M.D.* in the '80s, and *Doogie Howser, M.D.*, *Chicago Hope*, and *E.R.* in the '90s.

While visiting Walt Disney World near Orlando, Florida, guests can tour such areas as Fantasyland, Adventureland, Tomorrowland, and Main Street, U.S.A. Completed in 1971, this theme park was just one of the many spectacular creations of Walt Disney (inset).

Above, Snow White wakes to the delightful company of Dopey, Sneezy, Happy, Grumpy, Doc, Bashful, and Sleepy. Left, Jiminy Cricket helps Pinocchio wish upon a star.

Dr. Seuss's most popular character was the mischievous Cat in the Hat, who came to entertain two bored children on one "cold, cold, wet day."

## DR. SEUSS

Before Theodor Seuss Geisel gave himself the honorary title of doctor, he worked in advertising and used his talents in a campaign for Flit, a bug repellent. "Quick, Henry, the Flit!" was unmistakably a Seuss creation. When he began writing for children, people didn't believe there was an audience for his stories. His first book, *And to Think That I Saw It on Mulberry Street*, was turned down by 27 publishers.

Throughout his career, Seuss created stories that were more than delightful—they made learning to read easy and fun. *The Cat in the Hat*, published in 1957, was written as a primer and used only 225 simple words. But it told a story wild enough to tickle any child's imagination.

These and his 47 other books have become childhood classics. *How the Grinch Stole Christmas* was made into a television special that is still shown every December. Although the story always came first with Seuss, most of his books had a moral. *Green Eggs and Ham* taught that if you try something new, you just might find that you like it: "I like green eggs and ham! / I do! I like them, Sam-I-am!... / And I will eat them here and there. / Say! I will eat them ANYWHERE!"

## DO-IT-YOURSELF

When a faucet begins to drip, when paint peels from the wall, when a floorboard develops an annoying squeak, what can you do? You might let your fingers wander through the *Yellow Pages*, or you could follow the lead of more and more Americans who are tackling such jobs themselves. Some of these do-it-yourselfers are inspired to action because they don't want to pay high repair prices, while others take pride in showing off their handiwork.

Do-it-yourself projects can be very rewarding—if only there weren't so many of them, upstairs, downstairs, and all around the house.

As novice D-I-Yers undertake projects—and make mistakes—they gradually gain expertise and confidence. Fortunately, there are a wide variety of resources to consult. Home repair books, videos, and television shows stand ready to guide, and some companies even offer tools that are user-friendly and well suited to the all-thumbs market.

## DONNER PARTY

The tragic fate of the Donner Party is unequaled in the history of western migration. In 1846 a wagon train of 89 emigrants, led by Jacob and George Donner, decided to leave the traditional route to California and take the untested Hastings Cutoff. The shortcut looked good on paper, but it crossed such difficult terrain that by the time the travelers reached the base of the Sierra Nevada, they were exhausted and had fallen nearly one month behind schedule.

With no choice but to push on, they climbed high into the mountains, where the first winter storm hit and left them snowbound. Frightened, they huddled in makeshift shelters for weeks. Their supplies dwindled,

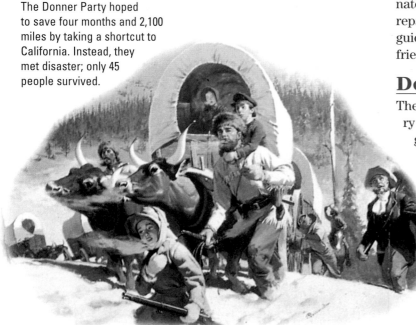

The Donner Party hoped to save four months and 2,100 miles by taking a shortcut to California. Instead, they met disaster; only 45 people survived.

and violent snowstorms buried them deeper and deeper. Finally, 15 of the strongest set out to get help. Hunger and the cold soon claimed four of them, and in a grim effort to stay alive, the starving survivors ate the dead, "averting their eyes from each other, and weeping." By the time they staggered into an Indian village, only seven of them were left.

Rescuers sent for the rest of the party found scenes of unforgettable horror. Nearly half had died, and the emaciated survivors had also resorted to cannibalism. Many recovered, although none was unmarked. "Never take no cut ofs," one survivor wrote home, "and hury along as fast as you can."

## DOOR-TO-DOOR SALESMEN

As American settlers ventured west, they were followed by enterprising traveling salesmen who carted goods to customers far away from stores. Along with their wares, these "drummers" brought news, gossip, and the excitement of a new face to isolated homesteads. At the same time, salesmen in cities and suburbs began going from house to house, using their charm to get their foot in the door.

The Fuller Brush man was the ultimate door-to-door salesman. Impeccably groomed and well mannered, he would mention a free gift, say "I'll step in," and be in the house to demonstrate his brushes in a flash.

By the 1950s and '60s, the salesperson at the door was likely to be a woman. Hundreds of thousands of women who wanted to work became Avon ladies. But as the number of women with jobs continued to rise, sales became more difficult—because fewer people were home to buy!

## DOO-WOP

Sung mainly by young black men, often on city street corners, doo-wop was an earlier form of rock and roll that was popular from the early 1950s to the early '60s. It combined gospel and rhythm and blues with jazzy four-part harmonies. Vowels were stretched, and nonsense syllables were sung in rhythmic patterns ("rama lama ding dong"). On most recordings, doo-wop had a gentle instrumental backup.

Some groups were made up of schoolboys (Frankie Lymon and The Teenagers), gang members (The Matadors), and girls (The Shirelles). Tough guys held singing contests. Lured by the dream of making a hit record, kids practiced in hallways, backyards, or garages, waiting for their lucky break. Bands took fanciful names, often those of cars (The Cadillacs, The Lincolns, and The Coupe De Villes) or birds (The Penguins, The Crows, and The Ravens).

Throughout the doo-wop era, these songs—simple, infectious, and usually about young love—poured from jukeboxes and radios wherever teens partied. Memorable doo-wop hits include "Crying in the Chapel" by The Orioles, "Only You" by The Platters, "Tears on My Pillow" by Little Anthony and The Imperials, and "Get a Job" by The Silhouettes.

Avon ladies are following their customers to their jobs. Currently, almost half of Avon's business is selling perfumes and beauty products in the workplace.

Doo-wop stars, The Penguins, borrowed their name from a character on a cigarette pack—Willie the Penguin.

"Will You Love Me Tomorrow?" asked The Shirelles, the first of doo-wop's girl groups. They also hit it big with "Tonight's the Night," "Mama Said," and "Soldier Boy."

Through an advertising blitz, which included posters like the one at left, the U.S. raised $17 billion in Liberty bonds. Americans also observed gasless Sundays, meatless Mondays, and wheatless Wednesdays in order to support the war effort.

## DOUGHBOYS

On the eve of America's entry into World War I, Uncle Sam's army was far from ready for combat. President Woodrow Wilson hastily conscripted an army of green recruits. The men were hurried through basic training, given a few lessons in French and in foot care, and shipped overseas to France.

Outfitted with soup-bowl helmets, choke-collared tunics, and bolt-action rifles, the troops arriving at the front lines left many unimpressed. "These men are not soldiers; they are a uniformed rabble," sniffed one French critic. In response to taunts of "Sammy" and "Teddy" from Allied soldiers, the Americans decided to call themselves *doughboys*, a term borrowed from Civil War slang. The rookies infused it with a pride that their bravery in battle would soon justify.

The doughboys took up arms in fields that were scarred with muddy trenches and snarled barbed wire—battlefields where millions of soldiers had already died. Between enemy lines lay no-man's-land, visited only by snipers and occasional patrols. Gunfire crackled, and heavy guns boomed. Poisonous gases sometimes wafted overhead.

But the doughboys didn't enter the war to crouch in trenches. At Belleau Wood, for example, waves of American infantrymen amazed German troops by charging across a wheat field into withering enemy machine-gun fire. The Americans plunged into the dense woods, taking out nests of German gunners, one by one, for 19 days. Few questioned the doughboys' tenacity after Belleau Wood.

Within months, the Allied armies had pushed the Germans back all along the western front, but at a terrible cost of life. British and French generals credited the heroic effort of the American infantrymen for the war's speedy end. Of the fruits of war, one doughboy recalled, "We came home on a beautiful luxury liner that we got from the Germans. Ate like kings.... And we danced with Red Cross girls."

## DRED SCOTT DECISION

In 1846 the slave Dred Scott sued his owner, the widow of John Emerson, for his freedom. He claimed in a Missouri state court that he had been freed when Emerson had taken him to live in territories where slavery was prohibited (by the Missouri Compromise). He won the case, but then lost in a higher court. In response, he appealed to the federal circuit court for Missouri.

The Supreme Court finally heard the case in 1856. In 1857 Chief Justice Roger B. Taney held that a "negro," whether a slave or a freedman, could not be a citizen and had no right to sue in a federal court. He also stated that Congress had no right to outlaw slavery in the territories. Pro-slavery forces hailed the decision, but anti-slavery forces were outraged. Like Congress, which had repeatedly dodged the issue, the Supreme Court was not going to resolve the problem, and war between the states became even more probable.

## FASCINATING FACTS

During World War I (1914–1918) the Central powers—Germany, Austria-Hungary, Turkey, and Bulgaria—fought the Allies—Great Britain, France, and Russia, with the U.S. joining the war in 1917.

Size of American armed forces in early 1917: 200,000

Size of American armed forces by war's end: 4.7 million

Men who registered for the draft (June 5, 1917): 9.5 million

Men drafted: 2.8 million

Draft dodgers: 160,000

Americans who fought overseas: 2 million

Americans who fought at the bloody battle of Meuse-Argonne, the last battle of the war (September to November 1918): 1.2 million

Americans who died in that battle: 26,000

Total American war deaths: 112,432

Total war deaths: nearly 10 million

## DREISER, THEODORE

With the kind of compassion for the down-and-out that can come only from experience, Theodore Dreiser wrote tragic novels of human weakness in the face of inescapable poverty. His own impoverished childhood in Terre Haute, Indiana, made Dreiser a scrappy survivor. Sympathetic but unsentimental in his view of human frailty, he felt that people were "too wise to hearken always to instincts and desires" but "too weak to always prevail against them."

Dreiser's skills as a journalist elevated a sensational, real-life crime into an enduring work of art that showed how the American dream of instant wealth can become a nightmare. Based upon the Gillette-Brown murder case of 1906, *An American Tragedy* (1925) tells of a former bellhop who plots the murder of his lover in order to marry a rich socialite. The novel pioneered an approach to literature in which a horrific crime is presented calmly and without comment. Decades later, Truman Capote would use this technique to write the spellbinding *In Cold Blood*.

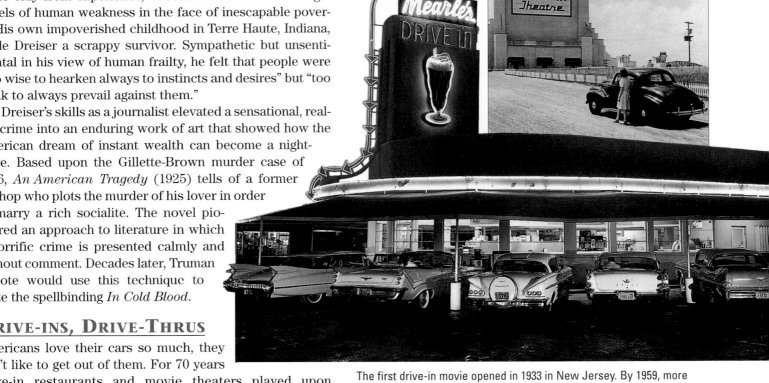

## DRIVE-INS, DRIVE-THRUS

Americans love their cars so much, they don't like to get out of them. For 70 years drive-in restaurants and movie theaters played upon Americans' devotion to their cars and became magnets for leisure seekers, especially during the summertime. The craze began in 1921, when two restaurants designed for in-car dining opened—Kirby's Pig Stand, between Dallas and Fort Worth, Texas, and White Castle, in Wichita, Kansas. Two years later an A&W stand hired "tray boys" to carry root beer to cars. "Tray girls" soon followed, as did the "running boys" at Hot Shoppe restaurants. As the trend continued, carhops, as these car-side servers came to be known, wore ever-fancier uniforms and, sometimes, roller skates.

After World War II, drive-in movies became popular with families, who paid by the car, not per person, and with teenagers, who usually ignored the movie. In the 1970s many theaters closed as gasoline prices rose and cars became more efficient but less comfortable. In addition, theater owners found that they could sell the large chunks of land to real estate developers for a fortune, making way, in some cases, for yet another car-related craze—mall shopping.

Although drive-ins didn't last, drive-thru windows have. Since the 1960s entrepreneurs have installed them in banks, bookstores, dry cleaners, and liquor stores. Parents of sick children, the disabled, and the elderly appreciate picking up their prescriptions at pharmacies with such windows. There are few limits to the things Americans can do while in the driver's seat—even some churches and funeral parlors have drive-thru windows.

The first drive-in movie opened in 1933 in New Jersey. By 1959, more than 4,000 dotted the U.S., some with rides to tire out small fry so they'd sleep during the film. Mearle's Diner (above), in Visalia, California, typified drive-in restaurants' neon-and-concrete decor.

Fast-food chains estimate that one diner in 10 eats in the car. These restaurants strive to complete each drive-thru transaction within a matter of a few minutes and are always looking for improved electronic-ordering gadgets.

Horseback riding is a favorite pastime at dude ranches. Guests can choose a short ride, such as the evening barbecue trip above, or a daylong pack ride. Either way, they are assured of sore muscles.

Isadora Duncan on her dancing: "For hours I would stand quite still, my hands...covering my solar plexus.... I was seeking and finally discovered the central spring of all movement."

Jimmy Durante's nose was insured by Lloyd's of London for a whopping $100,000. He would often sign off wistfully: "Good night, Mrs. Calabash...wherever you are."

## DUDE RANCHES

Even as the West was being won, Easterners—"dudes," as the cowboys called them—began to arrive, uninvited, with few survival skills but with the money to pay for a place to stay. The Eaton family of North Dakota was the first to turn rugged hospitality into a business. In 1882 they began charging guests $10 a week for the privilege of doing a ranch hand's job: branding a steer or fixing a broken fence.

By the turn of the century, dude ranching had become a full-fledged, if basic, vacation industry. Ranches in Wyoming, Montana, and the Dakotas provided such outdoor enthusiasts as Teddy Roosevelt with hot meals, horses, and guided tours of the Rockies. Today dude ranches attract families and groups of friends with package deals that include riding lessons, babysitters, fly-fishing, and white-water rafting, as well as horseback pack rides and a chance to lend a helping hand with a roundup.

## DUNCAN, ISADORA

Isadora Duncan, it is said, didn't dance *to* the music, she danced the music—letting a symphony of sounds spontaneously guide her body to graceful expression. Untutored in dance but determined to share the beauty of natural movement with the world, Duncan trained herself to express her innermost spirit to the strains of Beethoven and Wagner. Her simple yet charismatic performance of hops, skips, and leaps conveyed the carefree joy of childhood, while her dramatic poses reflected suffering universal to humanity.

Duncan flitted across America and Europe in bare feet and flowing Grecian-style tunics, her unrestricted style alternately scandalizing and mesmerizing buttoned-up turn-of-the-century audiences that were accustomed to "mechanical" ballet. The dance community had not seen the likes of her before, nor has it since. She left no choreography, no technique, no repertory, yet her idiosyncratic, instinctive approach to art freed the stage for generations of modern dancers who would follow in her steps.

## DURANTE, JIMMY

"I got a million of 'em, a million of 'em!" said Jimmy "The Schnozzola" Durante, and he did: jokes, songs, and fans. One of the best-loved entertainers of all time, Durante began his career at 17 playing ragtime piano. After his success in vaudeville, he arrived on Broadway in 1929. He made movies, such as *The Man Who Came to Dinner* (1942). He also cut records, did radio, and had his own TV show, *The Texaco Star Theater's Jimmy Durante Show*. He was sought-after as a guest star on TV shows and worked well into the 1970s.

Durante had a croaky voice and a host of endearing mannerisms. He never lost his earthy New York accent. When proper English actress Greer Garson once appeared on his show, he urged everyone to behave with decorum. Reviewing the script with her, he showed her where the laughs would come. "But what if they don't laugh?" asked Miss Garson. Replied The Schnozz: "Den we both go down the terlet."

## DUST BOWL

In the 1930s bad farming practices, along with nature's fickleness, produced the Dust Bowl—one of the worst environmental disasters in history. The Dust Bowl encompassed the panhandles of Texas and Oklahoma and sections of Kansas, Colorado, and New Mexico. During World War I, high grain prices had enticed farmers to chance the region's light soil and highly variable rainfall. These sodbusters plowed up millions of acres of grassland and planted wheat. In 1933 a drought that would last seven years arrived. The wheat stopped growing, leaving nothing to anchor the soil.

In the following years, heavy springtime windstorms scoured the plains, picking up loose topsoil and carrying it as far away as the East Coast. These smothering "black blizzards" clogged roads and disrupted train travel. People caught outside during a storm sometimes got lost or suffered "dust pneumonia." But it was the farmers who had hoped to profit who paid most dearly. Their livestock choked, and their farm machinery was buried under mounds of black grit. With little to harvest, they went bankrupt by the thousands.

Many packed their belongings into jalopies and headed to new lives in California, a harsh journey described by John Steinbeck in *The Grapes of Wrath*. With the help of the federal government, the farmers who remained learned how to slow erosion and protect the soil, a process that eventually meant restoring many of the wheat fields to grassland.

## DYLAN, BOB

Bob Dylan's brilliant song-poems, with their biting insights and mystical imagery, galvanized the antiwar and civil rights movements in the 1960s. Young Dylan idolized folk legend Woody Guthrie, and his early songs imitated Guthrie's talking style. The clear-voiced Joan Baez, an established artist, sang Dylan's protest songs and in 1962 took him on tour. His pale, scruffy figure and his rasping, intense style were soon famous.

When Dylan moved into rock in 1965, his folk-music fans booed him—and his electric guitar. Beset by controversy, he married secretly and sought privacy. In July 1966 he was seriously injured in a motorcycle accident near Woodstock, New York. Rumors of death and drug abuse abounded among Dylanologists.

When he recorded again in 1968, it was in Nashville. On *Nashville Skyline* (1969) his voice was smoother and his material more upbeat. Dylan toured successfully with The Band in 1974 and has appeared occasionally since then. At Woodstock II in 1994, he riveted the children of his '60s fans with "songs both apocalyptic and cautionary."

Such WPA photographers as Arthur Rothstein documented the tragedy of the Dust Bowl. He recorded this scene in 1935 in Cimarron County, Oklahoma.

### DYLAN MASTERPIECES

A Hard Rain's a-Gonna Fall
All Along the Watchtower
Blowin' in the Wind
Don't Think Twice, It's All Right
It Ain't Me Babe
Just Like a Woman
Knockin' on Heaven's Door
Leopard-Skin-Pill-Box Hat
Like a Rolling Stone
Masters of War
Mr. Tambourine Man
Positively 4th Street
Rainy Day Women
Subterranean Homesick Blues
The Times They Are a-Changin'

Bob Dylan wrote the song "Desolation Row" in the backseat of a taxi in New York City. "I try to write the song when it comes," he says.

Eakins painted portraits of people who interested him, such as scientists, musicians, and doctors. At right, a self-portrait.

*The Champion Single Sculls* (detail shown above) is thought to be a tribute by Thomas Eakins to his friend Max Schmitt (foreground), who won a race on the Schuylkill River in 1870.

At the controls: Amelia Earhart, who in 1932 became the first woman to make a solo flight across the Atlantic Ocean.

*"They have yarns / Of a skyscraper so tall they have to put hinges / On the top two stories so as to let the moon go by."*

## EAKINS, THOMAS

Thomas Eakins, like many great artists, was misunderstood, and even maligned, in his day. Yet he is now viewed as an important innovator of the late 19th century, for he pursued an original vision based on an appreciation of the everyday. His paintings depict both America and Americans with a sensitivity unmatched in domestic art.

In an era when Americans looked to Europe for all things cultural, Eakins cast his eye around his own backyard and chronicled the people and preoccupations of the middle-class Philadelphia neighborhood where he spent most of his 72 years. Whether modeling a cellist's delicate fingers or capturing boxing, hunting, and rowing scenes, Eakins used his superb drafting skills and knowledge of human anatomy. In an age when other artists were infatuated with soft, luminous Impressionism, Eakins was intent on painting somber, realistic canvases that not only recorded minute details with precision but also revealed insights into the sitter's personality.

## EARHART, AMELIA

When Amelia Earhart disappeared over the Pacific without a trace on July 2, 1937, during a daring attempt at a round-the-world flight, fans could scarcely believe the tragic news. The pioneer pilot with the engaging smile had come to be a symbol of the new American woman, capable of doing anything a man did, and possibly doing it better.

Over the years many theories evolved regarding Earhart's fate; along with plausible ones about her running out of fuel or crashing in a storm were tales of political intrigue and kidnapping by foreign powers. One such tale held that the Japanese had downed the plane and either executed Earhart as a spy or turned her over to Emperor Hirohito as a "love slave." But the discovery in 1992 of some metal fragments on an uninhabited coral atoll some miles off Earhart's charted course suggests a more mundane but realistic possibility: she simply lost her way.

## EARTH DAY

In 1969, when no one over 30 was supposed to have any innovative ideas (youth knew it all), 53-year-old Wisconsin senator Gaylord Nelson thought up Earth Day. He had become keenly aware that human carelessness was endangering the planet, and he wanted to galvanize Americans into action. When the first Earth Day dawned, on April 22, 1970, about 20 million mostly young citizens arose to gather trash, collect recyclables, and attend teach-ins. It was one of the largest peaceful demonstrations in U.S. history.

Such overwhelming concern inspired Congress. The Clean Air Act was passed, and the Environmental Protection Agency was created in the 1970s. Earth Day itself—a sometime annual event—continues to be a call to paint over graffiti, pick up litter, and get on with recycling.

## EASTWOOD, CLINT

"Go ahead. Make my day," taunts Harry Callahan in *Sudden Impact* (1983), one of Clint Eastwood's Dirty Harry movies. Eastwood's Harry is a tight-lipped tough guy who takes the law into his own hands. Although moviegoers loved him, the critics did not. Reviewing Eastwood's performance in *Dirty Harry* (1971), one critic said, "… one could hardly call him a bad actor. He'd have to *do* something before we could consider him bad at it." Harry, however, was a box-office smash.

Eastwood began portraying "economical characters," as he has called them, when he starred in the TV Western *Rawhide* (1959–66). But he has not fallen into the trap of playing only the macho type. He has also portrayed gentler, even comic characters. In *Every Which Way but Loose* (1978), his costar was an orangutan. In the '80s he concentrated on directing films and continued to surprise his fans. In his film *The Unforgiven* (1992), Eastwood played a retired gunslinger who is reluctantly drawn back into action. In *The Bridges of Madison County* (1995), he proved that a 65-year-old can be a romantic hero.

## EDISON, THOMAS ALVA

Thomas Alva Edison said that genius is "one percent inspiration and 99 percent perspiration." America's greatest inventor, he patented 1,093 inventions during his lifetime. He was dubbed the "Wizard of Menlo Park" for the frenetic pace at which creations poured out of his laboratory in that New Jersey town. He survived on little sleep, napping only when he had to, often on a table in the midst of employees working around him. Edison's achievements are all the more remarkable because he was hard of hearing from childhood and received formal schooling for only three months. Edison changed the lives of millions of people not just by his most famous inventions— the electric light and the phonograph—but also by improvements to inventions that might not have been feasible otherwise—the telephone, the electric generator, the typewriter, and the motion picture, to name a few. A practical man, he was irate when Congress rejected his vote-counting machine. Edison was not interested in invention for its own sake, and he vowed that he would "never again invent anything nobody wants."

Actor Richard Gere spoke to an audience on Earth Day in 1990. Founders of the movement can boast that 6,600 communities have set up recycling programs, most of them within the past decade.

In *The Outlaw Josey Wales*, Eastwood's character is embittered by the massacre of his family and seeks revenge.

To test his newly invented phonograph, Thomas Edison shouted verses of "Mary Had a Little Lamb" into the machine.

Thousands of names were considered for this car, including the Resilient Bullet and the Utopian Turtletop. The company finally settled on Edsel, the name of Henry Ford's only son.

When shown a compass as a small boy, Einstein realized that "something deeply hidden had to be behind things...." He later achieved "the greatest single stride science has ever made."

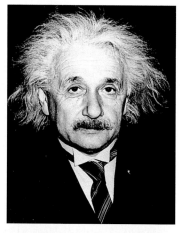

As a general, Eisenhower led the most powerful military force ever assembled. In the White House, his easygoing manner reassured the nation. He and his wife, Mamie, retired to their farm in Pennsylvania.

## EDSEL

The Edsel, which debuted in September 1957, was one of the worst marketing disasters in automotive history. Despite unprecedented advertising and promotion (marketers went so far as to stable a pony at every dealership to encourage families to stop in for a test drive), Americans refused to buy the car. Part of the Edsel's problem was timing. It was big at a time when people were turning away from large, ornate cars, and it was expensive when the country was entering a recession. And, according to many critics, the Edsel was just plain ugly. Its oval radiator grill was compared to everything from a horse collar to a toilet seat. On top of that, the Edsel was plagued with mechanical problems. Ford lost close to $350 million on the car, which was discontinued in November 1959. Ironically, because so few Edsels were produced, they are now valuable collector's items.

## EINSTEIN, ALBERT

Albert Einstein changed our sense of reality with a deceptively simple equation: $E=mc^2$. It states that energy (E) and mass (m) are aspects of each other. A teapot, in other words, is a ray of sunlight in disguise. Einstein also proved that the faster an object moves through space, the slower it moves through time, and that starlight bends as it nears the sun. That his descriptions of the physical world have been confirmed by experiments makes them no less perplexing. As the writer Aldous Huxley put it, "The world is not only queerer than we imagine, it is queerer than we *can* imagine."

Born in Germany, Einstein spoke haltingly until he was nine. He was considered a poor student, but when he dropped out of school for a brief period, he took the opportunity to teach himself calculus and higher mathematics. While working as a patent examiner at the Swiss Patent Office, he earned a Ph.D. from the University of Zurich and wrote four groundbreaking papers, one of which won him the Nobel Prize.

Einstein fled Nazi Germany in 1933 and settled in Princeton, New Jersey. In 1939, fearing Hitler's intentions, he wrote a letter to President Roosevelt, encouraging the development of atomic energy. That letter led to the creation of the atomic bomb. Einstein died in 1955, three years after declining the presidency of the new state of Israel. He once said, "Politics are for the moment. An equation is for eternity."

## EISENHOWER, DWIGHT DAVID

Once criticized by journalists as a passive president, Dwight Eisenhower has since come to be seen as one of our best chief executives. "Ike," as he was affectionately called, preferred to get things done without confrontation. He liked to pretend that he was not concerned about a problem while taking deft, behind-the-scenes measures to solve it.

As commander of the Allied forces in Western Europe during World War II, General Eisenhower forged armies from different nations into a united force that successfully invaded Europe and crushed the Nazis. "I am not one of the desk-pounding types…" he said. "I would rather try to persuade a man to go along…."

Eisenhower ran for president as a Republican and defeated Adlai Stevenson twice. He advocated middle-of-the-road policies, annoying both conservative Republicans and liberal Democrats. He held the line against communism abroad with military and economic foreign aid, and he resisted social changes at home. Only with reluctance did he force the racial integration of a high school in Little Rock, Arkansas, in 1957. Despite criticism by the media, Eisenhower was one of the most popular presidents in American history.

## EISENSTAEDT, ALFRED

The father of photojournalism, Alfred Eisenstaedt came to America in 1936 as one of four original staff photographers at *Life* magazine. There, "Eisie," as he was fondly known, had no use for the studio lights and heavy makeup of earlier artists. He favored the guise of a "casual visitor, who incidentally brought a Leica, three lenses, and a little tripod," thereby creating legendary shots of human interest.

Eisenstaedt's portraits of John F. Kennedy, Eleanor Roosevelt, and Marilyn Monroe are classics. In each instance he sought the essence of his subject and let it speak. Modestly (but truthfully) he said, "The important thing is not the camera but the eye." For "eye" one could read "heart," for he also said, "Whenever I photograph, I photograph as a friend."

## ELECTION DAY

"Turn out, turn out and save your Country from ruin!" was the urgent get-out-the-vote message of November broadsides in 1800. Ice, mud, and snow delayed a complete vote count until February, keeping the nation in suspense. Finally Jefferson's election was announced. By 1830 better roads sped election returns from Philadelphia to Washington in two days.

By the 1920s radio broadcasts of the returns had transformed election night into a ritual of alternating gloom and cheer. Elections had become like horse races, with pollsters predicting outcomes by percentage points. The biggest election-night upset came in 1948. The few polls that had been conducted showed Dewey far ahead of Truman. But pollsters had stopped querying voters weeks before Truman's late surge. After winning the election, Truman held aloft a newspaper mistakenly headlined "Dewey Defeats Truman."

In 1960 CBS blundered on election night, predicting a Nixon win at 7:15 P.M. Nixon's loss to Kennedy was revealed mid-morning the next day. In the 1980 presidential election, votes were tabulated so quickly that Jimmy Carter conceded the race to Ronald Reagan nearly two hours before the polls had closed on the West Coast. No other presidential candidate had ever conceded while citizens were still voting.

At the end of World War II, Eisenstaedt captured this world-famous image of a sailor sharing his euphoria with a passerby in Times Square. The photographer's portraits often caught their subjects in unguarded moments, revealing their true character.

Political discussions often generate a lot of heat but very little light. Breakfast may be the very worst time to try to get one's point across.

## ELEVATOR SHOES

Since 1939, American men who wanted to walk a little taller have known where to turn: the back pages of magazines in which the Richlee Shoe Company runs mail-order ads for its "Elevators." These height-enhancing shoes and boots conceal a built-in two- or three-inch booster, and are shipped in boxes that make no reference to the footwear's special nature. It's been claimed that Humphrey Bogart, Winston Churchill, Bing Crosby, Thomas Dewey, and Robert Kennedy all wore elevator shoes. There's no question that Mickey Rooney did—he was Richlee's spokesman during the 1950s and '60s. Although elevator shoes have long been a target for comics, there's a good case for buying them: surveys have shown that taller executives command higher salaries.

## ELIOT, T. S.

No poet today can claim to be free of the influence of Thomas Sterns Eliot, whose innovative writing style juxtaposed the commonplace with the fantastic and mixed lyrical rhymes with unwieldy fragments. While a student at Harvard, Eliot wrote "The Love Song of J. Alfred Prufrock," one of his most widely read poems, about a balding, timid man who "measured out [his] life with coffee spoons." Eliot's frustration with the spiritual emptiness of modern life found its most powerful expression in *The Waste Land*. This poem, which originally ran to twice its current length, benefited from Ezra Pound's blue-pencil editing. It is filled with historical allusions, for Eliot believed that history and literature are inextricably linked. *The Hollow Men* contains two lines that sum up his vision of the 20th century: "This is the way the world ends / Not with a bang but a whimper."

Eliot believed that poets must not "meddle with the tasks of the theologian" but instead should strive "to be something of a popular entertainer." To this end he wrote for the theater such verse dramas as *Murder in the Cathedral* and *The Cocktail Party*. He won the Nobel Prize for literature in 1948.

## ELLINGTON, DUKE

Duke Ellington was the most significant, and most recorded, composer and bandleader in jazz history. His 2,000 or so compositions were tailored to the specific talents of his players, some of whom remained with him for 20 years or more. Fellow composer Billy Strayhorn once remarked, "Ellington plays the piano, but his real instrument is the band."

Among Ellington's finest resources were saxophonists Johnny Hodges (alto), Ben Webster (tenor), and Harry Carney (baritone); trombonists Joe "Tricky Sam" Nanton and Lawrence Brown; and trumpeters "Bubber" Miley and "Cootie" Williams. The band's distinctive textures first became apparent at Harlem's Cotton Club in the late 1920s, where its trademark was the "jungle" growls produced by Nanton's and Miley's plunger mutes. "Mood Indigo," featuring

Eliot, who favored idioms and natural rhythms of speech, revolutionized the poetic conventions of his day. His *Old Possum's Book of Practical Cats* inspired the musical *Cats*.

Duke Ellington wrote hundreds of jazz standards; ironically, his band's theme, "Take the A Train," was by another composer, Billy Strayhorn. The band's sound was so distinctive that it could never be imitated.

Barney Bigard's clarinet, became a big hit in 1930. Ellington experimented with new combinations of instruments, including using the voice as a horn, and reached far beyond the usual jazz forms. His tone poem *Black, Brown and Beige* celebrated black American musical history. He also wrote many suites inspired by tours to Asia, Latin America, and Africa.

A butler's son from Washington, D.C., Ellington studied piano from the age of seven and was heavily influenced by the giants of stride piano. Because of segregation, his band, in its early days, had to travel in private Pullman cars. Elegant and sophisticated, Ellington, whose sad, pouchy eyes lit up when he smiled, charmed cheering crowds by calling out, "Love you madly!" His composition "It Don't Mean a Thing (If It Ain't Got That Swing)" gave the swing era its name.

## ELLIS ISLAND

They came from Dublin and Dubrovnik, Stockholm and Sorrento, churning up one of the greatest human waves in history. And they flowed, 12 million strong, in an unbroken stream over a small patch of land tucked in New York Harbor between the Statue of Liberty and the land of opportunity.

Beginning in 1892, Ellis Island was the primary port of entry for those seeking the promise of freedom. After journeying across the Atlantic in steamship steerage, arrivals inched their way toward a new life through the imposing brick Main Building. A melting pot for the citizens of 75 nations, the building poured out thousands of would-be Americans daily. (On April 17, 1907, a record 11,747 passed through.) The processing went quickly, with inspectors performing an initial six-second evaluation and branding with blue chalk those who required further examination: L for lameness, Pg for pregnancy, X for mental deficiency. Then followed the nerve-racking inquiry into age, finances, work prospects, and destination, during which any wrong response might lead to deportation.

For some, the Portal to Plenty became a Palace of Tears. Two percent of immigrants were turned away as carriers of infectious disease, subversive politics, or questionable morals. For the rest, the first taste of America that they had been served on Ellis Island—the hot dogs and hot showers, the electric lights and motion pictures—foretold the wonders awaiting them in their adopted home.

By 1924 the resettlement flood had slowed to a trickle; 30 years later Ellis Island was closed. Today, however, after a $160 million renovation—the most extensive and expensive ever undertaken in America—the receiving station again welcomes travelers. The Main Building houses the Ellis Island Immigration Museum, which hosts 2 million people annually—double the number of immigrants who were processed even in peak years.

Ellis Island was built to accommodate 5,000 people a day; but planners grossly underestimated the flood of immigrants that soon swept through.

In 1905 a wary Italian family wonders when they will see the rest of their baggage, some of which was lost while the mother and children were being processed.

Newly arrived "marriageable women" anxiously await the start of their new lives in America.

In this engraving a Union soldier reads to a group of slaves the document that granted them freedom and gave the Civil War a moral focus.

Nominated for a record 111 Emmys, *Cheers* won 26 of them. The only series ever to win more was *The Mary Tyler Moore Show.*

Candace Bergen won Best Actress in a comedy series for her role as the sharp-tongued broadcast journalist Murphy Brown.

## EMANCIPATION PROCLAMATION

President Lincoln's Emancipation Proclamation was just one of the steps that led to the end of slavery in the United States, but it has come to symbolize the whole process. Lincoln considered slavery "an unqualified evil." Still, he was bound by the Constitution to allow it in any state that wanted it. He could, however, confiscate property—including slaves—that contributed to war efforts against the Union. Two Union generals freed slaves in the areas they controlled, and many other slaves fled to the protection of the Union armies.

There was mounting pressure on Lincoln to free all slaves. On July 21, 1862, he told his Cabinet, "We must free the slaves or be ourselves subdued." His secretary of state, William H. Seward, advised him to wait; a declaration would have greater impact after a Union victory. In September, after winning the Battle of Antietam, Lincoln warned Confederate states that if they were still in rebellion at year's end, he would declare their slaves "then, thenceforward, and forever free." On January 1, 1863, the Emancipation Proclamation liberated slaves in rebel states as "an act of justice." But legally this was only a war measure. Lincoln then began to work on the Thirteenth Amendment, which ended slavery forever.

## EMERSON, RALPH WALDO

America's master of maxims, Ralph Waldo Emerson is one of our most widely quoted authors. "To laugh often and much;... To know even one life has breathed easier because you have lived; That is to have succeeded," he wrote. Emerson became known as the Sage of Concord when he took up Transcendentalism, which captivated New England freethinkers with its pro-democratic optimism and its celebration of the divine in every person. He called for an American literature equal to that of the Europeans but was nevertheless skeptical of wisdom that comes from books. "'Tis the good reader," he wrote, "that makes the good book."

Emerson's treatises "Nature," "The American Scholar," and "Self Reliance" exhorted Americans to trust their whims, even if they were contradictory. "A foolish consistency is the hobgoblin of little minds, adored by little statesmen," wrote this champion of individualism.

## EMMY AWARDS

From the first small ceremony in 1949, the Emmy Awards have expanded to a three-hour, star-studded telecast similar to the Oscar presentations. The Academy of Television Arts and Sciences, which runs the ceremony, has handed out a dazzling array of awards for prime-time shows including dramas, comedies, miniseries, and specials. Many repeat winners have featured strong ensemble casts, starting in the 1960s with the *Dick Van Dyke Show.* In the 1970s the British import *Upstairs, Downstairs* was a consistent winner. In 1977 the academy had to add a new category to acknowledge the miniseries *Roots*. Actors can win any of 20 different awards. Alan Alda of *M\*A\*S\*H* was the first to win Emmys for acting, writing, and directing. In the 1980s producer Steven Bochco was recognized for creating a new style of realistic drama series with *Hill Street Blues*, set in a gritty police precinct, and *L.A. Law*, about a firm whose lawyers grapple with the social issues of the day. The Emmy's cousin, the Daytime Emmy Award, honors soaps, talk shows, game shows, and children's programs, such as *Sesame Street*.

## EMPIRE STATE BUILDING

At 1,250 feet and 102 stories, the Empire State Building was the world's tallest skyscraper by far when it was completed in 1931. Although it has since ceded that title to other buildings, the slender steel-and-brick spire remains the preeminent symbol of architectural audacity. Construction began during the depths of the Depression, when many office buildings were vacant and the prospects for filling yet another skyscraper seemed poor. Driving the risky project was an investment group led by General Motors founder John Jacob Raskob. Raskob's motivation seems to have had to do less with future profits than with beating out Walter Chrysler's newly completed Chrysler Building, which rose 1,048 feet above 42nd Street.

With $50 million to spend and a two-acre plot at the corner of Fifth Avenue and 34th Street, Raskob gave architect William Lamb just 18 months to design and complete the new structure. Raskob insisted that the building's projected height—over 1,250 feet, plus a 200-foot dirigible-mooring mast—remain secret, lest Chrysler add a few feet to his tower at the last minute. Despite the difficulties of moving some 365,000 tons of materials through crowded midtown streets and working at dizzying heights (48 men died during the construction), the builders, who numbered in the thousands, finished ahead of schedule and $9 million under budget.

On May 1, 1931, President Hoover pressed a button in Washington, D.C., turning on the lights in the Empire State Building. The press dubbed the Art Deco masterpiece the "Eighth Wonder of the World." Despite the fanfare, the building stood nearly empty for a decade. A sluggish economy, perhaps coupled with a fear of working so high in the sky, kept prospective tenants away. But by the 1940s business had picked up, and so had confidence in the building's sturdiness. A tragic mishap in 1945 ended any doubts about its structural integrity. A B-25 bomber, off course in the fog, hit the skyscraper, hurtling one engine across the 78th floor and sending another down an elevator shaft. The three-man crew was killed, as were 11 office workers on the 79th floor. The building, however, stood staunchly intact.

On July 28, 1945, an Army Air Forces bomber, lost in the fog, crashed into the Empire State Building at the 79th floor, killing 14 people and leaving a gaping 18-by-20-foot hole.

The Empire State Building costarred with King Kong in the final sequence of a classic 1933 movie.

Publicity stunts held at the Empire State Building have included everything from Girl Scout slumber parties atop the tower to "run-up" races. The record for the ascent to the 86th floor is 10 minutes, 30 seconds.

## FASCINATING FACTS

**HEIGHT OF EMPIRE STATE BUILDING:** 102 stories above the street; 1,454 feet to top of television antenna.

**SIZE:** Area of site about two acres, or 79,288 square feet. Rentable area: 248,369 square feet.

**INSIDE STORY:** Building contains 1,060 miles of telephone cables; 2,500,000 feet of electric wires; 50 miles of radiator pipes; 73 elevators.

**VIEW:** On clear days, observation decks afford 360° panoramic views of portions of five states as far distant as 80 miles.

**TOWER LIGHTS:** Turn one 360° sweep each minute; visible to airplanes 300 miles away.

The *Enola Gay* was presented to the Smithsonian in 1949. After extensive restoration work, the front third was put on display in 1995.

The four-foot-deep canal could accommodate only flat barges drawn by horses walking along a towpath. For a while, it was the fastest, cheapest way to ship goods east and west.

The inventor of Eskimo Pies also pioneered the use of dry ice to refrigerate ice cream, thus making it possible to transport frozen desserts far and wide.

## ENOLA GAY

The B-29 bomber *Enola Gay* approached the skies over Japan on the morning of August 6, 1945. Its mission was so secret that only three members of the crew were aware of it. Once the plane was over Hiroshima, the bomb bay of the huge Superfortress opened and an atomic bomb hurtled to the earth. A blinding white light and an eerie silence was followed by an earthshaking blast that destroyed everything in the city's center and killed at least 78,000 people outright. From the plane, 11 miles away, the stunned pilot, Col. Paul W. Tibbetts, Jr., reported, "...we had seen the city when we went in, and there was nothing to see when we came back."

Military strategists saw the atomic bomb as the only way, short of a full-scale invasion of Japan, which was sure to cost hundreds of thousands of American and Japanese lives, to bring a quick end to World War II. Still, the decision to use the bomb was difficult to reach and remains highly controversial. Today the *Enola Gay*, named for the pilot's mother, is on display at the Smithsonian's National Air and Space Museum.

## ERIE CANAL

The Erie Canal, acclaimed in folklore and song, was once derided as "Clinton's Ditch." For years, politician DeWitt Clinton had promoted his plans for a waterway between the Great Lakes and the Atlantic Ocean. Many said it couldn't be built, and it was true that few of the farmers and Irish laborers who were recruited to build the canal had any experience, but they did have ingenuity. Remarkable men, such as Benjamin Wright and James Geddes, constructed aqueducts, invented machines to cut down trees and uproot stumps, and developed a new cement that would harden under water. For eight long years they toiled. When the canal was finally completed in 1825, the country exploded in a joyous celebration of this engineering marvel. "Canal fever" swept the U.S., and waterways were dug from Maine to Virginia.

## ESKIMO PIE

In 1920 Christian Nelson, a teacher and co-owner of the Nelson-Mustard Cream Company, a candy store in Onawa, Iowa, was inspired by a boy who had a terrible time deciding whether to spend his nickel on ice cream or a chocolate bar. After months of late-night experimenting, Nelson discovered a way to combine the two. He dubbed his invention the "I-Scream Bar." Next Nelson teamed up with Russell Stover, who later became famous for his chocolates and whose wife is credited with inventing the name Eskimo Pie.

Eskimo Pies were an immediate hit. Nelson was hailed as an all-American, rags-to-riches hero, although, in fact, the Eskimo Pie company was plagued by problems, especially unlicensed imitators. The Eskimo Pie remains one of America's favorite treats. Recently, sugar-free, low-fat, and yogurt Eskimo Pie products have been introduced.

## EVERGLADES

"Boo louder," said Marjory Stoneman Douglas to her jeering opponents during a 1970 debate on the fate of the Everglades marshlands. And they did. Known as the "Grandmother of the Glades," Douglas, then in her eighties, was no stranger to hostile receptions. She was, once again, fighting to save her beloved Everglades from destruction. Where critics saw a "wholly valueless" swamp, Douglas saw a unique river, 50 miles wide and six inches deep. Her landmark 1947 book, *The Everglades: River of Grass,* linked her name with a passionate movement to preserve the region and its wildlife long before *ecology* became a household word.

In the 1800s the United States Army had called the wilderness merely "a retreat for the rascally Indian." Over the next hundred years, engineers crisscrossed southern Florida with 1,400 miles of canals, which disrupted the Everglades's natural cycles. "The Everglades were dying," Douglas wrote. "The endless acres of saw grass, brown as an enormous shadow where rain and lake water had once flowed, rustled dry...." Thanks in part to Douglas, roughly 1.5 million acres of the Everglades were established as a national park in 1947.

Still, the fog-laced Everglades is not among the nation's 10 most-visited parks. Because summer temperatures reach 95 degrees, with 100 percent humidity, tourists prefer to visit from November to June. Roseate spoonbills and great egrets attract visitors, as do stunningly beautiful wild orchids, dense tree islands, and rare species of panthers, crocodiles, and eagles. Meanwhile, efforts continue to restore the natural flow of water in the Everglades. As Douglas is the first to admit, "There's a lot more work to be done."

The second-largest national park in the lower 48 states, the Everglades is host to an abundance of wildlife, including the great egret (above) and the American alligator (left).

## EVERLY BROTHERS

Bob Dylan once said, "We owe these guys everything—they started it all." The Everly Brothers, who combined tightly blended vocals with a full-bodied guitar, had a fresh energy and an infectious style.

Don and Phil Everly had had an early start in music—they spent their childhood summers touring with their country-singing parents. While in their teens, the brothers moved to Nashville, where they wrote songs for other singers, such as "Thou Shalt Not Steal," which became a hit for Kitty Wells. They also performed on their own, recording the songs "Bye Bye Love," "Wake Up Little Susie," "All I Have to Do Is Dream," and "Bird Dog." They charted an impressive 15 Top 10 hits between 1957 and 1962, including "('Til) I Kissed You," "Cathy's Clown," and "Crying in the Rain." Their glory days faded after Don's stint in the Marines, but they still toured and even hosted a TV show for ABC in 1970. The strain of work led to the breakup of the team in July 1973. They worked separately for a decade, then came together again. In 1986 they were inducted into the Rock and Roll Hall of Fame.

The Everly Brothers first appeared on radio when Don (left) was eight and Phil was six. The brothers were known for their close harmonies.

Lava lamps, Rubik's Cubes, and mood rings have sold in the millions. Other fads include fuzzy dice (hanging from a car's rearview mirror), beanbag chairs, pogo sticks, Day-Glo shoelaces, and black-light posters.

## FADS

Every now and again a fad sweeps the country. In 1958 millions of people suddenly had to have a Hula Hoop. The fad started when entrepreneurs at the Wham-O company heard that, in Australia, people twirled bamboo hoops using a hula-like hip motion. They experimented with wooden rings but opted to make hoops out of a plastic called Grex.

In the late 1960s no conversation pit was complete without a lava lamp. The brainchild of an Englishman named Craven Walker, the lava lamp was designed to entertain, not illuminate. When the lamp was switched on, colored fluids in a container above the lightbulb slowly flowed and changed shape, creating a "psychedelic" effect.

Two major fads were born in 1975: mood rings and pet rocks. Mood rings featured a "stone" that allegedly changed color depending upon the wearer's mood. It was actually a liquid crystal that reacted to changes in body temperature. Specially designed mood rings sold at department stores for as much as $250; cheap knockoffs sold for $2.

While mood rings were sold, in part, as aids to self-knowledge, pet rocks were pure silliness. They were started as a joke by an unemployed California advertising man, Gary Dahl. But, thanks in part to his clever packaging and witty manual, they became the hottest Christmas gift of the year.

In 1980 and 1981 the country became obsessed with Rubik's Cube, a devilishly challenging puzzle originally created to help students think in three dimensions. The cubes sold like crazy, and so did books offering systems for solving them. The reasons some fads take off while others fail remain as puzzling as Rubik's Cube itself.

## FALLOUT SHELTERS

They looked like prison cells and were about the same size, but a family of five was expected to live in one. A symbol of the Cold War era, these windowless concrete rooms were designed to protect people from the lethal fallout of a nuclear attack. They first appeared when President Truman began a civil defense program. President Eisenhower helped popularize them, but few shelters were built until after July 25, 1961, when President Kennedy, making a speech about the Soviet Union, encouraged people to build fallout shelters.

Instantly, shelter mania took off and contractors rushed to fill orders. Stocked with food, water, medicine, and other necessities, shelters were as standard in some suburban neighborhoods as patios or pools.

This 1951 fallout shelter, called the atomic igloo, looks like a mausoleum. The civil defense symbol (right) was used to identify public shelters.

## FAMILY REUNIONS

A bridge across time and distance, the family reunion is an American custom that keeps growing. Whether held by one of the country's famous clans or by just-plain-folks, reunions satisfy a need to belong and offer a chance to strengthen blood ties. "It's the kind of thing that should be happening all over the country," said one participant.

Reunions are as diverse as the families themselves. While many are hosted in private homes, others are held in parks, resorts, restaurants, and churches. Independence Day is a favorite get-together date, but reunions are also organized around birthdays, anniversaries, and other joyous occasions. And while reunions might include all manner of activities—from potato-sack races to marathon gabfests—they are generally centered around food, with members contributing dishes that are special to the family. One group put johnny-cakes on the menu because that was their immigrant ancestors' first American meal in 1800.

The desire to mingle with kin and to reminisce knows no bounds. And reunions seem particularly significant among blacks, many of whom were inspired to explore their heritage by Alex Haley's 1976 novel *Roots*. These events can assume added poignancy when descendants of slaves and slave owners, sharing the same name, join to close a historic gap. "What is a reunion," asked one North Carolinian, "but a whole that is divided and then comes back together?"

## FARMER, FANNIE

"It is impossible to raise cookery above a mere drudgery if one does not put heart and soul into the work," declared Fannie Merritt Farmer at the end of the 19th century. Farmer first found success in the classroom, running the famed Boston Cooking School. As the author of the celebrated *The Boston Cooking-School Cookbook* (1896), now known as *The Fannie Farmer Cookbook*, Farmer inspired generations of American housewives to become better, more imaginative artists in the kitchen.

In 1902 Farmer started her own school of cooking. Her recipes, not surprisingly, were from New England. Such regional favorites as codfish cakes, Boston baked beans, clam stew, and Parker House rolls were given places of honor. Her cookbook was also blissfully free of caloric concerns. She used sugar copiously, not only in the desserts and candies for which she is justly famous but in such bizarre-sounding combinations as steak with cherry sauce.

Fannie Farmer's most important influence on American cooking was her emphasis on scientific methods. In an era when most recipes were cobbled together with a pinch of this and a handful of that, and timed "by guess and by golly," Farmer insisted that precision was the cook's best friend. She was the first cookbook writer to call for measuring cups and has been called "The Mother of Level Measurements."

When it comes to family reunions, the bigger the better. To start your own reunion, choose someone who has the time and energy to act as chief organizer. Develop a plan a few months ahead of your target weekend. Use newsletters to spread the word.

Calories didn't count in Fannie Farmer's kitchen. The famous chef had a passion for white foods and might combine mayonnaise, whipped cream, bananas, and marshmallows in one triumphant trifle.

# Fashions
## OF THE 20TH CENTURY

*Styles change with dizzying speed. And despite small rebellions, many women accept the fashion industry's answers to the question: What should I wear?*

### TWENTY-THREE SKIDDOO
In the Roaring Twenties fashion was dashing, slim, and sophisticated even by day, as illustrated by this sporty three-piece tweed-knit suit from 1928.

### THE NEW LOOK
Christian Dior's 1947 collection introduced tiny waists, structured bodices, and voluminous skirts—a radical departure from the styles dictated by wartime fabric shortages.

### THE FEMININE FIFTIES
With the emphasis on home and family after World War II came fashions like this 1952 shirtwaist dress for the proper woman.

### CLOTHES SOBER UP
The Depression took a toll on 1930s fashion, which turned to dark colors, narrower skirts, and longer hemlines. Designers used more practical fabrics and lowered their prices as well.

### ART TO WEAR

The year 1965 saw the utterly new geometric look of Yves St. Laurent's famous "Mondrian" shift, an adventurous fashion in step with youthful spirits.

### SHORT, SHORTER, SHORTEST

Once worn only by the very young and very brave, the miniskirt was shown on the cover of *Life* in August 1969. It was soon followed by even shorter hot pants and the polyester pantsuits of the '70s.

### THE OVERDONE EIGHTIES

The decade of material excess meant exaggerated styles for both day and night. The fashionable woman's wardrobe featured short skirts, oversize jackets, and stiff shoulder pads.

### NEARING THE MILLENNIUM

As a new century approaches, fashion seems only to look backward, favoring a return to simple feminine lines that recall the fitted suits of the '50s and the short shift dresses of the '60s.

After a day of eating sensibly, working out, and listening to lectures on stress, many health-spa clients treat themselves to a massage, facial, or something more exotic—such as this skin-softening kelp wrap.

After traveling the world, William Faulkner returned to Mississippi, where he purchased the house Rowan Oak in 1930. Preferring old-fashioned ways, he never owned a TV or installed air-conditioning. "They're trying to do away with weather," he grumbled.

Renamed the Federal Bureau of Investigation in 1935, the FBI has been dramatized on radio (*Gangbusters*) and in countless TV shows and movies.

## FAT FARMS AND SPAS

When they stopped doing physical labor, Americans gained weight. Farm and factory chores kept people fit; office jobs and laborsaving devices did not. Portliness went from being a mark of prosperity to being a sign of weak character. When home remedies failed, people began going to fat farms for help. Usually, this meant following a ruthless regimen of diet and exercise. Health specialists now say weight control is not enough; any definition of fitness must include the building of strength and the control of stress. Compared with the boot-camp atmosphere of early fat farms, spas may seem luxurious. But their aim is quite ambitious—a change of lifestyle.

## FAULKNER, WILLIAM

Faulkner is famous for his page-long sentences and rich evocations of rural life in the Deep South. Relations among family members and small-town neighbors were Faulkner's great subjects, but his themes are far from local; indeed, his novels earned him the highest honors of any American writer, including the Nobel Prize. In *As I Lay Dying*, he experimented with 59 monologues by a variety of characters, each one revealing the frustrating lives within a single family. "I was trying to rid myself of a dream," Faulkner said of his unusual technique, "which would continue to anguish me until I . . . could gather the pieces together and fill in the gaps."

Always beset by financial difficulties, Faulkner occasionally worked as a Hollywood scriptwriter, reworking Hemingway's *To Have and Have Not* and Chandler's *The Big Sleep*. But in his own writing, he usually returned to his literary home, the fictional Yoknapatawpha County, where many of his stories are set. "I discovered that my own little postage stamp of native soil was worth writing about," he explained, "and that I would never live long enough to exhaust it."

## FBI

Dismayed by widespread immorality, President Theodore Roosevelt decided to create a federal detective service. Congress approved the plan in 1908 but, fearing an American secret police, restricted the new Bureau of Investigation to enforcing laws regarding pornographic books, condoms, and prizefighting movies. During World War I the Bureau watched enemy aliens, caught draft dodgers, and arrested alleged radicals. In the 1920s the role of the Bureau was changed from law enforcement to investigation. It recruited only lawyers and accountants, amassed the world's largest fingerprint collection, built a scientific crime-detection laboratory, and trained local police officers. During World War II the FBI fought enemy spies but tarnished its image with illegal wiretaps in a postwar drive against subversives. In 1960 the FBI strengthened its investigations of organized crime and later took on the growing threat of terrorism.

## FELIX THE CAT

Felix the Cat, who made his debut in 1919, was the first animated animal star. He was created by Otto Messmer, an artist who let his partner, Pat Sullivan, reap the praise. Felix was unbeatable. When forced to dig his own grave, he struck oil. He could think up question marks and shape them into an escape ladder. In a pinch, he could magically turn his tail into anything, from an umbrella to a fishhook.

Felix's films were enormously popular. In 1923 he began to appear in newspaper comics in England and the U.S. Later in the '20s, U.S. Fighter Squadron 31, the Tomcatters, painted him on their planes. A globe-trotting cat, he was also the mascot for Britain's polo team. In 1928, however, Felix's silent films were surpassed by a talking newcomer, Mickey Mouse.

## FERRIS WHEELS

Fairgoers walking through the 1893 World's Columbian Exposition in Chicago were dazzled by the spectacle of a giant, revolving steel wheel jutting into the sky. For 50 cents they could enter glass-enclosed cars on the wheel and be whisked up to the breathtaking height of 20 stories. Invented by a young engineer, George Washington Ferris, the wheel ushered in a new age of mechanical amusements.

Ferris's creation was the hit of the 1893 fair—more than 1.4 million people rode on it. Formed by two wheels with 36 cars in between, it could hold 2,100 people at a time. The axle connecting the two wheels was the largest single piece of steel forged up to that time and weighed 45 tons. Today's Ferris wheels are much smaller, usually rising about 40 feet. They also seem sedate when compared with such fast-paced, stomach-wrenching rides as the roller coaster. Still, Ferris wheels remain popular and are a staple at fairs, carnivals, and amusement parks throughout the country.

## FIBBER McGEE AND MOLLY

"By George, one of these days I gotta straighten out that closet!" If a hall closet can be said to have personality, then the hall closet at the McGee's address, 79 Wistful Vista, was loaded with it—and everything else but the kitchen sink. The radio audience knew that if an unfortunate should open the closet door by mistake, its bulging contents would tumble out with a gratifying assortment of thumps, crashes, and bangs. To this day "Fibber McGee's closet" is still used to describe any untidy storage space.

The closet was the most gleefully anticipated running gag on *Fibber McGee and Molly*, the Tuesday-night event of the 1930s and '40s. Jim and Marian Jordan (the couple's real names) were vaudeville performers until 1925, when they broke into radio on a Chicago station. Signed by the Johnson Wax Company in 1935, *Fibber McGee and Molly*, with its gentle, small-town humor and lovable characters, became one of radio's top four comedy shows.

A childhood favorite, Felix the Cat has taken a variety of forms on toys throughout the years. The one below was made in the early 1930s; the jointed toy at left is a modern reproduction.

At a breathtaking height of 265 feet, the first Ferris wheel towered over midway pavilions in 1893. Much larger than today's Ferris wheels, it had 36 cars and treated customers to a 20-minute ride.

Though Fiedler kept a hectic schedule, he found time to be an amateur firefighter and had a two-way radio in his car. For his 75th birthday, his family bought him a fire pump truck, which he proudly rode to rehearsal.

Fields, as Twilly (right) and Micawber (below), learned the art of the comic aside from his mother. She would often mutter comments while in casual conversations.

## FIEDLER, ARTHUR

At the helm of the Boston Pops Orchestra, the distinguished conductor known as "Mr. Pops" led enjoyable programs of light classics and popular favorites. Fiedler, who was trained at the Royal Academy in Berlin, made his debut as a violinist at the age of 17. But he wanted to conduct. In 1924 he formed the Boston Sinfonietta, a small orchestra, and soon organized free concerts on the Esplanade. When he joined the Pops in 1930, his life's path was set.

"Evening at the Pops" was a big hit with the public, and Fiedler rejected as snobbery criticism of his eclectic approach. The Fourth of July Bicentennial Esplanade concert in 1976 had a vast radio and TV audience, and some 400,000 people were present to cheer the Pops's signature song, the stirring "Stars and Stripes Forever."

## FIELDS, W. C.

"Are you fond of children?" "I am if they're properly cooked." To Fields buffs this exchange is rivaled only by the sight of the Great Misanthrope kicking bratty Baby LeRoy's bottom in *The Old-Fashioned Way* (1934) or as Egbert Sousé (with the imperishable accent over the *e*) ordering a Depth Bomb cocktail or as Cuthbert J. Twilly admiring Mae West's fingertips in *My Little Chickadee* (1940): "What symmetrical digits!" The choice of Famous Fields Moments is infinite.

William Claude Dykenfield began his theatrical career as a juggler in burlesque and vaudeville, and he used bits of his juggling acts in several of his movies. His transition from silents to talkies was successful; his idiosyncratic voice and line delivery, together with his bulbous nose and tiny, suspicious eyes, completed his comic character. Fields wrote several of his movie scripts under assumed names, such as Mahatma Kane Jeeves and Otis Criblecoblis. One of his best roles was that of Mr. Micawber in the superb *David Copperfield* (1935). In real life Fields was a complicated man, difficult, mistrustful, penurious, alcoholic, yet he died mourned by devoted friends. One final Fields Moment: mistakenly (and knowingly) in bed with a goat, he asks, "Ever thought of sending your nightgown to the cleaners?"

## FILIBUSTER

In 1853 a congressman criticized his colleagues' delaying tactics as "filibustering," a play on the word *filibuster*, the Dutch word for "pirate." The definition stuck, and today filibusters are used in the Senate to block legislation, usually via marathon speeches. The longest filibuster ever was by Senator Strom Thurmond, who spoke for 24 hours and 18 minutes. Senator Huey Long included a recipe for "pot likker." Other senators have been known to fill time by reading telephone directories and baseball statistics. Although much criticized, the filibuster is alive and well on Capitol Hill.

## FIRST LADIES

Neither elected, appointed, nor mentioned in the Constitution, the First Lady is nonetheless a potent force on the political scene. The role—whether assumed by a president's wife, sister, or daughter—has been defined as "hostess and helpmate." The "First Lady in the Land," as she was dubbed around 1863, is expected to entertain graciously, which Dolley Madison did with particular aplomb. As the president's wife, she assists with statecraft when foreign dignitaries visit the White House, supports administration policy, and sometimes attends Cabinet meetings. Some, however, do even more: "Presidentress" Edith Wilson practically took over the executive branch from her ailing husband.

First Ladies have always been subject to intense public scrutiny, from their wardrobe (Mary Lincoln's was deemed too lavish) to their drinking habits ("Lemonade Lucy" Hayes was a teetotaler). Although several entered public life reluctantly—"I am more like a State prisoner," complained Martha Washington—most have embraced their position enthusiastically, adopting socially relevant causes. They became more activist as women's place in society evolved in the mid-1900s. "President's wives have an obligation to contribute something," said Jackie Kennedy. Lady Bird Johnson, for example, advocated beautification, Betty Ford raised breast-cancer awareness, Rosalynn Carter stumped for mental health, Barbara Bush promoted literacy, and Hillary Rodham Clinton championed women's and children's rights.

## FITZGERALD, ELLA

"It isn't where you come from, but it's where you're going that counts," Ella Fitzgerald used to say. Her philosophy: "The only thing better than singing is more singing." A true musician, Fitzgerald was revered by her peers for her pure, almost innocently sweet tone, polished phrasing, and deep sense of swing. She could turn a popular standard into a triumphal arc of melody or turn songs like "Oh, Lady Be Good" into fireworks of jazz scat singing. "Her intonation was perfect," said her longtime accompanist, Tommy Flanagan. Mel Tormé, a lifelong fan, said, "She doesn't know how good she is."

"America's First Lady of Song" began her career at the age of 16, when she won an amateur contest at the Harlem Opera House and a chance to audition for Chick Webb, a top bandleader. With Webb she made several recordings, including an arrangement of a nursery rhyme for which Fitzgerald had written special lyrics. The 1938 "A-Tisket A-Tasket" established her as a first-rate singer. Over the years, she sang the music of Cole Porter, Rodgers and Hart, Duke Ellington, and the Gershwins. With Louis Armstrong she performed jovial duets. With Count Basie she sang such favorites as "Shiny Stockings." A major star worldwide, Fitzgerald toured almost nonstop with Basie, The Oscar Peterson Trio, and others, and she sang with more than 40 symphonies.

A locket with a portrait of Martha Washington was worn by her husband during the Revolutionary War.

In 1924 Howard Chandler Christy painted the stylish and fun-loving Grace Coolidge with her beloved collie, Rob Roy.

According to her husband, Lyndon, Lady Bird Johnson was "a woman of great depth and excellent judgment."

Ella Fitzgerald poses with jazz greats Louis Armstrong (left) and Lionel Hampton (right). Hampton began playing the vibraphone, an amplified xylophone, in a band that also featured Armstrong.

Scott Fitzgerald, Zelda, and daughter Scottie share a dance. Fitzgerald once said, "Sometimes I don't know whether Zelda and I are real or whether we are characters in one of my novels."

Woodrow Wilson pressed a button at the White House and lit up the Woolworth Building (right). One of the gargoyles of the "skyline queen" depicts the founder counting his coins. Below, goods are on display at the first Five-and-Ten.

## FITZGERALD, F. SCOTT

"So we beat on, boats against the current, borne back ceaselessly into the past." With these lines F. Scott Fitzgerald, one of the most gifted writers of his time, ended his masterpiece *The Great Gatsby* (1925). The novelist, who became the spokesman for the '20s, which he dubbed the Jazz Age, was born in St. Paul, Minnesota, attended Princeton University, and had his first success in 1920 with the publication of *This Side of Paradise*. That same year, he followed one of his own plots by marrying a beautiful Southern belle, Zelda Sayre. They proceeded to live an extravagant life in New York and Paris and at fashionable resorts, where they knew everybody and everybody wanted to know them. Their legendary glamour and charm and their mad pursuits ended with Scott's excessive drinking and Zelda's incurable schizophrenia.

Fitzgerald's books include *The Beautiful and the Damned* (1922), *Tender Is the Night* (1934), and innumerable short stories, many written to pay for Zelda's treatments. He ended his days as a screenwriter in Hollywood, the setting for his novel *The Last Tycoon*. Fitzgerald found some comfort in romance, but he remained preoccupied with Zelda. As he said in one of his stories, "There are all kinds of love in the world but never the same love twice."

## FIVE-AND-TEN-CENT STORES

The people who strolled into F. W. Woolworth's new store in downtown Lancaster, Pennsylvania, in the summer of 1879 had never seen anything like it. Woolworth had arrayed his wares in attractive displays and sold them for fixed, low prices. Customers could browse and ask to buy items they had never known they wanted (help-yourself shopping was some 40 years away). Thus a new form of amusement was born—shopping. Woolworth wanted the Five-and-Ten to feel like a fair with counters covered with "plums and corkers"— pie plates, bags of candy, and the glass Christmas-tree ornaments he first made popular. The new merchandising method was a huge success. By 1912 he was ringing up sales in 596 stores. The next year, he opened the opulent Woolworth headquarters in Manhattan, then the world's tallest building.

So strong was the Woolworth Company's commitment to five-and-ten-cent prices that it required a vote of the board of directors in 1932 to allow 20-cent items in the stores. Today Woolworth's retains a foothold in the market, along with a niche in our memory. Many Woolworth stores have closed— but other entrepreneurs have opened up 99-cent stores.

## FLAGPOLE SITTING

Americans have a penchant for stunts like flagpole sitting, a craze that started in 1924, when Alvin "Shipwreck" Kelly was paid to perch on a flagpole in order to attract crowds to a Hollywood theater. Imitators popped up, but it was hard to rise above Kelly. "The Luckiest Fool Alive," as he called him-

self, sat for 49 days on a pole in Atlantic City, drawing over 20,000 spectators. One year, he spent a total of 145 days aloft.

Other crazes have flourished among college students. In 1939 a Harvard student made a bet and swallowed a live goldfish in front of reporters. Students around the country followed suit and set new records for the number swallowed. Luckily for the fish, this fad soon died down. Twenty years later, 25 students in South Africa stuffed themselves into a phone booth; American students heard the call and also crammed into booths. After studying the physics involved, 19 MIT students squeezed in. At Modesto Junior College, 34 people were able to fit in by putting the booth on its back.

## FLAPPERS

The sheltered world of women ended with World War I, and the 1920s saw "flappers"—newly independent, unfettered, unchaperoned, and uncorseted women—emerge. Complicated dressing gave way, and it became chic to look sleek. As described by novelist Edna Ferber, a flapper wore a "smart slim dark tailleur [suit]… beige silk stockings, vivid scarf, mannish blouse; tiny cloche hat pulled well down over her ears." Her long tresses were trimmed to a layered bob.

No longer a fragile flower, the modern Bright Young Thing was adventurous: she raced cars, flew airplanes, wore makeup, smoked, drank, and swore. In Paris she admired Josephine Baker and Le Jazz Hot and danced the Black Bottom, the Shimmy, and the Bunny Hug. What does *flapper* mean? Some say it's a young duck trying its wings. Others believe the word celebrates her unfastened galoshes defiantly flapping. So what was a flapper? Why, a jazz-baby rebelling against the conventions of her parents, of course.

## FLASH GORDON

Setting out to destroy the earth, the evil tyrant Ming the Merciless asked, "Pathetic earthlings, who can save you now?" The answer for Depression-era moviegoers was Flash Gordon. A popular comic book character, Flash appeared on the silver screen in a 13-episode science fiction saga in 1936. With Buster Crabbe, a former Olympic athlete, as the hero, Flash battled Ming and his manlike monsters on the futuristic planet Mongo. At the end of each episode, Flash faced certain death, only to escape the following week and continue his fight to save the earth. The shows' rocket ships, technogadgetry, and cliffhanger format thrilled Saturday-matinee crowds. Joined by a female earthling, Dale Arden, and an eccentric scientist, Dr. Hans Zarkov, Flash eventually won over many of Ming's allies to Earth's side and in a final battle defeated the tyrant.

*Flash Gordon* was followed by many sequels. In the 1950s the serials were spliced together into single films that ran on late-night television and served as an inspiration for future sci-fi hits, such as *Star Wars*.

"Shipwreck" Kelly perches high above Union City, New Jersey, in 1929. He learned to nap for five minutes each hour. Stirrups and other safety devices kept him from falling.

The flapper (right) strikes a typical pose; a song of the day proclaimed: "She's the most heart-breakinest, shimmy-shakinest gal you ever knew!"

Dale Arden covers her ears when she hears the "fiendish screech" of Ming's deadly riot-ray. So enraged is Flash Gordon by Dale's pain that he "hears and feels nothing." Flash drives a crane into the riot-ray and destroys it.

## FLINTSTONES

The Flintstones gave us not only Fred's favorite expression—"Yabba-dabba-doo"—but the original friendly dinosaur, Dino.

*The Flintstones* is the story of a "modern Stone Age family." A parody of life in the suburbs based loosely on *The Honeymooners*, it was the first and the longest-running animated series on prime-time television. Rife with rock puns, the show ran from 1960 to 1966. Reruns still flourish.

Despite the prehistoric trappings, Fred and Wilma Flintstone live a middle-class life. They own a stone house in the town of Bedrock, drive a foot-powered car, and have a garbage disposal (a hungry buzzard), an indoor shower (an elephant), and a phonograph for playing "rock" albums. Fred belongs to the Royal Order of Water Buffalos, along with his neighbor, Barney Rubble. Wilma often embarks on shopping sprees with Betty Rubble. Their motto: "Charge... it!"

The series was the brainchild of William Hanna and Joseph Barbera, creators of the Oscar-winning *Tom and Jerry* cartoons. Spin-offs include *The Flintstone Kids*, featuring Pebbles and Bamm Bamm, and *The Jetsons*, set in the space age instead of the Stone Age.

## FLYING TIGERS

In 1941 a band of mercenary pilots secretly formed the American Volunteer Group in Burma. The daredevil fighting unit was part of an ambitious plan to help China defend her skies without officially involving the United States military in combat.

The pilots were led by retired air force general Claire Chennault, who taught them to "pass, shoot, and break away," and scrutinized their training maneuvers from a rickety bamboo tower. They went into action as the Flying Tigers, protecting Rangoon and K'un-ming, the terminus of the Burma Road. Their P-40 Tomahawks swooped close enough to enemy planes for the Japanese to get a good look at the jagged shark's teeth painted on their noses. Because they had fewer than 50 planes in flying order at any given time, the pilots resorted to changing the numbers on their fuselages at frequent intervals and giving orders over the radio to imaginary squadrons to make the Japanese think they were outnumbered. In seven months the Flying Tigers destroyed about 300 Japanese aircraft, boosting morale back home at a time when Japan's airpower seemed unstoppable.

The design on the planes flown by the Flying Tigers was created by Walt Disney Studios. The pilots were led by Gen. Claire Chennault, who was called Old Leather Face by the Chinese.

Modern folk medicine taps the healing properties of common plants and herbs, from peppermint, used to soothe the stomach, to echinacea, which stimulates the immune system.

## FOLK MEDICINE

American folk medicine ranges from sophisticated traditions imported from China to practices based on old wives' tales. Some treatments, such as drinking tea made from black-spruce needles (rich in vitamin C) to cure scurvy, are known to work. But the 19th-century technique of rubbing the head with onions to cure baldness has attracted few advocates.

The first Europeans to come to the New World were impressed by the Indians' good health. They adopted some of the Indians' simple herbal cures and sweat baths at a time when their own pharmacopoeias still called for mummy dust and dragon's blood. In the 19th century, people who didn't trust doctors or were too far from one used home remedies made from common herbs, roots, and bark.

In the 20th century folk medicine gave way to more modern practices. Still, in some pockets of the country, tobacco is still chewed to relieve toothaches, and "sweat herbs" are used to bring down fevers. Lately, many of the more reliable folk remedies have gained new respect. In fact, some medical schools include training in folk medicine in their curricula.

## FOLK MUSIC

Folk music is the people's music. Its sound is that of the human voice telling a story, often of work, love, death, or protest. Over time, authorship is forgotten. Every group that came to America brought its own songs, which were shared, reworked, and passed along. English, Scottish, and Irish ballads became Appalachian or cowboy songs. French, African, and Hispanic music evolved into Cajun, blues, rock, and Tex-Mex music.

With the advent of recording in the 1920s, the Carter family began to document traditional Appalachian songs. A wealth of black folk songs was recorded by the itinerant 12-string guitarist Leadbelly for the Library of Congress, which made them widely accessible for the first time. Woody Guthrie crisscrossed the country during the Depression with his guitar and harmonica, learning local songs and writing new ones in support of the downtrodden.

Actor and singer Burl Ives was the first folksinger to win a mass audience by performing on radio and television in the 1940s and '50s. Pete Seeger's quartet, The Weavers, sang a hit version of "Good Night, Irene" that helped spur the urban folk revival of the 1950s. Although most of their hits were apolitical, they were nevertheless blacklisted from many nightclubs for their leftist leanings. No one, however, objected to the clean-cut image of the Kingston Trio, a smoothly energetic group whose 1958 hit "Tom Dooley" further spread the folk craze among high school and college students.

In the early 1960s Joan Baez sang mournful ballads with a haunting, lyrical dimension. Folk music began to underscore the civil rights and antiwar movements. In 1963, on the day of the March on Washington, Baez led a crowd of 200,000 in Pete Seeger's song "We Shall Overcome." Peter, Paul, and Mary's version of Bob Dylan's "Blowin' in the Wind" also became a civil rights anthem. Folk turned more introspective in the late '60s and '70s. Judy Collins had a hit with Joni Mitchell's "Both Sides Now," and Simon and Garfunkel sang of a "Bridge Over Troubled Water." In the '80s and '90s a few singers carried the folk torch while folk-rock groups took the tradition in yet another direction.

Peter, Paul, and Mary reached millions of listeners with a host of television specials. Their hits include Pete Seeger's "If I Had a Hammer" and the children's favorite, "Puff the Magic Dragon."

Pete Seeger has been called America's tuning fork. Among his memorable songs are "Where Have All the Flowers Gone?" and "Turn, Turn, Turn."

Grave-mannered Joan Baez sang in a crystalline voice. For many she embodied opposition to the Vietnam War.

Joe Montana, the highest-rated quarterback in NFL history, was the king of comebacks for the San Francisco 49ers. He was famous for snatching victory from certain defeat.

Henry Ford (left) vowed: "I will build a motorcar for the great multitude." The Model T, or Tin Lizzie (below), was the first car that Ford's own workers could afford.

## FOOTBALL

On Thanksgiving, New Year's Day, and Super Bowl Sunday, millions of women become "football widows" as their men turn to watching football. Foreigners disdain the sport's lack of continuous action; they prefer soccer, which they call football. But for many Americans, there's sheer poetry and exquisite drama in the clash of two teams of 11 heavily padded titans fighting for control of the pigskin.

The challenge isn't all physical: players must master arcane rules that evolved to provide maximum excitement but minimal injury. (The forward pass was legalized in 1906 after Theodore Roosevelt threatened to outlaw the game if the number of fatalities was not reduced.) Players must know when and how they can hit another player or carry the ball. Pulverize a receiver a second after he touches the ball, and you're a hero; hit him a second before, and you're penalized.

Professional football began in 1920, when the association that became the National Football League was founded. Each NFL team, or "franchise," has its own character. The clean-cut Dallas Cowboys call themselves "America's team," while the Oakland Raiders are known as "outlaws." Rules for drafting college players allow teams with losing records first picks; still, some teams manage to dominate. The Pittsburgh Steelers were unstoppable in the 1970s, and in the 1980s the San Francisco 49ers could almost always manage to win during the last two minutes of a game.

Every year some parents object to the violence and expense of school football programs. But others echo the sentiment of legendary Green Bay Packer coach Vince Lombardi, who said, "A school without football is in danger of deteriorating into a medieval study hall."

## FORD, HENRY

On Christmas Eve 1893, Henry Ford fastened a small gasoline engine to the kitchen sink and tried to start it. The vibrating machine finally roared, shooting flames, belching smoke, and nearly tearing the sink from the wall. Ford's lifelong obsession with gadgets moved into high gear when motorcars appeared on American roads. By 1896 he had built his first automobile, the Quadricycle, inside a shed behind his Michigan home. Too late, Ford realized it was far larger than the shed's doorway. Taking an ax, he shattered the door's frame and broke out bricks until he'd freed the vehicle for a test-drive. It looked like two side-by-side bicycles on thin, spindly tires, and it frequently broke down.

Undaunted, Ford continued to refine his horseless carriage. In 1908, while most carmakers were building expensive cars for the rich, Ford brought out the Model T, a car for the masses. It was cheap, almost anyone could repair it, and rutted, rocky roads couldn't stop it. Ford amazed the business world again in 1914, when he offered workers the unheard-of wage of $5 a day, more than double the going rate. Hardly a soft touch, however, Ford was equally quick to slam the factory doors in the faces of union organizers.

In 1913 Ford pioneered the conveyor-belt assembly line, cutting the 12½ hours needed to complete a car to just 93 minutes. More than 15 million of his Model Ts had been sold by 1927, utterly transforming the lives of millions of people.

## FORD, JOHN

"My name's John Ford. I make Westerns." Despite this much-quoted introduction, what Ford made were some of the best pictures to come out of Hollywood. He began his career in 1917 directing silents, mostly Westerns. But with the advent of sound, he came into his own.

Ford's real name was O'Feeney, and several of his films, including *The Informer* and *The Quiet Man*, were set in Ireland, the country of his parents. His feeling for American history and the frontier spirit was expressed in such pictures as *Stagecoach*, *Young Mr. Lincoln*, and *Drums Along the Mohawk*. His empathy for the individual in conflict with society was illuminated by his Academy Award–winning direction of the saga of migrant workers, *The Grapes of Wrath*, which he filmed in naturalistic and gritty settings.

After World War II, Ford made his best-known Westerns. Nine of them were photographed in Monument Valley, a location now known as "Ford Country." There he filmed many of the beautifully composed panoramic shots of men and horses that give his films the Ford look. He had a coterie of favorite actors, including Henry Fonda, who starred in *My Darling Clementine*, and John Wayne, who appeared in *The Searchers*, considered by many critics to be one of Ford's best. Asked why Wayne looked so good in his pictures, Ford pointed out how few lines he had. "That's how you make good actors," he quipped. "Don't let them talk!"

## FORD'S THEATER

Ford's Theater in Washington, D.C., was the site of Abraham Lincoln's assassination on April 14, 1865. That night, as Lincoln and his wife watched the comedy *Our American Cousin*, actor John Wilkes Booth crept into the president's box and shot him in the back of the head. Lincoln was carried unconscious from the theater. He died the next morning.

John T. Ford, who owned the popular theater and was sympathetic to the South, was arrested for conspiracy. After he was cleared of the crime, Ford announced that he would reopen the theater. This caused such a public outcry that the War Department seized the building and sealed it. The federal government eventually bought the building, but the theater was not reopened to the public for more than 100 years. Today, faithfully restored to its original condition, it is once more the site of plays and other performing arts. The presidential box, however, has never been used again.

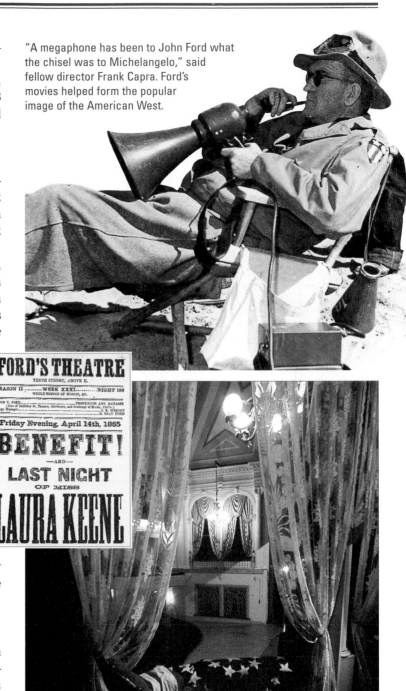

"A megaphone has been to John Ford what the chisel was to Michelangelo," said fellow director Frank Capra. Ford's movies helped form the popular image of the American West.

Lincoln was seated in this chair when he was assassinated by John Wilkes Booth, who then jumped onto the stage and managed to escape. Booth was shot and killed 12 days later in a Virginia barn. The playbill (above) was for the performance on that fateful night.

The gold bars in Fort Knox are 7 x 3⅝ x 1¾ inches each, only a bit smaller than an average building brick, but each weighs about 27.5 pounds.

Gold-hungry forty-niners came from across the country and from as far away as China, Peru, and Australia. Many worked on ships bound for San Francisco and then jumped ship once they were there.

Although Stephen Foster's songs were quite popular, he earned very little from them and lived on the edge of ruin. After his marriage broke up, he moved to New York City and died penniless at the age of 37.

## Fort Knox

Only once have visitors been permitted to see the 147 million troy ounces of gold stored in the U.S. Bullion Depository at Fort Knox, Kentucky. "We'll probably never do it again," a government official said, swinging open the vault's 22-ton door. Congressmen and journalists gaped at the golden bricks. Rumors of missing gold had prompted the 1974 congressional inquiry; the inspection ended the rumors.

The gold, valued at $6.2 billion in 1995, was first brought to Fort Knox when laws in the 1930s forbade the private hoarding of gold. The huge amounts turned in by citizens were melted down into ingots; these were held at Fort Knox and elsewhere. During World War II, it also safeguarded original copies of the Declaration of Independence, the United States Constitution, and England's Magna Carta.

## Forty-Niners

Within months of the discovery of yellow specks in the water near John Sutter's mill, the cry of "Gold!" rang from New York to Oregon. The California hills swarmed with thousands of would-be prospectors, called forty-niners after the year in which the biggest gold rush in history began in earnest. Some of the early arrivals struck it rich in a few months, but most found, in the words of miner William McCollum, that "the abundance of gold in California has not been as much overrated as the labor of procuring it has been underrated."

Days of backbreaking panning and digging often went unrewarded, and the forty-niners, struggling between hope and reality, soon hardened into lawless men who brawled over contested claims and settled arguments with guns. In the rip-roaring mining towns, some gambled fortunes on a single hand of cards, while the unlucky drowned their sorrows in whiskey. Store owners, ready to "fleece the golden fleecers," charged sky-high prices for clothing and supplies.

## Foster, Stephen

Stephen Foster, the composer of "Swanee River" and "Oh! Susanna," was torn between two musical styles—the respectable parlor songs he grew up with and the lively Negro, or plantation, songs that he loved. He was drawn to comic minstrel shows and even wrote songs for them, including "Old Uncle Ned" and "Camptown Races." In a move he would later regret, Foster arranged for Christy's Minstrels to perform and take credit for his minstrel songs, "owing to the prejudice against them by some, which might injure my reputation as a writer in another style." As the songs' popularity grew, he changed his mind but was not able to get credit for the songs during his lifetime.

In his most productive years, Foster wrote songs that would become American standards, including "Jeanie with the Light Brown Hair" and "Beautiful Dreamer." He also wrote "My Old Kentucky Home," even though he had never lived there. Ironically, the song became that state's anthem. His biggest success, "Swanee River," eventually sold more than 20 million copies. Foster's melodies are still published.

## FOURTH OF JULY

The Fourth of July has always been celebrated as America's birthday, even though the resolution for independence was passed by the Continental Congress on July 2, 1776, and most delegates didn't sign it until August 2. But it was on July 4 that the Declaration of Independence was adopted by the Congress and made official by John Hancock's signature.

At first, Fourth of July festivities had a stately tone. "It ought to be commemorated ... by solemn acts of devotion to God Almighty," wrote John Adams. "It ought to be solemnized with pomp and parade, with shows, games, sports, guns, bells, bonfires, and illuminations."

The first anniversary was indeed celebrated regally, with sermons, bonfires, and patriotic music. Ships in Philadelphia's harbor fired 13-gun salutes, and a captured Hessian band provided the music for an official dinner. In Boston the general court gave orders "for making every Preparation for drinking Success to the Thirteen United States," orders that were happily obeyed as far away as Charleston.

In 1788 Philadelphia introduced a "Federal Procession," and parades quickly caught on in other parts of the country as well. Over the years, preachers were replaced by patriotic orators, and picnics and such games as watermelon-eating contests, sack races, and three-legged races replaced many other activities. Fireworks became popular in 1777, but by the early 1900s many cities and states had prohibited their private use because of the hundreds of deaths and injuries the fireworks caused each year. In 1941 Congress finally voted to make the Fourth of July—the greatest patriotic holiday in the U.S.—a legal federal holiday.

## FRANKLIN, ARETHA

With her intense, radiantly powerful voice, Aretha Franklin can reach out and wrap listeners in the warmth of the gospel spirit. Or she can cut loose and set feet a-stompin'. Born in 1942 in Memphis, Tennessee, Franklin was one of five children of an evangelical minister. Her family moved to Detroit's East Side, where her father led a large church and became famous for his fiery sermons. Franklin sang in her father's church and toured with his gospel shows. She was acquainted with such gospel stars as Mahalia Jackson and Clara Ward. In 1960 Franklin went to New York, won a recording contract, and became a successful rhythm and blues singer.

Returning to her gospel roots in 1967, Franklin had her first big hits, including "I Never Loved a Man (the Way I Love You)" and "Respect." After a long and inspiring career—she won 15 Grammys and 24 gold records—she was inducted into the Rock & Roll Hall of Fame in 1987.

Different chemicals in the fireworks are what make the brilliant colors in a display. The sparkling gold and silver shimmers are created by adding metallic shavings.

In 1968 Aretha Franklin was featured on the cover of *Time* magazine and hailed in Europe as the new Bessie Smith. Franklin is widely recognized as "The Queen of Soul."

Benjamin Franklin proved that lightning is actually electricity—a fact unknown at the time—in a very dangerous experiment. Lightning struck his kite, traveled down the string, and caused an attached key to glow.

French fries are so named because they've been cut into narrow strips, or "frenched."

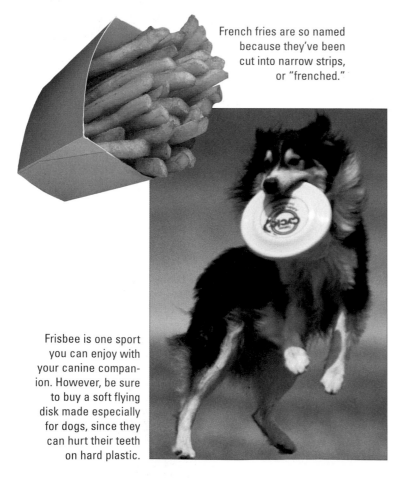

Frisbee is one sport you can enjoy with your canine companion. However, be sure to buy a soft flying disk made especially for dogs, since they can hurt their teeth on hard plastic.

## FRANKLIN, BENJAMIN

For all his folksy amiability, Benjamin Franklin was capable of subterfuge and intrigue. As relations became strained between England and the American Colonies, he anonymously planted in a London paper a satiric news item saying that a German king proposed to tax England because Anglo-Saxons had originally come from Germany. This irritated the followers of King George III, but to Franklin "it was a fair hit."

Franklin was immensely popular in colonial America. His humorous sayings were widely distributed in *Poor Richard's Almanack*. He was also a brilliant inventor. His discovery that lightning rods could protect homes saved many lives, but Franklin declined to patent the invention. "We should be glad of an opportunity to serve others by any inventions of ours," he explained. He also declined to patent two other inventions, bifocal lenses and the Franklin stove.

Despite a profound distaste for war, he threw himself into the fight to free the American Colonies from English rule by helping to draft the Declaration of Independence. When John Hancock boldly scrawled his signature on the Declaration, he announced, "We must be unanimous....We must all hang together." Franklin, picking up the pen to add his name, replied, "We must indeed all hang together, or most assuredly we shall all hang separately."

## FRENCH FRIES

When Thomas Jefferson served French-fried potatoes at the White House, they were an exotic European novelty that were believed to have originated in Belgium. Oddly enough, in England French fries are known as chips, but in Russia and China they are called American fries.

Today a hamburger, soda, and French fries have become the quintessential fast-food meal. Americans eat 5 billion pounds of fries a year. To the dismay of nutritionists, many teenagers, when low on cash, skip the burger and have only the fries, coated with salt and ketchup.

## FRISBEE

In the 1920s Yale students yelled "Frisbie" to signal that a pie tin from the Frisbie Bakery in Bridgeport, Connecticut, was skimming across the New Haven skies. In 1958 the Wham-O company adopted a respelling of that name, Frisbee, for the aerodynamic plastic disks they were marketing as "Flyin' Saucers" and "Pluto Platters."

Frisbees, in a variety of sizes and colors including glow-in-the-dark, rapidly became as popular as balls at beaches, playgrounds, and backyards. Players perfected backhand, sidearm, and overhand throws, as well as behind-the-back, between-the-legs, and single-finger catches. Frisbee games, like Frisbee golf, Guts Frisbee, and Ultimate Frisbee, soon developed. But the most popular Frisbee pastime remains the simple person-to-person or person-to-dog game of catch.

## FRONTIER

"It is a wandering people whom rivers and lakes cannot hold back," Alexis de Tocqueville observed of Americans, and history bore him out. From the arrival of the Franciscan missionaries in 1593, the American frontier—the line that separated settled regions from the wilderness—was never static for long. To the early colonists, the frontier was just beyond the Atlantic tidewater, but with the peace that came after the War of 1812, Americans began a steady migration across the Appalachians to the prairies, the "boundless regions of freedom." By 1850 the country was populated as far as the Missouri River, and within 50 years most of the vast Western plains had been settled. In 1893 historian Frederick Jackson Turner wrote that this continual movement west and the challenges of the frontier had created a unique character, "a new product that is American."

## FROST, ROBERT

Robert Frost's unmistakably American voice invested everyday observations with noble significance. His poem "The Road Not Taken," for example, begins with a simple story about reaching a fork in a road. Sorry that he cannot take both roads at once, the poet embarks on "the one less traveled." Frost's poem suggests that we can never return to our choices once we've made them.

The kindly, calm, wise voice in Frost's poetry was in many respects an alter ego for Frost, a literary version of the man he would like to have been but knew he was not. Unrecognized as a poet for 20 years, Frost struggled against poverty and family difficulties before Ezra Pound declared him a "VURRY Amur'k'n talent." The resulting recognition of such favorites as "After Apple-Picking" and "Stopping by Woods on a Snowy Evening" brought him financial security, but it was the invitation to read his poem "The Gift Outright" at John F. Kennedy's 1961 inauguration that secured Frost's reputation as our nation's best-loved poet.

## FULBRIGHT SCHOLARS

With superpower tensions growing after World War II, Senator J. William Fulbright decided that having students study and live in other countries would help promote world peace. "The best antidote for the poisonous relations between these two giants is a large dose of cultural exchanges," he said.

In 1946 Congress acted on his idea and created the Fulbright Scholars program. The first exchange took place the following year. A half century later, roughly 200,000 students from more than 140 countries have taken part. The program's alumni have become leaders throughout the world. One former scholar, Harrison Schmitt, said that his experience studying Norway's fjords pushed him toward a scientific career that eventually took him to the moon as a member of the *Apollo 13* space team.

Living precariously, with all their worldly goods in a rickety covered wagon, a pioneer couple pauses for a midday meal and a moment's respite in a Kansas meadow.

Daniel Boone (right) is portrayed blazing a trail through the Cumberland Gap, a rugged natural pass in the Appalachian Mountains where Virginia, Kentucky, and Tennessee converge.

Robert Frost dealt in poignant realities, as in the poem *Death of the Hired Man*. A husband and wife argue about their responsibility for an old farmhand: "Home is the place where, when you have to go there / They have to take you in."

Al Pacino (above, left) becomes the new Mafia don at the end of the first of Coppola's *Godfather* trilogy. Edward G. Robinson (right) and James Cagney were versatile actors, but they are best remembered as hoods.

Newspapers called Bonnie Parker "Suicide Sal" and pegged Clyde Barrow as the "Texas Rattlesnake." Here, she gets the drop on him.

*"In the United States there is more space where nobody is than where anybody is. This is what makes America what it is."*

GERTRUDE STEIN

## GANGSTER MOVIES

Americans flocked to gangster movies during the Depression, when the exploits of real-life gangsters in Chicago and New York filled the headlines. Unlike Westerns, which also pitted outlaws against the forces of order, gangster movies of the 1930s focused on the crooks, not the good guys. Crime ultimately did not pay for strutting racketeer Rico Bandello (Edward G. Robinson) in *Little Caesar*, pugnacious bootlegger Tom Powers (James Cagney) in *The Public Enemy*, or trigger-happy crime boss Tony Camonte (Paul Muni) in *Scarface*. Yet these characters had more vitality than the cops who toppled them. Whether they secretly envied the criminals' determination to "be somebody," or simply found them fascinating, moviegoers of the 1930s loved these film heroes.

More recently, actors like Warren Beatty, Faye Dunaway, Al Pacino, and Robert de Niro and directors like Martin Scorsese, Brian De Palma, and Francis Ford Coppola have made gangster films, adding graphic violence, sexual frankness, and psychological intensity to the classic formula.

## GANGSTERS

"Tell the public I don't smoke cigars. It's the bunk," said Bonnie Parker, who relished the newspaper headlines that made her and scores of small-time thugs into larger-than-life figures. The hard times of the 1930s spawned a new breed of gangster. They crisscrossed the country in fast cars, brandishing tommy guns and sawed-off shotguns and committing bank robberies, kidnappings, and murders. Bonnie and her partner, Clyde Barrow, "Pretty Boy" Floyd, and "Baby Face" Nelson were only a few of the more notorious gangsters.

Floyd's criminal career began with a $350 robbery; he gained publicity as a latter-day Robin Hood because he took the time during bank robberies to rip up the mortgages of farmers threatened with foreclosure. "I have robbed no one but moneyed men," he said. Nelson's youthful features earned him the nickname Baby Face, but no one dared call him that to his face. Nelson, who preferred to be called Big George, had a hair-trigger temper and clearly liked killing. After murdering an FBI agent, he delighted in another agent's curse that made the headlines—"IF IT'S THE LAST THING I DO, I'LL GET BABY FACE NELSON." The gangsters' folk-hero status had no effect on FBI chief J. Edgar Hoover, who said, "At heart they are all rats—dirty, yellow rats."

## GARBO, GRETA

"The woman nobody knows, the woman everyone wants to know." Garbo's Hollywood career, one of the strangest in screen history, lasted 15 years and comprised only about two dozen films. It came to a halt when, at 35, the star suddenly retired to spend the rest of her long life avoiding the public.

Swedish-born Greta Gustafsson arrived in the U.S. in 1925; her first MGM film established her as an electrifying presence appealing to both men and women. She costarred most frequently with John Gilbert, her ideal on-screen (and off) lover. A legendary recluse who hid under a slouch hat and dark glasses and who wore no makeup, she once rebuffed Groucho Marx, who had attempted to greet her. "Oh, pardon me, ma'am," he blurted. "I thought you were a guy I knew in Pittsburgh."

Garbo played opposite John Gilbert in *Flesh and the Devil* (above) and Charles Boyer in *Conquest* (left). Ads for her first talkie, *Anna Christie*, proclaimed, "Garbo Talks!"; her first comedy, *Ninotchka,* blared, "Garbo Laughs!"

## GARLAND, JUDY

Judy Garland, who was defeated by drugs, alcohol, five marriages, nervous breakdowns, and suicide attempts, was only 47 when she died. The Land of Oz eluded her. She started in vaudeville as Frances Gumm, was signed by Louis B. Mayer, and sang her first hit, "Dear Mr. Gable," in *Broadway Melody of 1938.* A year later came the movie that made her famous: *The Wizard of Oz.* Her exhausting work schedule at MGM apparently drove her to addiction to pills while she was still a teenager. Her second husband, Vincente Minnelli (father of Liza), directed some of her best movies, such as *Meet Me in St. Louis* (1944) and *The Clock* (1945). Fired from MGM in 1950, she made a stunning comeback in *A Star Is Born* (1954), for which she received an Oscar nomination. In 1961 she gave a legendary concert at Carnegie Hall. The audience was on its feet, shouting "Bravo!" when she took the stage and gave her many standing ovations during the show. She died of a sleeping-pill overdose in 1969. But to her fans, who revere her distinctive voice and movie persona, the vulnerable Judy lives.

In *A Star Is Born,* Judy Garland played an aspiring actress (right). Toward the end of her career, her role in *Judgment at Nuremberg* earned her an Academy Award nomination.

## GAS STATIONS

The first gas station opened in Pittsburgh in 1913 and sold only 30 gallons of gasoline its first day. Despite the slow start, the idea of a service station where motorists could get gas, an oil check, and a soda caught on quickly. Within a few years, gas stations were a familiar sight across the country. Even small roadside grocers hung out "Filling Station" signs.

As competition increased, stations had to offer more than just gas to attract customers. Some went in for wacky station designs, such as a giant teapot, an iceberg, a pagoda, a windmill, and even a dinosaur. Others turned to promotions; in the 1950s stations gave out green stamps, which could be redeemed for merchandise. By the 1970s and '80s, rising gas prices put the squeeze on the industry and self-service replaced full-service. Gas stations lost their pizzazz.

The Hats and Boots Gas Station, built in Seattle after World War II, had offices stowed under the hat. The restrooms were tucked into the boots.

A ballroom in New York City is aswirl with waltzing couples during the Gay Nineties. In this age of excess, Diamond Jim Brady owned a dozen gilded bicycles.

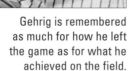

Gehrig is remembered as much for how he left the game as for what he achieved on the field.

A U.S. Indian agent recalled Geronimo at his capture in 1877: "Erect as a lodge-pole ... his form indicating strength, endurance, arrogance ... now under arrest but still defiant." Geronimo (left) posed for the camera in 1886.

## GAY NINETIES

The term *Gay Nineties*, which refers to the 1890s, was coined in the 1930s, during the Depression. A discouraged populace looked back with longing at "the good old days." Glorifying the past, they chose to remember the carefree bicycle craze that swept the nation in the early 1890s. They recalled the Colombian Exposition, a world's fair held in Chicago in 1893, where many saw their first, startling demonstration of electricity. An inventor (wearing cork-soled shoes) allowed 200,000 volts to course harmlessly through his body.

John Philip Sousa's "The Stars and Stripes Forever" seemed to reflect a nation brimming with confidence. The 1890s did indeed witness unprecedented industrial growth and the rise of great fortunes. The rich flaunted their wealth in mansions and with extravagant parties. Still, this was also a time of widespread labor unrest: poverty and despair were the lot of millions, for whom the times were anything but gay.

## GEHRIG, LOU

Forever in Babe Ruth's shadow, Yankee first baseman Lou Gehrig was quiet and reserved. While Ruth was boisterous and uninhibited, Gehrig's image was that of a Boy Scout in uniform. In comparing himself with Ruth, Gehrig once said, "Let's face it. I'm not a headline guy." At his retirement he was second only to Ruth in career home runs and runs batted in, but to most fans Gehrig was dependable rather than spectacular. His signature feat was his playing an astounding 2,130 consecutive games (a record broken in 1995 by Cal Ripken). Diagnosed in 1939 with amyotrophic lateral sclerosis, a fatal disease that has since been renamed in his memory, Gehrig reacted without bitterness. Instead, on Lou Gehrig Day, held at Yankee Stadium on July 4, 1939, he proclaimed himself "the luckiest man on the face of the earth."

## GERONIMO

General George Crook called the Apache Indians "tigers of the human race," and he considered the great war leader Geronimo the most vicious of them all. But it was a brutal act, committed by Mexicans—the killing of Geronimo's wife, mother, and three children in 1858—that instilled in him a lifelong hatred of white men.

Called Goyathlay ("One Who Yawns") by his Mimbreño Apache tribe, he became known to the world by his Mexican-given name of Geronimo. Although he married into Cochise's Chiricahua Apache tribe, he refused to follow Cochise to the misery of a reservation. Instead, for more than 15 years, he and a small band of Chiricahua renegades terrorized both sides of the Mexican border from their hideout in the Sierra Madres, periodically being captured and escaping again.

In 1886 Geronimo was finally persuaded to surrender. He lived out the remaining years of his life at a fort in Oklahoma, occasionally appearing at fairs and exhibitions to pose as the fierce warrior he had once been. This image resurfaced during World War II, when U.S. paratroopers took to yelling "Geronimo!" as they jumped from their planes.

## GERRYMANDER

In 1812, when Elbridge Gerry was governor of Massachusetts, state Republicans, hoping to wrest the state senate from the Federalists' control, redrew the electoral boundaries so that each area had a Republican majority. These machinations produced one district so oddly shaped that a political cartoonist drew it as a salamander. "Call it a Gerrymander!" another critic cried, even though Gerry had nothing to do with it. Nonetheless, the word is still used for this type of political manipulation.

Other states designed their own weirdly shaped districts. Iowa had one that resembled a monkey wrench, Mississippi had a shoestring district, and New Jersey carved a district into the shape of a horseshoe. In 1964 the Supreme Court ruled that all districts must be basically equal in population.

## GERSHWIN, GEORGE

"No matter what kind of revolution takes place in music," composer Nelson Riddle observed, "Gershwin has already been there ... and gone into the future." Indeed, Gershwin's jazz-inspired rhythms and colorful modern harmonies transformed musical theater, symphonic music, and even opera.

The Brooklyn-born pianist began his career as a plugger of other people's tunes, but when Gershwin turned to songwriting, his originality was clear. He wrote songs for more than 20 Broadway shows and in doing so defined popular music. He was only 25 when he wrote *Rhapsody in Blue*, a famous concert piece. With his brother, Ira, he won a Pulitzer Prize for *Of Thee I Sing* in 1932 and broke new ground with the black folk opera *Porgy and Bess* in 1935. Full of promise, Gershwin died of a brain tumor in 1937 at age 38.

## GETTYSBURG ADDRESS

When Abraham Lincoln delivered his famous speech at the dedication of Gettysburg Cemetery on November 19, 1863, he was not the featured speaker. That honor went to Edward Everett, a renowned orator; Lincoln was to give only "a few appropriate remarks." He drafted those remarks in Washington and not, as legend would have it, aboard the train to Gettysburg. After Everett's stirring two-hour oration, Lincoln rose haltingly (he was suffering from what was later diagnosed as smallpox). In less than three minutes he delivered his 10-sentence speech, which was greeted with only light applause. "That speech is a flat failure," Lincoln said afterward. Everett, however, recognized its genius, and wrote to Lincoln, "I should be glad if I ... came as near to the central idea of the occasion in two hours as you did in two minutes."

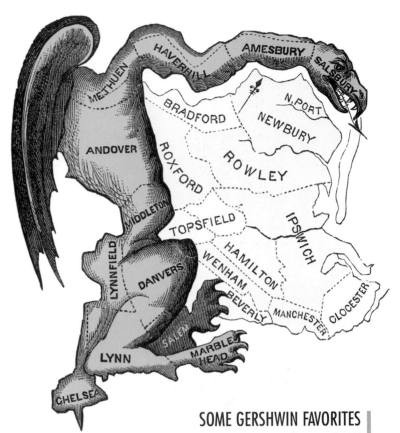

To draw the gerrymander "animal," a cartoonist of the day added a lizard-like head, wings, a tail, and talons to the map of Massachusetts.

### SOME GERSHWIN FAVORITES

Swanee (1919)
I'll Build a Stairway to Paradise (1922)
Fascinating Rhythm (1924)
Oh, Lady Be Good (1924)
Somebody Loves Me (1924)
The Man I Love (1924)
Someone to Watch Over Me (1926)
How Long Has This Been Going On (1927)
'S Wonderful (1927)
An American in Paris (1928)
Embraceable You (1930)
I Got Rhythm (1930)
Of Thee I Sing (1931)
Bess, You Is My Woman Now (1935)
It Ain't Necessarily So (1935)
Summertime (1935)
By Strauss (1936)
Let's Call the Whole Thing Off (1937)
A Foggy Day (1937)
Nice Work If You Can Get It (1937)
They Can't Take That Away from Me (1937)
Love Walked In (1938)

Gershwin said that he had more tunes in his head than he could write down in a lifetime.

Testimony to the optimism of a vanished time, weathered remains of towns dot the Great Plains and the Colorado Rockies.

A GI recruit gets his uniform (above). During training, GIs had to march in military cadence at 128 steps per minute and learn to assemble M-1 rifles blindfolded.

Among those marooned on *Gilligan's Island* were (left to right) Mary Ann, Gilligan himself, the Skipper, and the Professor.

## GHOST TOWN

In the second half of the 19th century, the mere rumor of a gold or silver strike could spawn a boomtown practically overnight. Prospectors rushed to the area, followed by the tradesmen, professional gamblers, and prostitutes who thrived on their business. According to one account, a typical mining town "opened up with a saloon to supply the necessities of life and later added a grocery store . . . for the luxuries." Frame houses and stores went up, and if the town lasted long enough, schools and churches were built.

Some of these towns, like Denver, evolved into cities, but most became "ghosts" once the precious metal gave out and the miners and camp followers moved on to the next El Dorado. In the 1870s and '80s, rich lodes of gold drew 10,000 miners to Bodie, California, but by the turn of the century, the ore—and the prospectors—were gone, leaving behind only decaying buildings.

## GI

"If you've got eyes, ears, and a throat, you're in," according to World War II barracks humor among army draftees. All were in basic training to become infantrymen—or GIs, as they came to be known. While some trace the origin of *GI* to *g*alvanized-*i*ron army garbage cans, others point out that G.I. (Government Issue) was stamped on everything, from underwear to tank parts, during WW II. On the front lines, WW II correspondent Ernie Pyle described battle-weary, unshaven GIs as "the mud-rain-frost-and-wind boys. They have no comforts, and they even learn to live without necessities. And in the end they are the guys that wars can't be won without." Many GIs didn't like being described as heroes at war's end. "We were a bunch of scared kids who had a job to do," said one. "We were in it to get it over with, so we could go home and do what we wanted to do with our lives."

## GILLIGAN'S ISLAND

Critics called it "TV's Titanic," and cast members called it "the longest three-hour tour in the history of television." CBS canceled it in embarrassment, but fans made *Gilligan's Island* a hit from 1964 to 1967 and have kept it in reruns ever since.

Before Sherwood Schwartz created *The Brady Bunch*, he stranded a bunch of sightseers on a desert island. The resourceful castaways tried to make a raft out of trees, a hot air balloon out of raincoats, a sail out of Mrs. Howell's wardrobe—but bumbling first mate Gilligan usually botched it up. The Laurel-and-Hardy antics of Gilligan and the Skipper (Bob Denver and Alan Hale, Jr.) were at the heart of the show's appeal. Some viewers, however, took the show so seriously, they wired the Coast Guard to "rescue those poor people before they starve to death." Finally, in a 1978 TV movie, the Coast Guard did rescue them. The castaways returned a year later, in yet another TV movie, to run a Club Med–style resort.

## GIRL SCOUTS

Inspired by Britain's Girl Guides, an offshoot of the Boy Scouts, Girls Scouts of the U.S.A. was founded in 1912 to promote ideals of service and self-respect. Besides teaching them household tasks, founder Juliette Gordon Low took her members hiking and camping. Today's five- to 17-year-old Girl Scouts do even more, earning badges for studying such subjects as science, computer programming, martial arts, and photography. At the same time, the girls learn confidence and self-reliance, as evidenced by the fact that the first woman Supreme Court Justice and six of the first nine women astronauts were once Girl Scouts.

## GISH, LILLIAN

Known as the First Lady of the Silent Screen, Lillian Gish started acting as a child. In 1912 Mary Pickford introduced young Lillian and her sister, Dorothy, also a budding actress, to the great silent-film director D. W. Griffith. Under his guidance Lillian starred in such movie classics as *Way Down East*, which featured the famous blizzard scene, filmed in a real blizzard, and the thrilling ice-floe scene, in which Gish spent a day floating on cakes of ice in a freezing river. She also starred with Dorothy in *Orphans of the Storm*, an epic about the French Revolution.

Gish made *The Scarlet Letter*, among other movies, for MGM but was let go to make way for up-and-coming star Greta Garbo. She headed for Broadway to play Shakespeare and Chekhov, occasionally appearing in supporting screen and TV roles. In 1970 Gish received a special Oscar for "superlative artistry," and in 1984 she received the Life Achievement Award from the American Film Institute.

## GOLDBERG, RUBE

When cartoonist Rube Goldberg invented an automatic stamp licker, it was anything but simple. First a small robot had to knock over a can full of ants, which would then crawl onto a page of stamps glue-side-up. Waiting nearby was a starving anteater who would lick them off. The stamps were then ready to use. Goldberg's comic contraptions, featuring Professor Lucifer Gorgonzola Butts, were so popular that Goldberg's name became synonymous with the complicating of a simple task. At Purdue University engineering students commemorate Goldberg in a contest each year, pitting Goldbergian-style inventions one against another.

Goldberg also created other comic strips. In 1915 he demanded and received the astronomical salary of $1,000 a week to draw several comics for New York's *Evening Mail*. One featured Boob McNutt, whose efforts to do good would lead to hilarious catastrophes. Goldberg also had a serious side and in 1948 won the Pulitzer Prize for a cartoon about the danger of atomic weapons.

Girl Scouts have always done more than sell cookies. During World War II they collected waste material for use in the war effort.

Although frail in appearance, Lillian Gish had great stamina and worked for decades. In 1987 she made her last movie, *The Whales of August*, at the age of 94.

Goldberg's barometer: Flash of lightning (A)... sends electrical vibrations (B) to magnetic spring (C) which contracts and causes knife (D) to cut cord (E) and release horseshoe (F), allowing it to drop on string (G) and pull trigger of cannon (H) which shoots a hole in the wall. Rat (I)... enters and is caught in trap (J) which springs and pulls rope (K) raising a storm signal flag (L). Ex-sailor (M)... hauls down sail (N), causing top boom (O) to strike against arrow (P) and swing it to position indicating storm.

Gold records are now issued in cassette form, too. Elvis Presley won the most gold records, with 110. The closest runner-up: the Beatles, with 47.

Gold panning lured optimists hoping to strike it rich; others worked for wages while bonanza kings reaped the big rewards. Wives were left at home by men who promised them a "pocket full of rocks."

A go-for-broke golfer, Arnold Palmer thrilled his army of fans with masterful shots when the chips were down. "He just seems to will the ball into the hole," said fellow golf champ Jimmy Demaret.

## GOLD RECORD

To most people, a gold record means one that has sold a million copies. Bandleader Glenn Miller was awarded a gold-sprayed copy of his 1941 hit "Chattanooga Choo-Choo" on a live radio broadcast. Bing Crosby's single "White Christmas" set a new high in sales at more than 30 million copies by 1968. In 1958 the Recording Industry Association of America (RIAA) began to certify singles as gold if they sold a million copies, and albums as gold if they grossed $1 million in sales—provided the record company was willing to open its books. To reward more contenders, the RIAA classified albums released after January 1, 1975, as gold if they sold only half a million copies. Albums and singles that sell more than a million copies now qualify as platinum.

## GOLD RUSH

From 1849 to 1899 thousands of prospectors chased dreams of riches from the gold fields of California to the mines of the Dakota Territory. In their wake cities sprang up and railroads were built, opening the land beyond the Great Plains decades earlier than would otherwise have happened.

The first and biggest rush began in 1848 when East Coast newspapers published reports from the American River in California that gold was being "collected at random and without any trouble." By 1852 the stampede for the precious ore had increased the state's population nearly twentyfold. When California's surface gold gave out, prospectors bitten by the gold bug rushed to the Comstock Lode in the Sierra Nevada. But these fabulous stores of gold and silver were rich men's diggings—too deeply embedded to mine without plenty of capital. Over the next 20 years, rumors of gold and silver strikes lured fortune hunters to the Black Hills of the Dakota Territory and to Pikes Peak and Leadville, Colorado.

In 1897 a ship docked in San Francisco, carrying two tons of gold from the Klondike River in the Canadian Yukon. This prompted 100,000 miners to head for "the golden Mecca of the North." Gold was soon found in Alaska, the site of the last—and one of the greatest—gold rushes.

## GOLF

With its manicured greens, tweed caps, and plus fours, golf was once the sport of choice among the privileged, played exclusively at private clubs. Today there are thousands of public golf courses. And some 10 percent of Americans—including welders, retired secretaries, and high school kids—can tell a birdie from an eagle, a gimmie, and a chip. Of the sport's new devotees, more than a third are women.

Many older amateurs are veterans of Arnie's Army, the passionate fans of Arnold Palmer, who came from behind to win the U.S. Open and The Masters in 1960. Jack Nicklaus succeeded him, becoming golf's biggest earner. Such players as Nancy Lopez have boosted the popularity of women's golf. But the most visible golfers aren't always the best. Even before so many voters played the game, being photographed while teeing up was a rite of the presidency, and winning was apparently a presidential perk. "A lot more people beat me now," confessed Eisenhower after he left the White House.

## GONE FISHIN'

The faster the world gets, the more people discover the slow, contemplative pleasures of fishing. In this battle of wits with an opponent hidden in a watery world, patience and observation become more important than technology or time. Presidents Franklin D. Roosevelt, Hoover, Eisenhower, Kennedy, and Carter fished for relief from the pressures of politics. Besides providing endless stories about "the one that got away," fishing has inspired novels by such authors as Mark Twain and Ernest Hemingway.

Debates rage among those who fish. Some fly fishermen look down on bait and bobbers, and surf casters are puzzled by freshwater fishermen. Those who eat their catch are perplexed by catch-and-release fishing. Still, most agree with the bumper sticker that reads "I'd rather be fishing."

## GONE WITH THE WIND

The greatest film ever to come out of Hollywood began in 1936 with Margaret Mitchell's best-selling saga of the Old South. It was brought to the attention of producer David O. Selznick by his secretary, and the rest is history. Competition was fierce for the plum role of the spitfire heroine, Scarlett O'Hara. Among those vying for the lead were Bette Davis, Joan Crawford, and Katharine Hepburn. Even Lucille Ball gave an audition. One rejected hopeful, determined to corner director George Cukor, followed him onto a train and forced him to escape to the coal wagon. The part went to the beautiful British unknown, Vivien Leigh. Clark Gable was the obvious choice for the worldly Rhett Butler.

The filming of *Gone With the Wind* used up three directors (Victor Fleming got the credit and the Oscar), 15 scriptwriters, hundreds of Walter Plunkett antebellum costumes, myriad extras, and millions of dollars. One scriptwriter, after being told the storyline because he hadn't read the book, commented, "That's the most involved plot I've ever heard. Can't you just throw it away and I write a new one?" But the efforts paid off. *GWTW* received an unprecedented 13 Academy Award nominations and won eight Oscars, including the first to be awarded to a black actor, Hattie McDaniel.

Although it was released back in 1939, *Gone With the Wind* endures as part of our lives. Its choicer lines ("Frankly, my dear, I don't give a damn!" and "Tomorrow is another day") have become part of our vernacular. A pallid sequel appeared in print and on television, only to be gone with the breeze. The Big Wind prevails.

Some say fishing lines have a worm at one end and a fool at the other. But to anglers, rod and reel—or pole and string—represent paradise.

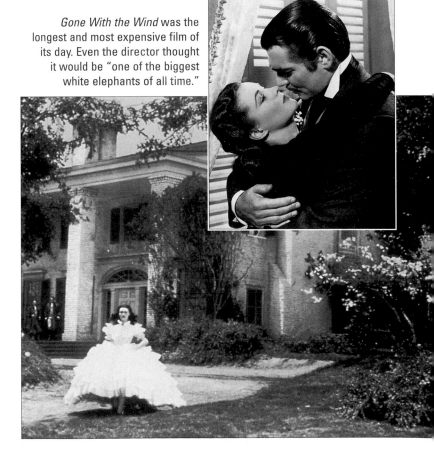

*Gone With the Wind* was the longest and most expensive film of its day. Even the director thought it would be "one of the biggest white elephants of all time."

A sure sign of spring was the first appearance of the Good Humor man. The spiffy vendors were instructed to raise their caps to women and offer men a friendly salute.

Blimps have no internal structure; their polyester skin is inflated with helium. Colored lights that cover the surface turn Goodyear blimps into programmable billboards.

Mahalia Jackson, the powerhouse "Queen of Gospel" with the vibrant contralto, sang at John F. Kennedy's inauguration and at Martin Luther King, Jr.'s funeral. She repeatedly refused offers to sing in nightclubs.

## GOOD HUMOR MAN

In 1920 Harry Burt, owner of an ice cream parlor in Youngstown, Ohio, invented a recipe for coating ice cream with chocolate. His daughter, the first to try it, liked the flavor but hated the chocolaty mess. Her brother, Harry Jr., suggested freezing the coated ice cream onto a popsicle stick, and the Good Humor Bar was born.

Burt drew attention to Good Humors by delivering them in white trucks, complete with bells, driven by men in white uniforms. The only people who didn't take an immediate liking to Good Humor men were some Chicago gangsters who, when refused protection money, blew up several Good Humor trucks. Fortunately the trucks were insured and the publicity helped popularize the treat. Affection for the Good Humor man is so strong that, when an antinoise ordinance threatened to silence the bells on Good Humor trucks, kids in Jackson, Mississippi, sued the city for a trillion dollars.

## GOODYEAR BLIMP

The Goodyear company has been known for its blimps since 1925, when it launched the *Pilgrim*. Goodyear blimps were used for reconnaissance during both world wars, but their main function has been to create publicity and goodwill for Goodyear. There are three Goodyear blimps based in the United States: one in Los Angeles, one in Pompano Beach, Florida, and one in Akron, Ohio. Among them, they hover over an amazing number of events of all kinds every year.

Under each blimp is a small gondola, in which the crew and occasional passengers ride. Suspended below that is a Gyrocam 360, a remote-controlled video camera that gives television viewers a bird's-eye view of major sporting events.

## GOSPEL MUSIC

A rousing hosanna to the heavens, gospel music has been ringing from choir lofts and meeting tents since the mid-1800s, transporting the faithful in righteous rapture. The songs, marked by messages of "good news" and driving, dynamic rhythm, developed from the joyful hymns commissioned by Protestant evangelists to enhance their sermons.

Around 1900, blacks added their traditions of stirring spirituals and lively call-and-response singing, transforming gospel into an exuberant testament of devotion. Usually accompanied by instruments and punctuated with spontaneous shouts, claps, and stomps, the music became integral to worship in black Pentecostal churches, where it served to invoke the ecstasy of possession by the Holy Ghost.

Gospel, popularized by such acclaimed talents as the Dixie Hummingbirds, the Edwin Hawkins Singers, and Mahalia Jackson, has won fans worldwide. Said Jackson of her calling, "As David said in the Bible, 'Make a joyous noise unto the Lord!' That's me."

## GOSSIP COLUMNISTS

In the late 1920s and '30s Louella Parsons, America's first queen of gossip, wielded power as the Hearst newspapers' Hollywood reporter, making and breaking stars by writing juicy personal scoops about them. Louella never pretended to be fair: she shamelessly boosted her friends and mercilessly harassed those who didn't tell her their news first. Celebrities were often too terrified to complain about her notoriously inaccurate stories. In 1937 she gave a particularly strong boost to someone from her hometown—she found a small movie role for an actor named Ronald Reagan.

A parade of gossip columnists have followed Louella, on radio and television as well as in print. Some tabloid newspapers are devoted almost exclusively to gossip, and many follow her tradition of preferring titillation to truth. Gossip columnists in major newspapers are more careful to stick to the facts. But if a star strays, it's a good bet that a columnist like Liz Smith will know and tell all.

Liz Smith, the "good ole gal" of gossip, dishes the dirt on celebrities while aiming to "tell the truth and be entertaining, and not be sued." Astronomical phone bills are one cost of being in the know.

## GRAHAM, BILLY

For half a century the Reverend Billy Graham has had the Word to spread—and the media attention to help spread it. After hearing him lead a 1949 revival meeting in Los Angeles, William Randolph Hearst ordered his newspapers to feature Graham, which made the young preacher an evangelical star. Since then, Graham has brought American revivalism into the age of mass communications with his movies, television appearances, radio shows, magazines, books, and syndicated columns.

Graham has shared podiums and private moments with every president since Harry Truman. After the 1968 election his friend Richard Nixon offered him a job in his new administration. Graham declined, saying, "When God called me to preach, it was for life."

## GRAHAM, MARTHA

"Out of emotion comes form," said choreographer Martha Graham. Her techniques differed radically from those of classical ballet, and infused 20th-century dance with new expressiveness and power. All her movements sprang from the contraction and release of muscles in the torso, which is central to breathing and, she believed, to inner feelings. Rather than daintily leaping and pirouetting, Graham's dancers hugged the earth and "carved a place for themselves in space."

Although she lacked the ballerina's elongated figure, Graham's long, pale face, black hair, deep-set eyes, and erect posture made her a commanding presence. She began training students at her New York studio in the 1920s. Her troupe's visceral style and frank sensuality disturbed some audiences. Yet such creations as *Clytemnestra* and *Appalachian Spring*, with its prizewinning score by Aaron Copland, became classics. Amazingly, she danced until the age of 75.

The most popular evangelist of our time, Billy Graham has delivered his message of personal salvation through faith and repentance to millions around the globe.

Graham continued choreographing until her death at age 96. She influenced such dance luminaries as Rudolf Nureyev and Mikhail Baryshnikov.

Michael Jackson won an unprecedented eight Grammy Awards in 1983, seven for *Thriller,* which sold more copies than any other album in history. The Grammy Awards took their name from the gramophone.

The Grand Canyon is grand indeed, but it is not America's deepest. Hell's Canyon beats the Grand's biggest drop—5,700 feet—by 2,200 feet.

## GRAHAM CRACKERS

Sylvester Graham, a self-styled naturopath and contentious clergyman, believed that the modest graham cracker offered salvation from a host of evils. He first developed his dietary theories to eliminate a craving for whiskey, which he viewed as one of many "abominations" separating Americans from God. Other evils included feather beds, meat, tobacco, and tight corsets. The staple of his own diet was coarsely ground whole wheat bread—eaten slightly stale to aid digestion.

In the 1830s Graham lectured widely and gained a large following of health-food faddists. Although his moralistic theories provoked some serious consideration, he was mocked in the press as the "Peristaltic Persuader." Today, ironically, graham crackers are often eaten in sugary cereals and made into s'mores, the popular campfire "sandwiches" filled with melted chocolate and marshmallows.

## GRAMMY AWARDS

The presentation of the Grammys, the most prestigious awards in the music business, has become a highly anticipated television event. Almost every year there are surprising upsets (the Beatles once lost to the Anita Kerr Singers) and bold fashion statements (Bette Midler once wore a Dell-Vikings single as a hat).

The Grammy Awards were conceived in 1957 by record-company executives who fretted over the impact rock and roll would have on the quality of popular music. Early awards went to such pop and jazz artists as Frank Sinatra, Barbra Streisand, and Ella Fitzgerald, but not to many of the most influential rock and rhythm and blues performers. Elvis did not win his first Grammy until 1967—for Best Sacred Performance. That same year, Aretha Franklin began a remarkable eight-year winning streak in the rhythm and blues category. Finally, in 1979 four rock awards were introduced, along with the first—and only—disco award, given to Gloria Gaynor for the number one single "I Will Survive."

A Grammy can boost an album's sales by up to 80 percent. In the 1980s Grammy recognition played a crucial role in the comeback stories of Marvin Gaye, Tina Turner, and Bonnie Raitt. But more important, according to five-time winner Dionne Warwick: "Being voted 'the best' by one's peers . . . is the greatest honor one can hope to receive."

## GRAND CANYON

For more than 10 million years the Colorado River has been eroding the land along its course in northern Arizona, creating the awesome landscape of the Grand Canyon. A 2-billion-year-old layer of rock lies at the bottom of the chasm; a mile above are petroglyphs carved by prehistoric Indians.

The first Europeans to see the canyon were members of the 1540 expedition led by the Spanish explorer Coronado. White men knew little about the region until 1869, when

Maj. John Wesley Powell and nine companions made a daring trip down the raging Colorado. "What a conflict of water and fire there must have been here!" he wrote.

A railroad spur line reached the canyon's south rim in 1901, and a hotel was opened at the line's terminus in 1904, turning the canyon into a tourist attraction. Theodore Roosevelt cautioned his countrymen to preserve the natural wonder, saying, "The ages have been at work on it, and man can only mar it." In 1919 Congress heeded his warning and created Grand Canyon National Park.

## GRANDMA MOSES

A housewife who began painting at age 76, Anna Mary Robertson "Grandma" Moses won unprecedented recognition for her joyful, brightly colored scenes of rural life. Born in Greenwich, New York, in 1860, Anna Mary married farmer Thomas Moses at age 27. After her husband died and her five children and 11 grandchildren moved away, Grandma Moses devoted more time to the embroidery and other fancywork she had always enjoyed. But arthritic fingers made needlework difficult, and she welcomed her sister's suggestion to try painting. Her first efforts were sold at a local shop, where a New York collector admired them and became determined to bring her to wider attention.

Moses's popularity owed much to her forthright, homespun personality. Unimpressed by fame, she said: "If I didn't start painting, I would have raised chickens.... I would never sit back in a rocking chair waiting for someone to help me."

## GRAND OLE OPRY

As a young reporter, George D. Hay spent an evening in the Ozarks listening to fiddlers at a hoedown. He never forgot the music, which he called "fundamental as sunshine and rain." In 1925 Hay went to work as a radio announcer at Nashville's WSM, where the *WSM Barn Dance* became a regular feature that followed a network program of classical music. Hay told listeners, "For the past half hour we have been listening to music taken largely from grand opera, but from now on we will present the Grand Ole Opry." The name stuck.

Local pride aroused, loyal audiences made the *Grand Ole Opry* the major force behind country-and-western stars and the vortex of a growing music industry in Nashville. A studio was built so that fans could watch live broadcasts of such fiddlers as Uncle Jimmy Thompson, harmonica player DeFord Bailey, and popular banjoist Uncle Dave Macon. Singer Roy Acuff and his band joined the cast in 1938, and Acuff hosted the show when it went national in 1939. Over the following years the cast included Ernest Tubb and his Texas Troubadours, Red Foley, Hank Williams, and Eddy Arnold. In 1974 the *Opry* moved from the well-worn benches of the Ryman Auditorium, its home for more than 30 years, to the new Opryland complex on the outskirts of Nashville.

With such paintings as "Sugaring Off," Grandma Moses aroused new interest in folk art, meanwhile demonstrating that it is never too late in life to begin creative work.

Minnie Pearl (right) rose to fame on the *Grand Ole Opry*—also called the "hillbilly Carnegie Hall"—the longest continuously running radio show in the country. Modern stars include singer Alan Jackson (above).

In 1940 Cary Grant starred with Katharine Hepburn in the comedy *The Philadelphia Story*—as her ex-husband, he thwarts her marriage plans.

The original members of the Grateful Dead (below) posed at San Francisco's famous crossroads in 1966. Left to right are guitarist Jerry Garcia, keyboardist Ron "Pigpen" McKernan, bassist Phil Lesh, guitarist Bob Weir, and drummer Bill Kreutzmann.

When bad investments bankrupted him, Ulysses S. Grant wrote his memoirs to save his family from financial ruin.

## GRANT, CARY

"You know what's wrong with you? Nothing!" says Audrey Hepburn to Cary Grant in *Charade* (1963), and who would argue? With his handsome face, cleft chin, navy-blue hair, perfectly fitting evening clothes, and witty way with a line, Grant was Mr. Perfect in everything from light comedies to Hitchcock thrillers. Who could forget him swaying atop a dinosaur skeleton in *Bringing Up Baby* (1938)? Or his famous long kiss with Ingrid Bergman in *Notorious* (1946), or risking his life on Mount Rushmore in *North by Northwest* (1959)? Born Archibald Leach in Bristol, England, his origins lingered in his speech, hilariously parodied by Tony Curtis in *Some Like It Hot* (1959). In 1970 he received a special Academy Award, and in 1981 he was a Kennedy Center honoree—elegant as ever. After all, it was to him that Mae West, in *She Done Him Wrong* (1933), made her celebrated suggestion: "Why doncha come up 'n see me sometime?"

## GRANT, ULYSSES S.

After failing at peacetime soldiering, farming, and business, Ulysses S. Grant found his true calling when the Civil War began. In 1862 he led the forces that captured Fort Donelson in Tennessee, where he won the first major Union victory—and the nickname "Unconditional Surrender Grant" for the terms he demanded. At Shiloh and Vicksburg, he again led the Union forces to victory, and in 1864 he was appointed supreme commander of the Union armies.

Grant's method of fighting was to hammer relentlessly at the enemy and never to back down (he had a lifelong superstition about retreating). Although he won battles this way, it cost the lives of so many thousands of soldiers that even the northern press called him "Grant the Butcher." When Robert E. Lee surrendered at Appomattox on April 9, 1865, however, Grant was hailed as a national hero.

He was elected president in 1868 and was reelected four years later. But his administration was plagued by corruption and cronyism. Grant acknowledged his mistakes, saying that it was his "misfortune to be called to the office of Chief Executive without any previous political training."

## GRATEFUL DEAD

Many rock groups build to a peak of popularity, stay there for a couple of years, then fade away. Not so the Grateful Dead. Decades after the band's start in 1965 in San Francisco's hippie community, they continued to pack arenas with multigenerational crowds of Deadheads, a family of fans that followed the band from city to city. The Dead generously allowed fans to record their live shows, at which favorite songs were often extended into enchanting improvisations.

Originally called the Warlocks, the band arrived at its final name when guitarist Jerry Garcia, a veteran player of bluegrass and country-flavored music, picked a page in a

Funk & Wagnall's dictionary and saw the term *grateful dead* (the name of a type of English ballad) under his finger. The band cut its first hit album, *Live/Dead*, in 1969. They went on to make such best-selling records as *Workingman's Dead* (1970) and *What a Long Strange Trip It's Been* (1977). Jerry Garcia's death in 1995 left the band and thousands of Deadheads to survive without their beloved leader.

## GRAUMAN'S CHINESE THEATRE

Grandiose movie palaces were already the rage when flamboyant showman Sid Grauman began building temples of entertainment in the motion-picture capital itself, Hollywood. His Chinese Theatre on Hollywood Boulevard was his most exotic, elaborate creation. It featured a copper pagoda-like roof and was decorated with bright red lacquered beams, genuine foo dogs, and huge silver dragons.

On the theater's opening night in 1927, a giant gong sounded, inviting the star-studded audience to watch a program of bizarre, vaguely biblical dances, followed by the premiere of Cecil B. DeMille's epic *King of Kings*. Shortly before the opening, a now-venerable ritual got its start. During construction of the theater, according to Hollywood historians, Grauman inadvertently stepped onto freshly poured concrete in the courtyard, leaving an indelible footprint. Instantly recognizing promotion opportunities, he invited Douglas Fairbanks, Mary Pickford, Norma Talmadge, and other stars to follow his example by recording impressions of their feet and hands in the wet concrete.

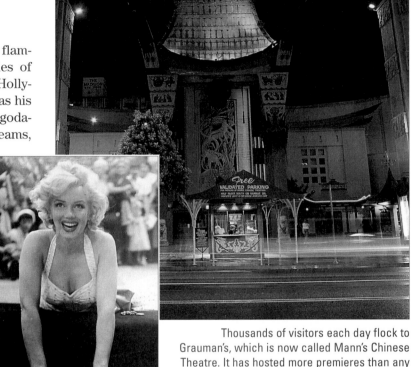

Thousands of visitors each day flock to Grauman's, which is now called Mann's Chinese Theatre. It has hosted more premieres than any other Hollywood movie house.

In addition to cement hand and foot prints of the famous, Grauman's has imprints of Trigger's hooves and Whoopi Goldberg's dreadlocks.

## GREASE

Word-of-mouth raves brought two New York producers to Chicago in 1971 to see an amateur, five-hour-long rock and roll musical comedy called *Grease*. Spoofing the Fabulous Fifties and shamelessly nostalgic, the plot centered on how innocent Sandy Dumbrowski breaks out of her square mold to win the heart of Danny Zuko, one of the Burger Palace Boys. After drastically trimming its length, the producers opened the play in New York the following year. Although it had a no-name cast, *Grease* played for seven years. For a time, it was the longest-running show on Broadway, with more than 3,300 performances.

*Grease*, starring John Travolta and Olivia Newton-John, finally hit the big screen in 1978. Both Frankie Avalon and the rock group Sha Na Na—pop-culture icons in their own right—were featured in cameo roles. Produced on a $6 million budget, the film was the biggest moneymaker of the year, earning $153 million. Audiences flocked to the show for its campy send-ups of such '50s teen-age concerns as bouffant hairstyles, black leather jackets, and who was taking whom to the high school prom.

By the end of *Grease*, no-longer-shy Sandy Dumbrowski (Olivia Newton-John) knows exactly how to get her boyfriend back. "You better shape up," she sings, "'cause I need a man, and my heart is set on you."

The Great Depression was the worst economic setback the U.S. has ever experienced. By 1932, 11,000 banks had closed their doors and millions had lost their savings. Soup lines and apple sellers became common sights.

So vast are the Great Lakes that lighthouses are needed to protect ships from the rocky shore. The Split Rock Lighthouse stands on the coast of Lake Superior. The Great Lakes join with the St. Lawrence River, creating a waterway that reaches the Atlantic Ocean.

## GREAT DEPRESSION

In 1928 Herbert Hoover stated that America was "nearer to the final triumph over poverty than ever before." In reality, the 1920s bull market concealed a depression in farming and other major industries. When the stock market collapsed in 1929, it set off a downward spiral of falling production, rising unemployment, and plummeting prices.

The breadwinners of one-third of American families lost their jobs. Farmers watched the prices of their crops fall at the same time they were hit by droughts, dust storms, and floods. President Hoover refused to authorize federal relief, so charities and local governments were quickly overwhelmed. In New York City, the average weekly relief payment was $2.39 for a family, for which there was a waiting list of 25,000 families.

In 1932 Franklin Roosevelt was elected president, and he declared, "This nation asks for action, and action now!" Although the Great Depression would linger until 1941, Roosevelt's New Deal programs of economic relief and social reform began to lead the country toward recovery.

## GREAT LAKES

The Great Lakes—Superior, Michigan, Huron, Erie, and Ontario—form an area so vast that early explorers thought they had found the fabled "Great South Sea" that led to Cathay. The first European to record his exploration of the region was Samuel de Champlain, who reached Lake Huron in 1615. Over the next 200 years, the Great Lakes were fought over by Huron and Iroquois Indians and, later, by France, England, and the U.S. The territory around the lakes was prized for its abundant natural resources, from animal pelts to iron and timber. Today the lakes' shoreline reaches from the skyscrapers of Chicago to the docks of Duluth to the untouched wilderness of Isle Royale in Lake Superior.

## GREAT PLAINS

The Great Plains encompass 10 states that were once rich natural grasslands. When Maj. Stephen Long explored the region in 1820, he named it the Great American Desert because it was "uninhabitable by a people depending upon agriculture for their subsistence." This description kept settlers away until 1862, when homesteaders began to arrive. Some were disheartened by the vast open spaces. "I never felt so strongly the sense of loneliness as here," said one.

After the Civil War, cattle ranchers used the Plains for grazing and farmers planted wheat. When drought struck in the 1930s, the overgrazed and overplanted land dried up and blew away, creating the Dust Bowl. In 1937 the federal government began soil-conservation measures to restore the Plains, and today the grasslands thrive once again.

Bison were hunted to near extinction in the late 1800s, but today they are hanging on. The Great Plains now support several protected herds.

## GREAT WHITE WAY

The Great White Way is Broadway, the theater district of Manhattan, street of dreams for actors, playwrights, and tourists. In reality, however, most of the theaters lurk in the side streets, and the movie palaces that once lit up the sky are gone. The year Broadway was nicknamed (1901), Sarah Bernhardt arrived with 50 trunks to play her repertory in French; when she forgot a scene, nobody could tell.

Times Square, of New Year's Eve fame, was established in 1904. A year later, George M. Cohan sent his regards you-know-where. The great impresario Florenz Ziegfeld, with three gold telephones on his desk, produced not only gorgeous Follies girls but also the original *Show Boat*, in 1927. The House of Barrymore—John, Ethel, and Lionel—trod the boards in classics, and in 1920 Eugene O'Neill's *Beyond the Horizon* marked the advent of modern American drama. The '30s welcomed Kaufman and Hart comedies, Cole Porter musicals, and clarion-voiced Ethel Merman.

During World War II Broadway ran the Stage Door Canteen for thousands of servicemen. *Mister Roberts* was the first play to win a Tony Award, in 1948; Arthur Miller's *Death of a Salesman* won the Pulitzer Prize a year later. The musical *Guys and Dolls*, inspired by Damon Runyon's colorful stories, appeared in '52. Lerner and Loewe's *My Fair Lady* made history in '56; so did Robert Preston in *The Music Man*, which began its impressive run in '57.

The '60s were enlivened by Edward Albee's *Who's Afraid of Virginia Woolf?* and the hippie musical *Hair*. *A Chorus Line* ran from 1975 to 1983, a record breaker until *Cats* scratched in '82; at press time it was still running. The '90s appetite for special effects has resulted in such stage spectaculars as *Beauty and the Beast*. It's a long way from Bernhardt to Disney, but Broadway beats on.

## GRIFFITH, ANDY

Andy Griffith proved that you can go home again when he introduced TV audiences to the small-town values of his childhood in *The Andy Griffith Show* (1960–68). There was no crime, no drugs, and no war in Mayberry, North Carolina, just a group of lovable eccentrics. Griffith, playing the resident philosopher, Sheriff Andy Taylor, surrounded himself with a cast of talented comedians, including Don Knotts as his bumbling deputy, Barney Fife, and Jim Nabors as the dim-witted Gomer Pyle. Andy was a widower raising his son, Opie (Ron Howard), with the help of Aunt Bee (Frances Bavier), whose pies he once set on the windowsill to trap a fugitive.

Griffith had won a Tony nomination for his first Broadway performance in *No Time for Sergeants* (1955–56), and another for his leading role in *Destry Rides Again* (1959–60). He left television to go to Hollywood but returned in 1986 as the canny defense lawyer Ben Matlock, a Southern successor to Perry Mason, in ABC's ongoing series *Matlock*.

Broadway has been the heart of Manhattan's theater district since 1895, when Oscar Hammerstein opened the Olympia. The area now attracts more than 9 million theatergoers every season.

Don Knotts (right) won five Emmys for his role as Deputy Barney Fife, the sheriff's less-than-capable sidekick. Poor Barney was allotted only one bullet at a time.

D. W. Griffith continued directing until 1931. He fell upon hard times and spent his last years ignored by the industry he helped create.

Marshall Matt Dillon's allies included saloon owner Kitty Russell and old Doc Adams (right).

Woody Guthrie wrote his songs as he traveled by "side door Pullman and sun-burned thumb."

## GRIFFITH, D. W.

Called the "King of Directors," David Wark Griffith innovated such film techniques as close-ups, long shots, intercutting, fade-ins, fade-outs, flashbacks, and mounting cameras on moving vehicles. Defending the close-up, he said, "If the face tells what I mean it to tell, an audience will forget about legs, arms, liver, and lungs."

Griffith trained his actors to use a restrained acting technique, and he developed a stock company that included the Gish sisters and Mary Pickford. His most famous and influential movie, *Birth of a Nation* (1915), a Civil War epic, established filmmaking as an art but was criticized for being racist. Stung, Griffith followed it with *Intolerance* (1916), a complex work about man's inhumanity to man.

## GUNSMOKE

*Gunsmoke* redefined the TV Western. Before *Gunsmoke*, Westerns were full of action, good guys in white hats, trick riding, and even singing cowboys. After the series's 20-year reign on television, Westerns were more likely to feature complex characters facing personal dilemmas.

*Gunsmoke* started out on radio in 1952, with William Conrad playing Marshal Matt Dillon. James Arness stepped in as the marshal when the show moved to television, and he spent 640 episodes, broadcast from 1955 to 1975, keeping the peace in the Dodge City, Kansas, of the 1870s.

## GUTHRIE, WOODY

"I'm out to sing the songs that make you take pride in yourself and your work," Guthrie would say to listeners across the land. America's legendary folksinger was a champion of the poor, playing at union meetings, rallies, migratory labor camps, churches, and saloons. The strongly evocative images in his songs raised people's spirits and motivated them to struggle for a better life. Of the more than 1,000 songs he composed or adapted, many are still being sung. "This Land Is Your Land" is often called "America's national folk anthem." The spark behind the folk movement of the 1950s, Guthrie also inspired Bob Dylan and the other singers who would lead the protest movement of the '60s.

"Woody could turn out two songs before breakfast," wrote his friend and fellow singer Pete Seeger. Among his best-known songs are "Union Maid," "This Train Is Bound for Glory," "So Long, It's Been Good to Know Ya," and "Reuben James." In 1940 he recorded the famous "Dust Bowl Ballads" series for the Library of Congress. He joined Seeger and The Almanac Singers in 1941 to tour and record, performing with such other activist singers as Huddie "Leadbelly" Ledbetter. Although he was hospitalized in 1957 with Huntington's chorea, a hereditary degenerative disease, Guthrie remained the core of American folk music until his death in 1967. His son, Arlo, carries on the family tradition.

> *"I know not what course others may take; but as for me, give me liberty, or give me death!"*
>

## HÄAGEN-DAZS

Long before yuppies and conspicuous consumption, there was Häagen-Dazs, the ice cream of the rich and famous. Indulgent, high-fat Häagen-Dazs, the perfect product for the 1980s, was introduced in 1960. The name promised quality in a vague, foreign-sounding way. But Häagen-Dazs doesn't mean a thing in any language. Its inventor, Reuben Mattus, made it up after hearing about a rich Danish ice cream.

By giving his product an upscale name and taste, Mattus found he could charge at least twice as much as his competitors did—and still gain customers at an astounding rate. In fact, Häagen-Dazs helped teach Americans to pay top dollar for imaginative names like Fruscn Glädjé, Godiva Chocolates, and Reebok Shoes, to list just a few.

## HACKERS

The first computer hackers were members of MIT's Tech Model Railroad Club, who in the 1950s and '60s discovered the fun they could have experimenting with the school's computer, which was available at night. Soon, because of the countless hours they devoted to programming, straggly, sleepless students at universities across the country knew more about using computers than did the companies that made them. They developed a counterculture based on a sharing of information and a scorn for authority.

Hacking began to seem more sinister in 1988, when Robert T. Morris, a 23-year-old computer-science graduate student at Cornell, created a "virus"—a destructive computer program—that spread through networks and erased vital information in military and academic computers. Nonetheless, while hackers have occasionally been harmful, more often they've been the pioneers of the computer age.

## "HAIL TO THE CHIEF"

Although most people would recognize "Hail to the Chief" as the music played to announce the president of the United States, few actually know the words. The first verse is "Hail to the Chief who in triumph advances! / Honored and bless'd be the evergreen pine. / Long may the tree, in his banner that glances, / Flourish, the shelter and grace of our line."

The words come from Sir Walter Scott's narrative poem *The Lady of the Lake*. The march was first used at the inauguration of Martin Van Buren in 1837.

The first batch of super-premium Häagen-Dazs was so high in butterfat (16 percent, as opposed to the usual 10 percent) that it actually turned to butter as it was being produced.

With the success of home computers in the 1980s, their great power became apparent. The 1983 movie *WarGames* startled audiences with a fictional account of a hacker who nearly causes World War III.

Gerald R. Ford became our 38th president on August 9, 1974. At his proud alma mater, the University of Michigan, the carillon played "Hail to the Chief" and "America the Beautiful."

# Hairstyles
## OF THE 20TH CENTURY

*Hairstyles, like hemlines, are in constant flux. Long or short, restrained or wild, different do's are shaped not only by combs and curlers but by the prevailing attitudes of the day.*

**THE CURLY BOB**
By bravely bobbing her hair, ballroom idol Irene Castle became the model for high-spirited women of the '20s, who by one estimate were copying the style at the rate of 2,000 a day.

**THE SLEEK BOB**
In the mid-'20s glamour girl Louise Brooks inspired the head-hugging, sometimes shingled bob—a perfect match for the cloche.

**THE SCULPTURED ROLL**
Longer hair, rolled close to the head in assorted formations, like this forward roll, was well groomed but chic for the more serious '30s.

**THE LONG PAGEBOY**
Defying wartime austerity, Veronica Lake hit the screen with blond hair falling eight inches below the shoulder and over one eye. Called the "sheepdog" or even the "bad girl" style, it recalled the luxuries of prewar life.

**THE UPSWEEP**
Practical but flattering, the '40s upsweep kept hair from flying away as women took on men's jobs. Hair was brushed up and fastened on top in loose curls or smooth coils, as shown here.

### THE BOUFFANT
A thick pageboy, the bouffant was set on large rollers, teased to create fullness, and sprayed heavily. Regular salon visits were a must.

### THE POODLE
This "casual" curlyhead style of the '50s, worn here by actress Rita Gam, was set with 125 curlers and required frequent permanents.

### THE BEEHIVE
The bouffant gone wild—teased hair piled so high it resembled a beehive—attracted teens and rock musicians of the '50s and '60s.

### THE AFRO
Actress Pam Grier displays the beauty of the afro, an outward symbol of inner black pride. Hair was combed straight out and sometimes professionally shaped.

### THE GEOMETRIC CUT
In the '60s British hairstylist Vidal Sassoon reinvented the bob. His abstract version was created to complement the miniskirt. It was an instant hit when launched by actress Nancy Kwan.

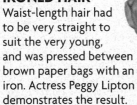

### IRONED HAIR
Waist-length hair had to be very straight to suit the very young, and was pressed between brown paper bags with an iron. Actress Peggy Lipton demonstrates the result.

### AU NATUREL
Emancipated from all care except possibly a permanent, the tousled look of the '80s and '90s was achieved by washing the hair and simply letting it dry, uncombed.

New York City honored Nathan Hale with a statue in 1890. The statement he is known for is a paraphrase from Joseph Addison's *Cato:* "What a pity is it / That we can die but once to save our country."

A young ghost walks (top); trick-or-treaters race to the next house (above); a pumpkin grimaces (right). In the 1800s, pioneers celebrated Halloween with a hayride or a taffy pull.

## HALE, NATHAN

When General George Washington asked for volunteers to spy behind enemy lines before the Battle of Harlem Heights, Capt. Nathan Hale was the first to step forward. In civilian disguise, he traveled in a roundabout way to the British encampment on Long Island, where he secretly gathered information about their defenses. However, just as he approached his own lines, he was captured.

His Tory cousin Samuel Hale allegedly betrayed him, and the British found incriminating papers on him. Hale was ordered hanged without benefit of a trial. "I only regret that I have but one life to lose for my country" are the heroic last words attributed to him. But according to the diaries of Capt. Frederick Mackenzie, a British officer at the scene, Hale really said, "It is the duty of every good officer to obey any orders given him by his commander-in-chief."

## HALLOWEEN

The origins of Halloween can be traced back to antiquity. In mid-autumn the Celts would don masks to scare away evil spirits. The Romans had a fall festival to celebrate harvest-time, hence our pumpkins and apple-bobbing. In the ninth century Pope Gregory IV designated November 1 All Saints' Day and October 31 a time of vigil, or "Hallowed Evening." Today children love the day because they can dress up and go from house to house collecting candy. Children tell each other eerie ghost stories, and some families turn their homes into haunted houses. Horror movies abound on television.

In recent years Halloween has become a social, and even a community, event—with costume parties, parades, and window-decorating contests. And with the multimillion-dollar Halloween costume and gewgaw business flourishing, one could say that Halloween is a season in its own right.

## HAMILTON, ALEXANDER

By the age of 20, Alexander Hamilton was already a trusted adviser to Gen. George Washington, and he would go on to a brilliant career in politics. He drafted the report that led to the Constitutional Convention of 1787, and he became a dynamic force in the Federalist movement, arguing for a strong central government. As the first secretary of the Treasury, he created the first Bank of the United States.

But when he resigned in 1795, "his best work had all been done; his cruellest errors remained to be committed," wrote historian Allan Nevins. Hamilton tried to influence Cabinet members during John Adams's presidency, which led to a bitter feud with Adams. Although he disliked Thomas Jefferson even more than Adams, Hamilton helped secure Jefferson's presidential victory in 1800 over Aaron Burr, whom he called a "dangerous man...who ought not to be trusted with the reins of government." In 1804 he blocked Burr's bid for governorship of New York.

Burr longed for revenge and challenged Hamilton to a duel. On July 11, 1804, Burr fatally shot Hamilton, who died the next afternoon at the age of 47.

## HAMMETT, DASHIELL

Hammett's eight years as a Pinkerton detective provided him with experiences to draw on when he turned his hand to writing his sophisticated crime novels, which critics have hailed as serious literature. His famous gumshoe, Sam Spade of Spade & Archer, was unforgettably played by Humphrey Bogart in the 1941 film version of *The Maltese Falcon*, named for the black bird coveted by the Fat Man. As an antidote to his usual hard-boiled prose, Hammett wrote *The Thin Man*, a lighter detective story. A moody man in private life, Hammett had a long relationship with Lillian Hellman. In 1951, during the McCarthy era, he was jailed because of his alleged membership in the Communist Party. In 1977 Jason Robards played Hammett in the movie version of Hellman's *Julia*.

## HAM RADIO

When disasters cut off telephone contact—as they do during hurricanes (such as Andrew in 1992), earthquakes, floods, and devastating fires—ham radio operators take to the airwaves and relay information into and out of the disaster site. Or, if all is quiet and weather conditions are right, one licensed "ham" can talk to another halfway around the world.

Another means of radio communication is the CB (citizens band) radio. These two-way radios, which have a range of only a few miles, were first used by farmers and truckers. But when the national speed limit was lowered to 55 miles an hour in 1973, millions bought CBs so they could hear truckers warn each other about the whereabouts of Smokeys, as they call state troopers, and speed traps.

## HAND GAMES

No matter where Americans grew up, they all seem to know the same hand games. Parents play Patty-Cake with babies; children love to create the wiggling finger-people of "Here is the church and here is the steeple"; adolescents learn strategy by playing Rock, Scissors, Paper; and people of all ages thumb wrestle. Hand games can also be a test of agility and nerves, as in Smash, which puts one player's palms gingerly atop another player's. The bottom hands try to slap the top ones, while those on top try to quickly pull away.

Hands are universal decision makers, too. To determine who gets to go first, the odds are that fists will be put in a circle and tapped to the chant of "one potato, two potato." To choose between two people, they're likely to "shoot" for it, calling "odd" or "even" and displaying one finger or two at the count of three. Then, just for fun, there is the Awful Egg Trick: tap the top of someone's head and lightly run your fingers down the person's hair, as if you've just broken an egg.

Asta the dog helped *The Thin Man*'s urbane Nick and Nora Charles (William Powell and Myrna Loy, above) solve cases. When Nora asked why he wouldn't take a case, Nick said, "I'm much too busy making sure you don't waste the money I married you for."

Hand games can have simple accessories, such as the string in Cat's Cradle (above). Shadow figures (left) are bound to appear in a room when a projector beam is left running without film. Hint: wiggle your fingers to make the ears wriggle. Below, a game of Pease Porridge Hot.

Handy's "Memphis Blues" had as its subtitle "or, Mr. Crump." He wrote hundreds of other blues, such as "Yellow Dog Blues," "Beale Street Blues," and "Aunt Hagar's Blues."

Even though the song is often sung off-key, it just wouldn't be a birthday without the familiar strains of "Happy Birthday to You."

The Happy Face has appeared on such diverse items as a cookie jar and a bath mat. One collector has an entire room filled with Smilie objects.

## HANDY, W. C.

W. C. Handy, known as the "Father of the Blues," might be better called the champion of the blues. He was the literate link who, by notating blues and incorporating them into popular songs, helped this form of music to spread and gain lasting popularity. Born in Florence, Alabama, in 1873, Handy was the son of a pastor who thought popular music was the devil's work. Despite his father's fury, Handy bought himself a trumpet. After graduating from college, he taught school and moonlighted on trumpet. He heard itinerant bluesmen and jazz bands playing ragtime, and he gravitated to the style.

In 1908 Handy wrote a campaign song for "Boss" Crump, who was running for mayor of Memphis. The song was "Memphis Blues," and Crump won. Unable to find a publisher for his next song, "St. Louis Blues," Handy started his own company, one of the first blacks to do so. He remained active with his band in New York until his eyesight failed in the 1940s. After his death in 1958, a film, *St. Louis Blues*, starring Nat King Cole as Handy, was made about his life.

## HAPPY BIRTHDAY TO YOU

No matter how you celebrate your birthday, the odds are that someone will sing "Happy Birthday to You." A 1995 survey found that 71 percent of Americans hear that song on their birthdays. The melody, now in the public domain, was published in 1893 with the words "Good Morning to All," written by sisters Mildred J. Hill, a church organist, and Patty S. Hill, a schoolteacher. The "Happy Birthday" lyrics written by the sisters were copyrighted in 1935. Until the copyright runs out in 2010, royalties must be paid for using these words at public performances. Fortunately, no fees are owed for singing them at private parties.

## HAPPY FACE

In 1971 a simple, sweet "happy face" began popping up everywhere. The N. G. Slater Company, which had been making Smilie buttons since 1969, started pasting it on dozens of other items as well. The face showed up on buttons, stationery, mugs, notepads, and clothes. Teachers used the face to reward good work, and waiters put it on checks. The fad lasted more than a year. Later in the 1970s the face came back again, this time accompanied by the slogan "Have a Nice Day." Soon renegade buttons with frowns, instead of smiles, began to appear—perhaps it's a sign of changing times.

## HARDY BOYS

A shriek in a haunted house, mysterious footprints near an old mill, secret passageways behind library shelves—if sleuthing is called for, Frank and Joe Hardy are the boys for the job. While their chum Chet sometimes lets his appetite for a third dish of ice cream win out over his taste for adventure, Frank and Joe never allow a case to go unsolved. It all started in 1927 with *The Tower Treasure*, followed by *The House on the Cliff*, *The Secret of the Old Mill*, and more than 100 other titles. Today the *Hardy Boys* series, in updated versions, continues to provide young readers with nonstop action and thrilling suspense.

Franklin W. Dixon is the name that appears on all the *Hardy Boys* books, but few readers know that it was the pen name of Edward Stratemeyer and his ghostwriters, who built a publishing empire based on dozens of juvenile series. Carolyn Keene was the pseudonym used for Stratemeyer's *Nancy Drew Mysteries*, which feature a squeaky-clean sleuth with titian hair and a nifty beau named Ned.

## HARLEM GLOBETROTTERS

America's most famous basketball team, the Harlem Globetrotters, also known as the "Ambassadors of Goodwill," have played before kings, queens, and popes in more than 100 countries on six different continents since 1927. During the 1930s and '40s, the all-black 'Trotters, who defeated the National Basketball Association's champion Minneapolis Lakers several times in exhibition games, might have been the best team in the entire country.

When the NBA became integrated in 1950, the best players went to the pros. So the Globetrotters's founder and owner, Abe Saperstein, changed the format to that of a carnival act. Playing to the infectious tune of "Sweet Georgia Brown," Meadowlark Lemon, Goose Tatum, and the nonpareil dribbler Marques Haynes toyed with their opposition—most often the inept Washington Generals. Passing the ball behind their back and between their legs, before scoring easy hoops, they piled up 8,829 consecutive victories over 24 years. Recently they have returned to serious basketball to boost attendance. And at the hands of a team of retired stars led by Kareem Abdul-Jabbar, they suffered a rare defeat.

## HARLEY-DAVIDSON

Bill Harley and the three Davidson brothers—Walter, Arthur, and William—founded their motorcycle business in 1903 in the Davidsons' Milwaukee backyard. Harley-Davidson has devoted customers who wouldn't consider riding another make. These fans have a vocabulary all their own, describing a Harley as a flathead, knucklehead, panhead, shovelhead, or blockhead, depending on the shape of its V-twin engine. They proudly wear Harley T-shirts, and some even sport Harley tattoos. Their motorcycles are often personalized with accessories and custom paint jobs.

Early Harley riders were likely to be mechanics who were proud of their ability to fix their often leaky engines. But today's Harley fans include RUBs (Rich Urban Bikers). The company sponsors H.O.G., the Harley Owners Group, a play on the fact that Harley's super-heavy-weight motorcycles are often called "hogs."

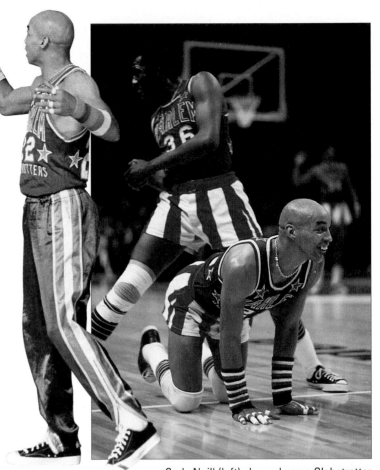

Curly Neill (left) showed some Globetrotter style when he spun a basketball on his finger. Above, Neill crawled through the legs of Meadowlark Lemon, just one of the unorthodox stunts of the 'Trotters's antic days.

The Harley-Davidson logo, here on a pin, proudly states that its motorcycles, such as the hog shown above, are "made in USA."

Silver-screen sex symbol of the 1930s, Jean Harlow was discovered by Howard Hughes, who cast her in his aviation drama *Hell's Angels*. In the mid-'30s Hollywood's Production Code forced MGM to tone down her image.

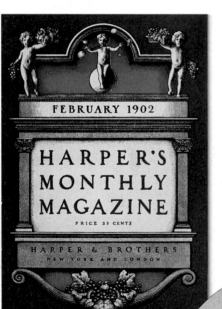

*Harper's* magazines were highly prized by readers. Pioneers heading west took along cherished copies, often bound in leather to protect them on the long journey. Gold seekers even made room for the magazine in their backpacks.

**FEBRUARY 1902**

**HARPER'S MONTHLY MAGAZINE**

PRICE 35 CENTS

HARPER & BROTHERS
NEW YORK AND LONDON

Bret Harte captivated the country with his sentimental tales. He continued to write stories about the West long after he'd moved back East.

## HARLOW, JEAN

He: "Let's take a drive in my car. I need the air." She: "Yeah? Well, I'm giving you the air." In this exchange from *Three Wise Girls* (1933), "she" is Jean Harlow, the original platinum Blonde Bombshell. With her spectacular figure and a sense of humor revealed by her good-natured grin, Harlow transformed her scant acting talent into an endearing and enduring comic presence. In *Red Dust*, playing opposite Clark Gable, she took a memorable bath in a rain barrel; in *Dinner at Eight*, she was hilarious as a newly rich wife with a questionable past; in *Bombshell*, she brilliantly parodied herself.

Harlow's private life was troubled. In a scandal that shook Hollywood, her husband of two months, Paul Bern, a top executive at MGM, committed suicide. At the age of 26, Harlow died of acute kidney disease, leaving a permanent void when it comes to delivering a sassy retort. "Don't worry, you'll get your fur coat," says her beau in *The Iron Man*. Answers Harlow, "Sure, if I go out and kill two cats."

## HARPER'S

Long cherished as a "mirror of American life and ideas," *Harper's Monthly* was founded by the noted book publisher Harper & Brothers in 1850. The magazine brought culture to a hungry public, serializing novels by Charles Dickens and publishing American luminaries from Mark Twain to Herman Melville. Woodrow Wilson, among others, contributed historical essays, and Winslow Homer was one of the illustrators.

Fletcher Harper, the youngest of the four brothers, managed the publication's early operation. Seeking to exert political as well as cultural influence, he inaugurated *Harper's Weekly* in 1857. Its strongest weapons were its artists, especially cartoonist Thomas Nast, who exposed and helped to topple New York's corrupt Boss Tweed. Although the *Weekly* folded in 1916, the monthly magazine has remained influential, introducing such 20th-century writers as Katherine Anne Porter, J. D. Salinger, and John Cheever.

## HARTE, BRET

While prospectors panned for gold in California's motherlode country, Bret Harte proved there was more money in writing about the '49ers. Stories like "The Luck of Roaring Camp" and "The Outcasts of Poker Flat," published in the *Overland Monthly*, made Harte a coast-to-coast celebrity.

Harte's characters quickly became part of American frontier lore. Mother Shipton, for example, is the original hooker with a heart of gold; Tommy Luck is the first stranger with a checkered past to swagger into town; and John Oakhurst is the first poker-faced gambler who can't bear to cheat a luckless greenhorn. Along with his friend Mark Twain, Bret Harte was one of a cadre of San Francisco writers called local colorists, whose tall tales helped to elevate the American West to the status of myth.

## HARVARD LAMPOON

A training ground for tomorrow's professional smart alecks, Harvard University's *Harvard Lampoon* has cheerfully abused the status quo for more than a century. The original editors' mission: to "have a cut at everything about us that needs correction." All affectation, all snobbishness, would be "set up as a mark for our darts of withering sarcasm and remorseless irony."

Such famous "Poonies" as George Santayana, Robert Benchley, and John Updike honed their tongue-in-cheek voices in the magazine's offices at The Castle, a mock Gothic fortress financed by William Randolph Hearst. There, someone dressed as a court jester always shows up for every important occasion, and editorial meetings often end in water-pistol fights. Recently, wisecrackers from the *Lampoon* have invaded late-night television as writers for such shows as *Saturday Night Live* and *The David Letterman Show*.

## HAWTHORNE, NATHANIEL

The word *adultery* never appears in *The Scarlet Letter*, but the flaming letter A that Hester Prynne must wear on her chest as punishment for her crime says it all. Nathaniel Hawthorne's best-known novel teaches us that love cannot be suppressed by public scorn; it has, in Hester's words, "a consecration of its own." The 1850 book was an instant success, and it remains in the first rank of American classics.

Guilt inherited from ancestral sin is a favorite theme of Hawthorne's. The novel he felt expressed it best, *The House of the Seven Gables*, is a Gothic tale of ghosts, speaking portraits, and haunting passions. Hawthorne once complained that he was "the obscurest man of letters in America." He was gratified when fame brought friendships with the likes of Henry David Thoreau and Herman Melville, who dedicated *Moby Dick* to Hawthorne.

## HAYES, HELEN

The "First Lady of the American Stage" said she learned early in life the three key words for success: discipline, discipline, discipline. Helen Hayes made her first Broadway appearance at the age of nine and at 18 was a Broadway star. In 1928 she married playwright Charles MacArthur, went with him to Hollywood, and in 1931 won an Oscar for her first film. Saying "I don't think I'm much good in pictures," she returned to the theater for one of the highlights of her career: the lead role in *Victoria Regina*, for which she was eminently suited.

Just over five feet tall, neither beautiful nor a sex symbol, Hayes had unfailing charm and a direct and appealing manner. No fashion plate, she prompted a friend to comment: "Helen doesn't dress badly, she just doesn't dress." She won a second Academy Award—and a lot of new fans—for her portrayal of a little old stowaway in the 1970 movie *Airport*.

*Harvard Lampoon,* the oldest college humor magazine in the U.S., is famous for publishing parodies of national magazines, such as these send-ups of *Mademoiselle* and *Life*. Other spoofs have included *Lampy's Home Journal* and a faux-*Newsweek* issue, which proclaimed: "Nuclear Arms and Terrific Legs: The Atomic Threat to America's Cover Girls." The *Lampoon* also publishes literary parodies, such as *Bored of the Rings,* a takeoff on Tolkien's classic.

In *Victoria Regina* Helen Hayes (with co-star Richard Burton) ascended the throne as Queen Victoria, perhaps her most famous role. In 1955 a New York theater was named for Hayes in honor of her 50 years on the American stage.

According to guidelines developed by the government, vegetables, fruits, and grains should now make up a larger part of our diets than in the past.

Hemingway (right), along with his friends Gary Cooper and Taylor "Bear Track" Williams, rests triumphant after a successful hunt in Sun Valley, Idaho, in 1939.

The great hemline debate has raged for decades as women have followed the ups and downs of fashion. In the 1960s the minidress was deemed appropriate for just about every occasion.

## HEALTH FOOD

As the government became involved in public health, people were urged to eat better by eating more, because many who had come to these shores were malnourished. In the 1890s, W. O. Atwater, a Department of Agriculture employee, created dietary standards that limited meat and dairy products, but his recommendations were dismissed because they might have encouraged people to eat less.

Still, there have always been people who champion different kinds of diets. Some, following the principles of naturopathy, have stressed low-fat, high-fiber diets. Recently, scientists have discovered a correlation between cardiovascular disease and the excessive consumption of fat. As a result, much of what was once considered health-food fanaticism is now accepted wisdom. Those who used to shop in health-food stores for grainy breads and mealy peanut butter can now go to regular supermarkets for tofu, organic produce, veggie burgers, and low-fat everything. And after endless study, the government has developed a "Food Guide Pyramid" remarkably similar to Atwater's guidelines.

## HEMINGWAY, ERNEST

"Mister Papa," as Ernest Hemingway often signed letters, was a burly man with 17-inch biceps and a fan-shaped beard. A consummate adventurer, he wielded a pen with the same bravado he used when aiming a Tommy gun on a battlefield, flourishing a bullfighter's sword, or anchoring a fishing line against a 450-pound fighting marlin. By the time *The Old Man and the Sea* appeared in *Life* magazine in 1952, Hemingway had become a celebrity. Never comfortable with fame, he wrote in "The Snows of Kilimanjaro" that a writer gets lazy and loses his talent if he trades on his reputation "instead of a pen or a pencil."

Arguably the most widely imitated American writer of all time, Hemingway perfected his famous unadorned style under the tutelage of Gertrude Stein and Ezra Pound in Paris during the 1920s. His novel *The Sun Also Rises* captured the disillusionment of youth in the aftermath of World War I. If young Hemingway was a good student, he was an even better teacher. He advised inexperienced writers to work every day, but to stop "when you are going good." That way, "you know what will happen next" and "you will never be stuck." Hemingway's favorite novel, considered his most mature work, was *For Whom the Bell Tolls*, an unparalleled study of epic courage and compassion set against the terrors of war.

## HEMLINES

For most of recorded history, women's hemlines were one length: long. Then came the 20th century. Skirts rose to just below the knee by the 1940s, lengthened again in the '50s, blasted about as high as they could go with the famous miniskirt of the '60s, and so on up and down.

What could this have to do with the stock market? In 1967 stock analyst Ralph Rotnem compared the fluctuation of hemlines and the Dow Jones Industrial Average since 1900 and found a remarkable pattern: the higher the hemline, the higher the market; the lower the skirt, the more figures fell. But the stock market and hemlines became an uneasy couple in the 1970s and '80s as women rebelled against designers' dictates and wore many different lengths. In 1990 the "Hemline Index" was pronounced (unofficially) dead.

## HEPBURN, AUDREY

Originally a ballet student in London, Audrey Hepburn's elegant dancer's body, long neck, and charming fawn face made her an ideal fashion model. After playing bit parts in British movies, she made her Broadway debut in *Gigi*. Her success led to a starring role in *Roman Holiday* (1953), for which she won an Academy Award. She went on to grace such films as *Sabrina*, *Love in the Afternoon*, and *Breakfast at Tiffany's*, and collected four more Oscar nominations.

Hepburn's friend and favorite designer, Hubert de Givenchy, created her much admired look. When, in 1964, Hepburn won the most coveted role since Scarlett O'Hara— Eliza Doolittle in the movie *My Fair Lady*—Givenchy flew to Hollywood to help with the fittings of her Cecil Beaton costumes. Hepburn eventually moved to Europe, returning for the occasional film role or to lend her presence to the PBS *Gardens of the World* series. In 1988 she was appointed an official spokeswoman for UNICEF and spent five years visiting children all over the world. One year before her death, in 1993, she received the Presidential Medal of Freedom.

## HEPBURN, KATHARINE

"There ain't much meat on her, but where there is, is choice," says Spencer Tracy of patrician Katharine Hepburn in *Pat and Mike* (1952), one of the nine pictures the two made together since they first teamed up in *Woman of the Year* in 1942. Hepburn's mother taught her that "independence is the only solution," and that "women are as good as men." Her free spirit illuminates her finest roles, including Jo in *Little Women* and Tracy Lord in *The Philadelphia Story*, two of the many films she made with director George Cukor.

Hepburn holds the record for Academy Award nominations (12) and has won the Oscar for Best Actress four times, the last in 1981 for *On Golden Pond*. While filming *The African Queen* on location with director John Huston, she balked at getting into the water: "The river's full of crocodiles!" Huston blithely replied that a few rifle shots would scare them away. "All right," said Hepburn, "but what about the deaf ones?" Her last film with Spencer Tracy, *Guess Who's Coming to Dinner*, was finished just weeks before Tracy died, in 1967. Of the man she never married she wrote, "We passed 27 years together in what was to me absolute bliss."

Audrey Hepburn sparkled as the eccentric Holly Golightly in *Breakfast at Tiffany's*, based on the Truman Capote novel. But it was her later role as UNICEF's Goodwill Ambassador that won her the most widespread admiration.

Katharine Hepburn played the spoiled socialite Tracy Lord with Jimmy Stewart in the 1940 classic *The Philadelphia Story*. In 1981 she portrayed an aging widow in the Broadway play *West Side Waltz* (inset) by Ernest Thompson, who also wrote *On Golden Pond*.

The Dagwood sandwich, created by Dagwood Bumstead, is an artful blend of whatever happens to be in the refrigerator—anything from lunch meats to leftovers.

Foil-wrapped Hershey's Kisses have changed remarkably little since they were first introduced in 1907. The Hershey's factory can produce 33 million of these tiny teardrop-shaped candies every day.

Henry Wadsworth Longfellow's epic poem, *The Song of Hiawatha*, borrowed the name of a Mohawk, but took its story from another tribe.

## HERO SANDWICH

Whether you call it a hero (coined because of the heroic appetite it takes to finish one), a sub, a zep, a grinder, or a hoagie, it's a slice of Americana. No one is sure of the origins of this larger-than-life sandwich, but in 1955 *The Saturday Evening Post* described it thus: "a noble edifice built of meats, cheeses, fish—preserved and pickled—and fresh vegetables and greens, all stuffed into a whole long loaf of bread and laved generously with oil, herb-flecked vinegar and other delicious lubricants." More than 40 years later, the hero is much the same. Only the price has changed. A sandwich that cost from 25 cents to a dollar in 1955 might cost more than $5 today.

## HERSHEY CHOCOLATES

Milton S. Hershey, originator of the American chocolate bar, was a producer of caramels until he saw some German chocolate-making machinery at an exposition. Fascinated, Hershey sold his caramel plant, bought the equipment, and with it created his first milk-chocolate bars and other novelties. In 1905 he opened a factory near his birthplace in rural Pennsylvania, near sources of the fresh milk essential to quality. Mass production of milk chocolate had begun.

Hershey Bars—later joined by rivals like Baby Ruth, Oh Henry! and Tootsie Roll—became a national obsession. They gratified the sweet tooth and provided quick energy. Handed out by chocolate-toting GIs during World War II, they became international symbols of America.

## HIAWATHA

Hiawatha is a heroic peacemaker in Iroquois legend, part historical figure and part myth. According to the legend, there was a time when the Five Nations of the Iroquois, who lived in what is now New York State, engaged endlessly in bloody warfare with one another. Deganawidah, a Huron Indian prophet, had a vision of the tribes united under the branches of a symbolic Tree of Great Peace. This vision so inspired Hiawatha, a Mohawk chief and medicine man, that he traveled among the tribes to spread the message of unity.

Some tribes were more easily converted than others: to win over the demonic Onondaga chief, Atotarho, Hiawatha is said to have had to straighten Atotarho's crooked mind and body and to have combed snakes from his hair. Around the year 1570, the chiefs of the five tribes gathered at a great council and formed the Confederacy of the Iroquois, which united the tribes but left them independent. To seal this pact, each tribe clasped the hands of the others "so firmly that a falling tree should not sever them."

The Confederacy of the Iroquois proved so effective that American statesmen used it as a model when they established a new government after the Revolutionary War.

## HICKOK, "WILD BILL"

James Butler Hickok's raucous life as a frontiersman and gunfighter earned him the nickname "Wild Bill" at a young age. In 1861 he got into an argument with David McCanles and killed him and two others—the first three of 36 deaths for which Hickok would later admit responsibility. He served as a scout and sharpshooter during the Civil War, and did so again during the Indian wars of 1868.

Hickok's reputation with a six-gun got him appointed marshal of the rip-roaring cattle town of Abilene in 1871. He lost the job when he fatally shot a rowdy cowboy and, by accident, one of his own deputies.

In 1876, while playing poker in a Deadwood saloon, he was shot in the back of the head by the notorious outlaw Jack McCall. He was buried at Mount Moirah Cemetery in Deadwood, near the grave of Calamity Jane, to whom, according to some accounts, he was secretly married.

## HINDENBURG

Before it crashed in Lakehurst, New Jersey, on May 6, 1937, the German-built *Hindenburg* was the largest, most luxurious aircraft in the world. Almost as long as an ocean liner, the cigar-shaped dirigible was held aloft by 16 huge hydrogen-filled balloons enclosed in a fabric-covered aluminum frame. The passenger quarters, lower in the hull, included 25 staterooms, an elegant 50-foot dining room, a lounge complete with grand piano, and a smoking room sealed against possible leakage of the flammable gas. Windows tilting downward offered breathtaking views of land and sea.

On its 11th transatlantic crossing, a three-day voyage, the giant airship carried 36 passengers and 61 crew members. Thunderstorms near Lakehurst delayed the craft's landing. Then, as it approached its mooring mast, watchers on the ground—including a horrified radio reporter—saw a sudden flash. In less than a minute, the entire airship was ablaze. Astonishingly, two-thirds of those on board survived. Although its exact cause was never determined, the disaster signaled the end of lighter-than-air travel.

## HIPPIES

With their celebration of free love, use of psychedelic drugs, and communal living, the hippies of the 1960s brazenly challenged the values of the "Establishment." Heirs to the "hipster" Beatniks of the previous decade, they first appeared on college campuses during the era of sit-ins and anti-Vietnam War protests. Their emphasis on environmental conservation, along with the communes they founded in San Francisco's Haight-Ashbury district, Manhattan's Lower East Side, and many rural areas, has led historians to compare hippies with 19th-century Utopian idealists. Many people dismissed hippies as dropouts, but to others they were the gentle conscience of a tumultuous period in our history.

Some passengers managed to escape from the stern of the *Hindenburg*, which settled downward while flames raced toward the nose. A cabin boy was saved from burning when a water tank burst above him.

Hippie clothing featured colorful tie-dyed T-shirts and such ethnic influences as sequined vests and the beaded jewelry of gypsy dress.

Scoring the final goal against the Soviets in the semifinals of the 1980 Olympics, Mike Eruzione (21) won a breathtaking underdog victory.

Allegedly the victim of a mob hit, Jimmy Hoffa was never found. Theories on his final resting place range from a field in Michigan to the swamps of New Jersey to the end zone of Giants Stadium.

Billie Holiday developed her performing style in the late 1930s, singing with a gardenia in her hair and snapping her fingers just behind the beat. She brought a sense of sadness and vulnerability to her music. "I've been told that nobody sings the word *hunger* like I do," she said.

## HOCKEY

The world's fastest team sport, hockey is an exciting blend of spectacular teamwork and jarring physical contact. The game grew up on the frozen ponds and rivers of Canada. Informal competition between teams became a ritual in 1893, when Lord Stanley of Preston bought a $49 punch bowl that became known as the Stanley Cup. Teams around the world have been vying for it fiercely ever since. The National Hockey League began in 1917 and has prospered; by the 1990s it had teams in such unlikely venues as Florida and Texas.

Today professional hockey is known for its furious rivalries, spontaneous action, and imposing stars. Fans of yesterday flocked to watch the goal-scoring prowess of Gordie Howe of the Detroit Red Wings and the two-way skills of Bobby Orr of the Boston Bruins. In the 1980s and '90s, Wayne Gretzky brought finesse and star appeal to the game.

## HOFFA, JIMMY

Jimmy Hoffa is best remembered not for his achievements as a labor leader but for his mysterious disappearance from a restaurant parking lot outside Detroit in 1975. An unpretentious Indiana native, James Riddle Hoffa started as a union organizer in Detroit during the Depression and became the Teamsters' president in 1957. He expanded the union's size and boosted pay and benefits for truck drivers, winning their loyal support. The government, however, believed he was a Mafia pawn who allied unions with organized crime. Convicted of jury tampering and fraud, he was imprisoned in 1967. Freed in 1971, Hoffa was trying to regain control of the Teamsters when he vanished.

## HOLIDAY, BILLIE

She couldn't read music, but when Billie Holiday reshaped a lyric with her small, plaintive voice and lazily released it, a pop song became an emotionally charged transmission of life experience. "What comes out is what I feel," explained Holiday. "I have to change a tune to my own way of doing it. That's all I know." As a child, she was moved by the music of Bessie Smith and Louis Armstrong. As an adult, she became "Lady Day," the essence of the jazz performer and an influence on nearly every major singer of her generation.

Born Eleanora Fagan in Baltimore in 1915, Holiday was the child of an unwed teenage mother and a guitarist, Clarence Holiday, who later deserted the family. Raised by other relatives, she went to New York in 1928 to find her mother. Because her mother couldn't support her, Eleanora was forced to work on the streets to survive. In the early '30s she took the name Billie, for the actress Billie Dove, and her father's last name, and began singing in small Harlem clubs. Producer John Hammond discovered her and got her some recording dates. These all-star sessions often included saxophonist Lester Young, whose airy improvisations were a perfect foil for Holiday's light voice. Many of these recordings, such as "What a Little Moonlight Can Do" and "I Wished on the Moon," became jukebox favorites.

Holiday was a sensation at the Apollo with Count Basie's orchestra in 1937. She joined Artie Shaw in 1938 and was one of the first black singers to work with a white band. Admired as a singer, she was nevertheless forced to use the back door and was unable to dine with the band. On her own, she gained a following at one of the first interracial clubs, the Café Society. She introduced the song "Strange Fruit" (about a lynching) and often sang her own compositions, such as "Gloomy Sunday," "God Bless the Child," and "Fine and Mellow." But alcohol, heroin addiction, and unhappy marriages dulled her voice, and she died at the age of 44.

Pranksters changed this famous sign to read HOLYWOOD during the pope's visit in 1987 and OLLYWOOD in honor of Lt. Col. Oliver North.

## HOLLYWOOD

When moviemaking was in its infancy, pictures were turned out on the East Coast. In 1913 Cecil B. DeMille went to Arizona to direct a movie called *The Squaw Man*, but he didn't like the scenery. He got back on the train and ended up in a place called Hollywood, the name that one Mrs. H. H. Wilcox had given to her husband's ranch in the late 1880s. DeMille found it a peaceful place. He converted a stable into a studio and started production. DeMille's partners were Jesse Lasky and Samuel Goldwyn; this was the beginning of what would one day be called Paramount Pictures.

Other producers followed the pioneers; they found California an ideal location for moviemaking. Its golden sunshine allowed them to film outdoors without artificial lighting, and weatherwise it beat the Bronx. By 1920 the industry was there to stay. Hollywood transcends its physical boundaries, and not every movie is made there, yet for decades the name has conjured up magic for millions. Not that everybody has stars in their eyes. W. C. Fields once complained, "It's hard to see where the D.T.'s end and Hollywood begins."

Attending a gala 1940 Hollywood premiere for *All This and Heaven Too* are Elsa Maxwell, Jack and Ann Warner, Norma Shearer, and David Lewis.

## HOMECOMING

Homecoming is an occasion for Americans to return to the scenes of their youth—to show off their mates, their offspring, their material success, and their expanded waistlines to old friends and classmates. As an autumn ritual, homecoming naturally inspires a certain amount of pomp and ceremony. Along with impassioned support for the home team during the big football game, and tailgate parties in the surrounding parking lots, most reunions reach a climax with the coronation of the "homecoming queen." Typically, this transient member of schoolyard royalty is chosen from the ranks of the current student body on the basis of popularity and comely appearance. The honor is perceived, in the words of one Texas Plains high school homecoming queen, as "the most exciting thing that will ever happen."

Wearing a formal gown and her glittering tiara, the homecoming queen often leads the homecoming parade in an open convertible.

Homer, inspired by the thundering surf, spent his last 27 years on the rocky Maine coast. "Eight Bells" (above) is one of his sea classics. "Autumn" (right), painted in 1877, shows an earlier style that documented everyday life.

Honeymooning, from left, are Ralph, Norton, Alice, and Trixie. Ralph thinks that he's the king of his castle and that the "I do" of the wedding vows should be the last decision a wife can make—but, in fact, Alice is the one in charge.

## HOMER, WINSLOW

One of the most powerful storytellers of the 19th century was Winslow Homer, whose medium was not prose but paint. In nearly 1,000 watercolors and oils, this taciturn, somewhat reclusive artist spoke volumes about his country, especially the outdoors that he loved. "The Sun will not rise, or set, without my notice and thanks," he wrote.

Homer first developed his narrative skill as a lithographer and illustrator. After covering the Civil War for the popular pictorial *Harper's Weekly*, he traded woodblocks for a paint box and began producing a poignant record of contemporary American life. Homer's early works are terse tales that demonstrate his genius for distilling the drama of a moment.

However, his later works—the marine paintings—are epics that pitch stout fisherfolk, sailors, and coast guardsmen in a never-ending struggle against the elements. His seascapes portray a world in which humanity is but a minor element overshadowed by gusting clouds, gale-driven waves, and the formidable forces of nature.

## HOME SHOPPING NETWORK

The debut in 1977 of Home Shopping Network (HSN), the nation's first cable-TV retailer, opened a new frontier for consumers. HSN offered Florida viewers 24-hour-a-day access to an array of merchandise—everything from costume jewelry and whoopee cushions to designer dresses, Ginsu knives, and toilet brushes. The concept was simple: get the customer where he or she lives—literally, at home in front of the TV—and make the experience fun. Choose an ebullient hostess and let her patter about each product as though she were a friend along on a shopping spree. Display a toll-free phone number and urge viewers to place their orders—quickly.

By 1987 HSN had some 25 million viewers nationwide. Imitators followed, most notably the QVC network. Together they sell more than $2 billion in must-have items each year.

## HONEYMOONERS

"In my part of Brooklyn, we had a million Ralph Kramdens," said Jackie Gleason about the bus driver from Bensonhurst trying to make a better life for himself and his wife, Alice. Along with his neighbor and best friend, Ed Norton, Ralph schemes to get rich quick. In one episode, Alice is hiding a dog from Ralph and stores some dog food in their icebox. Ralph discovers the bowl, samples it, and declares he can make a fortune selling "KramMars Delicious Mystery Appetizer." He's also always trying to get in good at work. At one point, he pretends to be a golfer, and his boss invites him to play. So Ralph tries to learn the game from a book. To help his buddy, Ed shows Ralph how to address the ball: he touches his hat and says, "Hello, ball!"

A roll of Alice's eyes is more threatening than Ralph's "Someday… Bang! Zoom! To the moon!" They battle fiercely but make up sweetly: he kisses her and says, "Baby, you're the greatest." TV audiences agreed. They watched various incarnations of *The Honeymooners* from 1950 to '66; the 39 episodes that were filmed from 1955 to '56 are still in reruns.

## HONKY-TONK

Sometimes a dance, more often a dingy "juke joint" lit up in neon at the border of "wet" and "dry" counties, honky-tonks were places where workers in oil-rich areas of Texas came to unwind, drink, and listen to some energizing twangy music in the 1930s and '40s. Glen Campbell later called them "the fightin' and dancin' clubs." To be heard in the raucous din, country bands added pianos, string basses, and occasionally drums to increase the rhythmic drive. Guitarists, who had taken to slapping the strings percussively, were delighted to change over to electric guitars, which were more powerful.

Thus the louder, insistently rhythmic country dance music, a cousin of western swing, became known as honky-tonk. While country pretties itself for commercial success, there are still hard bands playing honky-tonk in many a Southwestern town long about Saturday night.

## HOOD ORNAMENTS

The first hood ornaments functioned as radiator caps on early automobiles, and because they were highly visible, they were sculpted into many dramatic shapes. Soon both automakers and the buying public thought of them as status symbols. When the radiator cap was placed under the hood, the hood ornament became purely decorative. Dodge dreamed up the butting ram, Pontiac chose the chieftain, and Lincoln had the leaping greyhound. In the safety-conscious 1960s, protruding ornaments were deemed dangerous to pedestrians, so carmakers redesigned them. Most were scaled down into the logolike symbols we see today.

## HOOVER, J. EDGAR

Until his death in 1972, J. (for John) Edgar Hoover was the most feared and, by some, the most revered man in America. Hoover transformed the Federal Bureau of Investigation (FBI) almost single-handedly and ran it with determination for 48 years. A master of publicity, he kept the FBI's name in the news by chasing bank robbers, Nazi spies, and Soviet agents, and became known as the nation's "number one policeman." The FBI almost ignored organized crime until the Kennedy administration's initiatives forced Hoover's hand. (It was Treasury agents, not the FBI, who sent Al Capone to prison for income tax evasion.)

Hoover was pilloried for using the Bureau's mission against communist subversives to justify spying on Americans whose political views differed from his own. Still, his FBI is credited with developing the most effective methods of investigation of any law enforcement agency.

Packard buyers of the '30s could opt for a winged figure (above) instead of the standard cormorant (right).

The Cadillac shield (left) was framed by a laurel wreath in the Greco-Roman tradition.

J. Edgar Hoover mugs with a bulldog. The former had a reputation for being tenacious and powerful—the latter still does.

Hoover Dam contains 3.25 million cubic yards of concrete weighing 6.6 million tons. It cost $108 million to build. Utility customers repaid the sum, making the last payment in May 1987.

Hopalong Cassidy first galloped onto the television screen in 1948. By the '50s, *Hopalong* merchandise was in great demand.

Bob Hope (right) shares a joke. He often uses one-liners, such as his greeting to GIs at a remote base during World War II: "Greetings, fellow tourists."

## HOOVER DAM

If the arid states of the Southwest have brought forth avocados, lawns, the glitter of Las Vegas, and the desert megalopolis that has Los Angeles as its hub, it is thanks to the Hoover Dam. Begun during the administration of Herbert Hoover, the dam was inaugurated by President Roosevelt in 1935 as the Boulder Dam (Congress renamed it in 1947). This immense concrete faucet on the Colorado River provided drinking water, irrigation, cheap electricity, and security from floods to Arizona, Nevada, and southern California.

The dam became the flagship project of Roosevelt's New Deal and, ironically, was in the end a vindication of the much-criticized Hoover administration. For in the midst of the Depression, government and the private sector had collaborated to tame nature, raise standards of living, and create thousands of jobs—without raising taxes.

## HOPALONG CASSIDY

As a young actor, William Boyd was a favorite of Cecil B. De Mille, who gave him parts in several silent spectaculars. Unfortunately, there were two other actors named William Boyd and Bill Boyd, one of whom was involved in a gambling and liquor scandal during Prohibition. This made things awkward for Boyd. The upshot was that when he starred in a 1935 movie, *Hop-A-Long Cassidy*, he picked up the name, dropped the hyphens, and hastily learned how to ride Topper, the horse. He played in more than 54 Hoppy episodes until 1943. Later, having prudently acquired the rights to the character, Hopalong Cassidy made a fortune on television, showing the old films and making new ones.

## HOPE, BOB

"This is Bob Broadcasting from Camp Cooke Hope, telling all you soldiers to use Pepsodent.... Boy, is this camp tremendous... I never saw so many soldiers. They got five buglers here just to wake up the buglers!" During World War II, Bob Hope's Tuesday-night broadcast, often from army and navy bases, was the most popular comedy program on the home front, and his extensive overseas tours to entertain the troops made his reputation as comedy ambassador of goodwill.

As a song-and-dance man, Hope had starred on Broadway before getting his own radio show in 1938. His breezy monologues were written by a team of gagmen; his cast included the wide-eyed comedian Jerry Colonna. For Paramount he made many movies, among them the popular *Road* movies with Bing Crosby and Dorothy Lamour. He first appeared on TV in 1950 and has been doing specials ever since. A frequent Academy Awards host, he has won five Special Awards. He continued to entertain troops overseas through Desert Storm in 1990–91. In appreciation, his many fans would echo the theme song he has used for almost 60 years: "Thanks for the memory..."

## Hopper, Edward

The strongest presence in Edward Hopper's paintings is absence—of people, of connection, of personal interaction. A man of "semi-funereal solemnity," as a friend once remarked, the artist projected his own predilection for solitude onto his work, which forms an index of 20th-century alienation. Hopper adopted a spare, realistic style as the vehicle to transport his vision of the modern age. "My aim in painting has always been the most exact transcription possible of my most intimate impressions of nature," he said. And he chose commonplace subjects that let him show the superficial face of America while also exposing an intense emotional undercurrent.

There are houses without residents, stores without shoppers, and churches without worshipers—a reflection of Hopper's appreciation of architecture and his sense of isolation. A frequent traveler, especially when suffering from painter's block, Hopper conveyed a certain rootlessness with images of hotels, trains, gas stations, and especially roads. Intensifying the pervasive loneliness is Hopper's use of light, whether glaring to define every detail or fading to symbolize loss and despair.

The interior of the diner in Hopper's "Nighthawks" (above) is viewed from the outside looking in, which creates the sense of detachment and separateness that infuses his work.

## Hopper, Hedda

Just the words "This is Hedda Hopper's Hollywood" were enough to make radio listeners salivate. Formerly a supporting player in movies, Hedda Hopper began her 28-year journalistic career in 1938, dishing dirt on the stars in print and over the air. She fought for scoops with rival columnist Louella Parsons; both wielded such power over haute Hollywood that Hedda called her home "the house that fear built." Once, when she printed unkind remarks about Joan Bennett, the actress retaliated by sending Hedda a live skunk. Hedda acknowledged the gift in her column the next day, adding that she'd christened the skunk "Joan."

Hedda Hopper was famous for wearing enormous, flamboyant hats. She titled her autobiography *From Under My Hat.*

## Horne, Lena

She moves like a cat, graceful and poised. She doesn't sing the blues, but when performing a song like "Stormy Weather," her trademark, her voice changes from sweet to husky. Now in her seventies, Lena Horne is still a beauty. Born in 1917 into a socially prominent black family, Horne got a job as a dancer at Harlem's Cotton Club at age 16. She began singing in the mid-1930s and was the first black woman to sing with a white band at the Savoy-Plaza and the Copacabana. She also built a following at the Café Society Downtown. Recruited by Hollywood for roles in *Cabin in the Sky* and *Stormy Weather,* Horne became a star. On Broadway in the '50s, she had a two-year run in *Jamaica,* and in 1981 she was in *Lena Horne: The Lady and Her Music,* which ran for 333 performances, setting a record for a one-woman show.

A versatile artist with striking looks, Lena Horne escaped stereotyping with her charismatic singing style. In 1984 she received a Kennedy Center award.

Hot dogs got their strange name in 1906. A cartoonist saw a vendor's sign that read "dachshund sausage—red hot" and drew a picture to illustrate it.

## HOT DOGS

Sausages may come from Frankfurt or Vienna, as the names frankfurter and wiener imply, but the hot dog, a sausage served in a long bun, is an all-American creation. The first hot dog bun was actually a pair of cotton gloves that had to be returned to the vendor for the next customer. The bun we know today was probably born in the 1880s, when a St. Louis sausage vendor tired of giving his customers gloves and put his sausages on bread instead.

How many hot dogs do Americans eat? About 16 billion a year, or 65 per person. To keep up, the Oscar Mayer company rolls 36,000 franks off its "hot dog highway" every hour.

## HOT RODS

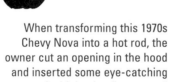

Beginning in the 1950s, generations of car-crazed craftsmen turned assembly-line automobiles into vehicles for self-expression. Teenagers learned to salvage jalopies headed for the junkyard and hot-rod them, or turn them into drivable art. They would install a more powerful engine, lower the chassis, strip off the chrome trim, and perhaps mount whitewall tires and paint flames on the hood. The goal was sleekness and power—the ability to accelerate from zero to 60 mph in four seconds and cover a quarter-mile drag-racing strip in 10 seconds. The ongoing passion for hot-rodding has inspired a magazine *(Hot Rod)* and popular songs, such as "Little Deuce Coupe" by The Beach Boys.

When transforming this 1970s Chevy Nova into a hot rod, the owner cut an opening in the hood and inserted some eye-catching fuel-injection "trumpets."

## HOUDINI, HARRY

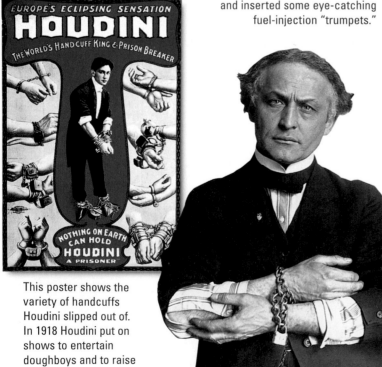

This magician, escape artist, and contortionist was, above all, a brilliant showman. Born in 1874, 17-year-old Ehrich Weiss took the name Harry Houdini and began performing magic in vaudeville. In his spare time he fiddled with handcuffs. He found that most used about a dozen designs and were no match for a few concealed keys and a bent-wire pick. Houdini was an astute promoter, too. He challenged police all over the world to keep him shackled. He broke out of leg irons, safes, coffins, straitjackets, even prisons. It took him just 27 minutes to escape from a lockup on "Murderer's Row," free the prisoners, and move them from one cell to another.

Houdini would hold an audience rapt as they watched the drawn curtain, the coffin, or the padlocked water tank on the stage. Before submerging himself in water in St. Louis, for example, he reminded his audience that he would drown unless he escaped in minutes and invited them to hold their breath, too. The tension rose quickly as one minute passed, then another. After three minutes, breathless spectators gasped in anxious anticipation. Just then, out sprang Houdini to thunderous applause. He died on Halloween in 1926. To this day, magicians annually assemble at the grave of the man whose name remains synonymous with the art of miraculous escapes.

This poster shows the variety of handcuffs Houdini slipped out of. In 1918 Houdini put on shows to entertain doughboys and to raise money for war bonds.

## HOWARD JOHNSON'S

For 60 years the familiar orange roof of a Howard Johnson's roadside restaurant gave truckers, salesmen, and families far from home the illusion of never having left. They might not know what state they were in, but at a Ho-Jo they knew exactly what to expect: 28 flavors of buttery ice cream, fried clams, and waitresses who were forbidden to chew gum, be grouchy, or tap their pencils while taking an order.

When entrepreneur Howard Johnson bought a soda fountain in Massachusetts in 1925, he tasted the vanilla ice cream served there and didn't like it. He replaced it with his own formula—a thick, rich ice cream that was an instant hit. Before long, he expanded his operation by franchising his name, the orange-and-aqua look, and the simple Yankee food. In the late 1970s, at the peak of the Ho-Jo era, more than 1,000 nearly identical restaurants served the country.

Orange roofs make the restaurants highly visible. Founder Howard Johnson used signature colors on his early ice cream stands as well.

## HOWARD UNIVERSITY

In the years immediately following the Civil War, a number of predominantly black universities were established. The largest was Howard University, acclaimed as "the capstone of Negro education." Howard was founded in Washington, D.C., in 1867 and named for Gen. Oliver O. Howard, a Union officer with an interest in the education of blacks. The university has graduated many of the country's black doctors, architects, and engineers. Alumni include Nobel laureate Toni Morrison and former New York City mayor David Dinkins. Of the illustrious company he shares, Dinkins said, "It is reassuring to know that I walk down freedom's road in the company of so many dedicated, courageous fellow foot soldiers."

Thurgood Marshall (right), shown here with Gov. Averell Harriman, was a Howard University alumnus. He became a judge for the U.S. Court of Appeals in 1962, and in 1967 he rose to the U.S. Supreme Court.

## HOWDY DOODY

When *The Howdy Doody Show* premiered on December 27, 1947, the star of the show was a disembodied voice in Buffalo Bob Smith's desk drawer. The first marionette was so ugly that it terrified children. But by the spring of 1948, Howdy had arrived. With Buffalo Bob's help, Howdy's TV show ran five days a week—live, before 40 lucky kids sitting in the Peanut Gallery. Clarabell's practical jokes kept the young audience screaming. In Doodyville, puppets outnumbered humans. Flubadub—six creatures in one—was the main circus attraction; Phineas T. Bluster was Howdy's archenemy.

For families all over America, the half hour before dinner was Howdy Doody time. Howdy went off the air in 1960, but his legacy continues: the cartoon strip "Peanuts" was named after the Peanut Gallery, and the creators of the Teenage Mutant Ninja Turtles borrowed "Cowabunga" from the greeting Buffalo Bob exchanged with Chief Thunderthud. Today Smith keeps Howdy in his study at home, and they go on nostalgia tours, to the delight of the Doodyville Historical Society.

This five-year-old won a Howdy Doody look-alike contest in the '50s, for which NBC received 17,000 photos. The grinning 26-inch puppet became one of television's first stars.

## HUDSON RIVER SCHOOL

The members of the 19th-century Hudson River School, the first distinctively American school of painting, were intoxicated with the American wilderness. They saw each plunging gorge, silvery stream, shimmering leaf, and fallen log of New York's Hudson Valley as an item of divine creation, which they rendered in reverent detail. Their view of painting as a form of prayer or praise—a kind of "visual sermon"—gave their work a moral purpose that won over an American public that was historically suspicious of art as useless, undemocratic, and effete.

The painters claimed to have learned more from the vistas they depicted than from any European master. For Thomas Cole, one of the school's founders, nature alone was "the star by which [the painter] is to steer to excellence in his art." His sketching partner, Asher Durand, exhorted aspiring artists to practice painting in the open air even before they sought any schooling. The only human intrusion in their landscapes was the occasional distant figure—"an Indian Hunter judiciously introduced...with his rifle leveled," suggested Cole.

## HUGHES, HOWARD

As dashing as Indiana Jones and as reclusive as the Wizard of Oz, the "bashful billionaire" has a special place in America's gallery of gifted eccentrics. Howard Hughes inherited the Hughes Tool Company by age 18 and left for Hollywood soon after. In six years he produced several legendary movies, including *Hell's Angels*, *Scarface*, and *The Front Page*.

Hughes then turned to aviation, a childhood passion. In 1935 he flew a record 352 m.p.h. in the technologically revolutionary H-1 racer, which he designed. Two years later, the plane streaked from Los Angeles to Newark in just under 7½ hours. In 1938 Hughes broke the round-the-world record in a Lockheed monoplane, flying 14,716 miles in three days, 19 hours, 8 minutes, and 10 seconds. One of his few commercial flops was the largest plane ever built, a troop transport called the "Spruce Goose" because it was constructed of plywood.

Never an extrovert, Hughes went into seclusion in 1950. Rumors abounded: he suffered from dementia; he secretly controlled a vast financial empire; his male aides were permitted to touch him only through multiple layers of Kleenex. When his million-dollar "memoirs" were revealed to be the work of forger Clifford Irving, the mystery only deepened. Emaciated and deranged, Hughes died in 1976 in an air ambulance returning to the U.S. from Mexico. He left no will.

## HUGHES, LANGSTON

Irresistible wit and restless exuberance made Langston Hughes a leader of the Harlem Renaissance writers. He captured on paper the sounds and rhythms of black speech and music, and he maintained throughout his career a balance between accessible simplicity and awe-inspiring profundity.

"In the pure blue sky is the highest sublime," wrote Thomas Cole, who preferred the cascade in "Genesee Scenery" to nearby Niagara Falls.

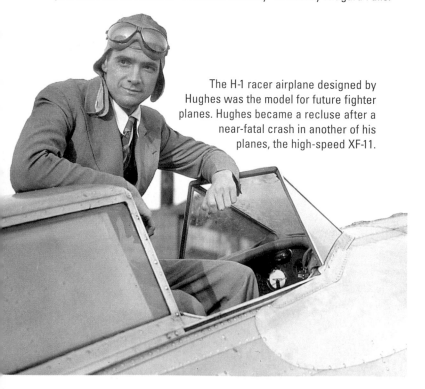

The H-1 racer airplane designed by Hughes was the model for future fighter planes. Hughes became a recluse after a near-fatal crash in another of his planes, the high-speed XF-11.

"I, too, sing America," wrote Hughes. Like the jazz music that inspired his rhythms, his poetry contains, as one reviewer wrote, "the same fire and steel" hidden in even the most jubilant Dixieland tune. From the drowsy, slow-burning passion of "The Weary Blues" to the frenetic "Montage of a Dream Deferred," Hughes wrote about people who, as he put it, are "up today and down tomorrow, working this week and fired the next"—ordinary people in "the quarter of the Negroes," where "The past has been / A mint of blood and sorrow— / That must not be / True of tomorrow."

## HUNTING

For a hunter, there's nothing better than waking before dawn and shivering silently in a damp duck blind, waiting for a migrating flock to land, or trekking for hours through thickets and forests in pursuit of prey that will be spooked if you get upwind, much less too close.

Opening day of hunting season is, for many, a chance to forget the rigors of the workplace and return to an earlier type of life in which survival was a matter of skill and daring. The ways of the woods—making campfires and telling stories, as well as tracking, shooting, gutting, and skinning—are often passed down from father to son. Comforts are few, but there is a unique camaraderie among men (and women) who pit themselves against beasts in the age-old ritual of the hunt.

## HUSTON, JOHN

One of the most flamboyant personalities in screen history, John Huston had the theater in his genes. His father was the distinguished actor Walter Huston, and his aunt was the voice teacher Margaret Huston Carrington, who trained John Barrymore for his celebrated 1922 Hamlet. But in his restless youth, Huston was a boxer, a reporter, and a cavalry officer in the Mexican Army before becoming a director.

Huston's first film was *The Maltese Falcon* (1941), considered by many the best detective movie of all time. In it, Huston's father can be glimpsed as the murdered sea captain. After the war, Huston won two Academy Awards, for writer and director of *The Treasure of the Sierra Madre*; another Oscar went to his father for best supporting actor. He went on to direct such memorable films as *The Red Badge of Courage*, *The Asphalt Jungle*, and *The African Queen*.

Huston's eventful private life included five wives (actress Anjelica Huston is the daughter of the fourth) and countless romances. In 1952, angered by Hollywood blacklisting, he moved to an estate in Ireland, where he enjoyed playing lord of the manor. A vivid fictionalized portrait of Huston on location in Africa while directing *The African Queen* was painted by Peter Viertel in his novel *White Hunter, Black Heart*, later made into a movie starring Clint Eastwood. In 1985 Huston directed daughter Anjelica in *Prizzi's Honor*, for which she won Best Actress. His last film was James Joyce's *The Dead*.

A trusty bird dog is a valuable companion for upland bird hunters. Other hunters rely on hound dogs to follow the scent of game animals.

Huston played the role of Noah (left) in the 1966 film *The Bible*, which he directed. Also a writer, he was the author of the screenplay for *Sergeant York*.

The arrival of the iceman was a happy occasion, especially for children, who enjoyed eating the ice chips that splintered from the big blocks.

"I scream, you scream, we all scream for ice cream"—whether in splits, in sundaes, or straight from the carton.

> *"And so, my fellow Americans, ask not what your country can do for you; ask what you can do for your country."*
>
> JOHN F. KENNEDY

## ICEBOX

An icebox was exactly what its name says: a box that held ice. For much of the 1800s and early 1900s, the best way to keep perishables from spoiling was to keep them, along with ice, in an insulated container. The system worked well, as long as one remembered not to open the box too often and to empty the drip pan before it overflowed.

At first, ice was quarried from northern lakes, ponds, and streams during the winter and stored in thick-walled ice-houses and in caves. The first ice-manufacturing plant was built in 1868 in New Orleans, and within a decade many restaurants and hotels had their own ice-making machines. Although refrigerators with electric and gas-driven motors have been a fixture in American homes since the 1920s, some people still slip and call them iceboxes.

## ICE CREAM

Ice cream is an American tradition. George Washington spent $200 on ice cream during the summer of 1790. Thomas Jefferson brought a recipe for ice cream, made with egg yolks and an exotic spice called vanilla, back from France, and First Lady Dolley Madison served it often at the White House.

In 1846 a woman named Nancy Johnson invented—but didn't patent—an ice cream freezer that made the making of ice cream at home practical, if not easy. A lot of ice, salt, and arduous hand cranking were required, plus a fair amount of patience while waiting for the ice cream to harden. Store-bought ice cream became available soon after. The treat was made even more convenient when it was first served in cones at the 1904 St. Louis World's Fair.

Vanilla, chocolate, and strawberry were the original options offered. Howard Johnson's upped the ante by advertising 28 flavors. Baskin-Robbins makes hundreds of flavors and has tried many others, including a 1965 blend made with gumdrops that never made it to the market: the frozen candies were hard enough to crack teeth. Whatever their favorite flavor, Americans eat about 14½ quarts of ice cream a year.

## ICED TEA

Iced tea was virtually unheard-of before 1904, when Richard Blenchynden added ice to his hot brew in order to make it more appealing to the sweltering crowds at the St. Louis World's Fair. Because it was nonalcoholic and refreshing, the drink became a favorite of the temperance movement.

Today in the South, sipping tall glasses of iced tea with friends is a ritual that rivals the English afternoon tea. Elsewhere in the country, the popularity of iced tea has soared, inspiring marketers to introduce herbal and fruit-flavored varieties. Because iced tea delivers a pleasant dose of caffeine with virtually no calories (unless you add sugar), it's a perfect drink for the weight-conscious. Some steep it in sunshine and garnish it with lemon, sugar, or mint, but those who can't wait can mix it from a powder.

With utmost grace, Kristi Yamaguchi captivated the world during the 1992 Olympics. She was the first female figure skater to win the gold for America since Dorothy Hamill in 1976.

## ICE SKATING

As a branch of competitive ice skating, figure skating has distinctly American origins. The English style of skating featured little more than figure-eight patterns. In the mid-1860s a young ballet dancer from New York named Jackson Haines revolutionized the sport by incorporating daring jumps into his free-flowing program. In 1937 a former Olympic champion from Norway named Sonja Henie made the first of a dozen Hollywood films that helped figure skating to become part of the American winter tradition. In recent years indoor rinks have been packed with skaters inspired by the heroes of the latest winter games.

Approaching speeds reached by thoroughbred racehorses, speed skaters compete in five events ranging from 500-meter sprints to 10,000-meter endurance races. During the 1980 Olympics, Eric Heiden made speed-skating history when he swept every race and won five gold medals. Bonnie Blair competed in the 1988, 1992, and 1994 Olympics to garner five gold medals—more than any other American woman.

Speed-skating favorite Dan Jansen poses with his daughter, Jane. The nation cheered when he captured the Olympic gold in 1994 after a series of heartbreaking losses.

## I LOVE LUCY

When Lucille Ball asked that Cuban bandleader Desi Arnaz play her husband in an upcoming television series, the network told her that no one would believe they were a married couple. "What do you mean nobody will believe it?" she replied. "We *are* married!"

*I Love Lucy*, starring Lucille and Desi as Lucy and Ricky Ricardo, with Vivian Vance and William Frawley as their best friends, Ethel and Fred Mertz, debuted in 1951. Most episodes began with a squabble over something Lucy wanted to do. Step by step, the situation would escalate into the crazy slapstick that made the show so popular. Lucy's wild-eyed celebrity hunting at the Brown Derby restaurant culminated in the dumping of a tray of desserts on William Holden. When returning from a trip to Europe, Lucy disguised a 25-pound hunk of cheese as a baby in order to smuggle it on the plane.

By its 26th episode, *I Love Lucy* had been seen on more than 10 million television sets (there were only 15 million in use at the time). In its second season, it made history again when Ball's pregnancy was written into the script. More people watched the episode in which Little Ricky was born than watched Eisenhower's inauguration two days later.

In a classic episode, Lucy rehearses a commercial for Vitameatavegamin: "It's so tasty . . . just like candy." The elixir, however, tastes awful, and, with 23 percent alcohol, it gets Lucy tanked before she can finish the taping.

VITAMEATAVEGAMIN
FOR HEALTH

In the words of Benjamin Franklin, nothing in this world is certain but death and taxes. Out of desperation, many taxpayers seek help from professional tax preparers.

High-octane gas, seat belts, and rear-view mirrors have all been tested at Indianapolis; but it's the race that draws the crowds. Pit crews (below) refuel the car and change its tires in a matter of seconds.

## INCOME TAX

"Taxes are what we pay for a civilized society," said Oliver Wendell Holmes. But Americans pay them with a reluctance deeply rooted in history. It wasn't until the Civil War that the first income tax was levied, and then only as a war measure. Congress tried to re-establish the tax during the depression of the 1890s, but the Supreme Court ruled that it posed a "communistic threat" to property, and was therefore unconstitutional. That barrier was removed in 1913, when the 16th Amendment to the Constitution was adopted, and a year later the income tax became a regular source of federal revenue.

The initial tax rate was only 1 percent on net income over $3,000 and 6 percent on net income over $500,000, but by World War I, the maximum tax had soared to 77 percent. Throughout the 20th century, taxes have risen sharply to pay the high cost of wars, then fallen during peacetime. This has resulted in so many changes to the U.S. Tax Code that it is now more than 2,000 pages long. Many Americans think their taxes are too high—not a new concern. "What is the difference between a taxidermist and a tax collector?" asked Mark Twain. "The taxidermist takes only your skin."

## INDIANAPOLIS 500

America's first auto race was run only nine years after a practical car was built. Six cars raced 54 miles through the snow-clogged streets of Chicago on Thanksgiving Day 1894. The average speed: 6.5 miles an hour. Even so, spectators P. E. Studebaker, Henry Ford, Alexander Winton, and Ransom E. Olds were encouraged to build automobiles. By 1909 Indianapolis was the center of the new industry, and it needed a high-speed test track to help improve its cars. The track, a 2½-mile rectangle with curved and banked corners paved with 3.2 million bricks, was called the Brickyard. Engineers figure that 200 laps equal 50,000 miles of highway driving, and what they have learned has shown up in new cars in the form of fuel injection, four-wheel brakes, and radial tires.

The track, which is used year-round for tests, hosts the 500-mile race once a year. On May 30, 1911, the first race was won, by a car called the Marmon Wasp going at an average speed of 74.6 miles per hour. The Indy hasn't changed much since then, although drivers now wear helmets and fire-retardant suits and drive a bit faster—about 230 mph.

## IN GOD WE TRUST

"In God We Trust" is the motto used on all U.S. currency. It first appeared on a bronze two-cent piece in 1864 in response to a swelling of religious sentiment during the Civil War. Secretary of the Treasury Salmon P. Chase chose the now-familiar epithet over several others, including "God Our Trust" and "God and Our Country."

The words were briefly removed at the suggestion of President Theodore Roosevelt, who believed that putting

God's name on a coin was a sacrilege. But in 1908 the motto was restored by an act of Congress. It wasn't until 1957 that the saying was first seen on paper currency. In the 1960s a whimsical takeoff began appearing in stores: "In God We Trust. All Others Pay Cash."

The 1864 two-cent piece (left) was the first coin to bear the U.S. national motto, "In God We Trust." The words occur in verse four of "The Star-Spangled Banner."

## INSTALLMENT PLAN

Paying for purchases on the installment plan is a perfect example of American optimism. Both sellers and buyers are betting that the economy will keep booming and employment will remain steady, so that making equal payments over time will be no problem. But the payments sometimes last longer than the pleasure, as Willy Loman lamented in *Death of a Salesman*: "I would like to own something outright before it's broken!" Nonetheless, the installment plan remains a primary tactic for "keeping up with the Joneses."

Originally, installment loans were offered by stores or banks on houses, vehicles, and appliances—things that could be repossessed if the payments weren't made. In the 1960s and '70s it became possible for Americans to "buy now, pay later" for almost anything, thanks to Visa, MasterCard, and American Express. Later, Discover and a host of other widely distributed credit cards were introduced. Most people handle the temptation well, but a few get carried away and end up consulting credit counselors, who generally order them to cut up their cards and buy only what they have cash for.

## INTERNET

In the 1990s, when people go surfing, they're most likely "surfing the 'net," short for Internet. After connecting, via your phone line, with millions of computers around the world, you can view up-to-the-minute news posted on bulletin boards, retrieve documents from libraries and databases, read your (electronic) mail, or talk, by keyboard, to other "Internauts" in chat groups on every imaginable topic.

It all started in 1969, when the Defense Department created the first big computer network, ARPAnet. This linked computers at several universities and military facilities around the country. The advantage of such a system was that because ARPAnet did not depend on a central computer, it was resistant to large-scale destruction, including nuclear attack. Soon other networks using the same technology were formed. When all these networks were linked, the result was the Internet, the "network of networks," available to any computer owner who subscribes to the service.

The Internet has developed its own "netiquette." Asking obvious questions is scorned and could get you "flamed," that is, insulted by others who are on-line at the same time. Typed language is made faster and more expressive by abbreviations that range from "LOL" for "laughing out loud" to "emoticons"—sideways faces, such as the smiley :-) or the more stressed-out =:-0.

"On the Internet, nobody knows you're a dog."

Coffee shop patrons in Cambridge, Massachusetts, can buy time in cyberspace on the Internet, with lunch on the side.

Published in 1952, Ralph Ellison's *Invisible Man* won the 1953 National Book Award for fiction. Suddenly famous, Ellison (right) became an effective spokesman for blacks. He is shown here with author John Cheever.

When Washington Irving's Rip Van Winkle woke up after a 20-year nap, he discovered that he was living in a new nation.

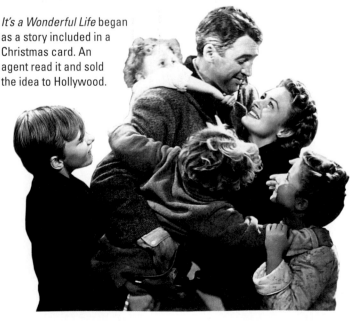

*It's a Wonderful Life* began as a story included in a Christmas card. An agent read it and sold the idea to Hollywood.

## INVISIBLE MAN

Widely regarded as one of the most influential novels on racism in America, Ralph Ellison's *Invisible Man* combines surrealism with folklore to show the experiences of people whose skin color has made them invisible to white society.

Again and again in the novel, the Invisible Man tries to make himself noticed, first by excelling academically, then by becoming a black nationalist, but he is repeatedly betrayed or ignored. "I have been called one thing and then another," he says at the end of the book, "while no one really wished to hear what I called myself." Painful though it is to exist without being seen, he discovers that "even an invisible man has a socially responsible role to play," as long as he chooses action over passivity and does not strive for "colorlessness."

## IRVING, WASHINGTON

Before 1820, American writers suffered an inferiority complex next to the great tradition of British literature. The pious moral tales and derivative poetry of the early republic did not reflect the new nation's exuberance. So when Washington Irving's whimsical tales appeared under the title *The Sketch Book of Geoffrey Crayon, Gent.*, readers on both sides of the Atlantic were astonished by his talent. Irving's subsequent publications, including *The Alhambra* and *A Tour on the Prairies*, earned him a vast fortune and introductions to American presidents and European aristocracy.

His two best-known tales are set in the Hudson River valley of upper New York. "Rip Van Winkle" is about a Dutch colonist who sleeps for 20 years, missing the American Revolution. "The Legend of Sleepy Hollow" presents a headless horseman who chases a country bumpkin named Ichabod Crane through the woods at night. Readers who are curious about whether true events inspired Irving's tales should note that Irving himself wasn't sure: "I am always at a loss to know how much to believe of my own stories."

## IT'S A WONDERFUL LIFE

Asked why this movie was his favorite, Jimmy Stewart replied, "It's based on a simple idea—you are not born to be a failure." No matter how you look at it, *It's a Wonderful Life* is one of the most cherished films of all time and is shown repeatedly on TV during the Christmas season.

It started with a fable written by Philip Van Doren Stern, an editor, Civil War historian, and—of all things—horror-story anthologist. Director Frank Capra, who also co-wrote and produced it, said of the lead, "I knew one man who could play it." It was Stewart, who won an Academy Award nomination in 1946 for his portrayal of family man George Bailey, who loses and regains his faith in life with help from his friends and an angel called Clarence. As a tribute, the Jimmy Stewart Museum, in his hometown of Indiana, Pennsylvania, is housed in a replica of Bailey's movie-set Building & Loan.

## IVY LEAGUE FOOTBALL

The Ivy League schools—Princeton, Dartmouth, Columbia, Harvard, Yale, Cornell, Brown, and the University of Pennsylvania—produce some of the country's best scholars and worst football teams. For the most part, the schools emphasize studies over sports, and they refuse to recruit athletes who can't meet their rigorous academic standards. In Ivy League football, winning isn't everything: tailgating and cocktails in the parking lots and tales of cleverly stolen mascots are also treasured.

In 1875, when Harvard and Yale started their gridiron rivalry—known to their alumni as "The Game"—few schools had teams, so they were among the best. For the Ivy colleges, whether they can beat outside teams is irrelevant. The question is whether they can beat each other.

## IWO JIMA

The battle for Iwo Jima, a volcanic island 660 miles south of Tokyo, was the most bitter in the Pacific. The U.S. wanted the eight-mile-square island as a base for air strikes against Tokyo and as an emergency-landing site for crippled B-29 bombers. But the Japanese were deeply entrenched, with over 600 gun positions and 10 miles of underground tunnels.

American warships bombarded the island for 75 days, and on February 19, 1945, 30,000 marines landed on the steep beaches. After five days of bloody fighting, where gains were measured in yards, the marines seized Mount Suribachi, the highest point on the island. They planted an American flag in the soft volcanic ash. A second flag raising later in the day, captured by Associated Press photographer Joe Rosenthal, became one of the most famous pictures of the war.

Mount Suribachi was captured, but the fight was only beginning. The battle raged across steaming sulfur pits and barren ridges for another month before the U.S. could declare Iwo Jima secured. Because both sides fought unflinchingly, casualties were extremely high: more than 6,800 Americans and nearly all of the 21,000 Japanese defenders died. It was a battle, said navy admiral Chester Nimitz, in which "uncommon valor was a common virtue."

## JACKS

Throughout U.S. history, kids have crouched on sidewalks, kitchen floors, and playground blacktops, bouncing rubber balls into the air and rushing to snatch up the six-pointed jacks.

Just as imaginative as the game's variety of moves—in which the players catch and toss different numbers of jacks with specified motions of the hand—are the names of these variations, or "fancies." In Raking Leaves, players rake the jacks with their hand one-by-one into a pile before picking them up between ball bounces. Other colorfully titled jacks games include Cherries in the Basket, Breaking Eggs, and King Cobra, one of the hardest of all the fancies.

Ivy League mascots include the Cornell bear, the Princeton tiger, and the Yale bulldog.

Iwo Jima was returned to the Japanese in 1968, but the U.S. flag still flies over the island four times each year: on Independence Day; Veterans Day; Memorial Day; and February 19, the date of the American invasion.

Jacks has its roots in ancient games called dibs and knucklebones, which were played with stones, bones, seeds, or little bags of sand.

## JACKSON, ANDREW

Andrew Jackson was the first frontier president, but his manner was that of an aristocrat. As a young man climbing the ranks of Tennessee politics, he still had rough edges. "I had a fight with Jackson," said Sen. Thomas Hart Benton. "A fellow was hardly in fashion who didn't."

In 1812 Jackson was appointed major general of the Tennessee Volunteers. He and his troops put down a Creek Indian uprising in the Mississippi Territory and defeated the British at the Battle of New Orleans, for which Jackson was hailed as the greatest hero of the War of 1812.

Jackson was elected the country's seventh president in 1828 and soon changed the course of national politics. He championed the cause of the common man, putting men of humble birth in high office and ruining the Second Bank of the United States because of what he considered elite interests. His critics called it "mob rule," but Jackson answered, "The great can protect themselves, but the poor and humble require the arm and shield of the law."

Still, while he supported the common man, he also favored the Indian Removal Act of 1830, which exiled several Indian tribes to Western lands at the cost of many lives.

## JAMESTOWN

Jamestown was the first permanent English settlement in North America, although its settlers were so unprepared that it hovered near extinction for years. In 1607, 105 English colonists enlisted by the Virginia Company of London landed on a peninsula in the James River, where they built Jamestown. The land was swampy, and within seven months more than 60 colonists had died, probably of dysentery and typhoid fever.

Most of the group were gentlemen adventurers, and, wrote Capt. John Smith, there was "no talke, no hope, nor worke, but dig gold, wash gold, refine gold, load gold." Instead of hunting or fishing, they ate up the ships' supplies and bartered for food with the increasingly wary Indians.

The colonists needed strong leadership, and in 1608 Smith took charge and made them plant crops and build houses. But when he returned to England the following year, work stopped. In the "starving time" during the winter of 1609–10, 90 percent of the settlers died.

Prosperity came in 1612, when John Rolfe introduced tobacco growing, which was so profitable that tobacco was grown even in the streets. Rolfe later married Pocahontas, the daughter of an Indian leader. The union helped bring peace between the settlers and the Indians.

The first legislative assembly in the New World met in Jamestown in 1619, but as the colony of Virginia expanded, the town lost its importance. Part of Jamestown was burned down in 1676, and in 1699 the capital was moved to Williamsburg.

After two terms in office, Andrew Jackson retired to the Hermitage, his vast cotton plantation in Tennessee, but he remained active on the nation's political scene.

This artist's rendition shows part of Jamestown as it may have looked in 1614. Today, remains of building foundations and the ruins of a church tower are all that can be seen of the original town.

# JAZZ

A uniquely American music, jazz developed into an improviser's art, built on the rhythmic play called "swing." The skill required to create melodies on the spot, while responding to the other players, put jazz at the cutting edge of music. Its intense pleasures can be sampled today in dark dives or on festival stages from New York to Bombay or Beijing.

Jazz was born in the brew pot of New Orleans at the turn of the 20th century, when slave chants and spirituals were mixed with European hymns and harmonies. In small bands, like that of Joe "King" Oliver, improvisations on cornet, clarinet, and trombone created the vibrant "New Orleans style." Piano "rags" by Scott Joplin had gentle syncopation, and "ragtime" started to swing with the springy piano playing of Ferdinand La Menthe (Jelly Roll Morton).

As jazz moved upriver to Chicago, Oliver's protégé, cornetist Louis "Satchmo" Armstrong, emerged as the first great jazz soloist. Among pianists, Chicago virtuoso Earl "Fatha" Hines, influenced by Armstrong, played trumpetlike lines.

In New York, James P. Johnson and Thomas "Fats" Waller played stride piano, which Art Tatum brought to the zenith of sophistication. Nat "King" Cole played a more modern swing. During the big band craze of the 1930s, ensembles led by Benny Goodman and Count Basie thrived. Coleman Hawkins established the tenor saxophone's role in jazz, and Basie's saxophonist, Lester "Prez" Young, inspired the "cool school" of the '50s with his zephyrlike phrasing.

After World War II the sharpening skills of improvisation reached a peak in "bebop," especially in the agile lines of alto saxophonist Charlie "Bird" Parker. Pianist Thelonious Monk's eccentric tunes became part of the bebop language. The next revolution came with saxophonist John Coltrane's "sheets of sound" approach in the '60s. By the mid-'90s, talented, academically trained young players, such as trumpeter Wynton Marsalis, mined earlier styles and sought the individuality that had characterized the greatest jazz innovators.

# JEEPS

In 1940 army brass ordered automotive engineers to come up with a no-nonsense, "low-silhouette scout vehicle." What they got, one journalist noted, looked like a "sturdy sardine can on wheels." The vehicle had dozens of nicknames, but "Jeep" was the name that stuck. Some claim the nickname was borrowed from Eugene the Jeep, a little creature in the *Popeye* cartoons. A more likely origin is the military's designation of "General Purpose" vehicle, shortened to G.P.

In 1951 a jeep was exhibited at New York's Museum of Modern Art, along with a Bentley, a Mercedes, and a Cord, as one of the world's automotive masterpieces. A museum curator explained that the jeep possessed "the combined appeal of an intelligent dog and a perfect gadget." Indeed, the WW II jeep served as a model for today's sporty, all-terrain vehicles.

Leading the pack in composition, arrangement, and personal style, Miles Davis (below) moved into jazz-rock fusion in the 1960s.

Jazz trumpeter Dizzy Gillespie (above) coined the term *bebop*. In the 1950s he toured the Middle East and South America as an ambassador of goodwill for the U.S.

William "Count" Basie's band, with its driving groove and bluesy horn riffs, set the style for the big jazz and swing bands.

The first jeep had no doors, and its only extras were a side-mounted shovel and ax.

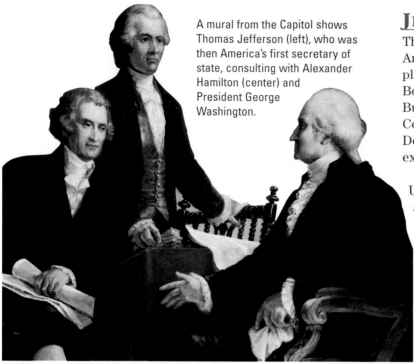

A mural from the Capitol shows Thomas Jefferson (left), who was then America's first secretary of state, consulting with Alexander Hamilton (center) and President George Washington.

## JEFFERSON, THOMAS

Thomas Jefferson was a true Renaissance man, one of America's most important statesmen as well as an accomplished architect and scientist and an ingenious inventor. Born in 1743, he was a member of the Virginia House of Burgesses by the age of 25. As a delegate to the second Continental Congress of 1775–76, Jefferson drafted the Declaration of Independence, in which he eloquently expressed the natural rights of man.

In 1800, Jefferson was elected the third president of the United States and was hailed as a "Man of the People" for advocating majority rule and the protection of civil rights. Throughout most of his political career, he also served as president of the American Philosophical Society, once calling the sciences his "supreme delight." "But," he said, "the enormities of the times in which I have lived have forced me to take a part in resisting them, and to commit myself on the boisterous ocean of political passions."

After two terms in office, Jefferson retired to Monticello, the home he had designed. Thereafter he devoted his attention to founding the University of Virginia.

## JELL-O

There's always room for Jell-O, especially when it's made into fun shapes like these "jigglers," introduced in 1990.

Jell-O, the first high-tech dessert, was so far ahead of its time, it had to wait for the infant refrigeration industry to catch up. In 1897 a LeRoy, New York, housewife, May Wait, and her husband bought the rights to a powdered gelatin mix based on an 1845 patent. They decided to add sugar to the mix and package it for sale. It was Mrs. Wait who came up with the now-famous name.

Without sufficient chilling, however, Jell-O took so long to firm up that demand was disappointing—so much so that in 1899 the discouraged Waits sold their product to marketing whiz Orator Woodward. Fortunately for Woodward, refrigeration was becoming more common in the average American home. Homemakers looking for a cool, light alternative to pies and cakes now bought Jell-O in droves. By 1906 sales reached the $1 million mark.

## JOGGING

"We can drain off tensions and negative emotions, heighten creativity, and enter altered states of consciousness," one runner proclaimed during the jogging boom of the 1970s. At its peak, some 40 million Americans striving for physical and mental fitness took daily trots around their neighborhoods. That almost anyone could run—regardless of age, gender, or athletic experience—added to the appeal of this activity.

Even nonrunners embraced "jock chic." Loose-fitting jogging suits—formerly known as sweat suits—became acceptable attire even at social gatherings. Community races attracted hundreds of joggers, many of whom entered just to get a T-shirt imprinted with the race logo.

As jogging took off in the 1970s, so did the price of running shoes, which reached $100 per pair.

## JOHN BROWN'S BODY

In 1859 abolitionist John Brown and a small band of followers seized the federal arsenal in Harpers Ferry, Virginia. They intended to provoke a slave insurrection in the South. Instead, they were quickly overpowered by a detachment of marines, and Brown was captured, tried, and convicted of treason. Within weeks he was hanged, which made him a martyr to northern abolitionists and a source of inspiration for generations to come.

After his death, the Second Battalion of the Massachusetts Infantry improvised the words of "John Brown's Body" to a revival hymn. "John Brown's body lies a-mouldering in the grave," it begins, and it became a popular marching song during the Civil War.

## JOHN HENRY

John Henry was "born with a hammer in his hand," says one ballad. He grew "almost as tall as a boxcar is long," declares a tall tale. In the early 1870s Henry (probably a real man) was one of hundreds of blacks hired in West Virginia to drive a railroad tunnel through a mountain. His foreman, calling him "the strongest steel-drivin' man alive," wagered $500 that Henry could hammer a spike faster and farther than a new automatic drill. Henry won the race but died of overexertion. Soon ballads and work songs about the duel between man and machine had spread throughout the South.

Since then, John Henry has been described as an American folk hero. By the 1960s there were approximately 50 recorded versions of "John Henry" available, sung by such artists as Harry Belafonte, Woody Guthrie, and Burl Ives.

## JOHNSON, LYNDON BAINES

When Lyndon Johnson became John Kennedy's vice president in 1960, he was already an experienced politician known for his powers of persuasion. Since 1937 he had represented Texas as congressman and later as senator. When Kennedy was assassinated in 1963, Johnson stepped into the role of president and a year later was elected to a full term by a landslide.

He called his ambitious domestic program "The Great Society," pushing through new civil rights laws, federal aid for education, and funding for a "war on poverty." But the escalation of the unpopular Vietnam War would be President Johnson's undoing. In March 1968 he called a partial halt to the bombing of North Vietnam to get peace negotiations started; he also announced that he would not seek re-election. Johnson died in 1973, and he is remembered today as he wanted to be: the president "who helped the poor to find their own way and who protected the right of every citizen to vote in every election."

Horace Pippin created several John Brown paintings, including "John Brown Going to His Hanging." The woman at the front right is Pippin's mother, who witnessed the execution.

According to tall tales about steel-driving John Henry, "When he brought his hammer down, folks three hundred miles away heard an awful rumbling sound."

During a British royal visit to Washington in 1965, President Lyndon B. Johnson danced with Princess Margaret at a formal reception in the East Room.

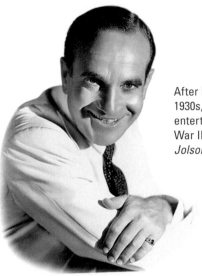

After his career declined in the 1930s, Jolson made a comeback entertaining troops during World War II. In 1946 the movie *The Jolson Story* was a big hit.

Janis once said: "If I'm going to do it, I'm going to do it for real. I can't... fake it [onstage]. I've got to let loose with what's inside."

Gracefully soaring in the air, his tongue wagging wildly, Jordan plays the game at his own speed, as if he were alone on the court. Above, he takes charge in Madison Square Garden in 1991.

## JOLSON, AL

Audiences of the 1920s adored Al Jolson's rich baritone, exuberant dancing, and magnetic personality. He once stopped during a Broadway show to ask, "Do you want the rest of this plot, or would you rather have me sing a few songs?" He sang, and the enthralled public refused to leave. "He was more than just a singer... he was an experience," recalled Eddie Cantor. Jolson is remembered for his starring role in Hollywood's first full-length talkie, *The Jazz Singer* (1927), which had a few spoken lines, including his trademark "You ain't heard nothin' yet!" and his renditions of "Mammy" and "Blue Skies."

## JOPLIN, JANIS

Electrifying rock and blues singer Janis Joplin, whose shrieking voice and uninhibited style made a song a gut-wrenching experience, had become a legend by the time she died at 27 of a drug overdose. "Janis Joplin sang with more than her voice," wrote one reporter. "Her involvement was total."

Joplin didn't fit into the humdrum world of Port Arthur, Texas, where she was born in 1943. She idolized Leadbelly and Bessie Smith, and went to Houston and San Francisco to sing in small folk clubs. Appearing with Big Brother and the Holding Company at the Monterey Pop Festival in 1967, she drove the audience into a frenzy with her shouted, danced, sweated-out version of "Ball and Chain." Soon she was leading her own band, then another one, the Full Tilt Boogie Band. After touring during the summer of 1970, the band went to Hollywood to record an album. Before it could be completed, Joplin was found dead in her motel room, victim of a heroin overdose. When the album, *Pearl*, was finally released in 1971, it rose to number one on the charts and stayed there for nine weeks. Joplin's life was dramatized in the 1979 film *The Rose*, starring Bette Midler.

## JORDAN, MICHAEL

Acclaimed by many as the greatest basketball player in the history of the sport, the Chicago Bulls guard Michael "Air" Jordan has phenomenal court skills and a superhuman physical presence. Few other players have ever matched his remarkable leaping ability and soft shooting touch. Driven to excel, he dominated the game by achieving seven straight scoring titles from 1987 to 1993, with an average of 32.3 points per game. He also led the Bulls to three consecutive National Basketball Association championships in the early 1990s. Teammate John Paxson once said of Jordan, "Night after night, year after year, he just carries this team."

Jordan transcends basketball, so much so that companies hire him to sell their sportswear, hamburgers, soda, and even underwear. His retirement from basketball in 1993 in order to play baseball stunned his fans. Yet his decision to fulfill a dream and attempt a new challenge kept fans following his progress. Jordan struggled for a season in minor league baseball but then gave it up. His simple statement "I'm back," when he returned to the Chicago Bulls in 1995, brought smiles to fans and advertisers around the world.

## JOSEPH, CHIEF

After six years of pressuring the nontreaty Nez Percé Indians to sign over the Wallowa Valley in Oregon, the U.S. Army finally forced them out in 1877. As the Indians were preparing to move to a reservation in Idaho, a handful of frustrated young warriors attacked local settlers, killing at least 18 of them. Knowing retaliation would come, Chief Joseph, one of the Nez Percé leaders, decided to flee to Canada.

He and other chiefs led a band of 150 men and their families on a fighting retreat across the mountains of Idaho, Wyoming, and Montana. For 1,500 miles they outmaneuvered and outshot the army, but when they were within 30 miles of safety, they were captured by Gen. Nelson Miles.

Although Joseph had been promised that his tribe could return to their home territory, the federal government sent them to Oklahoma, where many died. In 1885 some were allowed to go to Idaho, but Chief Joseph was sent to the Colville Reservation in northeastern Washington. He would later meet with Presidents William McKinley and Theodore Roosevelt, but he would never again see his beloved Wallowa Valley. Chief Joseph died at Colville in 1904.

Chief Joseph poses after his surrender in 1877. He spoke of his hopelessness—and that of other Indians: "I am tired.... I will fight no more forever."

## JUKEBOX

Whether in a 1930s speakeasy, a '40s soda fountain, or a '50s highway truck stop, the sound of a needle plunking down on vinyl meant one thing: your song might be next on the jukebox. A descendant of Thomas Alva Edison's phonograph, the first jukebox, called "Nickel-in-the-Slot," played one song, and only four people could listen at a time—by holding tubes to their ears. With the invention of the electric amplifier in 1927, jukeboxes became the ideal cheap entertainment for bars and diners. Soon there were more than 500,000 jukeboxes throughout the U.S., spinning dozens of records each.

In 1946 Wurlitzer rolled out the definitive jukebox, Model 1015, which had an arch of neon tubing and a shiny plastic-and-chrome exterior. Competition between Wurlitzer and its two main rivals, Rock-ola and Seeburg, resulted in ever more ornate jukeboxes with names like Luxury Light-Up, Spectravox, and Rocket. One over-the-top model earned the nickname Mother of Plastic.

This 1941 Wurlitzer was a forerunner of the classic Model 1015. By the 1950s, no diner worth its salt was without tabletop versions (below).

Bar owners have always taken great care hand-picking songs, frequently stocking the jukebox with singles by local bands. This practice helped R & B and country singers in the 1920s and rock and roll singers in the '50s. The first selection is usually reserved for the owner's favorite song. It's likely to be Patsy Cline's "Crazy" or Elvis Presley's "Hound Dog"—the two most popular jukebox songs ever.

Dolls (left to right): the Heart of Sky God holds sticks representing lightning; the horned doll takes part in a rite of initiation; Mudhead the clown plays games with children.

Boris Karloff and Elsa Lanchester (above) appear in *The Bride of Frankenstein.* The monster goes mad when his intended rejects him. Bela Lugosi as Dracula (left) stalks his prey in the 1931 film.

## KACHINA DOLLS

To the Hopi and Zuni Indians, kachinas are supernatural beings who live in the mountains of Arizona and ensure abundant harvests and fertility. Six months of every year, from the winter to the summer solstice, kachinas send their spirits to masked male dancers, who impersonate them. These kachina dancers perform ceremonies to bring rain, and give gifts and provide entertainment. At a young age, Hopi children are given kachina dolls—masked figures carved from cottonwood or cactus root that are decorated to resemble the dancers. These revered dolls help the children learn about the hundreds of different kachinas, from the frightening Natashka, who scolds misbehaving children, to the laughing Tcutckutu, a gluttonous clown. Today the dolls are considered folk art and are sought after by collectors and museums.

## KAISER, HENRY J.

Best known for the Liberty Ships he built to help America gear up for World War II, Henry J. Kaiser was the quintessential "can-do" industrialist. Kaiser, the son of poor German immigrants living in Upstate New York, began working at age 13. By age 20 he had saved enough money to buy the local photography shop, and he later moved to Washington State. In the rapidly industrializing West, Kaiser became a successful builder of urgently needed roads, bridges, and dams. He called problems "opportunities with their work clothes on" and solved them ingeniously. To transport cement over a mountain to a dam-building site, for example, Kaiser constructed a nine-mile conveyor belt. When he started building ships in 1940, Kaiser's novel use of prefabricated sections made it possible to complete a vessel in 4½ days. By war's end, his shipyards had built a third of the U.S. merchant fleet.

## KARLOFF, BORIS

Hailed as the king of Hollywood horror films, Boris Karloff won immortality as the hulking monster in the 1931 classic *Frankenstein.* Karloff was actually a mild-mannered, cultivated Englishman, christened William Henry Pratt, who was expected to become a diplomat. Instead, he turned to acting, adopted a Slavic-sounding name, and won the *Frankenstein* role when Bela Lugosi, star of the recent sensation *Dracula,* rejected it because it was a nonspeaking part.

To impersonate the lumbering creature brought to life by mad scientist Victor Frankenstein, Karloff endured daily four-hour makeup sessions, wore awkwardly shortened sleeves to make his arms look longer, and walked in heavily weighted boots. These devices and Karloff's expert pantomime made the movie—and Karloff—an instant hit. He played in two Frankenstein sequels and dozens more monster movies, occasionally appearing with Lugosi. Unlike Lugosi, however, Karloff also showed his versatility in some less horrific roles. Monster films have enthralled moviegoers since the silent era, when Lon Chaney, Sr., starred in early versions of *Phantom of the Opera* and *The Hunchback of Notre Dame*, among others. Why were these movies so successful? Clearly, people love to be scared.

Many of these spine-tingling tales had their roots in perennially popular legends about dead people restored to menacing life or living people transformed into fiendish beasts. But the most memorable monsters had another dimension: they were driven to violence by supernatural forces or by their pursuers' irrational hostility. Most of Karloff's voluminous fan mail showed compassion for Frankenstein's misunderstood monster. King Kong was another pathetic hunted figure. Even Dracula had been turned into a blood-sucking vampire by a cruel curse; the werewolf played by Lon Chaney, Jr., in *The Wolf Man* suffered a similar fate. Later monster movies, from *Invasion of the Body Snatchers* to *Alien*, have drawn audiences into their macabre worlds mainly through ever-more-spectacular special effects.

## KAZAN, ELIA

The foremost American director of his generation, Kazan is noted for his forceful, sometimes melodramatic style. Of his work he has said: "I've always been crazy for life. As a young kid I wanted to live as much of it as possible, and now I want to show it—the smell of it, the sound of it, the leap of it." In 1947 he institutionalized that creative energy when he co-founded the Actors Studio, where actors could study Method acting and learn to immerse themselves in their roles.

Kazan began as an actor with New York's Group Theatre, which produced realistic plays in the 1930s. In 1942 he made his first stage hit with Thornton Wilder's *The Skin of Our Teeth*. In the 1940s and '50s, Kazan divided his time between the stage and the screen. For the stage he directed award-winning productions, including *Death of a Salesman* (1949) and *Cat on a Hot Tin Roof* (1955). As a director of films, he brought some 20 actors to preeminence.

## KAZOO

Remarkably, the easy-to-play kazoo is descended not from an ancient toy but, rather, from a much-feared weapon of intimidation. The kazoo's African ancestor, an early form of flute known as a mirliton, was used by tribal chieftains to mask their voices and to create fearsome, unnatural noises that enemy tribes might take to be evil spirits.

Kazoos became important in early American blues and jazz; singers used them to make their voices loud enough to compete with stringed instruments. The cigar-shaped tube has a resonating membrane that covers a hole at the top. By singing or humming through it, players can create their own music, disguise their voices, or mimic other sounds. Versatile and fun to use, the kazoo is popular with just about everyone who can sing, hum, or speak.

Kazan cast Marlon Brando as Stanley Kowalski and Vivien Leigh as Stella in the 1951 film *A Streetcar Named Desire* (above). Kazan (right) won two Academy Awards for his film work.

Kazoos can take various shapes, as shown here. For a homemade instrument, wrap a tissue around a comb and blow through it.

In *Sherlock, Jr.,* Keaton steers the motorcycle from the handlebars after the driver falls off. His claim to fame: never cracking a smile, no matter how funny the scene.

Anne Sullivan gave Helen Keller the key to language—a manual alphabet. But she didn't want Keller to learn to speak. Only after the girl begged did Sullivan agree to teach her.

Audiences adored the sorry sight of Emmett Kelly's Weary Willie, who chased a patch of sunlight with an old broom as he swept the ring.

## KEATON, BUSTER

Joseph Keaton came from a family of acrobats and was nicknamed Buster by the escape artist Houdini. He began making silent two-reelers in 1917; within four years he was the star and artistic director of Buster Keaton Productions.

Known as "The Great Stone Face," Keaton's comic persona was a deadpan young man who, unlike his rival, Charlie Chaplin, stoically survived outlandish adversity and still managed to get the girl. Among his countless movies were *The General* (1926), a Civil War story in which he rescues a locomotive, and *Steamboat Bill, Jr.* (1928), in which a two-ton house falls on Keaton, who emerges through a window opening, impassive and unscathed. When his career declined in the 1930s, MGM gave him a small office, where he spent his days at a workbench, making ingenious props. The 1950s brought a Buster Keaton revival and, with it, the acclaim and appreciation due this great silent comedian.

## KELLER, HELEN

Blind, deaf, and mute from the time she was stricken with scarlet fever at 19 months, Alabama-born Helen Keller began to find her way out of darkness in 1887, when she was seven. Her parents, despairing of their wild, uneducable child, applied to Boston's celebrated Perkins Institute for the Blind in the hope that a specially trained teacher could be of help. Perkins appointed a recent graduate named Anne Sullivan, and within months the strong-willed teacher and the unexpectedly bright student were communicating by means of the manual alphabet and a rudimentary Braille-based vocabulary.

Over the next decade, Keller and Sullivan became inseparable as Helen progressed and her fame grew. In 1900 Keller applied and was admitted to Radcliffe College. With Sullivan as her interpreter and guide, she carried a full course load and graduated with honors. She then embarked on a career of writing and social advocacy, championing rights for the handicapped, militant feminism, pacifism, and civil liberties. To earn a living, Keller and Sullivan also appeared on the vaudeville circuit, and Keller became chief spokesperson for the newly established American Foundation for the Blind. Honored throughout the world for her courage in the face of severe handicap, Keller died in 1968 at the age of 87. Together with Sullivan she has been the subject of several books and of the play and movie *The Miracle Worker*.

## KELLY, EMMETT

"Send in the clowns!" orders the circus ringmaster in the event of mishap. The most famous clown of all was Emmett Kelly, whose stubble-chinned Weary Willie, with his battered derby, raggedy pants, and flapping shoes, was loved by young and old. A Kansas farm boy, Kelly was a sign painter, a cartoonist, and a trapeze artist; the Depression-inspired Willie did not appear in all his wistfulness until the early 1930s.

Kelly clowned his way up the circus ladder, reaching the biggest top of all when he became a major attraction at Ringling Brothers Barnum & Bailey Circus. In the 1950s he made two movies: *The Fat Man* and Cecil B. DeMille's star-studded *The Greatest Show on Earth*. In 1957 Kelly left the circus to be clown mascot for the Brooklyn Dodgers. He later did a nightclub act and television commercials, but the Big Top stayed in his heart. "The laughter of children is a sound no circus clown can ever forget," he said.

## KELLY, GENE

In *Singin' in the Rain* (1952), possibly the best movie musical ever made, Gene Kelly created art out of lousy weather. Kelly was brought to Hollywood by producer David O. Selznick after his Broadway success in *Pal Joey*. His first film, *For Me and My Gal* (1942), co-starring Judy Garland, was produced for MGM by Arthur Freed, who recognized Kelly's talents and made him a film choreographer.

Unlike pencil-slim Fred Astaire, Kelly was husky, an athletic rather than an elegant dancer. He was among the first to integrate dance into the narrative to advance the plot. For *Anchors Aweigh* (1945) he created an ingenious dance sequence with an animated mouse. When he directed *On the Town* (1949), he shot most of it on location in New York City, then considered a wildly innovative idea. *An American in Paris* (1951) ended with a 17-minute ballet choreographed by Kelly; that year he won a special Oscar for his achievements. In 1960 he was awarded the Chevalier of the French Legion of Honor for his choreography for the Paris Opera.

## KELLY, GRACE

Although she made only 11 films, Grace Kelly left some indelible screen images: her fashion-plate appearance in James Stewart's seedy apartment in *Rear Window*; groping for the scissors in *Dial M for Murder*; her love-scene fireworks with Cary Grant in *To Catch a Thief*.

Born into a wealthy Philadelphia family, Kelly attended private schools and an acting academy. Her good looks led to modeling jobs, Broadway, Hollywood, and her first starring role, in *High Noon* (1952). Only two years later she won an Oscar for *The Country Girl*. While filming on the Riviera, she met Prince Rainier III of Monaco, and in 1956, in the romantic setting of the ancient principality, the movie star became Her Serene Highness. Americans were swept up in the worldwide wedding fervor. To Alfred Hitchcock, who had cast her in three thrillers, her retirement meant the loss of his ideal "cool blonde"; he spent the rest of his life trying to replace her. (Kelly was grateful to Hitchcock, and invited him to her bridal shower. His gift: a shower cap.) As Princess Grace, she devoted herself to her family and to cultural and charitable interests. Her life ended too soon in a car accident on a treacherous mountain road on the Côte d'Azur.

Gene Kelly celebrates with joyous abandon in *Singin' in the Rain,* a spoof of Hollywood's transition from silents to talkies.

To many, Grace Kelly led a fairy-tale life even before becoming a princess. After marrying, she turned down all film roles, saying, "One cannot do everything."

Part of the attraction of the Kennedy administration was the presence of young children in the White House for the first time since Theodore Roosevelt was president.

## KENNEDY, JOHN F.

John F. Kennedy's election to the presidency in 1960 ushered in an era of high hopes and idealism. At 43, he was the youngest president the country had ever elected, and his youthful vigor was apparent from the start. "Let the word go forth from this time and place... that the torch has been passed to a new generation of Americans," he said in his stirring inaugural address, vowing to fight "the common enemies of man: tyranny, poverty, disease, and war itself." He established the Peace Corps, for which thousands of young Americans volunteered, expanded civil rights, and launched the race to put a man on the moon. In his first 100 days in office, Kennedy's popularity soared, boosted by his magnetic personality and the style and vitality of his wife, Jacqueline.

But international crises loomed. The Cold War mounted, leading to the building of the Berlin Wall, and Kennedy accepted blame for the disastrous attempted invasion of Cuba at the Bay of Pigs. He was lauded for his handling of the Cuban Missile Crisis and for negotiating the nuclear test ban treaty that was signed by the U.S., Great Britain, and the Soviet Union.

On November 22, 1963, Kennedy was assassinated in Dallas, and a stunned nation—and world—mourned his passing. Mayor Willy Brandt of West Berlin said, "A flame went out for all those who had hoped for a just peace and a better life."

## KENNEDYS

No family in America has earned as much public glory or suffered as much private sorrow as have the Kennedys. The marriage of Joseph P. Kennedy to Rose Fitzgerald in 1914 united two of Boston's most prominent political families. Kennedy vowed that he would be a millionaire by the time he was 35, and he was as good as his word, making a fortune in real estate and on Wall Street. From 1938 to 1941 he served as American ambassador to England.

Rose instilled in their nine children a sense of ambition and public duty, and saw them scale great heights. John was elected president, Robert became his attorney general, and Edward was a senator at the age of 30. But tragedy was never long at bay. Joseph Jr. died in battle in World War II, daughter Kathleen died in a plane crash in 1948, and both John and Robert were assassinated.

Rose lived to the venerable age of 104, long enough to witness the successes of the next generation of Kennedys. Caroline Kennedy Schlossberg became an author, Maria Shriver became a television journalist, and several other grandchildren followed their parents' path into public service.

In 1937 the Kennedy clan assembled in full force (left to right: Patricia, Joseph Jr., Robert, Kathleen, Rose, John, Rosemary, Edward, Joseph Sr., Jean, Eunice). Years later Ted said of Rose, "She sustained us in the saddest times—by her faith in God... and by the strength of her character."

## KENTUCKY DERBY

The Kentucky Derby is more than a race; it's an annual celebration of the lifestyle built around breeding and raising the world's finest racehorses in the bluegrass hills of Kentucky. The race has been called "the greatest two minutes in sports," but the television coverage lasts for hours and features gossip from the week's black-tie balls and reports about the steamboat race that is part of the festivities.

Although the race was inspired by England's Epsom Derby, its heritage is strictly American. It was started in 1875 by Meriwether Lewis Clark, Jr., the grandson of William Clark of Lewis and Clark fame, to promote his new track, Churchill Downs. At stake is one of the largest purses in horse racing, plus millions of dollars bet at the track and countless more wagered at mint-julep parties held on the big day.

## KERN, JEROME

Composer Jerome Kern, whom critic Alexander Woollcott called "that fount of melody," was responsible for the development of a distinctively American style of musical theater that flourished in the 1920s and '30s. Skimming away the froth from the Viennese operetta style that was popular until World War I, Kern created a new, more realistic form: the subjects were American, the stories were more serious, and the songs were organically tied to the story line.

Kern began his career as a song plugger, then became a "music doctor," adding songs to perk up European imports for American audiences. Among his most beloved contributions are "Smoke Gets in Your Eyes" from *Roberta*, "The Way You Look Tonight" from the film *Swing Time*, and "All the Things You Are" from *Very Warm for May*, which, for its daring yet logical and satisfying modulations, has been called "the greatest song ever written."

Kern's masterpiece was *Show Boat*. Based on the Edna Ferber novel and written with Oscar Hammerstein as the librettist, it is a modern romance that also touches on the troubles of black people. Kern encouraged younger composers, such as Harold Arlen, Richard Rodgers, and George Gershwin, to stretch beyond Tin Pan Alley. Gershwin's all-black opera, *Porgy and Bess*, was a direct descendant of *Show Boat*.

## KEWPIE DOLLS

Throughout much of this century, the most sought-after prize at carnival sideshow booths was a Kewpie doll. Kewpies are round-faced, big-eyed, winged baby imps named after Cupid. The difference, according to the Kewpies' creator, Rose O'Neill, was that Cupid was a troublemaker, while Kewpies were "always searching out ways to make the world better and funnier."

Kewpies first showed up in 1909 in a *Ladies' Home Journal* illustration. Dolls came on the market in 1912, and by mid-1913, 21 factories were busy making them. Kewpie dolls have become treasured collectibles. Fans comb flea markets looking for white-skinned, blue-winged dolls and the even harder to find black Kewpies with white wings. Avid collectors gather in Branson, Missouri, for the annual Kewpiesta and read the biannual "Kewpiesta Kourier."

The Kentucky Derby is nicknamed the "Run for the Roses" after the blanket of roses draped over the winning thoroughbred. In 1991 Strike the Gold carried the day.

*Show Boat* was the first musical to become part of an opera company's repertory. Still a stage classic, it has seen countless revivals.

### JEROME KERN MELODIES
They Didn't Believe Me (1914)
Look for the Silver Lining (1920)
Who? (1925)
Ol' Man River (1928)
My Bill (1928)
Can't Help Lovin' That Man (1928)
Why Do I Love You? (1928)
Make Believe (1928)
The Song Is You (1932)
Smoke Gets in Your Eyes (1933)
The Touch of Your Hand (1933)
A Fine Romance (1935)
The Way You Look Tonight (1935)
Pick Yourself Up (1935)
Never Gonna Dance (1935)
Bojangles of Harlem (1935)
All the Things You Are (1939)
The Last Time I Saw Paris (1941)
Dearly Beloved (1942)
Long Ago and Far Away (1944)

Kewpies graduated from drawings to Kewpie Kutouts to actual sculpted dolls. The dolls reappeared in soft-body form in the mid-1990s.

## KEYSTONE KOPS

Mack Sennett, who called himself "The King of Comedy," worked as an actor for director D. W. Griffith before becoming a director himself. In 1912 he formed the Keystone Company, which cranked out slapstick one-reelers, often at the breakneck rate of one a day. Keystone featured beautiful girls (like Gloria Swanson), inspired clowns (like Fatty Arbuckle and Charlie Chaplin), pratfalls, chases, and pies in the face. Most popular were the Keystone Kops, whose name is still synonymous with slack-jawed, bumbling inefficiency. Apparently, the Kops were a result of Sennett's belief that the boys in blue were good for a gag. Mack Swain was chief pie thrower; he later attained fame as the big-bearded baddie in all those Chaplin comedies. Why pie throwing? Filming a scene in a bakery, the Kops ran out of bricks and bottles, so one of them grabbed a custard pie, and you know the rest. Splat!

In 1937 Keystone Kop creator Mack Sennett received a special Oscar from W. C. Fields, who called Sennett a "master of fun" and "discoverer of stars."

## KIDD, CAPTAIN

William Kidd was a respectable Scottish-born shipowner living in New York City when, in 1695, he received two royal commissions from the colonial governor, the Earl of Bellomont. One directed "our trusty and well-beloved Captain Kidd" to fight piracy on the high seas, and the other hired him as a privateer—a government-supported sea raider—against the French.

Sailing in his ship, the *Adventure Galley*, Kidd headed for the east coast of Africa, but he found few French vessels to attack. There were plenty of ships from nonbelligerent countries, however, and their cargoes were too tempting for Kidd to resist. By 1697 he had turned pirate and forcibly seized as much as $400,000 in booty. Soon after he returned to New York in 1698, his murderous reputation caught up with him. The Earl of Bellomont ordered his arrest, and Captain Kidd was hanged in London in 1701.

Authorities recovered some of the gold Kidd buried at Gardiners Island off Long Island, and treasure seekers still dig for more. Although it's doubtful there is more to find, nobody can deny that the literary treasures inspired by the Kidd legend—including Robert Louis Stevenson's *Treasure Island* and Edgar Allan Poe's *The Gold Bug*—are worth discovering.

One American folktale—now known to be untrue—has it that Captain Kidd's treasure was uncovered in 1801 by John Jacob Astor, providing the basis of the Astor family fortune.

### KILROY WAS HERE

**MOST FAMOUS MAN OF WWII**

EVERYBODY knew the man by name. American servicemen in World War II carried his name to remote corners of the world. He was Kilroy, whose name GIs scrawled almost everywhere they went in the catch phrase, "Kilroy Was Here."

Was there really a Kilroy? Yes. He was James J. Kilroy, a shipyard worker from Halifax, Mass.

His widow recalls the ... of ... logan ...

would wait until the checker had gone off duty and erase the last mark. Another checker would come through again, and the riveters would get paid twice.

Just as he was going off duty one day, Jim heard his boss ask a riveter if Kilroy had been by checking rivets. The riveter said no.

When Jim heard that, he got angry because he had just checked those particular rivets. He took some chalk, went over to where the two ... en w... stand... and ...

After Kilroy began showing up everywhere during WW II, there were imitators, such as "Corduroy" and "Clem," but none was as popular as the original.

## KILROY WAS HERE

Kilroy was probably the most famous soldier of World War II. His name was scrawled on ship hulls, airplane fuselages, and latrine walls from Cherbourg to Okinawa, often accompanied by a rudimentary sketch of a bald man peering over a fence, only his long nose and grasping fingers visible. Kilroy represented every American GI who fought around the world, bragging that he had reconnoitered strategic areas long before the military brass arrived. "Kilroy was here" was even found written on Hitler's mirror at Berchtesgaden. Who was the original Kilroy? Never positively identified, he may have been a sergeant in the Air Transport Command or a foreman in a Seattle munitions factory, each of whom reportedly signed the equipment he checked. Or he may simply have been a boastful infantryman. Perhaps the most credible candidate was James J. Kilroy, a worker in a Quincy, Massachusetts, shipyard who in 1941 started marking the parts he had inspected for shipment overseas.

## KING, MARTIN LUTHER, JR.

On August 28, 1963, in Washington, D.C., Martin Luther King, Jr., held spellbound a quarter million protesters gathered in Washington, and a nation watching on television, as he spoke with a voice trained by years of preaching from pulpits. From the steps of the Lincoln Memorial, he declared, "I have a dream that one day on the red hills of Georgia the sons of former slaves and the sons of former slave owners will be able to sit down together at the table of brotherhood.... I have a dream that my four little children will one day live in a nation where they will not be judged by the color of their skin, but by the content of their character." He ended his speech by calling out, "Free at last! Thank God Almighty, we are free at last!"

In 1964 King won the Nobel Peace Prize in recognition of his leading the Montgomery, Alabama, bus boycott, founding the Southern Christian Leadership Conference, and calling for nonviolence, even when he was jailed during protests in Birmingham, Alabama. He described in his acceptance speech his philosophy, which combined Thoreau's emphasis on civil disobedience and Gandhi's insistence on nonviolence, saying, "Man must evolve for all human conflict a method which rejects revenge, aggression, and retaliation. The foundation of such a method is love."

King had enemies as well as admirers. He opposed the Vietnam War, and the FBI considered him a threat. Some black leaders denounced his commitment to nonviolence. His response to threats was, "If a man hasn't discovered something that he will die for, he isn't fit to live."

In 1968, while he was organizing a "poor people's campaign" to focus political attention on poverty, he traveled to Memphis, Tennessee, to support striking sanitation workers. On April 3, he told a crowd, "I've seen the promised land. I may not get there with you, but I want you to know tonight that we as a people will get to the promised land.... Mine eyes have seen the glory of the coming of the Lord!" The next day, King was assassinated.

King suggested in a 1968 sermon how he would like to be remembered: "Yes, if you want to say I was a drum major, say that I was a drum major for justice; say that I was a drum major for peace; I was a drum major for righteousness. And all of the other shallow things will not matter." In 1986, his birthday, January 15, was designated a federal holiday.

The main purpose of the 1963 March on Washington was to support the Civil Rights Act, which had stalled in Congress. It was passed at last in 1964.

The widowed Coretta Scott King spoke in her husband's honor at a 1983 Washington march.

## MARTIN LUTHER KING, JR.

Martin Luther King, Jr., called on his devout, scholarly background to inspire peaceful means of ending the nation's racial problems. Milestones of King's career include:

**FEBRUARY 25, 1949** After assisting his father, a pastor at the Ebenezer Baptist Church, King is ordained as a minister at age 19.

**JUNE 5, 1955** Having achieved top honors at Crozer Theological Seminary and applying his graduate fellowship to study at Boston University, he is awarded a Ph.D. in systemic theology.

**JANUARY 10, 1957** King is elected president of the Southern Christian Leadership Conference, which unifies several nonviolent civil rights groups.

**SEPTEMBER 17, 1958** He completes his first book, *Stride Toward Freedom*, a description of the Montgomery bus boycott.

**OCTOBER 16, 1962** King meets with President John F. Kennedy at the White House for a civil rights conference.

**APRIL 16, 1963** His "Letter from Birmingham Jail" is smuggled out and widely distributed. This eloquent manifesto allows him to continue to champion nonviolent protest from behind bars.

**JULY 2, 1964** King attends the signing by President Lyndon B. Johnson of the first bill of the Civil Rights Act, which bans discrimination in public facilities.

When *The Shining* by Stephen King (right) became a film, Jack Nicholson revealed the main character's dark psyche (below).

King got the idea for his first big success, *Carrie,* when he was a high school English teacher watching the pecking order among his students. The book sold more than a million copies and was made into a movie starring Sissy Spacek (left) in 1976.

After 30 years of trial and error, Richard King's ranch developed the first recognized American breed of cattle, the Santa Gertrudis.

## KING, STEPHEN

Stephen King's favorite holiday is Halloween. The blockbuster novelist believes that it's fun to be scared, and the phenomenal sales of such spine-tingling tales as *Skeleton Crew, The Dead Zone,* and *It* confirm that millions of fans agree. To King's mind, writing horror stories is not for dilettantes: "If you're not willing to go for the throat," remarks the master of the macabre, "you ought not to be in the business."

King's novels have topped best-seller lists almost as soon as they've been published. Hollywood versions of his works, including *The Shining, Christine, Cujo, Pet Sematary,* and *Misery,* have brought his fascinatingly creepy stories to even more viewers than readers. Asked why he writes horror fiction, King responds with a chilling question of his own: "What makes you think I have a choice?"

## KING RANCH

Texas's famous King Ranch was born when Richard King, a former riverboat captain, purchased 75,000 acres along the Santa Gertrudis Creek for only $300. King wanted to raise cattle, but the area was so inhospitable that most breeds couldn't survive. To remedy this problem, he crossbred Shorthorn cattle with Brahmans to produce his own hardy breed—the Santa Gertrudis. After he died in 1885, his wife, Henrietta, ran the ranch, which, by the late 19th century, had expanded to more than half a million acres. During the Great Depression, the ranch was teetering on the brink of bankruptcy when oil was discovered on its land. By 1951 more than 600 wells dotted the ranch. In the hands of King family descendants, it is now the largest privately owned ranch in the world, covering more than 1.2 million acres in Texas.

## KINSEY REPORT

Alfred C. Kinsey, America's leading demystifier of sex, was an unlikely pioneer in this sensitive field. A conservative Harvard-trained zoologist distinguished for his research on wasps, Kinsey remained married for life to the first girl he ever dated. When his zoology students at Indiana University began asking questions about sex, he looked for scientific information on the subject and was amazed to find that virtually none was available. At students' request, a course on sex and marriage was created; Kinsey, as principal lecturer, started his own research to remedy the lack of data.

Kinsey studied human sexual activity as thoroughly as he had studied insects. He and three assistants confidentially interviewed more than 11,000 men and women about their sexual practices and beliefs. They published their findings in two volumes: *Sexual Behavior in the Human Male* (1948), popularly known as the Kinsey Report, and *Sexual Behavior in the Human Female* (1953).

These reports revealed a startling gap between what people admitted to in public and what they did behind closed doors. Among the findings: sexual habits varied widely according to education and income level; premarital and extramarital affairs were unexpectedly common; masturbation was harmless and almost universal among men; and 4 percent of men interviewed were exclusively homosexual. Kinsey's interviewees may not have accurately represented the entire population, but later scholars applauded him for providing the first objective information on a subject previously obscured by myth and prejudice.

Kinsey's work, later continued by the institute he founded, heralded a new openness in America's attitude toward sex. The clinical experiments with couples later conducted by Dr. William Masters and Dr. Virginia Johnson have been widely discussed. And such radio and television personalities as Dr. Joyce Brothers and Dr. Ruth Westheimer find an eager audience for their honest advice on sex.

## KITCHEN CONVENIENCE

During the 1700s and 1800s, Americans patented a slew of mechanical kitchen gadgets, such as cherry pitters and apple peelers, but cooking still took muscle. In the 20th century, Americans, fueled by the desire to make life easier, created electrically powered devices for almost every kitchen chore, from opening cans to sealing leftovers.

In 1912 L. H. Hamilton and Chester A. Beach decided that they could increase the sales of a motor designed for sewing machines by providing attachments for sharpening knives, polishing silver, and mixing batter.

By the 1930s, gas and electric stoves had largely replaced ones powered by wood, coal, and oil. Later, pilot lights for gas stoves eliminated the need for matches, making roasting and baking as easy as turning a knob. The advent of the microwave oven in the 1970s (it was patented in 1945) made many cooking tasks faster, especially defrosting frozen food.

Refrigerators started replacing ice chests in 1918, when Kelvinator sold its first unit. Back then it was a luxury just to have a refrigerator; today it is highly desirable to have one that is quiet, has different temperature zones, and includes an ice maker and a water tap that allows kids to get a cold drink without opening the door.

## KLEENEX

Created during World War I as a substitute for cotton surgical gauze, it was sold as the "Kleenex Kerchief" in 1919. First marketed as a "sanitary cold cream remover," it won the endorsement of such stage and screen notables as Gertrude Lawrence and Helen Hayes. Kleenex buyers quickly found other uses for the product. Perhaps it was the growing awareness of germs, but to many these disposable tissues seemed superior to the pocket handkerchief when dealing with a runny nose. Customers also reported using Kleenex as a furniture duster and as a blotter for greasy French fries.

Although Kinsey's books were scholarly in tone, they set off a storm of controversy. Critics charged that he was undermining America's morals; defenders said that he was simply reporting behavior, not judging it.

Dr. Ruth Westheimer began her career giving sex advice on a radio call-in show. Known for her humor and sassy retorts, she is dedicated to educating people about sex.

When General Electric advertised this refrigerator in 1929, the company pointed out that it created no radio interference and never needed oiling.

By the time Evel Knievel retired in 1975, he had survived scores of jumps over buses, a hotel fountain, and other obstacles. He suffered 50 fractured bones, had 14 operations, and spent, all told, three years in the hospital.

Kodak made developing film easy. One simply mailed exposed film to the company and waited for the prints to return.

Telly Savalas shaved his head for a part in *The Greatest Story Ever Told* and found the look worked for him: "Once I became bald, women seemed to find me more attractive."

## KNIEVEL, EVEL

On September 8, 1974, a crowd of 14,000 watched Robert Craig "Evel" Knievel prepare to launch his Sky-Cycle X2 over the chasm of Snake River Canyon in Idaho.

This was not the stunt of some inexperienced daredevil. Knievel had cracked safes, played professional hockey, and won ski jump championships before turning to motorcycle jumping. The first success of his 16-year motorcycle career was a modest jump over two trucks. Over the years, he made an amazing $50 million in fees and product endorsements.

Although the Snake River Canyon jump carried Knievel to the peak of his fame, it did not carry him across the Snake River. One of his cycle's parachutes unfurled on the launch ramp, slowing his acceleration. He emerged from the canyon bloodied but wealthier.

## KODAK

George Eastman of Rochester, New York, introduced the Kodak camera in 1888. "Anyone who can wind a watch can use the Kodak," went the advertisement. Such a promise may seem modest today, but at the time, it was revolutionary. The camera was light, and its roll mechanism and flexible roll film replaced awkward glass plates. It cost $25 and came loaded with film for 100 pictures. With Eastman's introduction of the even smaller, lighter, and cheaper Brownie camera in 1900—it cost only $1 and sold by the millions—photography for the masses had come to stay.

Eastman coined the distinctive name Kodak because it was "short" and "vigorous," because it wasn't likely to cause trademark problems, and because he liked the letter K. To this day the Eastman Kodak Company is synonymous with film, equipment, paper, chemicals, and everything else photographers need to record the world around them.

## KOJAK

Television's Lt. Theo Kojak of the NYPD, who was on CBS from 1973 to 1978, was one of many idiosyncratic TV detectives who tended toward grit rather than glamour. Actor Aristotle "Telly" Savalas endowed Kojak with a host of endearing eccentricities: He shaved his head bald; his most visible prop was a lollipop instead of a revolver; he wore snazzy three-piece suits around the mean streets of Manhattan; and his standard greeting was a gruff "Who loves ya, baby?"

Several other TV detectives have become favorites. Peter Falk's Lieutenant Columbo shambled through his cases in a rumpled raincoat, exuding a deceptive air of bumbling geniality, while Sam McCloud, the cowboy cop from Taos, New Mexico, played by Dennis Weaver, charged around New York in a Stetson and a sheepskin jacket. In the 1980s, female cops Cagney and Lacey battled not just crime but their colleagues' sexism, and *Murder, She Wrote* featured Angela Lansbury as a schoolteacher turned mystery novelist and crime solver.

## K RATION

Every military strategist knows that "an army travels on its belly," and during World War II, the K rations that filled our soldiers' stomachs gave them something to fight for: home cooking. A daily ration contained three "meals" packed in cardboard. They were designed for easy storage and transportation: meat was canned, and coffee and juice were powdered. The chewing gum and cigarettes included in each box weren't nutritious, but they provided a needed diversion for soldiers under stress. Soldiers made fun of their monotonous fare, but they were often reminded of its value by local civilians ready to beg or trade for K rations.

## KRAZY KAT

Introduced on October 28, 1913, George Herriman's *Krazy Kat* enjoyed a 31-year run and universal acclaim as the greatest comic strip ever. Written in its own peculiar dialect that borrowed from Charles Dickens, Yiddish, and street slang, and set against an ever-changing desert backdrop, this strip broke all the rules. Looking back on it, Jack Kerouac said its humor and gently naive outlook contained "the glee of America ... its wild self-believing individuality."

Set in the enchanted Coconino County, *Krazy Kat* tells of an unlikely love triangle between a saintly cat of indeterminate gender (Krazy) enamored of an unsentimental, cat-hating mouse (Ignatz) whose efforts to "Krease that Kat's bean with a brick" are constantly thwarted by a club-wielding cop (Officer Pupp) struggling to protect the cat he adores. Ecstatic when brained by a brick, the love-blind Krazy sighs, "In my Kosmis there will be no feeva of discord ... all my immotions will function in hominy and kind feelings."

Other characters in the *Krazy Kat* menagerie included rakish Don Kiyote, wandering Bum Bill Bee, gossipy Mrs. Kwakk Wak, and the baby-delivering Joe Stork. The strip's enchanting but subtle humor confounded the uninitiated and earned cartoonist George Herriman a devoted following among the handful of readers who could grasp his genius. Fans included Pablo Picasso, Willem de Kooning, e. e. cummings, and (luckily) William Randolph Hearst, who, although there was no money in it, gave Herriman room to roam in his non-highbrow papers until the artist's death in 1944.

## KUKLA, FRAN AND OLLIE

*Kukla, Fran and Ollie* and the rest of the "Kuklapolitan Players" first went on the air in 1947. An immediate hit with youngsters, the show was on five nights a week from 1948 to 1957. Fran Allison, a former radio celebrity, played the human foil to two eccentric puppets: worrywart Kukla and lovable loafer Oliver J. Dragon (Ollie for short). Both were dreamed up by puppeteer Burr Tillstrom, who had a gift for creating unique personalities. "[Burr] never called Kukla and Ollie 'puppets,'" Hugh Downs recalled. "They were people."

K rations, designed by and named after physiologist Ancel Keys, weren't gourmet fare, but they accomplished their mission of keeping our troops strong and healthy.

Of the many animated cartoons based on Krazy Kat, the best were silent films supervised by George Herriman and released in 1916–17.

Left to right: Kukla, Burr Tillstrom, Ollie, and Fran Allison. Ollie couldn't breathe fire—an ancestor went swimming and drowned the family flame.

Having a car in L.A. is a necessity; having a fancy car is a common obsession. The average commute is over an hour each way.

Lewis W. Hine documented child labor in his photographs. Here he shows a 10-year-old at work in a cotton mill in North Carolina in 1909.

## L.A.

In the first half of the 20th century, buildings in Los Angeles were limited to a height of 150 feet as an earthquake safety measure. As a result, the city grew out, not up. Rather than a dense downtown area surrounded by suburbs, the city developed as a series of sprawling communities. As more people moved there seeking sunshine, it became, according to H. L. Mencken, "19 suburbs in search of a metropolis."

Los Angeles is tied together not by mass transit but by more than 900 miles of massive freeways. Starting in the 1940s, L.A. began suffering from serious air-quality problems: the exhaust from traffic was being trapped by the surrounding hills, causing smog to hang over the city. Auto-emission controls have alleviated the problem but have not solved it.

Life is less formal in Los Angeles; even businesspeople wear casual clothing better suited to the beach than the boardroom. The architecture is more open, and occasionally outrageous. The L.A. area embraces Hollywood, the historic capital of moviemaking, and Burbank, the nerve center of television production. Beverly Hills is a favorite place for stars to live, and Rodeo Drive is a top spot to shop. Indeed, L.A. has come a long way since Raymond Chandler called it a "city with no more personality than a paper cup" in 1949.

## LABOR MOVEMENT

Ever since the first recorded strike in America, by New York printers in 1768, the labor movement has been based on a single concept: individual workers—no match for the powerful owners of factories, mines, mills, and railroads—must unite in order to make their voices heard.

The right to organize and, if necessary, to strike was first officially recognized in 1842 by the Massachusetts Supreme Court, a milestone on the difficult and sometimes dangerous road to unionization. Bosses were often unscrupulous, even criminal, in their efforts to discourage the labor movement, summarily firing employees or beating them up for their organizing efforts. These same bosses were intent on making money and required all workers, including small children, to put in long, hard hours. Working conditions were often unsafe, and even life-threatening.

Real success came for the labor movement in the 1880s with the efforts of such groups as the Knights of Labor, the American Federation of Labor (AFL), and, in the 1930s, the Congress of Industrial Organizations (CIO)—all unions that were founded and perpetuated by dedicated, often charismatic leaders. Men like Samuel Gompers, an immigrant who brought respectability to the movement, and John L. Lewis, bookish and eloquent, struggled to introduce unity and equality to the American workplace. By the 1940s labor leaders had also waged and won a campaign against child labor, taking youngsters out of the factories and sending them to school.

## LACROSSE

The oldest known sport played in North America, lacrosse is a descendant of a rough, often brutal game played by Indian tribes and used as a means of training young warriors for battle. Disputes between tribes were often settled on the outcome of a single match, with as many as a thousand warriors taking part. Today lacrosse is played mostly in high schools and colleges throughout the Northeast. During a game, players vying for a solid rubber ball run on a 110-yard-long field. The ball is variously carried in the webbed pocket of a player's lacrosse stick, passed among teammates, knocked out of an opponent's pocket, and flung at the opposing team's goal. The free-flowing nature of the game, the players' constantly shifting from offense to defense, and the quick saves by the goalie, closely resemble those of soccer and ice hockey.

## LADIES' HOME JOURNAL

When Cyrus Curtis founded the *Ladies' Home Journal* in 1883, with the help of his wife, Louisa Knapp, he launched what would become a trendsetter among American magazines. With subscriptions starting at 50 cents a year, the *Journal* grew in just 20 years to reach more than a million faithful readers.

Edward Bok, who succeeded Knapp in 1889, filled the *Journal*'s pages with well-known fiction writers and features that broke new editorial ground—articles on home decorating and architecture, on sex education, and against patent medicines and alcohol had never before appeared in a women's magazine. But more important, the *Journal* and the many other women's service magazines like it—notably *McCall's*, *Good Housekeeping*, *Cosmopolitan*, and *Woman's Home Companion*—made it their business to give advice on "real womanhood" and on finding self-esteem within the often confining stay-at-home life of wife, mother, and homemaker. Readers responded to these articles by writing the editors nearly a million letters annually. They spoke from the heart about everything that troubled them, from their husbands' infidelities to their own weight problems.

The *Journal* and similar publications have changed markedly in recent decades, as have the women who read them. Many of today's "home book" readers are now self-reliant, career-oriented women, but they still want—and the editors provide—information, advice, and a forum for women's issues.

An attacker (in yellow) takes a swipe at the rolling lacrosse ball, and a defender (in red, at left) gives chase. The goalie (with neck guard) stands ready to catch the ball before it goes into the net.

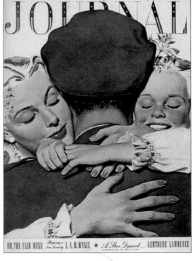

A *Ladies' Home Journal* cover is a snapshot of its time. Clockwise from top left: A 1912 cover pictures the telephone; the July 1945 issue shows a GI returning home, and the 1976 bicentennial issue carries a red, white, and blue theme.

Scrappy mutt Benji (right) charmed audiences with his heroic deeds. Although Lassie (below) is a female role, the dogs playing her have all been males.

For a time, Rin Tin Tin was Warner Brothers's biggest moneymaker and was given top billing.

When it was published in 1826, *The Last of the Mohicans* was considered controversial and drew criticism for its "idealized" and "sympathetic" portrayal of American Indians.

## LAFITTE, JEAN

Jean Lafitte, the "Pirate of the Gulf," had "a conscience as elastic as any politician could wish for." He was born in France around 1780, and by the early 1800s he led a notorious company of freebooters who raided merchant and slave ships. In 1814 U.S. naval forces razed his settlement at Barataria Bay, near New Orleans, and imprisoned more than a hundred of his men. Lafitte escaped, but when he learned of a British plot to attack New Orleans, he offered his services to Maj. Gen. Andrew Jackson in exchange for pardons. Jackson struck a deal and won the Battle of New Orleans with the help of Lafitte's "hellish banditti."

The pirates moved to Galveston, Texas, and Lafitte's new operation flourished until 1821, when the U.S. Navy ordered him out. Lafitte piled his plunder onto a ship and set sail for parts unknown. He is said to have died in 1826 in the Yucatán; no one knows, however, where he buried his treasure.

## LASSIE

Lassie and her four-legged peers bring a special canine charm to TV and movie screens. With all the attributes of human heroes but no human failings, these dog stars are the bravest and truest heroes around. Hollywood has found that each breed projects a type of heroism all its own.

The first furry matinee idol, Rin Tin Tin, was a muscular German shepherd that was never afraid of a fight. Rescued from a World War I trench and brought to Hollywood by Capt. Lee Duncan, "Rinty" was an immediate hit.

Asta, the wirehaired terrier of the *Thin Man* movies, was surely a lover, not a fighter. Elegant and somewhat highstrung (just like his owners, Nick and Nora Charles), Asta was top dog throughout the 1930s and '40s.

Lassie herself, a collie with a noble, maternal grace and a talent for rescues, has shown the most staying power. She appeared first in a 1940 novel and has starred in at least nine movies, one radio series, and three TV shows since. Like most dog "actors," each new Lassie is really a team of animals that take turns on camera.

Recent canine stars have tended to be less noble in looks if not in deeds, mixing humor with their heroics. Beethoven, a Saint Bernard, is clumsy but lovable. Like all dog stars, however, he is smart, brave, and loyal to the bone.

## LAST OF THE MOHICANS

*The Last of the Mohicans* is the hands-down favorite of all James Fenimore Cooper's *Leatherstocking Tales*. In the novel, Cooper pairs Hawkeye, the fearless frontiersman (who appears as Natty Bumppo in other Cooper stories), with Chingachgook, the last surviving chieftain of the Mohican tribe. The partnership of Hawkeye and Chingachgook, who clasp hands in the novel's triumphant closing chapter, served as the prototype for Westerns from dime novels to *The Lone*

*Ranger*, in which a white man and an Indian join forces to battle against the "wasty ways" of greedy settlers in the unfenced panorama of the American wilderness.

## LAS VEGAS

No place on Earth is quite like Las Vegas. With giant replicas of the pyramids, a volcano erupting every 15 minutes after dark, and other outlandish amusements, the "diamond in the desert" has become one of America's favorite vacation destinations. In a city where fortunes are made (and lost) in minutes, people want to believe that anyone can hit it big. The gambling, glitz, Hollywood star power, and extravagant splendor of Las Vegas create an almost irresistible picture of the good life awaiting the fortunate few. There are free drinks, of course, while you wait for Lady Luck.

## LATE-NIGHT TV

Where formerly only test patterns reigned, *Broadway Open House*, presented live on NBC, began entertaining insomniacs nightly at 11:30 P.M. in June 1950. Viewers were drawn to the chemistry between its host, comedian Jerry Lester, and his blonde sidekick, Dagmar. NBC had discovered a formula it would use to dominate the late-night time slot for decades.

*Tonight*, hosted by Steve Allen, debuted on NBC in September 1954. Producer Mort Werner's philosophy was "Let's get talked about on the commuter train tomorrow morning." Allen's replacement, Jack Paar, made *Tonight* his soapbox and made headlines in the news while keeping audiences in stitches with wicked double entendres.

When Johnny Carson took over *The Tonight Show* in 1962, he had already turned the job down once. He was afraid he'd grow stale being on TV every night. His fears were unfounded: his low-key personality, ribald wit, and goofy skit characters (Carnac the Magnificent, Aunt Blabby, and Floyd R. Turbo were the most famous) made him welcome in America's bedrooms for 30 years. Stars flocked to the show—being on Carson could make (or revive) a career. Politicians, on the other hand, probably felt relieved when Carson stepped down in 1992: his monologues unerringly found the soft spots in American politics. Of George Bush, Carson observed: "Read my lips. No new promises."

David Letterman spent 11 years pushing the envelope of late-late-night comedy with such features as Stupid Pet Tricks, Dave's Toy Shop, and Dave's-mom-in-the-street interviews. Long heir apparent to Carson, Letterman was passed over, in a surprise move by NBC, in favor of the more "accessible" Jay Leno. NBC's reign at the top of late night was challenged when Letterman moved to the 11:30 slot on CBS, in competition with Leno. Perhaps the era of a single personality (or network) ruling the wee hours is a thing of the past.

Towering neon sculptures give Las Vegas its flashy appeal. The city has more hotel rooms than any other city in the U.S.

Steve Allen was willing to do almost anything for a laugh—including dressing up in a suit made of tea bags and dipping himself in a very large cup of hot water.

Letterman (right) once dreamed of being on Johnny Carson's *Tonight Show.* Years later, Carson appeared on *Late Night with David Letterman.*

Arte Johnson was best known for his rendition of *Laugh-In*'s German soldier, who could be found lurking behind potted plants, murmuring the catchphrase "Verrry interesting!"

Some of the more famous members of the *Laugh-In* crew included (back row) Jo Anne Worley, Allen Sues; (middle row) Gary Owens, Mitzi McCall, Byron Gilliam; (front row) Ruth Buzzi, Dan Rowan, Dick Martin, Goldie Hawn; and (lying in foreground) Arte Johnson.

## LAUGH-IN

Nobody had ever seen anything like it. Beginning in January 1968, *Rowan and Martin's Laugh-In* tore through the limits of conventional television comedy. Here was a program that wasn't afraid to make jokes about social issues. Nor did it shy away from such ancient vaudeville gags as the pie-in-the-face or the fly-in-my-soup.

*Laugh-In*, like the sit-in and the love-in, was a reflection of its time—at least, as much as the censors would allow. The program was also the first to emphasize quick cuts, black-outs, and sight gags. Many lines became catchphrases: "You bet your sweet bippy," "Here come de judge," and "Welcome to beautiful downtown Burbank." Even Richard Nixon appeared on the show to say, "Sock it to *me*?"

The tuxedoed comedy team of Dan Rowan (the hand-some one) and Dick Martin (the slightly off-center loony) kept the action from seeming too subversive. Unknowns became stars: Lily Tomlin as Ernestine the telephone opera-tor, Gary Owens as the monotone announcer, Alan Sues as the grinning sports comentator, Goldie Hawn as the dumb blonde, and Judy Carne, who got it socked to her every week. Delighted audiences made the show number one in 1968 and 1969. However, the show's endless repetition of characters and catchphrases led to *Laugh-In*'s cancellation in 1973.

## LAUNDROMATS

The first coin laundromat, which opened in the Bronx in 1948, caused quite a stir—the police had to be called to restrain curious crowds. However, as more and more home-owners and landlords installed laundries in homes and apart-ment buildings, the commercial variety lost its luster.

Lately, some of that original excitement has returned. For many young urban singles, the local wash-and-dry has become the trendy place to meet people. Quick-thinking entrepreneurs have responded with a new breed of laundromat, where washing clothes is almost an afterthought. In some, well-groomed patrons nibble and imbibe while the machines churn. Other laun-dromats aim to please people who'd rather be doing any-thing else than laundry: they offer video rentals, office centers, poetry readings—even health clubs.

## LAUREL AND HARDY

"Here's another fine mess you've got us into!" Oliver Hardy would say to Stan Laurel. Hardy was the fat one with two chins, a toothbrush moustache, and a jacket three sizes too small. Laurel was the thin one with eyebrows like apostro-phes, an unruly cowlick, a beatific smile, and a tendency to sob like a baby when disaster loomed. Both wore derbys, and were introduced in their movies as Mr. Laurel and Mr. Hardy. Their film partnership began in 1927; over the next 20 years they made more than 100 movies. British Laurel was an understudy to Charlie Chaplin when their dance hall troupe toured the U.S. in 1910 and 1912. Like Chaplin, he stayed. After years in vaudeville, Laurel ended up in Hollywood, where film producer Hal Roach paired him with Hardy.

Their movie plots were simple: they got into trouble. If they cleaned house, Stan would burn it down; if they sneaked off to hanky-panky in Hawaii, their wives would see them in a newsreel; if they fixed a leak in a car radiator, they ended up with a tank full of rice pudding (don't ask). Their two-reelers are shown on TV and video, their fan clubs thrive, and no costume party is complete without a Laurel and a Hardy.

## LAWN ORNAMENTS

In the early part of this century, statues of saints and biblical figures began to appear on lawns around the country. Over time, lawn ornaments became more varied and whimsical. Today trolls sit on mushrooms, and vividly painted gnomes lurk by flower beds. Fuzzy sheep and pigs also put in an appearance. Dolphins do flips, horses rear, bikini-clad geese gather, and, of course, the stately pink flamingo poses elegantly. Some lawns even have a bust of Elvis. And it's easy to get carried away and overpopulate one's lawn. Even those who scorn the occasional concrete bunny may do a little something during the holiday season, when ornaments range from Santa and his sleigh to Mrs. Claus, Rudolph, Frosty, Jack Frost, candy canes, and large plastic candles.

## LEAVE IT TO BEAVER

The ideal families of 1950s TV were the Andersons, the Stones, and the Cleavers. *Father Knows Best* set the standard in 1954 with Jim Anderson, his wife, Margaret, and their kids Betty, Bud, and Kathy. In 1958 *The Donna Reed Show* proved that in the Stone family, the one who knew best was Mother. In between came *Leave It to Beaver*, starring a grammar-school boy who didn't know very much at all.

Sweet but gullible, Theodore (The Beav) and his older brother, Wally, were often bullied by Eddie Haskell, the neighborhood rascal. Eddie would scare Beaver out of doing the things he should do—like going to the dentist—and dare Wally to do things he shouldn't—like getting a silly haircut. Worst of all was that Eddie acted like an angel in front of grown-ups: "Wally, if your gunky brother comes with us, I'm gonna...Oh, hello, Mrs. Cleaver. I was just telling Wallace how pleasant it would be for Theodore to accompany us to the movies."

A decade later, when *The Brady Bunch* debuted, both parents were in their second marriage and the kids were much hipper. This polyester-clad stepfamily's biggest problem was how to get six growing children to share one tiny bathroom. With so many spin-offs (including a variety show, a play, and a feature-length movie in 1995), the Bradys became known as "the family that won't go away."

Although Hardy (left) was usually on the receiving end of Laurel's blows, he would occasionally get his jabs in.

Plastic pink flamingos can be seen strutting their stuff on lawns far from their Florida habitat.

Beaver Cleaver (Jerry Mathers, right) hated Brussels sprouts, girls, and homework, but he idolized his big brother, Wally (Tony Dow, left).

After he surrendered to Grant, Lee promoted reconciliation between the North and the South. He later became president of Washington College (now Washington and Lee University).

## LEE, ROBERT E.

Although the Confederate troops he commanded lost the Civil War, Robert E. Lee has been called "one of the greatest, if not the greatest, soldier who ever spoke the English language." Born into a prominent Virginia family, Lee won praise for his military skill in the Mexican War; he led the marines who captured John Brown at Harpers Ferry in 1859. At the start of the Civil War, President Lincoln offered Lee field command of the Union armies. Instead, Lee followed his native state and joined the Confederate side. "I have not been able to make up my mind to raise my hand against my relatives, my children, my home," he explained.

As commander of the Army of Northern Virginia, Lee devised a brilliant strategy for the Seven Days' Battles, which routed Union troops from Richmond's outskirts. In the Battle of Second Manassas, known as Bull Run by Union forces, he used a tactic that served him well throughout the war: a diversionary maneuver followed by front and flank assaults. After a decisive victory at Fredericksburg, Lee said, "It is well that war is so terrible—else we should grow too fond of it."

However, at Gettysburg Confederate casualties numbered 23,000 and victory shifted to the Union side. His troops decimated by Ulysses S. Grant's war of attrition, Lee finally surrendered at Appomattox Court House on April 9, 1865. Lee died in 1870, and he was hailed in both the North and the South as a hero. He is still revered as the "American Napoleon" for his courageous leadership and skill in battle.

## LEE, SPIKE

A friend once likened film director Spike Lee to "a pot at continuous simmer." Doubtless the description fits his movies. Credited with reviving black American filmmaking in the 1980s, Lee chooses as his subject not just racism but also the rest of black American experience in all its "great richness."

Lee learned his craft at New York University Film School, where his first, 10-minute project was a nervy satire of D. W. Griffith's *Birth of a Nation*. In 1986 his first commercial film, *She's Gotta Have It* (budgeted lower than low and edited in Lee's bedroom), won international acclaim. *School Daze* followed, then the breakthrough *Do the Right Thing*, about racial tensions in Brooklyn. After the jazz film *Mo' Better Blues* came *Jungle Fever*, a story of interracial romance, and the highly praised *Malcolm X* and *Crooklyn*. Lee, who acts in most of his films, has won major studio backing despite his criticism of Hollywood. He must be doing the right thing.

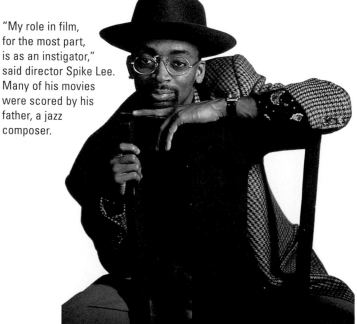

"My role in film, for the most part, is as an instigator," said director Spike Lee. Many of his movies were scored by his father, a jazz composer.

## LEISURE SUITS

The leisure suit was a true fashion nadir. First designed as casual clothing for the rich, these all-purpose outfits took off in the early 1970s, when, thanks to the miracle of cheap polyester knit, hundreds of styles were sprung upon an unsuspecting public. Available in an eye-popping array of pastels, the ensemble was a bizarre hybrid of safari suit and pajamas. Belted jackets featured boxy pockets, wide collars, and decorative seams; cuffs, lapels, and long sleeves were optional. Positioned between the formal business suit (too square) and the hippie look (too sloppy), the leisure suit was touted as the ultramodern sartorial solution for the guy on the go. It didn't work. Besides *Newlywed Game* contestants, only a few sports figures and entertainers wore leisure suits; the classy New York restaurant Lutèce banned them outright. Deep in the closets of lounge lizards and would-be trendsetters, however, specimens still lurk.

## LEMONADE STAND

A familiar sight in small towns on hot summer days, the lemonade stand has provided generations of youth with their first experience in the challenges of salesmanship and making small change. Erected on front lawns or sidewalks in sight of passersby and vigilant parents, these shaky monuments to free enterprise typically announce themselves with a large, hand-lettered sign. Seated behind the stands are fresh-faced future business leaders, eager to make a sale.

Over time, little about this picture has changed, except that today's lemonade is more likely to be made from frozen concentrate than freshly squeezed lemon juice. And the price has risen steeply: once, a penny would buy a puckery drink; now the going rate is a quarter or more.

## LEVITTOWN

*Life* magazine was dismayed by "these impassive rows of little houses," but veterans returning to a severe housing shortage after World War II snapped up the homes by the thousands. Regardless of how critics judged the mass-produced Cape Cod homes, culs-de-sac, parks, and shopping centers of Levittown, New York, nobody could deny that the development sparked a revolution in the American way of living.

William Levitt, a Brooklyn-born builder, saw the housing shortage as an opportunity to exploit the mass-production skills he had learned when erecting homes in the U.S. Navy Seabees. He raised Levittown in Long Island's potato fields in 1947 with a twist on Henry Ford's assembly-line system: instead of prefabricating houses in a factory, he brought the factory to the site. Teams of workers roamed the developing suburb, laying foundations, installing plumbing, and completing 24 other steps in sequence. Levittown grew by as many as 35 new homes a day.

Veterans loved the houses, which cost just under $7,000 (no down payment required) and were near planned shopping areas. Additional Levittowns sprouted in New Jersey and Pennsylvania, and copycat projects rose all over the country. The suburbs would never be the same again.

Leisure suits, usually made of wool gabardine, made their debut after World War II. They were intended as high fashion for the well-to-do. Polyester knockoffs in the 1970s tried to be groovy but didn't quite cut it.

Many Levittown residents did everything they could to distinguish their homes from their neighbors', from replacing the siding to adding dormer windows.

Sinclair Lewis, shown with his wife, Dorothy Thompson, was the first American to win the Nobel Prize for Literature.

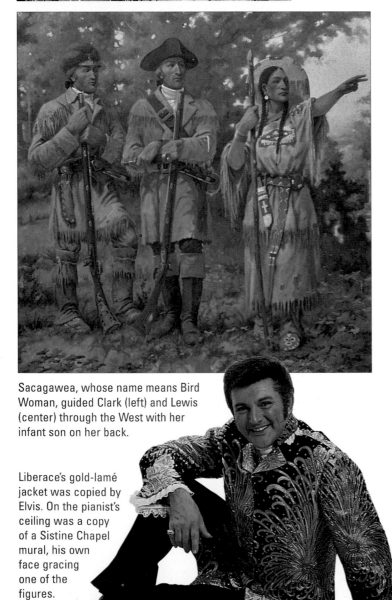

Sacagawea, whose name means Bird Woman, guided Clark (left) and Lewis (center) through the West with her infant son on her back.

Liberace's gold-lamé jacket was copied by Elvis. On the pianist's ceiling was a copy of a Sistine Chapel mural, his own face gracing one of the figures.

## LEWIS, SINCLAIR

Sinclair Lewis's 1920 novel, *Main Street*, hammers home the point that beneath the picture-perfect innocence of small-town America lies a close-minded resistance to new ideas. Its spirited heroine, Carol Milford, is unable to establish an avant-garde theater in the town of Gopher City, Minnesota, because of suspicion and gossip. Her eventual conformity to the town's antiprogressive values reveals Lewis's indignation at the narrowness of self-righteous naysayers.

Like *Main Street*, *Babbitt* was a popular social satire. The name Lewis gave to the main character, a middle-aged, middle-class conformist, has come to symbolize a slavish devotion to bourgeois values. Babbitt is, Lewis said, "all of us Americans at 46, prosperous but worried, wanting—passionately—to seize something more than motor cars and a house before it's too late." Babbitt's failure to break out of his rut is a warning against blind devotion to material goals.

## LEWIS AND CLARK

In 1803 President Thomas Jefferson persuaded Congress to approve a longtime dream of his: an expedition to explore the unknown West. Meriwether Lewis and William Clark, both experienced soldiers, were instructed to gather scientific information and to find trade routes.

In the spring of 1804, the 50-man Corps of Discovery started up the Missouri River. After wintering among the Mandan Indians in what is now North Dakota, they entered the wilderness, taking along a Shoshone Indian woman named Sacagawea as a translator. In the Rockies they bought desperately needed horses from her tribe, then crossed the Continental Divide and the treacherous Bitterroot Range— the most difficult part of the trip. In the fall of 1805, they descended the Columbia River to the Pacific. "Men appeared much Satisfied with their trip beholding with estonishment ... this emence Ocian," wrote Clark.

After a miserably rainy winter spent near the coast, the corps turned back, splitting into three groups to explore more of the country. The bedraggled party reached St. Louis on September 23, 1806, and was greeted with amazement, since nearly everyone except Jefferson had long assumed they were lost. The expedition was an extraordinary success. Meticulous journals of the trip added substantially to what was known of the region's inhabitants, geography, and wildlife. The first step had been taken toward opening the West.

## LIBERACE

Dressed in sequined capes and rhinestone suits, Liberace was the kindhearted king of the keyboard who wanted "to make people happy on an international scale." His rhapsodic and sometimes surprisingly brief renditions of popular classics (he liked to "leave out the dull parts") delighted millions of fans. His garish wardrobe included a

$300,000 fox cape complete with a 16-foot train, and a diamond watch shaped like a piano. His trademarks were a candelabra on the piano and jokes about his brother, George, a violinist who was also his bandleader. Liberace's success was nothing to laugh at: he reportedly earned about $5 million annually for more than two decades.

Born Wladziu Valentino Liberace, he began formal piano studies at age four and eventually soloed with the Chicago Symphony. But Liberace ("Lee" to his friends) made more money as a popular entertainer under the alias Walter Busterkeys. In 1952 he took his talent to television, starring in *The Liberace Show*. By the mid-1950s, the show was as popular as *I Love Lucy*. Liberace's concert at Madison Square Garden in May 1954 broke the attendance record set by his idol, the concert artist Paderewski.

## LIBERTY BELL

The Liberty Bell was ordered in 1751 for the 50th anniversary of William Penn's Charter of Privileges. It was cast in London by the renowned Whitechapel Foundry, but when it was tested upon arrival in Philadelphia, the 2,080-pound bell cracked. Philadelphia craftsmen had to recast the bell twice in order to give it a melodious sound.

The bell rang at the reading of the Declaration of Independence in Philadelphia, but it was hidden in an Allentown church during the years 1777 to '78 for fear the British would melt it down for ammunition. After the war, it tolled for many events, including Cornwallis's surrender at Yorktown, and for George Washington's death. In 1839 a group of abolitionists inspired by its inscription, "Proclaim Liberty throughout all the land unto all the inhabitants thereof," named it the Liberty Bell. By then the bell was showing signs of strain. During the celebration in 1846 of George Washington's birthday, it was damaged beyond repair. It was never rung again.

## LIBRARY OF CONGRESS

Today the Library of Congress contains more than 100 million items, but it began in 1800 with only 152 works and a few maps. The library, which was housed in the Capitol, was destroyed in 1814, when the British burned down the building. To rebuild the collection, Congress purchased Thomas Jefferson's personal library of more than 6,000 books, whose wide range of subject matter was called "admirably calculated for the substratum of a great national library."

In 1865 an act of Congress required that the library receive a copy of every book, map, piece of music, or photograph registered for copyright. Today the collection grows at the rate of 4,560 items each day. Among its diverse treasures are a perfect Gutenberg Bible printed on vellum—one of only three remaining—a recording made by Buffalo Bill Cody, photos of the Wright brothers' historic flight, and the "lost" episodes of *The Honeymooners*.

Since 1976 the Liberty Bell has been enshrined in a pavilion in Philadelphia's Independence National Historical Park.

Documents belonging to Frederick Cook, given to the Library of Congress in 1989, may help historians determine whether Cook was the first explorer to reach the North Pole.

The Library of Congress is the world's largest library, with materials in more than 400 languages. The librarian is appointed by the president.

This painted sculpture by Roy Lichtenstein, entitled "Goldfish Bowl II" (1978), was his interpretation of the style of Henri Matisse. Lichtenstein also created art in the manner of Pablo Picasso and Piet Mondrian.

## LICHTENSTEIN, ROY

In the early 1960s Roy Lichtenstein shocked the highbrow art world with paintings that borrowed from the comics and other lowbrow popular culture. Advertising imagery and everyday objects became important themes in such paintings as "The Refrigerator," "Bathroom," and "Hot Dog." Lichtenstein was even inspired by Bazooka Bubble Gum wrappers, on which comic book figures were printed. Critics turned up their noses, calling his work offensive and brash.

Lichtenstein said of his work, "We're not living in the world of Impressionist painting. The real American architecture is McDonald's and not Mies van der Rohe." His audacious sense of fun captured the essence of American culture—its bigness, vitality, violence, and power. And so the Pop Art movement, started chiefly by Lichtenstein, Andy Warhol, and Robert Rauschenberg, was a triumph.

## LIFE MAGAZINE

Photojournalism began on November 19, 1936, when the first issue of *Life* magazine hit America's newsstands. Big and bold, and full of candid pictures of the poor, the proud, and the secretive, it presented the world as no other publication ever had. America loved it. The first issue sold out in a single day. Four months later sales figures showed that the potential demand for *Life* was 5 million to 6 million copies a week, an amount the company would not produce for years.

For the first issue, Margaret Bourke-White was assigned to photograph construction projects in the Columbia River basin. Instead, the lives of WPA workers in Fort Peck, Montana, caught her attention. Her resulting nine-page photoessay on their dingy shanties, dance halls, and beer bars set a standard for photojournalism. Each week the arrival of the oversize *Life* magazine, with its huge cover picture, was eagerly awaited as mail carriers staggered under the load and newsstand operators apologized for having no copies left.

Henry Luce, founder of *Time* magazine, started *Life* because he felt that if he didn't launch a picture magazine, someone else would. His first choice of a name for the new publication was *Dime, the Show-Book of the World.*

## LIFE SAVERS

There was life before Life Savers, but who can imagine it? In 1912 a candy manufacturer named Clarence Crane (father of the poet Hart Crane) was looking for a summertime replacement for his melting chocolates. Mints, thought Crane. He hired a pill maker to press "Pep-O-Mints" into circles with holes. He noticed that the candy looked like a tiny life saver, and a marketing campaign was born. Crane presented Life Savers as the candy "for that stormy breath."

Life Savers were good, but in cardboard packaging they rapidly became stale. Luckily, Edward Noble, a New York adman, had bought a fresh box and went wild over them. Before long, Noble and a partner bought the company from Crane. They wrapped the candy in foil to preserve its flavor and promoted it not just in candy stores but in smoke shops, restaurants, and even barbershops.

Life Savers started out with one flavor—Pep-O-Mint. More than 30 flavors later (and counting), Life Savers are the best-selling hard candy in the country.

## LI'L ABNER

Hillbilly hero Li'l Abner burst into the comics in 1934 and enraptured Depression-era readers. The strip was carried for 34 years by newspapers throughout the country and inspired a Broadway musical, two films, and several animated cartoons. Abner himself, with his bulging muscles and slow-witted innocence, was everyone's favorite rustic. Other denizens of Dogpatch, his hometown, included his sweetheart, Daisy Mae; sultry Moonbeam McSwine; and such raffish characters as Hairless Joe and Marryin' Sam.

Daisy Mae's efforts to lead Abner to the altar were helped each year on Sadie Hawkins Day. On this terrible day—terrible for the single men of Dogpatch, that is—women had free rein to chase their fellas. The idea proved so popular that Sadie Hawkins dances became annual events at schools around the country.

## LINCOLN, ABRAHAM

A formidable figure at six-foot-four, spindly yet strong enough to hold an ax steady at arm's length, Abraham Lincoln is even larger in lore than he was in life. The 16th president, widely respected in his own era, is revered to this day as the homespun hero who saved the Union, freed the slaves, and made true America's favorite belief: anyone can become president. "I am a living witness," he told visitors to the White House, "that any one of your children may... come here, as my father's child has."

Lincoln's common touch was rooted in the Kentucky backwoods, where he was born to an "undistinguished" family. He overcame the poverty and privations of pioneer life through ceaseless work and sporadic schooling, and he often walked miles to borrow books. Honest, humble, and good-humored, Lincoln made his way on the frontier by working at everything from shopkeeping to surveying before discovering his calling: law and politics.

Years in the Illinois state legislature and courts honed Lincoln's storytelling skill to political poetry—especially when railing against injustice. "A house divided against itself cannot stand," began one memorable antislavery speech. His voice and views became more impassioned during seven debates with archrival Stephen Douglas, who opposed Lincoln for a seat in the U.S. Senate in 1858. Although Lincoln lost the seat, he won national attention and soon swept the Republican nomination and the presidential election.

Sworn in on the eve of strife over slavery and secession, Lincoln made his position clear in his first inaugural address. "We must not be enemies.... [But] the Union of these States is perpetual." For four years the Civil War tried Lincoln's courage and compassion. "This war is eating my life out," he said, his craggy face etched with sorrow. Lincoln was assassinated by Confederate sympathizer John Wilkes Booth only five days after the war had finally ended.

Al Capp's cast of irregulars included (left to right) Honest Abe Yokum; his parents, Daisy Mae and Li'l Abner; Mammy; Pappy; Salomey, the pet pig; and Abner's younger brother, Tiny. Two shmoos stand in the foreground.

The Lincoln Memorial statue was carved by Daniel Chester French. Lincoln's Gettysburg Address is engraved there, as is his second inaugural address: "With malice toward none, with charity for all, with firmness in the right as God gives us to see the right...."

John Lloyd Wright named Lincoln Logs after the 16th president and his log cabin birthplace. Wright claimed that the toy typified "the spirit of America."

After Charles Lindbergh made his nonstop, solo voyage from New York to Paris in 1927, Lindy-mania seized a public already entranced by the risk and romance of flight. Suddenly this lanky 25-year-old became an international superstar.

## LINCOLN LOGS

John Lloyd Wright spent his childhood in a playroom stocked by his famous father, architect Frank Lloyd Wright, with building blocks of every size and shape. As an adult, he watched the timbers for one of his father's hotels being hoisted into place and was struck with an idea for a children's toy. He sketched out the prototype for a set of miniature notched logs in only 10 minutes. Wright's toy perfectly matched the Progressive Era's celebration of the pioneer spirit and outdoor living. Since Lincoln Logs began selling in 1924, more than 100 million sets have transported countless junior Davy Crocketts to the rugged American frontier.

## LINDBERGH, CHARLES

Convinced that he could win the $25,000 prize for making a nonstop flight between New York and Paris if he had the right plane, Charles Lindbergh persuaded nine St. Louis businessmen to finance the compact, sturdy *Spirit of St. Louis*. He took off at 7:52 A.M. on May 20, 1927, having jettisoned both parachute and radio to make room for more fuel. His view obstructed by the extra tank, Lindbergh had to put his head out the side window to see where he was going. "Lucky Lindy" was greeted at Le Bourget airport 3,600 miles and 33½ hours later, at 10:22 P.M., by 100,000 cheering Parisians. "The boy is not our usual type of hero," gushed Will Rogers in his syndicated column. "He is all the others rolled into one and multiplied by ten."

A founder of the first passenger airline, Transcontinental Air Transport, Lindbergh pioneered many air routes with his wife, the poet and writer Anne Morrow Lindbergh. The kidnapping and murder of their two-year-old son, Charles Jr., was one of the most talked-about crimes of the century.

Criticized for his resistance to America's entry into World War II, Charles Lindbergh retired from public life, speaking out only many years later for nature conservation. "If I had to choose," said the great aviator, "I would rather have birds than airplanes."

## LIPPMANN, WALTER

Walter Lippmann was called "the dean of American newspapermen" for his long and influential career as a journalist and social philosopher. In 1914, at the age of 25, he helped to found the progressive *New Republic* magazine, but as he got older, his views became more conservative. In his book *Public Opinion*, he argued that average citizens were incapable of making complex public-policy decisions because the media gave them too little information. Government, he believed, should be in the hands of experts.

In 1921 Lippmann joined the New York *World* newspaper and a decade later began his widely syndicated column, "Today and Tomorrow," for the New York *Herald-Tribune*. His column and books were read by business leaders and politicians worldwide. Fellow journalist James Reston spoke for his colleagues when he said, "[Lippmann] has shown us how to put the event of the day in its proper relationship to the history of yesterday and the dream of tomorrow."

## LITTLE BIGHORN

In 1875 the U.S. Army, in violation of a treaty with the Sioux Indians, began to allow gold prospectors into the Dakota Territory. The outraged Sioux joined with the Northern Cheyenne and prepared to revolt. The army responded by sending in Lt. Col. George Armstrong Custer (he wasn't a general, as is popularly believed) and his 7th Cavalry.

On June 25, 1876, Custer and about 600 men located the Indian encampment on the banks of the Little Bighorn River in the Montana Territory. Scouts reported that the number of Indians was much higher than had been expected, but Custer was eager for a fight and ordered an immediate attack for fear the Indians would escape.

Dividing his troops into three major parties, Custer directed Capt. Frederick Benteen and 125 men to scout the hills, and he sent Maj. Marcus Reno and 115 men to approach the camp from the south. Custer took most of the remaining troops with him to attack from the north.

The battle went tragically wrong for the soldiers. When Reno's forces were overwhelmed by hundreds of Sioux, he panicked and led a wildly disorganized retreat. That left Custer's troops to fight unaided. Chief Gall and his warriors chased them back north, where Crazy Horse trapped them. Custer and all 196 men of his final command were killed.

The country was shocked by Custer's defeat and demanded revenge. Most of the Indians were quickly captured and killed or forced onto overcrowded reservations.

## LITTLE HOUSE ON THE PRAIRIE

The *Little House* books were written about early American life and family by a genuine pioneer. Laura Ingalls was born in a log cabin in Wisconsin and traveled throughout the West, homesteading in Kansas, Minnesota, and the Dakota Territory. She became a teacher at 16, married farmer Almanzo Wilder, and gave birth to a daughter, Rose. In 1894 they moved to a farm in Missouri, where Laura lived until her death at age 90.

Wilder was already an essayist when, at the urging of Rose and out of love for her prairie past, she began writing books at the age of 65. The first, *Little House in the Big Woods*, was published in 1932 and was followed by eight more, including *Little House on the Prairie* (1935), *On the Banks of Plum Creek* (1937), and *By the Shores of Silver Lake* (1939). Children are still happily reading them. A popular television series was created by Michael Landon and ran from 1974 to 1983. The series was followed by three television movies: *Look Back Yesterday* (1983), *Bless All the Dear Children* (1984), and *The Last Farewell* (1984).

Frederic Remington captured the heroism and hopelessness of the Battle at Little Bighorn in his 1891 painting "The Last Stand."

The *Little House* TV family included (clockwise from top left) Charles Ingalls, his wife, Caroline, and daughters Laura, Carrie, and Mary.

Patterned on professional baseball, Little League is scaled down for the younger player, with the baseball diamond about two-thirds the regular size and the games limited to six innings.

Readers couldn't get enough of Little Orphan Annie. She inspired a radio series, a Tony Award-winning musical, and three movies.

ARF!

LEAPIN' LIZARDS!

The first of three film versions of *Little Women* (1933) starred (left to right) Frances Dee, Katharine Hepburn, Joan Bennett, and Jean Parker.

## LITTLE LEAGUE

Organized baseball for boys ages 8 to 12 originated in Williamsport, Pennsylvania, in 1939. A childless factory hand named Carl Stotz came up with Little League as an activity to share with his nephews. From his first three all-boy teams, the program has grown to more than 6,500 U.S. leagues with chapters in 90 countries.

The 11- and 12-year-old All Stars of four U.S. and four international zones meet every August in Williamsport for round-robin play-offs. The U.S. winners are matched against the international champions for a single final game. Although recreation and sportsmanship have always been the stated goals of the organization, competition fever, often on the part of the parents, seems to be intrinsic to the sport.

## LITTLE ORPHAN ANNIE

"Leapin' lizards! A piece o' th' wall … movin' … just like a door …" That could be nobody other than Little Orphan Annie exploring a spooky house. In Harold Gray's long-running comic strip, Annie's exclamation "Leapin' lizards!" also resounds off alley walls, inside sinister dens of crime, in Oriental marketplaces, and in cruelly run orphanages as she explores the world with her dog, Sandy. Annie—the resourceful but parentless and pupilless girl who mixes periods of homelessness with reunions with her wealthy benefactor, Daddy Warbucks—is one of the best-known characters on the funny pages.

Gray originally conceived the strip in 1924 as *Little Orphan Otto*, about a boy. Following a publisher's request, Gray changed Otto to Annie, an independent and self-reliant red-haired waif. During the Depression, Annie grew into the embodiment of Gray's brand of anti-New Deal conservatism.

*Little Orphan Annie* survived virtually unchanged until Gray's death in 1968, after which other artists and writers took over the strip.

## LITTLE WOMEN

Generations of readers have been inspired by *Little Women*, the story of the struggle of the loving March sisters—Meg, Jo, Beth, and Amy—to make ends meet while their father recovers in a Civil War hospital. Hard times do not dampen the dreams of these girls as they grow into women. The most fondly remembered of the sisters is Jo, the tomboyish, high-spirited young woman who undertakes "a bold stroke for fame and fortune" by becoming a writer. Her literary efforts enable her family to overcome their financial difficulties, and she eventually marries and starts a school for boys.

Louisa May Alcott was as ambitious as her heroine—and as unorthodox. In the mid- to late 1800s, a time when jobs for women were scarce, this hardworking writer produced nearly 300 titles, the most popular of which were *Little Women* and its sequels, *Little Men* and *Jo's Boys*.

## LOMBARDI, VINCE

Vince Lombardi's coaching career was a prime example of "tough love." The Green Bay Packers's defensive tackle Henry Jordan once said that Lombardi "treated us all the same—like dogs," and star halfback Paul Hornung called him "probably the most hated man in pro football." When Lombardi arrived in Green Bay, Wisconsin, in 1959, he inherited a dispirited team that had won only one game the previous season. Lombardi's aggressive style soon prodded the Packers to the first of an eventual five National Football League titles in a seven-year period, a reign that included the first two Super Bowls in 1967 and 1968.

An intense man who motivated through fear, Lombardi believed that success depended on superior execution of fundamental tasks. Players who failed to sacrifice individual glory for team success didn't last long. For Lombardi, "winning wasn't the best thing. It was the only thing."

## LONDON, JACK

By the time 21-year-old Jack London arrived in Alaska's Klondike during the gold rush of 1897, he had already lived a rough life. As a boy in California, he worked several jobs. At age 16 he became an oyster pirate, then later rode the rails with other hobos. These experiences taught him the survival techniques he would apply in the lawless Alaskan territory. It wasn't only gold he was mining in the frozen wilderness, but stories—stories of heroic loners who struggle against brutal odds. *The Call of the Wild* was London's biggest success; *White Fang*, *The Sea Wolf*, and several other novels and short stories also contributed to his fortunes. He earned nearly a million dollars in his lifetime.

London wasn't prepared to deal with fame. Uneasy with success and plagued with health problems, he plunged into a depression. Some relief came, he said, through writing "stuff that is clean, alive, optimistic, and that makes toward life."

## LONE RANGER

For more than three decades, kids thrilled to the "William Tell Overture" and the stirring words "The Lone Ranger rides again." This fictional champion of the West was the brainchild of George W. Trendle, the owner of a Detroit radio station, who set out to create a larger-than-life, utterly wholesome Western hero, with a fiery horse named Silver and a faithful Indian companion named Tonto. The ultimate Good Guy, the Lone Ranger never drank, cursed, or shot to kill. This endeared him to parents, while young fans loved the nonstop action and simple plots in which the masked man forced "the powers of darkness into the blinding light of justice."

The radio show first aired on January 30, 1933, and was soon broadcast nationwide. *The Lone Ranger* was a hit half-hour television series from 1949 to 1957, and an animated version ran in the 1960s. "Hi-yo, Silver, away!"

Vince Lombardi had his own way of egging his players on. "If you aren't fired with enthusiasm," he said, "you will be fired with enthusiasm."

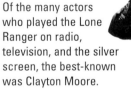

After being stolen from his comfortable home, Buck, the canine hero of *The Call of the Wild*, learns the ways of the fierce Alaskan sled dogs.

Of the many actors who played the Lone Ranger on radio, television, and the silver screen, the best-known was Clayton Moore.

Huey Long, one of the 20th century's most colorful politicians, vowed to redistribute wealth.

At Longwood Gardens, renowned glass conservatories include the East Conservatory (above), Fern Passage, and the Banana Room.

## LONG, HUEY

"In Louisiana they vote by electricity. It's a marvelous way to vote, but Huey runs the switchboard, so it don't matter which button the boys press, all the answers come out yes." So Will Rogers described the omnipotence of Huey Long, the populist governor of Louisiana from 1928 to 1932. The "Kingfish" himself, as he was known, had a favorite saying: "It ain't enough to get the breaks. You gotta know how to use 'em."

A drinker, womanizer, and spellbinding orator, Long was also an intuitive political genius who bribed, threatened, and charmed to get what he wanted: total control of the Louisiana government. He campaigned under the slogan "Every Man a King" and built schools, roads, and hospitals for his impoverished constituents. Elected to the U.S. Senate in 1930, the self-proclaimed "pore folks champion" gained national visibility with his radical Share Our Wealth plan, which proposed homestead allowances and a minimum annual income for every family. He hoped to challenge Roosevelt for the democratic nomination in 1936, but he was stopped when the son-in-law of one of his ruined political opponents shot and killed him in the Baton Rouge statehouse.

## LONGWOOD GARDENS

In 1906, to save a stand of rare trees near Philadelphia from the sawmill, industrialist Pierre S. du Pont purchased the first 200 acres of what was to become Longwood Gardens. Now considered one of the grandest of America's public gardens, Longwood's 11,000 ornamental plants grace 1,050 acres of formal gardens, conservatories, lakes, and woodlands.

Du Pont's aim was not to build a private retreat, but to provide beautiful vistas for the public to enjoy. A self-taught gardener, he designed Longwood to show that architecture and horticulture could function as pleasing extensions of each other. Influenced by the vast fountains he had seen in Chicago at the World Columbian Exposition of 1893, du Pont planned three water gardens at Longwood, with more than 1,700 separate fountain jets, some rising as high as 130 feet.

## LOONEY TUNES

Warner Brothers's Looney Tunes and Merrie Melodies animated series were created, in part, to showcase Warner's vast music library. But the spotlight was quickly stolen by a host of zany cartoon characters, from Bugs Bunny to Porky Pig, Daffy Duck, Tweety, and Sylvester. The Warner formula was to hire talented artists—including legendary cartoon directors Tex Avery, Friz Freleng, and Chuck Jones—and to put few restrictions on them beyond a tight budget and a requirement that the films be funny. Given that freedom, they salted the cartoons with irreverent wit and jokes aimed at adults.

Looney Tunes were unlike any cartoons that had gone before them. Thousands of drawings went into each feature, creating great subtlety of movement and expression.

Cinematic techniques—including the use of different "camera" angles—and crisp timing helped bring to life a unique cast of characters that went far beyond cartoon conventions. In one episode Bugs Bunny convinces a giant wrestler that his shorts are ripped, then assumes the role of a tailor, coaxes his opponent into a greatcoat, and literally pins his shoulders to the canvas.

Looney Tunes gave us such phrases as Bugs Bunny's favorite aside, "What a ma*roon*!" As often as not, the voices came from Mel Blanc, the man of a thousand voices. Blanc spoke for Daffy Duck, Elmer Fudd, Tweety, and Yosemite Sam. He coined Bugs Bunny's trademark "Ehhh, what's up, doc?" as well as Sylvester the Cat's "sufferin' succotash!" and Porky Pig's stuttering sign-off, "Th-th-th-that's all, folks!"

## LOST GENERATION

Many generations are given names—Baby Boomers and Generation X being two recent examples—but only the Lost Generation defined itself by those who were absent from it. Tens of thousands of young Americans, and millions of Europeans, lost their lives in World War I. The effect was a profound disillusionment and the erosion of moral bearings among those who survived, expressed most clearly by a loosely defined group of expatriates—bohemian writers and artists—living on the Left Bank in Paris during the 1920s.

Gertrude Stein coined the term *Lost Generation* in a conversation with Ernest Hemingway, and Malcolm Cowley defined it as "a craze," a popular lifestyle of casual intimacies, hard drinking, and risk taking. Hemingway, F. Scott Fitzgerald, e.e. cummings, and John Dos Passos formed the core of a group Thomas Wolfe mockingly dubbed "the what-is-the-use-we-are-doomed generation." For some, no trip to Paris is complete without a visit to one of the watering holes where this now-mythical group gathered.

## LOTTO

Lotto fever runs rampant in America, where a winning ticket can transform an ordinary Joe into an instant millionaire. Ever since Colonial times, lotteries have been used to raise funds for bridge building and other public projects. Even George Washington played the lottery. New Hampshire started the first statewide lottery in 1964, and 35 other states and the District of Columbia have since followed suit.

Promoters of government-run lotteries see them as a painless substitute for taxes. Ticket buyers are undaunted by an expert's estimate that their chances of winning are comparable to the likelihood of drawing four straight royal flushes in poker, all in spades, then running into four strangers with the same birthday. Players fantasize about being the big winner, especially when the jackpot approaches $118 million, the record sum won in a 1991 California lottery.

Said Chuck Jones, "When I look in the mirror, I see Daffy Duck, but when I look into my heart, I see Bugs Bunny." Both were hunted by the inept Elmer Fudd, top left.

The genius of the Warner cartoons was honored when they were shown in a retrospective exhibition at the Museum of Modern Art in New York City.

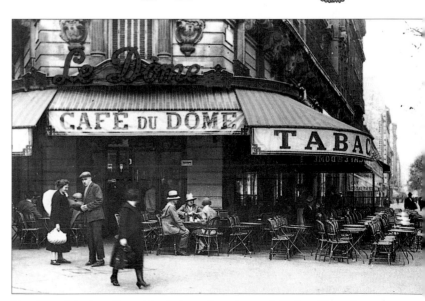

Members of the Lost Generation, who gathered at such Paris cafés as the Dôme, led lives like those depicted by Hemingway in *The Sun Also Rises*.

When Joe Louis's teacher said, "He's going to have to make a living with his hands," Joe's mother got her quiet son a violin.

The Louisiana Purchase doubled the size of the U.S. and provided access to ports at the mouth of the Mississippi. The French influence can still be seen in the architecture, cuisine, and culture of New Orleans.

## LOUIS, JOE

In the 1930s, a time when segregation was widespread and most sports figures were white, Joe Louis, perhaps the greatest heavyweight boxer ever, was the first black to become a hero for all of America. In 1936 the promising fighter, who had won 25 professional bouts, was knocked out by Max Schmeling of Germany. Blacks continued to revere him, but white America cheered his defeat. Just two years later—when Hitler's belligerent ambitions were clear—Louis decisively beat Schmeling in the first round. Radio listeners nationwide were thrilled that an American had beaten a Nazi, and the "Brown Bomber" became everybody's champion. In 1981 Louis died a hero: his flag-draped casket was buried in Arlington National Cemetery with a 21-gun salute, the sad notes of taps, and a eulogy by President Reagan. Joseph Louis Barrow, a sharecropper's son, had held the heavyweight crown for a record 12 years and defended it 25 times.

## LOUISIANA PURCHASE

The Louisiana Territory—the area between the Mississippi River and the Rocky Mountains—had been a political pawn for many years before the U.S. bought it in 1803. France had ceded it to Spain in 1762, but Napoleon, who had dreams of a French empire in North America, secretly got the territory back in 1800. Two years later the Spanish, who still administered it, cut off U.S. access to ports in New Orleans, which left American settlers without a way to get goods from the mouth of the Mississippi to markets on the East Coast.

In response, President Thomas Jefferson sent envoy James Monroe to France to offer the French as much as $10 million for New Orleans and the Floridas. By the time Monroe arrived, France had suffered heavy losses in a slave revolt in Haiti and was facing war with England. The French foreign minister astonished Monroe by asking what the U.S. would pay for the entire Louisiana Territory. After much haggling, they agreed on $15 million; with additional charges and interest, the cost of the land came to about four cents an acre.

## LUNCH BOXES

Each September, millions of schoolchildren demand a new lunch box. Last year's lunch box is outdated; and few parents can withstand the whimpers of children terrified that an old or hand-me-down box will label them as uncool.

The first tin lunch boxes, made in 1902, and the first lunch box decorated with Mickey Mouse, made in 1932, were both small and didn't have thermoses. "Real" lunch boxes—the metal ones with squeaky hinges and thermoses with glass linings that shattered easily—took off after a 1950 box was decorated with a Hopalong Cassidy decal. In 1959 vinyl-covered boxes, many featuring Barbie, were introduced, but they were never as popular as the metal ones. In 1972, when a mother brought a lawsuit claiming that they could be used as deadly weapons, metal boxes fell out of favor. Molded-plastic boxes and durable plastic thermoses gained popularity and soon became standard. Many old lunch boxes, including those featuring Gomer Pyle, The Monkees, and The Jetsons, have become collector's items.

## LUNT AND FONTANNE

Alfred Lunt and Lynn Fontanne (The Lunts) were the greatest acting team in the history of the American theater. Their friend Noël Coward (who wrote the comedy *Design for Living* for the couple and himself in 1933) said of them: "They are deeply concerned with only three things: themselves, the theater ... and food." British Fontanne and Milwaukee-born Lunt were already Broadway stars when they married in 1922. Their brilliance as a team was evident in the 1924 production of *The Guardsman*. From 1929 on, they worked together exclusively, directing themselves, choosing their casts, controlling their productions. So polished were their performances, so perfect their comic timing, that one critic marveled: "Their watches are synchronized."

Performing with wit and charm, they toured the U.S. constantly and played New York and London in *The Taming of the Shrew*, *Idiot's Delight*, and *There Shall Be No Night*, as well as lesser vehicles. When, in *Oh Mistress Mine*, Mr. Lunt lightly patted Miss Fontanne's fully draped bosom, a little old lady was heard to sigh, "How comforting to know they're really married!" The Lunts made their final stage bow in 1960 in *The Visit* and retired to their Wisconsin farm, having received every honor the theater can bestow.

## LYNN, LORETTA

Perhaps it was her clear country voice and the feisty, no-nonsense songs she wrote, or perhaps it was her almost magical rise from obscurity to stardom that made Loretta Lynn an idol of women whose lives left plenty to dream about. Born Loretta Webb, she was one of eight children born to a poor miner in Butcher Hollow, Kentucky. Married at 13, she was soon the mother of four. She took pleasure in singing for her children, which prompted her husband to give her a guitar. Recognizing her talent, he urged her to sing at local clubs, where she gained confidence and fans. Her first record, "Honky Tonk Girl," became a hit in 1960.

Befriended in Nashville by singer Patsy Cline and invited to sing on the Wilburn Brothers' syndicated TV show, Lynn joined the Grand Ole Opry in 1962. Her first No. 1 hit was her song "Don't You Come Home a Drinkin' (with Lovin' on Your Mind)." She had a stream of Top 10 hits throughout the 1960s and '70s, and her duets with Conway Twitty scored dozens more. Lynn was chosen as top female vocalist three times and was the first woman to be named Entertainer of the Year (1972) by the Country Music Association.

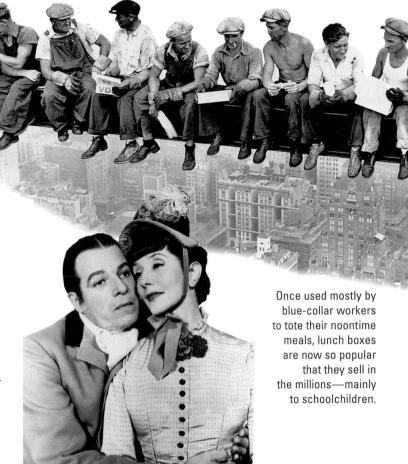

Once used mostly by blue-collar workers to tote their noontime meals, lunch boxes are now so popular that they sell in the millions—mainly to schoolchildren.

Recalling the acting career she shared with her husband (Alfred Lunt), Lynn Fontanne said, "We usually played two people very much in love," which paralleled their life offstage.

Loretta Lynn (left) entered the Country Music Hall of Fame in 1988. Her youngest sister, Crystal Gayle (above), is also a successful country music star.

Adding a cheese sauce to macaroni makes for a dish high in protein. Kids love its tangy flavor and its general gooeyness.

Of the men who died defending Bataan and Corregidor in the early days of World War II, Douglas MacArthur said, "They died hard, those savage men.... They were filthy.... And I loved them." Below, he waded ashore at Leyte in October 1944, fulfilling his vow to return at the head of a conquering army.

*"Sometimes people call me an idealist. Well, that is the way I know I am an American. America is the only idealistic nation in the world."*

WOODROW WILSON

## MACARONI AND CHEESE

No family shopping list is complete without macaroni and cheese. Having the makings on hand means there's a meal to serve even when the cupboard is nearly bare. Packaged macaroni and cheese dinners were invented by Harry Weishaar, a traveling salesman for Kraft, who boosted sales in his territory by attaching two-ounce packets of cheese to boxes of macaroni with rubber bands. Soon Kraft put the ingredients together in a blue box that promised "a meal for 4 in 9 minutes" for 19 cents. The price has risen, but the meal is still one of the fastest, most economical, and most popular around.

## MACARTHUR, DOUGLAS

A brilliant strategist and relentless self-promoter, Gen. Douglas MacArthur was one of America's most talented and controversial military leaders. First distinguishing himself in World War I, MacArthur became, at the age of 50, the youngest army Chief of Staff ever. He retired in 1937, only to be recalled to active duty in the Philippines at age 61 as war with Japan threatened. Ordered to escape to Australia—and ignoring suggestions that the collective "we" might be more appropriate—MacArthur swore, "I shall return."

After accepting Japan's surrender aboard the battleship U.S.S. *Missouri*, MacArthur presided over the occupation of Japan from 1945 to '50 as Supreme Allied Commander. His final campaign was in Korea, where he was dismissed by President Truman for publicly disagreeing with U.S. policy. Convinced, as always, that his strategy was right, the general defended it before Congress, closing with a line from an old barracks ballad: "Old soldiers never die; they just fade away."

## MACK, TED

Genial master of ceremonies Ted Mack was a struggling bandleader when he became an assistant to Edward Bowes, producer of *Major Bowes' Original Amateur Hour*, in 1935. This popular radio talent show attracted starry-eyed contestants from around the country who showed off their singing, mimicry, or harmonica playing in the hopes of a big break. Each week 20 out of some 700 contenders performed on the show; radio listeners then voted by mail or phone for the winner. Later the program moved to TV. Although few realized their dreams of stardom, those who did included singer Pat Boone, dancer Vera-Ellen, and, spectacularly, Frank Sinatra.

## MADISON, JAMES AND DOLLEY

James Madison was called "the master builder of the Constitution" for his pivotal role in its framing. At the Constitutional Convention of 1787, he worked tirelessly for a charter that would ensure a strong national government. To urge its ratification, he coauthored *The Federalist Papers*, and he later helped draw up the Bill of Rights.

The scholarly but introspective Madison was perfectly complemented by his flamboyant wife, Dolley. A vivacious socialite, Dolley created fashion trends by wearing Turkish turbans and high heels that made her tower over "the great little Madison." In 1801 Thomas Jefferson appointed Madison his secretary of state, and he asked Dolley to serve as his official hostess because both he and Vice President Aaron Burr were widowers.

Madison, aided by the popularity of "Queen Dolley," was elected president in 1808. He proved to be an indecisive leader, especially during the War of 1812. While he was at the front, the British sacked Washington, and Dolley gathered his papers and the Gilbert Stuart portrait of George Washington before she fled, thereby becoming legendary.

After eight years in the presidential mansion, the couple returned to their home in Virginia, where Madison died in 1836. A year later, Dolley rejoined the social whirl of Washington, where she reigned until her own death 12 years later.

## MAD MAGAZINE

In 1952, when William Gaines began publishing a spoof of horror comics called *Tales Calculated to Drive You Mad*, he never imagined that it would become the most successful humor magazine ever. The enthusiastic response turned *Mad* into a monthly pop-culture institution that ripped into every respected establishment and actively dissected every cherished belief in American society. Serving as cultural liberation in the form of parody, *Mad* was as titillating and taboo as *Playboy* for the millions of teenagers who grew up reading it in the 1950s and '60s. Today it still covers movies, music, politics, TV shows, and advertising campaigns. If something affects the national psyche, *Mad* is there to expose and ridicule whatever its writers, editors, and illustrators—"the usual gang of idiots"—view as institutional dishonesty.

Each issue of *Mad* contains more than a dozen features peopled by a cast of regular characters, including the "Spy vs. Spy" duo, cartoonist Don Martin's slack-jawed morons, and *Mad*'s grinning gap-toothed mascot, Alfred E. Neuman, whose motto is "What, me worry?" Nothing is serious and nothing is sacred, and by wrapping its derision in juvenile buffoonery, *Mad* has helped define a new audience—teenagers—and nurture a new outlook—rebellion—as a fundamental attitude of adolescence.

*Mad* magazine covers usually feature Alfred E. Neuman, a lovable delinquent who does the unexpected. Typical covers show him cutting class (top) and painting his own playing cards (bottom).

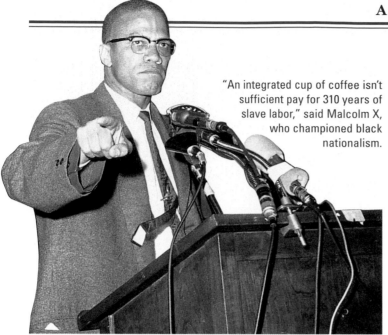

"An integrated cup of coffee isn't sufficient pay for 310 years of slave labor," said Malcolm X, who championed black nationalism.

## MALCOLM X

Malcolm X was a militant black leader who felt that nonviolent protest wasn't effective, and that if blacks could not cast a ballot, they would "have to cast a bullet." Born Malcolm Little, he became a thief, drug user, and pusher known as Detroit Red. While in prison, however, he re-educated himself and converted to the Nation of Islam. Upon his release, he dropped his "slave name" and, because his true family name had been lost through generations of slavery, called himself Malcolm X.

A provocative speaker, Malcolm X soon became the most prominent spokesman for the Black Muslims. Such statements as "You show me a capitalist, and I'll show you a bloodsucker" gained him a reputation as a revolutionary and a firebrand. In 1963, after he commented that President Kennedy's assassination was a matter of "the chickens coming home to roost," he was forced out of the Black Muslims by Elijah Muhammad, the leader whom he had started to eclipse.

After a pilgrimage to Mecca in 1964, Malcolm X again changed his name, to El Hajj Malik el Shabazz. He founded a new group, the Organization of Afro-American Unity, but was assassinated in 1965, before it had time to grow. Although he is remembered for his calls to violence, in his last year he had come to believe that a "bloodless revolution" was possible.

## MALL OF AMERICA

When the Mall of America opened in Bloomington, Minnesota, in 1992, it ushered in a new era in American commerce. The largest enclosed shopping center in the country, the mall contains more than 400 stores, dozens of bars and restaurants—including one in which a tropical thunderstorm erupts every 20 minutes—and 14 movie theaters. Some visitors rely on electric carts just to navigate the far-flung corridors.

Minnesota's steamy summers and frigid winters make climate-controlled shopping a popular idea with residents. The country's first enclosed mall opened in 1956 in nearby Edina, Minnesota. However, at only 400,000 square feet, it was tiny compared with the Mall of America, which sprawls over 4.2 million square feet—large enough to command its own zip code.

Visitors can do just about anything at the mall, from playing miniature golf on a bi-level course complete with waterfalls to getting married at the Chapel of Love, where the "Mega Wedding" package includes an Elvis impersonator, if needed. The mall's centerpiece is the seven-acre Knott's Camp Snoopy, the country's largest indoor theme park. Set amid 30,000 flowering plants, it has been likened to "a rustic clearing in the Great North Woods," albeit one with a roller coaster and a three-story inflated replica of Snoopy. Today the Mall of America attracts some 38 million visitors a year, making it a tourist attraction more popular than Disney World and the Grand Canyon combined.

At the Mall of America, visitors will find such themed shopping areas as upscale South Avenue, parklike North Garden, trendy East Broadway, and quaint West Market. A giant inflated beagle (right) welcomes kids to Camp Snoopy.

## MAMMOTH CAVE

It's mammoth, all right—294 miles of explored passages make Mammoth Cave the longest cave system in the world by far—yet the forces that created it are all but invisible. Rainwater, trickling through soil and vegetation, alters chemically to form mild carbonic acid. Seeping down through cracks in the 300-million-year-old limestone strata, the acid eats away the rock, enlarging cracks into tunnels, rooms, and, eons later, chambers and grottoes. Exploration continues; no one knows just how vast the cave system might be.

Located near Bowling Green, Kentucky, Mammoth Cave National Park offers such breathtaking subterranean sights as Bottomless Pit and Frozen Niagara. There are also archeological relics from human history, including woven slippers and bamboo torches of a prehistoric people who mined gypsum in the cave as long as 4,000 years ago.

## M&M's

War may be hell, but it was made a little sweeter by the introduction of M&M's in 1941. Armored with a candy coating, the chocolate pieces, included in C-ration packets, did not melt in the hands of American GIs. M&M's continued to be popular among those who wear uniforms: in 1982 NASA astronauts snacked on M&M's in space.

The rest of us seem to have a fascination with the M&M color scheme. We worried that red M&M's caused cancer and wondered if green ones were aphrodisiacs. We didn't care for violet (it was replaced by tan in 1949) and, in a 1995 national election held by the Mars candy company, voted to add blue to the mix. It's fitting that one of America's favorite candies now comes in America's favorite color.

## MANHATTAN PROJECT

The atomic bombs America used to end World War II were produced in a desperate race to build the weapon before Nazi Germany did. In 1939 physicists around the world realized that an atomic explosive was possible. A dramatic letter from Albert Einstein persuaded President Roosevelt to support research. (In fact, Germany was engaged in nuclear study, but was not yet working on a bomb.) An American program to build a bomb, code-named The Manhattan Project, was launched in 1942.

Speed required that several different methods and materials be tried simultaneously. A vast factory was built at Oak Ridge, Tennessee, to produce uranium; another, at Hanford, Washington, would produce plutonium. More than 100,000 specialists worked furiously in total secrecy. Finally, a bomb was built in a laboratory in Los Alamos, New Mexico. It was tested in the desert near Alamogordo, New Mexico, on July 16, 1945. Three weeks later a bomb was detonated over Hiroshima. Three days after that, a second bomb destroyed Nagasaki. After five days of bitter wrangling, Japan surrendered, and the world was left stunned by the power of nuclear weapons.

Rainwater continuously shapes Mammoth Cave. Variations in the amount of water and its speed have created canyonlike passageways and small shafts with flowstone formations (above).

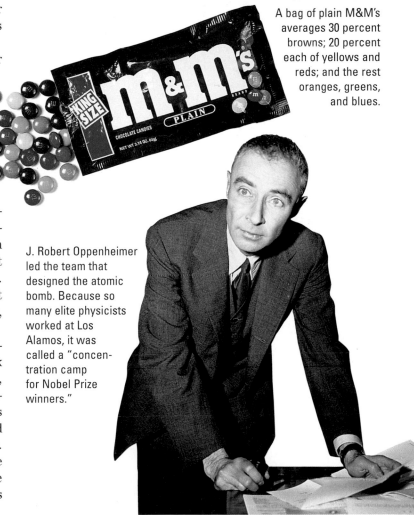

A bag of plain M&M's averages 30 percent browns; 20 percent each of yellows and reds; and the rest oranges, greens, and blues.

J. Robert Oppenheimer led the team that designed the atomic bomb. Because so many elite physicists worked at Los Alamos, it was called a "concentration camp for Nobel Prize winners."

Hawaii became a U.S. possession in 1898, largely at the behest of American sugarcane planters. It became the 50th state in 1959.

Yankee team publicists avidly measured Mickey Mantle's long clouts. (Previously, a home run was a home run, no matter how far over the fence it went.) One of Mantle's long drives traveled a whopping 565 feet.

## MANIFEST DESTINY

In the 1840s many Americans believed it was the country's God-given right to expand west to the Pacific and even beyond. Editor John O'Sullivan captured the national mood when he wrote in the *Democratic Review* that it was "our manifest destiny to overspread the continent allotted by Providence for the free development of our yearly multiplying millions." The slogan was picked up by expansionists, who were convinced that the country's "superior" talents and democratic government qualified it to influence other peoples. In a 10-year period, America acquired Oregon, annexed Texas, and bought California and the Southwest from Mexico after its defeat in the Mexican War.

The end of American expansion west came with the annexation of Hawaii in 1898. "We need Hawaii," said President William McKinley. "It is manifest destiny."

## MAN O' WAR

It was almost unfair. Man o' War was a god of a horse, with ground-gobbling strides, lungs like bellows, and charisma that captured the public imagination as thoroughly as Babe Ruth's and Jack Dempsey's had. Always the odds-on favorite, "Big Red" lost only one race—to Upset—because of confusion at the gate. Usually, in a sport in which one-fifth of a second equals one length, he'd win by two or three seconds.

Born on March 29, 1917, Man o' War retired to stud at age four. Such giants as Kelso, Hail to All, Forego, Seattle Slew, and Affirmed had Man o' War in their pedigrees. At 26 he suffered a heart attack and retired from stud. When the great horse died four years later, the entire nation mourned. He is buried at the Kentucky Horse Park in Lexington.

## MANTLE, MICKEY

When Mickey Mantle joined the New York Yankees in 1951, he followed a line of superstars that began in the 1920s with Babe Ruth and Lou Gehrig, and continued in the '30s and '40s with Joe DiMaggio. Mantle was the major league's first power-hitting switch-hitter. His combination of awesome strength and lightning speed made him—despite chronic trouble with his knees, which required extensive taping before each game—the sport's mightiest player.

Fans and the sports press did not immediately warm to this unsophisticated man from a small Oklahoma town; however, Mantle became a sympathetic figure when his dominance of the Yankees was threatened by the arrival of Roger Maris in 1960. In 1961 both men pursued Babe Ruth's record of 60 home runs in a single season, and the exploits of the "M and M" boys drew huge crowds. When Mantle became the underdog because of recurring leg injuries, his popularity soared. During the remainder of his career, his fans grew more devoted as his performance suffered. Upon his death in 1995, Mantle was deeply mourned by the whole nation.

## MAPLE SYRUP

When spring brings warm days and cool nights, the sap of the maple tree flows. Indians collected sap by gashing trees with hatchets and inserting a wood chip or a hollow reed to direct the flow into bark containers. They killed many trees in the process. European settlers used drills instead of hatchets, and they soon learned how much sap could be drawn without destroying the tree. In many northern communities, products made from the precious extract were the only sweeteners available; today a pancake is not a pancake without maple syrup. Networks of plastic tubing have replaced the buckets and horse-drawn sleds of yesteryear. But each spring people flock to local "sugaring off" celebrations to watch syrup being made the old-fashioned way.

## MARATHON

Officially 26 miles, 385 yards long, the marathon first gained popularity in the United States during the fitness boom of the 1970s. Prompted by Frank Shorter's 1972 Olympic gold medal in the marathon and Jim Fixx's best-selling *The Complete Book of Running*, the nation embraced marathon running as the ultimate physical challenge.

According to legend, the first marathon was run in 490 B.C., when a Greek messenger ran from the Plain of Marathon to Athens, gasped out the news of an unexpected victory over the invading Persians, then died of exhaustion. The story inspired Olympics officials to include a special race to commemorate his run when they revived the games in 1896. Enthralled by the event, Americans started their own race in Boston the following April, making the Boston Marathon the oldest of the annual marathons. More than 300 cities in the U.S. currently hold yearly races.

## MARBLES

Countless generations of American kids have shredded the knees of their knickers while knuckling down to a nerve-racking round of marbles. In schoolyards and farmyards, contestants with steely eyes and steady hands launched little globes in such age-old circle, chase, and hole games as Ringer, Rolley Hole, and Bounce Eye, often competing "for keeps," whereby the victor claimed the colorful spoils.

The prized playthings were crafted in glass, ceramic, steel, stone, or semiprecious gems like jade or onyx, and they had names as appealing as the marbles themselves. Rolling by the billions from German and American factories between the late 1700s and the 1950s came aggies—large agate orbs used as shooters or taws—and immies—streaked-glass spheres imitating agate—along with clam-broths and commies, mibs and marriddiddles, onion-skins and tigereyes. Real rarities include goldstones, made of glass with copper specks, and sulfides, with tiny clay figures encased in clear glass.

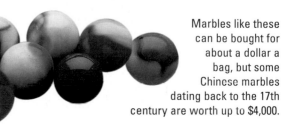

Some 25,000 runners streamed across the Verrazano Bridge (above) during the 1990 New York City marathon, the largest in the world. Family and friends can share the euphoria of the finish at the reunion area (right).

Marbles like these can be bought for about a dollar a bag, but some Chinese marbles dating back to the 17th century are worth up to $4,000.

The UCLA Bruins won the hearts of a cheering nation when they swept the games of March Madness in 1995 to claim their 11th NCAA championship. Senior Ed O'Bannon led the team to an 89–78 victory against the Arkansas Razorbacks in the final game.

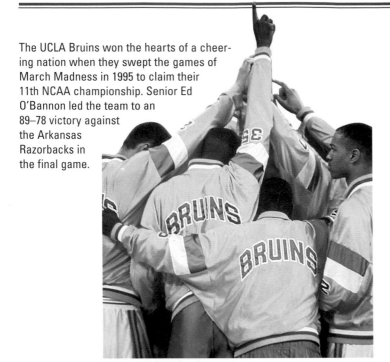

## MARCH MADNESS

The term *March Madness* was coined back in 1939 by H. V. Porter, an executive director of the Illinois High School Association, to describe his state's basketball tournament. In 1990 the NCAA adopted the term to describe its own 18-day-long annual competition, which has been thrilling hoop fans ever since. March Madness brings together 64 teams from across the country to determine the nation's number one college basketball team. Then, in exciting elimination rounds, the number of teams is whittled down to 32, then 16, 8, 4, and 2, until at last one team wins the final, breathtaking match.

Part of the drama of March Madness is its potential for David versus Goliath upsets. Unknown schools from obscure conferences may not only achieve stunning upsets against more heavily favored schools, but they may also heroically win the entire tournament. March Madness became such a popular event that CBS paid $2.7 billion for the rights to televise all tournament games until the year 2002.

## MARDI GRAS

New Orleans throws the best-known Mardi Gras celebration in the United States. Throngs of people wearing sequined clothes, feathered masks, and outlandish body paint dance down the street among the 20-foot-tall floats from which business and community leaders, costumed like mythical figures, toss trinkets to the eager crowds.

*Mardi Gras* is French for "Fat Tuesday," a Christian holiday, also called Carnival, on which people have one last party before the 40 somber days of Lent. The event also has roots in pagan agricultural festivals that mark the season of planting. It is celebrated in most parts of the world; Rio de Janeiro, for example, hosts an extravagant Carnival.

Mardi Gras came to New Orleans with the first French settlers. It became a bigger ritual in 1857, when a secret society of men called the Mystic Krewe of Comus first paraded in costume. Over the next few years, they were joined by the Krewes of Proteus and Nereus and by the Knights of Momus. Krewe members work all year to prepare their costumes and floats, hoping to outdo the other krewes.

New Orleans's Mardi Gras has grown into a citywide carnival that lasts nearly two weeks and features more than 50 separate parades. These are sponsored by scores of krewes and clubs. People take to the streets in dazzling sequined costumes like the one below.

## MARINES

Since the U.S. Marine Corps was established in 1775, "Send in the marines!" has been the signal that America means business. Marines have fought more often and in more places than has any other branch of the military, distinguishing themselves in battles from the American Revolution and the Boxer Rebellion to Desert Storm. During World War II, marines captured the island of Iwo Jima after five weeks of bitter fighting and heavy loss of life, and they were among the first American troops in Korea and Vietnam.

The "leathernecks" (so called because of the collars marines wore in the 18th century as protection from swords) are an elite fighting force trained for combat and military ceremony—"shoot and salute," as they call it. According to a former commandant, marines take pride in tackling "a life of hardship and the most hazardous assignments in battle."

## MARSHALL, JOHN

"If American law were to be represented by a single figure," said Justice Oliver Wendell Holmes, "the figure could be one alone, and that one, John Marshall." Although he had little formal education and studied law for only six weeks, Marshall was appointed chief justice of the Supreme Court in 1801. At the time, the Supreme Court was largely ignored and, without even an office of its own, was forced to meet in a tiny basement room in the Capitol.

Marshall devoted his judicial career to expanding and shaping the Constitution into what he believed was its true meaning. He discouraged individual opinions by the justices in favor of one "opinion of the Court"—often his.

Marshall dominated the Court for 34 years, longer than any chief justice before him or since. Thanks to his broad vision and tireless effort, today the Supreme Court is respected as the highest legal authority in the land.

## MARSHALL PLAN

At the end of World War II, Europe's economy was as ruined as many of its cities. In 1947 U.S. Secretary of State George C. Marshall announced a plan to restore "the confidence of the European people in the economic future of their own countries and of Europe as a whole." Called the Marshall Plan, or the European Recovery Program, it sent Europe more than $13 billion in farm and factory machinery, airplane parts, oil, and other goods over the next four years. The plan was hailed as a "lifeline to sinking men," and soon factories were reopened, electricity was restored, and roads were rebuilt. To achieve this, countries that had recently been enemies were forced to work together for their common good.

## MARTIN AND LEWIS

Soon after they joined forces in 1946, Dean Martin and Jerry Lewis became household names. The success of their nightclub routines attracted Hollywood, and within three years, they made their first movie, *My Friend Irma*. The two played off of their differences: Martin was the relaxed ladies' man and Lewis, his uptight, barely postadolescent sidekick. An early and often repeated routine had Lewis "helping" Martin with a song, whether upstaging the number, misleading the band, or croaking out a duet. While Martin usually provided direction for his less worldly pal onstage, Lewis took the lead offstage, writing and directing material for their act.

By their 10th year together, they had made 16 movies and several television appearances. At their peak, they were among the industry's highest-paid entertainers.

The marines's motto is *Semper Fidelis,* which is Latin for "Always Faithful." The emblem at right is worn on officers' dress uniforms.

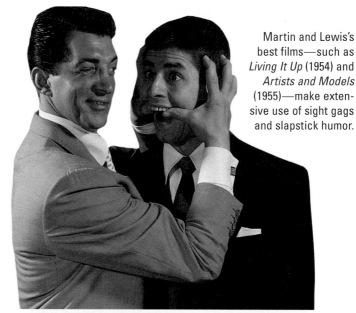

Martin and Lewis's best films—such as *Living It Up* (1954) and *Artists and Models* (1955)—make extensive use of sight gags and slapstick humor.

In *You're Never Too Young* (1955), Jerry Lewis played an apprentice barber trying to escape from a murderer by posing as a 12-year-old.

The Marx Brothers were (left to right) pointy-hatted Chico with the tutti-frutti accent, mustachioed Groucho with a cigar and a leer, and the silent, curly-wigged Harpo.

Mary Richards (right) was television's favorite career girl. Below, it's a very Mary Christmas with, left to right, Murray Slaughter, Rhoda Morgenstern, Lou Grant, Mary Richards, Ted Baxter, and Phyllis Lindstrom.

## MARX BROTHERS

Humorist Robert Benchley called them "cheerful maniacs." To watch them wreaking havoc in *A Night at the Opera* (1935) is to see them at their delirious best, although *Horse Feathers* (1932) is a delight, and *Duck Soup* (1933)—with Groucho as the Prime Minister of Freedonia, cavorting with Margaret Dumont, his perfect foil—exudes inspired zaniness.

Born in New York City, the brothers Marx were launched in vaudeville by their mother, Minnie, and finally made it to Broadway in 1924. They made their screen debut with a fourth brother, Zeppo, in *The Cocoanuts* (1929), but he dropped out after five films when the others left Paramount for MGM. After they made their last Hollywood movie together in 1950, Groucho wrote books and hosted a popular comedy quiz show, *You Bet Your Life*, on which he ad-libbed with abandon. The essence of a Marx Brothers movie? It's in one of Chico's lines: "There ain't no sanity clause!"

## MARY TYLER MOORE SHOW

"My forte is not being funny," Mary Tyler Moore said, "but reacting in a funny way to those around me." So the writers of her 1970s sitcom surrounded Mary with vibrant characters like her friend Rhoda. Always dieting, Rhoda once picked up some candy and said, "I don't know why I'm putting this in my mouth—I should just apply it directly to my hips."

A new style of sitcom, *The Mary Tyler Moore Show* dealt with such issues as the marital problems of Mary's boss, the gruff but tenderhearted Lou Grant, or the insecurities of news writer Murray Slaughter. Only Ted Baxter, the empty-headed anchorman, seemed to have his life in order: "I've got a good job, good health, a good wife, and a fantastic barber."

Mary herself really could turn the world on with her smile, as the theme song said. She was a liberated single working woman, holding together a loyal family of friends and coworkers until the series finally ended in 1977.

## M*A*S*H

Colonel Potter: "By the way, what war is this?" Hawkeye: "The latest war to end all wars." This dialogue, funny and cynical, is from *M*A*S*H*, the most popular series in sitcom history. Running on CBS from 1972 to 1983, it was watched weekly by a worldwide audience of 225 million viewers.

*M*A*S*H*, an acronym for Mobile Army Surgical Hospital, is based on the real-life experiences of Dr. Richard Hornberger, who served as a medic on the front during the Korean War. His war-is-hell novel was released in 1968 and was made into a hit movie in 1970, at the very moment that Americans were becoming critical of another war—Vietnam.

When *M*A*S*H* was adapted for television, Alan Alda contracted to play "Hawkeye" Pierce only after creator Larry Gelbart consented to include operating-room scenes in each episode to bring home the bloody reality of war. Other

M*A*S*H members included Margaret "Hot Lips" Houlihan, the prudish nurse with a liking for secret affairs, Radar O'Reilly, the clerk who knew what you were going to say before you said it, and Max Klinger, an operating-room assistant in drag who hoped he'd be sent home for insanity.

## MASON-DIXON LINE

The celebrated Mason-Dixon Line was the outcome of a simple—but bloody—border dispute. In the 18th century, the Penns and the Calverts, proprietors of Pennsylvania and Maryland respectively, often skirmished over the boundaries of their land. In 1750 the Court of Chancery in England ordered that a line be run between the two properties. Consequently, the families sent to England for surveyors who were "totally unbiased and unprejudiced on either side of the question." Two men, Charles Mason and Jeremiah Dixon, were dispatched. Between 1763 and 1767 they laid out the line to everyone's satisfaction. In the Missouri Compromise of 1820, the Mason-Dixon Line became famous as the northern boundary beyond which slavery would not be allowed.

## MASTERSON, BAT

Bat Masterson had such a daunting reputation as a lawman that a Denver newspaper once reported, "All the toughs and thugs fear him as they do no other dozen men." Born in 1853, he worked as a buffalo hunter and army scout until 1877, when he arrived in Dodge City and was elected sheriff. Within a month, he had captured the notorious outlaw Dave Rudabaugh, which boosted his fame as a gunfighter. Dressed in his signature black suit and bowler hat, Masterson discouraged other desperadoes with hours of public target practice and spread the word that he filed his gun's hammer until "the blamed gun would pretty near go off if you looked at it."

Masterson turned up in New York City in 1902, where he became a sportswriter for the *Morning Telegraph*. In 1905 President Theodore Roosevelt offered him the job of marshal of the Oklahoma Territory, but he declined, saying, "I would be a bait for grown-up kids who had fed on dime novels."

## MATHER, COTTON

Cotton Mather's birth united two of the most honored families in early New England, the Cottons and the Mathers. His grandfathers were Puritan leaders who helped develop the Massachusetts Bay Colony as a haven for Protestants escaping persecution in Britain. A child prodigy, Mather entered Harvard at age 12, studying to be a clergyman. Ten years later he was appointed a co-minister with his father, Increase Mather, of the Second Church of Boston. As a chronicler of his times, Mather wrote *Magnalia Christi Americana*, a massive history of New England. His *Bonifacius* inspired Benjamin Franklin to write later, "If I have been ... a useful citizen, the public owes the advantage of it to that book."

In the 1970 movie version (left to right), Trapper John was played by Elliott Gould, Frank Burns by Robert Duvall, and Hawkeye by Donald Sutherland.

M*A*S*H's TV cast included (clockwise from top left) Father Francis Mulcahy, Cpl. Max Klinger, Maj. Charles Emerson Winchester, Maj. Margaret Houlihan, Capt. Benjamin Franklin Pierce, Col. Sherman T. Potter, and Capt. B. J. Hunnicut.

In the early-1960s television series *Bat Masterson*, the legendary sheriff became quite a dandy and a ladies' man. Gene Barry, shown here, starred in the title role.

Bret Maverick (right) was a ladies' man, a gentleman gambler, and an antihero—he wasn't good with a gun and liked to take his "pappy's" advice to run in the face of danger. Brother Bart (left) was played by Jack Kelly.

## MAVERICK

It began in 1957 as a conventional TV Western. Then, one day, not long after the show went on the air, a bored scriptwriter slipped in stage directions for Bret Maverick, the main character: "Look at him with your beady little eyes." Happy to oblige, actor James Garner hammed up the scene, and American television's first satirical Western was launched.

*Maverick*, like the unbranded steer the word describes, was a loner among TV Westerns, going so far as to periodically spoof other Westerns, such as *Bonanza*, *Cheyenne*, and *Gunsmoke*. The show even satirized *Dragnet*, a non-Western.

The series went off the air in 1962. The character was reprised by Mel Gibson in a 1994 film version that featured James Garner in the role of Maverick's "pappy."

## MAYFLOWER

Many think that being descended from someone who came to this country in 1620 on the *Mayflower* is a sign of high status, but the people who made that trip were actually refugees who suffered a great deal of discomfort. During the two-month passage from Plymouth, England, to what is now Plymouth, Massachusetts, the weather was stormy, and so were conditions on the 90-foot-long ship, which was crammed with 101 passengers, a full crew, supplies, and livestock. Life on board was so unbearable that the Pilgrims decided to land as soon as possible rather than sail on to Virginia.

Shipboard tensions ran high between rival religious factions. This—coupled with the fact that the ship was landing in an area outside any government jurisdiction—prompted the leaders to draw up the Mayflower Compact. The document, the first by European settlers, established democratic rule in the New World. It is this form of government that was the *Mayflower*'s great gift to America.

## MAYO CLINIC

The Mayo Clinic, a world-famous medical complex that has treated presidents, kings, and movie stars, started out in 1889 as St. Mary's Hospital in Rochester, Minnesota. It had one operating room and three doctors: Dr. William Worrall Mayo and his sons, Dr. William James Mayo and Dr. Charles Mayo. In the early years, the Mayos performed all the surgeries themselves (more than 3,100 operations in 1904) and assumed the clerical duties as well.

By 1905, when the hospital became known as the Mayo Clinic, other doctors had joined the practice and new specialties were developed. Today the clinic has more than 1,000 physicians and scientists and offers the latest in medical technology. What makes this clinic unique is its high quality of patient care: there is close contact with patients, and tests and treatments are designed with a minimum of waiting and a maximum of caring. The legacy of the doctors Mayo is consideration for the patient's sensibilities and comfort.

No one is sure what happened to the original *Mayflower*; one theory is that it was dismantled, its hull used as a barn roof.

## MAYS, WILLIE

Able to run, throw, field, and hit with power, Willie Mays was a natural athlete whose enthusiasm for the game infected all who watched him play. The most exciting player of the 1950s and '60s, Mays running bases was a sight not soon forgotten: legs far apart, arms pumping furiously, head turned sharply to watch the flight of the ball, cap flying off his head, he whooshed around the bases. When the Giants moved west from New York to San Francisco in 1958, Mays adjusted his batting stroke. Previously a dead-pull hitter, he began hitting the ball to right field in order to take advantage of the strong winds at Candlestick Park. Mays is generally regarded as the greatest player of the second half of the 20th century.

## McCARTHY, JOSEPH R.

Senator Joseph R. McCarthy made front-page headlines on February 9, 1950, when, in a speech in Wheeling, West Virginia, he claimed to have a list of 205 State Department employees "who have been named as members of the Communist Party and members of a spy ring." A Senate sub-committee labeled his charges "a fraud and a hoax," but McCarthy had ignited the country's anxieties about communism. His unsubstantiated charges often cost the accused their jobs and reputations, yet his many supporters applauded these events in the name of national security.

In 1954 he accused the U.S. Army of treason; the Senate, fed up with his "witch-hunt," condemned him. After that, his power waned, and he died three years later. In his memoirs, President Dwight Eisenhower wrote, "McCarthyism took its toll on many individuals and on the nation. No one was safe from charges recklessly made from inside the walls of Congressional immunity... the cost was often tragic."

## McCORMICK, CYRUS

Cyrus McCormick's cumbersome and clattering horse-drawn reaper was first publicly demonstrated on a hot July day in 1831 in Virginia's Shenandoah Valley. For centuries, farmers had harvested grainfields with sickles and scythes. Using this method, it took two days for one man to cut down one acre of wheat. That afternoon, McCormick's still-crude machine harvested six acres. Eventually, he manufactured an improved reaper capable of cutting an acre of grain in less than an hour.

Employing such sales techniques as field trials, testimonials, and installment plans, McCormick made his invention a commercial success by the 1840s. He became one of America's wealthiest men, despite efforts by more than 100 competitors to take over his design after his original patent ran out in 1848. McCormick's invention earned international acclaim in 1851 during London's Crystal Palace Exhibition. The London *Times* declared that the revolutionary harvester was "worth the whole cost of the Exhibition."

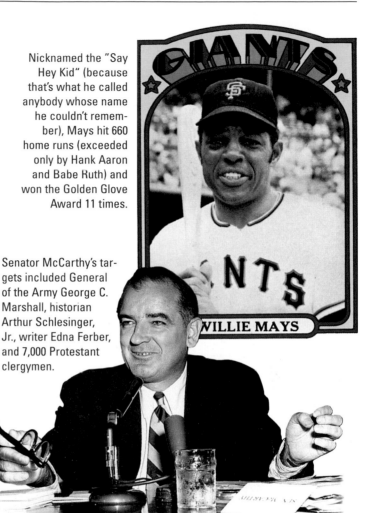

Nicknamed the "Say Hey Kid" (because that's what he called anybody whose name he couldn't remember), Mays hit 660 home runs (exceeded only by Hank Aaron and Babe Ruth) and won the Golden Glove Award 11 times.

WILLIE MAYS

Senator McCarthy's targets included General of the Army George C. Marshall, historian Arthur Schlesinger, Jr., writer Edna Ferber, and 7,000 Protestant clergymen.

For 20 years Cyrus McCormick's father tried (and failed) to invent a harvesting machine. Cyrus was just 22 years old when he succeeded.

In 1950 Mead warned Americans to avoid the urge "to overvalue youth, to undervalue the middle years, and merely to tolerate old age."

Home delivery of meals is a crucial service for the recipients. Meals-on-Wheels enables many people who are elderly or ill to live comfortably at home and have some independence.

Unlike other meats, a properly made meat loaf stays moist, thus providing a satisfying meal—and comforting leftovers—at all hours.

## MEAD, MARGARET

Margaret Mead was a pioneer in the field of anthropology whose study of primitive cultures gave Americans an insight into their own culture. In 1925, at the age of 24, she ventured to the remote Samoan island of Tau to study adolescent girls. She found that their relatively permissive society allowed them to maneuver adolescence with ease, unlike American girls of that period, who were encumbered by Victorian notions of behavior. The result was her first book, *Coming of Age in Samoa*, a classic of cultural anthropology.

In an attempt to determine whether human behavior is innate or ordained by society, Mead went on to study societies as different as those of the Soviet Union and the American Indians. She published 39 books and lectured all over the country, encouraging women to have careers as well as children. By the time she died in 1978, she had helped to guide American women to a larger role in the world.

## MEALS-ON-WHEELS

The Meals-on-Wheels program, which delivers nourishment and companionship to housebound people, is a joint venture between the U.S. government and private local groups: federal dollars help pay for the food; volunteers deliver it.

Volunteerism is strong in most communities. Many organizations provide critical services, such as cuddling attention-starved abandoned children and acting as Big Brothers and Big Sisters to troubled kids. Lawyers may offer their services pro bono (for free); retired executives join S.C.O.R.E., the Service Corps of Retired Executives, and donate their expertise to struggling start-up companies. Where there's a need, it seems, there is often someone willing to help.

## MEAT LOAF

Meat loaf developed an unfortunate reputation because it showed up in school and military cafeterias a day or two after the menu had featured a less mysterious form of meat, and because thrifty homemakers occasionally skimped on the meat and used too much filler. Recently, however, gourmets have rediscovered meat loaf and are making spicy variations, such as Cajun meat loaf, and using expensive ingredients, like veal. Whether gourmet or everyday, meat loaf has much to recommend it. It sticks to the ribs and it's fun to make: all but the finicky mush the ingredients together with their fingers.

## MEDAL OF HONOR

In 1782 George Washington created a badge for bravery in the form of a purple heart, but after the Revolution it was not awarded for 150 years. America's dislike of royal orders stood in the way of honoring heroism. It was not until the Civil War that a Medal of Honor for "gallantry in action and other soldierlike qualities" was authorized. A review of these awards in the early 20th century led to more than 900 cancellations—they had been given not for heroic deeds but, in some cases, for merely reenlisting. Notable recipients include Civil War assistant surgeon Dr. Mary Walker, the only woman to receive the medal; Charles A. Lindbergh, who made history with his solo flight over the Atlantic; and Audie Murphy, the most decorated soldier of World War II, who subsequently became an actor.

The Medal of Honor, our highest award for valor, has been given 2,611 times from the start of the Civil War through the end of the Vietnam War.

## MELVILLE, HERMAN

"I'd strike the sun if it insulted me," brags the egotistical Captain Ahab in *Moby Dick*, Herman Melville's bold epic pitting man against nature. At first Melville planned a conventional sea-adventure story, much like *Typee* and *Omoo*, two previous novels about exotic adventures in the South Pacific. However, when Melville introduced Ahab on the deck of his whaling ship and outlined the captain's obsessive quest to spear the white whale, *Moby Dick* began to take on darker tones. Melville created fantastical scenes of shipwrecking tempests, sharks' feeding frenzies, and mutinous harpooners.

His next novel, *Pierre*, which appeared just a year after *Moby Dick*, was universally panned. Unable to handle the criticism, he ended his writing career at age 36 and lived out the remainder of his days as a customs inspector in New York City. He died in 1891 at the age of 72, and it wasn't until *Billy Budd* was published, some 30 years after his death, that his place in American literature was secured.

## MERMAN, ETHEL

On opening night of *Annie Get Your Gun* (1946), a tremulous chorus member approached the star. "Oh, Miss Merman," she quavered. "Aren't you nervous?" "Why?" demanded the familiar brassy voice. "I know my lines." Born in Queens, New York, in 1909, the former stenographer performed in nightclubs before making her Broadway debut in *Girl Crazy* (1930). Not conventionally pretty and neither charming nor demure, she was instead a natural force whose clarion notes could rattle teeth in the top balcony, whose crystal-clear diction unabashedly proclaimed her "New Yawk" origins, and whose top-heavy build prompted one critic to marvel that she always appeared to be viewed from above.

In 1934 Cole Porter's *Anything Goes* perfectly showcased her brazen delivery in songs like "Blow, Gabriel, Blow" and established her as the reigning queen of Broadway musicals. *Red, Hot and Blue* and *DuBarry Was a Lady* were followed by *Annie Get Your Gun*, in which she introduced the backstage national anthem, "There's No Business Like Show Business." In 1950 The Merm won a Tony for *Call Me Madam*, and in 1959 she crowned her career as Mama in *Gypsy*. Her inimitable (and unamplified) voice endures on recordings, and she can be seen in more than a dozen movies.

The 1851 epic novel *Moby Dick* tells of an obsessed sea captain who drives his crew mercilessly in his quest for vengeance against the elusive white whale.

Born Ethel Zimmerman, Merman shortened her name because she was afraid it had too many letters to fit on a marquee. Commenting on Merman's unique style, Cole Porter once likened her to a brass band going by.

Cliff Palace, with 220 rooms, was the largest pueblo at Mesa Verde. The village included an intricate system of ditches for collecting rainwater.

## MESA VERDE

"It looks just like a palace," whispered Charles Mason to his companion, Richard Wetherkill. In 1888 the two were searching for stray cattle near Wetherkill's Colorado ranch when they stumbled upon a time capsule of sorts: the cliffside dwellings of a vanished people known as the Anasazi, or "ancient ones." The multistory city, complete with homes, meeting places, and ceremonial chambers, dates back to A.D. 1150. No one is certain why the tribe abandoned the site.

Wetherkill spent much of the rest of his life trying to unearth relics from the Anasazi culture. Although his work has been criticized because of his sometimes slipshod technique, it has provided valuable insight into the mysterious Anasazi. They were a fascinating people, skilled not only in building but in basket weaving, pottery making, and farming as well. Their city, sheltered from the elements, is so well preserved that it seems its inhabitants left only yesterday.

## METROPOLITAN OPERA

In the 19th century, New York City's freshly minted millionaires found that they were unable to buy box seats at the New York Academy of Music because the Old Guard had a monopoly on them. So they took matters into their own hands and built a new opera house. The Metropolitan Opera opened in 1883, and by the turn of the century, it was one of the world's great theaters, attracting such artists as conductor Arturo Toscanini and tenor Enrico Caruso. The Met became a national institution in 1931, when its Saturday-matinee performances were broadcast nationwide on the radio and brought opera live to the heartland. The broadcasts were a crucial source of revenue for the Met and kept it afloat throughout the Depression.

From the beginning, the Met focused on bringing international stars, such as Fyodor Chaliapin, Kirsten Flagstad, and Renata Tebaldi, to its stage. It wasn't until the late 1930s that the voices of many American singers began to be heard; thus began a parade of native talent that would include Risë Stevens, Leonard Warren, Richard Tucker, Roberta Peters, Leontyne Price, Sherrill Milnes, and Jerry Hadley. Since the 1970s, broadcasts on public television have featured both American and foreign artists, such as Luciano Pavarotti, Marilyn Horne, Joan Sutherland, Thomas Hampson, and Cecilia Bartoli, and have brought the Met bigger audiences than ever.

James Morris (left) made his debut at the Met at age 23. He is one of today's foremost Wagnerian singers. Maria Callas (below) was noted for her superb musicianship and dramatic flair. She spurred the revival of 19th-century bel canto operas.

Following her debut at the Met in 1975, soprano Beverly Sills was given an 18-minute ovation. But she is best known for her association with the New York City Opera.

## MGM

In April 1949 a movie studio threw a 25th-anniversary luncheon at which 58 of its 80 stars and supporting players posed for a historic group photograph. The guests had names like Barrymore, Astaire, Gable, Hepburn, Tracy, and Sinatra. Their boss believed in movie queens "looking right," and they did: there's beautiful Arlene Dahl dressed in high-fashion splendor; Angela Lansbury all gloves, glossy lips, and gleaming curls; even Lassie is fresh from a doggie makeover. The gents sport jacket and tie, short hair, and smooth chins. The gathering represented the most glamorous lineup ever controlled by one company: Metro-Goldwyn-Mayer.

MGM, a combination of Metro Pictures, Goldwyn Picture Corporation, and Louis B. Mayer Pictures, was established in 1924. As a subsidiary of Loew's, which had a huge chain of movie houses, it had a ready-made audience. By the early 1930s the MGM lion was roaring, and the studio's slogan, "More Stars Than There Are in Heaven," was almost true.

Diminutive Irving Thalberg, the "Boy Wonder" whose name (by choice) never appeared on the screen, was responsible for some of MGM's best pictures: *Grand Hotel, Mutiny on the Bounty*, and *The Good Earth*. Thalberg, who "looked and behaved like a prince," died at 37, leaving his widow, star Norma Shearer, in a studio controlled by Louis B. Mayer alone. Mayer thought of MGM as one happy family, with himself as Big Daddy, protecting and controlling his stars. Under Mayer, who tolerated no vulgarity in his pictures, MGM produced *The Wizard of Oz* and *The Philadelphia Story*.

In 1951 Mayer was replaced by Dore Schary. The following year Loew's was forced to divest itself of MGM. In the '50s the studio entered the golden age of movie musicals, which gave us *Annie Get Your Gun, Show Boat*, and *Singin' in the Rain*. In the 1960s MGM declined, and in 1970 it auctioned off hundreds of thousands of classic MGM props and costumes. By the late '70s the company had diversified; in 1986 Ted Turner acquired the huge library of MGM films. But regardless of how the company has changed over the years, what most people think of when they hear "MGM" is that star-spangled studio of the '30s and '40s,—and Louis B. Mayer's motto: "Make it good, make it big, give it class!"

## MIAMI BEACH

No two words conjure up images of surf, sand, spandex, and gold lamé more readily than *Miami Beach*. Ever since its first hotel opened in 1914, this Florida tourist mecca has cultivated a reputation for fun, fantasy, and perpetual sunshine.

A separate city from Miami, the "Beach" occupies 16 islands located 2½ miles off the mainland. The largest, a sliver of sand and pavement just seven miles long and 1½ miles wide, is where the action is. In the 1950s the island was best known for its Gold Coast hotels, including the flashy Fontainebleu, complete with a Frank Sinatra suite and a half-acre swimming grotto. In the 1980s the hot spot shifted to the island's tip, where newly renovated Art Deco hotels and buildings—sporting tropical colors, streamlined corners, and nautical motifs—line the streets. The 800-odd structures in the Art Deco Historic District constitute the largest concentration of such Depression-era architecture in the world.

MGM was famous for its grand roster of stars, which included Judy Garland (pictured here with Tom Drake in the 1944 musical *Meet Me in St. Louis*), and for the majestic roar of its mascot, Leo the Lion.

Often likened to the French Riviera, Miami Beach is a haven for sunbathers, celebrity hunters, and Rollerbladers.

Minnie Mouse has been at Mickey's side ever since the beginning. She loves and inspires her Mickey but will give him a scolding when he deserves it.

Before Microsoft, America's image of a billionaire was a gray-haired veteran of industry in a suit. Bill Gates changed that by becoming a billionaire at 31 and the richest man in America while still in his thirties.

## MICKEY MOUSE

Mickey Mouse debuted in *Steamboat Willie* in 1928, with his creator, Walt Disney, supplying his squeaky voice. Disney gave Mickey a sunny disposition and a trusting nature along with the courage to face opponents that towered over him. Mickey quickly became America's little hero and appeared on everything from lunch boxes to underwear. Mickey has starred in films and, on television, in the original *Mickey Mouse Club* and, more recently, the *New Mickey Mouse Club*. He's on hand to welcome guests to Disneyland, the Walt Disney World Resort, Disneyland Paris, and Tokyo Disneyland. He even has a multi-platinum record, "Mickey Mouse Disco," and a statue in Madame Tussaud's Wax Museum in London.

Pluto the Pup has been Mickey's pet since 1930. Pluto can't talk, so he can't defend himself when blamed for something he hasn't done. Not that he's always blameless; Pluto has a mischievous streak. Goofy, Mickey's best friend, was originally called Dippy Dawg. He greets his frequent failures, often due to his own clumsiness, with a hearty guffaw.

Donald Duck's distinctive voice and hot temper first appeared in *The Wise Little Hen* in 1934. Although it's often impossible to understand what Donald is saying, there's never any question about how he feels. He's jealous of any attention the others get, but he's made more movies than Mickey, including *Der Fuehrer's Face* (1943), which launched a best-selling record and won an Academy Award.

## MICROSOFT

At age 19, Bill Gates co-founded Microsoft, the company that created MS/DOS (the operating system that runs IBM and IBM-compatible personal computers) and Windows, the software that added on-screen symbols and point-and-click "mouse" commands to IBM PCs, making them almost as user-friendly as Macintosh computers. In recent years Microsoft has been developing multimedia and Internet software.

At Microsoft, located in Bellevue, Washington, there is no dress code, most workers are very young, and the competitive spirit is strong. Because of the long hours they put in, new employees are nicknamed "Microserfs."

## MILLER, ARTHUR

Says salesman Willy Loman, "He's a man way out there in the blue, riding on a smile and a shoeshine.... A salesman is got to dream, boy. It comes with the territory." *Death of a Salesman* (1949) established Arthur Miller as a leading playwright and earned him a Pulitzer Prize. *Salesman* was followed by *The Crucible*, a parable about McCarthyism set during the Salem witch trials, and *A View from the Bridge*, a tale about Italian Americans living in Brooklyn. In 1961 Miller wrote *The Misfits*, one of Marilyn Monroe's greatest roles. His marriage to Monroe, however, was disastrous and inspired *After the Fall*, a play he wrote after her death.

In the 1966 TV version of *Death of a Salesman,* George Segal (left) and James Farantino (center) played the sons of Lee J. Cobb's Willy Loman.

## MILLER, GLENN

Tall, lean, bespectacled bandleader Glenn Miller had a passion for precision and an ear for variety. The Glenn Miller Band, which played romantic, danceable ballads like "Moonlight Serenade" and "Fools Rush In" and catchy bounces like "In the Mood" and "Chattanooga Choo Choo," was one of the most beloved of the swing era.

Miller played with, and arranged for, Benny Goodman, Red Nichols, the Dorsey Brothers, and others. When he put together a band for visiting bandleader Ray Noble, he made his most important discovery—the distinctive sound of a clarinet playing the high notes over four saxophones, which became the Miller sound. In 1938 Miller's band captivated jitterbuggers and soon went to the top. In 1942 Miller enlisted in the air force and led the U.S. Army Air Force Band. When his plane went down over the English Channel on December 15, 1944, the whole nation mourned. After Miller's death, his band was kept alive by Tex Beneke and others.

## MILLS BROTHERS

For more than five decades, the warmly meshed voices of The Mills Brothers spun out popular melodies in cool, sophisticated harmony. The most successful male singing group in America, and the first black group to win a large white audience, the quartet was a model for later harmony groups. Of the group's 2,246 recordings, 71 were charted and five went to the number one spot, including "Tiger Rag," "Dinah," "You Always Hurt the One You Love," and "Paper Doll," which stayed at number one for a record 12 weeks and sold more than 6 million copies. "The Glow Worm" (1952) was made with a backup band instead of their own vocal riffs.

The brothers—John Jr., Herbert, Harry, and Donald—found their sound as teenagers practicing in their father's barbershop. After John Jr. died in 1935, his spot was filled by the boys' father, John Sr., until he retired in the '50s. The remaining brothers, unable to find a replacement who could produce the appropriate harmonies, carried on. Harry once remarked, "It's in the blood... it's a family thing."

## MINIATURE GOLF

Invented in 1916 by a wealthy Southerner who was entertaining guests at his weekend estate, miniature golf didn't became a national craze until about a decade later, when a Tennessee man added a course to his hotel. Americans eagerly accepted the challenge of putting a golf ball through or around miniature castles, waterfalls, and windmills before sinking it into a hole. Miniature golf was so popular in the '20s that postage-stamp-size courses even sprang up on the rooftops of Manhattan skyscrapers. In the '30s miniature golf tournaments encouraged friendly competition. Today some large malls include miniature golf courses as part of the shopping experience.

Born in Clarinda, Iowa, in 1904, Glenn Miller began performing with dance bands at age 16 and left college to play trombone professionally.

The Mills Brothers, a singing group that used their voices to imitate brass instruments, paved the way for the doo-wop sound of the 1950s.

In the '50s, teenagers flocked to miniature golf courses featuring such obstacles as grinning turtles, lighthouses, and sphinxes.

The Minuteman statue overlooking the town green in Lexington, Massachusetts, honors the men who fought in the first battle of the Revolution.

The first Miss America (above) was also the smallest: the 1921 winner was 5'1" and weighed 108 pounds. For today's winner, life is a whirl of interviews, speeches, and appearances. She travels all year long, always in the company of a female chaperone.

## MINSTREL SHOW

The first experience many whites had with black music and dialect were skits performed by white entertainers in "black-face"—their skin darkened by burned cork—who imitated black speech, dances, and songs. By the mid-1800s the skits had grown into "minstrel shows," or "Ethiopian operas," performed by such troupes as Christy's Minstrels, for whom Stephen Foster wrote many of his best-known songs.

The shows included crude parodies of such stereotyped characters as Dandy Jim, the city slicker, and Jim Crow, the plantation slave. Musicians stood in a semicircle and played fiddle, banjo, tambourine, and clappers, and accompanied a dancer. Between numbers, they exchanged jokes in dialect. The finale was a song-and-dance skit called a "walk-around." After the Civil War, blacks took up minstrelsy, adding spirituals and portraying the characters more sympathetically.

## MINUTEMEN

Before the Revolution, America had no army; the Colonies relied on militias made up of every able-bodied male between the ages of 16 and 60. As war neared, a third of them became Minutemen, armed and ready to fight at a moment's notice. On the night of April 18, 1775, 700 British soldiers left Boston to destroy military supplies collected at Concord. At dawn they reached Lexington, where 70 Minutemen faced them. Hopelessly outnumbered, the Minutemen were withdrawing when a weapon was fired—no one knows by which side. It was "the shot heard round the world." The nervous British killed eight soldiers and wounded ten.

The British continued on to Concord. On their return march, Minutemen fired into the column from behind walls and trees, in the guerrilla style of fighting they learned from the Indians. They could hardly miss the bright red British uniform coats, and 273 soldiers were killed or wounded. Only a British rescue force prevented total annihilation.

## MISS AMERICA

There she goes, and if it's September, it must be Miss America. The first Miss America beauty contest was dreamed up in 1921 as part of an effort to extend the tourist season in Atlantic City, New Jersey. To give the stage show more punch, the talent category was added in 1938. Controlled by modeling agencies and observed by Hollywood talent scouts, the contest judged beauty, voice, wholesomeness, and special talents, in that order.

Today the term *beauty contest* is a no-no—it's The Miss America Scholarship Pageant. All the competitors have a local and a state sponsor. They are judged in four categories: talent, swimsuit, evening gown, and interview, with talent accounting for half the points. Other qualities emphasized are intelligence, energy, poise, and oh, yes—attractiveness. The contestant's measurements are no longer divulged.

## MISSISSIPPI RIVER

The Mississippi, that "ol' man river," is the greatest river in the country, coursing 2,350 miles from Lake Itasca in northern Minnesota to the Gulf of Mexico. It meanders in its northern reaches, but after it meets the Ohio River, it winds so sinuously that it takes 1,500 miles to travel 600 miles as the crow flies. Along the way, its restless waters cut wide loops and horseshoe-shaped bends. Channels change course so often that the river must be constantly resurveyed.

For centuries the Mississippi was a major means of transportation. In 1811 the steamboat *New Orleans* set sail from Pittsburgh. By 1860 more than 1,000 steamboats plied the river's waters. Floods have always caused damage to farms and businesses, although, as Mark Twain saw it, the Mississippi "never tumbles one man's farm overboard without building a new farm just like it for that man's neighbor." Today, as towns sprawl onto the floodplain and homes are built on the river's banks, protecting property from floods has become an expensive—and controversial—proposition.

## MR. ED

In the 1960s some of the funniest television humor came from a horse's mouth: Mr. Ed's. Mr. Ed was an opinionated talking palomino who would converse only with Wilbur, played by Alan Young. The horse, whose deep voice was supplied by Allan "Rocky" Lane, caused trouble by reporting overheard conversations, typing letters that Wilbur got blamed for, and making demands, including the right to vote and a stall decorated in Chinese Modern style.

The horse who played Mr. Ed died in 1979 at age 33. But the show lives on in reruns around the world, each beginning with the theme song "A horse is a horse, of course, of course" that leads up to the horse's announcement: "I am Mr. Ed."

## MRS. O'LEARY'S COW

The Great Chicago Fire of 1871 started in a cow barn behind Mrs. Patrick O'Leary's cottage, but who or what started it is a mystery. At about 9:00 P.M. on October 8, a man noticed tiny flames coming from the barn, and his shouting woke up the neighborhood. Legend holds that Mrs. O'Leary was milking a cow, and it kicked over a kerosene lantern. Actually, she was sleeping when the fire started, but if a lighted lantern had been left behind, the cow could indeed have kicked it over.

The summer had been very dry, and almost every building in Chicago, as well as the sidewalks, were wooden. The O'Leary barn burned in minutes, and strong winds sent flaming debris flying from roof to roof. Firemen fought as heat warped their leather helmets and caused their uniforms to smoke. Four square miles burned for three days, killing nearly 300 and making 100,000 homeless. Losses bankrupted some insurance companies. Food, clothing, and money poured in from all over America and 29 foreign countries.

The Mississippi has more turns than the *s*'s in its name. During the flood of 1993, thousands in Des Moines, Iowa, lost their homes. The lucky managed to rescue their most precious belongings.

Mr. Ed was a voracious reader and a hypochondriac, too. His was one of the fantasy shows that pervaded the 1960s, along with *I Dream of Jeannie*, *Bewitched*, and *My Favorite Martian*.

## JASPER JOHNS
Johns said he chose to paint a familiar image in "Three Flags" (1958) "because I didn't have to design it.... That gave me room to work on other levels."

# MODERN AMERICAN

*European work once dominated the art world—even in America. But in the last half century, American artists have taken the lead, pioneering bold new styles.*

## GEORGE SEGAL
By placing his stark white figures in everyday situations, as in "Walk, Don't Walk" (1976), Segal called attention to the alienation that people can feel even on a crowded street.

## HELEN FRANKENTHALER
In such landscapes as "Flood" (1967), Frankenthaler used her "soak-stain" technique, in which colors soak into the canvas and form their own vague boundaries.

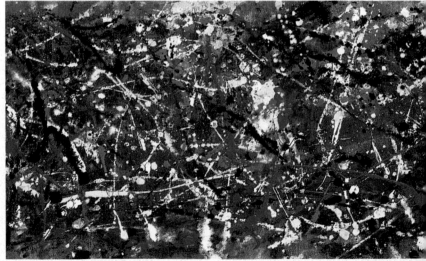

## HORACE PIPPIN

"Pictures just come to my mind, and I tell my heart to go ahead," Pippin said. Completely self-taught, he began painting at 42 and often found inspiration in family life, as with "Sunday Morning Breakfast" (1943).

## STUART DAVIS

Davis painted this "Abstract Vision of New York" for a museum show in 1932. He used his loose, jazzy technique to convey the energy and diversity of his hometown. The Empire State Building, one-year-old at the time, is seen in the background.

## CLAES OLDENBURG

By creating massive soft sculptures of everyday objects, such as "Giant Hamburger" (1962), Oldenburg showed his distaste for high art and his wariness of mass culture.

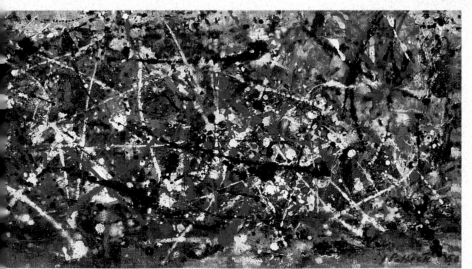

## JACKSON POLLOCK

In paintings like "Number 25" (1950), Pollock claimed that his unconscious mind took control of the work. He would stand over a canvas and carefully pour paint on it, "since this way I can walk around it, work from the four sides, and literally be in the painting," he said.

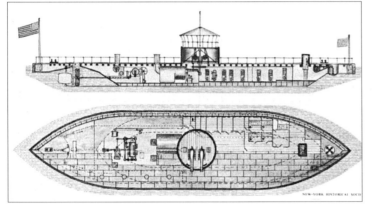

A Currier & Ives print (top) captured the battle between the *Monitor* (at left) and the *Merrimack*. The plan of the *Monitor* (above) shows the revolving turret in the center of the ship.

## MONITOR AND MERRIMACK

They were the most unlikely-looking saviors a navy had ever known. Union officers said the Confederates' ironclad, the *Merrimack*, resembled "the roof of a barn belching forth smoke from a chimney." Their own *Monitor*, with its cylindrical gun turret perched on deck, had been described as a "cheesebox on a raft" and a "tin can on a shingle." But for all their detractors, the first ironclad warships to meet in battle were fearsome secret weapons. In the summer of 1861, word had spread around Washington that the Confederates were raising a scuttled Union frigate and equipping it with impenetrable armor. President Lincoln, fearing the ship would lay waste to his naval blockade, ordered the production of an ironclad.

In 100 days, the *Monitor* was ready to sail, and just in time. On March 8, 1862, the *Merrimack*, renamed the *Virginia*, lumbered into Chesapeake Bay and demolished two Union warships. The next morning, when the ironclad headed for a third ship, it met the *Monitor* instead. At Virginia's Hampton Roads, the metal monsters passed and repassed, lobbing 150-pound shots at each other. It was a war of attrition, and after about four hours, the *Merrimack* limped off, taking in water and running out of fuel.

Neither ship would be effective in battle again. The Confederates destroyed the *Merrimack* when they evacuated Norfolk two months later. The *Monitor*, which rode just nine inches above the water, sank in a gale on December 31, 1862. By that time, two more Union ironclads had been built, and the age of wooden fighting ships had come to an end.

## MONOPOLY

In 1931 Charles Darrow, who was out of work because of the Depression, sat at his kitchen table and sketched on the oilcloth the design for a game he called Monopoly, which let players spend hours pretending to be real estate tycoons. Parker Brothers rejected the game, but changed its mind in 1935 after Darrow made his own copies and sold them with great success. The royalties made Darrow a millionaire.

Today many aspects of Monopoly—including the figure of the top-hatted tycoon in tails, the streets named after those of Atlantic City in its heyday, and the low prices on real estate—clearly come from another era. But the game remains popular. It brings out the ruthless capitalist in even the meekest player, allows one to accumulate colorful stacks of cash, and occasionally sends even the most skillful player to "jail."

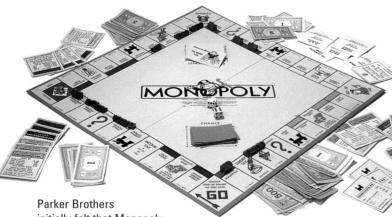

Parker Brothers initially felt that Monopoly was "terribly complicated" and that "the subject matter—real estate—was of no interest to anybody." Today the game is played worldwide.

## MONROE, MARILYN

Born in Los Angeles of uncertain paternity, Norma Jean Baker was consigned to an orphanage after her mother was institutionalized. Her looks were her salvation: after World War II she began a career as a model, became a Fox Film starlet, and changed her name to Marilyn Monroe. She played a variety of small roles before 1953, the year of *Gentlemen Prefer Blondes*, *Niagara*, and *How to Marry a Millionaire*. Monroe was a major box office attraction, and her pretty pout, sensational figure, and breathless little-girl voice abundantly compensated for her limited acting skills.

In 1954 Monroe married baseball legend Joe DiMaggio; the union lasted less than a year. Yearning for intellectual pursuits, Monroe took classes at the Actors Studio in New York. In 1956 she married playwright Arthur Miller; that year, she gave an irresistibly comic performance in *Bus Stop*.

By the time she filmed *The Misfits* (1961), written for her by her husband, Monroe had become increasingly difficult to work with. She was chronically late and was dependent on alcohol and sleeping pills. One week before the film's opening, she divorced Miller. She began a new movie in 1962 but was fired for habitual absence. A month later, she died of a barbiturate overdose, possibly a suicide. Since her death, there have been countless books, documentaries, and TV movies about the girl who paid the highest price for superstardom. As Elton John sang, "Goodbye, Norma Jean ... the candle burned out long before the legend ever did."

## MONROE DOCTRINE

In his annual message to Congress in 1823, President James Monroe boldly stated, "The American continents ... are henceforth not to be considered as subjects for future colonization by any European power." The declaration was prompted by Russian claims on the Oregon Territory, and by the fear that European nations would use force to help Spain reclaim her newly independent colonies in Latin America. The policy, in effect a warning to Europe, became known as the Monroe Doctrine. It wasn't exercised until 1845, when James Polk invoked it to annex Texas and lay claim to the Oregon Territory and California. For the rest of the 19th century, it was used to justify American expansion in the West.

## MONSTER TRUCKS

In 1974, when Bob Chandler of Hazelwood, Missouri, created *Bigfoot*, a souped-up pickup truck perched on four-foot-tall tires, he attracted some attention. A truck built that way could get sportsmen through the muddiest backwoods. But when he drove *Bigfoot* over a heap of junked cars, he launched the monster-truck fad. Fan clubs, magazines, and television specials soon followed.

*Bigfoot* is small compared with today's 15,000-pound monster trucks, which ride on six-foot-tall tractor tires and star in competitions at arenas around the country. The trucks sometimes race through deep mud pits, but their main attraction is their ability to crush cars. The violent spectacle is immensely appealing to anyone who has ever dreamed of escaping a traffic jam by cruising over everything in his path.

From *The Seven Year Itch*, the image of Marilyn Monroe standing over a subway grating has become a famous pinup.

Fans look on as a monster truck leaps from a ramp onto a row of cars. The trucks have 1,800-horsepower engines and names like *Nitemare II*.

The house that Jefferson built is considered one of the finest examples of Classical Revival style. The former president is buried on the grounds.

The buttes and pinnacles of Monument Valley were once part of a continuous layer of rock. Eventually they, too, will be worn away.

A moonshiner labors over his corn whiskey, which mountain folk still swear by as a cure for snakebite. Most stills consist of an airtight kettle connected by a copper coil to a barrel of cool water.

## MONTICELLO

Thomas Jefferson and Monticello: a pair for the ages. In no other presidential residence are the personalities of house and master so deeply intertwined. Jefferson was 25 when, in 1768, he began building his new house atop a small mountain near Charlottesville, Virginia. He scorned the stock Georgian designs so loved by his peers. And, distancing himself even further from the colonial nabobs of his day (who preferred their mansions facing broad, navigable rivers), Jefferson set his home—Monticello, Italian for "little mountain"—on a foothill of the Blue Ridge Mountains.

For 40 years Jefferson took delight in "putting up and pulling down," following his own designs. He built the kitchen, carriage house, and other service rooms under the long terraces on either side of the house. He believed that staircases should be inconspicuous; his were only 24 inches wide. In the 1790s Jefferson, inspired partly by mansions he had seen in France and partly by the domed Temple of Vesta in Rome, began a massive redo. Monticello was enlarged from eight rooms to 21 and arranged to disguise three stories behind a one-story facade. Today the house, which contains original furnishings and a host of mechanical gadgets devised by Jefferson, still reveals much about the man who built it.

## MONUMENT VALLEY

Visitors to Monument Valley Navajo Tribal Park may experience a sense of déjà vu—that odd feeling that they've been there before—and for good reason. Director John Ford used the area as the backdrop for many of his Westerns, starting with *Stagecoach* in 1939. It was also the setting for scores of other films, such as *She Wore a Yellow Ribbon, My Darling Clementine, How the West Was Won,* and *The Searchers,* prompting one reviewer to write, "Monument Valley is to the Western movie what Yankee Stadium is to baseball."

The "monuments" are red sandstone buttes and pinnacles, massive monoliths that rise from the desert floor. The tallest tower soars more than 1,000 feet and, like the others, was formed by erosion. This vast, sun-blasted area, part of the Navajo Reservation in northeastern Arizona and southwestern Utah, epitomizes the stark beauty of the Southwest.

## MOONSHINE

For years the best race-car drivers were mountain boys who learned their stuff outrunning authorities while delivering "moonshine," the raw corn whiskey brewed by the light of the moon in the backwoods of the rural South. Being chased by revenue agents is one of the hazards of making moonshine. Among the hazards of drinking the often 100 proof or more "likker" are illness, blindness, and the occasional death caused by batches made in poorly constructed stills. If the flavor doesn't live up to the promise of its other names— "white lightning" and "rotgut"—bootleggers have been known to boost their brew with everything from lye and Clorox to embalming fluid. Humorist Irvin S. Cobb commented that "when you absorb a deep swig of it you have all the sensations of having swallowed a lighted kerosene lamp."

## MORGAN, J. P.

The name J. P. Morgan is wrongly synonymous with avarice. John Pierpont Morgan, the most powerful financier in America from the 1870s until World War I, knew, and helped finance, many of America's greediest industrial tycoons. But Morgan, who was born rich, was not driven to make a fortune or to live ostentatiously. In a period of reckless speculation, he believed that worldly success had its obligations.

Morgan reorganized railroads, created General Electric and U.S. Steel, and controlled banks and insurance companies. He also talked bankers into helping bail the U.S. Treasury out of a crisis, stemming the financial panic of 1907. Taking long vacations in Europe—"I can do a year's work in nine months, but not in 12," he said—Morgan became an important collector of paintings and rare books.

## MORMON TABERNACLE CHOIR

Conductor Eugene Ormandy called the Mormon Tabernacle Choir the world's greatest choir; certainly, it is among the most famous. The choir's nondenominational weekly radio broadcasts from the enormous domed Tabernacle in Salt Lake City—an acoustically superb concert hall as well as a church—have been heard nationwide since 1929. The group's Christmas concerts are telecast around the world, and its tours are widely acclaimed.

The choir began in the early days of the Church of Jesus Christ of Latter-day Saints, with rich-voiced Welsh converts as its nucleus. Today more than 300 singers donate their time and talent. The group has appeared with leading orchestras and at presidential inaugurations. Its most popular recording, *The Battle Hymn of the Republic*, won a Grammy in 1959.

## MORRIS THE CAT

When the advertising agency for 9-Lives cat food wanted a new spokescat, animal trainer Bob Martwick showed them seven felines; but he knew all along which one they'd pick. Lucky, a big-headed orange cat with dark green eyes, a torn eyelid, and undeniable personality, became Morris. That Morris and the two that followed him (all adopted from animal shelters) are famous for being finicky about their food.

Morris is a true star. He flies first class and rides in limousines to personal appearances. He receives bags of fan mail. His face decorates everything from mugs to watches. Morris even ran for president in 1987, with Walter Mondale's daughter, Eleanor, as his campaign manager.

In 1907 J. P. Morgan raised $25 million in 15 minutes in order to save the Stock Exchange. His art and book collections form the core of the Morgan Library in New York City.

The acoustics in the Mormon Tabernacle are such that you can hear a pin drop 200 feet away.

Morris has been called "the Clark Gable of cats." He is said to be the inspiration for the macho feline in the comic strip *Garfield*.

Mother's Day greetings have become a major industry in America. We buy more than 150 million Mother's Day cards every year and make more than 100 million long-distance phone calls that Sunday.

## MOTHER'S DAY

Anna Marie Jarvis, a pious Methodist from West Virginia who revered her own mother's memory, was chiefly responsible for creating a special day to recognize mothers' contributions to society. The idea was not new. During the Civil War, Julia Ward Howe, author of "The Battle Hymn of the Republic," had suggested a mother's day dedicated to peace. But it was Jarvis's letter-writing campaign that led President Woodrow Wilson, in 1914, to declare the second Sunday in May Mother's Day, a national holiday. Jarvis envisioned a quiet tribute featuring church services and family reunions. However, the celebration grew extravagantly from its modest beginnings, encouraged by florists and greeting card manufacturers. Mother's Day today is a billion-dollar business as well as a welcome occasion for expressing gratitude and affection.

## MOTOWN SOUND

Motown, "the sound of young America," was a clever combination of black soul music, with its insistent beat, strong bass, and gospel-flavored backup singing, with the smoother sounds of Tin Pan Alley. This alchemy produced the "Motown Sound" and was the creation of ex-boxer turned songwriter Berry Gordy, Jr., and his team of songwriters and producers. Having started as a small Detroit record company, Motown Records became one of the country's most successful black-owned corporations by the mid-1960s.

Motown artists included Smokey Robinson, Marvin Gaye, Jackie Wilson, Mary Wells, The Temptations, Diana Ross and The Supremes, Stevie Wonder, Gladys Knight and The Pips, and The Jackson Five. The first indications of success were the 1960 hit "Shop Around" by Smokey Robinson and The Miracles, a million-seller that went to number two on the pop charts and number one on the R & B charts, and "Please Mr. Postman" by the Marvelettes, which hit the top spot on both charts the following year. Soon Motown was churning out hits with hip music that went to the hearts of American teenagers, both black and white.

Stevie Wonder was a musical prodigy when Motown signed him in 1961. His first album, *Little Stevie Wonder / The 12 Year Old Genius,* went to number one, as did his third single, "Fingertips."

The Supremes (left to right: Florence Ballard, Mary Wilson, and Diana Ross) put Motown on the map with hits like "Stop! In the Name of Love."

## MOUNT RUSHMORE

Mount Rushmore National Memorial is the world's largest sculpture. Its designer, Gutzon Borglum, a patriotic Danish-American artist, set out to create portraits of America's leaders so imposing "that there among the clouds they may stand forever, where wind and rain alone shall wear them away."

Borglum was already famous for his heroic sculptures when South Dakota's state historian asked him to create "a massive sculpture" in the Black Hills representing heroes of the American West. The sculptor chose instead to depict national figures: Presidents George Washington, Thomas Jefferson, and Abraham Lincoln—and Theodore Roosevelt, a onetime friend. Their faces, he announced, were waiting to be released from the granite of Mount Rushmore. Carving began in 1927. Borglum supervised operations from a sling seat suspended precariously on the mountainside; his principal tools were dynamite and pneumatic drills. Work continued for 14 years, punctuated by bitter disputes over control of the project, elaborate dedication ceremonies, and glowing endorsements from living presidents. The completed memorial, visible from 60 miles away, draws up to 3 million awestruck tourists every year.

## MOVIETONE NEWS

On May 20, 1927, when Charles Lindbergh took off from Long Island for Paris, *Fox Movietone News* cameramen filmed the historic moment for America's first significant sound newsreel. Moviegoers saw Lindbergh taxi down the runway and heard onlookers shout encouragement.

For more than four decades, until television assumed its role, newsreels brought the sights and sounds of noteworthy events to the public. Usually about 10 minutes long, the films were rushed twice a week to more than 15,000 movie theaters around the country. There they were screened along with feature films, cartoons, and short subjects. *Movietone News*, started by the Fox Film Corporation and featuring popular commentator Lowell Thomas, was the largest newsreel series. Its competitors included Pathé, Universal, Hearst, and Paramount.

Sports and fashion were perennial *Movietone* subjects. But the producers also filmed memorable interviews with world figures, including Italian dictator Benito Mussolini and British author George Bernard Shaw. *Movietone* newsreels reported the abdication of the Duke of Windsor, the birth of the Dionne quintuplets, and the Hindenburg disaster. During World War II, *Movietone News* cameramen were among those who covered crucial battles from Normandy to Iwo Jima.

## MTV

At midnight on August 1, 1981, the new Music Television cable channel broadcast its first video, a little-known novelty called "Video Killed the Radio Star." The song was prophetic. In a few years, bands would need to be seen on MTV, not just heard on the radio, in order to sell albums. Video jockeys—or "veejays"—introduced music clips 24 hours a day. Kids were hooked, and viewers whose cable companies didn't carry the channel cried, "I want my MTV!"

A typical video might show the performer in concert, dramatize the song's lyrics, or have nothing to do with the song at all. Most videos, however, featured what came to be known as "MTV-style editing"—cutting from image to image within seconds. As a result, MTV has been blamed for shortening the attention span of today's teens. Still, kids stayed tuned in long enough to make stars out of such MTV regulars as Madonna, Michael and Janet Jackson, and Paula Abdul.

Sculptor Gutzon Borglum was amazed by some of the early reactions to Mount Rushmore. Many people wanted to know how much concrete he had used.

Starting in 1935, *Movietone News* faced competition from Time, Inc.'s *March of Time*, which presented its stories in a snappy, journalistic style.

Madonna was the first MTV-savvy superstar. Videos made hits out of her first singles and then helped her change her image with each new album.

In 1901 President Theodore Roosevelt and John Muir (right) spent three days camping in Yosemite and sleeping under the stars. After Roosevelt returned to Washington, he authorized the completion of the park and eventually doubled the size of protected American forests to 75 million acres.

## MUCKRAKERS

In the early 20th century, a group of journalists began writing detailed exposés of abuses of power by big business and government at all levels. Being put down as "muckrakers" by President Theodore Roosevelt only seemed to whet their passion for social justice. Writers like Ida Tarbell, who wrote a series of articles condemning Standard Oil, and Lincoln Steffens, who revealed corruption in city and state politics, continued to alert the reading public to outrages.

Upton Sinclair's masterpiece of muckraking took the form of a novel instead of an article. In *The Jungle*, he told the tragic tale of the friends and family of Jurgis Rudkus, cruelly exploited immigrants who worked in the meat-packing plants of the imaginary Packingtown. His grisly, graphic descriptions of their working conditions aroused the public to push for the Pure Food and Drug Act, passed in 1906.

## MUIR, JOHN

John Muir became America's greatest conservationist by accident. Born in Scotland, he emigrated with his parents to a Wisconsin farm when he was 11. He was largely self-educated and became known as a rustic eccentric. While working in a wagon-parts factory in Indianapolis, Muir injured one of his eyes. During his long convalescence, he decided to take a sabbatical to enjoy nature. "I might have become a millionaire," he wrote, "but I decided to become a tramp."

In California Muir found his spiritual home in the Sierra Nevada mountains, which were for the rest of his life "a source of exhaustless and unmeasurable happiness." When Muir visited Mount Shasta, he was shocked to discover what lumbering had done to the forests. In 1889 Muir camped in Yosemite with Robert Underwood Johnson, editor of *Century Magazine*. They decided to campaign to turn the poorly managed state preserve into a national park. Muir wrote, "The ground is already being gnawed and trampled into a desert condition." The following year, Congress passed a bill making Yosemite a national park and outlawed sheep grazing and lumbering from its 1,500 square miles.

## MUPPETS

In 1955 Jim Henson took one of his mother's old coats, added two halves of a Ping-Pong ball, and created a puppet that would soon be known as Kermit the Frog. Henson's creations are best known for their longest-running gig—public television's *Sesame Street*—but from 1976 to 1981 they had their own *Muppet Show*. Viewers got to see Rudolf Nureyev dance "Swine Lake," Gilda Radner sing a duet with a tuxedoed carrot, and Dom deLuise have his head served up on a platter by the Swedish Chef. Backstage, host Kermit tried to duck the amorous advances (and karate chops) of prima donna Miss Piggy while bolstering the egos of such regulars as Fozzie, a bear comedian, and The Great Gonzo, a "whatever."

*The Muppet Show's* popularity led Jim Henson (above) to create a string of movies that offered such puppeteering feats as Kermit riding a Schwinn and Miss Piggy performing a water ballet.

## MURROW, EDWARD R.

Before the United States entered World War II, Edward R. Murrow, the European director for CBS news, assembled a staff of crack correspondents across the continent to provide timely, on-site radio broadcasts about the growing crisis. Murrow himself reported from London, and his deep baritone voice brought 1940's Battle of Britain, or "Blitz," live to millions of listeners. As one great building after another collapsed, he observed sadly, "A thousand years of history and civilization are being smashed."

Following the war, Murrow created important TV shows, including one that exposed the demagoguery of Senator Joseph McCarthy. Murrow is best remembered, though, for his celebrity-interview program, *Person to Person*, in which he and the viewer were invited into the homes of such luminaries as then senator John F. Kennedy and his wife, Jacqueline, Audrey Hepburn, and Marilyn Monroe. In 1961 Murrow was named head of the U.S. Information Agency.

"This is London" will always be remembered as the on-air signature of Edward R. Murrow, one of broadcasting's legends.

## MUSTANG

After World War II, Detroit produced big cars that provided space and safety for the families of newly returned soldiers. By 1964 kids from these families, and their parents, who could finally afford a second car, were ready for a little automotive excitement, and Ford gave it to them.

Launched with a public relations and advertising blitz that featured a mild-mannered Milquetoast named Henry Foster turning into a freewheeling playboy, the Mustang became a big success: in 1966, its peak year, 550,000 were sold. Since then, Mustangs have become bigger and less sporty. Ford redesigned the Mustang several times but never quite recaptured the "Mustang magic" of the mid-1960s.

At left, this version of the familiar charging-mustang logo decorated the grilles of early-1970s models.

## MUZAK

It may be "environmental music" to the people who make it, but it's "elevator music" to the rest of us. Muzak is music to be heard but not listened to. It's the blandly orchestrated pop music that sneaks into your brain when you're on hold, waiting in line, or in the dentist's chair.

Now playing to a captive audience of 80 million people in 12 countries, Muzak was invented back in 1934 by Gen. George Squier, head of the army's Signal Corps. His plan to transmit Muzak over a wire for a fee found a ready market in the late 1930s, when research revealed that music gets more work out of people. Piped into factories during World War II, Muzak increased production significantly, and a $100 million business was born. (Zealots claim that it also gets more milk out of cows and more mangoes out of mango trees.) Muzak's meticulously programmed Stimulus Progression speeds people up (on assembly lines) or slows them down (in supermarkets, which increases sales by up to 38 percent).

When it was introduced, the Mustang was fast, sporty, and, at $2,368, refreshingly affordable. Shown above are the 1964 Mustang convertible and the restyled 1994 model.

Ralph Nader is no longer on a one-man crusade. Through the decades, thousands have helped him "to give voice to voiceless people."

On the eve of the 1969 Super Bowl, Joe Namath guaranteed that his Jets would defeat the heavily favored Baltimore Colts. Namath's delivery of a 16–7 victory secured his reputation as the top quarterback.

## NADER, RALPH

Airbags. Padded dashboards. Seat belts. If not for Ralph Nader, none of these would be standard equipment in the American auto. His 1965 book, *Unsafe at Any Speed*, showed how carmakers profited from vehicles they knew weren't sound, and turned this reclusive consumer advocate into a household name. When a detective testified before the Senate that General Motors had hired him to "get something on this guy" (to no avail, since Nader's private life yielded no dirt), Nader received an apology and a $425,000 settlement.

By the late 1960s, Nader had single-handedly started a nationwide consumer-protection movement, soon joined by college students called "Nader's Raiders." When Sen. Robert F. Kennedy asked him why he was "doing all this," Nader replied, "If I were engaged in activities for the prevention of cruelty to animals, nobody would ask me that question." By 1973 he had initiated 25 major pieces of legislation regulating highway safety, public health, food additives, industrial pollution, and congressional reform. Without Nader, there might be no Freedom of Information Act, Consumer Product Safety Commission, or Environmental Protection Agency.

So far this tireless activist for the public interest has outlasted six presidencies and a dozen Congresses. "You've got to keep the pressure on, even if you lose," he maintains. "The essence of the citizen's movement is persistence."

## NAMATH, JOE

If you've got it, flaunt it. Flashy both on and off the football field, Joe Namath had great talent and an ego to match. A college hero at the University of Alabama, he signed a $427,000 contract to join the New York Jets in 1965. Having accepted the biggest contract in the history of professional football, Namath became an instant celebrity.

As a quarterback, Namath generated electricity every time that he trotted onto the field. He was an aggressive passer who disdained short throws in favor of rifling the ball downfield to his wide receivers.

Although football has seen many great players, Namath's off-the-field activities earned him even greater fame. In a newspaper poll taken in 1974, 90 percent of the women ranked "Broadway Joe" Namath as the sexiest athlete in sports. In a famous television commercial of the period, Namath poked fun at gender roles when he wore a pair of panty hose to advertise the product. Of all contemporary athletes, only Namath could have gotten away with such a stunt.

## NAPA VALLEY

Ever since the 1860s, when German wine makers like Charles Krug and Jacob and Frederic Beringer settled in, the fertile soil of California's Napa Valley has been devoted to growing grapes. The vineyards were nearly ruined by a pest called the vine louse in the 1880s, and they suffered a serious setback with Prohibition in the 1920s. Still, the valley's unique micro-climates, which range from hot hillsides to foggy flatlands, are so perfect for growing grapes that the industry endured.

Tastings at quaint wineries and the area's natural beauty have made the wine country (Napa Valley and neighboring Sonoma County) a magnet for tourists. Napa Valley is better known to the public, as it has been cultivated on a larger scale, but Sonoma County is home to many excellent wineries, including Buena Vista, the oldest in the region.

## NASA

On October 4, 1957, America's postwar confidence was shaken when the USSR launched *Sputnik*, the first man-made Earth-orbiting satellite. President Lyndon B. Johnson later spoke of "the profound shock of realizing that it might be possible for another country to achieve technological superiority over ours." Unwilling to let the Soviets dominate the space, Congress stepped up math and science programs in schools throughout the country and, in July 1958, created the National Aeronautics and Space Administration (NASA).

NASA, a civilian agency, didn't start from scratch. It took over the National Advisory Committee for Aeronautics (NACA), thus gaining five "installations," including the Langley Research Center in Virginia and the Ames Research Center in California. NASA also absorbed resources from the military, including the army's Jet Propulsion Laboratory in California and part of the army's Ballistic Missile Center in Alabama, from which they acquired the services of Dr. Wernher von Braun, the renowned German scientist.

Against a backdrop of escalating Soviet successes—including *Sputnik II*, which sent a dog into orbit, and the launch of a massive 3,000-pound satellite—the NASA team laid the groundwork for manned spaceflight and deep-space exploratory missions. In the 1960s America regained its sense of technological leadership, first catching up with the Soviets by sending the *Mercury* astronauts into orbit, and then taking the lead by putting the first man on the moon.

NASA's extensive experiments on Earth and in space have expanded our knowledge of the universe. Working in conjunction with large private contractors, NASA has also made advances in a range of technologies—including satellite communications, weather forecasting, and electronic miniaturization—that have been applied to consumer products and services. Despite this, the public's main image of NASA is that of the dedicated scientific and engineering geniuses who make spaceflight possible.

Grapes like Cabernet Sauvignon and Pinot Chardonnay thrive in Napa Valley's rich soil and ideal climate. Today Napa's wines rival those of older, larger European wine regions.

When the space shuttle *Columbia* was launched on April 12, 1981 (left), it ushered in a new era of space research. Other shuttles followed, including *Challenger, Discovery, Atlantis, and Endeavour.*

When his beloved Baltimore team lost the 1969 Super Bowl, Ogden Nash composed this lament: "I weep with the army of loyal dolts / Who gave 17 points and bet on the Colts."

"I cannot tell a lie—I did it with my little hatchet!" When Carry Nation laid waste to a saloon, billiard balls, brickbats, and even cash registers went flying.

The *National Enquirer* has often miffed celebrities with its gossipy headlines. Dolly Parton, for one, says she has considered suing the paper "for printing lies about me in the middle of the magazine instead of on the cover."

## NASH, OGDEN

Ogden Nash had a magical ability to combine easy-to-read couplets with a saucy drollery. His popular aphorisms, such as "Candy / Is dandy / But liquor / Is quicker," uplifted Depression-era readers of *The New Yorker*, and even today he is considered the most-quoted contemporary American poet. Typical of his pithy banter are observations of the animal world: "The turtle lives twixt plated decks," goes one of his rib ticklers, "Which practically conceal its sex; / I think it clever of the turtle / In such a fix to be so fertile." Even his more innocent jests are somewhat skewed: "The cow is of the bovine ilk; / One end is moo, the other milk."

"It would be better to be a good bad poet than a bad good poet," said Nash of his tendency to wax funny rather than philosophical. The success of his first collection of humorous verse, *Hard Lines* (1931), enabled Nash to leave his job as an advertising copywriter and work full-time composing his ditties. He collaborated with S. J. Perelman and Kurt Weill on a hit Broadway musical, *One Touch of Venus*, and published more than 30 books. A posthumous collection, *I Wouldn't Have Missed It*, was a fitting "monument ogdenational."

## NATION, CARRY

Carry Nation, a crusader against alcohol, was a favorite of cartoonists, often drawn as a frowning, witchlike woman who strode angrily into bars and smashed liquor bottles with a hatchet. The cartoons hardly exaggerated, but they ignored the specific evils she hated: alcoholism, wife beating, and the waste of family income on liquor. Nation powerfully preached her views all over America, Scotland, and England in the early 1900s. She also dedicated herself to taking care of poor and battered women, who called her "Mother Nation." Her extreme actions as well as her radical ideas—equal rights for women, sex education for children, and help for the homeless—cleared a path for reformers of the future.

## NATIONAL ENQUIRER

In 1952 Generoso Pope, Jr., bought a little-read tabloid, the *New York Enquirer* (changed to the *National Enquirer* in 1957), and filled it with gruesome tales of freaks, cannibalism, and sadistic murders. In 1969 he offered the newspaper for sale at checkout counters, but supermarkets refused to display it because of the shocking content. So Pope changed the *Enquirer*'s editorial direction to focus on celebrity scandals and medical marvels; sales soon reached 5 million a week.

The *Enquirer* is often ridiculed for its coverage of Elvis and UFO sightings and for such self-help topics as "Psychics say your grandparents may be from another planet: here's how to tell." Still, by deploying dozens of reporters on stories like the O. J. Simpson trial, and by paying its sources handsomely for scintillating scoops, the *Enquirer* has ensured itself an avid readership.

## NATIONAL GEOGRAPHIC

In 1888 Gardiner Greene Hubbard invited 33 gentleman geographers to form the National Geographic Society; they began publishing a scholarly journal that October. Hubbard's son-in-law, the famous inventor Alexander Graham Bell, took over as president in 1898. Bell had an egalitarian idea: to make the journal more accessible to the general public.

In 1902 *National Geographic*'s editor, Gilbert Hovey Grosvenor, requested that a scientific expedition be sent to the scene of a devastating volcanic eruption on the island of Martinique. Bell instructed Grosvenor to go to Martinique but to "Leave Science to ... others and give us details of living interest beautifully illustrated by photographs." From then on, that's just what Grosvenor did, with stunning pictorial essays on such exotic locales as the Tibetan city of Lhasa and the Galapagos Islands. Over the years, *National Geographic* has given its readers rare glimpses of wild animals and undersea life as well as breathtaking aerial views of faraway places. Today it has a worldwide circulation of more than 9 million, and no armchair traveler would stay home without it.

## NATIVE SON

If society so degrades a man as to turn him into a criminal, then is society responsible for his crimes? Richard Wright's 1940 novel, *Native Son*, examines this question through the character of Bigger Thomas, a scrappy survivor of a Chicago ghetto, who at every turn is treated like a pariah because of his black skin. After he accidentally kills a rich white girl, Bigger flees, knowing that his record and his race will prevent him from receiving due justice. A second murder arises from Bigger's frustration at living like a caged rat. He strikes back—tragically—at the society that imprisons him.

Wright himself transcended a childhood marked by poverty and racism. He published the autobiographical *Black Boy* in 1945 and, the next year, moved to Paris, where he joined the post-World War II expatriate movement.

## NAVAJO CODE TALKERS

In battle, quick communication is essential, but field telephones and radios are not secure: the enemy can listen in. The usual expedient is English peppered with slang and code words, but during World War II, the marine corps relied on 420 Native American code talkers. The remarkably difficult Navajo tongue, in which a single word could stand for a complete English sentence, baffled Japanese eavesdroppers.

Military officers first thought the Navajo code too simple until tests proved it unbreakable; combat experience demonstrated its speed. Code talkers detected radio messages sent by Japanese soldiers impersonating Americans, and they broke down stereotypes within their own troops. "When you started sending messages and everything was correct," one code talker recalled, "they started treating you like a king."

For more than 100 years, *National Geographic* has been America's lens on the world. Piled high in attics and basements, it's the magazine no one can bear to throw away.

By translating a string of unrelated Navajo words for "*Mouse Turkey Sheep Uncle Ram Ice Bear Ant Cat Horse Intestines,*" code talkers relayed the news of the victory at Mount Suribachi on Iwo Jima.

With his Greek-god profile, killer blue eyes, and laid-back humor, Paul Newman (right) could make even an out law like Butch Cassidy likable. Also starring in *Butch Cassidy and the Sundance Kid* were Robert Redford and Katharine Ross (below).

Newman starred in *Mr. and Mrs. Bridge* (1990) with his wife, Joanne Woodward, the only woman, he has said, he can dance with.

## NEW DEAL

In 1932, in the depths of the Great Depression, Franklin D. Roosevelt campaigned for the presidency with a promise of "a new deal for the American people." He was swept into office, and New Deal became the name of his unprecedented plan to get the country back on its feet.

During the first 100 days of his administration, Roosevelt proposed legislation to regulate the failed banking system, subsidize farmers, oversee the stock exchange, curtail unemployment, and harness the power of the Tennessee River. One stunned member of Congress said that the program "reads like the first chapter of Genesis."

In 1935 the WPA (Works Progress Administration) was established, creating millions of jobs in building and improving hospitals and schools. The same year, the landmark Social Security Act established old-age pensions, unemployment insurance, and welfare benefits.

Although the New Deal didn't end the Great Depression, it restored the nation's morale and greatly expanded the federal government's involvement in the welfare of its citizens and institutions.

## NEWMAN, PAUL

Actor-director-producer Paul Newman's screen career has lasted more than 40 years, and his recent film *Nobody's Fool* (1994) proves that his looks have, too. After being kicked off his college football team for rowdy behavior, Newman turned to acting to fill his spare time. He liked it so much that he joined a repertory company after graduation, but his acting career was cut short when his father died and he was called home to run the family's sporting-goods store. When the store was sold a year later, he immediately enrolled in the Yale University School of Drama. "I wasn't driven to acting by any inner compulsion," Newman was once quoted as saying. "I was running away from the sporting-goods business."

His many films include *The Hustler* (1961), *Cool Hand Luke* (1967), *The Sting* (1973), and *The Verdict* (1982). After six Academy Award nominations, he won his first Oscar for *The Color of Money* (1986). In 1958 he married actress Joanne Woodward, who had the title role in *Rachel, Rachel* (1968), the first movie Newman directed. Newman's hobby is sports-car racing, which he says he took up because he wasn't a natural athlete. Nobody's perfect.

## NEWPORT

With its harbor on Narragansett Bay, Newport, Rhode Island, was a prosperous seaport. It had its heyday between 1890 and 1914, when wealthy New York socialites summered in their Newport "cottages"—huge, often absurdly ornate mansions. It was here that Mrs. William Astor, considering the limited capacity of her ballroom, decreed that only the elite Four Hundred could be invited to her soirees.

Although its Gilded Age has passed, Newport remains a popular resort that boasts fine beaches, yacht races, and music festivals. Tourists can visit turn-of-the-century cottages and restored colonial homes and churches as well as the nation's first synagogue.

## NEWSPAPERS

In 1793 Noah Webster wrote that the newspaper circulation in America led that of the world. Every village seemed to have a paper, and most people read nothing else. Newspapers served as a national town meeting and helped democracy grow. As gold lured Americans to the West, hundreds of papers sprang up. Railroads, the telegraph, and aggressive newsboys began building mass circulation.

After the Civil War, such serious papers as *The St. Louis Post-Dispatch* and *The New York Times* thrived, while William Randolph Hearst, Joseph Pulitzer, and Edward W. Scripps sold the blue-collar dailies. During the late 19th century, Pulitzer and Hearst tried to outdo each other with sensational headlines, and entertainment began to take precedence over serious journalism. World War I saw a wave of mergers and closings that eventually left most cities with only one paper. In the 1920s such tabloids as *The New York Daily News* built big circulations with lively photos of crime victims, celebrities, and sports.

Radio didn't compete with newspapers, but post-World War II migration to the suburbs did. Commuters couldn't read while driving, and when at home, they turned to TV. While daily circulation stagnated, growing Sunday circulation showed the attraction of features and service. *USA Today*—a mix of facts, maps, and short news items—took only five years to become the second most read daily paper in America.

## NEW YEAR'S EVE

It's a night to make resolutions, to make merry, and to make noise. Perhaps the largest crowd of noisemakers can be found in New York City's Times Square, where some 300,000 celebrants attend a televised New Year's Eve party. The sweetest-sounding New Year's tradition began in 1929, when Guy Lombardo and the Royal Canadians first broadcast their rendition of "Auld Lang Syne" over the radio. In 1954 the band joined the televised festivities, and by 1977, when he died, Lombardo had helped America usher in the new year for 48 consecutive years.

For some people, watching the ball on TV while donning funny hats and downing champagne is not enough. More athletic revelers march in the Orange Bowl Parade in Miami, "shoot in the new year" with a musket salute in North Carolina, or join the Ad a Man Club (they add one member each year) in scaling Pikes Peak to set off Colorado's spectacular New Year's display of fireworks.

Circulation may be declining, but papers are still popular with those who commute to work by bus or train. Well into the 20th century, papers were sold on street corners by newsboys (or girls), who would shout out the latest headlines to entice readers.

Continuing a tradition begun in 1908, millions of people across the nation watch as the 500-pound illuminated sphere slides down a flagpole on the roof of One Times Square, dramatically marking the end of one year and the beginning of another.

## NEW YORK CITY

New York City isn't the capital of New York State, but residents of the "Big Apple" compensate for that fact by considering their city the capital of the globe. There's a good case to be made: New York is the home of the United Nations and an astoundingly diverse population, as well as the largest investment market in the world.

So many movies, books, plays, and television shows have been written about New York that even its street names are known nationwide. Wall Street is famous for finance, Madison Avenue means advertising, and Fifth Avenue stands for world-class shopping. New York's neighborhoods are also icons. Greenwich Village, or The Village, has fostered some of the world's great writers; SoHo is an enclave of artists; Harlem has a priceless musical heritage. The city is a feast for art lovers. The Guggenheim, the Metropolitan Museum of Art, and the Frick Collection line Fifth Avenue. And no trip is complete without a visit to the Museum of Modern Art.

Most of New York's skyscrapers are located on the island of Manhattan, including the Art Deco Chrysler Building and the twin towers of the soaring World Trade Center. Cultural landmarks include Carnegie Hall, Lincoln Center, Madison Square Garden, and the elegant Waldorf-Astoria hotel, where visiting presidents and royalty stay. New York's four other boroughs—Brooklyn, Queens, Staten Island, and the Bronx—don't always get their due. For instance, despite its famous zoo, Ogden Nash quipped, "The Bronx?/No thonx."

New York City's secret is the ongoing infusion of energy and talent it gets from the rest of the country and immigrants from around the world. Moss Hart observed, "The only credential the city asked was the boldness to dream. For those who did, it unlocked its gates and treasures, not caring who they were or where they came from."

## NEW YORKER

With equal measures of journalistic sass and editorial meticulousness, *The New Yorker* has been the standard-bearer of excellence in American magazines for more than 70 years. The magazine's founder, Harold Ross, a member of the Algonquin Hotel's famed Round Table, wrote in his prospectus that the integrity of the magazine "will be above suspicion" and that "it will hate bunk." Week after week *The New Yorker* has achieved this goal, presenting the best fiction and poetry, comprehensive profiles, and the most incisive commentary on books, the arts, and issues in the news.

Rachel Carson's *Silent Spring*, Truman Capote's *In Cold Blood*, James Baldwin's *The Fire Next Time*, and John Hersey's *Hiroshima* all first appeared in *The New Yorker*. In the 1990s the magazine's coverage has ranged from Henry Louis Gates's article on race in America to William Finnegan's firsthand reports on surfing. On the lighter side, *The New Yorker* also publishes a clutch of cartoons in every issue,

The Twin Towers (above, at left) crown New York's financial district. The excavation for these buildings provided the landfill on which nearby Battery Park City was built. Left, a 70-story building in Rockefeller Center overlooks the Lower Plaza, which becomes an ice-skating rink in winter. Below, the 1891 Memorial Arch in Washington Square Park is the gateway to Greenwich Village, one of the city's most historic neighborhoods.

which reads like a Who's Who of great cartoonists. Such favorite humorists as James Thurber and Charles Addams started their careers by enlivening the pages of the magazine with social satire, and the tradition continues today with George Booth, Edward Koren, Roz Chast, and many others. In fact, some readers confess to paging through the magazine in search of the cartoons before turning to the articles.

## NIAGARA FALLS

Niagara Falls became the honeymoon capital of the world shortly after Jérôme Bonaparte, brother of the French emperor, visited there in 1803 with his new wife. Today the site attracts nearly 50,000 newlyweds every year, as well as 10 million other tourists from around the world.

In the 19th and 20th centuries, the falls have been a magnet for daredevils. The most famous was a Frenchman known as the Great Blondin who, in 1859, walked a tightrope above the Niagara Gorge across the American Bridal Veil Falls and the Canadian Horseshoe Falls—a distance of 3,175 feet. On a later trip, he carried his shaking manager on his back. Before long, men and women were tumbling over the falls in barrels, suits made of India rubber, and life preservers. With the waters plunging 182 feet from their highest point, those who survived had the ride of their lives.

## NIXON, RICHARD M.

Richard Nixon was one of the most controversial American presidents, and an endless source of fascination. He honed his political skills during two terms as Dwight D. Eisenhower's vice president. After losing a close contest for the presidency in 1960 and the governorship of California in 1962, he finally reached the White House in 1968.

On the domestic front, Nixon created the Environmental Protection Agency and expanded the Social Security Administration. But it was as a skilled negotiator in the arena of world affairs that he made his most lasting mark. He began to withdraw American troops from the unpopular war in Vietnam, and he encouraged arms reduction in the U.S. and the Soviet Union. In February 1972 he traveled to China to reestablish diplomatic and trade relations, for which he was widely hailed. But his downfall came later that year, when the Watergate scandal broke. Faced with impeachment, Nixon resigned on August 9, 1974.

In semiretirement, Nixon gradually rebuilt his reputation. He published nine books, carried out personal diplomatic missions abroad, and advised presidents. When he died in 1994, President Bill Clinton said, "The enduring lesson of Richard Nixon is that he never gave up being part of the action and passion of his times."

The New Yorker was planned as a literary magazine for a small audience. When its circulation topped 300,000, founder Harold Ross said, "We must be doing something wrong."

Wrote an early missionary of Niagara Falls, "...the Universe does not afford its Parallel...." The falls are not the highest in the world but are rated the third most powerful.

Nixon, with his wife, Pat, stood on the Great Wall of China during his historic 1972 trip, which opened a new era in Chinese-American relations.

## SAGUARO

A saguaro can live for 200 years and reach a height of 50 feet. Likened to a massive sponge, this Southwestern cactus can absorb about a ton of water.

# North American
# PLANTS

*An important part of our American heritage is the wonderful diversity of our native plants. Thanks to public awareness, these national treasures are being preserved for future generations.*

## CRANBERRY

One of the first foods to be enjoyed by the Pilgrims, cranberries are fairly common in New England bogs, which are flooded at harvest time.

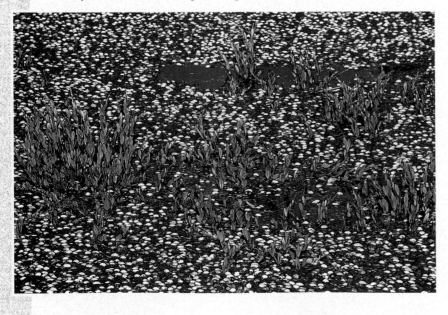

## BRISTLECONE PINE

Gnarled by severe weather, bristlecones are the world's longest-living trees, reaching ages of nearly 5,000 years.

## CALIFORNIA POPPY
These long-stemmed flowers bloom across Western hills and meadows, a colorful show that can last eight months.

## VENUS FLYTRAP
This insect-eating plant is found only in the Carolinas. When sensitive bristles on the leaves are touched by a fly or another insect, the leaves snap shut and digestion begins.

## SUNFLOWER
The sunflower is cultivated not only for its beauty but also for its edible seeds, which are made into cooking oils.

## LADY'S SLIPPER
A member of the orchid family, this flower is found in woodlands.

## GIANT SEQUOIA
Stands of this stately beauty, the most massive tree in the world, are found only in California.

Roald Amundsen's small ship, the *Gjoa,* was the first to cross the Northwest Passage. Eight years later, he would become the first man to reach the South Pole.

Celebrating the 51st anniversary of woman suffrage in 1971, women marched in New York City.

Widely praised for his unflinching stand at the Battle of the Bulge, Brig. Gen. Anthony C. McAuliffe was soon promoted to major general.

## NORTHWEST PASSAGE

The discovery by Europeans of North America started a 400-year search for a "Northwest Passage"—an ice-free water route from Europe to the Far East. Jacques Cartier mistook the St. Lawrence River for the Passage in 1535. In 1609 Henry Hudson thought it was a river in New York, which was subsequently named for him. In 1778 Captain James Cook declared that an ice-free route didn't exist. Sir John Franklin sailed past Greenland and found the Passage in 1845, but he and his crew died of exposure, and his discovery remained unknown for years. In 1903 Roald Amundsen of Norway became the first to sail through the Passage to the Pacific. The discovery of oil on the North Slope of Alaska in 1968 promised to make the Passage a commercial reality, but actual voyages proved too expensive because of the costly ice-breaking equipment needed on every ship.

## NOW

"I am woman, hear me roar," sang Helen Reddy in 1972. It could have been the anthem of the women's movement, which had shaken up America for much of the previous decade. At the forefront of that movement was NOW—the National Organization for Women—founded in 1966 by Betty Friedan, who was its first president.

NOW supported the Equal Rights Amendment, which was overwhelmingly passed by Congress in 1972—the same year Gloria Steinem's *Ms.* magazine hit the newsstands. NOW demanded better educational opportunities for women and encouraged more employment choices as well.

But as times changed, so did NOW. When the Equal Rights Amendment failed to be ratified by the states in the 1980s, NOW recruited women to run for political office to help get the ERA passed on its next attempt. Today, with a membership of 275,000, NOW continues to use politics and the courts to fight for women's rights. According to its president, Patricia Ireland, the organization works to make "today's radical issues . . . become tomorrow's givens."

## NUTS!

In December 1944 the U.S. 101st Airborne Division made a heroic stand during the Battle of the Bulge. The American troops, commanded by Brig. Gen. Anthony C. McAuliffe, held the strategic town of Bastogne, Belgium. On December 20, German troops completely surrounded the town. Two days later, their commander sent emissaries to McAuliffe with an ultimatum to surrender or face "annihilation." At first, McAuliffe refused to take the demand seriously, but he finally agreed to put his response on paper. His reply read: "To the German Commander: / Nuts! / The American Commander."

The next day, the fog lifted, allowing C-47s to airdrop supplies to the embattled GIs. The Americans held their position, and McAuliffe won acclaim for his grit.

*"This will remain the land of the free only so long as it is the home of the brave."*

ELMER DAVIS

## O'CONNOR, SANDRA DAY

At the confirmation hearings for her nomination to the Supreme Court, Sandra Day O'Connor was asked, "How do you want to be remembered?" "I hope [my tombstone] says, 'Here lies a good judge,'" she answered. "I hope I am remembered as the first woman who served on the Supreme Court." On September 25, 1981, she realized that hope when she became the first female justice in the court's 191-year history.

O'Connor began practicing law in the 1950s, first in private practice, then later as a judge on the Arizona bench. As a justice of the Supreme Court, she became a role model for, and a sign of changing public attitudes toward, women.

## O. HENRY

William Sydney Porter went into the Ohio State Penitentiary a literary amateur, but he emerged a star. While serving time for embezzlement, he wrote 14 stories under his pen name, O. Henry. With their surprise endings and light, swiftly moving plots, they became enormously popular.

In a sense, O. Henry's life had the same surprise ending as his tales. After his release from prison in 1901, he moved to New York, where he became the most sought-after story writer of his day. Known as the darling of the Sunday supplement, he was famous for his ability to write stories in just an hour. He gave us such favorites as "The Ransom of Red Chief" and "The Last Leaf," which "touched a magic democratic chord," as one critic put it, and earned him worldwide fame.

## O.K. CORRAL

The gunfire at the O.K. Corral lasted less than a minute, but it has echoed through Western history for over a century. On one side were the Earps—lawmen Wyatt and Virgil and their brother, Morgan, and Wyatt's friend Doc Holliday. On the other side were the Clanton and McLaury brothers, cattle rustlers who looked for trouble when they came to town.

On October 25, 1881, the Clanton gang rode into Tombstone, Arizona, and had several confrontations with the Earps. The next day, with the town a hotbed of rumors, both groups met in a vacant lot near the O.K. Corral. The outcome was trumpeted in the *Tombstone Epitaph*: "Three Men Hurled into Eternity in the Duration of a Moment." The unlucky three that day were Frank and Tom McLaury and Billy Clanton, but revenge killings followed for a decade.

Justice Sandra Day O'Connor earned a reputation as an independent thinker who believed that the courts should interpret the laws rather than change them.

In O. Henry's "The Gift of the Magi," a husband sells his gold pocket watch to buy combs for his wife's long hair. She sells her hair to buy a chain for his watch.

Burt Lancaster played Wyatt Earp in *Gunfight at the O.K. Corral* (1957), a Hollywood version of the famous shootout.

Georgia O'Keeffe's subjects ranged from the dazzling heights of big-city skyscrapers to the subtle beauty of flowers, such as *Yellow Calla* (1926).

Contrary to legend, you can't set your watch by Old Faithful. It tends to erupt roughly every 78 minutes, but it can take as long as 2 hours.

## O'KEEFFE, GEORGIA

As a young painter, Georgia O'Keeffe discarded her art training and decided "to accept as true my own thinking." The resulting collection of charcoal drawings so impressed photographer and gallery owner Alfred Stieglitz that he helped O'Keeffe launch her career. O'Keeffe moved to New York City in 1918, and the two were married six years later.

During her time in New York, O'Keeffe painted vibrant images of the city and large, sensuous depictions of flowers. It was during a trip to New Mexico in 1929, however, that she was inspired to create some of her best work. Trying to reproduce the beauty of the desert, O'Keeffe collected rocks, flowers, pieces of wood, and enormous sun-bleached bones, making them the subjects of her art. "I have used these things to say what is to me the wideness and wonder of the world as I live in it," she wrote. By the time she died at 98, Georgia O'Keeffe was known as a great painter, an inspiration to women, and a role model for older Americans.

## OLD FAITHFUL

There are bigger and more spectacular geysers in Yellowstone National Park, but none is as popular as Old Faithful. The geyser attracts many of the approximately 3 million visitors who come to the park each year because it erupts with great regularity. It was first recognized by members of the Washburn-Langford Expedition, who explored the Yellowstone region in 1870. After watching it for two days, they named it Old Faithful because it was so predictable.

The park boasts hundreds of geysers, created by millions of years of volcanic activity several miles beneath the Yellowstone Plateau. Each one behaves in a unique way. Old Faithful's outbursts last from two to five minutes, propelling more than 10,000 gallons of steaming water skyward in a fountain of breathtaking grandeur.

## OLD FARMER'S ALMANAC

From its beginnings in 1792, the *Old Farmer's Almanac* has provided readers with information on everything from sunrise schedules to home remedies for fingernail fungus. Starting with Benjamin Franklin's popular prototype, *Poor Richard's Almanack*, more than 20 spin-offs competed for readers in colonial America. The *Old Farmer's Almanac* led the pack with a whopping 9,000 subscribers. Today it retains a loyal audience and a large market share, selling nearly 4 million much-thumbed copies. The familiar yellow cover, with its antique typography and rococo scrollwork, has not changed in more than 200 years.

Then, as now, each issue follows its founder's dictum: "to be useful, but with pleasure." As a young lawyer, Abraham Lincoln certainly put the *Old Farmer's Almanac*'s reputation for accurate astronomical information to good use. In 1857, during a murder trial, he discredited a witness who claimed to have seen the crime "by the light of the moon." Lincoln, citing a copy of the *Almanac*, proved that on the night in question, the moon was just a sliver on the horizon.

The *Old Farmer's Almanac*'s reputation for precision in forecasting the weather, however, is notoriously poor. A "secret formula" was devised by the *Almanac*'s founder, Robert B. Thomas, who happened to be an amateur astronomer. Based on solar cycles, the formula claims to predict the weather correctly about 80 percent of the time. A study done by the Climate Analysis Center, however, puts the *Almanac*'s accuracy rate at fifty-fifty.

## OLD GLORY

The American Revolution was fought under many colors: the pine-tree flag was displayed on ships, while soldiers flew the rattlesnake banner ("Don't Tread on Me"). Gen. George Washington tried to end the chaos with the Grand Union, a red-and-white-striped flag with a British Union Jack in the upper-left corner. The Declaration of Independence in 1776 made such enemy symbols anathema. The Continental Congress approved the basic design of stars and stripes on June 14, 1777. It specified 13 stripes and 13 stars in red, blue, and white, but ignored the number of points on the stars and their arrangement; some flags had them in a circle and others in rows. In 1794 Congress specified a stripe for each of the 15 states and the same number of stars in five rows of three.

In 1870 descendants of Betsy Ross, a Philadelphia seamstress, claimed that she had designed and sewn the first flag, but historians give credit to Francis Hopkinson, judge, artist, and delegate to the Continental Congress. In 1818 the U.S. reverted to 13 stripes and four rows of five stars. Since then, there have been only minor changes. The flag we know today went into effect in 1960, when a star was added for Hawaii.

## OLMSTED, FREDERICK LAW

Frederick Law Olmsted, America's preeminent landscape architect, designed public parks to offer city dwellers "a sense of enlarged freedom" and a convenient way to escape from the crowding and confusion of city life. Central Park in New York City is Olmsted's jewel. At 843 acres, it is one of the largest city parks in the country.

But Olmsted had to spend as much energy defending it as he did building it. His vision—a rustic refuge arranged to make the city around it invisible—clashed with that of politicians who wanted buildings and amusement parks and developers who yearned to pave it over and build apartments. The battle continues. Over the objections of preservationists, the Metropolitan Museum of Art has built on park land. Baseball diamonds, tennis courts, and a zoo have also been added. After his New York period, Olmsted went on to design more than 80 other parks, the grounds of the U.S. Capitol, and the 1893 World's Columbian Exposition in Chicago.

Our flag has been known as Old Glory since 1824, when the name was coined by sea captain William Driver of Massachusetts.

Frederick Law Olmsted wanted Central Park to offer surprises around every corner. It should provide, he said, a "sense of mystery" to those who walk through its green meadows and thick woodlands.

"Babe" Didrikson Zaharias won the gold medal for the javelin throw and 80-meter hurdles in the 1932 games.

The 1996 Summer Games (held in Atlanta, Georgia) were the 100th anniversary of modern Olympic competition.

Women, inspired by her chic, imitated Jackie's sophisticated look: the bouffant hairdo, outsize sunglasses, and pillbox hats. The world was awed by her courage and composure in the face of tragedy.

## OLYMPIC HEROES

Since the birth of the modern Olympics, American athletes have performed remarkable feats. When Jim Thorpe won the pentathlon and the decathlon during the 1912 Stockholm games, Sweden's King Gustav proclaimed him "the greatest athlete in the world." Carl Lewis took that title at the 1992 Barcelona games, where he won his eighth gold medal, including his third straight in the long jump. Undoubtedly the greatest long jumper in history, Lewis broke Bob Beamon's 23-year record in 1991 with a jump of 29 feet, 4½ inches.

The 1936 Berlin games saw a great performance by Jesse Owens, who won four gold medals in the 100- and 200-meter dashes, the long jump, and the 4 x 100-meter relay, for which he anchored the team. Bob Mathias took the gold for the decathlon in 1952, and Bruce Jenner won it in 1976. During the 1960 Rome games, Wilma Rudolph won three gold medals. In Seoul in 1988, Florence Griffith-Joyner (Flo-Jo) won four medals in track and field; her sister-in-law Jackie Joyner-Kersee set a world record in the heptathlon. Four years later, in Barcelona, Joyner-Kersee again won the gold in the heptathlon and became the first woman to win consecutive Olympic multi-event titles.

Although Johnny Weissmuller swam from Olympic gold (in the 1920s) into a movie career as Tarzan in the '30s, it was Mark Spitz and Greg Louganis who highlighted America's dominance in swimming events. Spitz won seven gold medals at the 1972 Munich games; Louganis, the greatest American diver in history, won gold medals in both 1984 and 1988 for the springboard and platform events.

In the Winter Olympics, Americans have sparkled in figure skating. From Tenley Albright in 1956 to Carol Heiss in 1960, Peggy Fleming in 1968, Dorothy Hamill in 1976, and Kristi Yamaguchi in 1992, American women have captured the hearts of skating fans. America's greatest triumph in Olympic ice hockey came at Lake Placid in 1980, when the American team stunned the sports world by defeating the powerful Soviet Union team to capture the gold.

## ONASSIS, JACQUELINE KENNEDY

She reigned over Camelot with the dignity of a queen, and when the brief shining moment had ended, the public enthroned her in its heart.

Jackie, as she was affectionately called, leaped from the society page to the front page upon becoming one of our youngest First Ladies, and she set a new tone in America with her elegance, élan, and impeccable taste. Born to privilege and polished at white-glove finishing schools, she cut a confident, charismatic figure whether charming heads of state or spelunking through musty storerooms in search of antiques for her White House restoration project. Yet more than her style, it was her substance—her determination to lead a life of service on her own terms—that won respect. As a private citizen, Jackie supported women's issues and the arts and worked as a book editor. Her proudest accomplishment was providing a normal upbringing for her two children in spite of the scorching limelight. "The thing I care most about," she said, "is the happiness of my children. If you fail your children, then [nothing] else really matters."

## O'NEILL, EUGENE

"Born in a hotel room … and dying in a hotel room," raged the tormented O'Neill before his death. With his Pulitzer-winning play *Beyond the Horizon* (1920), the focus of American theater turned from formula comedies to realistic drama. Misanthrope, drunk, unfaithful husband, unloving father, O'Neill was one of the great playwrights of this century. Son of a popular romantic actor and a morphine-addicted mother, much of his work reflected his tumultuous family life (*Ah, Wilderness, Long Day's Journey Into Night*) as well as other facets of his life (*Anna Christie, The Iceman Cometh*). His five-hour-long *Mourning Becomes Electra*, however, is based on Greek tragedy. Although O'Neill's lines are not quotable and his dialogue is stuffed with repetition and archaic slang, his plays are powerful and unforgettable. O'Neill won three more Pulitzers and, in 1936, the Nobel Prize for literature.

## ON THE WATERFRONT

"I coulda had class. I coulda been a contenda … instead of a bum." Terry Malloy didn't even yearn for the championship, only to be a contender. Marlon Brando's poignant words to Rod Steiger during a taxi ride are so much a part of his image that we must remind ourselves that they were written by Budd Schulberg. The classic 1954 film won eight Oscars, including Best Picture, Best Director (Elia Kazan), Best Actor (Brando), and Best Screenplay—it even had a score composed by Leonard Bernstein. Although Terry Malloy is a hero of the '50s, the movie still packs a wallop.

## OREGON TRAIL

In the 19th century, thousands of restless settlers took the Oregon Trail to the land of opportunity in the West. Starting at Independence, Missouri, the trail ran more than 2,000 miles across the plains, over the Rocky Mountains, and down the mighty Columbia River to Willamette Valley in Oregon.

The first wagon train followed the trail in 1842, and the next year saw the "great migration" of nearly a thousand immigrants. The trail was soon littered with cast-off belongings and marked by thousands of graves. Mountain man and guide Jim Clyman wrote of the settlers, "The long tiresome trip from the States, has taught them what they are capable of performing and enduring." The trail was used until the 1870s, when railroads offered an easier way to travel.

In *On the Waterfront*, Marlon Brando (above) plays Terry Malloy, a misfit whose brother is involved in union racketeering. With support from his priest and his girlfriend (Eva Marie Saint, right), Malloy agrees to testify before a crime commission.

Said one traveler of the four- to six-month-long trip, "Don't live and die within sight of your Father's house, but take a trip to Oregon!"

Variations on Oreos have been tried (lemon-filled, for one), but the cookie-munching public prefers the original. More than 200 billion Oreos have been made since 1912, each one to precise specifications.

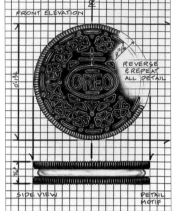

Most of the orphan train children flourished. Irma Schneiders, (shown above left, at about three) was sent to Missouri. Fondly recalling her childhood, Schneiders (above) says, "I was spoiled."

Although *Our Gang* debuted 70 years ago, the kids remain popular owing to videotape sales of the original films. Left to right: Spanky, Alfalfa, and Farina.

## OREOS

Oreos are America's favorite cookie. They have changed slightly in design since their introduction in 1912, but the recipe, which calls for pure Dutch cocoa in the crunchy chocolate wafers that are glued together with a vanilla-creme filling, has remained the same. Why change a formula that has sold more than 200 billion cookies?

At one point, Nabisco promoted Oreos with a commercial that pleaded, in vain, "Please don't fiddle with the Oreo middle." Nevertheless, those Americans who were not inclined to dunk their Oreos into tall glasses of ice-cold milk continued to pry apart the chocolate wafers so they could attack the filling first. Nabisco not only gave up the campaign but created "Double Stuf" Oreos with twice the filling, which rapidly became America's fifth-best-selling cookie.

## ORPHAN TRAIN

"WANTED: HOMES FOR CHILDREN" read posters throughout the West in the second half of the 19th century. The search was the brainchild of Charles Loring Brace, a pioneering social worker who was committed to helping the estimated 30,000 children orphaned or abandoned to the streets of New York City. In 1853 he founded the Children's Aid Society with the goal of finding these "little waifs of society" foster homes in the "pure country air."

The first orphan train took 46 hopeful boys (actually, 47; it picked up a street urchin along the way) to farming families in Dowagiac, Michigan. Within days, all of the children were placed in new homes. Soon thousands of children traveled every year to homes as far away as Florida and Texas—nearly 100,000 by the program's end in 1929. Today many Americans can trace their roots to the children who rode the orphan trains to new lives in the West and elsewhere.

## OUR GANG

Remember the dog with the black ring painted around his right eye? That was Pete, and he belonged to a bunch of mischievous kids who starred in countless short slapstick comedies bearing the name *Our Gang*. First produced by Hal Roach, who later sold the rights to MGM, the *Gang* survived until the 1940s; as the kids grew up, others took their place. Among the originals were fat Joe Cobb, curly-locked Mary Kornman, and freckle-faced Mickey Daniels. Among the alumni were Jackie Cooper, Scotty Beckett, Spanky McFarland, and Carl "Alfalfa" Switzer. Unlike most silent one-reelers of the era, *Our Gang* did not make fun of minorities; Farina's and Stymie's assimilation into the group was taken for granted. In 1936 the *Gang*'s "Bored of Education" won an Oscar. *Our Gang*, renamed *The Little Rascals*, made the leap to TV in 1955, when nearly 100 of the short comedies were aired. These shorts ran for about 20 years, to the delight of viewers of all ages.

## OUR TOWN

Since its first performance in 1938, Pulitzer Prize winner *Our Town*, one of the most endearing plays ever written, has become an American classic. The play, set in the fictional town of Grover's Corners, New Hampshire, covers the years between 1901 and 1913 and deals with the families of Editor Webb, Dr. Gibbs, and their friends and neighbors. In the second act, their children, Emily Webb and George Gibbs, grow up and marry. In the last act, Emily dies in childbirth and finds herself among the other dead of Grover's Corners, observing the living. In a wistful monologue, she speaks of the preciousness of life and the need to appreciate "every, every minute" of it. *Our Town* is intended to be performed on a simple set, with few props and little furniture. This, together with its large cast and life-affirming message, has made it a frequent choice of amateur groups.

Thornton Wilder (center) played the Stage Manager in the 1938 production of his play *Our Town*. Here he reviews the script with Dorothy McGuire (Emily Webb) and John Craven (George Gibbs).

## OUTLAWS

In the 19th century, the Western frontier was a breeding ground for gunslinging outlaws. Cattle towns and mining camps were notoriously freewheeling, and the line between lawman and desperado was easy to cross. Although dime novels romanticized outlaws as tough, daring free spirits, many were simply cattle rustlers or hired guns in range wars between wealthy ranchers.

Others came home from the Civil War with dangerous new skills. Frank and Jesse James and the Younger brothers, who had run raids on Union troops, joined forces to rob banks and trains. Starting in 1866, they stole more than half a million dollars, killing 21 men in the process. But few outlaws had a long career. Two weeks after holding up a bank in 1876, the Youngers were captured and jailed. The James brothers continued their reign of terror until Jesse was killed in 1882 and Frank turned himself in.

The James brothers' legend gave rise to a passel of imitators, including John Wesley Hardin, Tom Horn, and Billy the Kid. The most famous were the Dalton brothers, who were once lawmen but found holding up trains to be easy money. They kept this up for two years, until, in a headline-grabbing stunt in 1892, they robbed two banks simultaneously in their hometown of Coffeyville, Kansas. Their stage-whisker disguises fooled no one, and as they left the banks, four of the five gang members were gunned down.

Butch Cassidy led the last of the old-time gangs. Cassidy, whose WANTED posters described him as "cheery and affable," prided himself on avoiding bloodshed. In 1897 he merged his gang, the Wild Bunch, with Kid Curry's Hole in the Wall Gang to pull off one spectacular train robbery after another. Four years later, when things got too hot, Cassidy and Harry "Sundance Kid" Longbaugh retreated to South America. An era had ended in the West, but outlaws would provide inspiration for movies and novels throughout the next century.

Before her murder in 1889, it was Belle Starr's job to plan robberies and sell stolen goods for her gang. Jesse James (above), perhaps one of the most notorious of American outlaws, was the killer of an unknown number of victims.

Winning the gold medal in 1936 for a long jump of 26 feet, 5½ inches, Owens set an Olympic record that wasn't broken until 1960.

The Ozark region is famous for its handicrafts—pottery, quilts, weaving, dulcimers, rocking chairs, toys, jewelry, and leather goods.

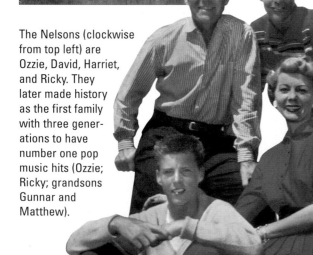

The Nelsons (clockwise from top left) are Ozzie, David, Harriet, and Ricky. They later made history as the first family with three generations to have number one pop music hits (Ozzie; Ricky; grandsons Gunnar and Matthew).

## OWENS, JESSE

Called the greatest American track and field athlete of the first half of the twentieth century, Jesse Owens captured America's attention while still an Ohio State student. At a Big Ten outdoor meet in 1935, he smashed three world records and tied a fourth—all with an injured back. After the race he explained, "My back hurt when I went to the starting crouch, but when the starter said, 'Get set,' I felt no pain at all." The following year Owens displayed his versatility at the Berlin Olympics. He became the first athlete to win four gold medals, taking the 100- and 200-meter dashes and the long jump, and anchoring the 400-meter relay team.

## OZARKS

The Ozark Mountains, often called a plateau, reach a maximum elevation of less than 2,500 feet—far more modest than the Appalachians to the east and the Rockies to the west. Yet their rounded, heavily wooded slopes are breathtakingly beautiful, with dramatic fall colors that rival New England's celebrated display. The Ozarks extend over several states, chiefly Missouri, Arkansas, and Oklahoma, and embrace a major national forest and the country's first national riverway. Their natural wonders include gushing springs and waterfalls, prehistoric caverns, and unspoiled lakes and streams teeming with trout and bass.

Although the name Ozark is probably derived from Aux Arcs, a French trading post, most early residents came from England and Scotland. Through years of isolation in rugged mountain hideaways, the descendants of these pioneers have kept their independent spirit and unique culture. They take pride in their handicrafts, and their foot-tapping bluegrass music is legendary. Once famous as the home of notorious outlaws, the region boasts the birthplaces of such distinguished citizens as scientist George Washington Carver and Presidents Harry S. Truman and Bill Clinton.

## OZZIE AND HARRIET

In the 1950s, when America moved to the suburbs, Ozzie and Harriet (and sons David and Ricky) were among our favorite next-door neighbors. Each week the Nelsons let us delight in a family in which all problems were minor and humor always triumphed. It was a formula that worked for 14 years (1952–66), making *The Adventures of Ozzie and Harriet* television's longest-running sitcom.

The set for the show duplicated the Nelson's own home—right down to the stuffed eagle over the fireplace. In the Nelson home, Harriet (always in pearls) could be counted on for a comforting smile and a cup of coffee; Ozzie was the well-meaning but fumbling dad who had no apparent job. In actuality, Ozzie led the show, acting as producer, director, editor, and writer. Harriet oversaw the children's wardrobes and designed many of the furnishings.

> *"America is a poem in our eyes: its ample geography dazzles the imagination."*
>
> RALPH WALDO EMERSON

## PAC-MAN

In the 1970s Namco, a Japanese computer company, developed a video-arcade game based on a legendary hero who liked *paku*—"to gobble." In 1980 Pac-Man came to the U.S. Within 18 months, these arcade machines had been fed $1 billion in quarters by players who guided Pac-Man as he gobbled up dots and fruits while trying to avoid falling victim to marauding ghosts. In 1982 Ms. Pac-Man joined the fun, and Atari introduced home versions of the game. Atari was soon competing in the home video game market with Nintendo and later Sega, which developed a portable handheld version. Every year the games become more high-tech, requiring more powerful equipment and new cartridges.

## PAIGE, SATCHEL

Pitching in the Negro Leagues and later in the major leagues for some 30 years, baseball star Leroy "Satchel" Paige liked to foster legends about his age and his pitching prowess. He gained legions of fans for his crack pitching, but he was also known to break contracts, alienate teammates, and demand a percentage of the gate receipts. A gifted phrasemaker, Paige renamed his breaking ball the "bat dodger" and his pause before throwing the "hesitation pitch." Paige's legacy included the oft-repeated maxim, "Don't look back; something might be gaining on you."

## PAINE, THOMAS

Born in England, Thomas Paine moved to Philadelphia in 1774. His widely read *Common Sense* galvanized citizens with its bold demand for immediate separation from British rule; George Washington called Paine's argument "sound doctrine and unanswerable reasoning." Seven months after the pamphlet was published, the signing of the Declaration of Independence solidified the colonists' resolve. After the war Paine returned to England, where his writings against the hereditary authority of kings, *The Rights of Man*, was labeled seditious and a warrant was issued for his arrest. He fled to France, where he was jailed for arguing against the beheading of King Louis XVI. While in jail, he wrote *The Age of Reason*, a scathing argument against institutionalized religion, which was received with hostility on both sides of the Atlantic. Upon being released from prison, he returned to America, where he was labeled an infidel and snubbed.

Pac-Man is in an "eat or be eaten" situation. The more dots he eats, the more points he scores. He avoids his enemies, the ghosts, but if Pac-Man gobbles up an "energy dot," the tables are turned and he gets to eat the ghosts.

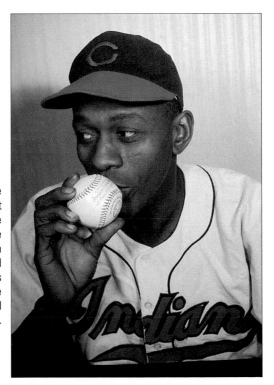

Statistics were poorly kept, but Satchel Paige estimated that he had played in 2,500 games and won 2,000. He was inducted into the Baseball Hall of Fame in 1971.

In order to pass through the Panama Canal, a ship must be lifted as high as 85 feet above sea level. This is accomplished with a series of locks—enclosed segments in which the water level is raised or lowered.

For many Americans, a festive breakfast (especially on Sunday) centers around hot, fluffy pancakes. Their popularity has inspired restaurant chains, such as the International House of Pancakes.

Wartime paper rationing put a damper on the production of paperbacks; afterward, they were more popular than ever. Today some books bypass the hardcover version and are published only as paperbacks.

## PANAMA CANAL

In 1513, when the Spanish explorer Balboa climbed a hill in Central America, he realized that the isthmus between the Atlantic and the Pacific was only 50 miles wide, and he visualized a shipping channel. Spain considered the idea but did not act on it. In 1881 Ferdinand de Lesseps of France—who had dug the Suez Canal through sand—began blasting a sea-level canal in Panama. Workers were overwhelmed by hard rock, yellow fever, and malaria, and the enterprise failed.

In 1898, the year of the Spanish-American War, the U.S. recognized the need to expedite the coast-to-coast movement of battleships. A canal through Panama, it was decided, would be the fastest route. With the backing of President Theodore Roosevelt, work began in 1904. Americans fought disease by draining the swamps that were havens to germ-carrying mosquitoes. The project was completed within 10 years. In 1977, after decades of dispute, the U.S. ceded jurisdiction of the 10-mile-wide canal zone to Panama. Control of the canal will go to Panama on December 31, 1999.

## PANCAKES

The French stuff all sorts of food into crepes; the Mexicans wrap savory fare with tortillas; and the Chinese use thin batter cakes in many dishes. But only in America are griddle-fried cakes, made with wheat, buckwheat, or cornmeal, the highlight of breakfast. Early pancakes, called hoecakes, were cooked over an open fire on the flat blade of a hoe. Johnny-cakes—durable disks that were cooked before a journey and carried in saddlebags—may have gotten their name from the Indian word *joniken*, or from "journey cake." Lumberjacks called pancakes flannel cakes, sweatpads, or flatcars. Today pancakes are sometimes called flapjacks or, if they're small, silver dollars. Popular toppings include berries and powdered sugar, but traditionalists insist on the cholesterol-and-calorie-laden combination of butter and maple syrup.

## PAPERBACKS

American paperbacks began as paltry dime novels in the late 19th century. The books later faded from sight. When paperbacks reappeared in 1939, they changed forever the way we read. Inspired by Britain's Penguin Books, Pocket Books issued paperbound reprints of classics and best-sellers, priced at just 25 cents. They were sold in bookstores and at newsstands, drugstores, and train stations. Critics doubted that Americans would buy them, insisting that "cheap books…must be of a low common denominator." Publisher Robert de Graff disagreed: "I…am prepared to prove my faith in the intelligence…of the American people."

De Graff's faith was amply justified. Readers snapped up his titles as soon as they appeared, beginning with Pearl Buck's *The Good Earth*. Other publishers joined the field, and sales of paperbacks skyrocketed. Today thrillers and romances with lurid covers attract buyers, but so do serious works. No longer 25 cents but still convenient, paperbacks make up some two-thirds of all books sold in the U.S.

## PAPER CUP

The paper cup, a boon for modern hygiene and purveyors of fast food, was the by-product of an unsuccessful marketing scheme. An entrepreneur named Hugh Moore, who founded the American Water Supply Company of New England in 1908, devised the first paper cup as part of his plan to sell water to thirsty travelers for a penny a drink. When the venture failed, Moore decided to sell his cups instead. In 1910 he started the Individual Drinking Cup Company, selling what he then called Health Kups. In search of a less clumsy name, he was struck by a sign on the office door of the nearby Dixie Doll Company. He asked the company's owners for permission to use the name, and in 1919 the Dixie Cup was born.

## PAPER DOLL

Looking for a paper dolly to call your own? There's a huge choice of modern ones, and many old favorites have been reprinted. The dolls, which debuted in Europe about 250 years ago, were once used as promotional giveaways for companies selling everything from corsets to coffee. In 1889 the Denniston Company introduced families of dolls, with instructions on how to dress them in crepe paper that could be pleated and ruffled. *McCall's* and *Ladies' Home Journal* included a detachable section of paper dolls. The dolls' clothes are a valuable historical record: Victory Dolls, for instance, came with 33 accurately rendered World War II uniforms—military and civilian—for men and women. Some dolls bear a likeness to movie stars; others wear clothes by famous designers. A 34-inch-tall cutout of Shirley Temple delighted children in 1936, and years later Marilyn Monroe, too, was immortalized in paper.

## PARKS, ROSA

On December 1, 1955, a black seamstress named Rosa Parks took a stand by keeping her seat on a Montgomery, Alabama, bus, thus defying a local segregation law. The law reserved the seats in the front of the bus for white people and also required blacks to give up their seats to whites. Parks was arrested, and her arrest led to an organized boycott. Blacks, who provided the bus system with some 70 percent of its revenue, chose instead to walk or to carpool. The bitter boycott lasted 381 days; it was settled when the Supreme Court declared Montgomery's seating laws unconstitutional.

The myth is that Rosa Parks was just too tired to move and was surprised by the furor that ensued. In fact, as the secretary of the Montgomery NAACP, she knew that refusal to move would lead to her being booked, fined, and jailed. She said, "The only tired I was, was tired of giving in."

Before the paper cup, communal drinking cups were in wide use—a health hazard that spread disease.

Former Mouseketeer Annette Funicello is just one of the many public figures who became paper-doll cutouts.

The day after the Montgomery bus boycott finally ended, Rosa Parks was photographed sitting in the seat of her choice.

# PATCHWORK QUILTS

*Quilts are part of America's past—and present. The colonists sewed them in order to salvage every scrap of fabric. Today quilting is a labor of love.*

## LOG CABIN DESIGNS

Country life inspired the themes of many log cabin piece quilts. The dark and light triangles of the Straight Furrow pattern (above) recall a freshly plowed field.

## QUILTS AS COMMEMORATIVES

This quilt was made to honor the 150th anniversary of a town in Michigan. It includes local scenes as well as the signatures of many residents.

## STAR POWER

Individual blocks in the classic Starry Path pattern have been turned into decorative pillows.

## FLORAL APPLIQUÉ

Trailing vines and pomegranates (right) are typical of mid-19th-century appliqué quilts. Irises bloom in the beautiful 1945 creation below. Both quilts feature trapunto, or stuffed appliqué.

## ANOTHER LOOK

Quiltwork is used here as a dramatic mirror frame. It can also be made into unique vests, jewelry cases, and other accessories.

## DOUBLE WEDDING RINGS

A bride's trousseau might include up to 12 Double Wedding Ring quilts. Made of tiny scraps pieced together to form rings, it was the most popular pattern of the 1920s and '30s.

## A NOT-SO-CRAZY QUILT

A passion for crazy quilts swept the nation in the late 1870s. Made of silk and exclusively for decoration, the quilts rejected the symmetry of geometric designs in favor of a kaleidoscopic effect.

Most patent medicines were shams. But some contained effective herbs that Native Americans and early settlers used successfully.

Tanks were Patton's specialty; "Attack, always attack" was his credo. His Third Army once advanced so far ahead of its supply lines that provisions had to be airlifted to reach them.

Paul Bunyan's appetite was heroic; the griddle used by his cook was greased by boys who skated over it with hams strapped to their feet.

## PATENT MEDICINE

Kickapoo Indian Oil, Pink Pills for Pale People, and Wilson's Panacea were 19th-century "patent," or proprietary, medicines, which often claimed to cure almost any ailment. Widely advertised and sold without a prescription, they were usually innocuous mixtures of water, alcohol, oils, and coloring agents. Buying a patent medicine from a peddler or at a medicine show was cheaper than visiting a doctor, who might do no more than dispense his own folk remedy.

Lydia E. Pinkham's Vegetable Compound, a remedy for women's reproductive complaints, was among the best-known patent medicines. Pinkham had given her concoction of alcohol, unicorn root, and pleurisy root to friends, but she began marketing it in 1875, after her husband lost all their money in real estate. Doctors ridiculed the compound as quackery, but modern-day herbalists say that some of the ingredients may actually have beneficial effects.

## PATTON, GEORGE

"Old Blood and Guts" was more complex than this appellation suggests. George Patton was ambitious yet self-destructive, egotistical yet riven with self-doubt. He wrote poetry, prayed on his knees, and wept over his fallen men. After graduating from West Point military academy in 1909, Patton received many honors for his service in World War I.

During World War II his 1st Armored Corps was bloodied in North Africa; his Seventh Army swept across Sicily with astonishing speed. There, victorious, Patton nearly destroyed his career when he publicly rebuked—and slapped with his gloves—a shell-shocked soldier in a hospital. Furious, President Eisenhower made Patton apologize to all concerned and let him languish until after D day. Patton then led the Third Army in Normandy and, during the Battle of the Bulge, relieved the siege of Bastogne with his signature speed of advance. His Third Army gained more ground and took more prisoners than any other army in history.

## PAUL BUNYAN

The origins of the Paul Bunyan legend are obscure. The first printed account appeared in a Michigan newspaper in 1906. But it took adman W. B. Laughead, a former woodsman himself, to spread the myth widely, using the brawny lumberjack to promote the Red River Lumber Company.

Bunyan's feats are impressive indeed. As an infant, one story goes, the folklore giant cleared four square miles of standing timber by rolling around in his sleep. His blue ox, Babe, "twice as big as all outdoors, and playful as a hurricane," could haul 640 acres of logs in one load to a river landing. And if the river twisted, Paul Bunyan and Babe would give it a mighty yank to fix a logjam. These outlandish stories celebrate the virtues of America's woodsmen, whose strength, ingenuity, and humor helped to build a nation.

## PAULING, LINUS

Linus Pauling made breakthrough discoveries in biochemistry that put him in a class with Newton, Darwin, and Einstein. His findings, controversial at the time, revolutionized the study of molecular chemistry, and he won the Nobel Prize in 1954. Pauling gained even greater fame when he presented to the United Nations a petition, signed by 11,000 scientists from 49 countries, that protested atmospheric nuclear testing. The gesture earned Pauling a second Nobel Prize, for peace. He was the first person to win two.

In the 1970s Pauling became the leading advocate of taking megadoses of vitamin C to prevent colds and even cancer. His own daily intake of the vitamin was equal to 240 oranges. Most doctors scoffed at the idea, but Pauling was unperturbed. "I'm accustomed to having my ideas received with skepticism," he said shortly before his death at age 93.

A famous chemist, Pauling opposed nuclear weapons. The U.S. revoked his passport in the 1950s; only at the last minute was he allowed to go to Sweden to accept the Nobel Prize.

## PEACEABLE KINGDOM

"The wolf shall dwell with the lamb" proclaims the Book of Isaiah. That prophecy of concord among all God's creatures inspired a series of at least 60 paintings, each entitled "The Peaceable Kingdom," by primitive artist Edward Hicks. Hicks was a Quaker minister who earned his living by decorating carriages and signs but who considered himself a "worthless, insignificant painter." The oils, created between 1820 and 1849, depict two separate scenes of amity: a child leading a menagerie of wild and domestic animals, and the Quaker William Penn signing a treaty with the Indians.

The paintings not only supplemented Hicks's income (each sold for about $20) but helped him to express what he called his "poor zig-zag nature." For although the Quakers eschewed ornament, Hicks was driven to create charming visual homages to Penn and his policy of religious tolerance, which embodied the divine promise of peace on Earth.

"The Peaceable Kingdom" series by Edward Hicks shows a world in which, as Hicks put it, "The beauteous leopard with his restless eye / Shall with the kid in perfect stillness lie."

## PEACE CORPS

In a 1960 campaign speech, John F. Kennedy said, "There is not enough money in all America to relieve the misery of the underdeveloped world in a giant and endless soup kitchen. But there is enough know-how and knowledgeable people to help those nations help themselves." Soon after he became president in 1961, Kennedy founded the Peace Corps.

Inspired by the idealism of the 1960s, 900 volunteers, many of them recent college graduates, signed up the first year. They were sent to Tanzania, Colombia, and other developing countries. After language and technical training—and classes on treating snakebite—they worked for two years at such jobs as establishing fishery programs, training health workers, and teaching English. Today's volunteers are often professionals who put their careers on hold, and older people—some in their eighties—lured by the appeal of sharing their skills with the world and learning from the experience.

In 1968 a volunteer tutors a child in Lobatsi, Botswana. By that time, the Peace Corps had more than 15,000 workers in some 50 countries.

*The Power of Positive Thinking,* said Norman Vincent Peale, "has sensible principles. If a person were to live by it, he wouldn't be free of trouble, but he'd know how to handle trouble."

By one estimate, the average American child wolfs down some 1,500 peanut-butter-and-jelly sandwiches before graduating from high school.

The *Peanuts* team of Shroeder, Lucy, Charlie Brown, Snoopy, Patty, and Linus gather on the mound. Alas! They have yet to win a baseball game.

## PEALE, NORMAN VINCENT

Methodist preacher Norman Vincent Peale was one of the most popular and influential American clergymen who ever lived. A dazzling orator who emphasized the benefits of faith and prayer, he was one of the first religious leaders to gain fame by using the mass media—newspapers, books, radio, and television—as well as the pulpit. His newspaper column appeared in nearly a hundred dailies, and millions nationwide listened to his weekly radio program.

His popularity was by no means a given. Peale described himself as having once been "a very shy, self-doubting boy." It was in the process of trying to understand and overcome feelings of timidity and negativity that he developed the principles of his tremendously successful book, *The Power of Positive Thinking.* Published in 1952, it begins: "Believe in yourself!" Today more than 15 million copies are in print.

## PEANUT BUTTER

Peanut butter is the fuel that most American children, and many adults, run on. Kids love its taste, and parents love that it's packed with protein and vitamins and that, thanks to stabilizers that keep the peanut paste and oil from separating, it can be safely left unrefrigerated for months. (Organic peanut butter has a shorter shelf life.)

Peanut paste, ground by hand, was for centuries a traditional food among Peruvian Indians as well as African tribes. In 1903 a St. Louis doctor, Ambrose Staub, invented a peanut mill to make a nutritious butter for elderly patients with poor teeth. No one knows who was the first to add jelly to peanut butter sandwiches, but he or she was surely a genius.

## PEANUTS

*Peanuts* is the most successful comic strip in history. It has inspired TV specials, books, dolls, posters, songs, and even a musical. And like Charlie Brown, the hero (and, more frequently, the goat) of *Peanuts,* the comic's creator, Charles M. Schulz, doesn't always get what he wants. He originally called his strip *Li'l Folks,* but despite his protests, the United Feature syndicate, which bought the strip in 1950, called his big-headed children "Peanuts," naming them after the tykes who sat in the "peanut gallery" of the *Howdy Doody* show's studio audience.

Charlie Brown and his friends inhabit a world free of adults but full of fears and anxieties. Charlie lives with the knowledge that the tree will eat his kite, Lucy will pull the football away before he can kick it, and he'll never impress the Little Red-Haired Girl. Linus can't cope without his security blanket. Lucy's attempts to help matters with a five-cent therapy booth never improve anything. Snoopy, the multitalented dog, provides a special flair with his imaginative adventures as a valiant World War I flying ace determined to gun down his nemesis, the Red Baron.

## PEARL HARBOR

President Franklin Delano Roosevelt summed up the sentiments of the entire nation when he called December 7, 1941, a "date which will live in infamy." In the early morning, Japanese airplanes took off from aircraft carriers for a bombing raid on Pearl Harbor, the site of a U.S. military installation on Oahu, Hawaii. The surprise attack came in two waves that included a total of 78 fighters and 272 bombers. It was a catastrophe for the U.S. because about half of the Pacific fleet was in port. Eight battleships were damaged or sunk, 164 aircraft were destroyed, and casualties—military and civilian—numbered more than 3,500.

The very next day, the U.S. declared war on Japan. From that point onward the initial sorrow associated with the attack on Pearl Harbor was transformed into an iron-willed resolve that would carry the nation to victory. Although Admiral Yamamoto was the mastermind of the Japanese attack, he had had misgivings about carrying it out, fearing that it would be suicide "to kick the sleeping giant."

## PENNSYLVANIA DUTCH

The people known as the Pennsylvania Dutch are not Dutch at all. They originally came from Germany, or Deutschland. The "Deutsch" was misunderstood by others as "Dutch," and the name stuck. They have faithfully kept alive their distinctive traditions since they began settling in southeastern Pennsylvania in the late 17th century. Fleeing religious persecution, the settlers included Lutherans and Reformed church members as well as the strict Amish and Mennonites. The hilly green countryside of Pennsylvania reminded them of the fertile Rhineland, and they quickly turned it into farmland. Their hearty cooking features dishes like sausage, sauerkraut, and shoofly pie—a molasses, sugar, and flour concoction probably named for the flies the baker had to chase away. When not busy farming or cooking, the Pennsylvania Dutch create fine furniture, textiles, and handicrafts.

## PENNY ARCADE

Early in the 20th century, the shooting galleries, freak shows, rides, and ball-pitching games in carnivals and amusement parks were supplemented by machines that didn't require an operator. They were bunched together in a penny arcade, where you could have your fortune told, test your grip strength, peep through a hole at moving pictures, play mechanical games to win candy, buy a postcard, or hear a song—all by dropping pennies into slots. During the Depression, penny arcades kept their name, but the price went up to a nickel. Next came pinball machines, which tested one's skill at using flippers and a bit of body English in order to maneuver steel balls through a maze of pins and holes. Today video games, costing a quarter or more to operate, have taken over the penny arcades.

During the Japanese raid on Pearl Harbor, an armor-piercing bomb penetrated to the forward magazine of the U.S.S. *Arizona* (above), igniting the munitions.

Clean lines and simple ornamentation characterize the crafts of the Pennsylvania Dutch. Hex signs (left) appear on barns.

Once an arcade's top attraction, peep shows portrayed historical subjects, natural scenery, comedy shorts, sports, and action sequences.

By offering breezy stories about celebrities like John F. Kennedy, Jr., Cher, and the stars of *Charlie's Angels*, *People* has made itself the most profitable of the Time-Warner magazines.

Blond bombshell Betty Hutton starred as Pearl White in *The Perils of Pauline* (1947), a big-screen biography of the silent movie legend.

Raymond Burr (right) resumed his old role of defender of the innocent in a series of television movies, beginning with *Perry Mason Returns* (1985).

## PEOPLE MAGAZINE

Although *People* devotes two-thirds of its articles to ordinary folks, the weekly chronicler of American pop culture is best known for its coverage of celebrities. Elizabeth Taylor's face has graced the cover almost 40 times, and Madonna's, more than 20. But it is Princess Di's storybook rise and fall in royal circles that remains the most popular subject of *People*'s shutterbug journalists. With what one critic has called a mixture of "supermarket sleaze and clever mass appeal," *People* reaches 35 million readers each week.

Declared an "overnight sensation" when it appeared in 1974, *People* practically invented star-watching journalism and has spawned a host of imitators.

## PERILS OF PAULINE

The heroine is tied to the railroad tracks—the train is approaching! Suddenly the action stops for the teeth-clenching message: "To Be Continued Next Week." Serial movies began in 1912, but it wasn't until 1914 that audiences were treated to the most famous cliffhangers in history, starring Pearl White, the undisputed "Queen of the Serials." A former child circus performer, silent-movie actress White got her break as the star of Pathé's sensational *Perils of Pauline*. Pauline's tribulations were endless: she struggled in quicksand; escaped white slavers; plummeted through trapdoors; survived explosions; and was swept away, gasping and gurgling, down a millrun. White usually performed her own stunts, but because of an early back injury, doubles (small men) were provided for the most strenuous bits.

The *Perils* villain seen most often was played by Warner Oland, a Swedish actor who specialized in portraying Asians and who ended up as hero detective Charlie Chan. Pearl White, an extremely popular star in her day, made enough money to retire to the South of France in 1924. She was the subject of two film biographies in 1947 and 1967.

## PERRY MASON

Contrary to popular belief, Perry Mason actually lost a case. In fact, during the nine-year run of the hit TV series *Perry Mason*, he lost three. The first time it happened, 30,000 fans sent letters pleading, "Don't do that again." They wanted to be sure that the real killer would confess in a dramatic courtroom outburst and that justice would be done every week.

Mason's winning ways began in a series of 82 novels by ex-lawyer Erle Stanley Gardner. After a few forgettable movies and a 12-year stint on radio, *Perry Mason*, starring darkly brooding Raymond Burr, became, during its 1957–66 run, "the longest-running, highest-rated lawyer show in TV history." Throughout, Della Street remained the charming helpmate; Paul Drake, private eye, never failed to find critical evidence to save the innocent defendant; and Hamilton Burger, hapless district attorney, always expected to win.

## PERSHING, JOHN J.

John "Black Jack" Pershing's career coincided with America's development as a world power. Born to a Missouri farm family, he won appointment to West Point and later earned a law degree. During the Spanish-American War, he gained a champion in President Theodore Roosevelt, who promoted him to brigadier general over 862 senior officers. President Woodrow Wilson sent him in pursuit of Pancho Villa during the Mexican Intervention of 1916. Pershing didn't capture Villa, but the chase gave him valuable field experience.

World War I had reached a bloody stalemate by the time the United States entered in 1917. Under Pershing's command, the American Expeditionary Forces brought crucial reinforcements and helped to turn the tide with such decisive victories as the one at Meuse-Argonne. Although Pershing was taciturn and aloof, his effective leadership embodied America's bold new international image.

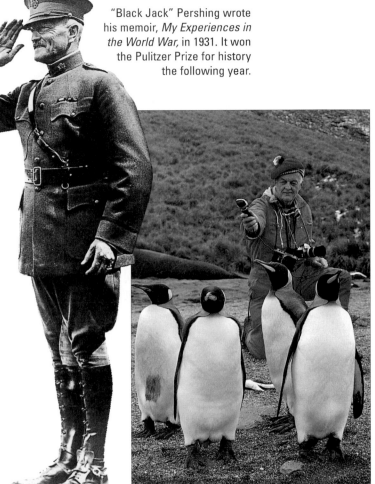

"Black Jack" Pershing wrote his memoir, *My Experiences in the World War,* in 1931. It won the Pulitzer Prize for history the following year.

## PETERSON, ROGER TORY

"Woods! Birds! Flowers! Here are the makings of a great naturalist." So reads the inscription under Roger Tory Peterson's 1925 high school yearbook photograph. Actually the "dean of bird watchers" got started as a child. He found a flicker, a small brown-and-yellow bird, in the woods. He thought it was dead, but when he stroked its feathers, it awakened and flew away. Thrilled, Peterson wanted to know all about birds.

Now often called the "second *Audubon*," Peterson's original 1934 *A Field Guide to the Birds* has sold millions of copies. Rejected as a manuscript five times, it was finally accepted by Houghton Mifflin, which printed an initial 2,000 copies. Within weeks it was completely sold out. Identification of birds had previously been time-consuming and tedious. Peterson offered an innovative system that grouped similar species together and used arrows to show where distinguishing marks could be seen. Peterson later adapted the method for spotting enemy aircraft during World War II.

Naturalist Roger Tory Peterson devoted his life to watching, painting, photographing, and recording the sounds of birds.

## PEYTON PLACE

Grace Metalious's 1956 novel about hanky-panky in a small town took the country by storm; thereafter, the mildest misbehavior in any community branded it "a regular Peyton Place!" It was made into a movie starring Lana Turner in 1957. In Peyton Place, she warned, "Two people talking is a conspiracy, a meeting is an assignation, and getting to know one another is a scandal." The book's sequel appeared in 1961.

Then came its golden age: *Peyton Place* was the first major American prime-time soap. It ran in half-hour segments twice each week from 1964 to 1969 and introduced two young actors: Mia Farrow and Ryan O'Neal. There was a sequel, *Return to Peyton Place* (1972–74), which ran as a daytime serial, as well as two TV movies in 1977 and 1985.

Ice-cold Constance MacKenzie (Lana Turner) danced with the new high school principal (Lee Philips) in the scandalous 1957 movie *Peyton Place.*

Avid Pez fans, some of whom own hundreds of dispensers, can subscribe to the newsletter *The Optimistic Pezzimist*.

When the Declaration of Independence was signed in Independence Hall in 1776, the Liberty Bell rang out, proclaiming the good news.

## PEZ

Americans find it hard to resist Pez; billions of the pastel-colored tablets are consumed each year. The appeal is not just the candy. It's also the plastic dispensers with little feet, topped with heads of characters that include Snow White, Uncle Sam, and the Creature from the Black Lagoon. Pez became a cultural icon when, in the nostalgic movie *Stand by Me*, one boy said, "If I could only have one food to eat for the rest of my life? That's easy. Pez. Cherry-flavored Pez."

Pez was created in 1927 in Vienna, Austria, when Eduard Haas III mixed peppermint oil with sugar to make a breath mint. (The name is derived from the German word for "peppermint," *Pfefferminz*). The first Pez dispensers—of plain design—appeared in 1948.

Soon after Pez arrived in America, in 1952, the candy was jazzed up with fruit flavors and colors. The first novelty dispensers were topped with Mickey Mouse heads. In the 1950s space guns that shot Pez "bullets" delighted children, and in the '60s Pez went "mod" with psychedelic flower dispensers. Many of the dispensers are now collectibles, and the rare "Make-a-Face" dispenser, with 18 interchangeable parts, sells for several thousand dollars.

## PHILADELPHIA

The streams of diversity and democracy that flow through America can be traced back to the headwaters of Philadelphia, the haven of equality and religious tolerance established as a "Holy Experiment" by the Quaker William Penn in 1682. "You shall be governed by laws of your own making, and live a free…and industrious people," he wrote. Penn's "greene Countrie Towne" welcomed the oppressed of many faiths, who created a peaceful, prosperous city.

The cobblestoned Colonial settlement, designed on a grid and dotted with parks, forms the core of today's multicultural metropolis. Close to the tidy Georgian town houses of Society Hill are the Victorian row houses of South Philly, an Italian community that launched the "cheesesteak" sandwich, and an open-air market where Sylvester Stallone's Rocky jogged (cheered on with the local greeting, "Yo!"). The neighborhood is also headquarters for the Mummers—bands of string musicians who don flamboyant costumes and dance their signature "strut" in daylong New Year's parades, as merrymakers did in Colonial times.

In Fairmount Park, America's largest landscaped city park, the stately manors of 18th-century aristocrats coexist with gingerbread Boathouse Row, the 19th-century base for a fleet of rowing clubs. On the site Penn designated as Centre Square stands the ornate City Hall, whose 550-foot-tall tower is topped by a bronze statue of William Penn himself. So broad-minded has his city become that in 1993, when rabid Phillies baseball fans in the grip of pennant fever had "Billy" Penn crowned with a huge team cap, no one batted an eye.

## PHILIP MARLOWE

Before Philip Marlowe came along in 1939, the typical hard-boiled detective in the world of pulp fiction was no better than the criminals he investigated. Like his predecessors, Marlowe rubs elbows with the lowlifes of L.A.'s lurid underworld, but through it all he remains a man of spotless integrity, conscience, and compassion. "Down these mean streets a man must go who is not himself mean, who is neither tarnished nor afraid," wrote Raymond Chandler about his hero in the essay "The Simple Art of Murder." In *Farewell My Lovely*, for example, Marlowe agrees to help an ex-con named Moose Malloy find his former sweetheart because he sympathizes with the isolated, heartbroken hoodlum.

Chandler didn't start writing detective stories until he was 45, and his scant output—just seven novels in 20 years—did not compare with that of his million-words-a-year colleagues in the pulps. But readers appreciated his unique style, and Hollywood paid him handsomely. Humphrey Bogart gave Marlowe a face and a distinctive voice in *The Big Sleep*, the 1946 classic directed by Howard Hawks.

Charlotte Rampling and Robert Mitchum starred in *Farewell My Lovely* (1975), a remake of the 1944 Philip Marlowe classic.

## PICKUP TRUCKS

When the automotive age arrived, the pickup truck replaced the horse as the rural individualist's favorite vehicle. The rifle was soon nestled in the gun rack across the rear window, instead of in the saddle, and dogs rode in back, instead of trotting alongside. The pickup was designed for rough work: its high clearance let it travel unpaved roads, and the open back could hold building materials and tools.

In recent years, a new breed of smaller pickups has become a status symbol for active city dwellers, and a popular suburban second car. The cabs have become fancier and more comfortable, and the cargo beds—perfect for transporting bikes and skis—are great for hauling bulky bargains back from discount warehouses.

"There used to be a stigma if you were seen in a truck," said one Chevy executive. "Now you see them in... affluent neighborhoods."

## PIKES PEAK

U.S. Army officer Zebulon Pike was not the first white man to see Pikes Peak, near present-day Colorado Springs, Colorado; the Spanish beat him to it by 27 years. Pike never even reached the top. He and his team of explorers tried to climb to its frigid 14,110-foot-high summit in November 1806; wearing only light summer uniforms, they nearly froze to death. Nor did he call it Pikes Peak; it was just "Grand Peak" to him. But Pike put the peak on the map when his account of his trip west became a best-seller.

Tourists have been drawn to the peak's massive rock formations, hidden lakes, and snow-covered crags ever since. One, Katharine Lee Bates, was so inspired by the mountain's majesty that she wrote "America the Beautiful" in 1893. On a clear day, you can actually see as far away as Kansas.

Pikes Peak looms over the sandstone formations of the Garden of the Gods—a landscape formed by sedimentary rock 65 million years ago.

Today pinball machines use flashing lights, sound effects, wild colors, and computer wizardry to draw a whole new generation to the game.

## PINBALL

Pac-Man tried, but he couldn't kill pinball. For a while, the game of flash, flip, and ching-ching-ching was hanging on for dear life. In 1983 only 5 percent of arcade cash was slipped into a pinball slot. Now many video arcades devote at least a third of their floor space to good old pinball—except there's nothing old-fashioned about today's high-tech machines.

Pinball's latest surge in popularity can be partly attributed to the 1993 Broadway musical *The Who's Tommy*, about a "deaf, dumb, and blind kid" who "sure plays a mean pinball." *Tommy*'s journey actually started in 1969, with a rock opera album and live performances by The Who. In 1975 a film version was made with Elton John as the Pinball Wizard.

Pinball itself began much earlier. A Cincinnati inventor patented the first primitive tabletop machine—a ball, plunger, holes, and pins for obstacles. The game didn't take off, though, until the Great Depression, when many saloons offered David Gottlieb's Baffle Ball (seven marbles for a nickel) to help the unemployed "rest their minds."

## PING-PONG

Legend has it that Ping-Pong started around 1890, when London gentlemen used cigar-box lids to bat champagne corks across a miniature tennis court. Flim-Flam, Klik-Klak, and Whiff-Whaff were some of the names the new sport went by, but Ping-Pong—the sound of a celluloid ball being bopped by a paddle—was the one that stuck. By 1900 it was a world-wide craze and the obsessed were diagnosed with "pingpongitis." Ping-Pong wasn't just chic, it was cheap, costing a fraction as much as lawn tennis, its full-scale predecessor. The sport peaked in the United States in 1902, but it went on to become an Olympic event and the most popular participant sport in the world. Just don't call it Ping-Pong in front of a table-tennis pro.

## PINUPS

During World War II, America's men were fighting for either "the girl they left behind" or the woman whose figure they admired the most: Betty Grable. A picture of Betty Grable in a bathing suit, smiling coyly as she looked back over her shoulder, was pinned up in almost every barrack and bivouac. Talking about her fame, Grable said, "There are two reasons why I'm in show business, and I'm standing on both of them." The combination of those legs and her all-American, wholesome face with its peaches-and-cream complexion drove the troops wild.

Grable, who once said, "I'm strictly an enlisted man's girl," made the most of her popularity with the troops in two 1944 movies: *Four Jills in a Jeep* and *Pin Up Girl*. Screenwriter Nunnally Johnson said of her, "I don't think Betty would want an Oscar on her mantelpiece. She has every Tom, Dick, and Harry at her feet."

Betty Grable (left) was easily the G.I.'s favorite pinup. Her famous legs were insured for $1 million with Lloyds of London. Other pinup stars included Rita Hayworth (above), Dorothy Lamour, and Lana Turner.

## PLASTIC

John Wesley Hyatt altered the course of the American marketplace forever when he developed the first plastic billiard ball. In 1870, while experimenting with celluloid—a combination of cellulose, nitric acid, and camphor—Hyatt realized that the material was soft when warm and rigid when cold. The possibilities for its use seemed endless, and by 1890 products made from celluloid, such as clock cases, dentures, toys, and combs, filled American homes. Despite being highly flammable, celluloid was marketed for the next 40 years. Gradually plastics became more versatile and colorful—Bakelite, rayon, acetate, and vinyl were in use before 1930; acrylics, Formica, and nylon were available by 1940.

Today plastic is made from synthetic resins derived mainly from coal, natural gas, petroleum, and limestone. Generally, manufacturers melt resins down to a syrupy liquid that can then be molded into virtually any shape imaginable. The resins can be compressed by machines, poured into a mold, or extruded through a tube. Machines can also coat sheets of paper, cloth, or metal foil with melted resin to strengthen and protect surfaces (a process called calendering). These methods help produce everything from football helmets to prostheses, playing cards to rocket parts.

No other material has the versatility of plastic. Hard plastics were used to make this chair, guitar case, and helmet, while transparent plastics were shaped to make the beaker and funnel.

## PLAY-DOH

Play-Doh's story began when a nursery school teacher from New Jersey wanted to give her students something easier to play with than conventional modeling clay. In 1955 the teacher's brother-in-law, Joseph McVicker of Cincinnati, Ohio, helped her by concocting a softer, more pliable clay—a grayish-white compound that was made mostly of flour and water. Yellow, red, and blue Play-Doh came out in 1957. At this time, Play-Doh also got its distinctive, vanillalike smell, an aroma so appealing that many kids were tempted to eat the stuff. The Play-Doh recipe soon included a hefty dose of salt—to preserve the compound's softness and to discourage children from taking a second taste.

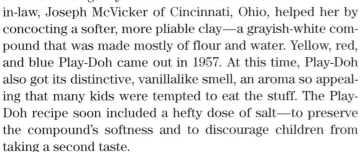

Among the first to test Play-Doh before it hit the stores was a blond-haired French boy sporting a beret. A drawing of that young lad has graced the 800 million cans of Play-Doh that have since been sold.

## PLEDGE OF ALLEGIANCE

Starting in 1892, the 400th anniversary of Columbus's discovery of the Americas, public school children began their day by standing and reciting a 22-word pledge of loyalty to the flag and the nation. The pledge had been written and published by an editor of *The Youth's Companion* in Boston, and reciting it quickly became as routine as singing the national anthem. In 1923 the words *the flag of the United States of America* were substituted for *my flag.*

Daily recitation of the Pledge of Allegiance was required in the schools of many states until 1943, when the Supreme Court ruled that such laws violated the First Amendment to the Constitution, which protects free speech.

The Pledge of Allegiance was last changed in 1954, when it became an official part of the U.S. Flag Code and the words *under God* were added.

It wasn't until 1820, when Daniel Webster said, "Beneath us is the rock on which New England received the feet of the Pilgrims," that Plymouth Rock became a historical icon.

Pocahontas met John Rolfe while she was being held prisoner by the colonists in 1613; a year later, she married him. In 1616 the Rolfes sailed to England, where Pocahontas commissioned this portrait of herself in English garb.

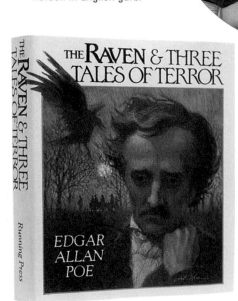

Remarking on Poe's work, D. H. Lawrence wrote, "He was an adventurer into the vaults and cellars and horrible underground passages of the human soul."

## PLYMOUTH ROCK

Legend has it that when the Pilgrims stepped off the *Mayflower* in 1620, they stepped directly onto Plymouth Rock. In fact, the Pilgrims' accounts tell only of their struggle for survival; they make no mention of a rock.

When patriots tried to move the 200-ton boulder in 1774, it split in half. The lower part remained at the shore, where it became part of a commercial wharf; the upper part was moved first to the town square, then later to Pilgrim Hall.

In 1880 the two halves were reunited and placed under a protective canopy. It wasn't until after a new structure was built in the 1920s (during which the rock—by this time in several pieces—was stored in a warehouse) that the rock was mortared together. Today Plymouth Rock is visited as a symbol of our nation's birth.

## POCAHONTAS

Pocahontas was the daughter of Algonquian chief Powhatan. When English settlers founded Jamestown in 1607, the spirited young girl became an emissary between the whites and the Indians. In his *Generall Historie*, Jamestown leader John Smith writes of how he narrowly escaped death after he was captured by Powhatan's warriors. Just as the chief was going to dash out Smith's brains with a stone club, Pocahontas put her head over his and begged her father to spare him. It's now believed that this was a ritual by which Smith was inducted into the tribe.

In 1614 Pocahontas took the name Rebecca and married John Rolfe—not John Smith, with whom she was just friends. Two years later Rolfe and Pocahontas (Rebecca) sailed to England, where she was feted as an Indian princess. As they were about to return to America, she contracted smallpox and died.

## POE, EDGAR ALLAN

For more than 150 years, schoolchildren everywhere have discovered the pleasures of poetry by reciting Edgar Allan Poe's strangely thrilling tale "The Raven," with its haunting refrain: "Quoth the raven, 'Nevermore.'" Just as well known are his terrifying short stories, such as "The Tell-Tale Heart" and "The Fall of the House of Usher." But few know that it was Poe who single-handedly defined the type of story that is now known as the detective thriller (he called them "tales of ratiocination") with "The Purloined Letter" and "The Murders in the Rue Morgue."

Although Poe led a troubled life—always in debt, moving from job to job—his lofty literary standards never wavered. Genius, he believed, could best be displayed in the form of a short story, "requiring from a half-hour to one or two hours in its perusal." Poe held his up own tales, along with those by Nathaniel Hawthorne and Washington Irving, as unmatched examples of greatness in American literature.

## POKER

Popularized by Mississippi riverboat gamblers, poker quickly became a favorite card game. To play, players bet that the value of their cards is higher than that of any other hand at the table. Usually, five cards are dealt and everyone puts a bet in the pot. In rotation, each player must equal or raise that bet to stay in the game. A player with a good hand or a bluffer may "raise" the bet still higher. If it's not matched, he wins without showing his cards. If another player "calls" him by equaling the bet, he must show his hand.

Poker was such serious business that shootouts often erupted between cowboys who thought someone was cheating. In 1876 U.S. Marshall James B. ("Wild Bill") Hickok was playing poker in Deadwood, in the Dakota Territory. He held two aces and two eights when he was shot in the back. Aces over eights is still called a "dead man's hand."

In the game of poker, having a "poker face"—being able to control signs of emotion—is more important than having good cards. In this spoof by Cassius M. Coolidge, the dogs practice their stoic expressions.

## POLAR EXPLORERS

In 1909, after many others had failed, America's Robert Edwin Peary and his associate, Matthew Henson, traveled by dog sled to the North Pole. Their success sparked international interest in polar exploration. Rear Adm. Richard Evelyn Byrd, a navy pilot famous for flying over the North Pole and the Atlantic in the '20s, led an expedition to Antarctica in 1928, where he set up a base camp called Little America; this began a 33-year career that made him the world's best-known polar explorer.

Byrd returned to Little America in 1933 to map and claim the land around the South Pole. He spent five months alone in a shelter 125 miles south of Little America and made observations and recorded conditions while suffering through low temperatures (-83°F and below) and nearly dying from carbon monoxide poisoning and frostbite. Byrd's third Antarctic expedition (in 1939) was sponsored by the U.S. government, but further exploration was interrupted by World War II.

At left, Admiral Byrd wraps a flag around a stone from the grave of fellow explorer Floyd Bennett. Byrd dropped the stone over the South Pole in honor of Bennett, who, after helping plan the expedition to the Pole, died before it began.

## POLAROID

While on vacation in 1943, Edwin Land was taking snapshots of his young daughter when she asked why she couldn't see the pictures right away. Why not indeed, thought Land, and he set out to satisfy her. Just over four years later, the inventor introduced the Polaroid Land camera—the first camera that let you see a picture soon after it was taken. Over the years, new and improved versions appeared, but it was the debut of the SX-70 in the 1970s that introduced true one-step photography. Because the film now contained its own processing materials, it was no longer necessary to peel away a layer of caustic chemicals. Ultimately, one-hour photo-processing stores and video cameras eclipsed Land's technological miracle, but it was the Polaroid that pioneered the way to the junction of "instant" and "photography."

At right, Edwin Land demonstrates the first Polaroid. Originally, the film and processing materials had to be peeled apart. Nowadays, the photo pops right out.

The National Foundation for Infantile Paralysis, founded in 1938 by Franklin Roosevelt, asked people to contribute just one dime each. The "March of Dimes" raised millions of dollars for polio research.

## POLIO VACCINE

When a polio vaccine was introduced by Dr. Jonas Salk in 1955, it was hailed as the most exciting medical breakthrough of the century. Fear of being paralyzed by polio had been sweeping the nation, and in 1952 the number of polio cases reached an all-time high. Nearly 58,000 Americans, many of them children, caught the virus, and some 3,000 died. Dr. Salk grew the virus in the lab, killed it with formaldehyde, and developed a serum that, when injected into the bloodstream, successfully prevented infection.

Salk's rival, Dr. Albert Sabin, believed that a living but weakened virus would produce more antibodies than a killed virus. In 1960 he came out with a vaccine that could be taken orally. Together the vaccines have practically eradicated polio throughout the world.

## POLITICAL PARTIES

John Adams once declared, "There is nothing I dread so much as the division of the Republic into two great parties." Yet George Washington had barely become president before the first political parties were formed. The Federalists, led by Alexander Hamilton, opposed Thomas Jefferson's Republicans, or Democratic-Republicans. Sixteen years after Jefferson's election in 1800, the Federalist Party had disappeared.

When Andrew Jackson was elected president in 1828, the two-party system was revived, this time between the Democrats and the Whigs. The first national nominating convention took place in 1832, and it was described by William H. Seward as a combination of "hustle, excitement, collision, irritation, enunciation, suspicion, confusion, obstinacy, foolhardiness, and humor."

The last shake-up of the two-party system came when the Democratic Party split in 1854. Antislavery Democrats joined Free-Soilers and Whigs to re-create the Republican Party, and they nominated Abraham Lincoln for president. Proslavery Democrats became the party of the South. After the Civil War, cartoonist Thomas Nast created the symbols of the elephant and the donkey, around which the parties rallied.

Minor parties have always existed on the political scene, from the Populists to Theodore Roosevelt's Bull Moose Party and the 1948 Dixiecrats. Infighting has taken place for just as long. In the early 20th century, the Democratic Party was so riven with feuding that Will Rogers joked, "I belong to no organized party. I'm a Democrat."

Pull the tail on this 1908 campaign card, and out comes a picture of Democratic candidate William Jennings Bryan.

Republicans showed support for presidential hopeful Wendell Willkie with a novelty license plate.

Hayley Mills played Pollyanna, a relentlessly cheerful orphan who prompts one adult to snap, "Glad this, glad that, you're glad about everything! What's the matter with you?"

## POLLYANNA

*Pollyanna*, Eleanor H. Porter's story of the "glad" girl, was first published in 1913 and was an immediate heart-warmer. Dramatized on the stage, *Pollyanna* went on tour in 1917. The heroine was played by young Helen Hayes, who hated the play, especially the end of the second act, when Pollyanna is carried onstage, both legs broken, and chirps,

"I'm so glad, glad, glad it happened! For you have to lose your legs to really love them!" Mary Pickford chose to play Pollyanna in the 1920 silent movie version, and in 1960 Hayley Mills won a special Oscar for her portrayal of the little sunbeam. The name Pollyanna has become synonymous with a goody-two-shoes kind of determined optimism.

## PONTIAC, CHIEF

The French and Indian Wars of the 1760s disrupted the lives of the Great Lakes Indians, among them the Ottawa tribe led by Chief Pontiac. When the British defeated the French, they did not continue the friendly relations that the French had cultivated with the Indians. Instead, the British enraged the Indians by moving onto tribal land, occupying old French forts, and infringing on their fur trade.

In May 1763 Chief Pontiac, who had won respect for his valiant but unsuccessful defense of Fort Detroit, decided to rebel against the British conquerors. He had been inspired by a Delaware prophet who urged the Indians to drive the British off their land. Pontiac's resolve was bolstered by rumors that the French would soon renew their fight against the British. Warriors from the Ojibwa, Potawatami, Huron, and other tribes joined the rebellion and mounted attacks on English forts from Niagara to Illinois. Eight forts fell and a ninth was abandoned; the settlers fled.

Fort Detroit, however, proved once again to be Pontiac's downfall. The British held out for almost six months, and when it became apparent that help from the French would not be forthcoming, Pontiac finally agreed to surrender. In 1769, his prestige gone, Pontiac was murdered by an Illinois Indian. His rebellion came to symbolize the Indians' spirited, but ultimately futile, resistance to European dominance.

## PONY EXPRESS

The Pony Express, which lasted just 19 months, was a brief but glorious adventure. Starting on April 3, 1860, it delivered mail 1,966 miles, between Missouri and California, in 10 days—lightning speed for that era. Newspaper ads called for "expert riders willing to risk death daily. Orphans preferred." Mounted on fast, sturdy horses, the scrappy young men changed horses about every 10 miles; riders switched about every 75 miles.

Desert heat, heavy Sierra snows, and hostile Indians made nearly every trip a trial of courage. Fifteen-year-old Buffalo Bill Cody once rode 322 miles when he found that the next man in line had been killed, and "Pony Bob" Haslam covered 380 miles in 36 hours while fighting a running battle with Paiute Indians. The Pony Express delivered 34,753 pieces of mail and lost only one sack of mail, but the new "talking wires" of the transcontinental telegraph made it obsolete by the end of 1861. Its dramatic legacy was the opening of the American West.

Chief Pontiac, at Lake Cuyahoga, warns British arrivals that their defeat of the French does not mean they can settle on the land.

The 1861 poster at left advertised the Pony Express's steep rates: one dollar for a letter weighing half an ounce or less.

Willie Mosconi (left) and Jimmy Caras compete in a 1946 billiards marathon. Mosconi was technical adviser for the 1961 movie *The Hustler*.

## POOL

When pool is mentioned in *The Music Man*, the citizens of River City know their children are in danger. Pool's reputation may reflect the fact that many billiard shots were first perfected by a French prisoner, or that pool was often played in smoky halls filled with disreputable characters. The ability to put "English" spin on a ball or run the table by sinking all 15 balls was thought to be the mark of an ill-spent youth. At the top of the sport in the mid-20th century was famed hustler Minnesota Fats; Willie Mosconi, considered the world's greatest player, once sank 526 balls in a row. Today the game is held in much higher regard, and it's often played in well-kept pool parlors and at home by the whole family. Pros include such fresh-faced women as Ewa Mataya and Loree Jon Jones, who toured in 1992 with her baby in tow.

## POOR RICHARD'S ALMANACK

When Benjamin Franklin introduced *Poor Richard's Almanack* in 1732, it was unlike anything the colonists had ever seen. In place of the usual weather, health, and crop predictions, Franklin, using the pen name Richard Saunders, wrote, "This year the stone blind shall see but very little," and, "As for oats, they'll be a great help to horses." He introduced his quarrelsome—and fictional—wife, Bridget, and peppered the pages with wry adages about human nature, such as "Three may keep a secret, if two of them are dead."

The *Almanack* was an instant hit. Within a few years it was the most popular book in the Colonies after the Bible, selling 10,000 copies a year. The last edition that Franklin himself wrote, published in 1758 and titled *The Way to Wealth*, was a compilation of his favorite advice in the form of a "speech" by a fictional Father Abraham. With epigrams like "Diligence is the mother of good luck," he popularized the notion that, with hard work, anyone can achieve success.

## POPCORN

A 5,600-year-old ear of popping corn was found in a cave in New Mexico. And it is said that Chief Massasoit's brother brought popcorn to the first Thanksgiving in 1621. But the popularity of popcorn didn't grow until owners of movie theaters discovered that they could make more money from selling popcorn than from selling sweets.

When the moisture inside a hard kernel of corn becomes steam, the kernel explodes into a soft, fluffy food. Air-popped and eaten plain, it is a high-fiber, low-calorie snack. The theater version—cooked in oil, coated with a butter-flavored topping, and salted to build soda sales—is better for the theater's health than for yours. (It was once estimated that, without their popcorn profits, half of the movie houses in the U.S. would close.) In 1976 Orville Redenbacher introduced microwavable popcorn, which made it even simpler to pop your own.

### POOR RICHARD'S ALMANACK

*Poor Richard's Almanack* featured Ben Franklin's philosophy of frugal living. Some of his oft-quoted adages:

"Early to Bed, and early to rise, makes a Man healthy, wealthy and wise."

"God helps those who help themselves."

"Well done is better than well said."

"If you would keep your Secret from an enemy, tell it not to a friend."

"Fools need Advice most, but wise Men only are the better for it."

"*Anger* is never without a Reason, but seldom with a good One."

"The worst wheel of the cart makes the most noise."

"You may delay, but *Time* will not."

"He is not well-bred, that cannot bear ill-Breeding in others."

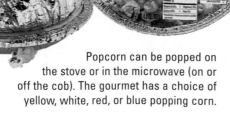

Popcorn can be popped on the stove or in the microwave (on or off the cob). The gourmet has a choice of yellow, white, red, or blue popping corn.

## POPEYE

In 1933 the Fleischer Studios put Popeye, a rowdy sailor from E. C. Segar's *Thimble Theatre* cartoon strip, into an animated short with Betty Boop. Popeye didn't fall for curvaceous Betty, but America fell for Popeye. He got his own series and his own girl, the reedy-bodied and reedy-voiced Olive Oyl. Other regulars included his nemesis, Bluto, and the moocher J. Wellington Wimpy, who offered, "I will gladly pay you Tuesday for a hamburger today."

Popeye's secret weapon was spinach; seconds after he poured a can of it down his gullet, his muscular arms turned into pile drivers, which he used to vanquish the brutish Bluto. After a fight he would dance a jig while singing in a croaking voice supplied by Jack Mercer, "I'm strong to the finich, 'cause I eats me spinach, I'm Popeye the Sailor Man." Parents may have hated his grammar, but they probably loved the fact that he inspired children to eat their greens.

## POPULAR MECHANICS

"Henceforth machinery will perform the heavy work now done by animal power." This provocative statement appeared on January 18, 1902, in a revolutionary new review of the latest advances in mechanical technology. The amazing article was entitled "The Beginning of the Horseless Age"; the publication: *Popular Mechanics*.

Henry Haven Windsor founded *Popular Mechanics* in Chicago with three employees and a belief that modern technology could be understood and enjoyed by average Americans if put in "plain, simple language ... condensed as much as possible." Readers learn how to build a house or put together an aquatic airplane from a kit. Writers take them along as they embark on firsthand risks and adventures. The future holds no fear for those who regularly read the "News of Tomorrow's Technology Today."

## POPULISTS

In the mid-19th century, many farmers blamed decades of falling agriculture prices on high freight charges, tariffs, and interest rates. In an effort to bring about change, they formed local alliances; and in 1891 the leaders of these groups unveiled the Populist—or People's—Party. In 1892 their presidential candidate, James B. Weaver of Iowa, drew about 8 percent of the vote.

In 1896 the Populists supported Democrat William Jennings Bryan for president because he favored increasing the money supply by coining a massive number of silver dollars—which the farmers championed as a way to help raise the prices of their goods. Bryan's defeat was the beginning of the end of the Populist Party. However, many of its seemingly radical ideas eventually became law, including the graduated income tax, the direct election of senators, and a government plan to help support farm prices.

When Popeye first appeared in animated cartoons, the sales of spinach soared. The squint-eyed sailor was also known for his signature phrase, "I yam what I yam."

From the start, *Popular Mechanics* was intended for the person "who has the type of mind that likes to know what is under the hood of an automobile."

In 1896 the Democrats nominated William Jennings Bryan on a Populist platform. In his most famous speech, he argued against the gold standard, saying, "... you shall not crucify mankind upon a cross of gold."

### COLE PORTER HITS

Let's Do It 1928
You Do Something to Me 1929
What Is This Thing Called Love? 1929
Love for Sale 1930
Night and Day 1932
Anything Goes 1934
I Get a Kick Out of You 1934
You're the Top 1934
Begin the Beguine 1935
Just One of Those Things 1935
It's De-Lovely 1936
Ev'ry Time We Say Goodbye 1944
It's All Right With Me 1953
All of You 1955

*Can-Can* composer Cole Porter once said, "I do the lyrics the way I'd do a crossword puzzle."

## PORTER, COLE

Wealthy, well-educated, and worldly-wise, Cole Porter made the sophisticated, cynical patter of his crowd into great fun for everyone by setting it to buoyant melodies. With lyrics full of double entendre and rhymes that ranged from witty to impertinent ("You're the top / You're a dance in Bali / You're the top / You're a hot tamale"), his songs became emblems of the 1930s. Too advanced for Tin Pan Alley (he himself used the word *Tinpantithesis*), many were hits in the more than 20 Broadway shows, and films, for which he wrote them.

Porter's career hit a high note in the '40s with his pièce de résistance, *Kiss Me, Kate*. More winners followed in the '50s, including *Can-Can*, *Silk Stockings*, and the film *High Society*, in which Bing Crosby and Grace Kelly sang "True Love," and Louis Armstrong and Crosby romped on "Now You Has Jazz." Porter was, in the words of biographer Robert Kimball, "the man who kept alive civilized entertainment."

## POST, EMILY

Yes, there really was an Emily Post. Born in Baltimore, Emily Price had a privileged upbringing. When her marriage to Edwin Post ended in divorce, she was forced to support herself and her two sons by writing novels. In 1922, at her publisher's suggestion, she wrote *Etiquette in Society, in Business, in Politics and at Home*, which featured such heady reading as "In arranging for the service of dinner the butler details three footmen to each table of ten." Topics included weddings, funerals, and the fundamentals of proper behavior, with which Post's name became synonymous.

*Etiquette* went through 10 editions and 89 printings during Post's lifetime. Today her etiquette books are written by others, but they are not always as gripping as the original: "In fashionable houses the butler does not put on his dress suit until six o'clock," and "If a visitor brings no maid of her own, the personal maid of the hostess always unpacks the bags."

## POST-ITS

In 1964, when Spencer Silver, a chemist at the Minnesota Mining and Manufacturing (3M) Company, concocted a particularly weak glue, the company thought it was useless. But Silver continued to work with his colleagues to find a use for his discovery. Ten years later, Arthur Fry, another 3M chemist, put the glue on paper to create bookmarks that he could stick to his hymnal and later remove. So the Post-it was born. Soon 3M employees were posting notes all over their offices. When 3M test-marketed its new memo pads by extolling their virtues, consumers couldn't imagine why they would want them. But when 3M gave out samples, people quickly discovered myriad uses for the removable "stickies," which now seem like one of life's essentials.

Emily Post offered the last word on questions of decorum. She had her own radio show and also wrote a syndicated newspaper column.

## POUND, EZRA

Many scholars believe the single most important influence on American poetry in the 20th century was Ezra Pound. He pioneered a thoroughly modern style, using brief, unrhymed lines and radically distilled images. His most famous poem, "In a Station of the Metro," consists of just two short lines: "The apparition of these faces in the crowd; / Petals on a wet, black bough." Pound was also famous for helping up-and-coming writers to sharpen their images and cut excessive length. T. S. Eliot, James Joyce, Robert Frost, Ernest Hemingway, and William Carlos Williams all learned from him.

Pound's opinions about politics were not as influential as his views on literature: he was arrested for treason in 1945 toward the end of World War II for broadcasting pro-fascist radio messages from Italy. He was found unfit for trial by reason of insanity and spent 12 years confined to a mental hospital, where he completed his masterwork, *The Cantos*.

## POWELL, COLIN

Colin Powell has been called "an African-American who transcends race; a public man who transcends politics." Born to poor Jamaican immigrants in Harlem, Powell found his calling when he enrolled in ROTC in college. His rise through the ranks of the army was meteoric; soon he was commanding troops in Vietnam, Korea, and West Germany. In 1989 Powell was named Chairman of the Joint Chiefs of Staff, the youngest officer and the first black ever to fill that role. As the mastermind behind Operation Desert Storm in 1991, he was catapulted to fame, becoming "the most celebrated general since Eisenhower." Since leaving the Joint Chiefs, he has published a memoir, been knighted by Queen Elizabeth, and wooed by politicians of all stripes. Through it all, he has embodied the distinctly American philosophy that, as he put it, "hard work generates good luck—and opportunities."

## POWWOW

*Powwow*, from the Algonquian word for "conjurer," originally meant the magic worked by a medicine man. In the early 20th century, it came to mean a gathering of American Indians. A tribe would discuss problems or consider a peace proposal by assembling around a fire, where they would sing songs, beat drums, talk, and pray. Powwows could also be exhilarating festivals of dancing and singing, which white men often mistook for war preparations.

Today American Indians celebrate their heritage through hundreds of annual powwows. The largest is the Gathering of Nations in Albuquerque, New Mexico. Singers and drummers perform old and new songs. Others compete in war dances, swirling and stomping in brightly colored costumes adorned with elaborate beading and eagle feathers. "We keep on dancing in order to set a path for our children," said one participant. "If we didn't dance, then our culture would be lost."

Colin Powell has been called "the most respected figure in American public life." Former national security advisor under President Reagan, he made his mark during the Gulf War.

A Shoshone man joins a powwow in Ethete, Wyoming. The events are "part family reunion, part cultural revival, part dance contest."

Conservationists have pledged to ensure that the remaining prairies—from the wetlands of North Dakota to the weed-filled lots of Chicago—will exist for future generations.

*The Official Preppy Handbook* taught people how to speak with Locust Valley Lockjaw and choose prep nicknames like Buffy and Biff.

In 1993 Bill Clinton (pictured here with Vice President Al Gore) became America's 42nd president and, at age 46, its third youngest. Teddy Roosevelt was 42 when he succeeded William McKinley, and John F. Kennedy was 43 at his inauguration.

## PRAIRIE

The largest prairie in the world was once found in North America: a vast, uninterrupted expanse that covered nearly 1,000 miles from the Mississippi Valley to the Rockies. Created by a windblown mixture of silt, sand, and clay, the prairie was where awestruck pioneers encountered terrain they had never seen before, a "sea of grass" that stretched to the horizon, blown by a wind "as if out of the lungs of the universe." Blazing stars, rattlesnake masters, and other wildflowers grew among its grasses, which nourished a wide diversity of wildlife, from pronghorn antelope to an estimated 60 millon to 70 million bison. Pioneers began to settle the prairie in the 1860s, building sod houses and one-room schoolhouses. Today, this region is a vast granary for the world, with only a few patches of original prairie left.

## PREPPIES

For years the graduates of such elite preparatory high schools as Phillips Exeter, Andover, and Emma Willard knew one another by their distinctive clothes and customs. Then, in 1980, *The Official Preppy Handbook* told the rest of the world how to look and act preppy. People across the U.S., tired of bell-bottomed pants and polyester disco outfits, started sporting "alligator" shirts, khakis, and boat shoes. Perhaps the biggest beneficiary of the fad was the L. L. Bean catalog, which suddenly became a national fashion resource.

## PRESIDENCY

America's Founding Fathers were so leery of an "elective monarchy" that the nation's first charter didn't even permit a president. It wasn't until the Philadelphia Convention of 1787 that an executive office was created, and it took two more years for George Washington to be elected to it.

Compared with today's chief executives, early presidents had few powers, and most serious issues were decided by Congress. In order to fight the Civil War, Abraham Lincoln assumed more power than had any preceding president, and a strong backlash followed. "The president should obey [Congress] and enforce the laws," declared Senator John Sherman; for a long time, presidents did just that.

Theodore Roosevelt boldly exercised "international police power," and he boasted when he left office that he made his most important decisions "without consultation with anyone." In 1917 Woodrow Wilson led a reluctant nation into World War I and increased the president's power during wartime. Franklin Roosevelt wielded an unprecedented amount of authority to do battle at home against the Great Depression and abroad during World War II.

Weak or strong, virtually every president has left his mark, and many have made history: Thomas Jefferson acquired the Louisiana Territory, and Abraham Lincoln freed the slaves and preserved the Union. Only David Rice

Atchison—president for one day in 1849—left barely a trace. James Polk's term in office ended at noon on March 4, but because it was a Sunday, Zachary Taylor wasn't sworn into office until the next day. For that 24-hour period, Senator Atchison of Missouri ran the country.

## PRESLEY, ELVIS

He was a smooth country Adonis, with a lock of hair falling on his brow and a sneer on his lip. When he sang "Heartbreak Hotel" or "Don't Be Cruel," he'd swivel his hips and twitch his legs, and when he crooned "Love Me Tender," the girls would swoon.

The sexy physicality of Elvis Presley's rockabilly performances brought the forbidden into the open for teens in the 1950s. His singing style bore the unmistakable stamp of black rhythm and blues. By carrying its message to a national audience, he changed popular music forever. Beatle John Lennon recalled, "Nothing really affected me until Elvis."

Elvis Aron Presley was born in Tupelo, Mississippi, in 1935. His close-knit family attended a Pentecostal church, where he first heard gospel music. Given a guitar at age 11, he picked up hillbilly songs and later, the blues. After graduating from high school, he worked as a movie usher and truck driver. One day he went into a Sun Records studio to make a recording for his mother's birthday. He caught the ear of the owner, who signed him to make other recordings, such as Arthur Crudup's "That's All Right (Mama)."

After acquiring a manager, Presley toured the South and signed with a major label. By 1958, when he joined the army, he had 14 consecutive million sellers (of his eventual 79) and had begun making Hollywood B movies, such as *Jailhouse Rock*, earning $1 million for each.

Personal excesses overtook Presley in 1977, when, at age 42, he died of a drug overdose. By then he had become one of the greatest stars of the 20th century. His home has become an international shrine. Sightings by the faithful continue.

## PRICE, LEONTYNE

In 1936, when Leontyne Price was a nine-year-old girl growing up in Laurel, Mississippi, she heard the great black contralto Marian Anderson give a recital in a nearby town. She began dreaming of singing opera herself one day.

Price was encouraged by her parents, and in 1953 she made her first major professional appearance as Bess in *Porgy and Bess*. The opera's European and American tours helped make her a star. Her later work with famed Austrian conductor Herbert von Karajan and with Rudolf Bing of the Metropolitan Opera helped boost her career on both sides of the Atlantic. Soon Price was singing Verdi in Vienna, London, Milan, and New York City. With her lustrous voice and powerful expressiveness, she became the first black diva, blazing a trail for later stars like Jessye Norman and Kathleen Battle.

Talking about his fame, Elvis said, "I was very lucky. The people were looking for something different, and I came along just in time."

Leontyne Price made her Metropolitan Opera debut in 1961, singing the role of Leonora, the female lead in Giuseppe Verdi's *Il Trovatore*.

Prohibition agents enforced the law by taking an ax to barrels of beer. In 1931 a government commission stated, "A violation [of the Prohibition law] in itself does not involve a sense of guilt; the only shame is in getting caught."

## PROHIBITION

The tide of immigration during and after the Civil War brought to America Europeans who were used to drinking beer, wine, and liquor, a habit widely deplored by rural and small-town people. County by county, temperance groups worked to outlaw these beverages. By the start of World War I, more than half the nation had adopted Prohibition. The war spurred the movement, with the federal government banning the use of grain to make alcohol. Many brewers were of German extraction, which made them and their beer unpopular. It seemed patriotic not to drink. On January 17, 1920, the Volstead Act banning beverage alcohol went into effect.

The law was a failure from the start: working-class immigrants continued to drink, joined by sophisticates for whom drinking had acquired a naughty attraction. In just a few years there were more illegal bars—or "speakeasies"—than there had been saloons before Prohibition. Breaking the law became something to brag about. Organized crime supplied the alcohol and started a pattern of political and police corruption. Illegal liquor fueled the roaring '20s. It also spurred Mafia power in America and created a climate of lawlessness and violence as mobsters fought one another over territory. In 1928 President Herbert Hoover was still calling it "a great social and economic experiment," but by 1932 both parties urged the repeal of Prohibition. Alcohol was legalized the following year, which forced mobsters to look elsewhere for business.

## PSYCHO

Released in 1960, *Psycho* remains perhaps the finest and most popular horror movie ever made. Viewers watch it repeatedly with undiminished fascination. Anthony Perkins is forever identified with his role as the outwardly ingratiating, inwardly tormented Norman Bates, owner of the motel where the ill-fated Marion Crane (Janet Leigh) seeks shelter.

The movie inspired two big-screen sequels and countless imitations. Yet none achieved the impact of the original *Psycho*, which relied more on subtle psychological twists than on gory special effects. Critics observe that the movie draws viewers into a troubling inner world, leading them to ponder their own darkest secrets. It also demonstrates director Alfred Hitchcock's masterful storytelling technique. The movie begins quietly with Crane's seemingly ordinary small-town life, then builds suspense almost unbearably toward a terrifying climax. But it does include comic touches: Bates's remark "Mother . . . isn't herself today" is the height of irony. The British-born Hitchcock used a similar blend of humor and terror in many classic Hollywood movies, from *Rear Window* to *The Birds*. "When employing suspense, you have to give the audience a chance to laugh," he said. "If you don't, they will anyway—because the human body cannot stand the strain—and the whole affair will become ludicrous."

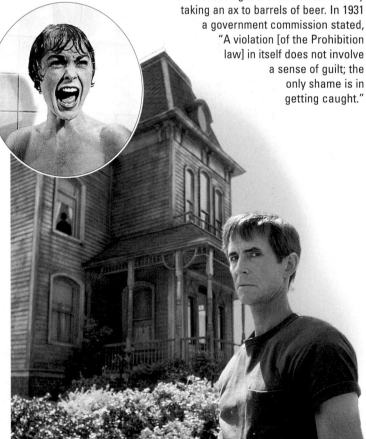

*Psycho*'s stabbing scene made many people, including Janet Leigh (inset), afraid to take showers. Anthony Perkins (above) repeated the role of Norman Bates in *Psycho II* and *Psycho III*.

## PARENT-TEACHER ASSOCIATIONS

More than 7 million parents, teachers, and other concerned citizens around the country belong to Parent-Teacher Associations. All are dedicated to helping children learn and grow. Said National PTA President Kathryn Whitfill, "When mothers and fathers are encouraged to be involved in their children's education, everyone benefits."

Volunteers in local PTAs may tutor students in reading or organize field trips, or donate special skills. PTAs also hold bake sales and bazaars to raise money for books, musical instruments, and other badly needed supplies. Although non-partisan, PTAs have political influence, too; they have lobbied for changes in everything from school-lunch menus to traffic safety. Since its founding in 1897, the PTA has helped pass such reforms as child-labor laws and the establishment of separate courts for juvenile offenders.

## PUBLIC LIBRARIES

Repositories of recorded knowledge, public libraries have been called the "people's university," where all can seek information among collections of diverse published works. "The Library belongs to every citizen," maintained the philanthropic Andrew Carnegie, who endowed 1,700 of them.

Before the first public library opened in New Hampshire in 1833, most libraries were private or charged a fee. The free-library movement spread rapidly throughout the century, serving an increasingly literate population and countless immigrants who wanted to learn about American culture.

So keen are Americans on their right to read that library outposts have been established in barbershops, firehouses, and gas stations. In 1903 Melvil Dewey, father of American libraries, predicted that "librarians of the future" would use "labor-saving...appliances" to provide "the best reading for the largest numbers at the least cost." In the Information Age, computers have made this come true.

## PUEBLO

The vibrant traditions of the Southwest's Pueblo Indians are much the same today as they were in centuries past. The conquistadores gave the name *pueblo* (Spanish for "village") both to the unique multistory dwellings that the Indians built and to the Indians themselves: Hopis, Zunis, and Rio Grande Indians. Then, as now, the Indians dug underground chambers called kivas for religious ceremonies, for which the men carved wooden masks and kachina dolls. The ancestors of today's Pueblo artisans are renowned for their intricate basketwork and beautifully painted pottery.

Today there is a renewed appreciation of their culture. Visitors flock to see the pueblos, where many Indians still live, and Pueblo crafts and ceremonial items have earned international recognition.

The first bookmobile was a horse-drawn carriage, which hit the road in 1904. Motorized bookmobiles came along a few decades later (above). At right, a stone lion guards the entrance to the New York Public Library on Fifth Avenue.

Since the days of the prehistoric Anasazi, the Indians of the Southwest have built stone or adobe pueblos with as many as five different levels connected by ladders.

Pulitzer ardently believed in the power of print in a free nation, and the prizes given in his name continue his legacy by rewarding excellence in all the arts.

## PULITZER PRIZE

Newspaper mogul Joseph Pulitzer, a vigorous, enterprising Hungarian immigrant, made his fortune by turning the *New York World* into a mouthpiece "of the common man." His thundering editorials spurred readers to action; it was one of his campaigns that led thousands to donate money to build the pedestal for the Statue of Liberty.

In his will, Pulitzer bequeathed an endowment for the Pulitzer Prizes. Since 1917 Columbia University, on the recommendation of a Pulitzer Prize board, has presented awards in journalism, literature, drama, and music. In journalism alone 14 prizes are awarded; it is the highest professional honor an American print journalist can attain. Political cartoonists like three-time winner Paul Conrad are also honored. The prestigious gold medal is given for meritorious public service by a newspaper. *The New York Times* received it for publishing the Pentagon Papers, and *The Washington Post*, for covering the Watergate scandal.

## PULLMAN CAR

Although George Pullman did not invent the sleeping and dining cars that made him famous, he perfected the notion of comfort and elegance on the rails—making his name synonymous with luxury train travel. For a modest supplement, passengers could enjoy the amenities of a first-class hotel en route. "If the traveling public thinks the beauty of finish and increased comfort are worth $2 per night," said Pullman, "there are my $24,000 cars all ready for them."

A self-taught engineer, Pullman launched the *Pioneer*—his first convertible sleeper, with ingenious fold-down and pull-out berths—from Chicago in 1865, and the *Delmonico*—a thoroughly equipped rolling restaurant—in 1868. They set the standard for his fleet, which featured such appointments as velvet draperies, walnut paneling, plush upholstery, and pile carpeting. Pullman quickly became the preferred purveyor of customized private cars for the Gilded Age society.

The interior of a Pullman car was lavish, and the service, first-rate. A cadre of meticulous porters would cater to a traveler's every whim—from shooing flies to shining shoes.

Said one rail traveler of his journey, "No royal personage can be more comfortably housed than the occupant of a Pullman car."

## PYREX

"Says a lady of deep penetration / I cannot see why in creation / You should bake in the dark / As they did in the Ark / When Pyrex permits observation." So went an early advertising jingle for Pyrex. Legend has it that a researcher at Corning Glass gave his wife the bottom of a heat-resistant glass battery jar to use when baking. The results were impressive: cooking time was reduced, the ingredients didn't stick, and the food could be seen as it baked. Corning went on to create a line of heat-resistant glass cookware. Not only did Pyrex become an essential part of the American kitchen, it was used to make laboratory equipment, telescope lenses, and insulation for power lines.

## QUEEN, ELLERY

"Ellery Queen is *the* American detective story," observed critic Anthony Boucher. He was more than that. Ellery Queen is the name of the detective as well as the pseudonym of his two authors: Frederic Dannay and Manfred Lee. The first EQ novel, *The Roman Hat Mystery*, appeared in 1929, and from then on EQ never had a dull moment. The team wrote scores of novels and short stories, anthologized their own and others' stories, and edited *Ellery Queen Mystery Magazine*. EQ gave and received awards, was heard sleuthing (with his father, Inspector Richard Queen) during radio days, appeared in nine movies, and starred in a TV series and a TV movie.

## QUIZ SHOWS

Quiz shows began on the radio with programs like *Break the Bank* and *Information, Please*, which awarded modest prizes to members of the audience or to brainy contestants who could correctly answer tough trivia questions. Television, however, vastly increased the stakes—*The $64 Question* suddenly became *The $64,000 Question*—and the 1950s became the heyday of big-prize shows.

But in 1958, when contestant Charles Van Doren admitted that the producers of *Twenty-One* gave him some questions in advance, the scandal almost knocked quiz shows off the air. They later regained popularity, but offered smaller prizes and demanded less brainpower.

*What's My Line?* for instance, presented a celebrity panel in pursuit of the contestant's occupation; *Let's Make a Deal* featured people who traded cash or prizes for whatever was behind the curtain; and *The Price Is Right* had contestants who guessed the retail price of selected items. Today only *Jeopardy!* has players with encyclopedic knowledge.

Some of the biggest winners were the show hosts—Bill Cullen, Art Fleming, Hugh Downs, Alec Trebek, Pat Sajak, and Vanna White to name a few—who became celebrities in their own right.

Viewers tuned in to *Hollywood Squares* (above) to see such favorite regulars as Paul Lynde, Nanette Fabray, and Charlie Weaver. Dr. Joyce Brothers (right) set a record as the top-ranking female contestant after winning $134,000 on quiz shows.

## QUONSET HUT

First built by the U.S. Navy in 1941 to provide living and storage quarters at the Quonset Point Naval Air Station in Rhode Island, Quonset huts quickly spread to other areas like an architectural virus. Military planners liked their inexpensive concrete base and corrugated-steel construction, prefabricated design, ability to withstand high winds, and the ease with which they could be shipped and assembled. The navy eventually raised 160,000 of them, and their occupants got used to the pings and pops of the metal walls when the temperature changed.

The end of the war didn't mean the end of the Quonset hut; its unusual shape soon became a common sight across suburban America.

The Quonset hut, with its half-cylinder profile, became post-World War II housing for vets, classrooms, dorms, even movie theaters and churches.

Before the advent of television, families would gather around the radio each night after supper to hear melodies crooned by Rudy Vallee, Bing Crosby, and that "Songbird of the South," Kate Smith.

Radio City's resident stars are the Rockettes, a troupe of 36 precision dancers whose eye-high kicks always wow the crowds.

## RADIO

During its golden age in the 1930s and '40s, radio was the most popular form of entertainment in America. Housewives would tune in to listen to such early soap operas as *Stella Dallas*, *John's Other Wife*, *One Man's Family*, *The Guiding Light*, and *The Romance of Helen Trent*. Every day millions of women identified with the beautiful Helen Trent as she struggled to prove "that because a woman is 35, and more, romance in life need not be over."

Children had their favorite after-school serials. *Jack Armstrong, the All-American Boy!* featured the superhero who, for 17 years, traveled across America in search of adventure. Later, *The Lone Ranger* was announced with the "speed of light, a cloud of dust, and a hearty Hi-yo, Silver!" Then there was *The Green Hornet*, who "hunts the biggest of all game, public enemies who try to destroy our America!".

The airwaves bubbled with hilarious skits performed by such comic greats as Eddie Cantor, Red Skelton, Ed Wynn, and Jimmy Durante. Husband-and-wife teams—Fred Allen and Portland Hoffa, Jack Benny and Mary Livingstone, and George Burns and Gracie Allen—were also hugely popular.

When television gained popularity in the 1950s, most of the radio stars moved over to the new medium. Today radio programming is devoted mostly to popular music, news, weather, religion, and call-in shows.

## RADIO CITY MUSIC HALL

When the 4,000-pipe "Mighty Wurlitzer" organ swells with music, the gold velour curtain rises from the 144-foot-wide stage, and 10,000-plus lights dazzle overhead, it's show time at "The Showplace of the Nation." Radio City Music Hall—America's largest indoor theater, with 5,900 seats—opened on December 27, 1932, as the centerpiece of Rockefeller Center. It soon drew 268 million patrons a year to its holiday extravaganzas, film premieres, concerts, and variety acts.

The opulent music hall, a showcase of Art Deco style, is spectacular. "We hope to impress the customers by sheer elegance, not by overwhelming them with ornament," said the interior designer. Restored as a national landmark in 1979, the limestone-faced theater is resplendent with sleek furnishings of Bakelite, aluminum, and other Machine Age materials; hand-painted murals; and an auditorium formed by a series of gilded arcs intended to evoke a sunrise.

## RAGGEDY ANN AND ANDY

Political cartoonist Johnny Gruelle's illustrations for his Raggedy Ann and Raggedy Andy books are so enchanting, it's no wonder their namesake dolls are dear to children's hearts. The Raggedys are designed to delight: their red yarn hair, shoe-button eyes, barber-pole legs, her pinafore and pantalets, and his blue button pants and little bow tie never fail to provoke a smile. Dozens of Raggedy Ann books were written; the text, although somewhat humorless, is upbeat. Gruelle's message is clear: Raggedy Ann's candy heart says, "I love you," and countless children have echoed the sentiment.

## RAGTIME

Ragtime is the name used for the melodious and catchy piano music from the turn of the century that is often associated with composer Scott Joplin. A forerunner of jazz, it blended syncopated, or "ragged," banjo rhythms with the contrasting elements of march music. While some players improvised "rags," others began to write them down. Kerry Mills's "At a Georgia Camp Meeting" was published in 1897, as was "The Harlem Rag" by Tom Turpin. Two years later Scott Joplin—considered the master of classic rags—published "Maple Leaf Rag." In New York, Ben Harney composed the "ragtime songs" that influenced Tin Pan Alley. Irving Berlin had his first big hit in 1911 with "Alexander's Ragtime Band."

The term *ragtime* was soon applied to singers, orchestras, dancers—the whole era, in fact. The stride style of such jazz pianists as Jelly Roll Morton, James P. Johnson, Fats Waller, and Eubie Blake incorporated elements of ragtime. In 1950 the book *They All Played Ragtime*, by Rudi Blesh and Harriet Janis, kindled interest in the real thing. Collections of Scott Joplin's rags, as he wrote them, came out in the early 1970s; in 1973 his rag "The Entertainer" (the theme of the film *The Sting*) became a million-seller, and his ragtime opera, *Treemonisha* (which was performed only once in his lifetime), finally came to Broadway.

## RAG TRADE

"To be out of fashion is to be out of life," said 18th-century fashion maven Colley Cibber. The rag trade—a vast army of fashion designers, manufacturers, retailers, and glossy magazines—is still trying to convince us of that notion. To tempt us, designers trot out a new line of fashion statements—from the prim to the absolutely outrageous—each season.

Until the 1850s, most clothing was homemade; only the wealthy could afford tailor-made outfits. The sewing machine created the ready-made-garment industry, cutting the time needed to make clothes. Paris was the mecca of fashion until the 1970s, when homegrown designers like Calvin Klein created clothes that had designer labels but were comfortable and more affordable. Others soon followed suit, and today American designers are highly regarded in the fashion world.

A doll made by cartoonist Johnny Gruelle's mother inspired the Raggedy Ann stories, which were first published in 1918. Andy appeared in 1920.

The "Maple Leaf Rag" was one of the most popular rags; some of the lesser known included "Dill Pickles," "Frog Legs," and "Carbalick Acid."

The fashion industry spends millions to entice you into buying the latest styles. If you need a bit more persuasion, take advice from Ralph Waldo Emerson: "There is one other reason for dressing well... dogs respect it, and will not attack you in good clothes."

"When I hear the iron horse make the hills echo with his snort like thunder...," wrote Henry Thoreau, "it seems as if the earth had got a race now worthy to inhabit it."

## RAILROADS

They carried strawberries to market and soldiers to battle, miners to goldfields and homesteaders to the heartland. Railroads united the United States, their iron rails binding the nation to its destiny of prosperity and mobility.

Ever since the first "iron horse" steamed out of Charleston in 1830, the persistent chug of the choo-choo has pulsed through the country like a heartbeat, pumping lifeblood into every aspect of daily life. As America's most extensive transportation network—once boasting 254,000 miles of track—railroads provided affordable, convenient travel for some 900 million passengers annually. Indeed, riding the rails on sleek trains like the *Twentieth Century Limited* and the *Super Chief* meant the utmost in luxury and comfort.

In their heyday, railroads fueled the economy, employing as many as 2 million workers a year. Today automobiles and airplanes have diminished the railroads' dominance. Still, Americans continue to have a romance with the rails, whether aboard the latest high-speed locomotives or the vintage short lines that recall the era when trains promised progress for boomtown and backwater alike.

## RAISIN IN THE SUN

The poem "Harlem" by Langston Hughes—"What happens to a dream deferred? / Does it dry up like a raisin in the sun...?"—inspired Lorraine Hansberry to write this warm and impassioned drama. In *A Raisin in the Sun*, a family rallies against prejudice and adversity in an attempt to realize its dream: escape from the Chicago ghetto. The first play by a black woman to be produced on Broadway, *A Raisin in the Sun* premiered in 1959, starring Claudia McNeil, Ruby Dee, Sidney Poitier, and Lou Gossett, and won the New York Drama Critics' Circle Award. In 1961 it was made into a film with the original actors. Tragically, Hansberry died of cancer at the age of 34. A self-portrait, *To Be Young, Gifted and Black*, was produced posthumously.

Of her play *A Raisin in the Sun*, Lorraine Hansberry said she tried to show "the unbelievable courage of the Negro people." Here, Sidney Poitier and Claudia McNeil share a moment of triumph as they enter their new home.

In a typical ranch house, picture windows and sliding glass doors let in light, and patios extend the one-level living space to the outdoors.

## RANCH HOUSE

From carport to conversation pit, it was the postwar American dream house. Designed for convenience and casual living, the large, rambling, one-story "ranch" was introduced in Los Angeles in 1937 and peaked in popularity in the 1950s and '60s. Cliff May, a pianist and amateur architect, took his inspiration from the Spanish haciendas of the colonial Southwest, with their shaded galleries and tiled roofs. Despite his lack of formal training, he was soon receiving commissions for ranch houses from all over the world. In the 1950s May designed or licensed the building of some 18,000 ranches. Eventually, "ranch house" became a generic label for virtually any single-level residence with a long, horizontal profile and a low-pitched roof.

## RAP

Rap is improvised patter in rhyme, chanted to a prerecorded beat. It is a sort of street poetry that follows in the long tradition of black rhetoric. It first caught on as a pop phenomenon among young African-Americans and Latinos in the South Bronx and Harlem in the late 1970s, when disco deejays like Grandmaster Flash and Kool D.J. Herc took up the Jamaican style of talking over dance music, or "toasting." Soon rappers were patching and mixing bits of older R & B, funk, and jazz instrumentals on tape into a rhythmic mélange known as "hip-hop."

In 1979 The Sugar Hill Gang's "Rapper's Delight" became the first rap record to make the pop charts, and in 1984 a video by the group Run-DMC made a stir on MTV. Recognizing the popularity of such verbal virtuosos as L. L. Cool J and Heavy D, major record labels got into the act. Although some rappers establish street credibility by bragging about violent acts and sexual exploits, others urge social change to combat racism. Rappers like Salt-n-Pepa and Queen Latifah preach female assertiveness and pride.

On her 1991 album, Queen Latifah warns potential suitors: "Easy love is something that I ain't. / Besides, I don't know you from a can of paint."

## RAY, MAN

Man Ray, born Emmanuel Rudnitsky in 1890 in Philadelphia, was one of the world's most inventive and imaginative photographers. Originally inspired by realist photographer Alfred Stieglitz and cubist painter Marcel Duchamp, Ray found a spiritual home in the Paris of the 1920s, then brimming with American expatriate artists. He became involved in the surrealist and dadaist art movements, which emphasized dreams and truths that lie beyond the real world. "I do not photograph nature," he said. "I photograph my fantasy."

Of his many experiments, Ray's cameraless prints are his greatest legacy. Ray placed ordinary objects directly on photographic paper and then exposed the paper to light. The resulting "Rayographs," with their delightfully unexpected shadows and abstract shapes, led French author and playwright Jean Cocteau to dub Ray "the poet of the darkroom."

The surreal "Tears" (1933–34), with its use of glass beads for teardrops, is one of Man Ray's most famous images.

## RAZOR BLADES

Men shave about 27½ feet of whiskers in a lifetime, and they're always looking for a better way to do it. Safety razors, with holders that shield the blade and prevent deep cuts, were a big improvement over straight razors, but they still required frequent sharpening; many men preferred to go to a barbershop rather than risk cutting themselves with a dull blade. In 1895 King Camp Gillette came up with the idea—while shaving—of a disposable razor blade, figuring that it would be easier to replace a blade than to sharpen one. By 1904 he was selling 123,000 blades a year, and soon shaving had become a home routine. World War I gave a big boost to the business when Uncle Sam issued millions of Gillette Khaki Razor sets to members of the armed forces.

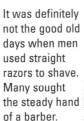

It was definitely not the good old days when men used straight razors to shave. Many sought the steady hand of a barber.

Lila and De Witt Wallace (right) presided over their publishing empire—located in Pleasantville, New York—into their eighties.

## READER'S DIGEST

Printed in 19 languages and 48 editions, *Reader's Digest* is read by more people worldwide than any other magazine. It began with one man's simple idea. Minnesota-born De Witt Wallace, who never finished college, took a job selling agricultural textbooks, which led him to compile a booklet for farmers summarizing helpful information available in government pamphlets. Could a similar approach be applied to general magazines? During World War I, while recuperating from war wounds, Wallace tested this idea. He combed countless periodicals and wrote out condensed versions of articles that interested him, using the authors' own words.

When publishers rejected his proposal, Wallace decided to sell the magazine himself. With borrowed money, he and his wife, Lila, set up shop in a basement in New York's Greenwich Village, and in February 1922 they mailed out the first issue of their pocket-size monthly. It presented articles "of enduring value and interest"—one for each day of the month—culled from leading periodicals. Covering a wide range of subjects, it emphasized information that was "quotable," "memorable," and "applicable." The response was overwhelming. The Wallaces soon moved to larger quarters and guided the phenomenal expansion of *Reader's Digest* over the next five decades.

Today the magazine contains about 50 percent original material and is known for inspirational and crusading articles, such as those that supported family planning and warned about the health hazards of smoking.

## REAGAN, RONALD

Few people would have predicted that a former movie actor could become a political hero to many Americans, but it happened to Ronald Reagan. Born in 1911 in Tampico, Illinois, Reagan began his professional life as a sportscaster. He moved to acting when he signed a Warner Brothers contract in 1937. He appeared in more than 50 films, including *King's Row, Desperate Journey, The Killers*, and *Knute Rockne—All-American*, and was married to actress Jane Wyman for nine years. In 1952 Reagan married Nancy Davis. Ten years later he underwent a political transformation from New Deal Democrat to a Republican foe of "big government."

A popular conservative spokesman, Reagan won two terms as governor of California starting in 1966. As the Republican presidential nominee in 1980, he defeated incumbent Jimmy Carter and embarked on a program of economic revitalization, anti-Soviet diplomacy, and the strengthening of national defense. His second-term win over Walter Mondale was the biggest landslide in U.S. history. In office, Reagan was called "The Great Communicator" for his ability to speak effectively to the public. He was unpretentious and fond of jellybeans and Western-style clothes. His expressions of patriotism struck an answering chord in the electorate.

Reagan was once described as the most popular president since Dwight D. Eisenhower. His wife, Nancy, was active in the war against drugs.

## RECREATIONAL VEHICLES

In the early 1910s a few wealthy industrialists, including T. Coleman du Pont and Henry B. Joy, president of Packard Motor Car, owned custom-built motor homes. Less affluent citizens soon followed their lead and purchased camping trailers and house cars. As demand for traveling homes rose, such companies as Prairie Schooner, Auto-Kamp, and Airstream sprang up to supply them. In the 1930s, however, when the Depression forced many families to live on the road, mobile life lost much of its glamour.

In recent decades mobile homes have regained their popularity and have been renamed recreational vehicles—"RVs" for short. Impressive "land yachts" like the Winnebago, introduced in 1966, are often loaded with options, including wall-to-wall carpeting, color televisions, VCRs, microwaves, ice makers, trash compactors, stereos, and dishwashers. Families vacation in them to avoid airfare and hotel costs. Some retirees take up full-time residence in their RVs and spend their golden years cruising America.

Some 9 million RV owners enjoy seeing the country from the road, often camping in national and state parks. In an RV with air-conditioning and a satellite dish, one is never far from the comforts of home.

## RED RIBBONS

Red ribbons are so universally recognized as symbols of the fight against AIDS that many people think they grew out of a spontaneous grass-roots movement. In reality, the ribbons were introduced in 1991 by Visual AIDS, a group of artists and others determined to heighten awareness of the disease. Noting the popularity of the yellow ribbons worn during the Persian Gulf War, they designed their own ribbon—a simple, folded red band—and sent it to organizers of entertainment events and other trendsetters. The emblem, first worn by actors at the Tony Awards ceremony and later by Oscar nominees in Hollywood, was soon seen throughout the world.

The ribbons helped bring AIDS into the open, and they have inspired innovative fund-raising efforts. Advocates of other causes have since adopted their own ribbons: pink for breast cancer research, purple for the fight against urban violence, and green for environmental concerns.

There's a ribbon for every cause, and not enough colors to go around: blue has been used to protest everything from child abuse to Internet censorship.

## RED TAPE

In 17th-century England, government clerks and lawyers often tied piles of documents and official papers together with pieces of narrow red ribbon. By the 1800s the term *red tape* had become synonymous with the maddeningly unhurried response of a bureaucracy to any question or problem.

Although red tape was not actually used in this country, Americans adopted the expression to describe official foot-dragging and the needless complexity of regulations, especially those of courts and government agencies. In 1855 the American author Washington Irving said of a bureaucrat, "His brain was little better than red tape and parchment." During World War I Americans again copied the British, who used the term to describe rigid military regulations.

Whimsical magnets have turned the fridge into a changing gallery of photos, reminders, newspaper clippings, and artwork.

## REFRIGERATOR MAGNETS

The refrigerator door is the ideal bulletin board for Americans who do more living in the kitchen than in the living room. When people got tired of scraping tape off the doors and trying to spell messages with the kids' magnetic letters, they turned to the kind of magnetic clips used to affix memos to office file cabinets, and put them to use at home. They were functional, but hardly exciting to look at. In 1964 Arlene and John Anasto of New Jersey started making magnets in the shapes of tea kettles, pots, pans, roses, and daisies. Next they added magnets with famous-brand logos. Refrigerator magnets became a new art form; some are now collectibles—whether they hold down notes or not.

## REMINGTON, FREDERIC

The most vivid portraits of the Wild West and the people who tamed it were made by a self-taught artist who spent most of his life in his native New York. Frederic Remington left home at 19 to seek adventure on the frontier. Throughout the 1880s he rode with cow punchers and cavalry units, joined wagon trains, and visited Comanche camps, sketching all the while.

Remington returned to the East with memories and drawings to last a lifetime. He used them to conjure the romance and spirit of the West in some 2,700 paintings and sculptures that are charged with vitality. His broncos thunder across sun-parched prairies with manes flying and muscles bulging; wary scouts slip over moonlit mountains to scan the horizon; and Indian hunters circle buffalo in a graphic hunting scene. Although the wilderness Remington loved soon vanished—"My West passed out of existence so long ago as to make it merely a dream"—his art keeps it forever fresh.

In such paintings as "Old Time Plains Fight," Remington captured the austere beauty of the land and the rugged character of its inhabitants.

A Revolutionary War hero, Revere was also a noted silversmith. Many of his bowls, utensils, and pitchers are now museum pieces.

## REVERE, PAUL

On the night of April 18, 1775, British troops prepared to seize a rebel arsenal of weapons in Concord, Massachusetts, and arrest Samuel Adams and John Hancock, leaders of the brewing Colonial rebellion. When silversmith and patriot Paul Revere learned of this, he volunteered to sound the alarm. The sexton of Boston's Old North Church agreed to signal the route taken by the Redcoats with lanterns hung in the steeple: "one if by land, two if by sea." When Revere saw two lanterns, he rowed across the Charles River, unseen by a prowling British warship, then leaped onto a waiting horse and sped through the countryside, yelling, "The regulars are out!" (not the much-quoted "The British are coming!").

In Lexington, Revere roused Adams and Hancock. Halfway to Concord he was captured by a British patrol, but when gunshots rang out, his captors fled. A jubilant Revere knew it was patriots' fire. The next morning the Minutemen routed the British at Concord, and Revere was hailed as a hero. His daring ride became popular legend through Longfellow's ballad "Paul Revere's Ride."

## REVIVAL MEETINGS

Revivalism in America has a long history as an exuberant religious celebration. In the early 18th century, itinerant preachers traveled the Colonies, threatening unrepentant sinners with fire and brimstone. After the Revolutionary War, a Great Revival took place in backwoods communities in Kentucky and Tennessee. People flocked by the thousands to camp meetings that lasted for days to hear Baptist, Methodist, and Presbyterian preachers exhort them to accept the "golden mantle of salvation." Whipped into an emotional frenzy, the crowds made barking noises that were said to "tree the Devil," and some even fell into trances.

In the 1920s preachers took their message to the cities. Billy Sunday scared sinners back to the straight and narrow with cries of "Hell will be forever for rent!" As the century progressed, revivalism was overshadowed by Sunday schools and church involvement in community problems.

## RFD

In 1896 the U.S. Post Office initiated what would become one of its great success stories: rural free delivery, which brought mail directly to country people. City dwellers had enjoyed this service since 1863, and now farmers, too, could receive daily newspapers with crop prices and the latest on national and world events. They could also receive mail-order catalogs, which gave rise to direct-mail marketing. A year after RFD began, Sears, Roebuck, and Company announced that it was selling a buggy every 10 minutes. When parcel post started in 1913, the mail-order business mushroomed.

RFD was so popular that the number of routes expanded from 8,000 in 1902 to 32,000 three years later. Roads were improved to accommodate mail carriers, and the value of farmland increased. But to rural folk the greatest benefit was the connection to the world beyond their own four corners.

## RHYTHM AND BLUES

*Rhythm and blues* is an umbrella term for several styles of black music, the wellspring of most popular American music. Black music began to cross racial boundaries in the 1930s and '40s. By 1949 the trade magazine *Billboard* had recognized this development by changing the name of its "race records" category, formerly marketed separately to a black audience, to "rhythm and blues." Whereas black jazz had been popularized by white bands, it was R & B performed by black artists that broke through to a mass audience.

As black bluesmen moved to the cities, they formed groups and began playing popular music as well as the 12-bar blues. The ensemble music, with the rollicking stamp of boogie-woogie, horn riffs, and heavily accented backbeats, was rambunctious and happy. The singers were strident rather than melancholy.

The Conway. FIVE ROOMS AND BATH
$1,614 MONTHLY PAYMENTS $30

Standard Built Homes From $520 to $1,041 Choice of 4, 5 or 6 Rooms With Bath
The Grant. SIX ROOMS AND BATH
$1,041 MONTHLY PAYMENTS $25

The Puritan. SEVEN ROOMS AND BATH
$2,504 MONTHLY PAYMENTS $40

In 1927 one could order these "permanent, high-grade homes" by mail through the Sears catalog. They included "all the material to build your house complete"—even heating and plumbing fixtures.

James Brown, once known as Mr. Dynamite, had 56 Top 10 R & B hits, including "Please, Please, Please" and "Papa's Got a Brand New Bag."

One of the greats of R & B in the mid-1950s, Bo Diddley was famous for his rhythmic guitar and a beat known as "shave and a haircut, six bits."

Among the pioneers were master guitarist T-Bone Walker in Los Angeles, urban blues "shouters," such as Big Bill Broonzy and Muddy Waters in Chicago, Amos Milburn in Texas, and B. B. King and Arthur "Big Boy" Crudup in the South. Some R & B performers were big-band belters like Jimmy Rushing, Big Joe Turner, Wynonie Harris, and Dinah Washington, or balladeers like Percy Mayfield. Others were saxophonist Louis Jordan, with his popular "jump" band, and doo-wop groups, such as The Orioles and The Platters.

In the early '50s such black R & B artists as Fats Domino, Chuck Berry, Little Richard, and Bo Diddley, featured by disc jockey Alan Freed, came to the fore. White kids stayed by their radios all night to hear the intense "new" sounds, which Freed called "rock 'n' roll." R & B favorites in the '60s were James Brown (the "King of R & B"), Sam Cooke, Aretha Franklin, Brook Benton, and Ray Charles, many of whom crossed into the gospel-flavored "soul" style.

## RICKENBACKER, EDWARD V.

Edward V. Rickenbacker lived the adventurous life small boys dream about. A world-famous auto racer, he drove in the 1907 Vanderbilt Cup races and the first Indianapolis 500, and he set a speed record of 134 miles per hour in Daytona Beach, Florida. An ace fighter pilot in World War I, he shot down 22 German planes and four observation balloons in seven months, winning the Congressional Medal of Honor.

In 1935 Rickenbacker joined Eastern Airlines, and he retired 28 years later as chairman of the board. Twice he escaped death as a civilian during World War II. In 1941 he was nearly killed in an Eastern plane crash. The following year, on a mission in the Pacific, Rickenbacker's plane was forced down, and he lived for 24 days on fish and rainwater in a small rubber raft. He died of pneumonia at the age of 83.

## RINGLING BROTHERS

Trapeze artists, lion tamers, clowns, trick cyclists, and big-top tents—these are the images that the name Ringling has conjured up in the minds of circus lovers for more than a century. There were seven Rungeling brothers (they later changed their name to Ringling), born between 1852 and 1866. Five of them—Albert, Otto, Alfred, Charles, and John—were so enamored of the Mississippi River circus boats they saw as children that they planned careers in the circus. As boys they staged shows with musical instruments and a ragtag menagerie that consisted of a pony and an old goat. By 1884 they were ready to manage a real circus; their first show opened in Baraboo, Wisconsin.

The early Ringling Brothers circus toured small towns, performing under a canvas big top. Their business grew and eventually included 1,000 animals and 1,500 workers. In 1907 the Ringlings

Captain Eddie Rickenbacker led the daredevil 94th Aero Pursuit Squadron. He was the most celebrated air ace of World War I.

Aerialists and elephants dazzle young and old in what has become the "Greatest Show on Earth." The performers travel and live in the world's largest privately owned trains.

bought the Barnum & Bailey Circus from Bailey's widow, creating a multimillion-dollar circus monopoly and making the brothers fabulously wealthy. The last brother died in 1936, but the Ringling Brothers circus lives on. In 1944 it survived a horrific tent fire in Hartford, Connecticut, which killed 168 people. Thereafter, the circus shifted to permanent indoor venues, and it remains the "Greatest Show on Earth."

## RIPLEY'S BELIEVE IT OR NOT!

Believe it or not, Robert LeRoy Ripley, famous for creating the longest continuously running syndicated newspaper cartoon, was on his way to becoming a major league baseball player when he hurt his arm trying out for the New York Giants. He turned to drawing sports cartoons, and in 1918 he drew a collection of sports oddities for the *New York Globe*, including a man who jumped rope 11,800 times in a row. The response was good. Soon Ripley was drawing other curiosities, such as people with incredibly long fingernails and vegetables that looked like humans.

In 1929 William Randolph Hearst's King Features signed Ripley to a $100,000-a-year contract and put his cartoons into hundreds of newspapers. Ripley also made film shorts and radio shows based on the strange truths he traveled the world to find. Today his discoveries are preserved in Believe it or Not! museums, and in the memories of people whose favorite part of the paper was his bazaar of the bizarre.

## RIVERBOATS

In the early 1800s a generation of pioneers, beginning with Lewis and Clark, headed west in long, wide keelboats and raftlike flatboats, many of them homemade. Legendary river men from Mike Fink (the keelboat king) to Mark Twain guided riverboats carrying passengers and trade goods up and down the Mississippi. As Twain recounts in *Life on the Mississippi*, pilots needed a detailed memory of the river's landmarks, including dangerous sandbars and ever-shifting shallows, and were paid huge sums. Twain tells how the cry "S-t-e-a-m-boat a-comin'!" roused even the sleepiest river town. Indeed, the boats were quite a sight, with two "fancy-topped chimneys," a gingerbread pilothouse, and handsome paddle wheels churning toward the levee.

The steamboat era reached its peak in 1870 with a race between two of the most luxurious steamboats ever built: the *Robert E. Lee* and the *Natchez*. Millions of dollars were bet on the outcome, and the competing captains set off from New Orleans for St. Louis. Driving their vessels at full throttle, they raced neck and neck for nearly 1,000 miles when fog dropped on the river. While the *Natchez* prudently waited for it to lift, the *Lee* inched forward. The dangerous maneuver paid off; the *Lee* reached St. Louis in a record 3 days, 18 hours, and 14 minutes. Ironically, the great days of the steamboat were nearing an end as railroads spread across the U.S.

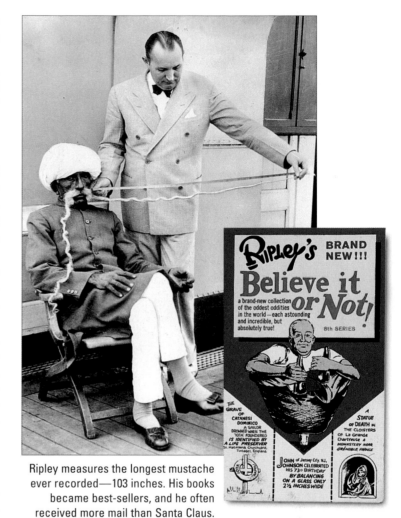

Ripley measures the longest mustache ever recorded—103 inches. His books became best-sellers, and he often received more mail than Santa Claus.

The legendary *Delta Queen* paddle wheeler, launched in 1927, still plies the Big Muddy. The river still shifts its course, but today the U.S. Corps of Engineers aids pilots by using buoys to signal any change in depth.

With this cover illustration for *McClure's* (right), John Held caught the exuberance of the era. In 1921 *The Sheik*, starring Rudolph Valentino and Anges Ayers, made millions of women swoon.

## ROARING TWENTIES

After World War I, America lurched headlong into an era characterized by restlessness and rootlessness combined with a surge of new energy. It began with the enforcement of Prohibition and passage in 1920 of the 19th Amendment: woman suffrage. That same year, hemlines rose so high that the town of Sunbury, Pennsylvania, issued an edict against short skirts, and the Shimmy, a popular dance, was condemned by an archbishop. Louis Armstrong arrived in Chicago with his trumpet; blues singer Bessie Smith recorded "T'Ain't Nobody's Bizness." In 1922 F. Scott Fitzgerald published *Tales of the Jazz Age*; he, Ernest Hemingway (chronicler of the Lost Generation), and writer Gertrude Stein were among the expatriate Americans living in Paris. H. V. Kaltenborn delivered the first NBC newscast, and a year later the first overseas radio broadcast was heard.

George Gershwin's "Rhapsody in Blue" premiered in New York, where you could see young Humphrey Bogart, the Barrymores, Al Jolson, and the Marx Brothers on Broadway. Al "Scarface" Capone was headquartered in Cicero, Illinois, where admirers flocked to shake his hand. In 1927 the nation cheered when Charles "Lucky Lindy" Lindbergh flew across the Atlantic. Babe Ruth hit 60 home runs; the first talking movie, *The Jazz Singer*, made history; and the stock market boomed. Duke Ellington played the classy Harlem Cotton Club, nationally syndicated newspaper columns were born, newsreels were a novelty, and so were Model A Fords. In 1929 the number of gangsters was depleted by seven on St. Valentine's Day; the toast of Tinsel Town was Clara Bow; and everybody Charlestoned. *Whoopee!* was the title of a Ziegfeld hit, and "whoopee!" it was until, with the great Wall Street crash, the dance ended and the orchestra went home.

## ROBBER BARONS

The gilded age of the late 19th century produced a new breed of industrialists—ruthless, driven men who amassed enormous wealth by monopolizing entire industries. Their ranks included financier J. Pierpont Morgan; Andrew Carnegie, who sold Carnegie Steel for $480 million in 1901; the Vanderbilts and their network of railroads; and John D. Rockefeller, who in 1879 controlled 90 percent of the country's oil industry. Their critics called them robber barons.

To their defenders, they were "industrial statesmen" who modernized industry and bolstered the economy. But while the robber barons lived in unparalleled luxury, their workers lived in squalid company towns. When criticized for insensitivity, William Vanderbilt roared, "The public be damned!"

These monopolies were disbanded when President Theodore Roosevelt, citing the Sherman Anti-Trust Act of 1890, stood up to these "malefactors of great wealth." Roosevelt went on to disband 45 illegal trusts, earning himself the nickname "trustbuster" and ushering in an era of reform.

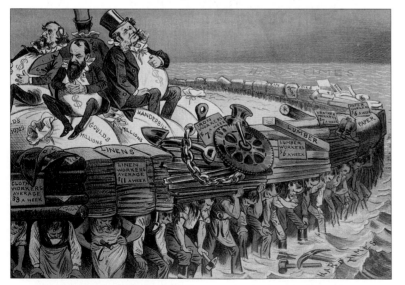

This cartoon from *Puck* (1883) shows robber barons as the public saw them: resting while their oppressed workers labored to make them richer.

## ROBESON, PAUL

Although Paul Robeson was an all-American football player, a Phi Beta Kappa graduate of Rutgers in 1919, and an alumnus of Columbia's School of Law, it was his voice that made him famous. His unforgettable "Ol' Man River" brought down the house night after night in *Show Boat*. As a member of the Provincetown Playhouse, he appeared in *All God's Chillun Got Wings*, *The Hairy Ape*, and *The Emperor Jones*.

During the Depression, Robeson's social conscience led him into politics. An adherent of "scientific socialism," he was an early campaigner for civil rights, and his open admiration for the Soviet Union drew criticism during the Cold War. He moved to England in 1958, where he wrote *Here I Stand*, a statement of his social beliefs. He returned to the U.S. in 1963, where he died in 1976.

## ROBINSON, JACKIE

On April 10, 1947, the Brooklyn Dodgers issued a press release that jolted the baseball world: "The Dodgers today purchased the contract of Jackie Roosevelt Robinson from the Montreal Royals. He will report immediately." With that short announcement, Robinson became the first black man to play in the major leagues since the 19th century. The president of the Dodger organization, Branch Rickey, insisted that Robinson turn the other cheek when confronted with racial abuse. Not only did this require exceptional courage of Robinson, but it demanded a shift in deportment for a man who was quick to protest injustice.

Despite having to play a new position in the field (first base), Robinson earned rookie-of-the-year honors—an impressive start toward a Hall of Fame career. In 1949 he won the MVP award, leading the league with a .342 batting average and 37 stolen bases as the Dodgers won the pennant. An outstanding batter, Robinson electrified crowds whenever he reached base, drawing his lead, feinting a start to the next base and then whoosh, pilfering the base.

## ROBINSON, SUGAR RAY

Called "pound for pound the best boxer" of his time, middleweight Sugar Ray Robinson drew fans away from the heavyweights. During his 25-year career Robinson won 175 of 202 bouts, 109 by knockouts. Born Walker Smith in 1920, Robinson decided to become a fighter after watching Joe Louis train. Too young to be a Golden Gloves amateur, Smith borrowed the papers of fighter Ray Robinson—then kept the name. He added "Sugar" when his style was called "sweet as sugar."

Robinson won the middleweight championship five times between 1951 and 1959. In 1947 he beat Jimmy Doyle, who died of his injuries the next day; Sugar Ray gave most of the purse to Doyle's family. Robinson retired in 1965; two years later, he was elected to the Boxing Hall of Fame.

In 1923 Paul Robeson starred in *The Emperor Jones,* a play in which an escaped convict flees to a remote island. There he tricks the natives into naming him emperor. Rumors of an uprising send the Emperor into the jungle, where he is forced to confront his past.

While in college, Jackie Robinson won a division scoring title in basketball, held the national record for the most punt returns in football, was active in track—and still found time to play baseball.

A generous man as well as an outstanding boxer, Sugar Ray Robinson made regular donations to charities. In 1951, after a bout with Kid Marcel in Paris, Robinson donated his purse to the Cancer Society of France.

John D. Rockefeller, Jr. (right), said his goal was to give away the fortune made by his famous father (left). He contributed to education and research and donated land for the United Nations headquarters.

One of the first influential rock stars, Buddy Holly (right) created such feel-good teen hits as "That'll Be the Day" and "Peggy Sue."

The legendary Jimi Hendrix (left) is remembered for his dazzling experimental guitar work as well as his outrageous live concerts.

## ROCKEFELLER, JOHN D.

John Davison Rockefeller, America's most efficient industrial buccaneer, lived to be 97, and his name became synonymous with enormous wealth. He began to build his fortune in 1858, when at the age of 18 he borrowed money from his father to begin trading in grain and meat.

After the first oil well in America began producing in 1859, Rockefeller and his partners went into the oil-refining business. A ruthless businessman, Rockefeller would drastically undercut his competition and drive them into bankruptcy. By age 38, he controlled 95 percent of American oil refining and was the richest man in the country. His Standard Oil Trust was set up in 1882; it was the nation's first monopoly. For nearly 30 years state and federal attacks on the Trust wound through the courts, and in 1911 Standard Oil was broken up into smaller companies. But Rockefeller had retired in 1897, devoting himself to philanthropy. In his lifetime he donated more than $500 million. He outlived his peers and in his final years gave away shiny dimes to children.

## ROCK MUSIC

It's hard to pinpoint exactly when rock 'n' roll was born. Rock music evolved gradually from the rhythm and blues of guitarists like B. B. King and Bo Diddley. It's safe to say, though, that by the mid-1950s, when disc jockey Alan Freed popularized the term *rock 'n' roll* on a Cleveland radio station and Elvis Presley's raucous numbers bumped pop tunes from the top of the charts, the rock era was well under way.

Rock 'n' roll owed its early success not just to Presley but to legendary showmen like Chuck Berry and Little Richard. In 1964 rock changed forever when English bands, such as The Beatles, The Rolling Stones, and The Kinks spearheaded the "British invasion." Their fresh, infectious music gave new life to the rebellious side of rock 'n' roll.

By the end of the 1960s, the upbeat tunes of rock 'n' roll gave way to harder-edged, more political music, now referred to simply as rock. From the hoarse folk-rock ballads of Bob Dylan to the acid-tinged fantasies of Jimi Hendrix and The Grateful Dead, songwriters expressed the turbulence of the times.

The '70s and '80s saw rock spin off in several directions: hard-edged rock surfaced in the heavy-metal music of Iron Maiden and Def Leppard and in the defiant lyrics of such punk bands as The Clash and The Ramones. At the same time, the softer side of rock brought the rise of singer-songwriters like James Taylor and Billy Joel, who crooned to stadiums full of swooning fans. Rock concerts became increasingly gargantuan spectacles, with enough props, lights, costumes, dance numbers, and smoke machines to put a Broadway show to shame. The members of Kiss hid their identities behind masks of extravagant make-up, while Michael Jackson dressed in glittery outfits and taught the world to do a gliding dance called the Moonwalk. In the '80s, music videos helped singers pave a new path to stardom. Madonna became a pop celebrity with slick, provocative productions. In a resurgence appealing to aging baby boomers, such early-era notables as Tina Turner and Eric Clapton proved that they could still rock on.

## ROCKWELL, NORMAN

Norman Rockwell is one of the most widely recognized and beloved of American artists and illustrators. He is best known for the 318 covers he painted for the *Saturday Evening Post*, a weekly magazine that for decades competed with *Life*. Millions of people saw his covers, which were so popular that the *Post* received requests for reprints years later.

From his very first *Post* cover in 1916 (he was 22), Rockwell hit upon a signature style that would flourish for 60 years. He did this by managing to suggest in a single, realistic image an anecdote with which the general public could identify. His first cover showed a young boy stuck with pushing his baby sister in her carriage, while his pals make fun of him on their way to play baseball. In his 1960 autobiography, Rockwell wrote, "I do ordinary people in everyday situations."

People enjoyed the benevolent humor and sincere affection with which Rockwell observed his subjects: a grandfather taking over his grandson's rocking horse at Christmas; a nervous but happy young couple waiting for a marriage license; a young man "breaking home ties" with family and his sad-eyed collie. Other favorite Rockwell pictures showed scenes from local barbershops and old swimming holes. His "Willie Gillis" series followed one young man through World War II, from Pearl Harbor to a return to civilian life. As a group, Rockwell's covers constitute an often patriotic, always nostalgic look at America. In 1977 Rockwell received the Presidential Medal of Freedom for his life's work.

## ROCKY

An unremarkable but determined Philadelphia boxer fights his way to the championship—and nearly wins. That's the plot that propelled Sylvester Stallone and the film he wrote, *Rocky*, to fame. "It was elegant in its simplicity," observed Burt Young, who played Rocky Balboa's friend. The 1976 film went on to capture the Academy Award for Best Picture.

For years, Stallone hadn't been able to interest studios in his screenplays. His hard-earned success in finally getting *Rocky* to the big screen mirrored the slug-it-out determination of his protagonist (as well as the victories of John Rambo in Stallone's later films). Like so many other movie underdogs, Balboa pulled viewers into his struggle and kept them cheering. The four *Rocky* sequels dimmed in quality, but moviegoers kept a warm spot in their hearts for the hero.

"Triple Self-Portrait," which ran on the *Saturday Evening Post*'s February 13, 1960, cover, wasn't the only time Norman Rockwell painted himself. He enjoyed sneaking his face into crowd scenes from time to time.

"The Italian Stallion," boxer Rocky Balboa (played by Sylvester Stallone), went a grueling 15 rounds with the champ.

Riding an unbroken bronco tests a cowboy's agility and strength. The roughest, toughest broncos often become famous in their own right.

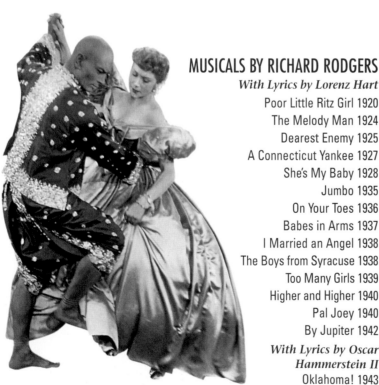

Yul Brynner set a record with more than 4,600 performances in *The King and I.* He also starred with Deborah Kerr in the film version (above).

## MUSICALS BY RICHARD RODGERS

*With Lyrics by Lorenz Hart*

Poor Little Ritz Girl 1920
The Melody Man 1924
Dearest Enemy 1925
A Connecticut Yankee 1927
She's My Baby 1928
Jumbo 1935
On Your Toes 1936
Babes in Arms 1937
I Married an Angel 1938
The Boys from Syracuse 1938
Too Many Girls 1939
Higher and Higher 1940
Pal Joey 1940
By Jupiter 1942

*With Lyrics by Oscar Hammerstein II*

Oklahoma! 1943
Carousel 1945
South Pacific 1949
The King and I 1951
Flower Drum Song 1958
The Sound of Music 1959

## RODEO

With a clang, the chute opens and out charges an angry-eyed, bucking Brahman bull. On its back, a rider struggles to hang on for the eight seconds before the buzzer sounds. Once the rider hits the ground, rodeo clowns scurry around the ring, waving gaudy flags to distract the bull from goring or trampling him. This is the rodeo, an event that combines athleticism, showmanship, and bone-crushing danger.

Many towns lay claim to the first rodeo, but it is certain that one was staged in Pecos, Texas, in 1883, when merchants invited local cowboys to display their roping and riding skills. The entertainment caught on quickly in the West. Rodeos gained international fame as part of Buffalo Bill's Wild West Show and its imitators. To trick roping and fancy riding were added steer wrestling and finally bull riding—the most popular of the events. Today the thrilling spectacle of rodeos attracts millions of people each year.

## RODGERS, RICHARD

A self-taught pianist with an uncanny ability to play by ear and improvise, Richard Rodgers composed the music for scores of America's most popular musicals. Librettist Alan Jay Lerner said of Rodgers's melodies that he had a "pipeline to heaven that runs through him." One year before he entered Columbia University, Rodgers met the down-to-earth, sardonic lyricist Lorenz Hart. Rodgers's early collaboration with Hart included the songs "Mountain Greenery" and "Manhattan" and the musical *Dearest Enemy.* They went on to write such standards as "My Funny Valentine," with Hart knitting his wry, offbeat lyrics to Rodgers's tunes.

In 1943, the year Hart died, Rodgers began collaborating with Oscar Hammerstein II. Their first production, *Oklahoma!*, ran on Broadway for five years, won the Pulitzer Prize for drama, and remains one of America's best-loved musicals. Of their many smash hits, Rodgers's own favorite was *South Pacific.* This Rodgers and Hammerstein musical and several others were later made into successful films.

## ROEBLING, JOHN

It was dubbed the "Eighth Wonder of the World," and when the Brooklyn Bridge opened on May 24, 1883, a holiday was declared on both sides of the East River. Schools closed, 14 tons of fireworks burst above twin 272-foot-high Gothic towers, and some 150,000 sightseers flocked to the bridge. This famed masterpiece was the work of John Augustus Roebling. It hung from a web of spun-steel cables, forming a graceful 3,456-foot-long arc between Brooklyn and Manhattan. Then the world's longest bridge, it carried an unprecedented 18,700-ton load and represented the first use of steel (rather than iron) in bridge building.

An immigrant from Prussia, Roebling had forged a brilliant career, patenting wire rope in 1842 and designing several important suspension bridges, including the 1855 span at Niagara Falls. Ironically, he never witnessed the completion of the Brooklyn Bridge. Just as construction began in 1869, Roebling's toes were crushed at the work site, and he eventually succumbed to tetanus. The job of chief engineer fell to his son, Washington, who supervised work from a bedside window after he himself was stricken with decompression sickness. After 14 years and some $17 million, the structure was completed, chiefly the work of immigrant labor. However, the crippled Washington, like his father, never set foot on the bridge that President Chester A. Arthur called "a durable monument to democracy."

## ROGERS, ROY

Roy Rogers proposed to Dale Evans as they galloped into the Chicago Stadium, he riding Trigger. Under the spotlight, she nodded yes. Dale Evans ("Queen of the West") was Rogers's leading lady at Republic Studios, where he made 81 B Westerns starting in 1943. The former migrant worker and founder of the singing group The Sons of the Pioneers, Rogers succeeded Gene Autry as "King of the Cowboys." At the height of his career, Rogers had 2,000 fan clubs, made hundreds of records, appeared on millions of cereal boxes, and starred in a radio show, a Dell comic book, and countless rodeos. As B pictures faded, he turned to television, making about 100 TV movies during the '50s and co-hosting a variety show with Evans. Rogers has been involved with many business enterprises as well as charitable causes. He and Evans have raised a large adopted family and have worked and played together since their marriage in 1947. Happy Trails!

## ROGERS, WILL

"This old country boy is doing pretty good," he told his son. Will Rogers was an American phenomenon: cowboy, mimic, comedian, stage and screen star, writer, speaker, political activist, humorist. While embodying unpretentious, honest values, he was on a first-name basis with the great and the famous, and he had entrée to the White House through five administrations. He so entranced the public that his account of his gall-bladder operation became a best-seller.

Part Native American, Rogers grew up in Oologah, Indian Territory (now Oklahoma). He was an expert rider and roper. Billed as "The Cherokee Kid," he twirled the lariat and made jokes in Wild West shows, vaudeville, and as a Ziegfeld Follies star. In the '20s he toured the country, speaking up for the common man and poking fun at bureaucracy. Millions listened to his CBS broadcasts, flocked to his movies, and read his unedited column (said *The New York Times*: "Will Rogers makes his own English"). In 1935 he and his friend, aviator Wiley Post, were killed in a plane crash in Alaska. The entire nation grieved for the good-natured cowboy who had once remarked, "I never met a man I did not like."

The centennial of the Brooklyn Bridge took place on May 24, 1983. Before it was built, a ferry linked Manhattan and Brooklyn.

Recalling their first film together, Roy Rogers said that Dale Evans "looked like she had just stepped out of the shower, real clean and fresh."

Speaking with a drawl and continually scratching his head, Will Rogers let fall such wry political gems as "It takes a great country to stand a thing like an election hitting it every four years."

Besides being fun, Rollerblades offer an aerobic workout. These days, it's common to see kids skating to school, adults blading to work, and couriers zipping through city streets, delivering packages.

What is it about roller coasters that keeps riders coming back? Says one fan, you "leave the cares of the world behind and laugh, whoop, holler, and just have a good time."

## ROLLERBLADES

For more than two centuries, the main challenge of in-line skating has been stopping. In 1760 Belgian violinist and inventor Joseph Merlin showed up at a London masquerade ball, fiddling and skating at the same time; then he crashed into a mirror. Other attempts to align wheels along the blade of ice skates fared no better. By the 1860s the safer but slower roller skate (with two pairs of wheels set side by side on the skate, instead of four in a row) had become popular, and in 1866 James Plimpton opened the first American roller rink. In 1935 Leo Seltzer brought excitement to skating with the roller derby, in which skaters tried to pass each other while zooming around an indoor track.

In the early 1980s, in order to practice during the off-season, hockey players started using in-line skates to simulate the feel and speed of skating on ice. The trend was picked up by skiers in Southern California, and it kept growing. By 1990 a million Americans were blading, and sales had soared to $150 million. Of course, the number of injuries has risen as well, to more than 37,000 a year. For safety's sake, skaters should wear a helmet, knee pads, and wrist guards.

## ROLLER COASTERS

The first American roller coaster was built in 1884 at New York's Coney Island by LaMarcus Thompson. It was a primitive device with cars that ran down rolling hills at the rate of six miles an hour; workers had to push the cars up the next hill. Nevertheless, the five-cent ticket brought in $700 a day. Fascination with America's favorite ride had begun, and thrill seekers never looked back.

Today's roller coasters offer drops of more than 200 feet and deep dips into pitch-black tunnels. On a few roller coasters, passengers ride standing up or are suspended from an overhead track. To ensure a stimulating ride, some roller coaster aficionados suggest sitting in the front (for the best view), while others prefer the back (the jerkiest ride); some parks accommodate different tastes by having separate lines for front and back seats. Real daredevils ride in the rain, which slicks up the track and increases speed. This allows for improved air time, or "negative gravity"— those few seconds when you are lifted out of your seat.

To many people, roller coasters are "magical places that … keep a part of your childhood alive." Ironically, some buffs claim they ride the "scream machines" to relieve stress.

## ROLLING STONE

From classic rock to the latest rap, Muhammad Ali to health clubs, *Rolling Stone* magazine has long been the icon of American pop culture. Established in the late 1960s in the epicenter of the counterculture movement—San Francisco—the magazine was started by college dropout Jann

Wenner to explore the messages that popular music was sending about relationships, politics, values, and authority. In its heyday, *Rolling Stone*'s thorough articles and thought-provoking photos so impressed one commentator that he referred to its editors, writers, and photographers as "literary hellcats" who ignore "journalistic conventions and social taboos to get at new ways of telling the truth." Although *Rolling Stone* still favors the young and the new, it has become more mainstream and has expanded its scope to include movies, television, and fashion.

Many famous personalities have graced the cover of *Rolling Stone,* including John Travolta (left), Richard Gere, Janis Joplin, The Beatles, Eric Clapton, Goldie Hawn, Bob Dylan, The Who, and Bob Hope.

## ROOSEVELT, ELEANOR

Eleanor Roosevelt was a great humanitarian and one of the most active First Ladies the country has ever had. Born in 1884 into a socially prominent New York family, Eleanor married Franklin Delano Roosevelt, her distant cousin, in 1905. As her husband advanced through Democratic politics, she raised their five children and gradually became active in the League of Women Voters and the Women's Trade Union League. In 1921, when Franklin was stricken with polio, Eleanor studied politics to help him keep abreast of the action. When he was elected president in 1932, she became her husband's "eyes and ears" while acting as an advocate for children, women, minorities, and the poor. For years she had her own radio program and a syndicated newspaper column, *My Day*.

When her husband died in 1945, Eleanor became even more active in public service, playing a major role in drafting the United Nations Declaration of Human Rights and remaining a strong Democratic supporter. "I suppose I should slow down," she observed at age 77, but she stayed active until her death, one year later. She once told Edward R. Murrow: "The important thing was that you never let down doing the best you were able to do."

## ROOSEVELT, FRANKLIN DELANO

Lyndon Johnson said that Franklin D. Roosevelt was "the one person I ever knew, anywhere, who was never afraid." Born in 1882 into a life of privilege, Roosevelt entered the tumultuous politics of the Progressive Era. In 1905 he married Eleanor Roosevelt, who proved to be a lifelong force in public and private events.

Roosevelt was stricken with polio in 1921, and he never walked again without the aid of braces and a cane. But with a determination fueled by his famously ebullient personality, he was elected governor of New York in 1928 and 1930.

Four years later he was elected president. Declaring that "the only thing we have to fear is fear itself," he took on the crushing economic and social problems of the Great Depression. Roosevelt created and implemented the programs of the New Deal and reassured the country with radio "Fireside Chats." In 1936 he was elected to a second term by

The Roosevelts posed for a family portrait in 1916 (left to right: Elliott, Franklin, Franklin Jr., James, John, Eleanor, and Anna). As First Lady (right), Eleanor traveled the country lecturing on social issues.

a landslide and would go on to be elected to record-breaking third and fourth terms. After the U.S. entered World War II, Roosevelt proved to be an effective wartime leader. In 1945, two months after the historic meeting at Yalta, he died. The nation mourned the man who had guided it through its darkest days, and Winston Churchill lauded him as the American president who had the greatest impact on world history.

## ROOSEVELT, THEODORE

"Get action, do things," Theodore Roosevelt advised. "Create, act, take a place wherever you are and be somebody." Roosevelt embodied this energetic philosophy, first entering New York politics at the age of 23, and later taking up mountain climbing, big-game hunting, and ranching in the Dakota Badlands. In 1898 he fought in the Spanish-American War, leading the Rough Riders in the famous charge up San Juan Hill. "Oh, but we have had a bully fight!" he said.

Elected governor of New York upon his return from the war, he became William McKinley's vice president two years later. When McKinley was assassinated in 1901, Roosevelt assumed the presidency.

Roosevelt's motto was "Speak softly and carry a big stick." While in office, he supported a Panamanian revolution, claimed the right to intervene in the affairs of Latin American countries, and mediated a settlement of the Russo-Japanese War in 1905. At home he was known as a trust-buster as well as an ardent conservationist (he doubled the number of national parks).

After seven years in office, he toured the world, ran unsuccessfully as a third-party candidate, explored Brazil, and led soldiers in World War I. But the death in combat of his son Quentin in 1918 and recurring bouts of malaria weakened him in body and spirit. Within a year, one of the most dynamic presidents this country ever had was dead.

## ROSEANNE

"I been married 13 years, and lemme tell you, it's a thrill to be out of the house," quipped Roseanne Barr during her first *Tonight Show* appearance, in 1985. "I hate the word *housewife*," she continued. "I prefer to be called 'domestic goddess.'" Roseanne was a teenager when she discovered that phrase in *Fascinating Womanhood*, a primer on acting like a lady and serving your husband. Roseanne didn't buy it; her own "goddess" character, brazen and forthright, was fodder for her stand-up comedy routines and became the basis of the top-rated TV sitcom that bore her name.

The show didn't shy away from such controversial subjects as lesbianism, abortion, and racism. No matter what domestic crisis arose, the working-class Conner family on *Roseanne* handled it with doses of sharp humor. Roseanne's TV sister once said of their close but bumpy relationship, "I'm just waiting for you to say, 'You may be right, Jackie.'"

Offering hope to those suffering during the Depression, Franklin D. Roosevelt said, "The test of our progress is not whether we add more to...those who have much; it is whether we provide enough for those who have too little."

"I took Panama!" declared Teddy Roosevelt. And, in a sense, he did. When Colombia refused his terms for building the Panama Canal (Panama was a Colombian province), Roosevelt encouraged a Panamanian revolution.

Roseanne replied, "Yeah, and I'm waiting for chocolate air." During many upheavals—loss of jobs, bankruptcy, starting their own business—the family retained its élan: "We are white trash, and we'll be white trash until the day they drag us to the curb."

## ROSE BOWL

Millions of football fans spend New Year's Day watching postseason college bowl games. Bowl games (which take place after the regular football season has ended) are played by college teams that take on opponents from outside their conferences in an attempt to determine the number one team in the nation. The oldest bowl, the Rose Bowl in Pasadena, remains popular because it combines football action with a spectacular parade—giving viewers in areas with gray winter skies an eyeful of California sun. The number of bowls keeps growing—some of the more famous ones include the Fiesta, Orange, Sugar, Gator, and Cotton Bowls—which creates dilemmas for football fans clutching their remote controls.

## ROSIE THE RIVETER

During World War II, 3.5 million American women entered the workforce to take over industrial jobs left vacant by men serving in the armed forces. While everybody knew that women could handle the desk jobs, women's ability to perform on production lines in the war plants and other heavy industry was a revelation. At first companies were reluctant to hire women, for fear that they were not physically up to the job. But necessity forced industry to view women as employees, and women proved to be as productive as men.

Many of these wartime workers were affectionately called "Rosie the Riveter," no matter what their real name or job was. The subject of a popular song, a Lockheed Aircraft poster, and a *Saturday Evening Post* cover, "Rosie" became the symbolic female production worker. Was there an original Rosie? Although no one knows for sure, it may have been Rose Balding, who started riveting for Lockheed in 1942.

## ROUTE 66

Among the highways that occupy a place deep in America's soul—the Natchez Trace, El Camino Real, the Texas Road—U.S. Route 66 is, as writer John Steinbeck once said, "the mother road." Built in 1926 and cutting a 2,400-mile arc through eight states and three time zones, this road, called the "Main Street of America," offers a nostalgic glimpse of the country before the advent of the great interstate highways. To savor the way America was, take a drive and stop at one of the many mom-and-pop diners along the way to taste a slice of cake baked by the person who serves it. First immortalized in song by Nat "King" Cole, then in a '60s TV series, the "Glory Road"—and our love affair with it—is kept alive by roadside museums and collectors of memorabilia.

The Conner family, clockwise from left: Becky (Lecy Goranson), Roseanne, Dan (John Goodman), D.J. (Michael Fishman), and Darlene (Sara Gilbert).

Wanting to support the war effort and show their pride in America, women became "WOWs"—woman ordnance workers.

One stretch of Route 66 follows the path of the Lightning Dromedary Express—a camel "pony express"—which carried mail to L.A. in the 1850s.

HISTORIC
ROUTE
66

Russell called himself an illustrator, but he was in fact the last great painter of the Old West, devoted to capturing a vanishing era.

Once called "the most gorgeous and desirable woman on the American stage," Lillian Russell "left a trail of affection wherever she passed."

## RUSSELL, CHARLES MARION

Admired by art critics and fellow cowboys alike, Charles Russell sketched, painted, and sculpted the American West that had enthralled him since childhood. In 1880 the 16-year-old greenhorn struck out for Montana, where he worked with a trapper, drove cattle, and became so respected among Native Americans that the Blood Indians adopted the "picture writer" into their tribe.

An eagle-eyed observer and natural draftsman, Russell wrangled art from the raw material of his life, capturing everything from high-spirited cowhands roping steer to a serene Plains chief in full regalia. The quintessential "cowboy artist" never romanticized the West, nor did he shy away from showing its seedy underside. His record of the West earned widespread acclaim: one panoramic mural adorns the Montana statehouse, and a bronze stands in the U.S. Capitol.

## RUSSELL, LILLIAN

She was a beautiful blue-eyed blonde with creamy skin; she weighed 160 pounds, and her sweet nature was as generous as her curvaceous figure. Lillian Russell was adored by all. Convent-educated, she aspired to grand opera, but she ended up in New York as a singing actress. She performed in plays as well as at the prestigious Weber and Fields Music Hall. In 1905 she made her vaudeville debut. Russell's great friend and admirer was bon vivant Diamond Jim Brady, who once presented her with a jewel-encrusted bicycle. She married four times, played poker, wore spectacular feathered hats, bet on horses, and had a cigar named after her. She is buried in Pittsburgh in a solid-silver coffin.

## RUTH, BABE

Babe Ruth transcended baseball. His celebrity equaled that of the president, and any Ruthian event—whether it was a majestic home run, his celebrated tummy ache in 1925, or his visits to children in hospitals—became news. In 1919 Ruth set a single-season record of 29 home runs for the Red Sox. In 1920, as a full-time outfielder for the Yankees, Ruth hit 54 homers, surpassing the totals of nearly every team in baseball. He went on to lead the American League in home runs for 12 straight years. Fans flocked to see Ruth play, and when the Yankees built a new stadium in 1923, it was called The House That Ruth Built. It took decades to topple Ruth's records. His lifetime total of 714 home runs remained unmatched until Hank Aaron hit number 715 in 1974—after batting 3,965 more times than Ruth had.

On April 27, 1947, later known as Babe Ruth Day, Ruth, weakened by throat cancer, made an appearance at Yankee Stadium. Praising his favorite sport, he said, "The only real game in the world, I think, is baseball."

Ruth was a hero to millions. An orphan himself, he established the Babe Ruth Foundation for underprivileged children.

*"No one flower can
ever symbolize this nation.
America is a bouquet."*

WILLIAM SAFIRE

## ST. LOUIS

Ever since 1764, when two French fur traders set up a trading post where the Missouri River meets the Mississippi, St. Louis has been the gateway to the West. In 1803 President Thomas Jefferson acquired the Louisiana Territory from Napoleon—doubling the size of the U.S. overnight. When Meriwether Lewis and William Clark set out to survey this vast region, they began their expedition in St. Louis. In 1904 the city hosted the World's Fair to commemorate the purchase. It was a wonderful party, at which ice cream cones, hot dogs, and iced tea were introduced.

In 1965 St. Louis captured its vitality and spirit in the towering 630-foot Gateway Arch, designed by Finnish-American architect Eero Saarinen. Visitors cram into a tiny five-seat elevator that zooms up the stainless steel leg in a mere four minutes. At the pinnacle, a magnificent 30-mile panorama greets the viewer until gravity pulls the little capsule down in a swift, three-minute descent.

The Gateway Arch in St. Louis was built to honor Thomas Jefferson and the country's westward expansion. The St. Louis World's Fair inspired the musical *Meet Me in St. Louis*.

## SALEM WITCH TRIALS

In the spring of 1692, a hysterical fear of witchcraft gripped the village of Salem, Massachusetts. A group of teenage girls, influenced by tales of voodoo told by a West Indian slave named Tituba, began to have violent fits. They thrashed and screamed that devils were pinching them and accused Tituba and other local women of bewitching them. Within a few months, they had accused hundreds of men, women, and even a four-year-old child. Those who admitted to being witches were not condemned; only those who maintained their innocence were executed.

A special court tried 27 of the accused. Bridget Bishop was convicted of witchcraft for possessing "lace clothes too elaborate for an honest woman," and was hanged along with 18 others. Giles Corey was crushed to death by weights for refusing to plead guilty or not guilty.

Villagers were afraid to condemn the witch-hunt for fear of being accused next. However, public officials and the clergy grew increasingly uneasy with the frenzied proceedings. In September Governor Sir William Phips banned the use of "spectral evidence" in the courts and put a halt to the trials. By May 1693 all those who had been imprisoned were acquitted and released. Thereafter, no one in America was ever put to death for the crime of witchcraft.

Historians link the Salem witch trials to enmity within Puritan society. The term *witch-hunt* is now synonymous with unfounded allegations.

From rather modest beginnings, the Salvation Army has expanded into a worldwide organization that offers its services in more than 80 countries.

The unique character of San Francisco is apparent at Lombard Street (above), which is known as one of the nation's steepest, twistiest roads. The Golden Gate Bridge (below) has an overall length that exceeds 9,200 feet; it links San Francisco with its northern suburbs.

## SALVATION ARMY

Although it's best known to Americans for bell-ringing Santas collecting donations at Christmastime, the Salvation Army is active throughout the year. Its members, who live frugally and avoid alcohol and tobacco, offer aid to all in need.

The Salvation Army began in 1865, when William Booth, a Methodist preacher, started urging London slum dwellers to embrace the Christian promise of salvation. Traditional churches rejected his tattered converts, so Booth created local missions, overseen by a quasi military organization. He called the group the Salvation Army; he became general, his followers soldiers. They ministered to both spiritual and physical needs. In 1880 Booth established the American branch, and in 1904 his daughter Evangeline became its commander. Met with ridicule and hostility at first, her troops won gratitude for handing out doughnuts during World War I and operating soup kitchens during the Depression.

Today the Salvation Army offers many social programs, including children's aid, hostels for the elderly, halfway houses for alcoholics, vocational training, prison work, shelters for the homeless, and relief for disaster victims.

## SANDBURG, CARL

Known as the "people's poet," Carl Sandburg appealed to the ordinary Americans he celebrated in verse: immigrant day laborers, factory girls, ditchdiggers, lovers of the open road. In the exuberant lines from his book *Chicago Poems*, Sandburg dared anyone to sneer at his "City of the Big Shoulders ... so proud to be alive and coarse and strong and cunning." He used slang, folk songs, and the rhythms of ordinary speech in his poetry. Subsequent collections, such as *Cornhuskers* and *The People, Yes*, solidified his status as one of the best-known American poets of the 20th century. Sandburg won two Pulitzer Prizes, one for his *Complete Poems* and the other for his biography of Abraham Lincoln.

## SAN FRANCISCO

San Francisco's past was shaped by gold and earthquakes. From its founding as Yerba Buena in 1776 by Spanish missionaries, San Francisco (don't call it "Frisco") remained a sleepy village of 800 until 1848, when the discovery of gold changed everything. In two years the population soared to 25,000. This was a lawless period when the city's Barbary Coast was home to raucous saloons and gambling halls.

On April 18, 1906, at 5:12 A.M., the San Andreas fault shifted, and San Francisco began to tremble. The earthquake lasted one minute; the resulting fires raged for three days, destroying much of the city. "It is as though a pretty, frivolous woman underwent a great tragedy," wrote a contemporary journalist. "She survives, but she is sobered."

San Francisco is a real working town, and one of the most livable. The weather is cooler than most tourists expect, and often foggy. Mark Twain said, "The coldest winter I ever spent was one summer in San Francisco." With its great bay, undulating hills, spectacular Golden Gate Bridge, the windswept Marin County headlands towering in the distance, and the fog dramatizing them all, San Francisco's setting ranks among the most beautiful in the world. Millions of tourists come to ride the cable cars, sample world-class cuisine, eat crabs at Fisherman's Wharf, and stroll the diverse neighborhoods of Nob Hill, the Castro District, North Beach, Chinatown, and Russian Hill. Most of these visitors leave their hearts in San Francisco.

## SAN SIMEON/HEARST'S CASTLE

"I'm tired of camping out on the hillside," said wealthy publisher William Randolph Hearst (1863–1951) to his architect, Julia Morgan. "I want to build something more comfortable." With a total of 56 bedrooms, 61 bathrooms, and 41 fireplaces, his multibuilding estate, called La Cuesta Encantada (The Enchanted Hill) was that, and more. Indeed, this oversize playground set on 127 lushly landscaped acres and perched 1,600 feet above California's San Simeon Bay is arguably one of America's greatest monuments to eccentricity.

In addition to two swimming pools (one indoor, one out), a private zoo, and three guest cottages, the estate includes Hearst's 60,000-square-foot "castle" (called Casa Grande), decorated with Greek vases, Flemish tapestries, and Italian Renaissance furniture. Here Hearst and his mistress, actress Marion Davies, presided over a steady stream of guests. By day, such stars as Clark Gable, Greta Garbo, Joan Crawford, and Cary Grant cavorted as they pleased, but each evening they sat down promptly at 7:30 to dinner in the baronial hall—the table set with paper napkins and jars of mustard. Begun in 1919, the estate was still unfinished when Hearst died; it was opened to the public as a museum in 1958.

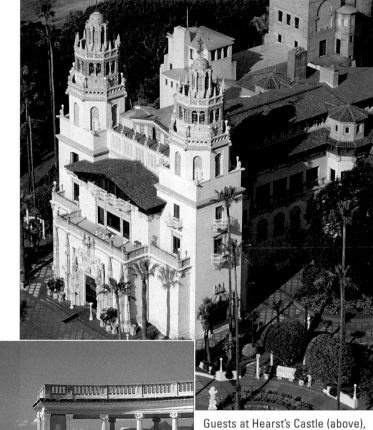

Guests at Hearst's Castle (above), a 100-room Spanish-style mansion, were given floor plans to help them find their way around. Classical marble columns, tiles, and statuary adorn the Neptune Pool.

## SANTA FE TRAIL

The legendary Santa Fe Trail was established by an accidental meeting. In 1821 William Becknell led a small party from Missouri to trade with the Plains Indians. Near the Colorado-New Mexico border, they happened upon Mexican troops, who told them that Mexico had overthrown the Spanish and that the town of Santa Fe now welcomed foreign traders. The party hurried to this potentially rich market with their goods and returned home with saddlebags loaded with Mexican silver. The route they took became known as the Santa Fe Trail.

The 800-mile trail soon attracted caravans of up to 100 wagons. Traders had to contend with rock slides, Indian raids, and exorbitant New Mexican tariffs, but with profits of 10 to 40 percent, it was well worth it. By 1880 the railroad had replaced the trail, but parts of it can still be traced through ruts worn deep in the prairie by wagon wheels.

William Randolph Hearst (second from the right) reveled in his role as host. He once said, "Pleasure is worth what you can afford to pay for it."

John Singer Sargent was never happier than when he was depicting close friends, such as the couple in *Paul Helleu Sketching With His Wife* (1889), above. The bulk of his work consisted of paintings commissioned by a wealthy clientele. This portrait, *Mr. and Mrs. Isaac Newton Phelps Stokes* (1897), left, is one.

When David Sarnoff was growing up, his father wanted him to be a businessman; his mother wanted him to be a scholar. Sarnoff combined the two, becoming one of television's great innovators.

## SARGENT, JOHN SINGER

John Singer Sargent, society portraitist without peer, held a mirror up to the glittering Gilded Age, reflecting not only the glamour of the leisure class but the measure of his own artistic virtuosity. "No one has been able…to seize the exact cachet of fashionable life," wrote an art critic in 1900, "or to render it in paint with [such] smartness and piquancy."

Sargent was born in 1856 in Florence, Italy, where his parents had settled after emigrating from Philadelphia. As a student at the Ecole des Beaux-Arts in Paris, he perfected techniques that brought spontaneity and daring to his art. Henry James, for one, marveled at "the slightly uncanny spectacle of a talent which on the very threshold of its career has nothing more to learn." For 30 years Sargent was engaged in the nearly nonstop portrayal of the rich and famous. His oeuvre grew to include some 600 portraits, and counted among the sitters were such notables as John D. Rockefeller, Theodore Roosevelt, and Claude Monet. Many of his works were obviously meant to flatter the sitter, yet even in those depictions one can discern Sargent's dashing brushwork, deft use of color, and ability to elicit individual character.

## SARNOFF, DAVID

David Sarnoff was manning the wireless station atop the John Wanamaker department store in New York City on April 15, 1912, when a dire message came through: "S.S. *Titanic* ran into iceberg—sinking fast." The 45,000-ton *Titanic* was the world's largest, newest, and most luxurious ship. Called "unsinkable," the ocean liner was on her maiden voyage when it hit an iceberg and literally split in two. In less than three hours, the *Titanic* had sunk and 1,513 passengers and crew had drowned, including many of the wealthiest of New York and Philadelphia society. The untiring Sarnoff stayed at his post for hours, taking the names of survivors relayed from rescue ships. The role of the wireless—the more impressive because the *Titanic* was so far away—heralded the dawn of a new age in communications.

Within the next three years, inventors created radios that could transmit complex signals, including the human voice. At this point, David Sarnoff realized the commercial potential of the wireless systems. He proposed a plan for a simple "radio music box" for use in the home—an idea that eventually led to the establishment of the broadcasting industry. By 1926 the farsighted Sarnoff was in charge of the newly formed National Broadcasting Company. He later became president of RCA, where he funded research aimed at joining pictures to sound. This technology went on display at the 1939 World's Fair, where Sarnoff appeared on a small screen and proclaimed the advent of television: "Now at last we add radio sight to sound."

## S.A.T.

Since 1926 high school seniors have dreaded the Scholastic Aptitude Test, an exam that measures mathematical and verbal skills. High scores—anything approaching 1600 points—can bring scholarship offers. Low scores restrict college options. The test isn't perfect: critics cite higher average scores for affluent white males as evidence of cultural, racial, and class bias. Also, coaching services regularly raise students' scores, showing that the test measures trainable skills as much as aptitude.

The S.A.T has changed in recent years. Nonmultiple-choice questions have been added to the math section, students can use calculators, and more time is allowed for the verbal section. But the test remains a daunting rite of passage: years after taking it, some people still have nightmares of starting the test without enough sharpened No. 2 pencils.

## SATURDAY EVENING POST

*The Saturday Evening Post* began in 1821 in Philadelphia as an unpretentious four-page weekly. The paper did fairly well at first, claiming among its contributors Edgar Allan Poe and Harriet Beecher Stowe, but then came years of struggle. It was bought in 1897 by Cyrus Curtis, the publisher of the highly successful *Ladies' Home Journal.* Curtis found a brilliant editor for the *Post*: George Horace Lorimer.

To distinguish it from the *Journal,* Lorimer decided that the *Post* should address a predominantly male audience. Young businessmen enjoyed its articles about captains of industry, but Lorimer's real genius was for choosing fiction. He published stories by William Faulkner, F. Scott Fitzgerald, Sinclair Lewis, and Edith Wharton. Will Rogers and Ring Lardner, among others, contributed humor pieces, while Norman Rockwell's quintessentially American covers caught the fancy of the nation. This mix made the *Post* one of the country's most popular magazines for nearly half a century.

## SATURDAY NIGHT LIVE

"I would like...to feed your fingertips...to the wolverines." So began the first broadcast of *Saturday Night Live* on October 11, 1975, giving notice of the irreverent, take-no-prisoners humor to come. *SNL*'s combination of satire and silliness (including movie parodies, fake commercials, and the Coneheads) was embraced by baby boomers. By 1979 some 25 million people were staying up late to watch the show.

*SNL*'s original cast featured some of the brightest lights on television: Dan Aykroyd and guest host Steve Martin played the Wild and Crazy Guys, Gilda Radner and Bill Murray were nerdy sweethearts Lisa and Todd, John Belushi was Samurai everyman, and Chevy Chase portrayed an ever-bumbling President Ford. Later years made stars out of Eddie Murphy, Mike Myers, Dennis Miller, and Dana Carvey—the Church Lady. Isn't that special?

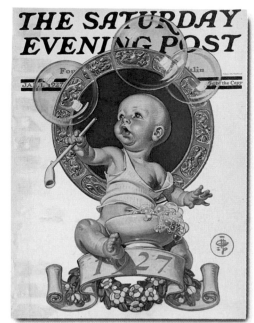

In 1927 illustrator J. C. Leyendecker used a baby to usher in the New Year. He painted 321 covers for the *Saturday Evening Post,* and his warm, anecdotal style was an inspiration for another *Post* artist, Norman Rockwell.

"Live, from New York, it's Saturday night!" The show's original cast members were (top row) Laraine Newman, John Belushi, Jane Curtin, Chevy Chase, Dan Aykroyd; (bottom row) Garrett Morris, and Gilda Radner.

While some sci-fi films have serious messages, others are strictly for laughs. Movies like *Plan 9 From Outer Space*, *The Day of the Triffids*, and *Queen of Outer Space* (at left, starring Zsa Zsa Gabor) have become camp classics.

One by one, the crew of the spaceship *Nostromo* fell to a gruesome invader in the sci-fi masterpiece *Alien* (1979), directed by Ridley Scott.

A Scrabble player's vocabulary should include the words *faqir, qaid, qoph, qindar,* and *qintar,* five English words you can play if you're stuck with a *Q* but no *U*.

## SCI-FI FILMS

Science fiction movies have thrilled audiences since silent-film days, when early classics portrayed mad scientists or the perils of a dehumanized future. During the 1930s adventurers like Flash Gordon found a place in Saturday-afternoon serials. But with the dawn of the space age, directors began creating sci-fi extravaganzas for a more adult audience.

Sci-fi films grew up during the 1950s. In such movies as *The Thing* (1951) and *The Blob* (1958), the enemies were hostile life-forms capable of overrunning the world. *The War of the Worlds* (1953) transplanted H. G. Wells's turn-of-the-century fantasy about Martian invaders to contemporary California. In *Invasion of the Body Snatchers* (1956), aliens changed the citizens of a small town into compliant zombies.

Sci-fi films also reflected our concerns about new technologies, especially nuclear weapons. In *Them!* (1954), radiation caused ants to grow to a giant size. *The Day the Earth Stood Still* (1951) introduced a benign interplanetary visitor who warned earthlings about the dangers of nuclear war.

Many critics consider *2001: A Space Odyssey* to be the greatest of all sci-fi films. Released in 1968, it sprang from a collaboration between writer Arthur C. Clarke and director Stanley Kubrick. The movie offers a poignant depiction of the conflict between HAL, a malfunctioning but almost human computer, and the crew of a spaceship bound for Jupiter. More recently, such directors as Steven Spielberg and George Lucas have brought technical wizardry to the genre, and movies like *Close Encounters of the Third Kind* (1977), *E. T.* (1982), and *Cocoon* (1985) have shown a new optimism about space and about our possible neighbors in the universe.

## SCRABBLE

Scrabble was created during the Depression by Alfred Butts, an unemployed architect. Butts covered a checkerboard in paper, drew a 225-square grid, and created 100 plywood letter tiles, assigning values to them based on how frequently the letters appeared on the front page of *The New York Times*. The name of the game was Lexico and, later, Criss-Cross; it was christened Scrabble in 1948.

In 1952 this new style of word game finally seized the country's imagination, and it remains a popular pastime even today. Fanatics spend hours hoping they draw one of the two blank tiles, which, because they can represent any letter of the alphabet, greatly increase the chances of building a word that covers a "triple word score" square or creating a seven-letter word for a 50-point bonus.

## SEARS, ROEBUCK CATALOGUE

One day in 1886, railway-station agent Richard Sears found himself with a refused shipment of gold-filled watches. They were inexpensive, so Sears decided to pay for the watches himself and try to sell them. He telegraphed up and down the railway line for buyers; the watches sold so quickly that Sears decided to buy more and go into business for himself.

Sears hired watchmaker Alvah C. Roebuck to help him with his new business. In 1893 they offered a wide array of articles in a 538-page compendium called the Sears, Roebuck Catalogue. This was the beginning of the mail-order business in America, and it was revolutionary. Virtually anything could be purchased from the Sears catalog: suits, dresses, fishing gear, guns, hunting and farm equipment, and furniture. No longer did people have to travel to towns to buy goods. Suddenly even farmers living far out in rural areas had access to quality merchandise at reasonable prices.

In 1970 Sears issued a facsimile edition of its 1927 catalog. Readers could marvel at a time when a bicycle cost $25, a set of silver cost $28, and a player piano could be had for less than $400.

## SEQUOYA

Sequoya, a Cherokee Indian of mixed race also known as George Guess, single-handedly created the Cherokee alphabet, the first written alphabet for a Native American tribe. Although he had no formal education, Sequoya was intrigued by reading and writing, and he believed that the white man's "talking leaves" were the key to their power. Around 1809 he began to invent a system of writing for his people. After years of frustration and being ridiculed, he created 86 characters, one for each syllable of the Cherokee language. In 1821 the syllabary was approved by the leaders of the eastern Cherokee tribes, and in a matter of months, thousands of Cherokee could read and write in their own language.

"The whole [Cherokee] nation became an academy for the study of the system," wrote one observer. Sequoya died in 1843, but the memory of his deeds lives on in the majestic trees named for him: the giant sequoias of California.

Owing to the work of Sequoya (shown at left with his 86-character syllabary), the first Cherokee newspaper, the *Cherokee Phoenix,* began publication in 1828.

## SESAME STREET

"Can you tell me how to get to Sesame Street?" For nearly three decades, millions of children worldwide have known the way. From *Sesame Street*'s beginning, its creators understood that the quick pace and catchy jingles of TV commercials appealed to children, so they used those techniques to teach the ABCs and 123s. They also created a neighborhood filled with people and puppets of all colors. Preschoolers count Elmo, Ernie and Bert, and that trio of blue monsters (Grover, Herry, and Cookie Monster) among their friends; adults get a kick out of Muppets named Flo Bear, Placido Flamingo, and Merrill Sheep.

But it's Big Bird, the eight-foot-tall canary with the heart of a six-year-old, who delivers the show's most compelling lessons. When cast member Maria had a baby, Big Bird found he was both happy and jealous. When the actor who played Mr. Hooper died, Big Bird learned about mourning for a friend. And when nobody believed in Big Bird's pal Snuffleupagus, the writers discovered they were sending the wrong message. "Children need to be believed," they conceded, and so the woolly creature was revealed.

During *Sesame Street*'s 25th-anniversary season, seven new Muppets, including childlike Elmo (left), joined such old favorites as Oscar the Grouch (center), and Big Bird (right).

The 7-Eleven name refers to the traditionally lucky numbers and to the store's original hours of operation, from morning to late night.

## 7-ELEVEN

The country's largest convenience-store chain, 7-Eleven was born in the 1930s when the Southland Ice Company in Dallas, Texas, started selling groceries. The 7-Eleven name came along in 1946; before that, the stores used an Alaskan totem pole as a logo and were called "Tote'm Serv-Ice Stations." In the 1960s Southland began buying up regional stores, including Minit Markets, Scotty Shops, Speedee Marts, Quick Marts, and Pak-A-Sak. The '60s also saw the introduction of two of 7-Eleven's trademarks: 24-hour-a-day operations (started in 1963 at the company's Las Vegas stores) and the Slurpee (a flavored ice drink introduced in 1965).

For people in a hurry to rent videotapes, use an automated teller machine, or buy beer, chips, milk, or aspirin, the 7-Eleven will likely suffice. Other convenience-store chains include Cumberland Farms, Circle K, and Stop N Go. And many gas companies have started their own convenience stores, such as Arco's am/pm stores. The prices may seem high, but the stores are designed to save time, not money.

## SEWARD'S FOLLY

In appointing William Seward as secretary of state, Abraham Lincoln chose a man of rare foresight. When Seward purchased Alaska in 1867 from the cash-strapped Russian government, critics called it "Seward's Folly," "Seward's Icebox," and "Walrussia." But at the bargain-basement price of $7.2 million, the secretary had bought a land of unimaginable beauty and natural wealth.

A stern-faced but affable man, Seward was an abolitionist and reformer. His nimble diplomacy kept Europe from siding with the Confederacy. As President Johnson's secretary of state, Seward tried to purchase the Danish West Indies (today's Virgin Islands) and also the Isthmus of Panama, but both proposals were rejected by the Senate. Seward did not live to see gold or oil discovered in Alaska or, of course, its statehood, but he probably wouldn't have been surprised.

## SEWING MACHINE

The desirability of a sewing machine was apparent to many people, but making one that would actually work proved difficult indeed. Mechanic Elias Howe achieved a breakthrough with a lockstitch sewing machine in 1846. This hand-powered contraption could sew an amazing 250 stitches per minute. It had two threads: one formed a loop in the fabric, and a second went through the loop, catching and securing it. Isaac Merrit Singer, a part-time actor, took the device further by adding a foot-operated treadle, which facilitated continuous stitching. Because Singer's machine used the lockstitch method, Howe sued Singer for patent infringement, winning the case in 1854. Several others, most notably A. B. Wilson, had added innovations that vastly increased the speed and practicality of the sewing machine. Altogether,

Its purchase once denounced as a folly, Alaska comprises 586,400 square miles of spectacular scenery, including pristine Wonder Lake and snow-covered Mt. McKinley.

The sewing machines of Isaac Merrit Singer were the most popular in the industry. He used wide-scale advertising, and his factories outproduced the competition.

some 800 patents were issued for various components—bobbins, needles, feeders, and the like. Apparently, no one manufacturer could produce an ideal machine without borrowing from others. Recognizing this stalemate, Orlando B. Potter, an attorney for one of the manufacturers, suggested a patent pool, and all the major innovators agreed to share their ideas. Nearly everyone did well under the new agreement, and the sewing machine brought speed and efficiency to both the garment industry and the home.

## SHADOW

"Who knows…what evil…lurks…in the hearts of men? The Shadow knows!" As any radio buff remembers, these are the opening lines of *The Shadow*, a radio mystery program of enormous popularity. The Shadow was an amateur detective who walked the streets as "Lamont Cranston, a man of wealth, a student of science, and a master of other people's minds." In the Orient the Shadow had acquired secret powers that allowed him "to cloud men's minds" and to become invisible. Only his "friend and constant companion, the lovely Margo Lane," knew the Shadow's true identity. Together they taught evildoers—crooks, tainted politicians, wicked doctors, and unscrupulous scientists—that "the weed of crime bears bitter fruit. Crime does not pay. The Shadow knows. Ha-ha-ha!" (*bloodcurdling laughter*).

From 1930 to 1954, fans eager for heart-stopping excitement tuned in, especially after a young actor, Orson Welles, became the Shadow in 1937. Unfortunately, after his "War of the Worlds" broadcast (in which he convinced millions of listeners that Martians were actually invading Earth), Welles had to leave *The Shadow* because his fame had become too great for a role that demanded anonymity.

## SHAKER FURNITURE

The founder of Shakerism was a visionary English Quaker named Ann Lee, who in 1774 led her followers to the Colonies. Shakers believed in communal ownership of property, celibacy, and isolation from the secular world. The sect peaked around 1840, with nearly 6,000 adherents in 18 communities. By 1987 Shaker membership had dwindled to about a dozen people. Their legacy of inventiveness can be found in the washing machine, the clothespin, and the circular saw.

The ascetic Shakers rejected ornamentation and intricacy in design; as Lee's successor Joseph Meachum put it: "All things ought to be made according to their order and use.… Plainness and simplicity in word and deed is becoming the people of God." Adapting these principles to prevailing designs, Shakers stripped away any of the superfluity that could disrupt efficiency. By reducing furniture and household objects to their basic forms, its members invented a distinctly modern look 100 years before the Bauhaus, the design school that had as its slogan "Form follows function."

Radio's highly rated mystery show *The Shadow* had countless fan clubs and its own best-selling magazine. In pursuit of criminals, the Shadow was "never seen, only heard, as haunting to a superstitious mind as a ghost."

Shakers hung their chairs on the walls so that rooms would be uncluttered and easy to clean. Baskets, such as the one at right, were once strictly utilitarian but are now prized for their beauty.

When this figurehead from a British ship was bought by Americans, she was given a U.S. flag.

# SHIPS ⚓ BOATS

*America began as a seafaring nation, and our affection for ships—particularly sailing vessels—runs deep.*

## FLYING CLOUD
During the Gold Rush, the *Flying Cloud* carried passengers from the East Coast around Cape Horn to the shores of California. The vessel twice made this perilous journey in just 89 days.

## U.S.S. CONSTITUTION
*Constitution* gained the name "Old Ironsides" in the War of 1812, when a heavy shot from a British man-of-war bounced off her thick oaken sides.

## AMERICA
The first America's Cup was held in 1851. In that race, this 100-foot schooner outsailed England's best yacht, thus initiating one of sport's longest winning streaks.

### CLERMONT

In 1807 Robert Fulton's paddle-wheel steamboat, the *Clermont,* traveled 150 miles up the Hudson River in 30 hours, helping to usher in the age of powered navigation.

### CHARLES W. MORGAN

This handsome whaler (shown as a model, left, and in scrimshaw, above) can be visited today at the Seaport Museum in Mystic, Connecticut.

### S.S. UNITED STATES

The fastest luxury liner ever built, the S.S. *United States* made her maiden voyage across the Atlantic in 1952. However, even at an average speed of 35 knots, she was no match for the jet airplane, which forced many of the stately transatlantic steamers into retirement.

Theda Bara starred in *Cleopatra* in 1917. One of the great silent-film stars, Bara created an aura of mystery by claiming to be the love child of an artist and by surrounding herself with snakes and human skulls.

## SILENT MOVIES

Piano chords pulsate as ardent hero carries swooning damsel to their bower. "My Beloved—At Last!" reads the title card, but horrors—what are her luscious lips saying? "Drop me, ya big ape, and I'll kill ya!" The silents were a feast for lip-readers. Subtitles conveyed everything from simple time lapse ("Came the Dawn ...") to succinct plot summary ("The Man Who Stole Her Father's Fortune Returns After 20 Years—'Call Me Uncle,'") and steamy commentary ("Passion, That Furious Taskmaster, Strikes Without Warning"). Occasionally, the captions got carried away. In one film, silent star Ramon Navarro, sweetheart clasped to bosom, canoes down the raging rapids. Subtitle: "Down the Virgin Falls."

The average silent consisted of about six 10-minute reels; when a projector broke down, a slide announced: "One Minute, Please." Other slides requested that ladies remove their hats, that gentlemen not drop peanut shells or spit on the floor, and that local businesses be patronized. Favorite piano accompaniments included "Poor Butterfly," "The William Tell Overture" (for exciting chase scenes), as well as staccato "Indian" music for Westerns. Some movies came with entire scores, but most pianists had to wing it. After the picture, you might hear "When You Come to the End of a Perfect Day" as the slide bade the audience "Good Night."

## SILICON VALLEY

California's Silicon Valley, a 25-mile-long valley that runs between Palo Alto and San Jose, has been the center of the computer industry since the 1960s. Home to industrial giants like Hewlett-Packard and Intel, "the Valley" takes its name from the element silicon, which is used to make microprocessor chips—the "brains" of computers and electronics.

The microprocessor chip, a piece of silicon smaller than a fingernail, can hold up to 100,000 transistors. It is these transistors that provide memory, complete the required functions, and handle the flow of data. The first microprocessor chips could handle between 50,000 and 100,000 functions per second; the latest generation of chips can manage up to 66 million functions per second.

These technological advances have created a unique business culture in which computer know-how is essential and a vision is more important than a formal education. The wizards of computer engineering are a new breed of employee, often working at night and shunning suits and ties for jeans and T-shirts. It's not all that unusual for a 30-year-old to be a multimillionaire—or a former multimillionaire.

This culture has spread to other areas, usually around universities, where brainpower and new ideas abound. Despite the attractions of other high-tech centers, such as North Carolina's Research Triangle, Oregon's Silicon Forest, and Manhattan's Silicon Alley, people still flock to California to cash in on the next technological innovation.

Because of their tiny size, microprocessor chips (above, shown enlarged; left, shown actual size) are used in everything from watches and video games to cash registers and gas pumps.

## SILLY PUTTY

In 1949 Peter Hodgson, a former advertising copywriter, realized that a useless silicone-based "bouncing putty" invented by General Electric in 1944 would make a great toy. He sold some through a toy store catalog, then named it Silly Putty, packaged it in plastic eggs, and sold it to Neiman Marcus and a Doubleday bookshop. In 1950, soon after Hodgson and his product were profiled in *The New Yorker*, people across the nation were rolling, stretching, bouncing, and using Silly Putty to pick up and distort newspaper photos and cartoons. *Apollo 8* astronauts reached for the familiar plastic egg of goo when they wanted to fasten down weightless tools during their spaceflight. Today Silly Putty has been joined by other pliable playthings, such as Goop and Slime.

## SIMON, NEIL

"People are always coming up to me and saying, 'Thanks for the good times,'" says Neil Simon. After 30 years and more than 20 Broadway hits, Simon has brought the good times to millions of theatergoers. Finding the humor in everyday situations is Simon's forte. His most famous play, *The Odd Couple*, in which the fastidious Felix moves in with his slovenly friend Oscar, had audiences rolling in the aisles.

In his early years, Simon sharpened his wit by working as a jokesmith for Sid Caesar's *Your Show of Shows*, and he learned his craft from such comic greats as Mel Brooks, Woody Allen, Jackie Gleason, and Phil Brooks. After *Barefoot in the Park* clinched his reputation as Broadway's rising star, he wrote hit after hit, including *Biloxi Blues* and *Lost in Yonkers*. He won four Tony Awards, two Emmys, and one Pulitzer Prize. Simon likens his creative process to playing a pinball machine, with ideas "bouncing off one neuron to another." He never knows if he has a hit until he hears the audience laughing and applauding on opening night.

## SIMPSONS

In December 1989 the Fox network presented an animated series about a "messed-up American family." With its smart-aleck, satirical attitude and its anything-goes spirit, *The Simpsons* soon broke into the Top 10, making it the first successful prime-time cartoon since *The Flintstones* went off the air some 24 years earlier.

Beer-bellied belcher Homer Simpson works in a nuclear power plant; his blue-haired, gravel-voiced wife, Marge, makes excuses for him; world-weary eight-year-old Lisa plays the saxophone; and baby Maggie silently gnaws on her pacifier. But it is Bart, the rebellious preadolescent son, whose mischievous antics have taken the nation by storm. Bart has a knack for finding trouble—whether he is at home, school, or even church. The secret of *The Simpsons*'s appeal? According to creator Matt Groening, it's that "you can still love the people who drive you crazy."

*The Odd Couple*, a TV series based on the Neil Simon play, starred Jack Klugman (left) as Oscar and Tony Randall as Felix. Oscar the slob and Felix the neat-freak had been ousted by wives fed up with their excesses.

The Simpsons (clockwise from left: Homer, Marge, Lisa, and Bart) live in Springfield, as did the Anderson family of *Father Knows Best*. The similarities end there.

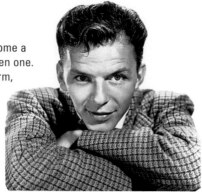

Frank Sinatra's decision to become a professional singer was a sudden one. After seeing Bing Crosby perform, Sinatra declared that he was "going to be a singer." He then quit his job and started working with local bands.

## SINATRA, FRANK

As a skinny kid with big ears, seemingly vulnerable Frank Sinatra touched the hearts of bobby-soxers, who swarmed to hear him sing at the Paramount Theater in New York. As he matured, his light baritone deepened, and his interpretive skills at the microphone made him the leading popular singer of the 1940s and '50s. Whether melancholy, as in "One for My Baby," or buoyant, as in "Come Fly with Me," Sinatra chose his models wisely: Billie Holiday and Mabel Mercer for interpretation, Tommy Dorsey for his controlled legato, and Bing Crosby for his conversational intimacy.

Born in the Italian section of Hoboken, New Jersey, in 1915, Sinatra started singing in the Demarest High Glee Club. He won an amateur radio contest and toured with The Hoboken Four. On his first job, at the Rustic Cabin in Englewood, bandleader Harry James heard and hired him; Sinatra then made his first records. By late 1942 he was a hot property, having spent two years with Tommy Dorsey's band and had his first number one hit, "I'll Never Smile Again." Going on his own, he played the Paramount and had a regular guest spot on radio's *Your Hit Parade*.

As wartime audiences aged and styles changed, Sinatra's popularity waned; he faced voice problems, management trouble, and divorce. Resurrected by his performance in the film *From Here to Eternity*, Sinatra soon had a new recording contract. His other films include *The Man with the Golden Arm*, *High Society*, and *The Manchurian Candidate*. After a brief retirement, "Ole Blue Eyes" returned in 1973, a tad gruffer but still America's top storyteller of song.

Proving that he is multi-talented, Frank Sinatra won an Oscar for best supporting actor in the 1953 film *From Here to Eternity*, which starred Donna Reed (above left) and Montgomery Clift (above right). Now in his eighties, Sinatra is still singing. Said longtime friend Bing Crosby, "There is only one guy who's the greatest singer in the whole world. His name is Sinatra."

## SINGING COWBOYS

No prairie has been more overgrazed than the American West of popular imagination, and no figure has been more glorified than the singing cowboy-hero in a ten-gallon hat. He was a man who rode the open range on a handsome horse and who was as likely to pull out a guitar as a gun.

Audiences loved the twangy sounds of songs like "Tumbling Tumbleweeds," "The Red River Valley," "The Yellow Rose of Texas," and "My Little Lady," with their images of wide-open spaces and starry skies, as well as poignant tales of loneliness, unrequited love, and death.

Early folk songs were originally sung by authentic cowboys. Carl T. Sprague, who made albums for RCA Victor records, learned his songs from his uncle on their Texas ranch; Jules Verne Allen, who sang on the radio in the '20s and '30s, was a working cowboy who covered the territory between the Rio Grande and Montana. But it was ex-railroad employee Jimmie Rodgers who made Western folk songs famous. Gene Autry started his singing career imitating Rodgers's style, then went on to star in more than 100 Western B movies. Another famous singing cowboy was migrant worker Leonard Slye, later known as Roy Rogers.

## SINGING TELEGRAMS

According to George P. Oslin, a former Western Union public relations director, it was he who arranged for the first singing telegram by talking an operator named Lucille Lipps into crooning birthday greetings to singer Rudy Vallee in 1933. The stunt was covered in Walter Winchell's column, and soon operators and uniformed messengers across the country were singing messages for all sorts of occasions.

Singing-message services are still popular. In many American cities it's possible to find musically inclined entrepreneurs who will deliver a message while dressed like a gorilla or a clown, or even while belly dancing.

## SITTING BULL

A revered Hunkpapa Sioux leader and medicine man, Sitting Bull was renowned for his courage in battle and considered "unfriendly" by the U.S. government. In 1876 he ignored an order to move his people onto a reservation, which led to the fateful encounter with General Custer at Little Bighorn. Before the fighting began, Sitting Bull had a vision of "dead soldiers ... falling upside down into camp," and his people believed that it was his "medicine making" that had led to their victory. (Although he led the Indians who fought Custer, he himself did not take up arms in the battle.)

Sitting Bull fled to Canada, not to return until 1881, when he was promised amnesty. He appeared in Buffalo Bill's Wild West show in 1885 but continued to resist white demands to sell the Sioux lands. On December 15, 1890, he was arrested on the trumped-up charge of causing an Indian rebellion by spreading word of a "Ghost Dance." In the scuffle that followed, Sitting Bull was shot and killed, ending forever the power of the great Sioux nation.

Resenting the government's image of Indians, Sitting Bull asked, "What treaty that the whites ever made with us ... have they kept? What white man can say I ever stole his lands or ... his money? Yet they say I am a thief."

## SKATEBOARDS

The California surfer who first attached rollerskate wheels to a piece of wood in the 1950s just wanted more "hang" time. He certainly never imagined that a sport inspired by his contraption would become a way of life for millions of kids. And who knew that the skateboarding superstars of the '80s would goofy-foot their way to doing movie stunt work and commercial endorsements?

Such technical innovations as smooth urethane wheels have made skateboarding more of an art form than a mode of transportation. Skaters can be seen doing flips and wheelies and even performing ballet routines on their boards. With practice, even a gawky teenager can make his board levitate over obstacles (an ollie) or slide down handrails (a railslide), among other amazing tricks. Because of the resulting danger to life and limb, skateboarders are urged to wear helmets and knee and elbow pads. And because of the danger to unwary pedestrians, "No Skateboarding" signs are now posted in parking lots and on sidewalks around the country.

Although skateboarders are a common sight today, there was a time when the sport was discouraged. In the 1960s some cities went so far as to confiscate skateboards, calling them a public nuisance.

Skelton was a master of pantomime. He became famous for his doughnut-dunking routine, in which he imitated the sloppy dunker, the fussy dunker, the well-mannered dunker, and the slosher.

Slinky, a simple "walking" spring, has captivated kids since the 1940s. Physicists have used the toy to demonstrate the properties of waves, and it has even been sent into space.

## SKELTON, RED

In the 1960s Red Skelton was America's most beloved clown. Millions tuned in to *The Red Skelton Show* every Tuesday night on CBS to watch him transform himself into such characters as Freddie the Freeloader, Clem Kaddidlehopper, the Mean Widdle Kid, and Cauliflower McPugg. Skelton would stop at nothing to get a belly laugh: he'd make faces, babble baby talk, or fall on his face. Even if the gags fell flat or he blew a line, he'd make us laugh about that: "If you send in three cents, we'll mail you a picture of that joke," he once ad-libbed. We were his partners in lunacy, and we loved it. Beyond the guffaws, though, viewers were drawn to the heart that Skelton was not afraid to wear on his sleeve. Anyone watching his famous (and often repeated) pantomime of a war veteran at a July 4th parade laughed heartily, but with sadness. His poignant sign-off, "Good-bye and God Bless," closed the show for the last time in 1971.

## SLANG

If you can remember when you first heard about an *attitude*, an *ego trip*, or someone who *freaked out*, you were *with it* in the 1960s. *Big daddy*, *sad sack*, and *jitterbug* take some of us back to the 1940s; *groovy* to the 1930s; and *bimbo*, *fence*, and *big shot* to the 1920s. Surprisingly, many slang expressions we think of as contemporary go way back: *kick the bucket* to the Civil War; *hush money* and *duds* to colonial times; and *beat it* all the way back to Shakespeare.

Slang is defined by J. E. Lighter, editor of the *Random House Historical Dictionary of American Slang*, as "novel-sounding synonyms for standard words and phrases." Coined by such groups as students, servicemen, athletes, musicians, and ethnic minorities, slang provides a way of being *in*. The colorful expressions are understood at first only by members of the group and are often irreverent. Slang words with a broader appeal and usefulness tend to endure, and some, such as *jazz*, *snob*, *bellhop*, and *blizzard*, eventually become accepted as correct English. Others that merely reflect a passing attitude, like *the bee's knees*, *skirt*, *wolf*, and *the cat's pajamas*, fade away.

Some 10 percent of words that Americans know are slang, and Americans, particularly men, use slang more than any other people. This may not be as bad as some purists might think, for slang is, according to renowned editor H. L. Mencken, "the most powerful of all the stimulants that keep language alive and growing."

## SLINKY

The recently introduced plastic Slinkys are colorful indeed, but most Slinky aficionados prefer the classic metal version, which clicks and chimes as you spill waves of coils from hand to hand, roll it on the floor, or make it perform its most famous stunt: descending stairs.

The Slinky, patented in 1947, was perfected by Richard James, a shipyard engineer who invented things in his spare time. His wife, Betty, named it Slinky after trying to find another word for *slithering*. At first it didn't sell. But when Betty persuaded Gimbel's department store to display the toy for one evening, their complete supply of 400 Slinkys was sold within 90 minutes.

## SMITH, KATE

"I'm big and I'm fat, but I have a voice, and when I sing—boy, I sing all over." The "Songbird of the South" weighed 235 pounds, had a hearty laugh, and no sex appeal. But from her trademark greeting, "Hello, everybody, this is Kate Smith," to her tagline, "Thanks for listenin'"—boy, everybody tuned in all over. After her radio debut, she made 15,000 broadcasts and 3,000 recordings, and she received 25 million fan letters. Her best-known song was "God Bless America"; she acquired exclusive rights to sing it on the air from the composer, Irving Berlin. During World War II Smith's honest and patriotic image raised millions of dollars for war bonds. In 1982 she was awarded the Presidential Medal of Freedom.

## SMITHSONIAN

It was America's great fortune that the nephew of English scientist James Smithson died childless. In that event, as Smithson's will stipulated, his estate was to be used to create a scientific institution in the United States devoted to "the increase and diffusion of knowledge." Congress didn't know quite what to make of such a gift, and it didn't act on the bequest until 1846—eight years after receiving Smithson's fortune, which totaled more than $500,000. In 1855 the Smithsonian's first home, the red sandstone building known as the "Castle," finally opened.

Today the Smithsonian has developed into a museum complex with a collection unrivaled in the world. Its cache of more than 140 million items is so large that its many buildings can exhibit only 1 percent of the museum's holdings at any given time. Some of the treasures in the "nation's attic" include the oldest American gunboat in existence, the first U.S. telegraph, the first cotton gin, the Wright brothers' *Kitty Hawk Flyer*, the ruby slippers from *The Wizard of Oz*, 16 million postage stamps, the Hope Diamond, and the *Apollo 11* command module. The National Zoo, also part of the Smithsonian Institution, is home to a famous giant panda.

Most of the Smithsonian museums are situated along the National Mall in Washington, D.C., including the National Air and Space Museum, the Natural History Museum, the American History Museum, the Arts and Industries Building, and six art museums. Other Smithsonian sites are the Museum of the American Indian and the Cooper Hewitt Museum in New York City and the Whipple Observatory in Tucson, Arizona.

Millions of devoted listeners tuned in to *The Kate Smith Show*, which began in 1930 and opened with Smith's signature song, "When the Moon Comes Over the Mountain." Smith and Jack Benny were the only two on radio with contracts that could not be canceled.

The "Castle" (top) now houses a visitors center. At the National Museum of American History are a printing telegraph (above) and a reproduction of the first incandescent lamp (right), both invented by Thomas Edison.

Smokey Bear, named for former fire chief "Smokey Joe" Martin, is recognized by about 98 percent of Americans.

According to a poll conducted by Hostess Cakes, Americans feel guiltier about snacking than about cheating on their taxes or lying to a friend. Pictured below are some of our guiltiest pleasures.

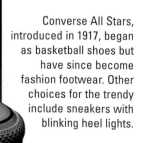

Converse All Stars, introduced in 1917, began as basketball shoes but have since become fashion footwear. Other choices for the trendy include sneakers with blinking heel lights.

## SMOKEY BEAR

America's most popular bear has his own zip code (20252), the better to handle the 75,000 or so letters that arrive for him each year. Smokey has been guarding our forests from careless humans since 1944, when the campaign to stamp out forest fires heated up owing to the importance of lumber to the war effort. At the behest of the U.S. Forest Service, the Advertising Council went to work on a symbol for forest-fire prevention; after considering a deer, a squirrel, and a flat-tailed beaver, the council finally settled on a bear.

Smokey's commanding radio voice was created by an announcer who spoke into a metal wastebasket. Since his introduction, Smokey has touched millions and has helped to reduce the area of burn by some 30 million acres annually. In 1950, when rangers rescued a tiny cub from a New Mexico forest fire, the bear became the living symbol of Smokey.

## SNACK FOOD

Among the crunchy, salty snacks Americans crave are pretzels, cheese curls, and tortilla chips. Most popular of all, however, are potato chips: we buy nearly $5 billion worth of them each year. According to legend, Cornelius Vanderbilt was dining at the Moon Lake Lodge in Saratoga Springs, New York, one night in 1853. The french fries were too thick for his liking, so Vanderbilt sent them back—several times. In retaliation, chef George Crum prepared a batch of fries so thin and crispy that they couldn't be eaten with a fork. Vanderbilt loved the new finger food, and the Saratoga chips, as they were then called, became a favorite of Northeasterners. With the invention of industrial potato peelers and slicers in the 1920s, the rest of the nation discovered potato chips. In the '50s the chips found their ideal companion: California dip, a combination of onion soup mix and sour cream. In the '70s potato chips were challenged by Pringles, saddle-shaped chips made of potato flour and water, which come stacked neatly in cardboard tubes.

Chips are the couch potato's snack of choice, but for many schoolkids, there's nothing that tops a Twinkie. The little golden cakes, injected with "creme" filling through three holes on the bottom, were invented in 1930 by James A. Dewar, a Chicago businessman. Around the same time, a Nebraska teenager named Edwin Perkins was hard at work in his mother's kitchen, concocting a drink he called Flavor Smack. It's now known as Kool-Aid, and Americans consume no less than 750 million gallons of it each year.

## SNEAKERS

With rubber soles so quiet as to suggest stealth, sneakers crept into the American wardrobe around 1868 as an all-around recreation shoe, their laced canvas uppers offering a lightweight, "breathable" alternative to leather. The versatile footwear's popularity soared in 1916, when U.S. Rubber introduced Keds. (The name is a takeoff on *ped*, a Latin prefix for "foot." Also considered were "Peds" and "Veds.") Goodrich's P.F. Flyers and Converse All Stars soon followed.

De rigueur for James Dean and other postwar rebels, pedestrian gym shoes were outpaced during the '70s fitness craze by myriad new sport-specific styles that were biomechanically engineered for top performance. Since then, many high-tech—and pricey—models, including one sneaker that can be "pumped up" with the press of a button for extra support, have stepped from the playing field to the fashion arena as runaway status statements.

## SOAPBOX DERBY

The All-American Soap Box Derby, an annual race of gravity-powered homemade cars driven by teenagers, began in 1934. News photographer Myron Scott conceived the idea after watching boys roll down a hill on crude wooden vehicles with baby-buggy wheels. For the first few years, the derby was run on a city street, but in 1936 it acquired its own "Derby Downs," a 953.9-foot sloping, three-lane concrete track next to the Akron, Ohio, airport. Derby contestants have always been required to build their own cars, although cars have been sold in kit form since 1976. The combined weight of the car and the driver is limited, and contestants seek advantage by weight distribution, steering skill, and the shape and finish of their car. Corporate sponsors of the derby award scholarships to the winners. In 1994 a 13-year-old girl became the first two-time winner in history.

## SOAP OPERAS

A Chicago schoolteacher named Irna Phillips created the first "true-to-life" daytime drama in 1930, a 15-minute segment on local radio called *Painted Dreams*. Almost immediately, soapsuds manufacturers, wishing to reach female listeners, began buying or sponsoring most of the new shows, which were soon known as soap operas. Phillips's later radio show, *The Guiding Light*, moved to television in 1952; by 1970 nearly 20 soaps aired on television daily, including *As the World Turns* and *Another World*, both owned by Proctor & Gamble, and *All My Children*. In 1973 a more glamorous soap, *The Young and the Restless*, was introduced in order to attract a younger audience.

Viewers who eavesdrop on daytime television's most intimate moments (love, villainy, mayhem, and ever-steamier sex) soon become wrapped up in the drama. Some fans are so devoted that they send sympathy cards when a character dies. Those who miss an episode can consult "fanzines," such as *Soap Opera Digest*, or even join a chat group in cyberspace. But they needn't worry too much: few problems are resolved at the end of an hour... or a week... or a year.

Part auto racing, part downhill sledding, soapbox derbies are serious contests. Some winners put as many as 1,500 hours of work into their racers.

In 1981 the largest soap audience ever (14 million) tuned in to watch Luke and Laura's wedding on *General Hospital*. Diehard fans can stay current via a host of supermarket magazines.

The soda fountain was the place for hanging out, as well as for ice cream sodas and, later, for sundaes and floats.

## SODA FOUNTAINS

In the 1800s drugstores began selling soda water, a tonic recommended for a range of ailments. People soon learned that the cool, bubbly water, often flavored with sweet syrups and cream, was as refreshing for the healthy as for the ailing. In 1874 Robert Green, a soda fountain operator, ran out of cream and slipped some vanilla ice cream into the sodas. Sales soared, and soda fountains became popular gathering places. When clergy members decided that sipping bubbly water on the Sabbath was sinful, soda fountains began serving "sundaes"—concoctions of ice cream and syrup without soda water. In the 1920s soda fountains benefited from another crusade against pleasure: Prohibition, which brought men to the soda shops. However, the shops were mainly the territory of teens, who would while away hours nursing a soda and watching the "soda jerk" work.

## SOD HOUSES

Free land offered by the Homestead Act of 1862 lured thousands of settlers onto the plains. Lumber and rock were scarce, so they built homes out of the only resource available: sod. Cut into blocks called "Nebraska marble," the sod was stacked to make walls, and the cracks were filled with dirt. Doors, windows, and rafters were ordered through the mail or bought in faraway towns. The houses were warm in winter, cool in summer, and withstood fire and windstorms. But, as many a prairie wife learned, they had their drawbacks. The ceilings and walls shed dirt, not to mention snakes, mice, and bugs. After a heavy rain, the roofs leaked so much that women were forced to hold umbrellas while they cooked.

A soddy could be put up in a week and was dirt cheap to build. As soon as settlers could afford a frame house, the humble soddy became a barn for livestock.

## SONDHEIM, STEPHEN

In 1962 Stephen Sondheim, the lyricist of *West Side Story* and *Gypsy*, tried his hand at writing both music and lyrics for *A Funny Thing Happened on the Way to the Forum*. The musical, which placed old vaudeville routines in the even older setting of ancient Rome, struggled through its pre-Broadway tryouts until Sondheim came up with "Comedy Tonight," an opening number that told the audience just what to expect and ensured the show's success. "Something familiar, something peculiar..." the song began; since then, Sondheim's audiences have come to expect the latter.

They've visited a Burlesque theater filled with ghosts (*Follies*) and a Freudian forest filled with fairy-tale characters (*Into the Woods*). They've watched a quack psychiatrist turn sane people into loonies (*Anyone Can Whistle*) and a murderous barber turn people into meat pies (*Sweeney Todd*). They've seen a musical written entirely in waltz time (*A Little Night Music*) and a musical that moved backward in time (*Merrily We Roll Along*). About the only thing they haven't seen is a Sondheim musical that plays it safe.

Bernadette Peters (left) has starred in several plays by Sondheim (right), including *Sunday in the Park with George*. Based on a painting by Georges Seurat, the play won the Pulitzer Prize in 1985.

## SOONERS

On April 22, 1889, some 60,000 settlers lined up for the first great land rush in the West. President Harrison had recently authorized white settlement of unoccupied parts of the Indian Territory, now called Oklahoma. At stake that day was a 2-million-acre tract called the Unassigned Lands, and whoever got there first could claim a town lot or 160 acres of farmland for a mere $15. Troops patrolled the borders to keep out those who tried to "jump the gun," but many of these "sooners" managed to sneak in ahead of the starting time and stake a claim.

At noon a shot was fired, and hordes of would-be landowners rushed across the plains on horseback, in wagons—even on bicycle and on foot. The land was snapped up, and towns like Oklahoma City and Guthrie sprang to life. Although most of the sooners lost their claims, they gave Oklahoma its nickname: the "Sooner State."

Known as the "March King," Sousa (center) composed 136 marches, 12 operettas (one included the hit *El Capitán*), 11 band suites, and 70 songs. He even invented an instrument, the sousaphone.

## SOUSA, JOHN PHILIP

"The Stars and Stripes Forever," wrote the *Philadelphia Public Ledger* in 1897, "is stirring enough to rouse the American eagle from its crag, and set him to shriek exultantly." The song became America's most famous patriotic march. Other Sousa march favorites were "The Washington Post," "The Thunderer," and "Semper Fidelis," which became the official march of the U.S. Marine Corps.

Sousa was born in Washington, D.C., in 1854. He studied brass instruments and apprenticed with the U.S. Marine Band for seven years, but his preferred instrument was the violin. Nevertheless, at age 25, when he was offered a job as director of the U.S. Marine Band, he accepted. Twelve years later he resigned to form his own concert band, which made four tours of Europe and a world tour and became what has been called the most celebrated band in history.

*Grits* is the Southern term for hominy (dried corn with the hulls removed) ground into meal. It is often boiled and eaten for breakfast—drowned sinfully in butter and syrup—or served as a side dish.

## SOUTHERN COOKING

Southern cooking produces a wealth of tantalizing delights meant to be slowly savored in good company. Honeyed ham and fried chicken are Sunday staples, but there are tasty dishes that include almost anything that swims, flies, or walks. Catfish is breaded, ducks are baked, beef and pork are barbecued, crabs become gumbo, and squirrels are turned into a tasty stew. Southerners also like their sweets: pies are stuffed with home-grown pecans and peaches, and local berries are served with buttery pound cakes.

While each Southern cook has treasured family recipes, and each geographical area has its specialties, corn is a constant. It's turned into bread, muffins, fritters, cornmeal sticks, and dumplings. Corn grits are served with butter at breakfast and with gravy at every other meal. As humorist Roy Blount, Jr., says, "True grits. / More grits, / Fish, grits and collards. / Life is good where grits are swallered."

Crayfish, also called crawfish or crawdads, are a staple of Cajun cooking. The Deep South also fosters an appetite for okra and sweet potatoes.

NASA's Hubble Space Telescope (left) took this picture (above) of gaseous pillars in the Eagle Nebula. The eerie columns of cool hydrogen gas and dust act like incubators for new stars.

## SPACE EXPLORATION

For centuries humankind has marveled at the mysteries of outer space, and today we are using science to investigate them. Despite the mind-boggling distances involved, space exploration presents an irresistible challenge, for in space we may be able to discover the origins of our universe.

Our knowledge of the cosmos has been growing steadily as unmanned space probes fly deeper and deeper into space, transmitting data back to Earth. For example, *Pioneer 11*, launched in 1973, flew by Jupiter in 1974 and reported unexpectedly strong radiation. The probe then continued on toward Saturn, where it discovered a ring and two moons that no astronomer had ever seen before.

Despite the bad publicity that the Hubble Space Telescope received for its initially faulty optics, this technological wonder, launched in 1990, has succeeded in providing dazzling pictures of distant galaxies. Among its discoveries was the first conclusive evidence of the existence of black holes—immense high-gravity areas that suck in everything that passes near them, including light. Scientists are fighting for funds to support continued space exploration, including a base on the moon, a manned mission to Mars, a Pluto flyby, and ambitious, decade-long projects that might determine whether there is life in those disks of dust around faraway stars that the Hubble telescope has discovered.

## SPAM

Spam isn't really "mystery meat." Its name is a shortened version of "spiced ham," and that's just what it is: a simple combination of ground pork shoulder, ground ham, salt, sugar, water, and sodium nitrate. It was introduced by the Hormel Foods Corporation in 1937, just in time for it to become a mainstay of the diets of World War II troops, allies, and civilians, who appreciated its remarkable ability to keep, without refrigeration, as long as the can stayed sealed.

Spam's popularity didn't end after the war. Some soldiers had learned to like the stuff, and because it is fully pre-cooked, homemakers embraced it as a convenience food. During the Cold War, stocks of Spam were stashed in fallout shelters. Spam may never become chic, but the introduction of Spam Lite has made it healthier fare, and the fact that it stays fresh makes it an essential for camping trips.

Although Spam is often the butt of jokes, 5 billion cans have been sold since 1937. In South Korea, the highly prized luncheon meat is sold in fancy gift boxes.

## SPCA

Americans are animal lovers. The country's oldest humane society, the American Society for the Prevention of Cruelty to Animals (ASPCA), was founded in 1866, 10 years before the founding of the American Society for the Prevention of Cruelty to Children. The ASPCA launched an ambulance service for injured horses two years before the country's first ambulance service for people was formed. Its agents have the authority of police when enforcing humane laws. Local

SPCAs (*SPCA* is an umbrella term for any society concerned with the well-being of animals) run animal hospitals and provide humane education and animal birth control programs.

Other important humane societies include the Humane Society of the United States (HSUS), the largest organization of its kind in the nation, and the American Humane Association (AHA). Their activities on behalf of animals range from saving creatures endangered by natural disasters to promoting vegetarianism. The AHA publishes a list of "unacceptable" films, which includes *Lawrence of Arabia*, during the filming of which horses and camels were harshly treated.

Many humane societies promote the adoption of homeless animals, including cats and dogs and even hamsters and guinea pigs. Some also offer foster-care services and dog-training classes.

## SPECIAL OLYMPICS

Since 1968 the Special Olympics has been proving that participation in high-level sports can benefit everyone, regardless of ability or disability. Under its auspices, mentally retarded athletes from eight years old onward compete in 23 sports, from alpine skiing to aquatics, to taste not just the thrill of victory but also the exhilaration of personal achievement. The program's motto states: "Let me win. But if I cannot win, let me be brave in the attempt."

The Special Olympics was the brainchild of Eunice Kennedy Shriver, who grew up with a retarded sister and became a tireless advocate for the handicapped. "The mentally retarded must have champions of their cause," she wrote in 1962, "the more so because they are unable to provide their own." Guided by her compassion and commitment, the organization has evolved into an international entity with 1 million athletes and half a million volunteers in 146 countries. Besides hosting biennial world games, the Special Olympics sponsors year-round programs to promote fitness, fair play, and the opportunity to excel for the 190 million mentally disabled worldwide.

Eunice Kennedy Shriver started a day camp in her backyard for the mentally retarded; it grew to become the Special Olympics.

## SPELLING BEES

The auditorium is quiet as the child onstage begins to spell: "m-i-l-l-e-n-n-i-u-m." The judge nods, and the audience applauds. Another school-spelling-bee winner has been found. Ever since Noah Webster's *American Spelling Book* standardized American spelling in the 18th century, spelling bees have tested children and adults alike. They remained popular into the 20th century, and in 1925 the *Louisville Courier Journal* began a National Spelling Bee, which won the sponsorship of the Scripps Howard newspapers in 1939.

At local spelling bees, such words as *millennium*, *ecstasy*, *mausoleum*, *parenthetical*, and *recurred* are usually hard enough to separate the winner from the losers, but in national competition the words must be even tougher. Champions of the National Spelling Bee have earned their laurels for correctly spelling stumpers like *insouciant*, *vouchsafe*, *staphylococci*, *odontalgia*, *milieu*, *luge*, *Purim*, *psoriasis*, *sycophant*, and *elegiacal*.

Winner Scott Isaacs of Colorado slumps with relief after the tension of the final round. He correctly spelled *spoliator* to win the National Spelling Bee in 1989.

In *E.T.* Henry Thomas plays a 10-year-old who befriends a visitor from outer space. In one scene, alien and boy take a magical, moonlit bike ride (above).

Steven Spielberg (above) searches for the perfect camera angle. In *Indiana Jones and the Temple of Doom,* Harrison Ford (left) wields a giant machete.

In Steven Spielberg's *Jurassic Park,* an entrepreneur builds an amusement park on a remote tropical island, complete with live dinosaurs.

## SPIELBERG, STEVEN

Movie genius and head of a huge entertainment enterprise, Steven Spielberg has created several of the most successful films of all time. He began making movies in childhood, using a camera borrowed from his father, an electrical engineer. A self-styled "nerd" in high school, he used the camera to escape classroom pressures.

Spielberg was only 27 years old when he directed his first blockbuster, the suspense film *Jaws*. Not long afterward, he started his own production company. Spielberg's movie fantasies often rely on dazzling special effects, but they have a human dimension as well. In the cliffhanger *Raiders of the Lost Ark*, daring archaeologist Indiana Jones rescues the Ark of the Covenant from Nazi agents. The warmhearted *E.T. The Extra-Terrestrial* features an endearing alien who, with the help of his young friends, strives to get back to his own planet. In another spectacular movie, *Jurassic Park*, dinosaurs are resurrected from DNA found in amber. When the dinosaurs escape, human beings must run for their lives.

To some critics, Spielberg seemed like a talented child at play. Then came *Schindler's List*, the true story of a German businessman who saved thousands of Jews from Nazi extermination camps. *Schindler's List* won Academy Awards for best picture and best director and was called the finest film yet made about the Holocaust. Spielberg shot it in stark black and white. The project took 10 years—time, Spielberg said, he needed to grow up and face this dark side of history.

## SPIES

In America spies have always been with us. Without the help of a spy named John Honeyman, the ragged troops led by George Washington might not have surprised the Hessians during their Christmas revelry at Trenton, an event that turned the tide of the Revolution. A secret agent in James Fenimore Cooper's novel *The Spy* resembled Honeyman and enthralled early-19th-century readers with his exploits. Teenage Belle Boyd, who had passed valuable information on to Confederate officer Stonewall Jackson, was romanticized by the Civil War press. Julius and Ethel Rosenberg were accused of selling nuclear-bomb secrets to the Soviets and were executed in 1953. Forty years and a Cold War later, CIA agent Aldrich Ames tried to live like James Bond by using more than $1 million of KGB money. His personal spy thriller earned him a sentence of life in prison.

## SPOCK, DR.

Dr. Benjamin Spock's famous book, *Baby and Child Care*, is the second-best-selling book in history (the Bible is the first). Published in 1946, *Baby and Child Care* was the essential child-rearing manual for the postwar baby boom. Spock gave reassurance to anxious parents; the book's first words are "You know more than you think you do." He then went on to answer hundreds of questions about child development and raising children, with chapters on medical care, feeding, thumb sucking, toilet training, schools, and first aid. Critics claimed its emphasis on the child's psychological needs led to excessive permissiveness. But Spock's book usually just offers advice; parents are left to make their own decisions.

As the times have changed, so too has *Baby and Child Care*, which is published with revisions about every 10 years. Recent editions of the book have recognized the increased role of fathers and day-care centers in bringing up Baby.

## SPOON RIVER ANTHOLOGY

Deacon Taylor, a prohibitionist and upright citizen of Spoon River, was believed to have died from eating watermelon. Not true; he had cirrhosis of the liver from 30 years of noontime nipping. The unfortunate deacon is one of the 244 souls who speak to us from the Spoon River cemetery, where "The weak of will, the strong of arm, the clown, the boozer, the fighter / All, all are sleeping on the hill."

Edgar Lee Masters had never had a literary success before he wrote this collection of brief, free-verse monologues. They reveal the secret lives and thoughts—often at odds with their epitaphs—of the inhabitants of an apocryphal small Illinois town. "It takes life to love life," proclaims a character who was inspired by Masters's grandmother. The publication of *Spoon River Anthology* was a sensation, and it made more money than had any previous book of American poetry. In the late 1960s it was adapted as a theater piece interspersed with songs, and it endures as a favorite of school and community players.

## SPRINGSTEEN, BRUCE

With mournful, rambling lyrics about blue-collar life in small towns and long, fiery performances with his E Street Band, singer-songwriter Bruce Springsteen won an ardent following in the 1970s. After one of his concerts, one critic wrote, "I saw rock and roll's future, and its name is Bruce Springsteen." His third album, *Born to Run*, rose to number three on the charts, and cover stories in both *Time* and *Newsweek* touted him as the most influential new rock star.

Springsteen, who grew up on the New Jersey shore, began playing the guitar at age 13. He formed his own band while still in his teens. Working solo in New York's Greenwich Village, he was signed by Columbia. His early narrative style gave way to a terser, more dramatic rock approach, as in the song "Born to Run." His first number one album was *The River*. In 1984 *Born in the U.S.A.*, his most successful album, climbed to the top spot, stayed on the charts for more than two years, and sold some 15 million copies. *Live 1975–1985* also topped the charts. Springsteen participates in benefit concerts for Amnesty International, and he won an Oscar for writing the theme song for the 1993 movie *Philadelphia*.

Child-care expert Dr. Spock emphasized the fact that "every child is different, every parent is different, every illness or behavior problem is somewhat different from every other."

In 1915 many readers were shocked by the blunt treatment of sex and immorality in Edgar Lee Masters's *Spoon River Anthology*, yet the book sold extremely well.

A generation of fans has grown up with Bruce Springsteen, whose themes have ranged from youthful rebellion to mature introspection.

Today square dancing cuts across social boundaries: anyone willing to learn the many movements and don the right duds can join in the fun.

After being banned in Britain in 1963, Lenny Bruce (top) flashed a victory sign to his supporters. The movie *Richard Pryor Live on the Sunset Strip* (1982) showed Pryor (above) at his best. Jerry Seinfeld (right) entertained at the 1992 Emmy Awards.

## SQUARE DANCING

While dance fads have bowed in and out of fashion faster than the Texas two-step, one style has held the floor for 300 years: square dancing. Based on traditional Irish jigs and English reels that were brought to the colonies by settlers, square dancing flourished at barn raisings, husking bees, and church socials. At one time, a square dance was the most popular and eagerly anticipated opportunity for people in isolated communities to socialize and make merry.

Square dancing is defined not by footwork but by floor pattern: Four couples "square the set," then form an ever-changing kaleidoscope of figures prompted by the driving cadence of a caller. An opening chant of "Allemande left your corner maid, swing your partner and promenade" might set dancers to weaving a star or cloverleaf interspersed with sashays, twirls, and do-si-dos. Square dancing also includes round dances and line dances. The movements are traditionally performed to such toe-tapping tunes as "Turkey in the Straw" and "Oh, Susannah!" plucked out on a fiddle or banjo.

## STAND-UP COMICS

Funny just ain't what it used to be. Time was, all a comic had to do was stand on a stage and tell jokes. "Things were rough when I was a baby. No talcum powder!" joked Henny Youngman. Until the 1950s, American stand-up comedy was innocent: social issues were rarely mentioned, and no one was offended, except perhaps a mother-in-law.

Then came Mort Sahl. Audiences howled with delight as he skewered the sacred cows of '50s politics, often taking his topics directly from the newspaper: "I'm for capital punishment. You've got to execute people.... How else are they going to learn?" By the end of the decade, such comics as Shelley Berman had built successful careers by applying Sahl's comedy of reality to the basic irritations of daily life— like getting spinach caught between your teeth on a date or not getting all the pins out of a new shirt.

For Lenny Bruce, also known as "Dirty Lenny," this new freedom to tell the truth meant that nothing was off-limits. By finding humor in life's darkest corners, Bruce broke down the last barriers to social satire. Largely because of Bruce, stand-up comics like Richard Pryor and George Carlin found growing enthusiasm for their irreverence, which was punctuated by the frequent use of "words you can't say on TV."

But it was television that made in-your-face stand-up comedy such an immensely popular form of entertainment. In the 1980s cable stations that needed to fill airtime opened the door to comics of all stripes, drawing huge audiences in the process. Comedy clubs boomed in every major city across the country. With the runaway television success of former stand-up comics, such as Roseanne and Jerry Seinfeld, network sitcoms are now teeming with stand-ups, too.

## STARS AND STRIPES

*Stars and Stripes*, the army's newspaper, was launched on November 9, 1861, when Union soldiers seized a printing press in Bloomfield, Missouri, and published a sarcastic attack on the Confederates. Nineteen days later, Confederate prisoners in New Orleans responded with their own insult-filled *Stars and Stripes in Rebeldom*. During World War I *Stars and Stripes* was revived. Its staff, based in Paris, allowed no one above the rank of sergeant through the door.

During World War II the paper became famous for Bill Mauldin's cartoons of grubby soldier life. But Gen. George S. Patton thought that Mauldin's sloppy Willie and Joe characters were bad for morale. He was particularly incensed by a cartoon that showed a column of dejected and muddy German prisoners escorted by Joe, who looked just as downtrodden as they did. That cartoon went on to win a Pulitzer Prize in 1945. *Stars and Stripes* continues to be published in Germany and Japan for U.S. armed forces serving overseas.

## STAR-SPANGLED BANNER

September 13, 1814, found America at war. With Washington, D.C., still smoldering from British torches, the only thing standing between Baltimore and an English invasion was Fort McHenry. Francis Scott Key, a lawyer and part-time poet, was aboard a British schooner, negotiating the release of a prisoner, when the fort fell under attack. He was detained on the ship during the 25-hour bombardment and chronicled the siege. The poem he wrote focused on a massive banner flying above the fort. That banner was the American flag, and Key's poem, set to an English tavern song, became our national anthem in 1931. Since then, the "Star-Spangled Banner" has undergone its own bombardments by those who say it's too hard to sing and impossible to march to. Nevertheless, it continues to pass the goose-bump test.

## STAR TREK

*Star Trek* lasted for only 78 episodes between 1966 and '69, but it influenced two generations of "Trekkies" and inspired six movies, a children's cartoon, and three other TV programs. "Making entertainment history was the furthest thing from our minds," recalled William Shatner, who played Capt. James T. Kirk. "Back then, it was day-to-day survival."

Created by Gene Roddenberry and set in the 23rd century, *Star Trek* was rejected by CBS but was picked up by NBC. At various times the crew of the U.S.S. *Enterprise* fought invisible Romulan attackers, watched Mr. Spock fall under the spell of the Vulcan mating cycle, and fought a virus that broke down people's inhibitions.

*Star Trek* fans have become famous for their dedication to the show. One paid $9,350 at an auction for one of Kirk's phasers, which originally cost less than a dollar. Yearly conventions attract Trekkies from around the globe.

While in the army as a newspaper man, *Stars and Stripes* cartoonist Bill Mauldin often visited the front so his humor would ring true.

*"Now that ya mention it, Joe, it does sound like th' patter of rain on a tin roof."*

When Francis Scott Key saw, "...by the dawn's early light," the American flag still flying, he was inspired to write "The Defense of Fort McHenry," later renamed "The Star-Spangled Banner."

On an intergalactic mission, Capt. James T. Kirk, Dr. Leonard McCoy, and Mr. Spock were under orders "to boldly go where no man has gone before."

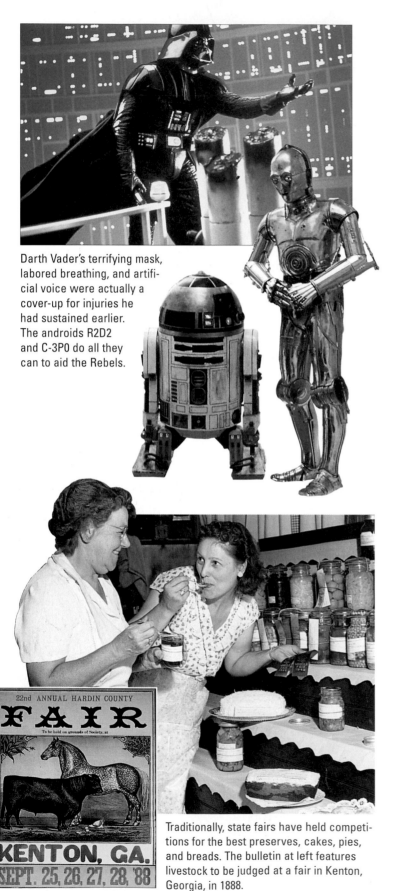

Darth Vader's terrifying mask, labored breathing, and artificial voice were actually a cover-up for injuries he had sustained earlier. The androids R2D2 and C-3PO do all they can to aid the Rebels.

22nd ANNUAL HARDIN COUNTY

FAIR

To be held on grounds of Society, at

KENTON, GA.

SEPT. 25, 26, 27, 28, '88

Traditionally, state fairs have held competitions for the best preserves, cakes, pies, and breads. The bulletin at left features livestock to be judged at a fair in Kenton, Georgia, in 1888.

## STAR WARS

The action takes place "a long time ago in a galaxy far, far away." All that stands between the crushing domination of the evil Empire and a free galaxy is the beautiful Princess Leia and her allies. To the rescue come Luke Skywalker, a young farm boy; his Jedi mentor, Obi-Wan Kenobi; a swashbuckling pirate, Han Solo; Chewbacca, Solo's shaggy first mate; and a pair of androids, the beeping and whistling R2-D2 and the fussy, easily frazzled C-3PO. A rapid-fire succession of action-packed scenes propels the narrative: alien riffraff swilling drinks in a cantina on the planet Tatooine, an infinitude of stars streaming past as spaceships make the jump to lightspeed, and deadly duels with "lightsabers"—a Jedi's weapon of choice.

Filmmaker George Lucas, whose previous titles included *American Graffiti* and *THX 1138*, directed the space epic. It was released in 1977 and has thus far generated two impressive sequels. In *The Empire Strikes Back*, Skywalker learns the ways of a Jedi Knight from the small and unassuming Jedi Master, Yoda; he also finds out the staggering truth about his father. *Return of the Jedi* features the crime lord Jabba the Hutt. On the Forest Moon of Endor, we meet its furry inhabitants, the huggable Ewoks. Ultimately, Han Solo destroys the force field that protects the evil Empire's seemingly impregnable space station, the second Death Star, thus bringing about its ultimate destruction. Lucas foresees other *Star Wars* sagas: May the Force be with him.

## STATE FAIR

In 1841 the New York Agricultural Society sponsored the first state fair. Over the years these gatherings multiplied in number and in importance. Their scope also increased as politicians took to the stump, farm-equipment manufacturers hawked their wares, and crowd-pleasing entertainments, such as horse races, were held. After the 1893 Chicago World's Fair set the standard, state fairs added midways complete with rides, games, and sideshows. Today the festivities are a beloved tradition, and each summer millions of Americans turn out for the wholesome, sometimes wacky fun.

## STATUE OF LIBERTY

For European immigrants arriving in New York Harbor, the Statue of Liberty was a welcoming beacon of freedom. A gift to America from France to celebrate the love of liberty shared by both nations, the statue was built with $400,000 donated by French citizens. Americans contributed nearly $300,000 for the 89-foot pedestal. Sculpted by Frédéric Auguste Bartholdi, the statue was so enormous that, even though its copper skin was hammered to a thickness of less than one-eighth of an inch, the figure weighed 225 tons. In order to keep it upright, an iron framework was designed by Gustave Eiffel, who would later create the Eiffel Tower. The statue was completed in 1884 in Paris, then taken apart and shipped to New York. "Liberty Enlightening the World" was dedicated on October 28, 1886, on Bedloe's Island, now called Liberty Island.

The Statue of Liberty became a major tourist attraction, and today it draws more than a million visitors a year. Sightseers can take an elevator to the top of the pedestal, where they can view the harbor, or they can climb a spiral staircase all the way to Liberty's crown. The moving inscription on the statue's pedestal, a sonnet by Emma Lazarus, closes with the words: "Give me your tired, your poor, / Your huddled masses yearning to breathe free, / The wretched refuse of your teeming shore. / Send these, the homeless, tempest-tost to me, / I lift my lamp beside the golden door!"

## STEICHEN, EDWARD

One of the greatest portrait photographers in the world, Edward Steichen produced compelling, elegant pictures of such celebrities as Greta Garbo, Charlie Chaplin, and George Gershwin for *Vogue* and *Vanity Fair*.

As director of photography at New York's Museum of Modern Art from 1947 to 1962, Steichen is probably best remembered for his 1955 exhibition, "The Family of Man." This collection of photographs showed humankind's joys and sorrows: a mother's tender love for her baby, small children walking hand in hand through the woods, families on picnics, and finally images of war and its inevitable heartrending grief. Indeed, every emotion common to humanity could be found in the show, which was so popular that it traveled worldwide. The companion book is still in print.

## STEIN, GERTRUDE

*The Autobiography of Alice B. Toklas* sold out within days of its publication in 1933, making its author, Gertrude Stein (whose autobiography it really was), an overnight celebrity. Everybody wanted to read her breezy account of the famous artists and intellectuals who gathered in her Left Bank salon in Paris. Of the apartment she shared with her lifelong companion, Alice Toklas, Stein wrote, "It was the heart of the movement." Pablo Picasso and Henri Matisse met there, and writers Ernest Hemingway, F. Scott Fitzgerald, Thorton Wilder, and Sherwood Anderson were frequent visitors.

In her life and in her work, Stein embraced the avant-garde. In most of the 500 titles she produced in her lifetime, for example, she would have nothing to do with customary punctuation, and her dizzying experiments with word repetitions left some readers baffled. "There is no there there" was her description of Oakland, California, her childhood home. Among her best-known works are *Three Lives*, a collection of stories; *Tender Buttons*, a book of experimental writing ("a verbal collage"); and a libretto for an opera, *Four Saints in Three Acts*, with music composed by Virgil Thomson.

The Statue of Liberty celebrated its centennial on October 28, 1986. From the tip of the torch to the foot, the figure measures 151 feet.

Edward Steichen was a painter as well as a photographer. His haunting photo of the Flatiron Building in New York City (right) is as evocative as an Impressionist painting.

Not one to feign modesty, Gertrude Stein proclaimed her own importance: "Think of the Bible and Homer, think of Shakespeare and think of me."

In the movie *The Grapes of Wrath,* Tom Joad (Henry Fonda), his mother (Jane Darwell), and his children (Shirley Mills and Darryl Hickman) pack up and head to California in search of a better life.

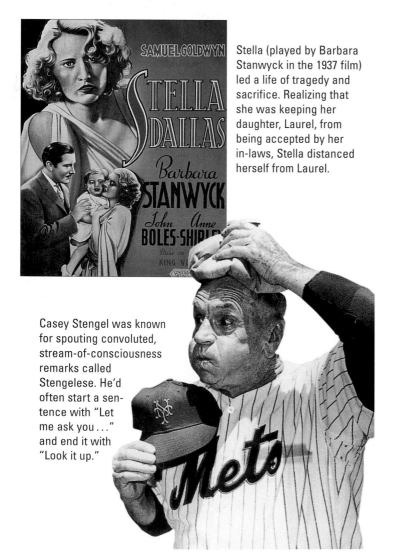

Stella (played by Barbara Stanwyck in the 1937 film) led a life of tragedy and sacrifice. Realizing that she was keeping her daughter, Laurel, from being accepted by her in-laws, Stella distanced herself from Laurel.

Casey Stengel was known for spouting convoluted, stream-of-consciousness remarks called Stengelese. He'd often start a sentence with "Let me ask you . . ." and end it with "Look it up."

## STEINBECK, JOHN

At the center of John Steinbeck's literary vision is the quiet dignity of the poor or oppressed. Even in defeat, his characters are heroic. The Nobel laureate's best-known book, *The Grapes of Wrath* (1939), is about a family's trek from the Oklahoma Dust Bowl to the migrant farmworkers' camps in California. Under the harsh conditions of the Great Depression, Tom Joad and his family suffer unremitting loss, but they are unified by their longing for a home and by a common belief in justice and decency. "Maybe . . . a fellow ain't got a soul of his own," Joad speculates at the end of this American classic, "but on'y a piece of a big one."

In *Of Mice and Men*, George is a migrant farmworker who is charged with the guardianship of Lennie, a mentally retarded giant. In spite of George's efforts, Lennie's life ends tragically. *Cannery Row* and its companion novel, *Sweet Thursday*, are about social outcasts, idlers, and nonconformists living near the canning factories on the Monterey peninsula. These dropouts are outrageously eccentric but harmless; and like all of Steinbeck's most memorable characters, they are generous, honest, and caring.

## STELLA DALLAS

"I would give up everything I own to make *Stella Dallas*," vowed Barbara Stanwyck in 1937. Others snickered at Louis B. Mayer's decision to make the old tearjerker, but our Babs knew a surefire part when she saw one. *Stella Dallas* started out as a 1922 best-seller by Olive Higgins Prouty. It became a play, then a successful silent film.

It's the story of good-hearted but uneducated Stella, who marries a blue blood. Alienated by her unrefined taste, he leaves her and their daughter, Laurel. Realizing that she's a social millstone, Stella withdraws from Laurel's life. She ends up standing outside in the rain, watching Laurel's classy wedding through a window. Gulp.

Stanwyck is unforgettable as Stella: all totsy curls, tacky prints, and jangling bangles, but she lost the Academy Award to Luise Rainer (ironic aftermath: Rainer disappeared, Stanwyck soared). The movie inspired a long-running radio soaper of the same name. The self-sacrificing mom was last seen in *Stella*, the 1990 update that starred Bette Midler.

## STENGEL, CASEY

As baseball's master impresario, Casey Stengel occupied center stage for more than five decades both as a player and as a manager. Managing losing teams in Brooklyn and Boston in the 1930s and '40s led Stengel to quip to his barber one day, "Don't cut my throat. I may want to do that myself later."

Although many baseball observers regarded his on-field antics as clownlike, he skippered the New York Yankees to 10 pennants in 12 years (1949–60), and his idiosyncratic managing methods won him grudging admiration. In New York he instituted a system of platooning his players, inserting them into the game when he considered it most propitious. Invariably, his hunches worked. Cut loose by the Yankees after the 1960 World Series because of his age, Stengel remarked, "I'll never make the mistake of being 70 again." Stengel returned two years later as manager of the expansion New York Mets, one of the worst teams ever, leading him to lament, "Can't anybody play this here game?"

The fabled "ten-gallon" hat refers to the Spanish *sombrero galón*, or "hat with braids"—not to its capacity for holding water.

## STETSON

It's been said that, next to the Statue of Liberty and the flag, the cowboy hat is the most famous symbol of America. The felt hat with the high crown and the wide brim has been worn by cowboys to protect them from sun and rain since the West was settled. It's a descendant of the higher and wider sombrero worn by Mexican horsemen. In the 1850s John Batterson Stetson, a hatter from New Jersey, traveled to Missouri and Colorado. After returning to the East, he opened a small factory in Philadelphia in 1865 and made the kind of hats he'd seen cowboys wearing. His quality and design made Stetson, or the "John B.," synonymous with the cowboy hat.

## STEWART, JIMMY

Ann Miller, his longtime friend, once said of Jimmy Stewart, "He stood for everything that was good." A lanky young Princeton graduate with a beguiling stammer and straight-arrow good looks, he was signed by MGM in 1935 and thrived in the studio system. He played the lead in the Frank Capra films *You Can't Take It with You* and *Mr. Smith Goes to Washington*. In 1940 Stewart won an Oscar for *The Philadelphia Story*. After flying 20 bombing missions for the air force during World War II, he graced Capra's *It's a Wonderful Life*, made four Hitchcock films, including *Vertigo* and *Rope*, as well as 17 Westerns. Stewart is both a Kennedy Center and a Lincoln Center honoree, and in 1985 he received the Medal of Freedom. On-screen and off-, his strength, sweetness, and decency made him a beloved figure.

In the 1954 Alfred Hitchcock thriller *Rear Window*, Jimmy Stewart played a photojournalist who detected a murder from his apartment window.

## STIEGLITZ, ALFRED

Alfred Stieglitz, an important photographer himself, actively championed the idea that photography is an art form, as deserving of recognition as painting. Sharing the vision of Picasso and the Cubists, who explored in painting what he did with photography—that form conveys emotion—he analyzed the visual world in terms of its underlying shapes.

In 1905 Stieglitz and a group of photographers, including Edward Steichen, opened the 291 Gallery on New York's Fifth Avenue. Here they showed their own work and that of such photographers as Ansel Adams and Paul Strand. Stieglitz also presented such modern artists as Pablo Picasso, Auguste Rodin, and Paul Cézanne. It was there that Stieglitz discovered the work of Georgia O'Keeffe, whom he married in 1924.

For the 1893 photo "Winter, Fifth Avenue," Alfred Stieglitz waited patiently until "everything was in balance." Later he favored a more spontaneous approach, rapidly capturing the shapes in a scene.

During the rationing of World War II, stockings were "made" with foundation and eyebrow pencil.

The oldest hopscotch grid known to us is 2,000 years old—it was carved into a street in ancient Rome. Newer versions of the game include water hopscotch and snail hopscotch (no water or snails needed.)

Barbra Streisand, one of the most powerful women in the entertainment industry, includes among her screen credits the roles of performer, director, and producer.

## STOCKINGS

At the 1939 World's Fair in New York City, nylon stockings were touted as the product of the future: "Shrink proof, moth proof, non-allergic, resists mildew, warm as wool." Moreover, they were supposed to last practically forever. The stockings first appeared in department stores on May 15, 1940—"Nylon Day"—and women stampeded to buy them. During World War II, however, nylon was needed for ropes, tents, and parachutes; women had to make do with such clumsy substitutes as rayon. Black market nylons sold for up to $10 a pair.

Pantyhose, which eliminated the need for girdles and garters, were invented in 1959, but they didn't become a true necessity until 1965, when British designer Mary Quant introduced the miniskirt. The pantyhose story doesn't end there: they have been used to dry onions, stuff pillows and quilts, strain lumps from paint, and enhance photos with a soft-focus look. They've even been used as a spare dog leash.

## STREET AND PLAYGROUND GAMES

In the days before TV and video games, city kids hardly ever complained that there was nothing to do. Traffic was slow, so playing in the street was less dangerous, and families were large, so there were always plenty of children to play with. The rules of stickball and stoopball were passed from boy to boy. Girls chanted singsong rhymes as they jumped rope or played hand-clapping games. Parents rarely had to tell a child to leave the hot, crowded house to go out and play; the problem was getting the kid back in by bedtime.

Fewer children play in today's faster streets, but the traditions live on. Kids in playgrounds reach new heights by climbing slide ladders or pumping swings, but they also play time-honored equipmentless games like Red Rover, Simon Sez, leapfrog, tag, and hide-and-seek. Stray cans are kicked, and bits of blackboard chalk are used to draw hopscotch boxes. Balls are thrown, caught, bounced, and batted. Children still learn complicated double Dutch rope jumping and the involved rituals for choosing teams. And they still beg to stay out when it's time to go home.

## STREISAND, BARBRA

Barbra Streisand never learned how to type; she was afraid if she had something to fall back on, she would. It was the first of many savvy career moves. Within five years of winning a talent show at a Greenwich Village bar in 1959, Streisand had made her first record, won her first Grammy, and had her first starring role in a Broadway show, *Funny Girl*. In 1968 she made her Hollywood debut in the film version of *Funny Girl*, for which she won an Oscar. Three decades in show business have not dissipated Streisand's incredible energy. In 1993 she overcame severe stage fright to begin a world concert tour—the first time in two decades that fans got to hear her sing live. Tickets sold for hundreds of dollars each.

## SUBWAYS

As a means of safe, cheap, speedy travel, subways have no equal. The nation's first subway, built in Boston in 1898, was one and a half miles long. New York City's system opened in 1904, with 22 miles of track. It is now the largest in the world, with the most stations and cars and a whopping 722 miles of track—enough to extend from New York to Chicago; it accommodates 3.5 million people each weekday.

At the beginning of the 20th century, New York's subways were seen as "chariots for the poor." They enabled thousands of people to reach the outlying suburbs and quickly transformed these underdeveloped areas into bustling neighborhoods. The success of New York's businesses is so closely linked to the subways that Mayor Fiorello LaGuardia once remarked, "Any time we don't have crowding during the rush hour...New York will be a ghost town."

Today straphangers can take the El in Chicago, the BART in San Francisco, the Metro in D.C., or the MARTA in Atlanta; Baltimore and Philadelphia also have subways. As for the future, scientists propose a high-speed subway system linking such cities as New York, Dallas, and Los Angeles.

## SULLIVAN, ED

Aware that he lacked talent himself, Ed Sullivan, Broadway columnist for the New York *Daily News*, knew that he could spot it in others. He thus propelled his trailblazing variety show into a Sunday-night institution and one of the most successful programs in TV history. Originally titled *The Toast of the Town*, *The Ed Sullivan Show* premiered on June 20, 1948; on the bill was the TV debut of Dean Martin and Jerry Lewis. Others who dipped a toe into TV for Sullivan were Maria Callas and Elvis Presley, who was exhibited only from the waist up to spare the public the sight of his gyrating loins. The Beatles, introduced to a grateful nation in a memorable early-'60s show, were largely inaudible because of the hysterical screams of the audience. Sullivan's wooden delivery, awkward gestures, and idiosyncratic pronunciation ("rilly big shew") were catnip to impressionists—the best of whom he booked. The "shew" breathed its last in 1971.

## SUPER BOWL

The Super Bowl, held each January to determine the top professional football team, is the most-watched sports telecast of the year. People who skip it may feel left out of the conversation for weeks. Corporations reward top salespeople and important clients by giving them hard-to-get tickets and treating them to a long, lavish weekend of pregame festivities. In Las Vegas and around the world, hundreds of millions of dollars are wagered. In living rooms across the country, people gather to drink beer and crunch pretzels while they watch the game, the gaudy halftime show, and the expensive commercials that sometimes outshine the on-field action.

Next stop, 168th Street—one of the 469 stations that make up New York City's subway system, whose labyrinthine map can be worn as a necktie (right).

Said pianist Oscar Levant of Ed Sullivan (left), "He will last as long as somebody else has talent." *The Ed Sullivan Show* presented some of the brightest stars from the worlds of comedy, opera, ballet, Broadway, and rock.

## GREAT SUPER BOWL MOMENTS

**1969** "Broadway Joe" Namath makes good on his boasts and proves that the American Football League (AFL) is equal to the National Football League (NFL) by leading the New York Jets to an upset victory in Super Bowl III.

**1971** Long-haired rookie Jim "Lassie" O'Brien kicks a field goal to win the close, error-filled Super Bowl V—remembered as the "Blunder Bowl" or the "Blooper Bowl"—for the Baltimore Colts.

**1974** Diminutive Miami Dolphin field goal specialist Garo Yepremian makes a disastrous attempt to pass the ball after a kick is blocked, showing average viewers what it would look like if they were in the big game with the big guys.

**1976** Pittsburgh Steeler wide receiver Lynn Swann soars to catch a pass from quarterback Terry Bradshaw, who is clobbered as he throws. Bradshaw doesn't see the reception that wins Super Bowl X.

With her magic lasso and bullet-deflecting bracelets, Wonder Woman (left) appeared in 1941, providing girls with a superhero role model.

Millionaire Bruce Wayne became Batman (left) to avenge his parents' death, while a lab experiment turned Steve Rogers into Captain America (above).

Surfing became a major fad in the 1960s, and hotdoggers spent sun-drenched days practicing handstands, "leanbacks," and "spinners."

## SUPERHEROES

Jerry Siegel—a skinny, bespectacled kid who spent his spare time reading the exploits of Tarzan, Buck Rogers, and Flash Gordon—changed comic books forever in 1938 when he teamed with artist Joe Shuster to create a caped crime buster named Superman. Kids all across the country went wild for the "Man of Steel," who was first seen holding a car above his head on the cover of *Action Comics #1*. Superman (aka Clark Kent, a mild-mannered reporter) was able to fly, to see through walls, and to survive a hail of bullets as he fought for "truth, justice, and the American way."

In 1939 Bob Kane of *Detective Comics* created the character called Batman, who wore a shadowy black costume because "criminals are a superstitious, cowardly lot." This masked crime fighter had an array of gadgetry at his disposal in order to outwit and defeat the villains of Gotham City. Subsequently, a profusion of superheroes began to turn up in the pages of comic books. Many were based on ancient myths: Wonder Woman was an Amazon aided by Aphrodite, and Captain Marvel drew his power from the word *Shazam!* (an acronym for "Solomon Hercules Atlas Zeus Achilles Mercury!"). Heroes also reflected our national concerns, as when Timely Comics's Captain America clashed with Nazis.

As sales of superhero comic books plummeted after World War II, many crime fighters were put out of business. It was the TV series *The Adventures of Superman* (1953–57) that helped rejuvenate the genre. A host of new and revived superheroes soon starred in their own titles. Stan Lee's Marvel Comics hit it big with fresh characters, such as the Fantastic Four, the X-Men, and Iron Man. Marvel heroes dealt with realistic, everyday problems while helping to save the universe. Spider-man was simply an awkward teenager until he was bitten by a radioactive arachnid.

In later decades superheroes have appealed to kids and adults alike. A series of Superman and Batman movies in the 1970s, '80s, and '90s were box-office blockbusters.

## SURFING

When The Beach Boys sang, "Let's go surfin' now, everybody's learnin' how," they turned an obscure California pastime into a pop phenomenon, bringing new terms—*wipeout, hang ten, shooting the curl*—into the language. But surfing itself is ancient, a Hawaiian practice that was first reported by Capt. James Cook in 1778. The sport caught on in the 1950s, thanks in part to the development of wet suits and light polyurethane-foam boards, which replaced 15-foot wooden "backbreakers." Surfing has since evolved into a million-dollar enterprise. On the pro circuit, which has dozens of international competitions, the top surfers display fantastic physical prowess as they maneuver along the turbulent surf. As a rule, the biggest waves are found near remote Pacific islands.

> *"One cannot be an American by going about saying that one is an American. It is necessary to feel America, like America, love America, and then work."*
>
> GEORGIA O'KEEFFE

## TALK SHOWS

"My Mother Is a Party Animal." "My Daughter Is a Tramp." "My Sister Stole My Man." Anything goes in the world of daytime talk TV, in which hosts vie for the attention of living-room rubberneckers. Today's "exploitalk" is a far cry from the more genteel entertainment once provided by Mike Douglas, Merv Griffin, and Dinah Shore, who in the 1960s and '70s interviewed celebrities and sang musical numbers.

In 1967 Phil Donahue created a forum for more serious discussion: he booked such guests as Bella Abzug, Ralph Nader, and Gloria Steinem, and he encouraged audience members to ask their own questions. But it was *The Oprah Winfrey Show*, which debuted in 1986, that really started the talk show boom. Warm and compassionate, Winfrey bonded emotionally with her guests and with viewers nationwide.

Among newer hosts, Geraldo Rivera has a more confrontational style and Ricki Lake reflects the attitude of a younger crowd. Critics feel that talk shows go too far. Says Winfrey: "When I began my talk show,...I never thought about [TV's] tremendous influence....Now I feel both the power and the enormous responsibility that comes with it."

## TAMMANY HALL

By the mid-1800s, several American cities were under a system of political domination known as bossism, which featured an all-powerful figure (the boss) and an affiliated band of underlings (the machine). One such organization, the Tammany Society in New York City, was characterized by its ability to control large blocs of voters—a power base consolidated through the use of ward heelers, who in times of trouble aided the poor, especially newly arrived immigrants. Grateful, the people voted for Tammany's candidates.

The list of corrupt Tammany officials was long, but none was greedier than William Marcy "Boss" Tweed. Taking advantage of a new law, Tweed gained access to New York City's treasury, then skimmed millions of dollars. His looting went unchecked until members of the media mounted a campaign against him in 1870. George Jones, a reporter for *The New York Times*, wrote a series of articles that revealed the scope of the graft, and cartoonist Thomas Nast lampooned Tweed in the pages of *Harper's Weekly*. These efforts prompted state officials to collect evidence, and in 1873 the once-omnipotent Tweed was convicted of fraud and sent to jail.

Someone was usually in the kitchen with Dinah. In this case, Peter Ustinov helped Shore prepare a recipe on her 1970s daytime talk show, *Dinah's Place*.

Phil Donahue knew when to let his audience do the talking. As he put it, "They stood and said what they had to say. And they were smart."

Oprah Winfrey is famous for telling audiences her own problems—such as her fight to lose weight and her efforts to deal with childhood abuse. By the mid-1990s, she was the highest-paid woman on television.

Jessica Tandy (above, with Morgan Freeman) followed up her Oscar-winning role in *Driving Miss Daisy* (1989) with outstanding performances in *Fried Green Tomatoes* and *Nobody's Fool*.

Bill "Bojangles" Robinson could really think on his feet: he was famous for carrying on a line of patter while he danced. Above, Ann Miller rat-a-tat-taps for her country in the 1944 movie *Carolina Blues*.

## TANDY, JESSICA

"Everything this actress does is so pure and right," gushed one reviewer in *The New York Times*, "that only poets, not theater critics, should be allowed to write about her." A leading classical actress in her native England, Tandy emigrated in 1940 to New York, where she met her husband-to-be, Canadian actor-director Hume Cronyn. The two moved to Hollywood and played opposite each other in the World War II movie *The Seventh Cross*. Tandy then played a number of bit parts until Cronyn directed her in a stage production of an early Tennessee Williams play, *Portrait of a Madonna*. Upon seeing it, Williams declared that "Jessica was Blanche [du Bois]" and cast her in *A Streetcar Named Desire*. Tandy's shattering performance earned her a Tony Award, her first.

Among the couple's many joint successes were *The Gin Game* (1978) and *Foxfire* (1983); Tandy won Tonys for both. Aging gracefully, she was increasingly in demand for screen roles. Tandy won the Drama Desk four times; she and Cronyn were 1986 Kennedy Center honorees, and in 1990 they received the National Medal of Arts.

## TANG

Most Americans associate Tang, the substitute orange juice drink, with the *Gemini* space flights of 1965 and the *Apollo* astronauts' trip to the moon in 1969. General Mills first launched Tang in 1959 as the fruit-juice answer to instant coffee, touting its payload of vitamins as "Nutrition in Disguise." Still, it wasn't until the space age that jars of "breakfast beverage crystals" began taking off from supermarket shelves.

In order to make Tang drinkable in the weightless environment of a space capsule, the astronauts used a $5,000 high-tech water pistol, designed by the Whirlpool Corporation, to inject water into the laminated pouches that contained the orangy powder. They would then knead the pouches until the mix was liquefied and could be easily quaffed through a special opening. After watching spacemen consume Tang, kids everywhere were eager to drink theirs.

## TAP DANCING

Tap, with its rhythmic, staccato clatter, is a purely American style of dance. It was created when black Americans took older dances—the hornpipe, the Irish jig, and the clog dance—a few steps further. They added the glide from the catwalk and the buck, the wing, and other steps, as well as expressive upper-body movements. They put metal strips on the heels and toes of their shoes, and soon soft-shoe gave way to fiery, percussive, and sometimes acrobatic tap. Tap's many variations have included flash, legomania, comic, classical, and rhythm tap, which ultimately led to jazz tap.

A highlight of minstrel shows, vaudeville, and revues, tap was performed by such legendary dancers as Bill "Bojangles" Robinson, who danced on his toes in wood-soled shoes.

"Hoofers" danced in small clubs and music halls; among the best were John Bubbles ("The Father of Rhythm Tap"), Bunny Briggs, Baby Laurence, Sandman Sims, and Honi Coles. The Nicholas Brothers were child stars who performed at the Cotton Club; they later appeared in the 1943 film *Stormy Weather* with Robinson. Other memorable dancing film stars of the '30s and '40s were Ruby Keeler, Ann Miller, and the elegant Fred Astaire, whose partners included Ginger Rogers and Eleanor Powell. Gene Kelly tickled the pavement in *Singin' in the Rain* in 1952. During a tap revival in the '70s and '80s, brothers Gregory and Maurice Hines scorched the floor in the Broadway revues *Eubie!* and *Sophisticated Ladies* and in the film *The Cotton Club*.

## TARZAN

Who was the first screen Tarzan? Wrong, it was not Johnny Weissmuller. Tarzan, who began life as the hero of popular stories by Edgar Rice Burroughs about a boy who has been raised among animals in the African jungle, was first played by Elmo Lincoln in 1918. The 200-pound, paunchy Lincoln had the title role in the silent *Tarzan of the Apes*; this was followed by two sequels and a serial. It wasn't until 1932 that Tarzan's trademark yell was ululated by former Olympic champion swimmer Weissmuller, who for 16 years flexed his muscles and grunted through 12 pictures. Weissmuller was rumored to have lost money playing gin rummy on the set with a chimpanzee. In the total 40-odd Tarzan movies, the tree swingers included Buster Crabbe, Bruce Bennett, Lex Barker, and Ron Ely. Recent years have seen TV Tarzans, and in the 1984 film *Greystoke: The Legend of Tarzan*, the ape-man had a French accent. *Moi* Tarzan?

## TATTOOS

Tattoos tell the world that the wearer is a great deal bolder than average, and certainly braver in the face of pain. A practice that dates back to the Stone Age, tattooing involves the introduction of pigments into the deepest layer of skin by means of a sharp instrument. During World War II, servicemen usually opted for such simple designs as anchors, hearts, and names of loved ones ("Mom" was a favorite). Seamen, longshoremen, truckers, and others kept the practice alive with statements of patriotism (an eagle or a flag) and affiliation (a fraternity letter or union motto).

In the 1960s hippies and bikers got themselves "inked" with designs that ranged from flowers and butterflies to fierce animals and macabre images. Rock and roll musicians—Cher, for one—made tattoos their personal fashion statement. Then punk rockers took up the practice, covering their bodies with tattoos of skulls with mohawk hairdos, and the like. Today tattoos can be seen on people from all walks of life—celebrities, models, athletes, doctors, lawyers—anyone who is a rebel at heart.

A Tarzan family portrait (left to right): Maureen O'Sullivan, Johnny Sheffield, Johnny Weissmuller, and Cheetah the Chimp.

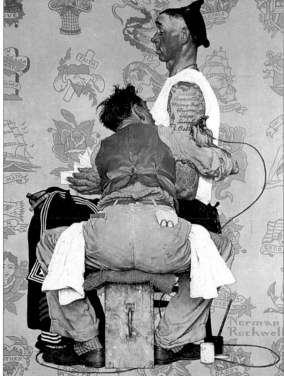

For people who may have second thoughts about their tattoos, there are now a number of removal techniques, including dermabrasion and lasers. In this Norman Rockwell illustration, a sailor takes the easy way out.

In *National Velvet* (above), Liz Taylor, hoping to pass for a jockey, got a haircut from trainer Mickey Rooney. A grown-up Liz (left) played the alluring wife of a rich rancher in *Giant*.

The steamroller of justice finally caught up to the perpetrators of the Teapot Dome scandal, an instance of federal corruption.

## TAYLOR, ELIZABETH

Although she hasn't made a Hollywood film since 1980, Elizabeth Taylor is still considered the quintessential movie star. She has had eight marriages, seven husbands, and since 1947 she has been hospitalized about 75 times. "I have never, God knows, done anything by half measures," she says.

Guided by a stage mother, British-born Taylor became a child of the MGM studio system, where she made her first big hit, *National Velvet* (1944). Almost overnight the violet-eyed actress became one of the world's most celebrated women ("I had no childhood"). She illuminated the screen in such films as *A Place in the Sun* (1951), *Giant* (1956), *Butterfield 8* (1960), and *Cleopatra* (1963). On-screen, her professionalism earned her the respect of fellow actors. Off-screen, every facet of her life has been of interest to the press and public: her turbulent life with Richard Burton (whom she wed twice), illnesses, drug and alcohol addictions, lavish lifestyle, fabulous jewels, fund-raising, even her weight. Says the still lovely Liz: "I want my tombstone to say, 'She lived.'"

## TEAPOT DOME

In 1924 the sensational news broke that someone in the administration of President Warren G. Harding had taken bribes to lease naval oil reserves to private interests. The scandal involved Teapot Dome, the name of an oil reservoir in Wyoming. After Harding's death in 1923, the Senate authorized an investigation, and the full story emerged.

Secretary of the Interior Albert Fall had gained control of government oil reservoirs, or domes, from the secretary of the navy. He then secretly leased Teapot Dome to Harry Sinclair's Mammoth Oil Company, and the Elk Hills fields in California to his friend Edward L. Doheny. In exchange, Fall received gifts and "loans" of more than $400,000. The oil fields were returned to the U.S. government in 1927. Fall was imprisoned for accepting bribes, Sinclair received a short sentence for criminal contempt, and Teapot Dome became synonymous with government graft and corruption.

## TECUMSEH

Tecumseh was a great Shawnee chief who led a crusade to unite a number of separate tribes against white encroachment on Indian lands. He fought against the incursions of the U.S. Army and its militias, and he denounced any tribe that sold its land. "Sell a country?" he asked. "Why not sell the air, the clouds, and the great sea?" In 1805 Tecumseh's brother began to have visions that Indians should return to traditional ways and avoid whites. Tecumseh turned this message into a political one, traveling throughout the Midwest to enlist others into his union. In 1811 his brother ordered an attack on Gen. William Henry Harrison's forces. The clash, called the Battle of Tippecanoe, was indecisive, but it nonetheless dealt a severe blow to Tecumseh's crusade. Undeterred,

Tecumseh fought on the British side in the War of 1812, but during the Battle of the Thames, he was killed. With him died the dream of an Indian confederation.

## TEDDY BEARS

President Theodore Roosevelt can take credit for inspiring the creation of this beloved stuffed animal; in 1902, while on one of his many hunting trips, he spared the life of a baby bear. President and cub were sketched in a cartoon that took the public's fancy, and "Teddy's Bear" became the big hit of the 1903 Toy Fair in Leipzig, Germany. Teddy emigrated when Americans abroad brought him back to the States in 1904 (a prototype is enshrined in the Smithsonian). True teddy bears have plush fur, glass eyes, movable arms and legs, and the distinguished profile so perfectly captured in Ernest H. Shepard's illustrations for A. A. Milne's *Winnie-the-Pooh*.

## TEFLON

One of the slipperiest substances in the world, Teflon is the trade name for tetrafluoroethylene, a plastic that is virtually impervious to other chemicals. Used as a lining for tubes and as a coating for conveyor belts, it is also known to cooks as the substance that makes pans stick-free. Shortly before World War II, Dr. Roy Plunkett, a chemist, was tinkering with coolant gases. He was shocked to discover one morning that he did not have a cold gas, as he expected, but a waxy solid. Teflon, as it was called, was kept secret by the U.S. military and was used to store U-235, the principle component of the nuclear bomb. Recently Teflon has taken on a metaphoric use. Someone who blunders but seems to escape criticism may be called, for example, a Teflon politician or celebrity.

## TELEPHONE

In a period when several inventors (including Thomas Alva Edison) were working frantically toward more effective communication by wire, Alexander Graham Bell, a teacher of the deaf, came in first with his invention of the telephone. It was his fascination with the human ear, especially the way sound waves cause the soft membrane of the eardrum to vibrate, that led him to believe that voices could be sent mechanically. "At once, the conception of a membrane-speaking telephone became complete in my mind," the inventor said. The patent was granted on March 7, 1876. Three days later, Bell's assistant, Thomas H. Watson, became the first person to receive a phone call. Bell, who had spilled acid on his clothes, called over the phone, "Mr. Watson, come here. I want you."

Just over a year later, the first telephone line was installed, followed by the first rental of equipment. Bell eventually sold his interest in the company that bore his name. A wealthy man, he tinkered with other inventions while his telephone transformed the world.

Teddy bears have colonized much of the world. Whatever your teddy's origin, treasure him, for he may indeed be a treasure: one vintage Steiff bear recently sold at auction for $171,000.

Telephone operators, who were spoofed by Lily Tomlin on the TV show *Laugh-In*, are a dying breed. More and more, they are being replaced by electronic instructions: "For our billing department, press one...."

The stars come out to help Jerry Lewis raise money for the Muscular Dystrophy Association. Above, Lewis is joined by strongman Mr. T.

In 1954 the Swanson Frozen Foods Company introduced the TV Dinner—just the thing for families who spent their evenings in front of the tube.

## TELETHONS

Telethons combine a little bit of Vegas with a whole lot of heart, bringing together singers, musicians, and comedians to raise money for charitable causes. As early as the 1950s, when television was still a novelty, charities began using it to raise funds. Over the years, the National Easter Seal Society, public-television stations, AIDS organizations, and other groups have persuaded viewers to phone in pledges.

Since 1965, when Jerry Lewis hosted his first nationally broadcast Muscular Dystrophy Association Telethon, this annual Labor Day event has raised well over $1 billion. It has also become the biggest and best-known telethon around. While it has occasionally drawn protests against the image it projects of disabled people, Lewis's songs, stories, and persuasive appeals have touched millions of lives.

## TELEVANGELISTS

Religious programs have been on the air since TV began, but it wasn't until 1952 that Bishop Fulton J. Sheen emerged as the first star preacher. His sermons resembled classroom lectures, and an "angel" erased the blackboard whenever it was off-camera. Rex Humbard built his Cathedral of Tomorrow as a television studio. Oral Roberts took the camera out of the church and into "the World's Largest Gospel Tent," where he performed healing miracles and encouraged viewers to place their hands on the TV set so that they, too, could be healed.

In 1963 Pat Robertson started the *700 Club*, named for the 700 monthly pledges of $10 each that were needed for the show's operating budget. Indeed, fund-raising has become central to religious programs, and—Jim and Tammy Faye Bakker's personal expenditures aside—most of the money goes toward buying more airtime. Electronic churches now claim a national congregation of 13.3 million viewers.

## TELEVISION

In the years since the first telecasts were aired in 1936, television has become an ever-present mirror—and often shaper—of American culture. Early television's picture quality was crude, offering little more than the actors' silhouettes. However, just over one decade later, television had created stars who were recognized throughout the world.

Sincerity counted more than glamour did in TV's early days. Audiences trusted newsman Walter Cronkite to tell them "the way it is" each evening. Ed Sullivan hosted the longest-running variety show ever. In the first partially televised presidential campaign, the voters of 1948 preferred homespun Harry Truman to New Yorker Thomas E. Dewey.

That year marked the start of television's golden age, when we thrilled to live dramas on *Studio One* or *Playhouse 90*, learned to appreciate music with conductor Leonard Bernstein, and laughed at our favorite comedians, including Milton Berle ("Mr. Television") and Jack Benny.

Television also showed us world events with startling immediacy. We were there when men walked on the moon, when President John F. Kennedy was assassinated, and when the Berlin Wall came down. Television coverage contributed to the downfall of Sen. Joseph McCarthy, the resignation of President Richard Nixon, and the end of the Vietnam War.

Today the average American watches seven hours of television each day. Cable television, pay-per-view, and other innovations have greatly expanded viewers' choices. On-air violence and sex have also increased, fueling concerns about television's social and moral influence. Such criticism is not new. In 1961 Federal Communications Commission chairman Newton Minnow excoriated American TV as a "vast wasteland." Yet the medium deserves praise for bringing together a nation of diverse people, for giving us shared memories that will endure long after videotapes of the last sitcom are rerun.

## TEMPLE, SHIRLEY

"I don't live in the past. I live for today," said former child star Shirley Temple. Discovered at the age of three, her career at Fox was managed by her formidable mother. The mighty moppet, whose namesake ginger ale cocktail is still requested, could sing, act, and dance well enough to partner Bill "Bojangles" Robinson. She had personality, curls, dimples, and a sunny disposition. The world-famous tot was tops at the box office. Such films as *Little Miss Marker*, *The Little Colonel*, *Wee Willie Winkie*, and *Heidi* cheered the public during the Depression years of the 1930s. The "Good Ship Lollipop" belter eventually retired from the screen, raised a family, and, as Shirley Temple Black, began a career in politics that has included two ambassadorial appointments.

## TENNIS

When sportswoman Mary Ewing Outerbridge set up the first U.S. tennis court on the grounds of the Staten Island Cricket and Baseball Club in New York in 1874, she never imagined that she was launching what would become one of America's most popular sports. A recreational game enjoyed by more than 20 million men and women, tennis is played in public parks and private clubs across America. The United States Tennis Association (USTA) sponsors tournaments throughout the year for players as young as 12 and as old as 75.

Since the 1970s, TV has played a key role in boosting the popularity of the game's more colorful players, such as Jimmy Connors, Billie Jean King, Martina Navratilova, Chris Evert, and John McEnroe. The U.S. Open, the fourth and final leg of the Grand Slam, attracts thousands of fans, who come to watch the world's finest players compete for the top prize of more than half a million dollars. Played annually in Flushing Meadows, New York, the two-week tournament is watched on TV by more than 500 million people worldwide.

Shirley Temple became the youngest person to receive an Oscar when, at age six, she was given a special award for her "outstanding contribution to screen entertainment."

Jimmy Connors (below) showed his powerful two-handed backhand at the 1991 French Open.

Above, a triumphant Billie Jean King holds the winner's plate after a Wimbledon victory. King won a record-breaking 20 Wimbledon titles throughout her career while fighting to bring women's tennis to a new level.

Nachos, a pile of crispy fried tortilla chips—plus cheese, beans, spicy beef, salsa, guacamole, or sour cream—have migrated from the Tex-Mex border to the rest of the country.

## TEX-MEX

Combine the staples of the Mexican diet (corn, chili peppers, beans) with ingredients that are common in America (beef, wheat), add a dash of Texas ingenuity, and you have the makings of a Tex-Mex feast. What started out as simple Mexican fare evolved into Tex-Mex cuisine when Texans began adding new ingredients, trying new cooking techniques, and substituting readily available spices for the more unusual ones. And probably because Texas is cattle country, Tex-Mex dishes often contain beef.

Meals in the Lone Star State are likely to include quesadillas (thin cornmeal pancakes stuffed with cheese), fajitas (a sizzling mix of steak, onions, and peppers), and refried beans (pinto beans that are boiled, mashed, and combined with lard). And no meal is complete without a "bowl o' red," or chili con carne. Invented by cowboys, this mix of meat, beans, and chili peppers is a good example of a Tex-Mex dish.

## THANKSGIVING DAY

Contrary to legend, the Pilgrims weren't the first colonists to share a meal of thanks with Native Americans. That honor belongs to the settlers of St. Augustine, Florida, who ate hardtack and beans in September 1565. The celebration at Plymouth in the fall of 1621 was a three-day event to give thanks for a bountiful harvest. It included "as much fowl as [ordinarily]... served the company almost a week."

The Macy's Thanksgiving Day parade, which began in 1924, remains an annual event even though the store declared bankruptcy in 1992. Below, a Norman Rockwell painting captures the essence of Turkey Day.

George Washington proclaimed the first two national days of Thanksgiving, but these were one-time affairs. Our nationwide celebration owes its existence to one woman's 40-year campaign; in 1863 Sarah Josepha Hale finally persuaded President Lincoln to set aside the fourth Thursday in November as a national day of thanks. Only once has the tradition been tampered with: in 1939 President Franklin D. Roosevelt moved Thanksgiving to the third Thursday in November. Why? To accommodate merchants who wanted to increase the number of shopping days between Thanksgiving and Christmas. This decision was so unpopular that in 1941 Roosevelt moved the holiday back to where it originally was.

## THEME SONGS

The strains of "Lara's Theme" from *Dr. Zhivago*, "The William Tell Overture" from *The Lone Ranger*, and the "Ballad of Joe Clampett" from *The Beverly Hillbillies* are icons of our shared pop culture. How many have heard (and can remember) the words "Here's the story of a man named Brady" or "He was born on a mountaintop in Tennessee"?

Some theme songs, such as *The Third Man* and *Never on Sunday*, became hits; others were recycled ("Unchained Melody" from *Unchained* became the theme of the film *Ghost*). Some are high art, some campy, some plain silly, but quality doesn't matter, because, like old photos, theme songs transport us back to moments from our own past.

## THOREAU, HENRY DAVID

Although he died young (age 45), Henry David Thoreau wrote with the wisdom of the ages. "Time is but the stream I go a-fishing in," he wrote in his most famous work, *Walden.* "Its thin current slides away, but eternity remains." *Walden*, an unparalleled book by a man of principle, chronicles four seasons spent by a pond in a cabin Thoreau built by himself with a borrowed ax and hand-hewn lumber. Of his hermitlike devotion to self-reliance, Thoreau said, "If a man does not keep pace with his companions, perhaps it is because he hears a different drummer. Let him step to the music which he hears, however measured or far away."

An ardent abolitionist, Thoreau once refused to pay his poll tax because he did not want to support the government of a nation where "a sixth of the population...are slaves." He went to jail, then recounted his experience in "Civil Disobedience." Mahatma Gandhi and Martin Luther King, Jr., put Thoreau's tactics to the test in their struggles, proving that unjust laws can be changed by passive resistance.

## THORPE, JIM

Jim Thorpe, a Sauk and Fox Indian, dominated the pentathlon and decathlon events at the 1912 Stockholm Olympics. The next year, Thorpe admitted that he had broken his amateur status back in 1909 by playing minor league baseball, and the Amateur Athletic Union stripped him of his two gold medals. Thorpe spent his lifetime trying to regain them, but they were returned only in 1982, 29 years after his death.

Thorpe's athletic talents extended to football and baseball as well as to track and field. He was considered the best college football player in the nation while at the Carlisle Indian School in Pennsylvania. He played professional baseball from 1913 to 1919. In 1920 Thorpe was named the first president of the organization that later became the National Football League. His story was made into a movie, *Jim Thorpe—All American* (1951), starring Burt Lancaster.

## 3-D

In the early 1950s Hollywood studios, bruised by the popularity of television, turned to the technological novelty of 3-D films. 3-D (also known as stereoscopy) prompts the brain to merge a pair of flat images into one three-dimensional image. To do this, two slightly different versions of the same picture are projected; special glasses allow each eye to see only one picture. Your brain does the rest.

3-D had been tried for more than a century; but in 1952, a movie marketing blitz that promised "a lion in your lap" lured people to the 3-D horror flick *Bwana Devil*. The film's success inspired a slew of other 3-D films. At first, donning glasses to watch gimmicky action films was fun, but the thrill was gone within two years. 3-D didn't disappear, though; virtual reality computer games have kept the magic alive.

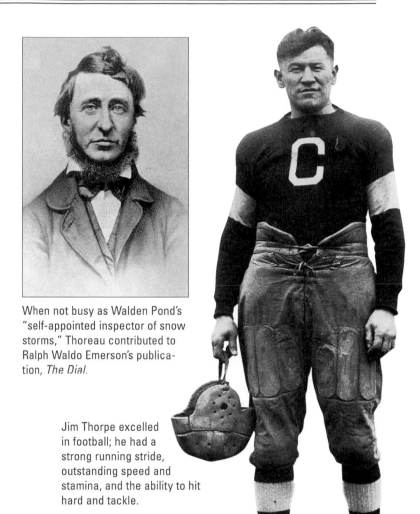

When not busy as Walden Pond's "self-appointed inspector of snow storms," Thoreau contributed to Ralph Waldo Emerson's publication, *The Dial.*

Jim Thorpe excelled in football; he had a strong running stride, outstanding speed and stamina, and the ability to hit hard and tackle.

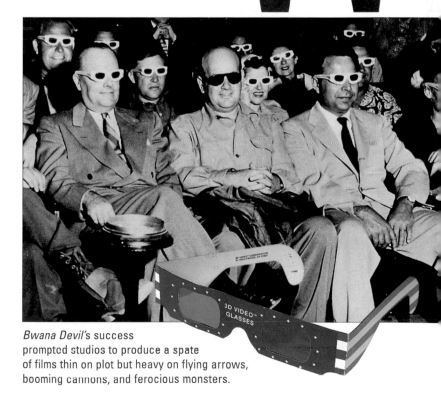

*Bwana Devil*'s success prompted studios to produce a spate of films thin on plot but heavy on flying arrows, booming cannons, and ferocious monsters.

The Three Stooges were at their best when they were up to no good for no good reason. "You do a lot of dumb stuff in this world," says one fan, "but when you see these guys, you feel like a genius."

A ticker-tape parade, New York's unique way of celebrating momentous events, was held in 1991 for the return of troops from the Persian Gulf.

## THREE STOOGES

Originally a vaudeville team, the Stooges played second banana to comic Ted Healy on stage and screen, with little to do but set up gags for him. In 1934 the Three Stooges—Larry Fine and Moe and Curly Howard—came into their own; during the next 30 years, they made a staggering 190 short movies for Columbia and about a dozen features. (In 1946 Curly retired, and his brother Shemp joined the act.) Their specialty was broad, vulgar, violent slapstick, complete with kicks, smacks, jabs, slaps, and conks on the head, all underscored by vivid sound effects, such as ratchets to simulate the sound of an arm being twisted. Their dialogue consisted mainly of old burlesque jokes. The Stooges weren't to everybody's taste, but their popularity got a boost in 1958, when their shorts were released to TV (Their shorts? Hey, whaddabout their socks? *Pow!*) and a whole new generation of kids fell (*splat!*) for the energetic clowns. *Boing!*

## THURBER, JAMES

"I like people and hate them at the same time," said *New Yorker* contributor James Thurber. "I wouldn't draw them … if I didn't think they were horrible, and I wouldn't write about them if I didn't think they were wonderful." Thurber always struck a funny bone with his whimsical drawings, which usually showed well-meaning husbands bedeviled by sharp-tongued wives or reproached by sad-looking pets. His books for children, *The Thirteen Clocks* and *The Wonderful O*, became instant classics, and his collaboration with E. B. White produced the hilarious *Is Sex Necessary?*

But his warm humor sparkled in his stories. "The Secret Life of Walter Mitty" was one of Thurber's most popular tales, made even more famous by the 1947 movie starring Danny Kaye. Mitty is bored running errands for his wife, so he compensates by imagining himself to be the fearless commander of a navy hydroplane or the greatest pistol shot in the world. When Mitty steps into these fantasies of heroism and derring-do, his wife thinks he is just being absentminded and promises to take his temperature when he gets home.

## TICKER-TAPE PARADE

For more than a century, New York City's sincerest form of adulation has been the ticker-tape parade, which consists of throwing tons of paper from Manhattan office windows onto the hero and the cheering crowds along the canyons of lower Broadway. Originally the ticker tape came from brokerage-house machines that printed market "ticker" prices on thin ribbons of paper. Now that Wall Street has gone electronic, New York buys special inch-wide paper strips from a company in Connecticut for just this purpose.

New Yorkers first tossed the ticker tape in 1886, when the Statue of Liberty arrived in New York Harbor. In 1910 Theodore Roosevelt's return from a 15-month trip to Africa prompted the first *official* ticker-tape parade. Subsequent parades have honored Charles Lindbergh, in 1927 for his solo transatlantic flight to Paris; Gen. Dwight D. Eisenhower, in 1945 for bringing home the troops at the end of World War II; the three astronauts who landed on the moon, in 1969; and the Mets baseball team that finally won the World Series that same year. But the biggest parade of all—at least in terms of paper thrown, all 971 tons of it—was for the triumphant return in 1981 of the U.S. hostages held by Iran. Ticker tape, yellow ribbons, and American flags fluttered through the air as America poured out its heart in joy at their long-awaited return.

## TIFFANY'S

The store was founded in 1837 by Charles Tiffany, and its first catalog included hairpins, perfume, cuspidors, furniture, and moccasins. In 1848 the Manhattan emporium found its identity when it mysteriously acquired the French crown jewels and the press dubbed Mr. Tiffany "the King of Diamonds." The store that sells more engagement rings than any other single establishment in the world was once jeweler to Queen Victoria and the czar of Russia. J. P. Morgan ordered his yacht stationery there, and Sarah Bernhardt, a giant silver washbowl. Tiffany boxes have held wedding presents for generations of brides, china for the White House, and a full-size silver football trophy. The 1961 movie *Breakfast at Tiffany's* still has tourists asking where the restaurant is; there isn't one, but visitors are welcome to browse.

## TIME MAGAZINE

*Time* first hit the stands on March 3, 1923. The brainchild of Henry R. Luce and fellow Yale classmate Briton Hadden, the magazine was published out of a tiny Manhattan office on a shoestring budget. It currently dominates its rival national newsweeklies with a circulation of 4.1 million.

Luce focused on the personalities behind the news. "People just aren't interesting in the mass," he said. "It's only individuals who are exciting." Far-flung correspondents gathered insights and colorful quotes from news makers, which gave *Time* its distinctive point of view. "Show me a man who claims he's completely objective," said Luce, "and I'll show you a man with illusions." Eventually a "*Time*style" evolved: vivid, succinct, and lively. Writers sprinkled articles with such invented words as *cinemactress* and *radiorator*, and they often reversed subject and verb. As one wag put it, "Backward the sentences rumbled in *Time*."

The Luce empire soon included the button-down business magazine *Fortune* (first published in 1929), *Life* (1936), and *Sports Illustrated* (1954). *People* and *Money* were created after Luce's death in 1967. In 1989 Time Inc. merged with Warner Brothers to create Time Warner, one of the largest media conglomerates in the world.

While Charles Tiffany (below) specialized in gems and precious metals, his son Louis made a name for himself with spectacular stained-glass lamps (left) and windows, many of which are on exhibit at the Metropolitan Museum of Art.

Tiffany & Co.'s distinctive blue box with the white satin ribbon is a symbol of luxury recognized throughout the world.

From authors to athletes and astronauts, from presidents to prime ministers and prima donnas, from scientists to statesmen and movie stars, the world's news makers have made the cover of *Time*. At right, *Time* tackles a newsworthy social trend.

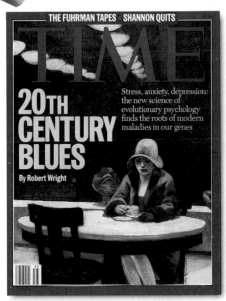

During the 1950s, the Tinkertoys Company awarded a $1,000 bond and a trip to New York City to the kid who created the year's most imaginative design. A simplified Ferris wheel, such as the one shown at right, can be built in a matter of minutes.

The sheet-music publishers of Tin Pan Alley were quick to discover that appealing covers spurred sales. To this end, some of the era's top lithographers and illustrators—Norman Rockwell, for one—were brought in to design covers for new scores.

## TINKERTOYS

Children like to learn, but they don't like to be taught: this was the belief of Charles Pajeau, the inventor of Tinkertoys. Inspired by kids playing with pencils and empty spools of thread, the stonemason from Evanston, Illinois, devised a rounded block of wood with eight holes around the edge; children could fit sticks in snugly and construct their own contraptions. Sales didn't take off until 1913, when Pajeau displayed a Ferris wheel made from Tinkertoys in a drugstore window. Large crowds gathered to see the new toy, and within a year some 900,000 sets of Tinkertoys were sold.

In the 1920s and '30s, Tinkertoys expanded its product line, including a train set called Choo-Choo Tinker Railway and a balancing toy called Tilly Tinker, the Talented Toe Dancer. Pajeau was also interested in the figures that kids came up with themselves. Each child who submitted a new idea was given a junior engineer's certificate.

## TIN PAN ALLEY

By the early 1900s, the music-publishing industry in New York City was the center of unceasing activity, creating and promoting new songs. Originally, music publishers were located near vaudeville houses around 14th Street and Union Square. When theaters moved uptown in the 1890s, so did the publishers, who set up shop around Broadway and 28th Street. There the clamor of the many song pluggers playing their latest offerings to prospective clients led composer Monroe Rosenfeld to liken the sound to the rattling of tin pans. Hence the name Tin Pan Alley—the place where tunesmiths prospected for golden phrases and melodies.

Tin Pan Alley songs, distributed through music stores or by mail, often sold a million copies. In the 1920s the Alley again moved farther uptown, centering in the Brill Building at 1619 Broadway, near 50th Street. Alas, with the advent of rock and roll, Tin Pan Alley faded.

## TIPPECANOE AND TYLER TOO!

"Tippecanoe and Tyler Too!" was the 1840 campaign slogan of presidential candidate William Henry Harrison, the U.S. commander at the 1811 Battle of Tippecanoe, and John Tyler, the vice presidential aspirant. The slogan was typical of their campaign, which avoided the issues and instead focused attention on Harrison's ability to quell Indian uprisings.

Throughout American history, presidential slogans have served as emotional rallying points for voters. "A Full Dinner Pail," was the prosperity-promising catchphrase of William McKinley's 1900 campaign. The word *new* is a natural for candidates. In 1912 former president Theodore Roosevelt campaigned for reelection with the slogan of "New Nationalism," which, he said, "puts the national need before sectional or personal advantage." Woodrow Wilson opposed him with a campaign for the rights of the common man, labeled the "New Freedom." Wilson won handily. In 1928 Herbert Hoover's campaign promised "A Chicken in Every Pot." (It later came to light that Hoover himself never said those words.) Franklin D. Roosevelt won four years later by offering a "New Deal" to desperate Americans, especially "The Forgotten Man," meaning the millions of unemployed.

Some memorable presidential slogans took time to evolve. Lyndon Johnson started out by promising a "Better Deal," then moved through a "Glorious Kind of Society" to a "Greater Society." It wasn't until he had been in office for several months that he finally hit on the slogan with which he is still associated: the "Great Society."

## TOCQUEVILLE, ALEXIS DE

In 1831 the French government sent Alexis de Tocqueville to the United States, ostensibly to report on prison conditions. His actual purpose, as he revealed in his book *Democracy in America*, was much broader. Indeed, he had come to study the very nature of American democracy, "its inclinations, its character, its prejudices, and its passions, in order to learn what we have to fear or to hope from its progress."

De Tocqueville believed that the spread of democracy was inevitable, that America was its new proving ground, and that democracy's specific form would vary according to the environment and the character of its practitioners. His great contribution was his ability to cut through distractions and nonessentials to get at democracy's central concept, the "principle of equality." He warned that as America matured, as notions of social virtue strengthened, individuality might be quashed by a "tyranny of the majority."

More than 150 years later, *Democracy in America* remains one of the most insightful studies of the American political system and its effects on the lives of citizens.

## TOMB OF THE UNKNOWN SOLDIER

In Arlington National Cemetery, a plain white marble sepulchre stands over the grave of the Unknown Soldier. The tomb is always guarded by a white-gloved army sentry in dress uniform who marches 21 paces, faces the tomb for 21 seconds, and resumes marching. The marble is inscribed: "Here rests in honored glory an American soldier known but to God." The unknown soldier was chosen at random from four unidentified World War I dead in France and buried at Arlington on Armistice Day—November 11, 1921—in tribute to the 116,708 Americans who died in the war. The marble tomb was completed above the anonymous soldier's grave in 1932. Since then three more unknowns, representing casualties of World War II and the Korean and Vietnam wars, have been placed in crypts in front of the tomb. The memorial is now called the Tomb of the Unknowns, a change that was inaugurated in 1958 by President Dwight D. Eisenhower.

Campaign slogans appear mostly on buttons, but Nixon's "Click with Dick" was on a cricket; "I Like Ike," on a key ring; and "Go Goldwater," on paper spectacles.

Each Veterans Day, thousands of Americans join the lone sentry at the Tomb of the Unknowns to pay homage to our fallen servicemen.

## TONY AWARDS

The first Tony Awards ceremony, to honor "distinguished achievement" on Broadway, was held at midnight on Easter Sunday in 1947 at the Waldorf-Astoria Hotel in New York. Best Actresses Ingrid Bergman and Helen Hayes received initialed sterling silver compact cases, and Best Actors Jose Ferrer and Fredric March took home gold money clips. Special recognition was given to a Mr. and Mrs. Katzenberg, who were cited for having attended opening nights for 30 years, and to restaurateur Vincent Sardi, for "providing a transient home and comfort station" for theater folk. Best Play was not awarded until 1948, and it was not until 1949 that winners were given medallions, designed with the comedy-tragedy mask on one side and the winner's name on the other.

The Tony Awards were established by the American Theater Wing and named for its president, actress Antoinette "Tony" Perry. Like the Pulitzer Prize and the New York Drama Critics Circle Award, the Tony is a prestigious theatrical honor. Since 1967 the ceremony has been nationally televised and has, like the Academy Awards, become a high-profile, star-studded TV event.

## TOOTH FAIRY

Sometime before age seven, the average child's "baby" teeth start loosening. Left alone, they would eventually drop out to make room for "grown-up" teeth. But they're never left alone; children accelerate the process, wiggling teeth with their tongues until they can yank the teeth out and place them under their pillow for the tooth fairy to exchange for cash.

The tooth fairy tradition may have been started by parents eager to offer children some consolation for the loss of a tooth and in the hope of preventing children from swallowing the tooth when it came out. Whatever its origins, the tradition has worked well: now children are eager to lose teeth. The event is considered a rite of passage and a sign of maturity. The challenge for parents is deciding how much to give—and making the exchange without being discovered.

## TOP 10 LISTS

The number 10 has a certain practical allure—after all, the first counting machine must surely have been our own fingers. The first well-known Top 10 list was J. Edgar Hoover's of the 10 most wanted fugitives, an inventory of the country's most villainous outlaws.

Quick to the point and easy to remember, Top 10 lists have been compiled for movies, TV shows, video rentals, books, albums, vacation spots, and stocks, as well as for the best-dressed (and worst-dressed) men and women.

Everyone, it seems, is choosing favorites. Friends do it and strangers on the street do it, but perhaps David Letterman does it best. The late-night talk-show host first tried it out as a comedy gag in 1985 at the suggestion of one of his

Mary Martin, Jackie Gleason, and Ann Bancroft (above) show off their Tony Award medallions in 1960. Glenn Close (right) won the Tony Award in 1995 for her role as Norma Desmond in *Sunset Boulevard*. In 1968, the Tony Award was mounted on a pedestal (bottom right) to make it easier to see on television.

When a tooth comes out, a child can't wait to show off: the gap is proof that he is growing up, and the cash-dispensing tooth fairy is expected.

writers, Steve O'Donnell. A wild mix of silliness and sarcasm—often biting if you happen to be famous or in the news—Letterman's list comes complete with a drumroll and a grand finale, and the topics know no limits. Take, for example, one of the "Top 10 Bad Things About Living Longer: shoulder-length ear hair"; or the "Top 10 Signs That You Have No Friends: You are one of the five best solitaire players in the world." For office workers, the "Top 10 Unpleasant Things to Hear on an Elevator" include: "'Does this look infected to you?'" and "'The acoustics in this elevator are perfect for yodeling.'"

## TOTEM POLES

Northwest Coast Indians have long been renowned for their intricately carved and painted totem poles. Made from the trunks of cedar trees by master craftsmen, the imposing columns sometimes rose as high as 60 feet. Like European coats of arms, their presence in front of homes announced the importance of the family within. But even more than that, the stylized figures of animals and people represented spirits who had guided the family's ancestors.

Some totem poles were designed to hold the ashes of dead chiefs or other nobility, and others were "shame" poles, carved to embarrass people who broke their word. Early missionaries mistook the sculptures for pagan religious symbols and destroyed many of them. Fortunately, artists from the Haida tribe began to revive the art of totem-pole carving in the 1960s. In 1969 the first Haida totem pole carved in 90 years was raised, to joyous celebration.

## TRACY, SPENCER

In a riveting scene in *Bad Day at Black Rock* (1955), Spencer Tracy, using his character's one good arm, pulverizes sadistic villain Ernest Borgnine with karate chops delivered suddenly, silently, and with deadly accuracy. In this scene, as in all his scenes, Tracy was a controlled, concentrated actor. Neither slim nor handsome (he avoided ladies'-man roles, anyway), he was a master at playing the incorruptible hero, unpretentious and quietly amused.

Originally a Broadway performer, Tracy won Oscars for two of his early MGM pictures, *Captains Courageous* (1937) and *Boy's Town* (1938), as well as Oscar nominations for seven other movies, including *Inherit the Wind* (1960), *Judgment at Nuremberg* (1961), and *Guess Who's Coming to Dinner* (1967).

Moody and alcoholic in private life, Tracy relied on the stability and devotion of Katharine Hepburn, with whom he shared a 27-year romantic partnership. His style was straight-from-the-hip, and when asked, "What do you look for in a script?" he replied, "Days off." *Judgment* co-star Richard Widmark commented, "He doesn't talk much about acting, but he knows it all."

When a family raised its totem pole, a feast called a potlatch was often held. Gifts were given to all who came to acknowledge the family's elevated status. Above, a totem pole in Saxman, Alaska.

Spencer Tracy and Katharine Hepburn (above) made classics out of the nine films in which they costarred, including the 1957 movie *Desk Set*.

# Famous TRADEMARKS

*Instantly recognizable, these inspired characters are no longer mere advertising icons; they are part of the American tradition.*

## CHICKEN OF THE SEA

This little mermaid made the transition from magazine advertisement to label logo in 1952. Except for a slightly new hairstyle, the appealing tuna fish trademark has remained unchanged.

## GERBER BABY FOOD

It was Mrs. Gerber's idea to can strained baby foods. The familiar baby picture, sketched by an artist, was first placed on the label in 1932, and it has remained there to this day.

## PILLSBURY DOUGHBOY

Created for a television ad, the Pillsbury Doughboy made his debut in 1966. His voice and bounciness were so appealing that he became the trademark for an array of Pillsbury's products.

## OLD DUTCH CLEANSER

Resolutely chasing dirt for half a century—until she was replaced by an updated symbol—the little Dutch girl was introduced in 1906. She reflected the reputation for cleanliness enjoyed by the housewives of Holland.

## THE JOLLY GREEN GIANT

The giant first appeared in 1925, but he didn't turn green until a decade later, when the Minnesota Valley Canning Co. gave him a jolly expression, green skin, and a leafy outfit.

## FISK TIRE BOY

Time to Re-Tire? The Fisk Tire Boy first asked that question on a 1907 poster. He showed up again in a 1914 ad and was a symbol of Fisk tires from then on.

## SUN-MAID RAISINS

Since the 1915 San Francisco Panama-Pacific International Exposition, the ever-cheerful Sun-Maid girl has worn the red bonnet and white blouse trimmed with blue.

## UNDERWOOD DEVILED HAM

This particular devil, the oldest registered food trademark in the U.S., has been modified several times. The design was first registered in 1870.

## BUMBLEBEE TUNA

This logo has evolved from the depiction of a real bumblebee through several stages. It no longer has its natural stripes, but sports a striped shirt.

*M'm! M'm! Good!*

## CAMPBELL'S SOUP

In 1904 the chubby-cheeked Campbell Kids made their debut in an ad in *Ladies' Home Journal*. The cherubs have been boasting that their soup is "M'm! M'm! Good!" ever since.

## MORTON SALT

Although she's changed her dress to keep up with styles, the Morton Salt girl has been carrying the same umbrella for decades, and she continues to advertise Morton's container-with-a-spout: "When It Rains It Pours."

1921    1933    1941    1956    1968    TODAY

A 1957 oil painting by Pawnee artist Brummett Echohawk of the Trail of Tears depicts the eviction of the Cherokee from their native lands.

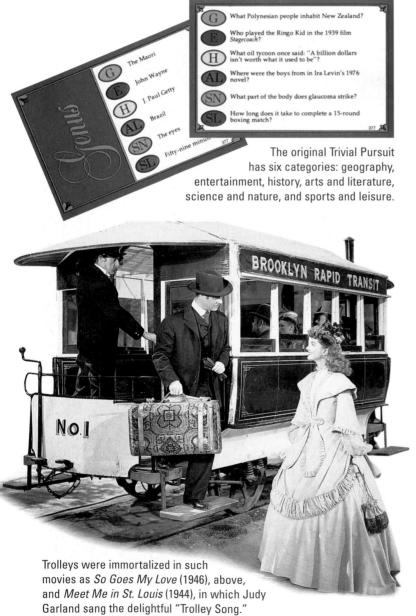

| G | What Polynesian people inhabit New Zealand? |
| E | Who played the Ringo Kid in the 1939 film *Stagecoach*? |
| H | What oil tycoon once said: "A billion dollars isn't worth what it used to be"? |
| AL | Where were the boys from in Ira Levin's 1976 novel? |
| SN | What part of the body does glaucoma strike? |
| SL | How long does it take to complete a 15-round boxing match? |

| G | The Maori |
| E | John Wayne |
| H | J. Paul Getty |
| AL | Brazil |
| SN | The eyes |
| SL | Fifty-nine minutes |

The original Trivial Pursuit has six categories: geography, entertainment, history, arts and literature, science and nature, and sports and leisure.

Trolleys were immortalized in such movies as *So Goes My Love* (1946), above, and *Meet Me in St. Louis* (1944), in which Judy Garland sang the delightful "Trolley Song."

## TRAIL OF TEARS

The Trail of Tears was one of the saddest episodes in the history of the American Indian. Since the late 18th century, the state of Georgia had tried to force the Cherokee to sell their tribal lands, but the Indians took the dispute to court. Finally, in 1835, federal authorities pressured a minor chief into signing the lands away. U.S. troops immediately descended on the Cherokee, and local settlers scattered the Indians' livestock and burned their homes. The Indians were herded into camps in Tennessee, and in 1838 they were forced to walk more than 800 miles to the Indian Territory (now Oklahoma). This route was called the Trail of Tears.

The journey began in the middle of a severe winter, and many Indians became ill and died. There were not enough supplies, and the troops hurried the Indians along, refusing to allow them to help the sick or bury the dead. Of the 15,000 who began the journey, 4,000 died—more than a quarter of the entire Cherokee nation. In spite of the tremendous hardships, those who survived the trip managed to rebuild their nation in the West. In 1907 Cherokee and whites worked together to bring Oklahoma into the Union.

## TRIVIAL PURSUIT

America's most enduringly trivial parlor game was created by two guys from Canada. Scott Abbott and Chris Haney, journalists and roommates, were accustomed to whiling away the dreary Montreal winters by challenging each other to board games. In 1979 they decided to create one of their own. Within 35 minutes, according to Abbott and Haney, Trivial Pursuit was born.

Word of the brain-bending new pastime spread quickly, especially among bright young overachievers. Six thousand questions, from silly to mind-boggling, were asked and answered in the first, or Genus, edition: What was the name of Dick and Jane's cat? (Puff.) What did Stan Mott drive around the world? (A go-cart.) What animal does a hippophobe fear? (The horse.) In 1984, at the height of trivia mania, 19 million sets were sold.

Trivial Pursuit has mutated into editions for every obsession, including TV, Vintage Years, 1960s, and All-Star Sports. The game is now available on CD-ROM, and there are even Trivial Pursuit travel packs for on-the-road trivialization.

## TROLLEYS

In 1887 Richmond, Virginia, became the first U.S. city to install a practical electric network of trolleys, or streetcars. Soon hundreds of electric trolley systems were being built around the country.

Trolleys were different in design and "feel" in each city; riding them became a distinctive part of the urban experience. In New York for example, Brooklynites developed a reputation as "trolley dodgers," hence the name of their baseball team. Some trolley lines, equipped with dining cars and movie projectors, ran between cities, and by 1913 a traveler could take the trolley from Waterville, Maine, to Sheboygan, Wisconsin—a distance of more than 1,000 miles—with just a few short gaps in the route.

Cities began dismantling their trolley lines in the 1930s to make way for the increasing numbers of cars and buses. Some retired trolleys became houses, restaurants, or storage bins. San Francisco's cable cars, which are among America's oldest trolleys, survived and are now a cherished tourist attraction. In the '70s new light-rail technology made it possible for trolleys to return to several other American cities.

## TRUCKERS

In such movies as *Smokey and the Bandit*, truckers are portrayed as freewheeling cowboys of the open road. However, truckers actually lead a hard life. Driving a 40-ton rig with 13 forward gears demands constant attention and exertion. Lots of long-haul truckers push to travel as many miles as they can during the 60 hours that regulations allow them to drive each week. They sleep in the cab of their truck to stay close to the cargo and to save on motel expenses. Truck stops provide them with showers, big parking lots, hearty food, and diesel fuel—not to mention phones for calling home.

Above, a convoy of trucks thunders along the highway. Says one driver, "You're *up* there, and you have a sense of cars swimming frantically around you, like minnows."

Truckers have developed a culture all their own. They use their CB radios to warn each other about smokies (the state police); chatter about the relative merits of Peterbilt, Mack, and Kenworth trucks; and tell tales like the one about the time a reefer (a refrigerated truck) broke down, leaving the driver with thousands of defrosting chickens.

## TRUMAN, HARRY S.

The day Harry Truman was sworn in as president, he told reporters, "Boys, if you ever pray, pray for me now." Yet the unassuming man from Missouri led the country so ably that Winston Churchill later credited him with saving Western civilization. Truman became president on April 12, 1945, after Franklin D. Roosevelt died in office. He made the difficult decision to drop the atomic bomb on Japan, which ended World War II. Truman's G.I. Bill welcomed the troops home and enabled some 12 million veterans to start small businesses, learn trades, and even go to college—a privilege that, before the war, had been reserved for the well-to-do.

Truman won praise for supporting the Marshall Plan for the economic recovery of Europe. It was an unprecedented effort on the part of the victors to aid the vanquished after a war. Still, he was criticized for the fall of China to communism and for the Korean War. His motto became "If you can't stand the heat, stay out of the kitchen." Truman retired after two terms in office, and within a decade he was being called one of the country's greatest presidents.

On the eve of the 1948 election, newspapers predicted a win for Thomas E. Dewey, but "Give 'Em Hell" Harry prevailed. Assessing his presidency, Truman said, "I did my damnedest, and that's all there was to it!"

Instead of wearing our hearts on our sleeves, we wear 'em on our T-shirts. Want one with a unique sentiment? Have it made to order.

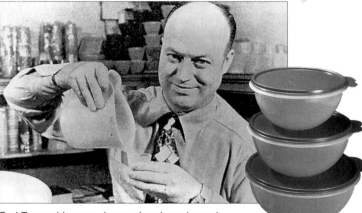

Earl Tupper hit on a winner when he salvaged material left over from oil refining. It became Tupperware.

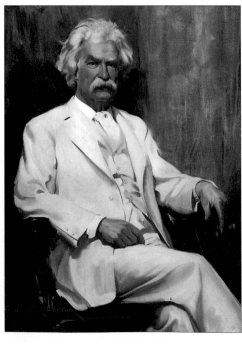

According to Ernest Hemingway, "All modern American literature comes from one book by Mark Twain called *Huckleberry Finn*." Twain was indeed a master of American vernacular.

## T-SHIRTS

They began as cotton underwear carried home from France by doughboys after World War I. Then they became workers' garb. When James Dean wore one in *Rebel Without a Cause*, T-shirts became a statement of youthful rebellion. Finally, beginning in the 1960s, they were adopted as personal billboards, places to display allegiance to favorite causes, sentiments, teams, schools, and brands of foods and beverages, or to broadcast affection for pets.

Why are T-shirts so appealing? Part of their charm is that in order to express an opinion, all you have to do is slip one on and, presto, you're a walking advertisement. Popular T-shirt messages include "Keep on Truckin'," "Bad Hair Day," "My Parents Went to Las Vegas and All I Got Was This Lousy T-Shirt," "Everything I Need to Know I Learned from my Dog," "Born to Shop," and "Hand Over the Chocolate and No One Will Get Hurt."

## TUPPERWARE

In 1946, when chemist Earl Tupper tried to sell his sleek, flexible food-storage containers in retail stores, hardly anyone was interested. Shoppers thought his claims that the plastic would not shatter, leak, or smell were too good to be true. Moreover, customers could not figure out the secret of Tupper's "burpable" seal, which preserved freshness. After spending three days learning how to burp a container, Tupperware distributor Brownie Wise started giving demonstrations in her home. Sales zoomed, and in 1951 Tupperware parties were born.

With visions of superorganized kitchens dancing in their heads, partygoers found themselves buying Tupperware in enormous quantities. Here were seemingly indestructible containers for every conceivable need—even ones people didn't know they had. Today Tupperware continues to sell at "sales events," often held at the workplace. The result? Ninety percent of American households use Tupperware.

## TWAIN, MARK

Samuel Langhorne Clemens grew up on the banks of the Mississippi in the years before the Civil War. Although he ventured far from home, recording humorous anecdotes of his adventures in such books as *The Innocents Abroad* and *Roughing It*, his best writing focused on the "majestic Mississippi, rolling its mile-wide tide along." Even his pen name—Mark Twain—came from a term he knew from his days as a riverboat pilot, meaning "two fathoms deep," which, for a riverboat, is safe water.

Twain's best-known characters, Huck Finn and Tom Sawyer, are perhaps the most rascally yet charming boys ever to appear in American literature. Whether trying to get out of whitewashing Widow Douglas's fence or playing robbers in a cave, these boys lived in a mythic world of endless summertime exploits and terrors. *The Adventures of Huckleberry Finn* has been called America's greatest book because it is eloquent without being pretentious, humorous without being vulgar, and wise without being condescending. Readers of all ages have been moved by the irresistible mixture of Huck's sly wit and his utterly generous heart.

A witty public speaker, Twain delighted audiences with his deadpan delivery of such quips as "There are three kinds of lies. Lies, damned lies, and statistics."

## TWILIGHT ZONE

"You unlock this door with the key of imagination. Beyond it is another dimension...." So began *The Twilight Zone*. Guided by Rod Serling, its narrator and creator, viewers "entered a magical reality, where dreams...and nightmares...come true." For the most part, the show featured ordinary people with ordinary dreams caught in extraordinary circumstances. In "A Stop at Willoughby," an overworked ad exec, Gart Williams, dreams that his commuter train is taking him back to the gentle life of 1880, to a serene town called Willoughby. At the end of the show, Williams, in a moment of final desperation, jumps from the train to his death, shouting something about Willoughby. Later his body is loaded onto a hearse—from Willoughby Funeral Home. In one of the more surreal episodes, viewers meet the Kanamits, humanoid giants from outer space whose credo is stated in a book entitled *To Serve Man*. Only at the last minute do the humans realize the aliens' bible is a cookbook!

In its initial incarnation *The Twilight Zone* lasted only five years (1959–64). But as long as the show—and its 1983 spin-off movie—are rerun on late-night TV, its eerie theme music will remain our anthem of the weird.

## TYPHOID MARY

Everywhere Mary Mallon went, typhoid fever was sure to follow. "Typhoid Mary" may have been responsible for infecting more than 1,400 people. But because she never became ill herself (she was only a carrier of the disease) she refused to give up her beloved profession: cooking for some of New York's wealthiest families. Unfortunately, typhoid is spread by contaminated food and water. Mallon must have suspected that something was amiss, for she would always change jobs whenever typhoid struck in her vicinity.

Finally identified as a carrier after a 1906 outbreak, Mallon was confined to a cottage on North Brother Island, near the Bronx. Soon William Randolph Hearst's newspapers were screeching about "the most dangerous woman in America." Nevertheless, Mallon was released in 1910 after promising never to cook for anyone again. She promptly found work in yet another unsuspecting kitchen. A few outbreaks later, Mallon was returned to her island home. She died in 1938, still refusing to believe that she had caused any trouble.

*The Twilight Zone* was created, hosted, and often written by Rod Serling (left). The show's surprise endings gave Serling a reputation as "the O. Henry of outer space."

In the episode "Time Enough at Last," Burgess Meredith plays the last man left on Earth.

Mary Mallon blamed the drinking water for the cases of typhoid that erupted where she worked. She once spent months caring for a family that she had made sick; many of them simply got worse.

'TYPHOID MARY' DIES OF A STROKE AT 68

Carrier of Disease, Blamed for 51 Cases and 3 Deaths, but She Was Held Immune

Mary Mallon, the first carrier of typhoid bacilli identified in America and consequently known as Typhoid Mary, died yesterday in Riverside Hospital on North Brother Island. With the exception of a five-year period from 1910 to 1915, this isolated spot in the East River had been her home since 1907 when she

Such rare but naturally occurring phenomena as comets, ball lightning, lens-shaped (lenticular) clouds, and the aurora borealis have all been mistaken for UFOs.

## UFOs

America's fascination with the unknown finds its ultimate expression in unidentified flying objects (UFOs). According to surveys, half of us believe in the existence of UFOs, millions claim to have sighted flying oddities, and thousands report that they have actually been abducted by aliens.

The number of sightings has increased tremendously in the past 50 years, but descriptions of otherworldly visitations date back to ancient times. Early extraterrestrial travelers typically flew in chariots borne aloft by winged horses. Today a flying machine of unrecognized origin is likely to be metallic, but there is variance in shape: cigars, saucers, footballs, spheres, bells, and oozy globs have all been reported.

The skeptics say that many sightings are actually projections of the unconscious mind. They also seek to explain away UFOs, citing uncommon weather phenomena, weather balloons, meteorites, advertising planes, hoaxes, and top-secret military designs. (Saucer-shaped aircraft have, in fact, been tested by military researchers since World War II.) However, even the debunkers admit that some evidence defies explanation. For example, there are unretouched photographs that depict flying objects that no one has been able to identify. For many, UFOs will remain an enigma until the government releases the 20,000 pages of related information that it has accumulated since the 1940s.

## UNCLE SAM

"Uncle Sam," the cartoonist's personification of America, is believed to have originated during the War of 1812. One Sam Wilson, who lived in Troy, New York, and who supplied the army with provisions, is said to have stamped beef with the letters *U.S.* to signify U.S. government property. But Wilson's friends had always called him "Uncle Sam," and the moniker quickly became the symbol of America, as "John Bull" was the personification of Great Britain.

The definitive image of Uncle Sam—a white-bearded man with a star-spangled top hat and vest—was created by political cartoonist Thomas Nast shortly after the Civil War. He drew Sam tall, thin, and elderly—but strong. Later images of Uncle Sam depicted him as younger and more vigorous. His most famous appearance was in a World War I recruiting poster by James Montgomery Flagg: a serious Uncle Sam points a finger, saying, "I Want You for U.S. Army."

During World War II, Uncle Sam took on heroic proportions as he sternly urged Americans to do their part by buying war bonds.

# UNCLE TOM'S CABIN

Most Northerners had little firsthand knowledge of slavery and so were relatively indifferent to it. This changed with the publication of *Uncle Tom's Cabin*, a novel by Harriet Beecher Stowe that revealed the horrors of the institution in heartfelt human terms. The author painstakingly researched Southern plantations and drew her characters from real life. Readers of her story cannot easily forget the cruel fate that Uncle Tom, a devout, compassionate slave, suffers at the hands of his master, Simon Legree.

*Uncle Tom's Cabin* was first serialized in an abolitionist magazine, then published as a book in 1852. Its success was phenomenal, with hundreds of thousands of copies selling within a year. Stowe's powerful plea for emancipation did more to prick the nation's conscience than had all previous abolitionist propaganda. President Lincoln himself was aware of the novel's effect on public opinion. When Stowe visited the White House during the Civil War in 1862, Lincoln greeted her by saying, "So you're the little woman who wrote the book that made this great war."

# UNDERGROUND RAILROAD

Slaves in the pre-Civil War South knew that the way to freedom was the Underground Railroad, an informal network of paths and safe houses located about a day's journey apart. The slaves traveled on foot, navigating by the stars at night and hiding during the day. The Underground Railroad had "conductors," courageous souls who risked their lives traveling through the South, recruiting and guiding slaves on their trek to freedom. The most famous, Harriet Tubman, escaped the savage abuse of her owner by hiding in caves and graveyards and wading up streams to throw bloodhounds off her trail. Rather than resting, she went back south 19 times, freeing her own family and more than 300 other "passengers."

# UNITED NATIONS

The United Nations rose from the ashes of World War II as "a world family of democratic nations" that, the Allies hoped, would prevent another war. On April 25, 1945, representatives from 51 countries met in San Francisco to adopt the U.N. Charter. Its far-reaching aims included protecting human rights, fostering peace, mediating international disputes, and encouraging social and economic development. The U.N. is open to all "peace-loving states" that agree to the charter. Today nearly all independent nations are members.

The U.N. has had many successes, from peacefully ending the Cuban Missile Crisis to resolving conflicts in the International Court of Justice. Its peacekeeping forces are increasingly called on to oversee cease-fires and to act as a buffer between hostile armies. Also, there are more than 50 U.N. agencies, including UNICEF, which provides needy children in Third World countries with food and medicine.

Harriet Beecher Stowe's book *Uncle Tom's Cabin* was the first American novel to sell more than a million copies; it has also been translated into more than 20 languages.

It has been estimated that prior to the Civil War, some 75,000 runaway slaves were able to reach freedom via the Underground Railroad.

More than 180 countries have signed the United Nations Charter, thereby pledging to "practice tolerance and live together in peace."

The U.S. Constitution begins with words that many of us know by heart: "We the People of the United States, in Order to form a more perfect Union...." Delegates used the inkstand below to sign the document.

## U.S. CONSTITUTION

America's first governing document, the Articles of Confederation, gave so little power to the federal government that by the mid-1780s the country was in disarray. Delegates of the Continental Congress met in Philadelphia's Independence Hall on May 25, 1787, to write a constitution. After a long summer of contention and compromise, the delegates finally arrived at a "supreme law of the land" that called for a strong central government with separate legislative, judicial, and executive branches. "Our new Constitution is now established," wrote Benjamin Franklin, "and has an appearance that promises permanency."

By the summer of 1788, two-thirds of the states had voted their approval, and the Constitution went into effect. However, the Constitution said little about individual rights, and some states, such as Virginia and New York, balked at ratification. Their support was won with the promised addition of the Bill of Rights (the first 10 amendments). Congress held its first session on March 4, 1789, but it wasn't until after the Bill of Rights was in place that the last two states ratified the Constitution.

## USO

Stars like Bob Hope and The Andrews Sisters braved mud, bugs, and sometimes bombs to bring entertainment to American troops during World War II. Marilyn Monroe gave up her honeymoon with Joe DiMaggio to entertain in Korea. And Jay Leno amused the troops during Desert Storm. Since 1941, USO shows have been boosting morale on the front lines and in the middle of nowhere, anyplace where a makeshift stage can be set up—and even where one can't.

The United Service Organization (USO) was born less than a year before the bombing of Pearl Harbor. With war in the air, the six founding organizations concluded that they could better serve America's armed forces by pooling their resources. President Roosevelt offered his personal blessing, along with funds to create some 300 USO centers. USO centers around the world have since become a "home away from home" for millions of military personnel.

## U.S. 1

U.S. 1—the highway that runs from Calais, Maine, to Key West, Florida—reprises the history of our Atlantic seaboard. It traces part of Paul Revere's 1773 gallop from Boston to Philadelphia. It passes Virginia's Fredericksburg battlefield. It goes through St. Augustine, Florida, America's oldest continually inhabited city. Part of it runs along the Post Road, which connected New York and Philadelphia by stagecoach in 1756. Segments of the highway were the routes of horse-drawn railcars in the early 1800s. When steam trains appeared, stretches of the road went unused until state road building began some 50 years later.

Hollywood went all out to entertain troops during World War II. USO-planned appearances by such actresses as Rita Hayworth (above) were met with warm enthusiasm.

U.S. 1 received its designation in 1925. Like all other federal highways that run north–south, U.S. 1 is an odd number; east–west routes have even numbers.

## UTOPIAN COMMUNITIES

America has always been a land of refuge for the persecuted, a new world for those seeking to practice their principles. Some visionaries came with the hope of establishing utopian communities based on specific theories, usually a turning away from materialism toward spirituality. The first was founded in 1663 in Delaware by Dutch Mennonites, but it lasted only a year. More successful was Pennsylvania's Ephrata Cloister, settled by German pietists in 1732 and continued into the 1780s. Brook Farm, an economic cooperative begun in 1841 in Massachusetts, was noted for the people it attracted, such as Nathaniel Hawthorne. And the Oneida Community in Upstate New York prospered between 1848 and 1881.

Many of the beliefs of these utopias and others have been criticized. Still, as the French scholar Charles Gide pointed out, "there is something touching and instructive in the spectacle of these colonies, for they embody an ideal—a longing that is always being born afresh for a Promised Land."

For centuries, people have been "saying it with flowers." The rose (the redder, the better) is the ultimate symbol of love on Valentine's Day.

## VALENTINE'S DAY

A holiday for romantics, Valentine's Day is linked to the legend of a martyred Christian saint named Valentine. On the day of his execution, February 14, A.D. 270, he sent a note of friendship to his jailer's daughter—an act that inspired our celebration of *amour* and affection.

Americans have been exchanging sentimental gifts and greetings on the saint's day since the late 1700s, when special cards first appeared commercially. Those valentines were fashioned by hand and embellished with paint, stenciling, or scissor work. Early Americans also gave such tokens of love as fancy gloves and scrimshaw corset stays—the forerunners of today's long-stemmed roses and heart-shaped candy boxes.

Cornelius "Commodore" Vanderbilt (above) began his empire with a $100 loan. His granddaughter Gloria (left) celebrated her 18th birthday with Morton Downey.

## VANDERBILT FAMILY

"Hain't I got the power!" crowed the founder of the fortune, Cornelius Vanderbilt (1794–1877), who began by running a ferry service between Staten Island and Manhattan, ended up running the N.Y. Central Railroad, and bequeathed an estate worth $100 million. His son, William Henry, lined Fifth Avenue with Vanderbilt mansions and left $200 million to his eight children. One of them, William K., built Marble House, a 70-room "cottage" in Newport, Rhode Island, in 1888. Not to be outdone, brother Cornelius II put up The Breakers, at which imperial Russian Grand Duke Boris goggled, saying, "I have never seen such luxury!" In Alice Vanderbilt's mansion 200 dinner guests ate off of gold plates; her son, Reginald, inherited $7 million and fathered Gloria Vanderbilt (Little Gloria), subject of a notorious custody battle. The family founded Tennessee's Vanderbilt University; they have also donated to several other educational institutions, as well as to hospitals, libraries, opera houses, museums, and churches.

George Washington Vanderbilt's Biltmore Estate, located in Asheville, North Carolina, has 250 rooms and an exterior of hand-carved limestone.

For nearly 50 years, vaudeville theaters could be seen in cities throughout the nation. Typically, they had grand marquees and advertisements that screamed out the headline acts.

Sarah Vaughan played to large club audiences in the 1950s. Later, she held fans spellbound with renditions of "Misty" and "Send in the Clowns."

## VAUDEVILLE

In the 1800s beer halls across the country put on entertainments of a rip-roaring, bawdy sort not suitable for genteel audiences. It wasn't until 1881 that minstrel singer Tony Pastor advertised a "straight, clean variety show" in New York City. The age of vaudeville thus began, and others copied Pastor's programs of short, unrelated acts: dog performances, flea circuses, contortionists, cartoonists, comedy teams, musical virtuosos, acrobats, and singers. Hundreds of vaudeville houses sprang up. Indeed, vaudeville became the most popular form of entertainment from the 1880s to the early 1930s. Vaudeville's mecca, the Palace Theatre in New York, was turned into a movie house in 1932, and soon vaudeville was displaced by radio and motion pictures. However, the stars of vaudeville survived. Among the entertainers who made the transition were Will Rogers, Fred Astaire, Mae West, W. C. Fields, Bob Hope, the Marx Brothers, and George Burns and Gracie Allen. Vaudeville had taught its players an important lesson. As Jimmy Durante put it, "Broadway and New York ain't the whole world. There's a great big country outside of it, and each place has a solid humor of its own."

## VAUGHAN, SARAH

Although her supple, sultry voice was operatic in power and range (three octaves), Sarah Vaughan devoted herself to jazz and pop. Her sensuous vibrato and precise control of pitch gave ballads an original sheen. "She had the best vocal instrument of any singer working in the popular field," said singer Mel Tormé. To Ella Fitzgerald, "Sassy" was the world's "greatest singing talent." To her fans, she was the Divine One.

Born in Newark, New Jersey, in 1924, Vaughan began her singing career in a church choir. Both her parents were musical, and she studied the piano from the age of seven. When she entered an Apollo Theatre amateur night in 1942, she sang "Body and Soul" with Earl Hines's band. Hines's vocalist, Billy Eckstine, persuaded the bandleader to hire her. In 1944 she joined Eckstine's big jazz band and proved to be an outstanding bebop improviser as well as a proficient pianist. Moving toward pop, her recordings of "Tenderly," "Nature Boy," and a classic version of "It's Magic" became hits in the late '40s. Hits in the '50s included "Whatever Lola Wants" and "Broken-Hearted Melody." "Nothing ever quite matches the feeling I get inside when an audience really shows me that they care for me," said Vaughan. "I sure care for them."

## VCR

Who would have thought that the cumbersome, $2,300 home videotape machine introduced by Sony in 1975 would become as indispensable as toasters and hair dryers? Sony claimed that its machine emancipated viewers from the tyranny of TV programming. However, most of the millions of people who bought VCRs over the next decade used them not to record TV programs (maybe because only rocket scientists could figure out how to program them) but to watch movies rented from the local video store.

As legions of couch potatoes succumbed before the "home entertainment center," the experience of watching movies was transformed. Another unanticipated effect, thanks to the increasingly portable camcorder, has been the creation of home movies that enable families to revisit birthday parties and vacations over and over and over again.

When VCRs appeared, film companies fought to outlaw the technology. Now, with large profits from tape sales and rentals, producers delight in giving their movies a second life.

## VFW

The charter of the Veterans of Foreign Wars (VFW) declares that "the purpose of this corporation shall be fraternal, patriotic, historical and educational; to preserve and strengthen comradeship among its members; to assist worthy comrades; to perpetuate the memory and history of our dead and to assist their widows and orphans; to maintain true allegiance to the Government of the United States." The organization's first members were veterans of the Spanish-American War, a conflict in which, for the first time, large numbers of soldiers were sent overseas to fight—specifically, in Cuba and the Philippines. Membership has since been open to Americans who have participated in military campaigns on foreign soil or in hostile waters. The American Legion, which was founded after World War I, is a similar organization, except that overseas military service is not a condition of membership.

The VFW helped World War I veterans get pension and hospital benefits and lobbied for the GI Bill of Rights for soldiers of World War II and the Korean and Vietnam wars. In 1931 the VFW persuaded Congress to adopt "The Star-Spangled Banner" as our national anthem. Today the group awards scholarships, provides disaster relief, sponsors Boy Scout troops, and helps with the Special Olympics.

Well into their eighties, these World War I veterans, the surviving members of a drum and bugle corps, met to play the old tunes.

## VICE PRESIDENCY

"I do not propose to be buried until I am really dead," Daniel Webster remarked when he turned down the Whig nomination for vice president in 1848. If the names Elbridge Gerry, Richard M. Johnson, William R. D. King, Hannibal Hamlin, Levi P. Morton, and Garret A. Hobart don't sound familiar, it is probably because they were all vice presidents.

Before 1804 the vice president was the presidential candidate who received the second-highest number of electoral votes. But after Thomas Jefferson and Aaron Burr tied in the race for the presidency, the 12th Amendment to the Constitution changed the procedure to require separate balloting for each office. Despite the secondary position's lack of luster (John Nance Garner, vice president from 1933 to 1941, said the office was "not worth a pitcher full of warm spit"), the death or resignation of the commander in chief quickly brings about a reversal. Indeed, nine vice presidents have succeeded to the presidency after the loss of the incumbent.

After serving as vice president in the Johnson administration, Hubert Humphrey made his own bid for the presidency. He lost, but only by one of the slimmest margins ever.

During World War II, the government ran a poster campaign urging people to plant victory gardens. One such poster went so far as to tell citizens that they could help "beet the enemy."

Americans were captivated by the talking machines made by Victor, but no one listened more intently than Nipper, the fox terrier.

Maya Lin, the designer of the Vietnam Veterans Memorial, called black "a soothing, deep, deep color because you can look into it forever."

## VICTORY GARDENS

With the entry of the U.S. into World War II, food rationing went into effect on the home front. Supplies of meat, butter, sugar, and coffee were regulated, and the armed forces were given priority. Produce was also scarce because of the loss of farm workers. The victory garden, an idea proposed in 1941 by Secretary of Agriculture Claude R. Wickard, was a practical response to the shortage of vegetables. Citizens eager to do their part in the war effort planted some 20 million gardens, which sprouted in backyards, vacant lots, and parks. The program's success became apparent in 1943, when the gardens yielded 40 percent (more than a million tons) of the fresh vegetables consumed throughout the country. After the war, many people continued to grow their own vegetables.

## VICTROLA

The Victrola, a trade name so famous that it became synonymous with the phonograph, was developed by Eldridge Johnson, a machinist whose "inventive and business genius made it possible...for good music to be heard in even the most humble home." (Thomas A. Edison had invented a phonograph earlier, but his version was in the form of a cylinder.) When Eldridge Johnson perfected the disk-playing machine in 1906, replacing the unwieldy exterior horn with a small interior one, the phonograph became more popular for home use. The revolutionary design was called the Victrola, and Johnson's Victor Talking Machine Company produced 112 different models, along with recordings by the era's foremost musicians, from Enrico Caruso to John Philip Sousa.

## VIETNAM VETERANS MEMORIAL

One of the most moving monuments in the nation's capital, the Vietnam Veterans Memorial consists of two polished black granite walls engraved with the names of some 58,000 dead or missing American service men and women of the Vietnam War. Of 1,421 designs submitted for the memorial, the one chosen was by a 21-year-old architecture student, Maya Ying Lin. Her design was highly controversial, called by some "a black gash of shame." The nation had been deeply divided by the Vietnam War, whose veterans had not had the hero's welcome accorded to the G.I.s returning from World War II. With this tangible public recognition in the form of a memorial, the country at last honored the sacrifices of the fallen of Vietnam. At the dedication in 1982, one veteran gave voice to the sentiments of the others, "We waited 15 years to get here, man. But it's not too late."

Thousands of visitors file by the monument every day to touch the names of loved ones, make a wall rubbing, or leave gifts or cards. "Tomorrow is your birthday," said one letter. "The only present I can give you is to have your family come to this memorial . . . and to remember you." Mementos are not discarded—the National Parks Service keeps them.

## VOGUE

The first issue of *Vogue* appeared on December 17, 1892. A weekly magazine costing 10 cents, *Vogue* was founded by Arthur B. Turnure as a mainly pictorial "dignified, authentic journal" of society and fashion. In 1909 it was acquired by publisher Condé Nast, who eventually launched the British and French *Vogue*s as well as Vogue Patterns. Under his aegis *Vogue* developed into a leading fashion bible. The prestigious publication has presented the photographs of Horst P. Horst, Edward Steichen, Baron De Meyer, and Irving Penn (Cecil Beaton's photographs first appeared in British *Vogue*), as well as the work of many notable contemporary English and American writers. Its editors have included Edna Woolman Chase, who organized the first American fashion show, and the flamboyant Diana Vreeland, later consultant to the Costume Institute of New York's Metropolitan Museum of Art.

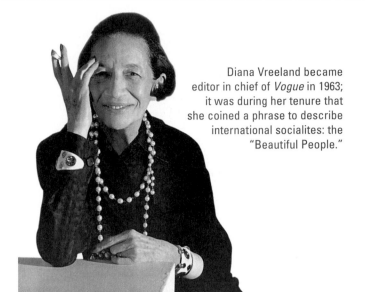

Diana Vreeland became editor in chief of *Vogue* in 1963; it was during her tenure that she coined a phrase to describe international socialites: the "Beautiful People."

## VOLUNTEER FIRE DEPARTMENTS

Since 1736 Americans in villages and cities alike have relied on volunteer fire departments to protect their lives and property. In the early days of the republic, few municipalities could afford to maintain a standing fire department. Yet long after police departments and other public institutions turned professional, and mechanized equipment lessened the number of "smoke eaters" required, volunteer departments endured—proud of their traditions and honored place in the community. Their firehouses are centers of social activity, from carnivals to chowder parties, and their members—whether their "day job" is banker or butcher—make up a respected fraternity.

"Volunteers in the service of beneficiaries are the glory of civilized life," said a firefighter in 1809. So entrenched is this conviction that 75 percent of the nation's 30,500 fire departments remain volunteer.

In the mid-1800s steam-powered fire engines, such as the Silsby Steamer (right), had come into use, replacing hand pumps and bucket brigades.

## VOTING

Voting is a right that many Americans take for granted, but in the 18th century it was a privilege granted only to free, white, property-holding males. It wasn't until 1860 that all white men became eligible to vote, and it would be another 10 years before suffrage was guaranteed regardless of "race, color, or previous condition of servitude." Even then, poll taxes and literacy tests kept blacks from voting in some states.

Until the 20th century, women were thought to lack the intellectual capacity to vote. (One exception was in New Jersey, where women were enfranchised from 1776 to 1807.) By the early 1900s, the woman suffrage movement, championed by Susan B. Anthony and Elizabeth Cady Stanton, was gaining ground, and in 1920, the 19th Amendment gave women the vote. The landmark Voting Rights Act, passed in 1965, provided increased protection for black voters. For the first time, equality at the polls applied to all Americans.

In 1776 New Jersey's constitution did not specify that a voter had to be male. This oversight gave women, for the first time, a chance to vote.

*"I hear America singing,
the varied carols I hear."*

WALT WHITMAN

Commotion reigns on the trading floor of the New York Stock Exchange, the largest securities marketplace in the world. The Wall Street district also includes the American Stock Exchange, the Federal Reserve Bank, trust companies, brokerage firms, and investment banks.

This war bonnet from the 1880s, made of eagle feathers, wool cloth, and weasel skins, is at the Buffalo Bill Historical Center in Cody, Wyoming.

Obsessed with the idea of fame, Warhol turned average people into so-called superstars (a term he popularized) through his many underground films.

## WALL STREET

When the business community speaks of Wall Street, it is referring to America's financial center, named after the New York City street where high finance was born. Legend has it that bills of lading, checks, and notes were once traded in Wall Street coffeehouses. This all changed in 1792, when 24 brokers met under a buttonwood tree to establish a market with regular hours and common trading practices. That market became the New York Stock Exchange.

Wall Street developed an image of ruthlessness during the post-Civil War boom as speculators fought for control of railroads, manipulated the price of gold, caused bank failures, and brought on recessions. In 1929 the infamous Black Tuesday market crash gave Wall Street a negative image that lasted for decades. In the 1960s many brokerages began moving uptown, but they're still considered "Wall Street" firms.

## WAR BONNET

Only the most courageous Indian war leaders were given the honor of wearing war bonnets into battle. Whether elaborate feathered headdresses or skin skullcaps, war bonnets could inspire bravery or call on the spirits for help. Whoever wore one was pledged to fight fiercely and be the last to retreat. Cheyenne and Blackfeet war bonnets traditionally had feathers that stood straight up; some tribes wore caps of animal fur. Only warriors in the highest positions donned headgear with buffalo horns. In 1867 the Lakota Indians chose Sitting Bull as their war chief and gave him a war bonnet of eagle feathers that reached all the way to the ground. Because each feather represented an act of bravery by a Lakota warrior, Sitting Bull carried into battle the courage of the entire tribe.

## WARHOL, ANDY

The father of pop art, Andy Warhol gave up his career as an advertising illustrator to churn out oversize silk screens of paper money, Coke bottles, and Campbell's soup cans, as well as silk-screen reproductions of photographs of such people as Marilyn Monroe and Elvis Presley. The highly impersonal prints shocked critics and the public alike. Warhol explained that pop art celebrates ordinary things— "comics, picnic tables, men's trousers, celebrities, shower curtains, refrigerators"—in other words, everything that abstract art doesn't. The silk screens, many of which depicted commercial products, were like commercial products themselves, printed in endless variations, often by studio assistants. Warhol's 1981 series glorified such symbols of America as Howdy Doody, Greta Garbo, Superman, and even himself. Usually dressed in black, the platinum-blond Warhol liked to surround himself with "beautiful people." The cult of celebrity that he generated led him to predict that "in the future, everyone will be famous for 15 minutes."

## WAR MOVIES

Almost immediately after the start of World War II, Hollywood began making war movies. MGM's poignant *The Mortal Storm* (1940), which depicted the horrors of Nazi Germany, flopped at the box office. Later, six studios vied for the title *Remember Pearl Harbor*, but not one produced it. Things changed after the American landing in North Africa a week before the release of *Casablanca* (1942). People flooded the theaters. *Mrs. Miniver* (1942), a tribute to British grit in the face of Nazi bombings, broke attendance records.

As actual battle footage reached Hollywood, combat films began to proliferate. Clark Gable and Lana Turner were war correspondents in *Somewhere I'll Find You* (1942); Humphrey Bogart was a merchant marine in *Action in the North Atlantic* (1943); Robert Taylor braved the burning sands of the back lot in *Bataan* (1943); Robert Montgomery and John Wayne manned PT boats in John Ford's *They Were Expendable* (1945). Courageous cameramen filmed documentaries, such as William Wyler's *The Memphis Belle* (1943), a salute to B-17 bombers. Wyler also directed the postwar classic *The Best Years of Our Lives* (1946), about three vets colliding with the realities of civilian life.

## WARNER BROTHERS

"I don't want it good. I want it Tuesday," ordered production chief Jack Warner. He often got both. The four Warner brothers began their careers by running a nickelodeon with chairs borrowed from an undertaker. In 1927 they made history by producing the first talkie, *The Jazz Singer*. In the early '30s Warner released a series of spectacular Busby Berkeley musicals, including *42nd Street*, which boasts the line "You're going out a youngster, but you've got to come back a star!"

Warner's "fast and cheap" philosophy led to the development of the crime movie. The studio turned out gritty yarns of social disintegration: *Little Caeser*, *The Public Enemy*, and *I Am a Fugitive from a Chain Gang*. Tough guys like Edward G. Robinson and Jimmy Cagney were a specialty ("Women love bums!" Warner announced); Humphrey Bogart played gangsters before attaining immortality in *The Maltese Falcon*. Bette Davis, star of *Dark Victory*, was queen of the lot until Joan Crawford showed up as a fugitive from MGM.

Warner's faltering fortunes were restored in the 1970s by Clint Eastwood films and other series. In 1989 Warner was acquired by Time Inc., creating the Time Warner empire.

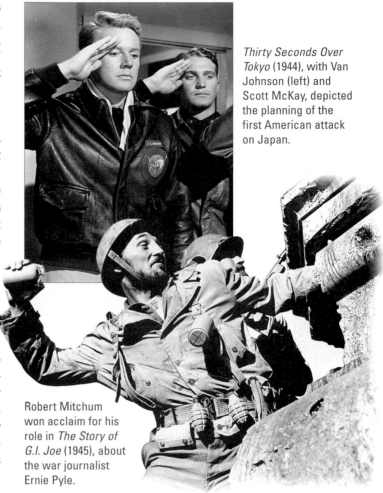

*Thirty Seconds Over Tokyo* (1944), with Van Johnson (left) and Scott McKay, depicted the planning of the first American attack on Japan.

Robert Mitchum won acclaim for his role in *The Story of G.I. Joe* (1945), about the war journalist Ernie Pyle.

Joan Crawford (left) played the self-sacrificing mother of Ann Blyth (right) in Warner Brothers's glossy 1945 film *Mildred Pierce*.

This famous photo by Robert H. Jackson captures the moment Jack Ruby (right) shot accused presidential assassin Lee Harvey Oswald (center).

This monument to Booker T. Washington, at Tuskegee University, shows the educator "lifting the veil of ignorance from his people."

Thomas Jefferson wrote of Washington, "Never did nature and fortune combine more perfectly to make a man great, and to place him in... an everlasting remembrance."

## WARREN COMMISSION

Did Lee Harvey Oswald shoot President John F. Kennedy? Did he act alone, or as part of a conspiracy? Did Jack Ruby shoot Oswald to keep him quiet? A week after Kennedy's assassination on November 22, 1963, the Warren Commission was established to find the answers to these questions and many others surrounding the tragic events in Dallas.

The seven-member commission, headed by U.S. Chief Justice Earl Warren, pored over volumes of reports and photographs and heard the testimony of 552 witnesses. After 10 months, it concluded that Oswald was the lone assassin, that he did shoot Kennedy and the policeman who tried to arrest him, and that Ruby acted alone in killing Oswald. At first, the Warren Report was widely hailed. But over the years, hundreds of books and articles have challenged the commission's findings. Later investigations have proved inconclusive, and, in the minds of many, the full story of John F. Kennedy's assassination remains a mystery.

## WASHINGTON, BOOKER T.

Booker T. Washington was born a slave, but he grew up to be the most influential black leader of his day. After the Civil War, young Booker worked long hours at salt furnaces and in coal mines while going to school. He then attended Hampton Institute, where he worked as a janitor to pay his tuition.

In 1881, at the urging of Hampton's founder, the 25-year-old Washington started the Tuskegee Institute in Alabama; under his leadership, it became one of the country's most prestigious vocational colleges. Tuskegee students were taught to take pride in their appearance and health and to find dignity in labor. They perfected trades and acquired the skills needed to design and erect most of the institute's buildings. Washington believed that, in the struggle for advancement, tangible accomplishments like these were more powerful than political agitation. Dissenters, however, felt that his focus on vocational training would turn blacks into second-class citizens. William E. B. Du Bois, in particular, wrote that education should produce not laborers but leaders.

## WASHINGTON, GEORGE

"First in war, first in peace, and first in the hearts of his countrymen," said Col. Henry Lee of George Washington in a fitting tribute to the man who would be remembered as the father of his country. Washington's leadership qualities were apparent at the First and Second Continental Congresses, and in 1775 he was elected commander of the Continental Army. On Christmas night 1776, he and his men rowed noiselessly across the Delaware River to capture some 900 Hessians at Trenton, and he went on to brilliant victories at Princeton and Yorktown.

By the end of the Revolutionary War, Washington enjoyed such prestige that in 1789 the electoral college unanimously chose him to be America's first president. Committed to a strong central government, he established the country's financial structure, upheld America's neutrality in the war between France and Britain, and quashed the Whiskey Rebellion of 1794. After two terms in office, he retired to Mount Vernon, where he died in 1799.

## WASHINGTON, D.C.

It's fitting that the Capitol lies at the heart of Washington, whose grand boulevards radiate from it like the spokes of a wheel. The city was conceived and developed to revolve around the federal government, the hub of the country. The site, an area of swampland on the Potomac River, was chosen by George Washington in 1791, and it was designed to rival the splendor of Paris. "The plan should...leave room for that aggrandizement and embellishment which the increase of wealth of the nation will permit...." said the architect, Maj. Pierre Charles L'Enfant.

Two centuries later, the riches of the nation built a city where America's story is written in marble and bronze. Street after street of august edifices—from the "President's Palace" to "Congress Hall" (as the White House and the Capitol were once known)—house the civil servants who turn the gears of government. Mile upon mile of monuments honor our heroes and history. Some 50 institutions, including the famed Smithsonian, showcase our cultural riches.

A site for pageants and protests, the federal city is diverse and residential, although much of its population changes with each administration. Ever since President John F. Kennedy rode up decaying Pennsylvania Avenue on the day of his inauguration and barked "Fix it!" to an aide, Washington has been undergoing radical renewal. The colonial port of Georgetown, which had deteriorated, is again the most coveted address, while row houses throughout the historic neighborhoods are being renovated to befit L'Enfant's dream for a city "magnificent enough to grace a great nation."

## WATER BED

In 1968 Charles P. Hall, a San Francisco State graduate student, got an *A* for his design of a bed with a water-filled mattress, which he then proceeded to patent and market. The concept was simple: a large mattress-shaped bladder to hold water, a heater to keep it from being unbearably cold, and a frame with a liner to stop leaks from becoming disastrous. As long as you remembered to put bleach in the mattress to keep it from growing algae, and eliminated all the air pockets that could cause sloshing noises, water beds could be remarkably comfortable. They were marketed, however, as the perfect setting for sensual escapades; during the '70s no swinger wanted to be without one. Recently, water bed owners are more interested in just getting a good night's sleep.

The Jefferson Memorial (above) is situated so that the 19-foot-tall sculpture of Thomas Jefferson inside overlooks the Potomac River. At about 555 feet, the Washington Monument (left) is the city's tallest structure. It took more than a hundred years to complete: the idea was proposed in 1783; the monument was opened to the public in 1888.

The Capitol, Congress's meeting place, was set on fire by the British during the War of 1812. Soon afterward, the building was restored and the central dome was added.

Ethel Waters (right) starred with Julie Harris in the play and the movie *The Member of the Wedding*. Waters's autobiography, *His Eye Is on the Sparrow,* was a best-seller.

Wayne didn't talk much on-screen; but, as John Ford noted, "What he said *meant* something." He was paired with Maureen O'Hara in *The Quiet Man* (above). His performance in *The Searchers* (left) is considered one of his best.

## WATERS, ETHEL

Born into deep poverty on the outskirts of Philadelphia in 1896, Ethel Waters sang the blues "out of the depths of the private fire in which I was brought up." Billed as "Sweet Mama Stringbean," 21-year-old Waters first sang at Baltimore's Lincoln Theater "from nine until unconscious," for the sum of nine dollars a week. She went on to headline at Harlem's Cotton Club, singing moving renditions of "Stormy Weather" and "Dinah."

In 1933 the smoky-voiced singer became a Broadway star in Irving Berlin's enormously successful musical *As Thousands Cheer.* But singing was not her first love. "I'd rather act," said Waters. And act she did. In 1950 she played the cook in *The Member of the Wedding*, which earned her rave reviews, a role in the movie version of the play, and her second Academy Award nomination. Though hard up in her later years, the great performer never lost the faith expressed in one of her favorite songs: "I sing because I'm happy, I sing because I'm free. His eye is on the sparrow, and I know he watches me."

## WAYNE, JOHN

Never mind the names of his films; to his fans, they were all John Wayne Movies, featuring the swagger, drawl, and square-dealing decency of the quintessential American screen hero. In a career that spanned almost 50 years, "Duke" made more than 175 movies and was one of the biggest box-office attractions of all time.

A college football star, Wayne worked summers for movie director John Ford, began playing bit parts, and made low-budget "quickie" Westerns until 1939, when Ford cast him as the Ringo Kid in *Stagecoach*, and Wayne's career took off. Among other films he made for Ford were *She Wore a Yellow Ribbon*, *The Quiet Man*, *Fort Apache*, and *The Searchers*. Wayne specialized in playing a leader of men, a cowboy, and a cavalry officer. In *True Grit* (1969) he played an old Western marshal complete with eyepatch, and at last he won an Oscar. A staunch conservative, Wayne helped found the Motion Picture Alliance for the Preservation of American Ideals. In 1968 he co-directed *The Green Berets*, his tribute to the Vietnam War. Wayne faced death from cancer with admirable courage; shortly before he died, Congress awarded him a special gold medal.

## WEATHER

"Everybody talks about the weather, but nobody does anything about it," wrote Charles Dudley Warner in the *Hartford Courant* in 1897. Even in places where it rarely rains and where the temperature hardly varies—elevators, air-conditioned offices, Los Angeles—the weather is the small-talk subject of first resort. For some people it has even become a hobby. The Weather Channel on cable television claims some

50 million viewers. Computer users with modems can log on to learn the atmospheric conditions in any part of the world. And growing numbers of storm chasers, armed with video cameras, actually seek out nature's most violent tempests.

Americans feel strongly about the people who tell them about the weather, and many television forecasters are highly paid celebrities. CBS anchor Dan Rather got his start on national television reporting on a hurricane in Houston. In 1911 one hapless amateur weather watcher was lynched for failing to predict the snow that ruined a July Fourth crawfish festival in Mobile, Alabama, as well as for omitting from his forecast mention of a total eclipse of the sun.

## WEATHER VANES

Centuries before satellites, radar, and weather balloons, a simple rooftop device supplied the forecast for seafarers, farmers, and anyone else who needed to know which way the wind was blowing. Weather vanes, which indicate wind shifts that often precede changes in weather, were the surest way to become weather-wise.

These instruments, crafted from colonial times to the late 1800s, provided information on more than just meteorology. In the hands of imaginative wood-carvers and metalsmiths, the vanes became iconic sculptures that might advertise a trade, support a cause, or express a sense of whimsy. All manner of handwrought and molded shapes—from leaping stags to prancing steeds, Lady Liberty to the archangel Gabriel—decorated barn roofs, housetops, and churches around the country. The copper grasshopper fashioned in 1742 by artisan Shem Drowne for Faneuil Hall still seems poised to spring over Boston. Covetously collected, weather vanes today herald another current: a newfound appreciation of American folk art.

## WEBSTER, NOAH

The last word of the Declaration of Independence is *honor*, not *honour*—a deliberate departure from British spelling, which told the world America was ready to manage its own language as well as its own political destiny. Noah Webster was the man responsible for defining and codifying American English, the new language of the fledgling republic. He proposed a simplified spelling system based on common speech, then invented a new way to teach it: the spelling bee. His blue-backed speller is one of the most successful books of all time, as familiar to early Americans as the Bible. Beginning in 1783 it sold more than 80 million copies.

Webster worked on his dictionary daily for 25 years, producing a 70,000-word rule book based on his battle cry: *Usus est norma loquendi,* or "Common usage is the basis for any grammar." Some of his spelling innovations—*ake* for *ache, crum* for *crumb*—never caught on, but his influence on the standardization of our national language is incalculable.

For a growing number of storm chasers, tornadoes are the stuff dreams are made of. Weather buffs can subscribe to such magazines as *Weatherwise* and join clubs like the International Weather Watchers.

"Cocks have always been seen, but never so well as in American weather vanes," wrote Pablo Picasso, the great Spanish painter.

Noah Webster's 1828 *American Dictionary of the English Language* included some 5,000 slang words and a brief history of the world.

Lawrence Welk is perhaps best remembered for his cue, "A-one, a-two..." His show was decidedly wholesome; at one point, he fired singer Alice Lon, the original Champagne Lady, for exposing her knees on camera.

West often delivered her double-entendres with a suggestive swivel. "It's not what I say," she explained. "It's the way I say it."

## WELK, LAWRENCE

Folksy and fatherly, accordionist and bandleader Lawrence Welk was the host of the longest-running television variety show in history, the *Lawrence Welk Show*. Welk cheerfully presided over his "boys and girls"—dancers, instrumentalists, and singers, such as "da lovely Lennon Sisters." He offered viewers what he called "Champagne Music," a middle-of-the-road potpourri of popular songs that to some people sounded more like "pink lemonade for the ears." The show was a Saturday-night institution on ABC from 1955 to 1971, and it continued in syndication until 1982. Welk's band also played at President Dwight D. Eisenhower's inauguration in 1957 and made hit records, including *Calcutta* in 1961. A successful businessman, Welk wrote several books, among them a best-selling autobiography, *Wunnerful, Wunnerful*.

## WEST, MAE

A lifelong champion of longline corsets, Mae West cautioned, "You got to have something to put in 'em. Know what I mean?" We sure do, Mae; the British Royal Air Force didn't name an inflatable life jacket after you for nothing. The paragon of sex parodists, West, with her rolling eyes, swaggering walk, and nasal voice, has been endlessly imitated. In 1926 she wrote, produced, and starred in a Broadway play succinctly titled *Sex*. It was banned after 11 months, and West was sent to the workhouse in her $200,000 Isotta-Fraschini car. After her next hit play, *Diamond Lil*, she made her first film, *Night After Night*, for Paramount, where she won artistic control over the nine comedies she made during the '30s.

West was noted for her one-liners ("I'm a girl who lost her reputation and never missed it"), and her steamy delivery could remove wallpaper. After her movie career ended, she kept her legend alive with stage revivals and nightclub tours, adorning the cover of *Life* magazine at age 76. Rarely linked romantically, she purred, "It's not the men you see me with, it's the men you don't see me with." Know what she means?

## WESTERNS

Only historians grumble that the Hollywood version of the Wild West is inaccurate. Others revel in the heroic exploits of rough-riding cowboys—men whose independence and grit loom large in our vision of America. One of the first movies ever made was a Western, *The Great Train Robbery*; audiences in 1903 were amazed by the nonstop action sequences showing good guys in white and bad guys in black settling their differences with six-shooters. By the '20s "horse operas" made up nearly a third of all feature films, and several new stars, including Tom Mix and William S. Hart, had emerged.

During the Depression, low-budget B Westerns featuring predictable plots and plenty of gunfights entertained millions of Saturday-matinee goers. The heroes were worshiped for their dead-eye accuracy and suspenseful administration of justice. Westerns were reinvented in 1939 with John Ford's masterpiece, *Stagecoach*, which launched the career of John Wayne, the ultimate Western hero. Wayne gave one of his best performances in *Red River* (1948), directed by Howard Hawks. By the time Gary Cooper starred as Marshal Will Kane in *High Noon* (1952), the Western had risen to a higher level of sophistication. *Shane* followed the next year.

The Western prevails as a framework for everything from comic parodies to dark dramas. In the tongue-in-cheek 1969 classic *Butch Cassidy and the Sundance Kid*, starring Paul Newman and Robert Redford, Redford asks, "Why is it, everything I'm good at is illegal?" In 1992 Clint Eastwood's stark revisionist film, *Unforgiven*, won Oscars for best picture and best director.

## WESTERN UNION

In 1861, five backbreaking years after construction began, the first transcontinental telegraph line was completed. The Western Union Telegraph Company was the driving force behind the monumental task. Thereafter, it continued to lay new telegraph lines across the country and under the Atlantic Ocean. Hundreds of Western Union offices appeared in cities, towns, and outposts, connecting the nation. Operators tapped out messages first by Morse code, then with teletype machines.

When the telegraph was eclipsed by the telephone and wireless radio, Western Union was overshadowed by its competitors. The company's decline in the second half of the 20th century was due largely to a mistake made in 1876, when it passed up an offer to buy all of Alexander Graham Bell's telephone patents. William Orton, then president of Western Union, reportedly said, "What use could this company make of an electrical toy?"

## WESTINGHOUSE, GEORGE

After the Civil War, a frenzy of transcontinental railroad construction began, accompanied by frightful train wrecks. Many accidents occurred because brakemen had to apply the brakes in each car by hand in order to stop the train. In 1869, 22-year-old George Westinghouse made train travel safer by inventing an air-brake system that was controlled from the cab of the locomotive. It made him a millionaire. Stopping trains was only half the problem; in the 1880s Westinghouse developed automated signals to tell engineers *when* to brake.

Westinghouse became interested in the use of electricity; this led him into competition with Thomas Edison, who was working with direct current (DC). Westinghouse made generators that produced an alternating current (AC). When his rivals spread the word that AC was dangerous, citing the fact that it powered the electric chair, the setback was temporary; Edison's DC system eventually faded away.

Gary Cooper won an Oscar for his role as a lone sheriff fighting for his life in *High Noon* (right). In *Unforgiven* (below) Clint Eastwood played a temporarily reformed trigger-happy killer.

When uniformed Western Union messengers arrived on foot or by bicycle, people braced themselves for important news: a wedding, a death in the family, the birth of a baby.

The West Point honor code, which is upheld by the cadets themselves, is a vow not to lie, cheat, or steal, or to let others do so.

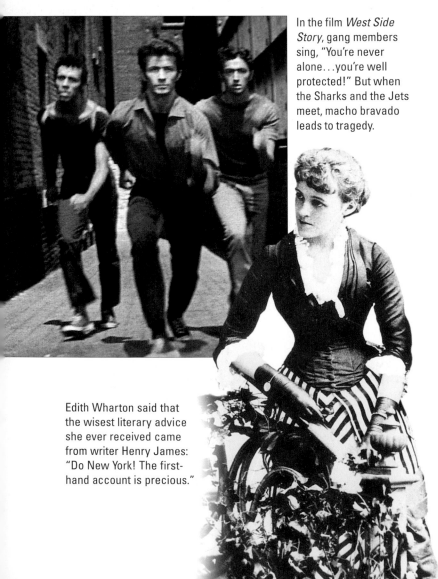

In the film *West Side Story*, gang members sing, "You're never alone…you're well protected!" But when the Sharks and the Jets meet, macho bravado leads to tragedy.

Edith Wharton said that the wisest literary advice she ever received came from writer Henry James: "Do New York! The first-hand account is precious."

## WEST POINT

As far back as 1776, Gen. George Washington supported a proposal for a national military academy, but Congress was distrustful of standing armies. However, treaty violations by the British after the Revolution, Indian wars, and boundary disputes persuaded Congress that Washington had been right. In 1802 the U.S. Military Academy was established at West Point, a fortification 50 miles north of New York City.

The academy didn't really take shape until 1817, under the leadership of Maj. Sylvanus Thayer. He established the honor code and strict standards for students, which cadets sometimes objected to as being too harsh. He also expanded the faculty and curriculum. For many years the academy was the only American engineering school; West Point graduates planned many of our major roads, railroads, and canals.

The leading generals on both sides of the Civil War were West Pointers, as was Jefferson Davis, the Confederate president. The academy dominated the top ranks of the army until World War II, and now one quarter of army officers hail from West Point. Since 1976 women have been appointed to the academy and currently make up 12 percent of the cadets.

## WEST SIDE STORY

*West Side Story*, a contemporary adaptation of Shakespeare's *Romeo and Juliet*, premiered on Broadway in 1957. In it, the Sharks and the Jets are rival street gangs in New York; Tony, a Jet, falls in love with Maria, sister of the Sharks's leader. Gang warfare erupts; Tony kills Maria's brother, and as with Romeo and Juliet, the young couple's fate is sealed.

The show was conceived by Jerome Robbins, who also did the choreography. The music was composed by Leonard Bernstein, and the lyrics were written by Stephen Sondheim; it played 734 performances and won two Tony Awards.

The movie that followed, filmed against gritty, realistic mean streets, was showered with 10 Oscars at the Academy Awards in 1962, including those for best picture, director, supporting actor, and supporting actress, as well as an honorary award for Robbins. *West Side Story*, with its exciting, tension-filled dance numbers, soaring score, and vibrant characters, still packs a wallop. Its list of ever-popular hit songs includes "America," "Tonight," "Maria," "I Feel Pretty," and "Somewhere." The musical has enjoyed many revivals and has proved to be a big success overseas.

## WHARTON, EDITH

Born into Old New York society, Edith Wharton grew up in an airless world of Victorian drawing rooms, gilt-edged calling cards, and 14-course dinner parties. Wharton's novels, written with tart wit and laced with revealing details, attack the hypocrisies of the suffocating society from which she came. *The Age of Innocence*, for example, scrutinizes the cruelties of upper-crust New Yorkers, who "dreaded scandal more than disease." *The House of Mirth* follows Lily Bart in her disastrous efforts to marry upward in a snobbish society.

No slave to convention, Wharton divorced her husband in 1913, seizing control of her finances and career. With shrewd marketing, her books sold fabulously well, expanding her already sizable income. She made some 60 Atlantic crossings in her lifetime and enjoyed nothing as much as a fast drive in an open motorcar with her friend Henry James. Volunteer work during World War I earned her the prestigious Chevalier of the Legion of Honour, and in 1921 she became the first woman to be awarded a Pulitzer Prize.

## WHEATIES

Wheaties made a modest debut in 1924; sales soared a few years later thanks to the world's first singing radio commercial. In 1933 Wheaties started its association with sports by sponsoring the radio broadcasts of the Minneapolis Millers, a baseball team. Knox Reeves, who worked for the company's ad agency, created the slogan "Breakfast of Champions" for a billboard at the baseball park. Endorsements from such sports stars as Jack Dempsey, Johnny Weissmuller, Bruce Jenner, Pete Rose, Chris Evert, and Walter Payton made the cereal a classic. Even European animal trainer Maria Rasputin has endorsed Wheaties. In the 1950s, as a marketing test, the Lone Ranger and Mickey Mouse replaced athletes on the box. When cereal sales dropped 10 percent, sports heroes were brought back.

## WHISTLER, JAMES

With his sharp tongue, quick wit, and natty attire—complete with monocle—James Whistler was as celebrated for his eccentric personality as for his extraordinary paintings. The expatriate artist, who lived primarily in London, rebelled against the detail-rich narrative style of his era by emphasizing mood over moralizing. "Art should be independent of all clap-trap," he said, "… and appeal to the artistic sense of eye or ear." Celebrating "art for art's sake," Whistler abandoned the telling of stories in favor of arousing sensation. He used muted colors and abstract forms to suggest atmosphere. His best-known work, popularly called "Whistler's Mother," is a study in gray and black. The economical lines of his portraits, landscapes, and nocturnal scenes show the influence of Japanese art; several works depict kimono-clad figures and Oriental porcelains.

Irrepressible and prolific, Whistler created not only oils but some 400 etchings, along with lithographs, watercolors, and interior designs—including the resplendent Peacock Room at the Freer Gallery in Washington, D.C.

Artist William Merritt Chase said there were two Whistlers: one, "in public—the fop, the cynic, the brilliant, flippant, vain and careless idler; the other was Whistler of the studio, the earnest, tireless, somber worker."

Aspiring athletes ate lots of Wheaties—not only to grow big and strong but to collect premiums like this bowl featuring their favorite sports heroes (left).

The original owner of the Peacock Room disliked the way James Whistler covered every inch of the leather walls to match his painting *Princess from the Land of Porcelain* (above). Still, it was a tour de force of which the artist was particularly proud. Whistler painted this self-portrait (right) in 1872.

The murder of Stanford White (top right) by Harry K. Thaw (left), husband of Evelyn Nesbit (bottom right), was called the "crime of the century." "He ruined my wife, and I got him," said Thaw.

"May none but honest and wise men ever rule under this roof," said John Adams, the first president to live in the White House. Above is the South Portico as it looks today; at right, the Blue Room.

## WHITE, STANFORD

Remembered as much for his libertine lifestyle as for his richly ornamented buildings, Stanford White personified both the excess and the elegance of the Gilded Age. A man of intellect and powerful bearing, this preeminent American architect was the most visible partner in the firm of McKim, Mead & White, and he moved with ease among its high-society clients. While the lavish mansions and clubs he designed displayed a taste for monumental columns, marble, and gilding, he also had a penchant for showgirls—most notably the lovely Evelyn Nesbit. His scandalous end came on June 25, 1906, at New York's second Madison Square Garden (which he had designed). As White enjoyed a revue called *Mamzelle Champagne*, Nesbit's deranged husband approached the architect's stage-side table, pulled out a pistol, and shot him dead.

## WHITE HOUSE

When Thomas Jefferson quipped that the famed mansion at 1600 Pennsylvania Avenue was "big enough for two emperors, one Pope, and the grand Lama," it may have been sour grapes: Jefferson is believed to have entered—and lost—the design competition for the official residence. The 1792 commission went instead to James Hoban, an Irish builder who modeled his design on a Georgian-style mansion in Dublin.

The house was still under construction when the earliest occupants, John and Abigail Adams, arrived in November 1800. (Abigail used the then unfinished East Room, now the elegant setting for concerts, balls, and official ceremonies, for drying clothes.) The building had to be completely restored after British troops torched it during the War of 1812. Among the many subsequent additions and alterations were the semicircular South Portico (1824), bathrooms (circa 1878), refurbished interiors by Louis Comfort Tiffany (1882), and electricity (1891). The name "White House" was officially designated by President Theodore Roosevelt in 1901. The West Wing and the Oval Office were designed by McKim, Mead & White one year later. Today a housekeeping staff of 17 keeps its 132 rooms in order.

## WHITMAN, WALT

The first edition of *Leaves of Grass* begins with "I" and ends with "you," and what comes between is Walt Whitman's gift to readers—intimate, generous expressions that convey some of the most unreserved poetry written in the English language. "I celebrate myself," announced the poet in the opening lines of "Song of Myself," "And what I assume you shall assume / For every atom belonging to me as good belongs to you." Readers of the mid-1800s didn't know how to react to Whitman's bold, irregular, unrhymed lines. Describing himself as "an American, one of the roughs, a kosmos, / Disorderly fleshy and sensual," Whitman was stung by critics who called his poetry "uncouth and grotesque...

indecent." In fact, the book cost him his job as a government clerk because of what were called "immoral passages." But when the most influential critic of the day, Ralph Waldo Emerson, found "incomparable things said incomparably well" in *Leaves of Grass*, Whitman's legacy was assured.

Whitman had started out writing temperance tales and political diatribes for the *Brooklyn Daily Eagle*. After he spent a short time in New Orleans, his writing underwent a profound change; for the rest of his life, he devoted himself to poetry that would plant, he said, "companionship thick as trees." As a nurse in a Washington, D.C., hospital during the Civil War, Whitman experienced firsthand the horrors of battle, sights that inspired his haunting collection *Drum-Taps*.

## WHITNEY, ELI

Eli Whitney gained a reputation for inventiveness at an early age. By 12, he had constructed a passable violin; two years later he started his own nail-making business. A more exacting test of his talents came on a visit to Georgia in 1792; his hostess said to a gathering of farmers, "Gentlemen, tell your troubles to Mr. Whitney. He can do anything."

At that time cotton was harvested laboriously by hand, and seeds had to be picked out of the cotton bolls one by one. After 10 days' work, Whitney unveiled his cotton gin, a contraption that dragged cotton through a wire screen, stripping away the seeds in the process. Suddenly, a worker armed with Whitney's machine could do the work of 50 people.

Whitney obtained a patent for the cotton gin, but the news of his invention had spread, and others duplicated the design. The machine that was to bring wealth and strength to the South brought little but disappointment to its inventor.

While a lesser man might have given up, Whitney had another idea in mind. He was soon in business building muskets for the government, speeding the process with his ingenious system of making uniform, interchangeable parts.

## WHO'S AFRAID OF VIRGINIA WOOLF?

Edward Albee's first big hit, *Who's Afraid of Virginia Woolf?* erupted on Broadway in 1962, stunning critics and audiences alike with its relentless ferocity. It's about a long and drunken evening in a small college community during which an older couple gradually involves a younger pair in the complicated games that have thus far sustained their marriage. So fever-pitched is the dialogue that to this day the script is reputed to be packed with obscenities; in reality it is not. Albee's three-hour sparring was a shocker in the early '60s; the play was also the hit of the season, winning the Critics Circle Award as well as five Tonys.

Asked about the play's title, Albee replied, "Who's afraid of the Big Bad Wolf means 'who's afraid of living life without illusions?'" The question is answered by Martha in the play's last line: "I am, George, I am."

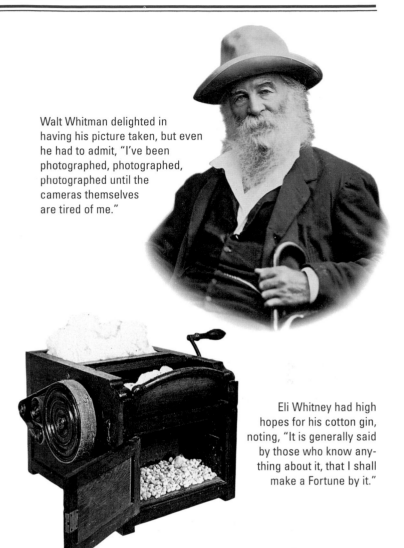

Walt Whitman delighted in having his picture taken, but even he had to admit, "I've been photographed, photographed, photographed until the cameras themselves are tired of me."

Eli Whitney had high hopes for his cotton gin, noting, "It is generally said by those who know anything about it, that I shall make a Fortune by it."

The movie version of *Who's Afraid of Virginia Woolf?* (1966) starred Richard Burton and Elizabeth Taylor, and won five Academy Awards.

# Wildlife
## of North America

*Home to some 2,000 species of mammals, birds, reptiles, amphibians, and fish, North America has many unique species. Some of them, including several shown here, are on the endangered list.*

**GRIZZLY BEAR**

This bear is called "grizzly" because of its silver-tipped coat. Males, which can weigh more than 1,000 pounds, require a range of about 400 square miles.

**MANATEE**

Manatees are one of the few mammals who spend their entire lives in the water. They are giants, reaching 15 feet in length, but gentle ones who eat only aquatic plants.

**WHITE-TAILED DEER**

Deer have few enemies, except for hunters—and suburban gardeners, whose flowers they nibble. When startled, these deer flash their bushy white tails, a sign of alarm to their companions.

**ALLIGATOR**

A living link to dinosaurs, the alligator has changed little in 150 million years. Like other reptiles, it is an efficient feeder, able to subsist on one meal a month.

### WILD TURKEY
Mostly forest dwellers, wild turkeys are hardy and agile. At mating time, males inflate their red wattles and fan their tails, gobbling all the while.

### SANDHILL CRANE
This majestic bird's elaborate courtship dance includes acrobatic leaps and bows. Mates often pair for life, a span of about 30 years.

### ARMADILLO
The armadillo is the only American mammal to have an armored shell. Females often give birth to quadruplets.

### PUMA
Other names—cougar, panther, mountain lion—are used for the puma. Solitary except when breeding, this big cat can prey on species much larger than itself.

### AMERICAN BISON
Fifty million bison, their massive bodies darkening the grasslands of the Great Plains, once roamed North America. Nearly extinct by 1890, they have made a comeback at wildlife preserves.

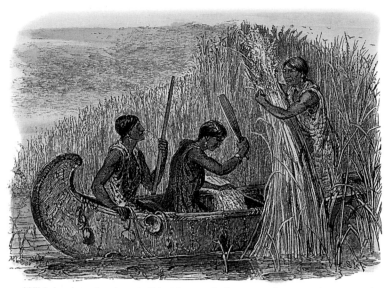

Wild rice is not a rice at all but the seed of an aquatic grass that grows in marshy areas and can reach a height of 10 feet.

In his autobiography, Williams wrote his own epitaph: "There goes Ted Williams, the greatest hitter who ever lived."

Burl Ives plays Big Daddy, a rich plantation owner, and Judith Anderson is Big Mama in the 1958 film version of Tennessee Williams's *Cat on a Hot Tin Roof.*

## WILD RICE

Wild rice, which is indigenous to the marshlands of Minnesota and Wisconsin, is a favorite food of Indian tribes living in the Great Lakes region. The rice is harvested by such tribes as the Menominee, whose full name, Menominiwok, means "wild-rice men." In late summer, when the stalks of grass are full of seeds, teams of three Indians paddle through the tall reeds in canoes and beat the stalks with sticks, causing the seeds to spray out. At least half the seeds drop into the shallow water, where they become the source of next year's crop. The harvested rice is taken ashore, dried, threshed from the husk, and served in a stew or boiled and seasoned with maple syrup, a traditional Indian dish.

## WILLIAMS, TED

Ted "The Splendid Splinter" Williams was an outspoken, opinionated perfectionist who called hitting "the hardest single feat in sports." Although he patrolled left field for the Boston Red Sox, he was more at home in the batter's box. Blessed with phenomenal eyesight and great coordination, Williams almost never swung at a bad pitch, and if he didn't swing, umpires rarely called it a strike.

Contentious with sportswriters and fans, Williams had a love/hate relationship with the city of Boston, where the press focused on his surly behavior and the team's inability to win a championship. Yet Williams's accomplishments are legendary. On the final day of the 1941 season, with a batting average of .39955, Williams decided to play rather than accept an adjusted .400 average. He played both games of a doubleheader, collected six hits, and finished at .406—the last player to do so.

After Williams returned from service in World War II, he stubbornly refused to alter his batting style when Cleveland manager Lou Boudreau instituted the so-called Boudreau shift, in which he stacked as many as six fielders on the right side of the diamond to field any balls Williams hit. Rather than try to direct the ball to an open spot on the field, Williams continued to swing away as always.

## WILLIAMS, TENNESSEE

Speaking of life, Tennessee Williams once cautioned, "Every minute is good-bye." Williams began writing to escape a difficult childhood. As a teenager, he fled St. Louis and drifted from job to job, accumulating experience on which to draw for his plays. In 1945 *The Glass Menagerie*, a memory play about his mother and beloved schizophrenic sister, Rose, was a brilliant Broadway success. A playwright known for his "poetic realism," Williams, unlike such realists as Clifford Odets and Arthur Miller, infused his plays with delicate imagery. His masterpiece, *A Streetcar Named Desire*, the knockout of the 1947 season, won the Pulitzer Prize. By the time he was 50, Williams was one of the world's best-known dramatists, his work translated into many languages. His output includes *Summer and Smoke, Cat on a Hot Tin Roof, The Rose Tattoo, Sweet Bird of Youth,* and *Night of the Iguana*—all of which were made into films. In the '60s personal problems and alcohol took their toll, and Williams's talent began to wane, but he gallantly continued to write. Williams was a Kennedy Center Honoree in 1979, and the following year he received the Presidential Medal of Freedom.

## WILLIAMSBURG

Virginia was England's largest colony in North America, and its onetime capital, Williamsburg, basked in an 18th-century golden age. A center of power and fashion, Williamsburg was home to wealthy colonial leaders, who resided in handsome town houses. Shops on the mile-long Duke of Gloucester Street bulged with stylish imports, while Williamsburg's cabinetmakers, tailors, and musical-instrument makers crafted products that were equal to those of London's masters.

As political conflict with England grew, a sense of destiny radiated from the pastel-brick capitol and spilled over into taverns, where such patriots as Patrick Henry, George Washington, and Thomas Jefferson held caucuses and debated the colony's future. Meanwhile, the royal governor looked on with Olympian detachment from his elegant Georgian mansion. In the 1920s John D. Rockefeller funded the restoration of the capitol, Raleigh Tavern, and Governor's Palace, and today Williamsburg stands hardly changed from its glory days.

## WINCHELL, WALTER

"How do I know? I read it in Winchell!" The 1957 movie *Sweet Smell of Success* perfectly conveys the terrifying power wielded by a ruthless columnist, unmistakably modeled on Walter Winchell. The most widely read and avidly listened-to commentator of his day, he gave his public a nonstop personality peep show: Broadway, Hollywood, and society gossip; news items; innuendos; political diatribes; and patriotic sentiments. As in the movie, his after-dark office was the Stork Club, a fashionable nightspot where the eager approached him at table 50 to offer the latest. As sweating press agents knew, a mention from Winchell (protected by contract from libel suits) could make or break a reputation.

A former vaudevillian, Winchell wrote showbiz gossip and chronicled Prohibition gangsters until William Hearst lured him to the *Daily Mirror,* whose publisher so loathed him that he once smashed Winchell's typewriter. But readers loved such Winchellisms as "makin' whoopee," "blessed event," "gone phffft," and "debutramp." A lone wolf who occasionally dabbled in romance, the journalist's true love was The Column, as he reverently referred to it. In 1967 his long career with Hearst papers ended, leaving him column-less. According to his daughter, he died of a broken heart.

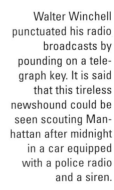

Hundreds of exhibition rooms filled with antiques and demonstrations of 36 historic trades make today's Colonial Williamsburg one of America's most popular year-round vacation destinations.

Walter Winchell punctuated his radio broadcasts by pounding on a telegraph key. It is said that this tireless newshound could be seen scouting Manhattan after midnight in a car equipped with a police radio and a siren.

Above, Dorothy and company finally make it to the Emerald City, despite the evil interventions of the Wicked Witch (played by Margaret Hamilton, right).

Since the 1950s, watching *The Wizard of Oz* (with Ray Bolger, Jack Haley, Judy Garland, and Bert Lahr) on TV has been a cherished family event.

## WIZARD OF OZ

In 1900 L. Frank Baum wrote a story about a little girl from Kansas who gets swept away by a tornado and wakes up in the land of Oz. With the help of her friends—the Scarecrow, the Tin Man, and the Cowardly Lion—she bests the Wicked Witch and makes her way home. In 1939 *The Wizard of Oz* ushered in MGM's golden age of musicals, and it has remained an all-time favorite movie classic.

Oz starred 16-year-old Judy Garland, tightly strapped into the dresses of little Dorothy (the studio had failed to get 10-year-old Shirley Temple). The movie went through four directors, hundreds of actors, 60 sets, and 124 midgets who, playing Munchkins, wore costumes with huge belts and vests to make them look even smaller. At a time when an eight-week shooting schedule was the norm, *Oz* took 22 weeks. It lost Best Picture to *Gone With the Wind* but won an Oscar for the song "Over the Rainbow," by Harold Arlen and E. Y. Harburg. That song became Garland's lifelong anthem, as indelibly associated with her as the famous ruby slippers.

## WONDER BREAD

America's best-selling bread was introduced in the early 1920s by the Taggart Baking Company of Indianapolis. Elmer Cline, a Taggart executive, came up with the name for the bread when he saw a sky filled with balloons and was filled with wonder. The balloons still adorn Wonder Bread's wrapper, leading some people to call it "balloon bread." Sliced Wonder Bread came along in 1930, and in 1941 extra vitamins and minerals were added as part of a government-supported bread-enrichment program; for many years ads claimed that Wonder "helps build strong bodies 12 ways." What really sells the bread to shopping moms, however, is that children love its sweetness and the way it can be rolled into spongy balls.

## WOODSTOCK

The three-day Woodstock Music and Art Fair in August 1969 gave baby boomers a new identity: "Woodstock Nation." Before it started, the festival was moved from Woodstock, New York, to Max Yasgur's 70-acre dairy farm in nearby Bethel; during the event, rain poured down. None of this mattered. Hundreds of thousands found their way to the new site; when faced with mud, they played in it. The Band, Santana, Jefferson Airplane, Sly and the Family Stone, Country Joe and the Fish, and Crosby, Stills, Nash and Young were among the musicians who rocked. The crowd joined in, celebrating peace, love, and hedonism. Jimi Hendrix gave the "Nation" its own version of the national anthem. Millions who weren't there feel like, and occasionally claim, they were.

Twenty-five years later, Woodstock II was organized. A few critics called it "Greedstock" because ticket prices were high and corporate sponsors were involved, but crowds came anyway. Joe Cocker and a few other veterans from Woodstock I returned, but most of the performers, including Melissa Etheridge, Metallica, Nine Inch Nails, Salt-n-Pepa, and Arrested Development, were younger. Once again it rained, and once again almost no one minded.

## WORLD SERIES

Each fall the winning teams from both professional baseball leagues face one another in the World Series, and during those four to seven championship games, it seems that every TV and radio in America is tuned in to the action. Since the World Series began in 1903, the New York Yankees have won it a record 22 times; Yankee catcher Yogi Berra played 75 games in 14 series, more than any other player.

The World Series suffered a terrible blow in 1919, when it was discovered that the games had been fixed by gamblers. To the dismay of fans, the 1994 series was canceled because of a strike by players against team owners. But sports fans are still electrified by the World Series, which in the past has yielded some of baseball's most unforgettable moments.

In game six of the 1975 World Series, Carlton Fisk of the Boston Red Sox hit a homer at the bottom of the 12th inning to win the game against the Cincinnati Reds and tie the series 3–3. And in 1986, during an at bat that seemed to last forever, Red Sox pitcher Bob Stanley threw Mookie Wilson of the New York Mets nine pitches—three balls, two strikes, and four pop fouls—before Wilson hit the grounder that enabled Ray Knight, on second base, to score the winning run.

But only one player has fulfilled the ultimate baseball fantasy of hitting a home run to win the entire series— Pittsburgh Pirate Bill Mazeroski, in 1960. Even Casey Stengel, manager of the Yankees, whom the Pirates beat that year, conceded that the play was "downright amazin'."

## WORLD'S FAIR

The World's Fair is an opportunity to commemorate America's history and to showcase its latest innovations, all the while entertaining millions of visitors. The theme of Chicago's Columbian Exposition of 1893, which celebrated the 400th anniversary of Columbus's discovery of America, was electricity. President Grover Cleveland opened the festivities from the White House, some 700 miles away. He pressed a button to turn on the power, which, thanks to Thomas Alva Edison's lightbulb, lit the buildings of the fair's "White City."

St. Louis's 1904 World's Fair commemorated the Louisiana Purchase and introduced 20 million Americans to such marvels as the telephone and a variety of fast cars. In 1939, 150 years after George Washington took the presidential oath, New York held its "World of Tomorrow" fair. The highlight was General Motors's Futurama exhibit: in the comfort of upholstered chairs mounted on a conveyor system, visitors glided through a huge diorama of the ideal 1960s city.

**THREE DAY TICKET**
Aug. 15, 16, 17 1969
**$18.00**
01921

The ticket stub at right is from Woodstock '69; the dog-tag necklace, from Woodstock '94. Above, a reveler uses body paint to bridge the two festivals.

At New York's 1939 World's Fair, the Perisphere symbolized "the world about us," while the 610-foot-high Trylon represented "aspiration."

While professional wrestlers have gone showbiz, amateur wrestling remains a serious sport. Above, Li-Hak Soon of North Korea comes to grips with Zeke Jones of the U.S. at the 1992 Olympic games.

Fallingwater, built atop a waterfall in Pennsylvania in 1936, seems to defy gravity. Workers feared that the huge horizontal elements would collapse, but Frank Lloyd Wright's famed creation remains upright.

## WOUNDED KNEE

In 1889 a Paiute prophet foretold a time when the white man would disappear and the Indians would be reunited with their dead ancestors. His message spread like wildfire among the Plains Indians, who were living on crowded reservations. Soon a cult based on the mystical Ghost Dance sprang up.

White officials feared this powerful new religion and, in December 1890, ordered the arrest of Chief Sitting Bull for encouraging it. A struggle followed in which Sitting Bull was killed; his people fled, and soldiers pursued them. After two weeks on the run, the Indians surrendered at Wounded Knee in South Dakota. As the soldiers searched them for weapons, a shot rang out, and the tense troops in the surrounding hills opened fire. An estimated 150 to 300 Indians were killed, as were 25 soldiers. A gravedigger said of the carnage, "It was a thing to melt the heart of a man, if it was of stone."

## WRESTLING

Wrestling has a long history that goes back to antiquity. Native Americans enjoyed wrestling long before Columbus landed, and each group of colonists brought with them their own style of unarmed combat. In the late 1800s Tom Jenkins, a mill worker from Cleveland, Ohio, popularized a catch-as-catch-can kind of wrestling, in which all grips, except the stranglehold, were legal. Frank Gotch, a daring lightweight, won the title from Jenkins in 1905 and ushered in the heyday of professional wrestling. Television brought wrestling back as entertainment: a carnival of fighters—including some former professional football players—with exotic names, glitzy costumes, and a no-holds-barred style of wrestling. The violence, complete with pulled punches and faked kicks, is a sham; the audience is large and loyal.

## WRIGHT, FRANK LLOYD

A master manipulator of space who believed that a building should integrate form, function, and site into an organic whole, Frank Lloyd Wright is widely considered to be America's greatest modern architect. Throughout his seven-decade career, this Wisconsin native rejected conventional European influences in a quest for an original style rooted in native traditions and materials. He emphasized human scale, designing buildings with economy, comfort, and convenience in mind.

Formally trained as a civil engineer, Wright learned his craft as an apprentice in Louis H. Sullivan's architecture firm in Chicago. Wright opened his own office in 1893 and focused on the freestanding suburban house. His Prairie house echoed the flat Midwestern landscape with its strong horizontal profile and open floor plan, where simple partitions and built-ins replaced traditional walls. Wright also designed office towers, hotels, and university buildings. He deemed his last work, the spiraling 1959 Solomon R. Guggenheim Museum in New York City, his true masterpiece.

## WRIGHT BROTHERS

Only a few spectators, mostly local fishermen, watched as Wilbur and Orville Wright tested their new flying machine on a cold, windswept sand dune at Kitty Hawk, North Carolina, in 1903. Made of fabric, wood, and wire, their double-winged contraption was nearly rattled to pieces by the 12-horse-power onboard engine and the spinning of the twin propellers. Lying flat on his stomach to reduce wind drag, Orville gripped the steering cables while his brother cast off the restraining wire and ran alongside, steadying the wingtip, until the improbable bird rose into the air, achieving a height of 10 feet and a distance of 120 feet in 12 seconds. Human-kind's long-held ambition to fly had finally been achieved.

The Wright brothers went on to build a better version of the Wright *Flyer* and were soon circling a cow pasture out-side Dayton, Ohio, for hours at a time. Word of their inven-tion reached the ears of presidents, prime ministers, and kings, who were eager to see the incredible flying machines made by these two former bicycle repairmen. The Wrights graciously accepted awards, such as a congressional medal in 1909, but they never let fame go to their heads. With char-acteristic single-mindedness, they were interested only in improving upon their inventions.

## WYETHS

A tiny hamlet amid the tidy farms and rolling hills of rural Pennsylvania has been the home and creative heart for three generations of artists: N. C., Andrew, and Jamie Wyeth.

Newell Convers, or N. C., was a gregarious giant of a man who came to the Brandywine River valley in 1902 to study with the illustrator Howard Pyle. N. C. stayed on and became the foremost illustrator of his era. His rich oils of such liter-ary classics as *Robin Hood* and *Treasure Island* depict imag-inary worlds, but their vibrant realism is rooted in a profound appreciation of nature and the surrounding countryside.

Andrew Wyeth inherited his father's powers of observa-tion and technical precision; he was educated at home and became an apprentice in N. C.'s studio at age 12. Unlike the elder Wyeth, Andrew chronicles personal stories of country life, exploring the unspoiled land and unpretentious people of Pennsylvania and around his summer home in Maine. His dry-brush watercolors and egg temperas are nearly photo-graphic in detail and contemplative in tone. A stolen moment in a forest or field is elevated to a timeless poignancy. "A man can only paint that which he knows more than intimately," he said. "And to do that he has to ... be a part of it."

Andrew's son, Jamie, also began painting at an early age. He turned his brush to probing yet playful portraits of both the celebrated and the commonplace. Whether painting President Kennedy or a rumple-snouted sow, the younger Wyeth perpetuates the family heritage of capturing living memories that open a window on their world.

N. C. Wyeth illustrated 25 books for Charles Scribner's Sons, includ-ing a 1913 edition of Robert Louis Stevenson's *Kidnapped*, in which "On the Island Earraid" (above) appeared. "Maga's Daughter," at right, was painted by Andrew Wyeth in 1966.

"What I like about piggies is that they can be very difficult," said Jamie Wyeth. He painted "Portrait of a Pig" in 1970.

The word *xerography* (Greek for "dry writing") was used to describe Chester F. Carlson's new process of copying. This 1977 ad by Xerox introduced a machine that could produce two pages a second.

## Introducing the Xerox 9400. Will miracles never cease?

When people saw all the incredible things our Xerox 9200 could do, they called it a miracle. But, at Xerox, we never rest on our miracles.

Introducing the Xerox 9400 Duplicator. It does everything the 9200 does and more. With its automatic document handler you can feed and cycle up to 200 originals at a time. (Even difficult originals like paste-ups.) With our density control dial, you can make copies lighter or darker without having to interrupt the job.

You can even correct most problems yourself with the help of our new self-diagnostic system which constantly monitors the machine.

And if all this wasn't enough, the Xerox 9400 can automatically copy on both sides of a sheet of paper at the same incredible speed of two pages a second.

You see, we believe that one good miracle deserves another.

**XEROX**

American soldiers adopted "Yankee Doodle" as a marching song during the Revolution. Norman Rockwell featured him in a mural (above).

In 1991 American troops went off to fight in the Persian Gulf. Citizens back home, expressing their hopes for the soldiers' safe return, tied yellow ribbons to trees throughout the nation.

## XEROX

In his work at a small office in Queens, New York, Chester F. Carlson became aware of the need for a new way to make copies of documents. Carbon copies and mimeographs were laborious, and photostating (the only way to copy illustrations) was expensive. After experimenting for several years, Carlson produced the first "electrophotographic" copy, on October 22, 1938. The process involved a metal plate coated with sulfur and a piece of glass inscribed with writing. After the metal plate was electrically charged, the glass was placed against it. Then both were exposed to light. When Carlson separated the glass from the plate and sprinkled dye on it, an image formed on the plate. Next he pressed waxed paper against the plate and peeled away a copy of his writing.

Carlson was delighted, but the companies he approached were unimpressed. He finally sold an interest in his process to Battelle Memorial Institute; it, in turn, cooperated with the Haloid Company in developing the product. Haloid eventually became the Xerox Corporation.

## YANKEE

The origin of the term *Yankee* is uncertain, but there is no doubt it began as a disparaging nickname. In 1755 a British soldier jotted down a few light stanzas making fun of a rag-tag regiment of Colonial soldiers. Set to an old-fashioned jig, the song was called "Yankee Doodle." It is a testament to the patriotic pride of the revolutionaries that they embraced this song, originally composed to mock them.

*Yankee* has had different meanings at different times in our nation's history. After the Revolution, a Yankee was a shrewd, often shady, individual from New England. In the years following the Civil War, Southerners took the word to mean a carpetbagger, a Northerner who went south to take advantage of the postwar economic upheaval. Today Southerners still refer to most Northerners as Yankees, but many Americans use the term to mean a New Englander. To foreigners, however, all U.S. citizens are "Yanks."

## YELLOW RIBBONS

When Americans want someone to return home safely, they display yellow ribbons. The earliest instance of this practice dates from the Civil War. The sweethearts of Union soldiers would wear in their hair yellow ribbons that matched the yellow neckerchiefs of the soldiers' uniforms. The practice hit the silver screen in the 1949 John Ford movie *She Wore a Yellow Ribbon*.

The tradition behind today's ribbons is more recent. In 1971 *New York Post* columnist Pete Hamill wrote up a story he had heard about an elderly man riding a bus after a stint in prison. The man had written to his wife in Brunswick, Georgia, telling her to put a yellow handkerchief on a tree in the middle of town if she wanted him to get off the bus and come home. As everyone on the bus saw, and as everyone knows who has heard Tony Orlando and Dawn's number one hit, "Tie a Yellow Ribbon Round the Ole Oak Tree," the tree was covered in dozens of yellow handkerchiefs.

## YELLOWSTONE

Before Yellowstone, parks were small, manicured plots of land. But the desire to preserve Yellowstone's magnificent wilderness for future generations moved Congress in 1872 to declare it the country's first national park. Its terrain was carved by volcanic eruptions hundreds of thousands of years ago. As naturalist John Muir marveled, "The park is full of exciting wonders. The wildest geysers in the world, in bright triumphant bands, are dancing and singing in it amid thousands of boiling springs...." Old Faithful, the most famous of the park's active geysers, may not spout with the regularity of clockwork, as some say it once did, but it does "play" about every 78 minutes, sending a plume of water and steam more than 100 feet into the sky for two to five minutes.

In addition to its geothermal wonders, Yellowstone is home to elk, moose, pronghorn and bighorn sheep, black bears, and grizzly bears. Every year the park attracts 3 million campers and tourists from around the world.

## YOGI BEAR

In real life, bears hunting for food can be scary. But in the cartoons, there are few characters friendlier than Yogi Bear, who devoted himself to getting hold of tourists' "pic-a-nic" baskets in Jellystone National Park. Essentially a nonviolent bear, the ever-hungry Yogi cooked up elaborate schemes to outwit his nemesis, Park Ranger John Smith. Yogi's sidekick, the naive Boo Boo, had misgivings about Yogi's plots but always gave in to the irrepressible Yogi and became an accomplice.

Yogi, created by William Hanna and Joe Barbera, first appeared in 1958 in one of their Huckleberry Hound cartoons. His name was a tribute to Yankee baseball star Yogi Berra, while his distinctive voice was provided by Daws Butler. A half-hour Yogi Bear show often included cartoons featuring Snagglepuss, Yakky Doodle, and Chopper. After a few years off the air, Yogi returned to television in 1973 in *Yogi's Gang*, a show that added Wally Gator, Squidly Diddly Duck, Magilla Gorilla, Touché Turtle, and Peter Potamus to his cast of lovable, mischievous buddies.

Yellowstone extends into three states— Idaho, Wyoming, and Montana. Dramatic landforms at the park include Lower Falls on the Yellowstone River (above) and a hot spring, Morning Glory Pool (right).

Gone fishin': Yogi Bear and Boo Boo have reeled in a picnic basket. Now they'd better watch out that Ranger Smith doesn't catch them.

Alvin York usually avoided the limelight, but he allowed a movie to be made about his life when America entered World War II. Gary Cooper played the title role in *Sergeant York* (1941), winning an Academy Award. Joan Leslie played his sweetheart.

## YORK, SERGEANT ALVIN

Alvin Cullum York was an unlikely candidate to become one of the greatest heroes of World War I. Raised in the hill country of Tennessee, he earned a reputation for drinking and carousing—and for being the best shot around. His wild ways ended in 1915, however, when he embraced religion during a revival meeting.

When America went to war, York tried to avoid the draft because of his religious beliefs, but his request was denied. "I had had fighting and quarreling myself. I had found it bad," he said. "I just wanted to be left alone to live in peace and love." But in boot camp an officer convinced York that the Bible did not condemn fighting when done in defense of liberty.

In October 1918 York's battalion was stationed in France, where they tried to capture a strategically placed German machine gun nest near the Argonne Forest. Using his sharpshooting skills, York kept fighting even when most of his companions were down. He killed at least 20 enemy gunners with one shot each, and the 132 survivors were persuaded to surrender. Gen. John J. Pershing considered York the outstanding soldier of the American forces. When he returned to America in 1919, York was honored with a massive ticker-tape parade in New York City. The Tennessee state legislature awarded him 385 acres of land in the hill country that he loved.

## YOSEMITE

By the mid-1800s, people realized that industry, agriculture, and unchecked commercialization could destroy the nation's natural beauty. The great eastern-seaboard forests were gone, and Niagara Falls had become a huckster's paradise. The defilement of Niagara, more than anything else, gave rise to the concept of preservation by federal decree. In 1864 President Abraham Lincoln established Yosemite Valley as a state park; in 1890 it became part of a national park.

Yosemite lies in the heart of California's Sierra Nevada. The Sierras are not a chain of individual mountains but a single block of granite 50 to 80 miles wide that was scoured first by glaciers, then by the Merced River. Yosemite, which means "dancing waters," offers a waterfall extravaganza in the spring. Yosemite Falls—at 2,425 feet the height of 13 Niagaras—is the highest in North America, but others, such as Ribbon and Bridalveil Falls, are equally spectacular.

Today Yosemite is threatened by its own popularity. In summer its roads are choked with traffic and favorite sites reach capacity before noon. Travelers should try to visit in the off-season, reserving campsites two months in advance.

## YOUR HIT PARADE

On April 20, 1935, *The Lucky Strike Hit Parade* began its run as the most successful song showcase in history. This legendary radio program spotlighted each week's top seven

Yosemite Valley's western end is marked by El Capitan, one of the world's largest masses of unbroken granite, which stands 3,600 feet high.

songs, performed by the show's regular cast of singers. If a song remained popular for several weeks, the singer and the treatment would vary. The rating system of *Your Hit Parade* was a tally of record and sheet-music sales, radio airplay, and requests to bandleaders. The show became a bellwether for other rating lists and charts. Lingering favorites or novelty songs were added as "extras." On the first show, the No. 1 hit was George and Ira Gershwin's "Soon," which was dislodged the following week by Jerome Kern's "Lovely to Look At."

In 1950 *Your Hit Parade* moved to TV, where its regular singers were Dorothy Collins, Snooky Lanson, Gisele MacKenzie, and Russell Arms. Top songs included "Too Young," "Because of You," and "Hey There." The show hit a snag in the mid-'50s when rock and roll became popular. Rock hits were strongly linked with the original performers and lacked luster when "translated" by the show's regulars. The program made its last stand in 1959, giving way to Top 40 radio.

## Yo-Yo

In 1929 David Duncan bought the rights to the yo-yo, a popular toy in the Philippines. To promote it, he hired Filipino yo-yo experts to tour the country and demonstrate the toy in schoolyards, candy stores, and playgrounds. Since then, generations of kids have spent hours progressing from simple up-and-down yo-yoing to "sleeping" a yo-yo—making it spin in a loop at the end of its string. Once they trim the string to the right length for their bodies, well-coordinated children can master advanced tricks like walking the dog, skinning the cat, rocking the baby, and going around the world.

Some people, comedian Tommy Smothers for one, have kept playing into adulthood. Collectors have also started paying good money for well-made old wooden yo-yos, plastic models in unusual shapes and colors, and novelty models that whistle, make music, shoot sparks, or glow in the dark.

## YUPPIE

In the early 1980s, marketers set their sights on a new breed of superconsumers: the Young Urban Professionals, labeled "Yuppies." Yuppies had good jobs with high incomes but few responsibilities because they had put off having children. They sunk their spare cash—plus the credit that banks were eager to give them—into status symbols like expensive stereos and foreign cars, particularly sporty Saabs and BMWs. They dressed in designer clothes, wore Rolex watches, and vacationed on exotic islands. Because they didn't have to worry about school systems and were too busy for long commutes, they bought lofts in cities and installed elaborate kitchens that they rarely got around to using.

The cover of *Newsweek*'s December 31, 1984, issue announced "The Year of the Yuppie," but the trend soon died. As their biological clocks ticked on, yuppies plunged into parenthood and started saving almost as hard as their parents had.

### YOUR HIT PARADE FAVORITES

*In addition to featuring seven songs a week, Your Hit Parade chose one song as the top hit of the year. Here is a sample:*

In a Little Gypsy Tea Room (1935)
September in the Rain (1937)
My Reverie (1938)
South of the Border (1939)
I Hear a Rhapsody (1941)
White Christmas (1942)
People Will Say We're in Love (1943)
I'll Be Seeing You (1944)
Till the End of Time (1945)
They Say It's Wonderful (1946)
Peg o' My Heart (1947)
Buttons and Bows (1949)
Goodnight Irene (1950)
Tennessee Waltz (1951)
Cry (1952)
Little Things Mean a Lot (1954)
Love Letters in the Sand (1957)
It's All in the Game (1958)

Tommy Smothers, of the Smothers Brothers comedy team, usually plays the fool, but when he gets a yo-yo in his hands, he's a wizard.

Mike and Joanie, characters in Garry Trudeau's comic strip *Doonesbury*, try to keep up with the times. At right, they donned the correct apparel and helped *Newsweek* announce "The Year of the Yuppie."

The *Ziegfeld Follies* girls (above) represented the height of fashion. Flo Ziegfeld (right) spared no expense on the show and was known to cut, after only one performance, scenes that had cost him a small fortune.

The ubiquitous zipper was invented by an engineer who also held patents for engines and transmissions.

## ZIEGFELD FOLLIES

Wrote Florenz Ziegfeld in 1926, "The ideal woman must have: Native refinement. Where that exists, education is not necessary." With *The Follies of 1907*, America's most famous theatrical producer introduced a new kind of entertainment to Broadway: the revue. Four years later he added his name to the annual series, and the famous *Ziegfeld Follies* was born.

A collection of songs, skits, comedy, and historical pageants, the *Follies*'s greatest attraction was what the extravagant showman called "the glorification of the American girl." Ziggy interviewed thousands of hopefuls every year, looking for his ideal (bust, 36; waist, 26; hips, 38, among other qualities). A Ziegfeld Girl's salary averaged $75 a week, but there were perks—parties, presents, and glory. Nudity was used only in the tableaux, and a nude showgirl was forbidden to move a muscle; in public she was expected to appear as modestly dressed as a debutante.

The *Follies* was famous for its opulent scenery and costumes and for introducing such major talents as Fanny Brice, Sophie Tucker, Eddie Cantor, W. C. Fields, and Will Rogers, as well as a bevy of hit songs, including "A Pretty Girl Is Like a Melody" and "By the Light of the Silvery Moon." The show ran regularly until 1925 and sporadically until 1931; it inspired Stephen Sondheim's 1971 musical, *Follies*.

## ZIPPER

Aside from a few enthusiastic quick-change artists, nobody knew what to do with Whitcomb Judson's new invention, the Hookless Fastener, which went on the market in 1904. Accustomed to buttons, hooks, buckles, and pins, people had never conceived of dressing any other way. Judson's early zipper never caught on, and his company went broke.

It took World War I to spark people's interest: air corpsmen found it handy to zip into windproof suits. Soon, tobacco pouches featuring the Hookless Fastener were selling at a rate of 7,000 a week. When the president of the B.F. Goodrich Company renamed his galoshes Zipper Boots, the public suddenly woke up to the ease and convenience of the product that sounds like its name. Within a decade, 20 million zippers a year slid off the production lines, fastening everything from elegant gowns to motorboat engine covers.

## ZOOS

America's first zoo, short for zoological garden or park, was chartered in Philadelphia in 1859. Chicago's Lincoln Park Zoo and the Cincinnati Zoo opened in 1874, and New York's famous Bronx Zoo opened its doors in 1899. Visiting the zoo quickly became a popular family pastime. Adults welcomed the chance to see and hear the exotic animals they had read about, and children loved commenting on the various smells, making faces at the monkeys, and taunting the fierce lions, tigers, and gorillas trapped behind bars.

Although entertaining for people, these early zoos weren't particularly comfortable or healthy for the animals. The Saint Louis Zoo (1921), the Detroit Zoo (1928), and Chicago's Brookfield Zoo (1934) became the first in America to use more humane, spacious enclosures that approximate the animals' natural habitats, instead of cramped cages. Many older zoos followed suit by remodeling. The Bronx Zoo set the standard for these exhibits with its African Plains.

Today such zoos as the world-renowned San Diego Zoo and its 1,800-acre Wild Animal Park focus on education as well as entertainment. Children learn about the animals' natural behaviors and habitats while petting everything from frogs to African goats. Zoos also play an important role in protecting and breeding species, such as the giant panda, whose homes are being destroyed by development.

## ZOOT SUIT

In the early years of World War II, some teenagers and even a few grown men attracted attention by wearing zoot suits. The outfits combined a long padded jacket with absurdly wide lapels and billowy high-waisted pants that bagged at the knees and tapered to narrow cuffs. "Zoot-suiters" also wore garish ties, extra-long watch chains, and wide-brimmed hats. The look may have been started by gangsters who hid guns under their spacious "threads"; it was perfected by "hepcats," like Cab Calloway, who liked to flash yards of fabric as they "jived" with their "jills."

There's debate about where *zoot* comes from; it may be rhyming slang for *suit*. The suits themselves were controversial. In 1943 fights broke out in New York and Los Angeles between servicemen and zoot-suiters. The War Production Board ended the craze by issuing regulations that kept suits smaller and saved fabric for the war effort.

## ZORRO

In the late 1950s, boys who were tired of playing cowboys would use the nearest stick as a sword and carve Zs in the air. They were imitating Zorro, the hero of the TV series of the same name, which ran from 1957 to 1959. The show, starring Guy Williams, retold the tale of Don Diego de Vega, who pretended to be a coward so that no one would discover who he really was: the masked El Zorro ("the fox"), who battled injustice in California during the 1820s. Zorro outsmarted and out-dueled his adversaries, Captain Monastario and Sergeant Garcia, aided by Bernardo, a crafty manservant, and two stallions. The local ladies, including Anita Cabrillo (Annette Funicello), scorned Diego and swooned over Zorro.

The character Zorro first appeared in 1919 in "The Curse of Capistrano," a story by Johnston McCulley that ran in *All Story Weekly* magazine. He was also the subject of a host of movies, including *The Mark of Zorro* (1920), starring Douglas Fairbanks, Sr., and a 1940 remake with Tyrone Power.

Crowds adore the cuddly-looking giant panda, but the panda population is tenuous. Zoos are still struggling to breed the animals in captivity.

At a game farm on New York's Long Island, one young animal lover makes a furry friend.

Sammy Davis, Jr., models a zoot suit. Some suits were so narrow at the ankle that men with big feet could not get them on.

Guy Williams starred in the 1960 movie *The Sign of Zorro.* In 1990 Zorro rode again in a series on The Family Channel.

Numbers in **boldface** refer to illustrations.

Numbers in **boldface** refer to illustrations.

Numbers in **boldface** refer to illustrations.

Numbers in **boldface** refer to illustrations.

# C R E D I T S

**Key:** Bettmann=The Bettmann Archive. FPG=FPG International. TIB=The Image Bank **Front Cover** *clockwise from top*: FPG; Monopoly ® is a registered trademark of the Tonka Corporation for its real estate trading game and elements © 1993, Parker Brothers, a division of Tonka Corporation, used with permission/Photo by Noel Alum; FPG; Wurlitzer Jukebox Company, Moonachie, NJ/Photo by Steven Mays, *The Encyclopedia of Collectibles*, published by Time-Life, Inc., courtesy of Rebus, Inc., NY, 1978; FPG. **Back Cover** Photo courtesy of the Norman Rockwell Museum at Stockbridge. Printed by permission of the Norman Rockwell Family Trust © 1960 the Norman Rockwell Family Trust. **Title Page** *background* by Eliot Bergman, *photo* by Henryk T. Kaiser/Envision. **6** *top* American Automobile Association, used by permission; *center* The Curtis Publishing Company; *bottom* Focus on Sports. **7** *top & center* Photofest; *bottom* Culver Pictures. **8** *top left & right* Library of Congress; *bottom* Arthur Grace/Sygma. **9** *top* Drawing by Charles Addams © 1951, 1979 The New Yorker Magazine, Inc. All rights reserved; *center* Cover drawing by Charles Addams © 1959, 1987 The New Yorker Magazine, Inc. All rights reserved; *bottom* Bachrach Photography. **10** *top* Ralston Purina Company; *center* Giorgio Beverly Hills; *bottom* A registered trademark of Schering-Plough HealthCare Products, Inc., USA. Reproduced with permission of Schering-Plough HealthCare Products, Inc., the trademark owner. **11** *top* H. Armstrong Roberts; *bottom* Archive Photos. **12** *top* David Muench; *center* U.S. Naval Academy Museum, Annapolis, MD; *bottom* Patti McConville/TIB. **13** *top & center* Culver Pictures; *bottom* © Al Hirschfeld. Drawing reproduced by special arrangement with Hirschfeld's exclusive representative, The Margo Feiden Galleries, NY. **14** *top* Bettmann; *center* Steve Jackson/Ali Collectibles, Hackensack, NJ; *bottom* Culver Pictures. **15** *top* Globe Photos; *center* "Inside Woody Allen" comic strip by Stuart Hample © 1978 IWA Enterprises, Inc.; *bottom* Peter Fox. **16** *top* Paul Schutzer, *Life* Magazine © Time, Inc.; *center* "American Gothic" by Grant Wood, American, 1891–1942, oil on beaver board, 1930, 74.3 cm. x 62.4 cm., Friends of American Art Collection, 1930.934/Photo © 1994, The Art Institute of Chicago. All rights reserved; *bottom center* EPA Journal cover by Nathan Davies, 1979, courtesy of the U.S. Environmental Protection Agency; *bottom right* William Scahill Purdom; *bottom left* Richard Hess. **17** *top* Archive Photos; *center* Sally Samins; *bottom right* Guy Gurney. **18** *top* Mel Horst Photography; *center* Library of Congress; *bottom* Kobal Collection. **19** *top* Nabisco/Photo by Noel Alum; *center* Marty Katz/Gamma Liaison; *bottom* Courtesy of Uncle Milton Industries. **20** *top* Albert Squillace/ESTO Photographics; *center* Shinichi Kanno/FPG; *bottom* Zefa/Stock Market. **21** *top* Steven Needham/Envision; *center* Stephen Snider; *bottom* CBS, Inc. **22** *top* Philadelphia Museum of Art: Louise and Walter Annenberg Collection; *center The New York Times* © 1913; *bottom* Eliot Elisofon/Time-Life Picture Agency. **23** *top* Simon Bruty/Allsport; *center* Archive Photos; *bottom* Collection of Whitney Museum of American Art, NY/Photo by Sheldon C. Collins. **24** *top* Focus on Sports; *center* Lester Glassner Collection/Neal Peters Collection; *bottom* Courtesy of Astrodome USA. **25** *top* Mark Rossotto/Stock Market; *center* Neal Peters Collection; *bottom* Lester Glassner Collection/Neal Peters Collection. **26** *top left* Reproduced by permission of Charles Atlas Ltd., New York, NY 10159; *top right* Photofest; *center* Collection of the New York Historical Society; *bottom* Library of Congress. **27** *top* Uniphoto; *center* Albert Squillace/ESTO; *bottom* Archive Photos. **28** *top* Jeff Foott/Bruce Coleman; *top left* Kevin Schafer/Tony Stone Images; *bottom left* Milt & Patti Putnam/Stock Market; *bottom right* Noel Alum. **29** *top* Culver Pictures; *center* Spencer Jones; *bottom* UPI/Bettmann. **30** *top* Al Azzarello/Archive Photos; *center* Courtesy of *Barbie Bazaar, The Barbie Collector's Magazine*; *bottom* Courtesy of Mattel Toys. **31** *top & bottom* Culver Pictures. **32** *top* Culver Pictures; *center* American Red Cross; *bottom left* Transcendental Graphics; *bottom right* Al Tielemans/Duomo. **33** *top, center left & right* National Baseball Library & Archive, Cooperstown, NY; *bottom* Focus on Sports. **34** *top* Bettmann; *center* Frank Driggs Collection; *bottom* Culver Pictures. **35** *top* Noel Alum; *center* Globe Photos; *bottom* Bettmann. **36** *top* Courtesy of Anheuser-Busch, Inc.; *center* Movie Star News; *bottom* Archive Photos. **37** *top* St. Louis Art Museum, Purchase; *bottom left* Frank Driggs Collection; *bottom right* Archive Photos; *second from bottom* Museum of the City of New York; *third from bottom* Frank Driggs Collection. **38** *top* UPI/Bettmann; *center* Culver Pictures; *bottom* Photofest. **39** *top Encyclopedia of Collectibles*, published by Time-Life, Inc., courtesy of Rebus, Inc., NY, 1978; *bottom* Photofest. **40** *top* Burt Glinn/Magnum; *center* Ray Skibinsky; *bottom* Culver Pictures. **41** *top* Photo Patterson/Glimlin © 1968 Dahinden; *center* Noel Alum. **42** *top left* Beinecke Rare Book & Manuscript Library, Yale University; *top right* Culver Pictures; *bottom left* Sobel/Klonsky/TIB; *bottom right* Noel Alum. **43** *top* Bettmann; *center left* Culver Pictures; *center right* Shooting Star International; *bottom* Phillip Hate for Columbia Records. **44** *top* Frank Driggs Collection; *center* Eli Reed/Magnum Photos; *bottom* Steven Nau/Deborah Wolfe Ltd. **45** *top left* From *Bowl-o-Rama*, Abbeville Press; *top right & center left* Boy Scouts of America; *center right* Art from the Archives of Brown & Bigelow, Inc. © 1959, and by permission of the Boy Scouts of America; *bottom* H. Armstrong Roberts. **46** *left* Peter Mauss/ESTO Photographics, Inc.; *top right* Ron Schramm; *center left* Berenholtz Photography; *center right* Vladimir Pcholkin/FPG; *bottom right* Steve Gottlieb. **47** *left* Pereira & Associates; *top center* D.C.Lowe/FPG; *right* FPG; *bottom right* Peter Gridley/FPG. **48** *top* Photofest; *center* Richard Hamilton Smith/FPG; *bottom* Reader's Digest. **49** *top* Stephen Wade/Allsport; *bottom* Ray Skibinsky. **50** *top* Culver Pictures; *center* Photofest; *bottom* White House Photo/Black Star. **51** *top* Noel Alum; *bottom* Photofest. **52** *top* University Press of Mississippi; *center* Collection of the Whitney Museum of American Art, NY/Photo by Geoffrey Clements, NY; *bottom* Collection of the Whitney Museum of American Art/Photo by Jerry L. Thompson, NY. **53** *top* Scott Gordley/The Penny & Stermer Group; *bottom* Culver Pictures. **54** *top* Jim Turgeon; *center* Culver Pictures; *bottom* Photofest. **55** *top* Steve J. Sherman; *bottom* Photofest. **56** *top* The Granger Collection, NY; *center* Townsend Dickinson/Comstock; *bottom* Photofest. **57** *top* Reuters/Bettmann; *center* U.S. Postal Service; *bottom* Photofest. **58** *top* Bettmann; *center* Noel Alum; *bottom* Photofest. **59** *top* Brown Brothers; *center* National Museum of American Art, Washington, DC/Art Resource, NY; *bottom* Photofest. **60** *top* Painting by W. H. D. Koerner, 1878–1938; *center* Photo courtesy of the Norman Rockwell Museum at Stockbridge. Printed by permission of the Norman Rockwell Family Trust © 1961 the Norman Rockwell Family Trust; *bottom left* Noel Alum. **61** *top* Brown Brothers; *top right* Superstock; *bottom* Pepsi Cola Company/Photo by Timothy White. **62** *top* Photofest; *center* Mitzi Trumbo/Shooting Star; *bottom* Noel Alum. **63** *top* Bettmann; *bottom* Stephen Dunn/Allsport. **64** *top & center* Jeffrey Tennyson; *bottom left & right* Ron Schramm. **65** *top* Ira Wyman/Sygma; *center* Joe DiMaggio; *bottom* Motion Picture & Television Archive. **66** *top left* Max Romine/Superstock; *top right* Noel Alum; *center* © 1985 Dover Publications, Inc.; *bottom* Noel Alum. **67** *top left & right* Photofest; *bottom* Photo courtesy of The Norman Rockwell Museum at Stockbridge. Printed by permission of the Norman Rockwell Family Trust © 1961 the Norman Rockwell Family Trust. **68–69** *all* Nicky Wright. **70** *top* Bettmann ; *top left* DowBrands; *center right* Courtesy of Faultless Starch/Bon Ami Company/Photo Noel Alum; *bottom* Bettmann. **71** *top* Photo courtesy of Curtis Publishing Company; *center* © 1991 Cable News Network, Inc. All rights reserved; *bottom* Bettmann. **72** *top left & right* Courtesy of the Archives, The Coca-Cola Company; *bottom right* Pepsi Cola Company; *bottom* Bettmann. **73** *top* Culver Pictures; *bottom left* Brown Brothers; *bottom right* Collection of William L. Simon. **74** *top* Regis Bossu/Sygma; *center* J. Langevin/Sygma; *bottom* Photofest. **75** *top Pogo* cartoon by Walt Kelly © 1950 *Los Angeles Times*. Reprinted by permission; *center left* Noel Alum; *center* U.S. Postal Service; *bottom left & right* © United Features Syndicate, Inc./Noel Alum **76** *top left* FPG; *top right* Bettmann; *bottom right* Ray Skibinsky; *bottom* FPG. **77** *top* Britt Erlanson/TIB; *center* Noel Alum; *bottom* Library of Congress. **78** *top* Bettmann; *center* Viacom/Shooting Star; *bottom* Photofest. **79** *top* Archive Photos; *bottom* Jack E. Davis. **80** *top* G.T. Pugh/Globe Photos; *center* William Campbell/Sygma; *bottom left* Ken Nahoum/Sygma; *bottom right* Stephen Trupp/Globe Photos. **81** *top* Sygma; *center* Lawrence Fried/TIB; *bottom* Courtesy of Frederic Remington Art Museum, Ogdensburg, NY. **82** *top* Stark Museum of Art, Orange, TX; *center & bottom left* Wesley S. Johnson; *center right* Noel Alum. **83** *top* © 1982 Reader's Digest Association, Inc.; *center* Brown Brothers; *bottom* Hiroji Kubota. **84** *top* Richard Sexton; *center & bottom* Photofest. **85** *top left* © Columbia Records; *top right* © RCA; *center* Globe Photos; *bottom* FPG. **86** *top left & right* Noel Alum; *center* Bettmann; *bottom* Collection of the New York Historical Society. **87** *top* Nancy Ellison/Gamma Liaison; *bottom* Photofest. **88** *top* Culver Pictures; *center* Superstock; *bottom* Steve Hopkins/Black Star. **89** *top* Bettmann; *center* Brown Brothers; *bottom* Movie Star News. **90** *top* National Archives; *center* Superstock; *bottom* Everett Collection. **91** *top* Steve Gottlieb; *center* Linda & Gene Kangas; *bottom* The Shelburne Museum, Shelburne, VT. **92** *top* Photofest; *center* James M. Kelly/Globe Photos; *bottom* Motor Books International. **93** *top* Courtesy of Katz's Deli, New York, NY; *center* Photofest; *bottom* Culver Pictures. **94** *top* From *The New We Look And See* by William S. Gray, A. Sterl Artley and May Hill Arbuthot. Illustrated by Eleanor Campbell © 1951 by Scott, Foresman and Company. Reprinted by permission; *center* Amherst College/Robert Frost Library, Special Collections & Archives; *bottom* Photo courtesy of the Norman Rockwell Museum at Stockbridge. Printed by permission of the Norman Rockwell Family Trust © 1953 the Norman Rockwell Family Trust. **95** *top* Bettmann ; *center* Photofest; *bottom* Collection Virginia Museum of Fine Arts. **96** *top left* Michael Ochs Archive; *top right* Kobal Collection; *bottom* Archive Photos. **97** *top* Suzanne Brookens/TIB; *center left* © Walt Disney Company/Photofest; *center right* AP/Wide World; *bottom* Photofest. **98** *top The Lorax* by Dr. Seuss © Dr. Seuss *top left Green Eggs and Ham* by Dr. Seuss © 1960 Random House, Inc.; *top center One fish two fish red fish blue fish* by Dr. Seuss © 1960; *top right The Cat in the Hat* © 1956 by Dr. Seuss/*all* Noel Alum; *center* Drawing by Mort Gerberg © 1974 The New Yorker Magazine, Inc. All Rights Reserved; *bottom* "The Donner Party" by William Reusswig, *True* Magazine, Collection Edward Cerullo. **99** *top* Avon Products; *center* Archive Photos; *bottom* Globe Photos. **100** *top* Bettmann; *center* Imperial War Museum, London. **101** *top right* Archive Photos; *center* Cindy Lewis. All rights reserved; *bottom* Tim Bieber/TIB. **102** *top* Joe Viesti/Viesti Associates; *center* Brown Brothers; *bottom right* Bettmann. **103** *top* Library of Congress; *bottom* Movie Star News. **104** *top* The National Academy of Design, New York, NY; *center* The Metropolitan Museum of Art, Purchase, The Alfred N. Punnett Endowment Fund and George D. Pratt Gift, 1934; *bottom* Schlesinger Library, Radcliffe College. **105** *top* Mark Reinstein/FPG; *center* Kobal Collection; *bottom* Bettmann. **106** *top* George Rosario/Stock Market; *center* Bettmann; *bottom* AP/Wide World. **107** *top* Alfred Eisenstaedt/*Life* Magazine © Time Warner, Inc.; *bottom* Printed by permission of the Norman Rockwell Family Trust © 1948 the Norman Rockwell Family Trust. **108** *top* Patrick Litchfield/Globe Photos; *bottom* Bettmann. **109** *top* Max Hilaire/TIB; *center* Bettmann; *bottom* Library of Congress. **110** *top* Library of Congress; *center* NBC/Globe Photos; *bottom left* Photofest; *bottom right Movie Star News*. **111** *top left* Bettmann; *top right* Motion Picture & Television Photo Archive; *bottom* Richard Laird/FPG. **112** *top* UPI/Bettmann; *center* Bettmann; *bottom left & right* Courtesy of The Eskimo Pie Corporation. **113** *top left* Peter Beney/TIB; *top right* Bill Terry/Viesti Associates; *center* Cralle/TIB; *bottom* Globe Photos. **114** *top all* Noel Alum; *bottom right* Civilian Defense; *bottom* Loomis Dean/1961 Time Inc. **115** *top* Bob Daemmerich/Stock Boston; *bottom left* Bettmann; *bottom right The Fanny Farmer Cookbook* by Marion Cunningham, Alfred A. Knopf, 1995. **116** *top right* NYPL Picture Collection; *left* © 1935 Paramount Pictures, Inc./NYPL Picture Collection; *bottom center* Willy Maywald/ADAGP; *bottom right* Fashion Institute of Technology. **117** *top left* Peter Knapp/SCOOP; *top right* Vernon Merritt/*Life* Magazine © Time Warner; *bottom right* NYPL Picture Collection; *bottom* Eugen Gebhardt/FPG. **118** *top* Miguel/TIB; *center* Courtesy of John Lawrence; *bottom left* UPI/Bettmann.; *bottom right* Federal Bureau of Investigation. **119** *top* Noel Alum; *center* © Felix the Cat Productions/Photo by Steven Mays, *The Encyclopedia of Collectibles*, published by Time-Life, Inc., courtesy of Rebus, Inc., NY, 1978; *bottom* Bettmann. **120** *top* Costas Manos/Magnum; *center & bottom* Bettmann. **121** *top* The Mount Vernon Ladies Association of the Union, Mount Vernon, VA; *center left & right* The White House Collection; *bottom* Rick Maiman. **122** *top* Bettmann; *bottom left* Courtesy of Woolworth Corporation; *bottom right* A. M. Rosario/TIB. **123** *top & center* Brown Brothers; *bottom* King Features Syndicate. **124** *top* Turner Home Entertainment/Photofest; *center* Imperial War Museum, London; *bottom* Ira Block. **125** *top* Jack Stroh/Globe Photos; *center* Peter Arnold/Globe Photos; *bottom* Dennis Brack/Black Star. **126** *top* Focus on Sports; *center* Brown Brothers; *bottom* Bettmann. **127** *top* Bettmann; *center* New York Historical Society; *bottom* Williams Weems/courtesy of National Geographic Society. **128** *top left* H. Armstrong Roberts; *top right* Lawrence Hughes/TIB; *bottom* Courtesy of John Hancock Life Insurance Company. **129** *top* Jeff Hunter/TIB; *center* Milt/Patti Putnam/Stock Market; *bottom* NBC/Globe Photos. **130** *top* Philadelphia Museum of Art: Mr. & Mrs.Wharton Sinkler; *center* Chris Collins/Stock Market; *bottom* Focus on Sports. **131** *top* Kansas State Historical Society, Topeka, KS; *center* Washington University Gallery of Art, St. Louis. Gift of Nathaniel Phillips, 1890; *bottom* National Portrait Gallery, Washington, DC/Art Resource, NY. **132** *top left & right* Photofest; *bottom* Bettmann. **133** *top* Bettmann; *center left* Photofest/Jagarts; *center right* Photofest; *bottom* John Margolis/ESTO. **134** *top & bottom* Bettmann; *center* Photofest. **135** *top* Bettmann; *bottom* Archive Photos. **136** *top* David W. Hamilton/TIB; *center* AP/Wide

World; *bottom* Archive Photos. **137** *top* Courtesy of Girl Scouts of the U.S.A. Archives; *center* Culver Pictures; *bottom* Rube Goldberg, property of and © Rube Goldberg, Inc., distributed by United Media. **138** *top* Noel Alum; *center* Denver Public Library, Western History Collection/Photo by L. McClure; *bottom* Duomo. **139** *top* Bettmann; *center & bottom* Photofest. **140** *top* © Good Humor; *center* Jon Reis/Stock Market; *bottom* Driggs Collection. **141** *top* Gwendolyn Cates/Sygma; *center* UPI/Bettmann; *bottom* Martha Graham, "Letter to the World" ("Kick") 1940 © Willard & Barbara Morgan Archives. **142** *top* UPI/Bettmann; *center* Archive Photos; *bottom* Superstock. **143** *top* Grandma Moses, "Sugaring Off," Copyright © 1996 Grandma Moses Properties Co., NY/Photo, Edward Owen/Art Resource, NY; *center* Gaylord Entertainment; *bottom* Globe Photos. **144** *top* Photofest; *center* U.S. Postal Service; *bottom* Herb Green. **145** *top* Ira Block/TIB; *center & bottom* Photofest. **146** *top* Bettmann; *top right* Culver Pictures; *center* Tom Till/Tony Stone Images; *bottom* Frank Oberle. **147** *top* J. Barry O'Rourke/Stock Market; *bottom* Photofest. **148** *top & center* Bettmann; *bottom* Photofest. **149** *top* Gabe Palmer/Stock Market; *center* Photofest; *bottom* UPI/Bettmann. **150** *top left* Culver Pictures; *center right* Bettmann; *bottom left* Superstock; *bottom right* Photofest. **151** *top left* Photofest; *top center* UPI/Bettmann; *top right* Photofest; *center left* Culver Pictures; *center right & bottom center* Photofest; *bottom right* Courtesy of Judith Carmel. **152** *top* Grace Davies/Envision; *top left* Randy O'Rourke/Stock Market; *bottom left* George Silk/*Life* Magazine © Time Inc.; *bottom right* Pamela Zilly/TIB. **153** *top* Culver Pictures; *center* Ellen Senisi/The Image Works; *bottom right* Granitsas/The Image Works; *bottom* © Running Press. **154** *top* Bettmann; *center* Paul Barton/Stock Market; *bottom* Noel Alum. **155** *top left* Photofest; *top right* Focus on Sports; *center* Marvy!/Stock Market; *bottom* Alan Levenson/Tony Stone Images. **156** *all* Culver Pictures. **157** *top* © *Harvard Lampoon*; *bottom* Photofest. **158** *top* Christel Rose/TIB; *center* UPI/Bettmann; *bottom* Courtesy of Lord & Taylor. **159** *top* Photofest; *center* Culver Pictures; *bottom* UPI/Bettmann. **160** *top* Rick Ostentoski/Envision; *top left* King Features Syndicate; *center* Noel Alum; *bottom* Culver Pictures. **161** *top* Bettmann; *bottom* Dick Snyder. **162** *top* Neil Leifer; *center* UPI/Bettmann; *bottom* Photofest. **163** *top* Jeff Hunter/TIB; *center* Culver Pictures; *bottom* Bruce Wodder/TIB. **164** *top* Addison Gallery of American Art, Phillips Academy, Andover, MA; *center* National Gallery of Art, Collection of Mr. & Mrs. Paul Mellon; *bottom* Photofest. **165** *top* Shirley Rosicke/Stock Market; *center left* Courtesy of General Motors Corporation; *center right* Seth Goltzer/Stock Market; *bottom* AP/Wild World. **166** *top* Tom Bean/Stock Market; *center* Kobal Collection; *bottom* © CBS, Inc. **167** *top* The Art Institute of Chicago. All rights reserved; *center* Archive Photos; *bottom* Photofest. **168** *top* Michael Skott/TIB; *center* David Fetherston; *bottom left The Encyclopedia of Collectibles*, published by Time-Life, Inc., courtesy of Rebus, Inc., NY, 1978; *bottom right* UPI/Bettmann. **169** *top* Lake County Museum/Curt Teich Postcard Archives; *center* UPI/Bettmann; *bottom left* Courtesy of NBC; *bottom right* NBC/Globe Photos. **170** *top* Museum of Art, Rhode Island School of Design; *bottom* UPI/Bettmann. **171** *top* Bob Woodward/Stock Market; *center* Kobal Collection; *bottom* UPI/Bettmann. **172** *top* Library of Congress; *bottom left* Derek Murray/TIB; *bottom right* Stephen Marks/TIB. **173** *top left* AP/Wide World; *top right* Clive Brunskill/Allsport; *bottom* from *For the Love of Lucy* by Ric B. Wyman, Abbeville Press, 1994. **174** *top* Printed by permission of the Norman Rockwell Family Trust © 1948 the Norman Rockwell Family Trust; *center* Michael Dunn/Stock Market; *bottom* Focus on Sports. **175** *top* Larry Stevens/Nawrocki Stock; *center* © The New Yorker Magazine, Inc.; *bottom* Brooks Kraft/Sygma. **176** *top* UPI/Bettmann; *center* U.S. Postal Service; *bottom* Photofest. **177** *top* Cornell University Photo; *center* National Archives; *bottom left* L. Kolvoord/The Image Works; *bottom right* Noel Alum. **178** *top* David Pollack/Stock Market; *center* Metropolitan Museum of Art, Harris Brisbane Dick Fund, 1964 (detail); *bottom* National Parks Service. **179** *top left & right* David Redfern/Retna Ltd.; *center* Starfile; *bottom* National Archives. **180** *top* Architect of the Capitol; *bottom left* Chuck Solomon/Focus on Sports; *bottom right* Noel Alum. **181** *top* Pennsylvania Academy of Fine Arts; *center* Stephen Snider; *bottom* Mark Kauffman/*Life* Magazine © Time Inc. **182** *top* Brown Brothers; *center* Elliot Landry/Magnum Photos; *bottom* Jack Ballett/UPI/Bettmann. **183** *top* Photo by John H. Fouch, courtesy of Dr. James Brust; *center* Wurlitzer Jukebox Company, Moonachie, NJ/Photo by Steven Mays, *The Encyclopedia of Collectibles*, published by Time-Life, Inc., courtesy of Rebus, Inc., NY, 1978; *bottom* FPG **184** *top* Maxwell Museum of Anthropology; *center & bottom* Kobal Collection. **185** *top* Photofest; *center* Globe Photos; *bottom right & left* Noel Alum. **186** *top* Movie Still Archive; *center* Library of Congress; *bottom* Photofest. **187** *top* Photofest; *bottom left* Photo by Philippe Halsman © Halsman Estate; *bottom right* Popperfoto/Archive Photos. **188** *top* The John F. Kennedy Library; *bottom* Bachrach. **189** *top* Neil Leifer; *center* Martha Swope/The Gershwin Theatre; *bottom* © B. Shackman Company, Inc., NY. **190** *top* Culver Pictures; *center* "Buried Treasure—The True Captain Kidd" by John D. Hamplin, *Harper's* Magazine, Dec. 1902; *bottom* © The New York Post, Sept. 11, 1981; **191** *top* Frank Miller/*Life* Magazine © Time, Inc. 1963; *center* Samuel Yette. **192** *top left, top right & center* Photofest; *bottom* Courtesy of the King Archives. **193** *top* UPI/Bettmann; *center* Steve Friedman; *bottom* Culver Pictures. **194** *top* Peter Lake/Globe Photos; *center* George Eastman House; *bottom* Doc Pele/Stills/Retna Ltd. **195** *top* Culver Pictures; *center* "Krazy Kat" (detail), original watercolor, c. 1925. Gift to Carl Harbaugh/Courtesy of Murray Harris; *bottom* Photofest. **196** *top* Greg Christensen/TIB; *bottom* Courtesy of George Eastman House. **197** *top* George W. Disario/Stock Market; *center left, center right & bottom* © 1912, 1945, 1976 Meredith Corporation. Used with the permission of *Ladies' Home Journal*. **198** *top & center* Kobal Collection; *bottom left* Brown Brothers; *bottom right* Steven Mays, *The Encyclopedia of Collectibles*, published by Time-Life Inc., courtesy of Rebus, Inc., NY, 1978. **199** *top* Paul Steel/Stock Market; *center* Culver Pictures; *bottom* Photofest. **200** *top* Everett Collection; *bottom* Photofest. **201** *top* Digital Archive; *center* Richard Pasley/Stock Boston; *bottom* Photofest. **202** *top* Library of Congress; *center* Courtesy of Appomattox Courthouse, National Historic Park; *bottom* Photofest. **203** *top* Marshall Fields Catalogue, 1975; *bottom* New York Times Pictures. **204** *top* Bettmann; *center* Montana Historical Society; *bottom* Photofest. **205** *top* Peter Gridley/FPG; *center* Jonathan Wallen; *bottom* Michael Freeman. **206** *top* courtesy of Roy Lichtenstein; *center & right Life* Magazine © Time Warner; *bottom* Noel Alum. **207** *top* Capp Enterprises, Inc. All rights reserved; *bottom* Jeff Spielman/Stock Market. **208** *top* Noel Alum; *center* Culver Pictures. *bottom left* Henry Groskinsky; *bottom right* Brown Brothers. **209** *top* Wooloroc Museum, Bartlesville, OH; *bottom* Photofest. **210** *top* Ed Bock/Stock Market; *center* Chicago-Tribune-New York News Syndicate, courtesy of Woody Gelman and Nostalgia Press; *bottom* Kobal Collection. **211** *top* Neil Leifer; *center* L. Grant/FPG; *bottom* Photofest. **212** *top* FPG; *bottom* L. Albee/Longwood Gardens. **213** *top* Photofest; *center left & right* Looney Tunes characters, names, and all indicia are trademarks of Warner Brothers © 1996; *bottom* Collection Viollet. **214** *top* Superstock; *center left* The Granger Collection, NY; *bottom* David Hamilton/TIB. **215** *top & center* UPI/Bettmann; *bottom left & right* David Redfern/Retna Ltd. **216** *top* Ross Whitaker/TIB; *center & bottom* UPI/Bettmann. **218** *top* UPI/Bettmann; *bottom left & right* Bob Firth. **219** *top* William Strode/Woodfin Camp & Associates; *center* Noel Alum; *bottom* UPI/Bettmann. **220** *top* William Waterfall/Stock Market; *bottom* AP/Wide World. **221** *top* David Madison/Duomo Photography; *bottom right* Courtesy of Judith Carmel; *bottom* Superstock. **222** *top* Rich Clarkson; *center left* John M. Roberts/Stock Market; *bottom right* Mitchell Osborne. **223** *top* Department of the Navy; *center & bottom* Photofest. **224** *top* Culver Pictures; *center* Photofest; *bottom* CBS-TV/Kobal Collection. **225** *all* Photofest. **226** *top* Warner Brothers/Kobal Collection; *bottom* Bettmann **227** *top* National Baseball Hall of Fame; *center* AP/Wide World Photos; *bottom* Bettmann. **228** *top* UPI/Bettmann; *center* Meals on Wheels America; *bottom* Dennis Galante/Envision. **229** *top left* Schaeffer, illustrator, 1943, Dodd Mead; *top right* courtesy of Evans Kerrigna, author, *Guidebook of U.S. Medals; bottom* Culver Pictures. **230** *top* Win Swaan/FPG; *center left* Beth Bergman; *center right* Cecil Beaton/Camera Press/Retna Ltd.; *bottom* Globe Photos. **231** *top* MGM, Inc. © 1944; *center* Photofest; *bottom* David Noble/FPG. **232** *top* Disney characters © Disney Enterprises, Inc./Noel Alum; *center* Allan Levenson; *bottom* Globe Photos. **233** *top* Photofest; *center* FPG; *bottom* Bob Daemmrich/Stock Boston. **234** *top* Peter Gridley/FPG; *center* UPI/Bettmann; *bottom* Adam Scull/Globe Photos. **235** *top* Nathan Benn/Woodfin Camp & Associates; *center* John Gaps/AP/Wide World; 235 *bottom* Globe Photos. **236** *top left* © 1995 Whitney Museum of American Art. 50th-anniversary gift of the Gilman Foundation, Inc., The Lauder Foundation, A. Alfred Taubman, an anonymous donor, and purchase; *center right* © 1996 Whitney Museum of American Art, NY. Purchase, with funds from the Friends of the Whitney Museum of American Art collection; *bottom left* © 1996 Whitney Museum of American Art. Purchase, with funds from the Louis and Bessie Adler Foundation, Inc., Seymour M. Klein, President, the Gilman Foundation, Inc., the Howard and Jean Lipman Foundation, Inc. Photography by Jerry L. Thompson, NY; *bottom* Hirshhorn Museum and Sculpture Garden, Smithsonian Institution. Gift of Joseph H. Hirshhorn Foundation, 1966. Photo by Lee Stalsworth. **237** *top left* Norton Museum of Art, West Palm Beach, FL; *top right* Private collection, courtesy of Galerie St. Etienne, NY; *center right* Art Gallery of Ontario, Toronto. **238** *top* Library of Congress; *center* Collection New York Historical Society; *bottom* Monopoly ® is a registered trademark of the Tonka Corporation for its real estate trading game and elements © 1993, Parker Brothers, a division of Tonka Corporation, used with permission/Noel Alum. **239** *top left* Culver Pictures; *top right* Doc Pele/Stills/Retna Ltd.; *bottom* Luke Frazza. **240** *top* Gary Cralle/TIB; *center* Travelpix/FPG; *bottom* Culver Pictures. **241** *top left* Brown Brothers; *top right* Alex Webb/Magnum; *bottom* Courtesy of Star-Kist Foods, Inc. **242** *top left* Private collection; *top right* Card courtesy of Hallmark Archives, Hallmark Cards, Inc.; *center* Mauro Carrard/Gamma Liaison; *bottom* Archive Photos/Frank Driggs Collection. **243** *top* Kunio Owaki/Stock Market; *center left* Smithsonian Institution; *center right Life* Magazine © Time Inc.; *bottom left* Lynn McAfee/Retna Ltd.; *bottom right* MTV: Music Television, logo used by permission. MTV Networks, a division of Viacom International, Inc. © 1995 MTV Networks. All rights reserved. **244** *top* Culver Pictures; *bottom* Kobal Collection. **245** *top* UPI/Bettmann; *center & bottom left* Nicky Wright. **246** *top* George Lange; *bottom* Walter Iooss, Jr./*Sports Illustrated*. **247** *top* Kunio Owaki/Stock Market; *center* Stephen Wilkes/TIB; *bottom left* NASA. **248** *top right* Henry Groskinsky/*Life* Magazine © Time Inc.; *center* Culver Pictures; *bottom National Enquirer*. **249** *top left* © 1994 *National Geographic*/Dave Harvey; *top right* © *National Geographic*/Mitsuaki Iwago; *center* © *National Geographic*/Frans Lanting; *bottom* National Archives. **250** *top* Kobal Collection; *center* Everett Collection; *bottom* Miramax/Kobal Collection. **251** *top* NYDEX; *center left* Alice Austen Photo; *bottom right* George Obremski/TIB. **252** *top* Lance Nelson/Stock Market; *center* Patti McConville/TIB; *bottom* Gail Greig **253** *top left* Cover art by Charles Saxon © 1972 The New Yorker Magazine, Inc. All rights reserved; *top right* Cover art by Peter Arno © 1964 The New Yorker Magazine, Inc. All rights reserved; *center* Piotr Kapa/Stock Market; *bottom* AP/Wide World. **254** *top* Charles Gurche/The Wildlife Collection; *right* Tom Bean/DRK Photo; *bottom left* Clay Myers/The Wildlife Collection. **255** *top left* Inga Spence/Tom Stack & Associates; *center left* Hal Horwitz/Photo/Nats; *center right* David M. Dennis/Tom Stack & Associates; *right* Sydney Karp/Photo/Nats; *bottom center* John Gerlach/DRK Photo; *bottom right* D. Cavagnaro/DRK Photo. **256** *all* UPI/Bettmann. **257** *top* Reuters/Bettmann; *center* Bettmann; *bottom* Culver Pictures. **258** *top left* UPI/Bettmann; *top right* National Museum of American Art, Washington, DC/Art Resource, NY. **259** *top* Sumo/TIB; *center* Bart Barlow/Envision; *bottom* Richard Laird/FPG. **260** *top* UPI/Bettmann; *center* Noel Alum; *bottom left* Jacques Lowe; *bottom right* UPI/Bettmann. **261** *top* Culver Pictures; *center* Springer/Bettmann; *bottom* Butler Institute of American Art. **262** *top right* Michael Hostovich; *center left* Family of Irma Schneiders; *center right* Christopher Kean; *bottom* Archive Photos. **263** *top* UPI/Bettmann; *center & center left* Bettmann; *bottom right* Western History Collections, University of Oklahoma Library. **264** *top* UPI/Bettmann; *center left The Ozarks Mountaineer*, U. of Mississippi Press; *bottom* Michael Ochs Archive. **265** *top* © 1982 by Publications International Ltd.; *bottom* UPI/Bettmann. **266** *top* UPI/Bettmann; *center right* Rudy Muller/Envision; *bottom* Noel Alum. **267** *top* Bettmann; *center* Private collection; *bottom* UPI/Bettmann. **268** *top right* Reprinted by permission. From *Better Homes and Gardens Creative American Quilting* © 1989 by Meredith Corporation. All rights reserved; *center* America Hurrah, NY; *bottom left* Signature quilt by Caron L. Mosey, The Flushing Michigan Historical Society, from *America's Pictorial Quilts* by Caron L. Mosey, American Quilter's Society, Paducah, KY; *bottom right* Steven Mays. **269** *top left* Shelburne Museum, Shelburne, VT/Photo by Ken Burris; *top right* Reprinted from *Better Homes and Gardens Creative American Quilting* © 1989 by Meredith Corporation. All rights reserved; *center left* Dr. Jeannette Dean Throckmorton, American, Des Moines, IA, 1883–1963, bedcover (Blue Iris), cotton, plain weave, pieced; quilted, pattern outlined in pencil, heavily padded in parts; appliquéd with cotton, plain weave, printed, backed with cotton, plain weave, inscribed lower center: 1945, Dr. Jeannette, 246.6 cm. x 183.8 cm., Gift of Dr. Jeannette Dean Throckmorton, 1959.329.; *center left* Museum of American Folk Art, NY; Gift of Robert Bishop 1993.04.31; *bottom right* America Hurrah, NY. **270** *top left* Bettmann; *top right* University of Oklahoma Library Manuscripts Division; *center* UPI/Bettmann; *bottom* James Bernardin. **271** *top* Joseph McNally; *cen-*